MEDICAL ANTHROPOLOGY

A Biocultural Approach

FOURTH EDITION

ANDREA S. WILEY

INDIANA UNIVERSITY, BLOOMINGTON

JOHN S. ALLEN

INDIANA UNIVERSITY, BLOOMINGTON

NEW YORK   OXFORD

OXFORD UNIVERSITY PRESS

Oxford University Press is a department of the University of Oxford.
It furthers the University's objective of excellence in research, scholarship,
and education by publishing worldwide. Oxford is a registered trade mark of
Oxford University Press in the UK and certain other countries.

Published in the United States of America by Oxford University Press
198 Madison Avenue, New York, NY 10016, United States of America.

For titles covered by Section 112 of the US Higher Education
Opportunity Act, please visit www.oup.com/us/he for the latest
information about pricing and alternate formats.

Library of Congress Cataloging-in-Publication Data

Names: Wiley, Andrea S., 1962- author. | Allen, John S. (John Scott), 1961- author.
Title: Medical anthropology: a biocultural approach / Andrea S. Wiley,
  Indiana University, Bloomington, John S. Allen, Indiana University,
  Bloomington.
Description: Fourth edition. | New York : Oxford University Press, 2020. |
  Includes bibliographical references and index. | Summary: "This is a
  medical anthropology textbook"—Provided by publisher.
Identifiers: LCCN 2020025286 | ISBN 9780197515990 (paperback) | ISBN
  9780197516003 (ebook)
Subjects: LCSH: Medical anthropology—Textbooks.
Classification: LCC GN296 .W55 2020 | DDC 306.41/61—dc23
LC record available at https://lccn.loc.gov/2020025286

Printing number: 9 8 7 6 5 4 3

Printed by Sheridan Books, Inc.,
United States of America

In memory of Roy J Wiley (1930–2019)

CONTENTS

CHAPTER 3   Healers and Healing   *40*

CHAPTER 4   Diet and Nutrition in Health and Disease   *79*

CHAPTER 5   Child Growth and Health   *117*

PREFACE

A BIOCULTURAL APPROACH TO MEDICAL ANTHROPOLOGY

The field of medical anthropology embraces a wide range of perspectives as it seeks to understand human health and illness as fully biocultural phenomena. Medical anthropology emerged as a distinct topic of interest in anthropology in the 1970s and has grown tremendously since then. The Society for Medical Anthropology, a unit of the American Anthropological Association, is one of the largest sections of the association. Anthropologists from across the four subdisciplines (archaeological, biological, cultural, and linguistic anthropology) have contributed to making medical anthropology a vital and essential part of anthropology.

Our interest in writing this text grew out of our dissatisfaction with the existing texts on the market. We struggled to find a text that matches our pedagogical approaches and our students' backgrounds and interests. We each patched together appropriate readings, but felt the need for a book that could be the core of the course, one that provided both an overview of the field and a clear orienting focus. This is a tall order, but the range and diversity of medical anthropology makes the task of textbook writing an exciting challenge. In this fourth edition, we have built on and revised the book to reflect trends in the field and current urgent health concerns (e.g. the COVID-19 pandemic, which is ongoing as we write) and to reflect student feedback as we and colleagues have used the text in the classroom.

To present the field's wide range of content and perspectives in one textbook, it is necessary to develop a cohesive approach; ours is explicitly biocultural. Health and disease have both biological and cultural causes and consequences. An ailment is likely to have a physiological foundation, but its meaning is subject to cultural interpretation and its causes more often than not stem from sociocultural conditions. A biocultural perspective draws on the breadth of anthropological research on health and attempts to articulate and synthesize the ways in which biological and cultural factors interact and affect health.

Our approach is to first present basic biological information on a particular health condition and elaborate from there. We then expand our analysis to include evolutionary, historical, and cross-cultural perspectives that enrich our understanding of particular health conditions. Our emphasis is on understanding biological and socio-cultural sources of variation in health within and between populations and through time; as such, this book makes use of the holistic perspective of four-field anthropology. In our approach, we do not mean to privilege physiological explanations of disease, but we have found that expanding from a biological foundation to the social and cultural aspects of health and disease is a pedagogical strategy that works well for students. Many students come to medical anthropology from the health and biological sciences, and students in the social sciences and humanities, also find that their perspectives mesh well with the biocultural approach we present.

We attempt to present a holistic view of medical anthropology, but we recognize that we cannot do justice to the full range of the field. Given that teachers of medical anthropology come from diverse perspectives, this text is best used in conjunction with additional resources. After each chapter we list some options for ethnographies or other related texts that would be complementary to the material covered in the chapter. Furthermore, we feature the work of applied medical anthropologists—those who are making use of anthropological perspectives to design, implement, or evaluate health interventions or policies.

WHAT IS DISTINCTIVE ABOUT THIS TEXT

Each of the chapters of this book is organized around a topic central to medical anthropology. The basic biology will be presented and then contextualized by the relevant evolutionary, historical, and sociocultural factors that shape it. In addition, the intersections between the biocultural perspective and other approaches in medical anthropology, especially the political economy of health and applied medical anthropology, will be highlighted.

- *An explicit biocultural focus to each chapter.* Each chapter starts with the basic biology of an ailment and expands the analysis from there to include historical, sociocultural, and political–economic factors that somehow influence it.
- *Holistic anthropological analysis.* The strength of anthropology in general and medical anthropology in particular derives from a broad and inclusive perspective. We include relevant work from all of the subdisciplines of anthropology, but most especially biological and cultural anthropology.
- *Examples of "anthropologists in action."* We highlight anthropologists who make use of their skills to create, evaluate, or implement health policies, both within their home country and across the globe.
- *Accessibility and relevance to students in the biological sciences and social sciences.* Students from both areas learn how biology and culture are essential to understanding health.
- *Up-to-date data.* Research in the health sciences changes rapidly, and we have made every effort to ensure that the biological understanding of disease is current. Similar efforts were made to make certain that anthropological analyses likewise reflect contemporary understandings.

- *Use of both contemporary and historical examples.* Students will see ways in which current health problems are either unique or similar to patterns that have existed in the past.
- *Use of both local and global examples.* The scope of this text is global, and many of our examples are drawn from anthropological research in non-Western cultures. We also draw extensively on work done in the United States (as well as Canada and Europe), which demonstrates to students that the anthropological perspective is as useful in industrialized and Western societies as it is in non-Western or low- or middle-income countries.
- *Has a strong evolutionary component*, based on new work in Darwinian or evolutionary medicine.
- *The links between the biocultural approach and interventions to improve health* are considered throughout the text.

WHAT IS NEW IN THIS EDITION

Based on reviewers' and users' (both students and instructors) comments, we have revised this text for the fourth edition in the following ways:

- All research updated to include the latest findings and new approaches
- More discussion of the importance of causation in healing, training in alternative medicine, decision making in transplant patients, and the concept of cultural safety in health-care delivery
- A new box on gender and living donation of organs
- Updated discussion of the vaccination and anti-vaxx movements, including cross-cultural perspectives
- Chapter on diet and nutrition substantially revised—organized around major transitions in prehistory and history, and around population variation in diet and nutrition
- More material on diet, health, and sustainability concerns
- Elaborated material on the gut microbiome
- A new box on the exposome
- New material on menstrual health
- New material on obstetric violence
- A new box on the anthropology of disability
- Updated discussion of allergies and asthma, including a biodiversity framework
- Expanded consideration of climate change and infectious disease, and human–animal interactions related to infectious disease
- Reflections on the COVID-19 pandemic, unfolding in real time
- Elaborated discussion of intersectionality and structural discrimination/racism and its relationship to stress and health disparities
- A new box on transgender health
- A new box on patienthood
- Expanded discussion of community mental health centers, and stigma and mental illness

OUTLINE OF THE BOOK

Chapter 1 provides a brief introduction to the field of medical anthropology. Chapter 2 discusses the concept of health as the key issue for medical anthropology. A biocultural perspective on health is explicated, and other more culturally focused approaches to medical anthropology are introduced.

Chapter 3 provides a discussion of healing systems across cultures, including those of small-scale societies and textual traditions of complex societies. It considers the role of traditional healers and heath care within these societies and how they attempt to provide a system of explanation and therapeutic methods for local health problems.

Health at different times in the life cycle is the focus of Chapters 4 through 7. The life cycle includes gestation, birth, growth and development, reproduction, aging, and death. Chapter 4 outlines the relationships between nutrition and health. Nutrition is fundamental to health throughout life, but each life stage has particular needs and is affected by nutritional deficiencies or excesses in different ways. Across diverse populations, nutritional problems underlie many common diseases, from outright protein-energy undernutrition to coronary heart disease deriving in part from chronic overconsumption.

Chapter 5 focuses on child growth. Since children's bodies are literally being constructed from the earliest stages of embryological development through adolescence, the dietary and environmental conditions to which they are exposed (including chronic over- and undernutrition) will shape their growth trajectory and ultimately affect adult body shape, size, function, and, of course, health.

In Chapter 6 we explore reproductive health with a focus on how conception, pregnancy, and "mothering" are important biological phenomena with clear links to health and how they are heavily influenced by cultural context. Men's reproductive health has been relatively understudied, and here we discuss two pertinent issues facing contemporary men: declining sperm counts and erectile dysfunction.

In Chapter 7 we present an overview of the aging process and its relationship to health and disease. Aging is a biological phenomenon that is strongly influenced by cultural patterns, such as diet, smoking, stress, and social status of the aged, and variation in these factors contributes to substantial population variation in the experience of the aging process.

In Chapters 8 and 9 we explore the range of infectious diseases and their impact on human health cross-culturally. Chapter 8 provides basic relevant information on the taxonomy of pathogens that infect humans and how they cause disease in the body. An overview of the human immune system is also necessary because it will influence the symptomatology of the disease. There is also consideration of how evolutionary factors have influenced the spread, virulence, and human responses to infection.

In Chapter 9 we discuss specific examples of the ways in which human behavior–environment interactions cause infectious diseases to "emerge" as important diseases in human populations both in the past and in the present. Malaria, cholera, schistosomiasis, human immunodeficiency virus, and tuberculosis are described in detail.

Chapters 10 and 11 consider stress, stress-related disease, and mental health. Chapter 10 focuses on the biology of the stress response, the conditions that activate this response, and the health consequences of chronic stress. This chapter will also consider the relationships among race, racism, and disease risk, with a focus on the United States and how these relationships may work through stress-mediated pathways.

Chapter 11 explores mental illness from a cross-cultural and evolutionary perspective. It asks whether mental health problems are similar or significantly different across cultures in their symptomatology and epidemiology and what role predispositions to mental illness might have had in human evolution.

The book concludes with a short epilogue that provides resources for students who want to continue to explore some of the themes and topics raised in this book. Each chapter contains a number of case studies or examples that demonstrate how a medical anthropological perspective sheds new light on a particular health condition. In many instances this perspective provides opportunities for a fuller understanding of the factors that contribute to the disease and, as a consequence, new approaches to more effective prevention and/or treatment. We hope that this text will illustrate the ways in which medical anthropology has the potential to help improve the health of populations throughout the world.

ACKNOWLEDGMENTS

Much of the material we cover in this book arose from classes we have taught over the years. JSA thanks his former students at the University of Auckland and the University of Iowa, whose keen interest in a range of medical anthropological topics stimulated his own work in this area. ASW thanks her students at the University of Iowa, Binghamton University, James Madison University, and Indiana University, whose feedback in medical anthropology classes has been invaluable. At Indiana University, special thanks go to Jennifer Cullin, whose careful reading of the third (and second!) edition and helpful suggestions greatly improved this new edition. ASW also recognizes her graduate student colleagues from the UC Berkeley/UC San Francisco medical anthropology program, who have been a continual source of support and inspiration. Many thanks go to those who so generously contributed photographs for the text.

Thank you also to those whose comments contributed to the revision process for the fourth edition:

HM Ashraf Ali, Grant MacEwan University
Leslie Dawson, MacEwan University
Roberta Fiske Rusciano, Rider University
Catherine M. Fuentes, University of North Carolina at Charlotte
Barbara R. Hewitt, University of Manitoba
Melissa Melby, University of Delaware
Susan Saul, California State University Los Angeles
Merav Shohet, Boston University
Amanda Thompson, University of North Carolina Chapel Hill
Lianne Tripp, University of Northern British Columbia
Heather S. Williams, Metropolitan State University

CHAPTER 1

Introduction

A Biocultural Approach to Medical Anthropology

Chapter Goals
- To gain an initial understanding of medical anthropology as a field
- To become familiar with the history of anthropology and its four subdisciplines and how medical anthropology is connected to these subdisciplines
- To gain an understanding of a biocultural approach to health and how it differs from biomedical approaches
- To gain an understanding of how health is related to culture, the environment, human history, and prehistory

You wake up one morning with a headache and the sniffles and swallow a pill composed of an anti-inflammatory, antihistamine, and decongestant. You feel better and are ready to go about your day. Somewhere else, a young girl wakes up behaving oddly; her parents take her to a local diviner, who ascertains that she is possessed by one of the local temperamental goddesses, who is offended by the lack of recent offerings. A friend's grandmother is diagnosed with breast cancer, which is treated by specialized physicians called oncologists who cut out the tumor and subject the remaining tissue to strong radiation while the woman's relatives pray for her. Yet someone else dies hemorrhaging from their orifices, a victim of the lethal Ebola virus, or on a ventilator from COVID19, while a middle-age and otherwise healthy man seeks out a shaman—a practitioner with powers to harness forces of the supernatural—for the loss of his soul. A toddler dies quietly on her sleeping mat while her mother is at work, done in by the combined effects of not enough food and dehydration caused by a bacterial diarrheal disease resulting from her family's lack of access to clean water and food.

How can these diverse experiences be understood? Do they have anything in common? Although the details of each example differ, the experience of suffering is shared by all individuals, and all human societies have methods to diagnose and treat ill health. Indeed, collecting and transmitting knowledge about health and illness has probably characterized human cultures over our entire history as a species.

For better or worse, disease is a human universal. Everyone gets sick, not once but many times during their lives. Yet some people get sick more often or die prematurely, whereas others remain relatively healthy and have long lives. Diseases common in one population may be rare or nonexistent in another. Similarly, attempts to prevent, cure, or lessen the effects of disease also exist in every culture, and these medical traditions exhibit great diversity. Medical anthropologists work to understand the factors influencing variability and universality in health and disease experiences across human populations and across time.

WHAT IS ANTHROPOLOGY?

Anthropology is a discipline that investigates the nature and causes of human variation and those aspects of life that are common to all of humanity. Anthropologists seek to understand similarities and differences in behavior and biology across cultures and populations and how these dimensions change over historical and evolutionary time scales. Hence, all aspects of human behavior, such as language, kinship, economic and political systems, subsistence, religious beliefs, and healing practices, among others, are topics for anthropological research.

As an academic field anthropology has its roots in the early twentieth century, amid colonialism and widespread migration. These processes put exposure to non-Western cultures front and center and raised questions about the scope, causes, and meaning of cultural diversity. Anthropologists took these on as their central questions, and the foundations were laid for contemporary cultural anthropology. It was also recognized that cultural variability coexisted with linguistic and biological diversity, leading to similar types of questions about language and biological variation. Work from the eighteenth and nineteenth centuries on human variation tended to emphasize race (idealized "types" of humans) and the evolution of cultures from simple to complex (Stocking Jr and Stocking 1982).

Anthropology in the United States was substantially reshaped by Franz Boas (1858–1942), a German-born physicist and geographer who immigrated to the United States. During his geographic work in the Arctic, he became intrigued by the lifeways of local peoples and began to advocate for systematic and long-term fieldwork to best understand peoples from different cultures. Boas included language, biology, and archaeology (which provided information on cultural histories) in his research, thus setting the stage for an integrated, holistic anthropology to understand the human condition in its entirety. Moreover, he insisted on rigorous methods and data collection, which informed theories that could be tested by further data collection. This set the standard for ethnographic fieldwork, during which anthropologists would collect data on mythology and tribal lore, religion, social taboos, marriage customs, physical appearance, diet, handicrafts, means of obtaining food, etc.

One of Boas's major contributions was the concept of **cultural relativism**, which means that cultures must not be evaluated in relation to another that is judged superior (which was often "Western" civilization), but rather understood or "made sense of" on their own terms. In other words, he did not view cultural change as a progression from "primitive" to "civilized" or peoples whose society differed from Europeans as inferior. Instead, he saw them as uniquely adapted to their own particular circumstances, a concept that applied to biology, culture, and language. This was a critical point, and anthropology has become a discipline known for overturning views of racial and cultural superiority/inferiority (for a recent insightful book on Boas and his students, see King 2019).

The burden of collecting multiple kinds of data that required training in numerous methodologies and analytic techniques ultimately led to specializations within the field of anthropology, and four distinct subfields emerged: cultural, linguistic, biological, and archaeological anthropology. These subfields can be found in most contemporary American four-field anthropology departments. Briefly, cultural anthropologists study human behavior in the context of societies, their traditions, and their institutions, whereas linguistic anthropologists focus on language, including its evolution,

FIGURE 1.1   Ale

Alexandra Brewis (right) is a biocultural anthropologist who investigates how stigma, poverty, and other social exclusions complicate and undermine global health efforts. She has conducted long-term fieldwork in the islands of the Pacific, in Mexico, and across the United States. Her research in the last decade has focused on how stigma worsens global efforts to address obesity and chronic disease, as well as those to bring safe water and sanitation to low-resource communities. Most recently she has been working with public health experts at Haramaya University in eastern Ethiopia to understand how water insecurity, food insecurity, disease, and stigma interact and compound each other. Here she is with her Ethiopian colleagues, testing electronic blood pressure monitors about to be deployed in a longitudinal study of 5,000 rural Ethiopian households. *Credit:* Photo courtesy of Alex Brewis.

structure, social uses and its relationship to cognition. Archaeologists study material remains to understand the behavior of past populations in both the prehistoric and historic periods. Biological anthropologists are concerned with human biology and how and why humans are biologically similar or different across groups. They also seek to understand how humans are similar to or different from other species (especially those most closely related to humans, the primates) and how humans have changed biologically over the past hundreds, thousands, or millions of years.

Regardless of their area of specialization, anthropologists are united by a comparative perspective—whether it be across cultures, time periods, or species. This allows anthropologists to understand and appreciate the many ways in which humans vary and at the same time ascertain the characteristics that humans share. Furthermore, anthropology as a field is committed to understanding the "whole" of the human experience, or "humankind in all of its aspects." Although not all anthropologists engage in scholarship that is explicitly holistic, many work collaboratively and adopt theories and methods from other subdisciplines in their research. A focus on a particular topic is one of the most useful ways to employ this holistic approach, and health is one such topic. Anthropologists studying health/disease often find it useful to understand the underlying biology, psychological aspects, its relationship to the natural environment or how it arises under certain social conditions, or how cultural behavior impacts risk or treatment. Understanding all of these aspects may require familiarity with research in other disciplines, or collaborations with other scholars from within or beyond anthropology.

THE DEVELOPMENT OF MEDICAL ANTHROPOLOGY

Anthropologists working in the early twentieth century often collected data on health and described healing traditions and concepts of disease causation as well as their relationship to religious beliefs and local medical systems, including knowledge of the medicinal properties of plants or animals. Furthermore, many early anthropological investigations in non-Western or tribal societies were conducted by physicians involved in colonial health care (see Chapter 9 for further discussion), and they gravitated to the study of these health-related aspects of culture. By the mid-twentieth century, especially during World War II and its aftermath, there was growing employment of anthropologists to better understand the health and nutrition of populations in the United States and abroad, not only to ascertain the "fitness" of Americans for war but also to address the wretched health conditions and lack of public health infrastructure faced by countries newly independent from their colonial rulers. With the creation of the World Health Organization in 1948, anthropologists were hired to help understand (and break down) "cultural barriers" to health promotion campaigns and craft ones that were more "culturally appropriate" (Castro and Farmer 2007), and they often served an important role in countering the prevailing public health views that resistance to biomedical interventions was the result of ignorance, superstition, or stubbornness that needed to be overcome among non-Western populations. George Foster, one of the major figures in the founding of medical anthropology, worked with international public health organizations to demonstrate the utility of anthropological knowledge to enhance the efficacy of any health intervention, be it admonitions to "boil water" or accept vaccinations.

Foster's colleague, Benjamin Paul, argued in his 1955 book of anthropological analyses of successful and failed health interventions, "If you wish to help a community improve its health, you must learn to think like people of that community. Before asking that community to assume new health habits it is wise to ascertain the existing habits, how these habits are linked to one another, what functions they perform, and what they mean to those who practice them" (Paul 1955, 1). For example, in Edward Wellin's contribution to the book he describes resistance to using boiled water among residents of a Peruvian village. Although this may seem like a reasonable intervention, the health worker's attempts to get villagers to boil water were often met with resistance, despite public health lectures about the health benefits of doing so. Wellin was able to ascertain the cultural logic of this resistance: water was needed during the heat of midday and needed to be cool by that time, yet the only time available for boiling it was after breakfast, when women were busy with other tasks. Access to fuels needed for boiling were scarce, and the village's relative isolation often resulted in suspicion of outsiders and their ideas, although in this case the health worker was generally well liked. Others rejected the idea that there were invisible waterborne germs that could cause disease. As some villagers commented, "There are enough *real* threats in the world—'cold' and 'airs' and poverty and hunger—without bothering oneself with animals that one cannot see, hear, touch, or smell" (Wellin 1955, 92). In other words, what may have appeared to be "irrational beliefs" by villagers were made sense of by an anthropologist who had taken the time to ascertain how this new public health message related to other established priorities, beliefs, and behaviors.

Medical anthropology in the mid-twentieth century centered around two different, although related, topics: **ethnomedicine**, including formal medical systems with written treatises and training institutions as well as those of smaller-scale or tribal groups that were passed down through oral traditions, and **international health**. In other words, from its inception, medical anthropology had an academic mission as well as an applied one, with the latter focusing on efforts to enhance health across human populations through more effective policies and interventions. In 1970 the Society for Medical Anthropology was formed as a section of the American Anthropological Association, and it is now one of the largest of these sections, with many subsidiary interest groups. Medical anthropology is also well represented in the Society for Applied Anthropology, and many medical anthropologists continue the tradition of working with national, international, and nongovernmental organizations in designing, implementing, and evaluating health programs.

WHAT IS MEDICAL ANTHROPOLOGY?

So, what is this field and what are its objectives for the twenty-first century? **Medical anthropology** is the study of health, illness, health care, and related topics from a broad anthropological perspective. More specifically, the Society for Medical Anthropology defines medical anthropology this way:

> Medical Anthropology is a subfield of anthropology that draws upon social, cultural, biological, and linguistic anthropology to better understand those factors which influence health and well-being (broadly defined), the experience and distribution of illness, the prevention and treatment of sickness, healing processes, the social relations of

therapy management, and the cultural importance and utilization of pluralistic medical systems. The discipline of medical anthropology draws upon many different theoretical approaches. It is as attentive to popular health culture as bioscientific epidemiology, and the social construction of knowledge and politics of science as scientific discovery and hypothesis testing. Medical anthropologists examine how the health of individuals, larger social formations, and the environment are affected by interrelationships between humans and other species; cultural norms and social institutions; micro and macro politics; and forces of globalization as each of these affects local worlds. (Society for Medical Anthropology, 2017)

Medical anthropologists investigate health and disease experience, comparing and contrasting sociocultural situations to illuminate the underlying causes of variation or similarity. What factors contribute to differences in disease patterns or to variation in responses to disease? There are many possibilities: social arrangements, living conditions, subsistence practices, economic resources, hygiene, gender roles, religious practices, access to medical institutions or healers; ecological conditions such as climate, altitude, aridity, plants and animals in an environment; biological factors such as genes, nutritional status, immunological competence, age, or sex; and many others.

FIGURE 1.2 The anthropologist Virginia Vitzthum (center) studies reproductive health in the Bolivian Andes. She is the director of Project REPA (Reproduction and Ecology in Provincia Aroma), a longitudinal study of reproductive functioning and health in the rural Bolivian highlands. The project's main purpose is to test hypotheses regarding the environmental, behavioral, and biological determinants of variation in fertility (e.g., reproductive hormone levels, the probability of conception, the probability of pregnancy loss). This is the first study in any population to have investigated reproductive functioning in women at the peak of their fecundity (their 20s and 30s) and again 14 years later as they experience the perimenopausal transition. Here she is pictured with her long-term collaborator, Esperanza Caceres, and one of the women who participated in her study.
Credit: Photo courtesy of Virginia J. Vitzthum.

The list above is long and wide-ranging—which factors are most important? That depends on the specific health condition and on the context because each community has a unique combination of cultural, economic, ecological, and biological characteristics. Even within a group whose members live in the same basic natural environment and are biologically similar, both subtle and more obvious behavioral differences contribute to health disparities. For example, there may be occupational variation that leads to different risk of job-related accidents, exposure to toxic chemicals, or infectious diseases. These may correlate with economic status or ethnicity. Or, it might be that there are groups with similar cultural attributes who live at slightly different altitudes or with access to different natural resources (water, marine resources, woodlands, pasturage, etc.), which, in turn, contribute to variation in disease vulnerability. Finally, groups with evolutionary histories that have resulted in genetic variations can have similar behavioral patterns and live in the same place but face a different array of disorders that derive from these genetic variations. Thus, it is important to consider the broadest range of possible factors to ascertain which are the most significant contributors to variation in health within or between groups. Comparative analysis highlights the ways in which different combinations of factors affect health, whether they are local social processes or configurations, a population's evolutionary history, or whether there are universalities that stem from a common evolutionary history or forces of capitalism or globalization.

THE CULTURE CONCEPT

Patterns of behavior that are common to a group are referred to as **culture**, a key concept in anthropology. Culture includes the beliefs, values, practices, and traditions of behavior of a group. These include subsistence and economic practices, social organization, rituals, diets, and healing practices, among many others. It is important to recognize that although many aspects of cultural behavior persist over generations (and thus are referred to as "traditions"), culture is not static. Instead, it is dynamic and creative, changing and reforming in a historical and geographic context, as its members simultaneously enact and change it through their unique experiences and behaviors.

To adequately understand the complexities of culture, anthropologists often engage in long-term fieldwork in a society. This is called **ethnographic fieldwork**, (*ethnography* refers to the systematic description of human culture). Fieldwork often requires residing in a community, speaking the local language, and participating in daily life as a member of that community, as Boas urged back in the early twentieth century. **Participant-observation**—the active participation in social and cultural life along with open-minded, non-judgmental observation of a group's behavior—is a hallmark of this kind of research. Participant-observation provides both an insider's and an outsider's perspective. The insider's view is referred to as an **emic** perspective, which is that of members of the society. An emic account is how a member of the group would describe or interpret the behavior of group members. In contrast, an **etic** viewpoint is that of an outsider, observing behavior as if from a distance and with no prior knowledge about its emic meaning.

One way in which medical anthropologists explore the "emic" and "etic" perspectives is through definitions of health (discussed further in Chapter 2). For example, Naomi Adelson, a medical anthropologist who has worked extensively with the Cree, an indigenous population of northern Canada, describes how the Cree use the term *"miyu-pimaatisiiun"* to describe health, more accurately translated as "being alive well" (Adelson 2000). Being alive well encompasses protection from the cold, physical activity, and eating distinctively Cree bush foods, which come from hunting and gathering. Thus, it more broadly references the quality of the land that provides them with this food, their history, and the social relations that supported their livelihoods as hunters. In the context of political struggles over land rights and incursions of "white man's foods" in local stores, *miyupimaatisiiun* is difficult to achieve. An etic description of health among the Cree might include standard biomedical measures such as levels of cholesterol, body mass index, or prevalence of hypertension, but an emic description in this context provides a richer understanding of how the Cree view their health, or state of being alive well. There are many such examples within the field of medical anthropology.

Anthropologists thus have a unique dual perspective that allows them to describe and understand the emic worldview but also allows for cross-cultural analysis. In practice, separation of these two perspectives is not easily maintained, nor is it necessarily desirable. Anthropologists are drawn into intracultural dynamics and bring to the

FIGURE 1.3   The medical anthropologist Bill Dressler (right) with a family in Brazil. Dr. Dressler studies the cultural dimensions of stress and stress-related diseases. He has developed an important model in wide use in medical anthropology called cultural consonance, which predicts that stress results in individuals who do not conform to prevailing cultural ideals or who cannot attain cultural norms because of economic or other constraints. He has also contributed in key ways to discussions of the utility of ethnicity, race, or culture as variables in public health research and policy making. He is currently overseeing a project in Brazil on the relationship among cultural consonance, depression, and genetic variation in serotonin receptors. *Credit:* Photo courtesy of M.C. Balieiro.

ethnographic encounter their own set of biases that preclude an objective view; they also bring with them a status (e.g., foreign, economic, ethnic, gender) that influences the way people interact with them. For example, it is not unusual for anthropologists working in cultures with limited access to Western medical care to be asked for help in treating common ailments. Anthropologists can thus become part of a complex cultural dynamic that is altered to some extent by their participation.

Careful observation of behavior within a community makes it possible to ascertain local patterns of disease, their likely causes, and the ways in which people respond to threats to their well-being. These are likely to depend, in part, on the environment in which they live, which can be described in part by *abiotic* (physical, climatic) and *biotic* (living forms) features that constitute part of the context for local disease patterns. Aridity and humidity, presence of fresh water, seasonality in temperature and light cycles, barometric pressure, and local flora and fauna, to name a few, are important in determining what kinds of health problems are likely to be faced by the population. However, the extent to which these factors actually impact health is related to how the population interacts with them, which in turn are strongly influenced by cultural practices that play out within socioeconomic structures. Thus, although ecological conditions play an important role in disease, they are never the sole determinant of disease in a population.

A BIOCULTURAL PERSPECTIVE

In this book we take a **biocultural perspective** on health, which considers the social, ecological, and biological aspects of health issues and how they interact within and across populations. It is a uniquely anthropological and holistic view of health, incorporating these different aspects of the human experience. Ecological conditions include the natural environments in which humans live. The social world includes all of the human modifications of those environments and the social institutions that form the structure of social life; these in turn have been shaped by historical processes. The body has also been shaped by a history—an evolutionary history—during which it has been molded by changing environmental conditions. Thus, a full biocultural analysis considers the global and local historical processes that have given rise to current health problems. This is, of course, an enormous project, and researchers often find that some aspects are more relevant to the topic at hand than others. Furthermore, a biocultural approach is but one of several that medical anthropologists bring to the study of health. Although this approach tries to be broadly holistic in its consideration of both biology and culture as important to health, many medical anthropologists focus their analysis on the sociocultural factors affecting health.

Human bodies, culture, and history have complex interactive relationships. For example, not all individuals are equally at risk of disease, despite location in a similar cultural context. Why is this? As noted earlier, it is partly the result of genetic and behavioral characteristics that are unique to individuals and that derive from their unique life histories and genealogies. Furthermore, to get beyond the simple exercise of "cultural feature *X* increases or decreases the risk of disease *Y*," it is useful to ask these questions: *Why* this particular disease? *Why* this particular cultural factor? These questions, like those pertaining to individual-level variation, require a more historical view. Biocultural

FIGURE 1.4 The applied medical anthropologist Crystal Patil (second from left) celebrating with a family in Tanzania. As a Fulbright-Hays fellow, Dr. Patil conducted biocultural ethnographic research in rural Tanzania that allowed her to deeply understand household health and the various ways that families access health systems. She learned about pregnancy, women's work, childbirth, food, and infant and child feeding, as well as the joys and difficulties of women's lives. From on this foundational experience, her research path went in an applied direction. Currently, she is a professor in the College of Nursing at the University of Illinois at Chicago and the principal investigator on an NIH-funded study assessing whether group prenatal care improves maternal, infant, and family health outcomes. This study is both a clinical trial with individual level randomization and a close examination of the contextual factors affecting implementation processes in Blantyre District, Malawi. She plans to expand this group healthcare model to include postpartum and well-baby care.
Credit: Photo courtesy of Crystal Patil.

analysis is inherently historical, seeking the roots of cultural behavior. At the same time biocultural analysis employs a longer-term evolutionary perspective that considers the forces that have shaped human biology and population biological variation. Given the intrinsic biocultural nature of health and disease, cultural, historical, and evolutionary factors must be taken into consideration.

Biocultural analysis considers the individual body as a starting point. In many ways, human bodies are similar, but they also vary tremendously in the particulars. Some of this variation is patterned across populations, but even within populations there is a great deal of diversity. Just as the anatomy of individuals is visibly different, so is the anatomy of the organs, which are only visible through imaging techniques. As Roger Williams (1956) so elegantly demonstrated in his book *Biochemical Individuality*, individuals differ in their biochemical processes, nutritional requirements, and internal

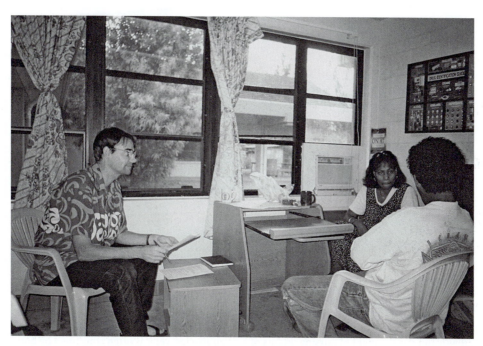

FIGURE 1.5   The anthropologist Roger Sullivan (left) studies mental health in Palau, Micronesia. Here, he and a social worker interview a patient. His work is discussed further in Chapter 11. *Credit:* Photo courtesy of Roger Sullivan.

anatomy. Although individual variation is interesting and it is important to never lose sight of its significance to individual health and clinical practice, it is not something that anthropological analyses frequently address. After all, anthropologists are more interested in group-level health phenomena.

One of the first tasks of medical anthropology is to define health in a way that both acknowledges different cultural models of health and allows for comparative analysis. Disease processes alter biological function in more or less predictable and measurable ways. Although populations differ in their patterns of health conditions, the way maladies unfold physiologically is fairly consistent even though there is variability in individual experience. In a biocultural analysis, it is possible to make use of these regularities, which are well described in the biomedical literature. Hence, there are some intersections between the biocultural approach and that taken by **biomedicine**. Biomedicine developed out of the scientific tradition in eighteenth-century Europe; as such, it is a medical system that arose out of a particular cultural context. It views disease as having a unique biological cause within the body, whether it be a microorganism causing infection, the growth of malignant cells, the deficiency of a nutrient, or the failure of an organ because of repeated insults (such as alcohol consumption). It has a well-developed and widely applicable set of diagnostic criteria used to describe a large number of disease states that are codified in the International Classification of Diseases (ICD), which is maintained by the World Health Organization (WHO) (https://www.who.int/classifications/icd/en).

FIGURE 1.6 The medical anthropologist Andrea Wiley studies the impact of cow's milk consumption on different aspects of child growth in the United States and India. She is interested in how milk might have some unusual effects on human biology, given that it is produced for calves, not humans. Furthermore, milk is produced by mammals specifically to support the growth and development of nursing infants of a given species, yet it is often consumed by both children and adults. She is also concerned with how milk drinking came to be a normative part of childhood diets in many parts of the world and how ideas about milk's relationship to child growth inform peoples' decisions to feed their children cow's milk. Her work also investigates the well-described variation in the ability to digest milk in adulthood across human populations, and how this intersects with widespread promotion of this food for individuals of all ages. Her work is discussed further in Chapters 4 and 5.
Crdit: Photo courtesy of Richard Lippke.

Biocultural analyses most often utilize biomedical categories of disease as a standard that can be used for cross-population comparison of health and disease. It is extremely important to have some sort of common standard by which to do comparative analysis precisely because understandings of health and disease vary significantly across cultures. Thus, although a syndrome that is well described by one culture may have no apparent analogue in another, a biocultural approach to disease that employs local cultural models and biomedical measures may nonetheless be used to frame a comparative analysis. That said, it is important to note that biocultural approaches differ from those based in biomedicine. Clinical biomedical understandings of disease tend to privilege the body as the only relevant site for understanding disease causation, which gives rise to the view that individuals are uniquely responsible for their health (McKeown 1979). As described previously, a biocultural approach looks beyond the body to its interactions with the social and natural environment to ascertain the broader causes of disease.

LOOKING AHEAD

The chapters of this book are organized around a series of topics central to medical anthropology. Each is presented from a biocultural perspective, highlighting uniquely anthropological insights into these health topics. The basic biology will be presented and then contextualized by the relevant evolutionary, historical, and sociocultural factors that shape it. Our emphasis is on understanding sources of variation in health, both within and between populations, and through time. In addition, the intersections between biocultural and other perspectives in medical anthropology, especially the political economy of health, are emphasized, and we discuss other approaches in medical anthropology in more detail in Chapter 2. The practical implications of this approach to each topic are also addressed—that is, how can this perspective be used in the development of policies to enhance health? Thus, the links between the biocultural approach and interventions to improve health are specified, and starting with Chapter 3, chapters feature the work of an applied anthropologist. We hope that this text illustrates the ways in which medical anthropology, whether practiced in universities, research centers, public health institutions, or nongovernmental or global health organizations, has the potential to help improve the health of populations throughout the world.

STUDY QUESTIONS

1. What is anthropology and how did it become established as a viable field of study?
2. What is medical anthropology and what do medical anthropologists study? How does the history of medical anthropology relate to the history of anthropology as a field?
3. What are the advantages and disadvantages of ethnographic fieldwork as a method for studying human behavior?
4. What are the diverse kinds of information that the biocultural perspective takes into account to explain human health and disease?

CRITICAL THINKING AND DISCUSSION

1. In what ways do you think your own health status is a product of your biology and in what ways is it a product of your culture? Is it possible to make such a distinction?
2. Check out the International Classification of Diseases (ICD) (https://www.who.int/classifications/icd/en). How is disease described? At this initial point, can you think of ways that a biocultural analysis of disease might make use of these descriptions but also offer a different perspective? The WHO website also provides previous versions of the ICD—what are some ways in which they have changed over time?

CHAPTER 2

Anthropological Perspectives on Health and Disease

Chapter Goals
- To understand the concept of health and the challenge of defining it as a universal concept
- To be able to distinguish among disease, illness, and sickness and their relationship to each other
- To understand the concept of adaptation in relation to health and disease
- To become familiar with the major cultural approaches to the study of health
- To become familiar with standard epidemiological concepts and terminology

The term "leper" refers to someone with leprosy (Hansen's disease) or, more generally, to someone who is an outcast, excluded from participation in social life for fear of contamination. Ronald Barrett, a medical anthropologist, describes working with patients with leprosy in India: although their disease is curable (it is caused by the bacterium *Mycobacterium leprae* and treatable with antibiotics) and not particularly contagious, "the social stigma of leprosy furthers its physical stigma, which returns to reinforce individual and collective models of discrimination" (Barrett 2005, 225). In other words, the social consequences of the disease far exceed its biological capacity to harm, especially in the age of antibiotics. Barrett's work with leprosy patients in India reveals how health and disease have meanings that are cultural and biological, and in this chapter we provide some conceptual anthropological and epidemiological tools for understanding health and disease.

DEFINITIONS OF HEALTH

The first task in this survey of medical anthropology is to define concepts of health and disease. It turns out that this is tricky, because health has many dimensions. In a famous pronouncement from the Alma Ata conference in 1978, the World Health

Organization (WHO)—the international organization based in Geneva, Switzerland that oversees health problems and interventions around the world—defined health as *a state of complete social, psychological, and physical well-being.* Although this definition is useful to the WHO, which has the laudable goal of achieving health for all of the world's citizens, it begs the question of what exactly is this state, and is it something that would be universally recognized? That is, does this sense of well-being in one society differ significantly from well-being in another? With respect to physical well-being, for example, having a substantial amount of body fat might be seen as a sign of excellent health in one population but defined as "obesity" and needing medical intervention in another. Depressed behavior may be seen as a cause of hospitalization in one culture but evidence of the power of witchcraft in another. Or, a hemoglobin reading of 17 mg/ dl might be seen at sea level as evidence of polycythemia, a condition in which an individual has too many blood cells and thick blood, whereas at 15,000 feet above sea level the same reading would be evidence of a beneficial adaptation to hypoxia, the relatively low oxygen pressure of high-altitude environments. There is also variation in what constitutes "healthiness" within populations. A body weight considered healthy for a man may be considered overweight for a woman; pregnancy in a 25-year-old woman may be seen as entirely routine, whereas pregnancy in a 45-year-old woman may be considered "risky." Hence the concept and appropriate measure(s) of well-being are specific to, and meaningful within, local conditions.

In research on health, medical anthropologists find it useful to make a distinction among three terms, which are often used interchangeably in popular language: disease, illness, and sickness.

Disease

Disease refers to a physiological alteration that impairs or has the potential to impair function in some way. Descriptions of disease processes largely derive from Western biomedical science. Disease is a more or less "objective" measure of health that should be universally applicable. However, as the earlier hemoglobin example demonstrates, what constitutes "disease" in one environment may in fact enhance function in another. Disease categories are a useful starting point because they describe alterations in biology and physiological function, but it is important to be careful about ascribing them the same meaning across populations and environments.

Here we list some common disease types and their causes. Most of these are not unique to humans, and several may co-occur simultaneously or derive from interactions among causes.

1. *Injury.* All organisms are vulnerable to injury or damage to some part of the anatomy as a function of random accidents, living in a dangerous environment (on a cliff, in a neighborhood with many hazards), behavior that increases the risk (driving recklessly, consuming a lot of alcohol), or some combination thereof (having a job in a factory working with heavy machinery).
2. *Infection.* Infectious disease derives from microorganisms that spread from one individual to another and compromise function in some way. Infectious diseases can be caused by viruses, bacteria, protozoa, or multicellular organisms (such as worms) and vary from those that cause relatively little harm (such as

rhinoviruses that cause the common cold) to those that cause permanent disability (such as the Zika virus) or that are potentially fatal (such as malaria. Anthrax, or COVID-19).

3. *Malnutrition.* These are physiological disorders that stem from the lack or surfeit of nutrients, including vitamins, minerals, carbohydrates, protein, and fat. A lack of food in general contributes to protein-energy malnutrition, and micronutrient deficiencies can contribute to specific disorders (e.g., scurvy from vitamin C deficiency). In contrast, long-term overconsumption can contribute to chronic diseases such as diabetes, cardiovascular disease, and some forms of cancer.

4. *Genetic.* In the process of sexual reproduction, **mutations** may occur in the formation of egg or sperm. These mutations can ultimately create alterations in fetal development or contribute to some forms of impairment after birth. Any given genetic disorder occurs relatively rarely at the rate of mutation (often estimated at about 1 in 10,000 genes), but may become more common when passed down in reproductively isolated and inbred populations or when the disorder confers some other biological benefit, as in the case of sickle-cell hemoglobin, which seems to protect against deadly forms of malaria.

5. *Chronic.* Some forms of chronic disease stem from genetic factors, but most result from lifelong behaviors. Included in this category is cardiovascular disease, which is related to long-term dietary and activity patterns, cancers such as those related to smoking or exposure to toxic compounds, and type II diabetes, which is in many cases related to long-term overconsumption, lack of activity, or both. Importantly, these forms of disease are by and large absent in wild-living organisms, although they do manifest in domesticated pets or zoo animals. They are also relatively absent from human populations engaged in subsistence agriculture or hunting and gathering. Many diseases can be chronic, such as allergies (immune responses to benign foreign substances) or autoimmune disorders (immune responses to one's own body tissues), or be long lasting if not effectively treated.

6. *Psychological or behavioral.* These forms of disease are also relatively absent from wild organisms, but they have come to be common among humans in industrialized societies. Depression, anxiety, and attention deficit disorder, among others, are increasingly diagnosed in countries such as the United States. These complex disorders are caused by many factors, both biological and social, that are incompletely understood. They increasingly are treated with medications that alter the balance of neurotransmitters such as serotonin in the brain.

As is evident from this list, different social environments, patterns of behaviors, and ecological conditions all give rise to variation in the risk of any of these disorders across human populations.

Illness

The term "illness" is used to describe the subjective experience of symptoms and suffering, often motivating changes in behavior to alleviate the discomfort (such as altering the diet, resting, or seeking professional help). Arthur Kleinman, a medical anthropologist (see Figure 2.1), distinguishes **illness** from disease in the following way:

> Illness complaints are what patients and their families bring to the practitioner. Indeed, locally shared illness idioms create a common ground for patient and practitioners to understand each other in their initial encounter. For the practitioner, too, has been socialized into a particular collective experience of illness. Disease, however, is what the practitioner creates in the recasting of illness in terms of theories of disorder. (Kleinman 1988, 5)

The subjective experience of suffering is informed by an individual's cultural context; that is, there are culturally specific and culturally appropriate ways of being ill and expressing that experience. In a successful therapeutic encounter, there is a close match between the articulation of illness and the diagnosis of disease. However, in many cases, the fit may not be good. The clinician may fail to find objective evidence of disease or declare a diagnosis that reflects an incomplete resolution of the patient's complaints. In other words, a patient may present his or her "illness problem" and receive the diagnosis that "nothing is wrong." Conversely, a person feeling well (i.e., not exhibiting illness behavior) might, through a chance clinical encounter, discover that he or she has a serious disease, such as a symptomless early-stage cancer.

Because illness reflects a set of individually experienced symptoms of discomfort, the disease diagnosis may not fully—or even partially—resolve these feelings. As Kleinman noted, "When chest pain is reduced to chronic coronary artery disease for which calcium blockers and nitroglycerine are prescribed, while the patient's fear, the

FIGURE 2.1   Medical Anthropologist and Psychiatrist Arthur Kleinman.
Credit: Photo courtesy of Arthur Kleinman /©Torben Eskerod.

Anthropologist in Action: Arthur Kleinman

The medical anthropologist Arthur Kleinman holds an M.D. and a master's degree in anthropology. He is a professor of psychiatry, as well as a professor of medical anthropology, at Harvard University and has made fundamental contributions to the field of medical anthropology, while maintaining a psychiatric practice until recently. Dr. Kleinman has worked in the United States and has carried out extensive research in Taiwan and China. He has been active as a consultant for the WHO, working on global mental health issues as well as issues related to infectious diseases, such as SARS and AIDS.

In his early work, Dr. Kleinman developed the concept of the explanatory model—what individuals construct to interpret and "make sense" of their experience of maladies, describing them in what he called "illness narratives" (Kleinman 1988). These illness narratives and explanatory models stem not only from an individual's cultural context but also from his or her own life history, family and community, and belief systems. In an article outlining the relevance of these models for clinical practice, Kleinman, Eisenberg, and Good (1978) suggest asking: (1) What do you think has caused your problem? (2) Why do you think it started when it did? (3) What do you think your sickness does to you? How does it work? (4) How severe is your sickness? Will it have a short or long course? (5) What kind of treatment do you think you should receive? (6) What are the most important results you hope to receive from this treatment? (7) What do you fear most about your sickness? What are the chief problems your sickness has caused for you?

In this work and throughout his career, Kleinman has been concerned with improving the doctor–patient relationship to best alleviate not only the physiological symptoms of disease but also the multiple social dimensions of patient suffering. As a psychiatrist, he has seen how the "routine" health crises that people inevitably face (for themselves or

loved ones) often precipitate a medical diagnosis (depression or anxiety), yet he argues that the moral issues that suffering brings to the fore should not be medicalized or turned into "disease" (see Q&A with Arthur Kleinman, *The Boston Globe*, July 23, 2006).

In recent years, Kleinman has turned to the consideration of how caregiving must be fully integrated into medical education, such that the diagnostic/technological aspects of medicine are not cleaved from the humanistic and moral aspects of patient care. As he writes,

> I do believe that what doctors need to be helped to master is the art of acknowledging and affirming the patient as a suffering human being; imagining alternative contexts and practices for responding to calamity; and conversing with and supporting patients in desperate situations where the emphasis is on what really matters to the patient and his or her intimates. . . . The implementation of useful programmes will require parallel attention to the structural and cultural barriers that undermine caregiving in practice settings so as to encourage the experience of caregiving as core to the professional and personal life of the doctor. This will also mean that students and practitioners acquire those interpretive skills of critical self-reflection that enable them to understand and respond to all those barriers that cause doctors to fail at the art of healing. (Kleinman 2008, 23)

This concern with care is taken up in his new memoir *The Soul of Care* (2019), in which he reflects on his own training as a physician in relation to his personal experience as a long-term caregiver of his wife, who suffered from early-onset Alzheimer's disease.

---

family's frustration, the job conflict, the sexual impotence, and the financial crisis go undiagnosed and unaddressed, it [the disease diagnosis and treatment] is unsuccessful" (Kleinman 1988, 6). Hence, a focus on disease is often considered reductionist; that is, it reduces the illness experience to a physiological locus. Treatment of an identifiable disease may or may not resolve the experience of illness, either for patients or for their loved ones. Illness is closely tied to the sense of well-being, as the WHO definition of health indicates, and there are psychological, social, and physical aspects of illness that must be addressed to achieve health. Illness is thus a more holistic concept than disease because it links the individual, his or her lived experience, cultural orientation, and social environment.

Sickness

Sickness is another term that is used in relation to health. Sometimes it is equated with disease, illness, or both, but it has a sociological meaning as well. Talcott Parsons, a famous medical sociologist, coined the phrase the "**sick role.**" What Parsons meant is that there is a socially recognized set of expectations for "sick" individuals (Parsons 1979). These expectations may include being exempt from occupational work, household tasks, or the other obligations expected of "well" individuals. To be able to take on the sick role, one must have an illness that is recognized as legitimate by the social group. Legitimacy may require documentation by a health expert, such as a clinician. Doctor's notes are often required in industrialized societies to exempt a person from work or to allow him or her to receive what is called in the United States "worker's compensation," financial compensation for wages missed while the worker is sick. Given that an individual can benefit from assuming the sick role, it can be abused. Among students, it is not uncommon for sickness to be used as an excuse for missing assigned work or an examination; documentation from a clinician is often required to legitimize the excuse.

Although in these contexts adopting the sick role provides some relief from obligations, the sick role may also be associated with stigma, which in turn triggers additional suffering. Afflicted individuals may be avoided or even ostracized, especially when the symptoms are visible, as in the case of leprosy. In her 1978 book *Illness as Metaphor*, Susan Sontag (who died of cancer in 2004) discussed the ways in which cancer is perceived as mysterious and generates fear, such that patients may be "shunned by relatives and friends and are the object of practices of decontamination by members of their household, as if cancer, like TB, were an infectious disease. . . . [Cancer] is felt to be obscene—in the original meaning of that word: ill-omened, abominable, repugnant to the senses" (Sontag 1978, 6, 9). In this case, individuals with cancer may not wish to take on the sick role out of fear of being stigmatized.

In the sick role, the distinction between illness and disease becomes relevant. In societies such as the United States where biomedically trained clinicians have authority in health matters, clinical evidence of a disease often must be presented to authenticate a patient's claim to the sick role. If not, the sick role may not be legitimated, even if the person continues to complain of feeling unwell. In most, if not all, societies, healers may need to "vet" a person's health status if he or she is to continue in a sick role, exempt from normal responsibilities.

These are useful terminological distinctions to make, but they do not answer the question of what defines health. Disease, illness, and sickness are all related to the WHO's definition of "social, psychological, and physical well-being." They are each an important aspect of health and point to the fact that health cannot simply be defined as the *absence* of disease, illness, or sickness. However, many people may not have a sense of complete well-being, but would not classify themselves as ill or seek the sick role or the services of a healer. For example, a person who is chronically sleep deprived because of the demands of work or an overactive social life may not feel particularly well but is unlikely to seek medical attention. Under these conditions, a person is able to carry out his or her normal functions, albeit with the sense that all is not as well as it could be. So, perhaps health is better described as being able to carry out normal functions to one's satisfaction. Only when the routines of "normal" life are disrupted by an increasing or acute sense of "dis-ease" does a person recognize that he or she is suffering from poor health.

In the WHO definition of health, "social well-being" is specifically included. What does this mean? In one society it may mean being inextricably embedded in a complex network of kin relations; in others it may mean autonomy or self-reliance. For the patients with Hansen's disease in India, social well-being was severely eroded through discrimination and permanent untouchable status, even after they were cured of the disease. They both continued in the sick role and expressed illness symptoms, even going so far as to further disfigure themselves as the physical confirmation of their internal suffering (Barrett 2005). Another example comes from the work of Naomi Adelson with the Cree described in Chapter 1. Adelson notes that "Of course, the ideals that comprise 'being alive well' (*miyupimaatisiiun*) cannot always be met, and one may then not 'be alive well.' This does not always necessarily imply a pathological condition of the individual, however, so much as it might of society" (Adelson 1998, 11). The Cree recognize that being alive well is not merely about the absence of an individual pathology; it involves the integrity of a whole society and way of life.

If you are used to thinking about health as having an exclusively bodily locus, it may seem odd to consider social well-being as an aspect of health. Indeed, for biocultural analysis, the body is often the focus of investigation. Yet as anthropologists understand and as other social and medical scientists are increasingly aware, social networks seem to have a great deal of relevance to health. People with well-developed sources of social support often get sick less, recover faster, or live longer than those with less support. A review of 148 studies encompassing more than 300,000 participants showed that having strong social support networks of various kinds resulted in a significant increase in the likelihood of survival (Holt-Lunstad et al. 2010). As Figure 2.2 shows, overall there was a 50% increase in odds of survival among individuals with stronger social relationships. Multidimensional assessments of social integration that included supportive social interactions and perceptions of social support (i.e., "functional" social support) as well as integration in social networks ("structural" social support) resulted in a 91% increase in the odds of survival. Figure 2.2 illustrates that the magnitude of the effect of social support on survival is potentially greater than that of well-known risk factors such as smoking, body mass index, or physical activity, among others. The results were consistent across adult ages, gender, initial health status, follow-up period, and cause of death.

THE LOCUS OF HEALTH: THE BODY AND SOCIETY

In a seminal paper in *Medical Anthropology Quarterly*, Nancy Scheper-Hughes and Margaret Lock (1987) argued that there are three bodies to be considered in the analysis of health and disease: the individual body, the social body, and the body politic. The *individual body* ("self") has been privileged in Western biomedical praxis as the sole locus of disease. A separation of the mind and body, the legacy of Rene Descartes's attempt to separate the "intangible mind" from the material body, has resulted in the latter being privileged over the mind in the search for the cause of a particular ailment. The extent to which people recognize social or psychological phenomena to be aspects of health is highly variable across cultures.

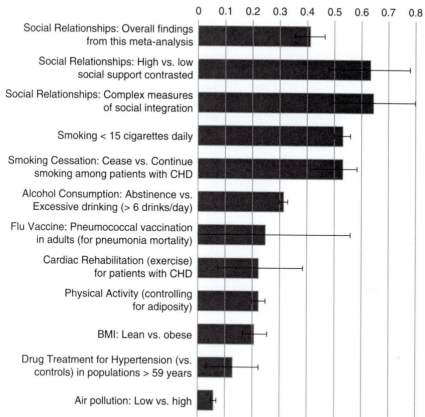

FIGURE 2.2   Comparison of odds of decreased mortality across several conditions associated with mortality. Zero indicates no effect.
Source: Holt-Lunstad J, Smith TB, Layton JB (2010) Social relationships and mortality risk: A meta-analytic review. PLoS Med 7(7): e1000316. doi:10.1371/journal. pmed.1000316.

Health, Ethics, and Cultural Relativism

The WHO's definition of health as a state of complete social, psychological, and physical well-being raises some ethical questions for medical anthropologists. One of the hallmarks of anthropology is the concept of "cultural relativism"—the idea that the elements of each culture must be understood on their own terms, without judgements based on norms derived from other cultures. However, if a particular practice (such as female genital cutting or maternal detachment from their infants, as discussed in Chapter 6) is physically harmful, yet enhances a person's social or psychological well-being, is this practice "healthy?" If it is accepted that a universal component of well-being is freedom from physical pain and suffering, but also that well-being encompasses social and mental attributes, what is an appropriate medical

anthropological interpretation or action? There is no clear answer to this question, and medical anthropologists take a variety of stances. Some use their research as a way of helping to understand these paradoxes; others adopt a "harm reduction" approach, and work to find ways to reduce or minimize physical suffering while preserving the cultural meanings or integrity of a practice; others seek to effect cultural change, regardless of what social benefits might come from physical suffering; still others use their writing to bring these complexities to a broader audience, including policy makers.

One important anthropological contribution is to bring to light the ways in which health is not evenly distributed across cultures and to clarify the ways in which local culture

(*continued*)

(continued)

is implicated in improving or worsening health and the ways in which larger political and economic forces contribute to health differentials. As Paul Farmer (2001) has argued, it should not be assumed that poor health is somehow an intrinsic part of a culture, such that there is little to be done about it without "disrupting" cultural integrity. Instead, medical anthropological analyses should elucidate the various local, historical, and more global factors that contribute to variation in health across cultures. As Farmer notes, what people with poor health tend to have in common around the world is poverty; despite very different cultural attributes, the common denominator to low life expectancy or high infant mortality, for example, is being at the low end of the economic hierarchy (this is covered in more detail in Chapter 10). Moreover, just because biomedicine is derived from Western culture (suggesting that its introduction might undermine local ethnomedical traditions) does not mean that it cannot be extremely effective in treating many diseases, and such resources should be made universally accessible.

Whether social or other forms of external forces (e.g., supernatural) are recognized as valid causes of illness or disease is also highly variable. Scheper-Hughes and Lock described the *social body* as the seam between the physical body and the social world of the individual. The ills of society may be inscribed on the body via disease; individual wellness in turn may be, at least in part, reflective of a harmonious social world. A society rife with social divisions, inequality, or conflict harms individual health (e.g., via stress, increased exposure to infection, or violence); in contrast, well-integrated or egalitarian societies should generate improved health for their members (see Chapter 10; Marmot 2015; Pickett and Wilkinson 2015). Lastly, the *body politic* refers to the ways in which social and political forces exert control over the bodies of individuals in a society and thereby constrain opportunities for optimal health for all.

Considering health in relation to all three "bodies" makes clear the ways that individual health is connected to larger social conditions and how individuals come to "embody" the conditions of their social worlds. **Embodiment** refers to the ways in which the environment in which humans live leaves sometimes quite profound traces in human biology, or alters biological development in children. In the context of biomedicine, it is fair to say that health has come to be exclusively the concern of medical practitioners and its links to larger social phenomena are not made explicit (Farmer 2001). Indeed, in biomedicine, as well as in other medical traditions, there is a tendency to medicalize conditions that have clear social roots. **Medicalization** refers to the defining of a condition as a disease, or in need of medical surveillance. It often occurs in situations in which medicine and medical practitioners have social and cultural authority or when there is resistance to seeing health as closely tied to social conditions.

Pregnancy and childbirth, which can certainly be considered intrinsic to the female life cycle, are good examples of life cycle processes that have been medicalized over the twentieth century. It is widely held that pregnancy should be monitored by clinicians and that birth should occur in hospitals (see Chapter 6). Similarly, depression, which in many cases is related to an individual's satisfaction with his or her life and social network, has come to be considered predominantly a biological disease and is treated accordingly with pharmaceuticals (see Chapter 11, as well as the box about Arthur Kleinman). How social forces increase the risk of such conditions is often not explicit in the biomedical literature, although it is widely appreciated by epidemiologists (e.g. Marmot 2017a), and the focus turns toward how to best "treat" these diseases. Thus, ills of the social body come to be treated as diseases of the individual body. This may result in inappropriate or ineffective treatments that sidestep the underlying cause; in other words, the focus is on biomedical *treatment* rather than social policies that might *prevent* the condition, reduce its frequency, or ameliorate suffering from it.

There is an important distinction to be made between a biocultural and a biomedical perspective on disease. Both take the body as their focus and assume that a cause or locus of disease can be found there. But this is a *starting* point for biocultural analysis rather than an *end*point, as it is in biomedicine. A useful distinction between the two is to consider the **proximate** and **ultimate** causes of disease. "Proximate" literally means nearby, and in this case it refers to the immediate cause of some physiological disruption. It could be a bacterial infection that is the proximate cause of a high fever, too little thyroid hormone causing lassitude, or cancer cells growing in the lungs causing shortness of breath. This is where biomedical analysis often stops.

In contrast, biocultural analysis also investigates the more distant or "ultimate" causes of the disease. It asks why—why this individual, in this population, living under a set of household, community, regional, national, or global conditions, each of which has been shaped by historical and evolutionary forces. What factors put the individual at risk for the bacterial infection? Was it the lack of attention to hygiene in a nursing home, and why was the person there to begin with? Was the individual exposed to asbestos in the course of his job as a demolition worker, and how did he end up with that job? Ultimate factors can also be locally defined and include supernatural forces that are believed to cause disease, such as witchcraft, sorcery, or some other form of divine intervention.

BIOLOGICAL NORMALCY

Biocultural analyses (and medical anthropological analyses in general) try to get at these more "distant" or ultimate causes of a malady. They cast a critical eye on Western biomedical definitions of health. The example described earlier of hemoglobin levels in sea-level and high-altitude populations is illustrative of this. Another example is that standards for growth (weight or height-for-age) routinely used in cross-population analysis used to derive from U.S. Centers for Disease Control and Prevention (CDC) growth charts. When used in this way, frequently it appeared that a population being compared with the CDC standards was "failing" to achieve the same age-specific body size. Figure 2.3 compares the CDC charts for growth in weight among boys against the new WHO standards published in 2007. In general, the WHO standards are lower than the CDC standards, especially from ages 6 months to 32 months. The WHO standards are based on healthy children from diverse populations and call into question the CDC standards as the global norm for "optimal" growth (de Onis et al. 2007).That is, contemporary children in the United States may in fact be over-nourished and able to grow at rates that are historically unprecedented, and are now manifesting increasing rates of what used to be considered adult-onset diseases such as diabetes. This specific topic is taken up in more detail in Chapter 4.

A question raised by these examples is: what is biologically *normal*? This is a crucial issue because "normal" tends to be equated with healthy. **Biological normalcy** refers to the ways in which the statistical distributions of biological traits in a population, which include measures of central tendancy and variance such as means, medians, and modes, and standard deviations, are related to normative views about what bodies "should" be like or what people in a given society consider to be a "normal" human body (Wiley and Cullin, 2020). Ideas about what is "normal" are often related to health—i.e. "normal" equals healthy and "abnormal" indicates pathology. Thus, it is crucial to have good evidence supporting a relationship between a trait and an increased or decreased risk of disease (Williams 2000). As the examples above also indicate, both the distribution of a given biological trait and cultural beliefs about that characteristic are likely to vary across societies, and the relationship between the trait and risk of disease may also vary. It is also the case that what people observe around them (i.e. the statistical norm) may influence their ideas about what is "normal" (see examples of obesity and lactose intolerance in Chapter 4). Furthermore, the language that is used to describe variation often reveals the ways that "non-normal" bodies are seen as deviant, problematic, or inferior. This bias has been termed "**ethno-biocentrism**" (Wiley 2016), which refers to the denigration or pathologization of biological variation that doesn't conform to people's beliefs about what is "normal" or "better" human biology.

The concept of biological normalcy can also be applied to conditions for which there is no known cause or cure within a given society, which are thus labeled normal. For example, the dowager's hump, now known to be caused by osteoporosis of the spine, long described a "normal" aspect of aging among women in Western societies. Barbara Mintzes (2002) noted the pernicious effects of direct-to-consumer drug advertising as a

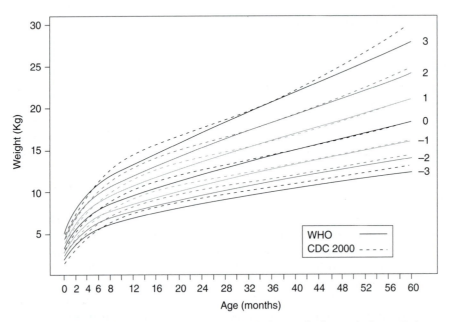

FIGURE 2.3 The CDC and WHO growth standards for weight for age for boys. Units are z scores, which represent deviations from the population mean. Note that the CDC standards are higher at almost every age, but especially so from ages 6 months to 32 months.
Source: de Onis, Mercedes, et al. 2007. "Comparison of the WHO child growth standards and the CDC 2000 growth charts." *J. Nutr* 137:144–148. Reprinted with permission from American Society for Nutrition.

way to encourage individuals who might have considered themselves relatively healthy (i.e., normal) to see themselves as at risk and in need of pharmaceutical treatment.

Thus, although in this book descriptive measures of bodily states (e.g., height, weight, parasite load, blood pressure) are used, their meaning will be subject to investigation, with no prior expectation that they will be associated with the same risks or derive from the same causes across populations or that they are considered problematic within any given society.

The issue of biological normalcy is especially relevant to our understanding of human biological variation. There are some well-known biological differences across human populations, and historically these were understood as aspects of **race**. Races were seen as different "types" of humans, with each type having some unique set of biological characteristics (e.g. skin color, hair form, nose or eye shape, etc.) that differentiated it from others. Anthropologists now understand that these differences are in degrees of frequency rather than simply all members of one population having a trait that is not found in another (the topic of race and health is considered in detail in Chapter 10). Some of these genetic differences can be understood as the outcome of variation in the diseases faced by populations and they therefore have health significance. Thus, to understand the sources of this biological variation among human populations, it is necessary to outline an evolutionary perspective on health. Biocultural analyses often make extensive use of evolutionary perspectives in efforts to understand how culture—especially as it affects interactions with the natural environment—has long-term consequences for the body.

EVOLUTIONARY PERSPECTIVES ON HEALTH

To start, evolutionary theory is a set of well-supported hypotheses that explains how biological systems came about, how they change over time, and how they are maintained. Evolutionary theory is the overarching paradigm for all of the life sciences—those branches of science that are concerned with living organisms. The core principles of evolutionary theory are straightforward and have clear relevance to health, and trace back to the pathbreaking work of Charles Darwin (1809–1882) in the nineteenth century. Darwin, along with the less-celebrated Alfred Russell Wallace, provided a process—**natural selection**—that could explain how organisms came to have their traits and how these traits were closely related to the environment in which the organisms lived. Simply put, within populations individuals vary in their characteristics, and many of these variations are heritable (capable of being passed on to offspring via DNA). Because resources such as food, space, mates, protection from predation or climate, and so on are usually limited, there is often competition among individuals for those resources. Individuals with characteristics that give them some advantage will get more resources, which in turn will provide those individuals an advantage in survival, reproduction, or both. For example, individuals who have some trait that allows them to better resist infection or metabolize energy more efficiently have an advantage in environments characterized by infectious disease or food shortages. Ultimately, they likely will have more offspring than those without these favorable traits. Over time, such favorable traits should spread in the population, and the characteristics of that population, as evident in the frequency of those traits, will have changed, as illustrated in Figure 2.4. This is **evolution**: changes in the characteristics of a population over time. Natural selection is a mechanism by which such changes can occur.

The traits that confer some survival or reproductive advantage are referred to as **adaptations**. Importantly, an adaptation is specific to an environmental context; what provides an advantage in a tropical forest may not be at all adaptive in an Arctic environment. Predators, food resources, and infectious diseases are problems that all organisms must solve, but the particularities of those problems and their adaptive responses vary by environment. Adaptive responses can occur throughout the body—natural selection may favor more acute vision, blood cells that do not allow infection by a parasitic disease, darker or lighter skin, larger or smaller intestines, or a bowl-shape pelvis for upright walking versus a flat pelvis that serves quadrupedalism well. Bodies can thus be thought of as bundles of adaptations. Keep in mind that although natural selection is often interpreted as "the strongest survive," the adaptation of interest often has nothing to do with strength per se and the "competition" may be invisible to us.

Adaptations are measured by the **fitness** of the individuals who possess them. Fitness is defined as reproductive success (how many offspring or grandoffspring, etc., you have). To have fitness, you must survive to reproductive maturity or make some contribution to the reproductive fitness of close biological relatives (this is known as *inclusive fitness*). Because the strict measure of fitness is often difficult to assess, especially in humans with their long generation times, measures of health are often used as proxies for fitness—that is, for the assessment of adaptations. By definition, these are linked—either directly or indirectly—to survival and reproduction. Standard biological measures

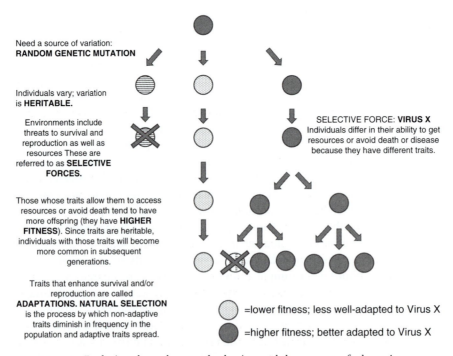

Need a source of variation:
RANDOM GENETIC MUTATION

Individuals vary; variation is **HERITABLE.**

Environments include threats to survival and reproduction as well as resources These are referred to as **SELECTIVE FORCES.**

SELECTIVE FORCE: **VIRUS X**
Individuals differ in their ability to get resources or avoid death or disease because they have different traits.

Those whose traits allow them to access resources or avoid death tend to have more offspring (they have **HIGHER FITNESS**). Since traits are heritable, individuals with those traits will become more common in subsequent generations.

Traits that enhance survival and/or reproduction are called **ADAPTATIONS. NATURAL SELECTION** is the process by which non-adaptive traits diminish in frequency in the population and adaptive traits spread.

=lower fitness; less well-adapted to Virus X

=higher fitness; better adapted to Virus X

FIGURE 2.4 Evolution through natural selection and the concept of adaptation.

are frequently used: hemoglobin status, infectious disease status or parasite load, child height and weight, blood pressure, reproductive outcomes such as miscarriage, or birth weight. All of these signal something about health that has significance for survival chances and overall reproductive success. Ideally, these measures can be linked together in a prospective study—that is, by assessing individual health characteristics and following an individual over longer periods of time to assess his or her fertility and survival (or age at death). Prospective studies are difficult to do because they require monitoring of individuals over long periods of time, so more often than not health measures are used as proxies for adaptation if they are known to affect survival or reproduction.

Selective forces are environmental factors that ultimately challenge survival and reproduction, but more immediately endanger health and well-being. They are sometimes referred to as **stressors**. Exposure to pathogens, lack of food or specific nutrients in the diet, or overexposure to heat or cold, among many others, all serve as selective forces, and individuals with characteristics that help them cope with these stressors have higher fitness and likely better health than others. Those characteristics then get passed on with greater frequency to the next generation of the population. Natural selection acting on organisms living in different environments contributes not only to variation between species but also to variation observed between populations within a species that inhabits a broad geographic range, such as humans. Hence, an evolutionary perspective is relevant to investigations of health, especially those that consider population differences in health.

Natural selection is a slow process, producing a gradual change in the frequencies of adaptive traits over generations. When environmental changes are relatively rapid, however, natural selection must play "catch-up." Genetic adaptations evolved in response to the previous environmental conditions; when environments change quickly relative to generation time, there will be a period of time during which there is a mismatch between the population's genetic characteristics and the environment. This time is likely to be characterized by higher rates of morbidity and mortality.

This mismatch may have a major implications for health among contemporary populations (Gluckman et al. 2019; Nesse and Williams 1994). Cultural change is rapid relative to genetic change, and the historical changes in lifeways that have occurred over the past hundreds of years have resulted in most contemporary humans living in environments that differ substantially from those in which we evolved. For some 2 million years, members of our genus *Homo* were hunter-gatherers, eating a diverse diet of wild plants and animals; living in small, mobile, kin-based groups; and engaging in energetically demanding activities. Few human groups live by subsistence hunting and gathering anymore, and most rely on the products of agriculture, which differ from wild foods. Furthermore, in industrialized or highly urbanized societies, work patterns are no longer shaped by foraging or food production but are often sedentary in nature. Combined with urbanization, which creates large, dense accumulations of people, this creates a set of environmental or lifestyle conditions at odds with those that prevailed during much of our genetic evolution. The types of diseases that prevail among industrialized societies are likely to reflect this mismatch, at least in part. The field of evolutionary (Darwinian) medicine and "Paleo" approaches to diet and health investigate such mismatches and propose that adopting behaviors more similar to those of our ancestors might mitigate the risk of some common contemporary diseases (see more on "Paleo" diets in Chapter 4).

Adaptability

Adaptations derived from natural selection are based on heritable variation, and they are therefore accompanied by genetic changes in DNA that are passed from generation to generation. There are other forms of adaptations, such as physiological plasticity or **adaptability**, which are shorter-term, nonheritable changes that occur in individuals when they are confronted with immediate challenges to their survival. The capacity for specific adaptability responses has a genetic foundation, but the engagement of that response depends entirely on individual environmental exposure. For example, in response to a sudden drop in temperature, an individual shivers to generate heat, and vasoconstriction (narrowing of the blood vessels) occurs to reduce heat loss. Likewise, when bacteria or a virus infects tissues in the body, the body responds by raising body temperature. To the individual, this manifests as fever, but to the bacteria this is a severe obstacle to reproduction. As soon as the challenges have passed, the individual reverts to physiological baseline. Note that these short-term responses are meant to be just that—of short duration—because they are expensive to maintain in terms of bodily resources and are inefficient and can be deleterious over the long term.

For stressors that persist over longer periods of time, the body engages more efficient adaptive responses. If cold stress continues, the body shifts to alternating constriction and dilation of the blood vessels. In the context of an infectious disease threat, other arms of the immune response are engaged (see Chapter 8). When individuals increase weight-bearing activity, bones increase in density to match the new load; when individuals travel to high altitude, they build more red blood cells to more adequately take up and deliver oxygen. These responses are entirely reversible: bone density declines with less activity, and red blood cell production goes back to baseline levels when the individual returns to sea level.

Other adaptability responses that are less reversible, but more efficient, are those that occur during the early periods of growth and development, when the body is most malleable. If a stress is encountered routinely during this period, growth and development can be fundamentally altered in ways that increase survival and reproduction under those conditions. For example, if undernutrition is encountered chronically in utero or during early childhood, growth in height will be stunted to preserve the development of more critical physiological systems such as the brain. Or metabolic functions may become more efficient to conserve energy. These kinds of alterations (as forms of embodiment) are often permanent, and they can be beneficial if the future environment is characterized by the same kinds of stressors, such as chronic food scarcity. However, as we will see in Chapter 5, these also come with costs to individual health that may manifest during childhood or later in life. Thus, whether these are adaptive or problematic (or both) is subject to differing interpretations (Schell and Magnus 2007).

Behavioral Adaptability

There are also behavioral adaptability responses, and these are likely to be especially important for a large-brained, cognitively astute species such as *Homo sapiens*. Cultural traditions may function as adaptability responses because groups have been exposed to different threats to their health over time as a result of their different historical and ecological circumstances. For example, differences in homebuilding styles may reflect differences in exposure to malaria. Researchers have shown that building houses high off the ground can reduce exposure to malaria-carrying mosquitoes that have a low flight ceiling (Charlwood et al. 2003). Healing traditions likewise reflect local health threats and may be adaptive in that context. Furthermore, unlike genes, which can only be passed from one generation to the next, behaviors can be transferred quickly across individuals or populations. However, there are barriers to the transmission of behaviors: those strongly linked to a specific cultural or religious tradition may be less likely to be transferred in the absence of migration, war, colonization, or proselytizing.

In many cases, behavioral adaptations involve modification of the environment itself. That is, instead of adapting to the environment, the environment is modified, and the latter has been a key part of the human adaptive behavioral repertoire. Most often this takes the form of buffering us from health threats: building shelters, separating drinking water from wastewater, building houses high off the ground, or using mosquito netting are all examples of this kind of environmental modification. Using insecticides to control insect-borne diseases or fertilizer to increase crop productivity also fit into this category, as do medical systems that effectively prevent or reduce mortality from life-threatening diseases. All reflect the creative abilities of *H. sapiens* to modify the environment in ways that reduce threats to survival, health, or well-being.

There is an important caveat to these kinds of technological innovations: although they may solve a particular problem, especially in the short term, it is also possible that they disrupt some other part of the environment such that a new challenge emerges. Building dams for irrigation or hydroelectricity can increase agricultural or economic productivity, but also changes the ecological conditions such that new disease vectors can flourish. When the Aswan Dam was built to create Lake Nasser in Egypt, the lake became home to *Bulinus* snails, which carry the helminthic infection schistosomiasis, a debilitating disease associated with blood loss and scarring of the blood vessels surrounding the liver, intestines, or bladder. When people started using the still water for a variety of activities (fishing, washing, playing), they were exposed to these helminthes, which are parasitic worms (Desowitz 1991; see also Chapter 9). Thus, environmental modifications can have unforeseen consequences for health, and they may also contribute to the problem of genetic–environment mismatch mentioned previously.

These examples illustrate another important point: all adaptations are in some way *compromises* (Wiley 1992). This means that there are both benefits and costs to changes made in response to a health challenge, regardless of whether the adaptation is genetic, developmental, a short-term physiological alteration, or a behavioral change. Sickle-cell hemoglobin may be a genetic adaptation to malaria, but it increases the frequency of sickle-cell anemia, a life-threatening disorder of red blood cells. Fever helps limit bacterial infection but requires many cellular resources and may be destructive to an individual's own cells. Insecticides may kill mosquitoes initially, but over time mosquitoes evolve resistance and are able to resurge.

There are thus two dimensions of investigation in biocultural analysis: one considers local adaptive responses to health challenges (genetic, physiological adaptability, or behavioral adaptability), which we have just described, and the other considers the nature of those specific challenges and how they became threats to health in that population (Wiley 1992). Many of these challenges are likely to be derived from historical processes that have altered the social environment in ways that result in ill health. The colonial era had a particularly deleterious effect on local health patterns when new modes of employment, including the shift away from subsistence agriculture to commodity production for export, new forms of stratified social relations, and ecological changes derived from new modes of production and transportation all fundamentally altered health conditions in colonized areas. One outcome of this was an improvement of health in many European countries as their economies expanded and new supplies of food were available, even as the colonies experienced a decline in health conditions. In the Americas, indigenous population numbers plummeted because of exposure to new infectious diseases from Europeans, and a legacy of major health disparities between native and European-derived populations persists well into the twenty-first century.

Disparities in health across the globe came to be more distinct during this time, and these persist today. These are evident in huge differences in **life expectancy** among countries around the world—from a low of just over 50 years in some sub-Saharan countries to 85 or older in Sweden, Australia, South Korea, and Japan, as shown in Table 2.1.

TABLE 2.1   Life Expectancy and Income across Countries, 2017–2019

	Life Expectancy at Birth		Gross National Income, Purchasing Power Parity, Per Capita
	Females	Males	
Central African Republic	54	50	$870
Sierra Leone	55	53	$1,520
Haiti	66	61	$1,870
Afghanistan	66	63	$1,960
Ethiopia	68	64	$2,010
Bangladesh	74	71	$4,560
Pakistan	68	66	$5,840
Palestinian Territory	75	73	$5,990
Bolivia	76	69	$7,670
India	70	67	$7,680
Philippines	75	67	$10,720
Brazil	79	72	$15,820
Costa Rica	83	78	$16,670
China	79	75	$18,140
Thailand	80	73	$18,160
Russia	78	68	$26,470
Turkey	81	76	$28,380
Greece	83	78	$29,600
South Korea	86	80	$40,450
Japan	87	81	$45,000
United Kingdom	83	79	$45,660
Canada	84	80	$47,280
Australia	85	81	$49,930
Sweden	85	81	$53,990
United States	81	76	$63,390

Source: Population Reference Bureau, 2017 and 2019 World Population Data Sheets. http://www.prb.org.

Life expectancy is the average length of life in a population and, as such, is strongly affected by levels of mortality early in life. Variation in life expectancies reflects differences in disease burdens, especially early in life, and years of life lost as a result of these diseases. Thus, global and local political economies, which have taken shape under specific historical conditions, have been important forces producing variation in health.

In the context of poverty, opportunities for adaptation may be severely constrained. All adaptive responses require resources of some kind, and if they are not available, the ability to adapt can be seriously compromised, leading to a downward spiral of health. Impoverished living conditions generate multiple stressors that challenge health and well-being, including crowding, unclean water or contaminated food, insufficient heating or cooling mechanisms, lack of access to health care, and increased levels of violence, among many others, such that not only are resources scarce, but also challenges to health exist on multiple fronts. Poverty is a root cause of health differentials within and between populations. Wealthier individuals have more resources and hence more adaptive options while also facing fewer challenges to their health and well-being. It is tempting to consider the relatively poor health often seen among impoverished populations as evidence of "failure to adapt," but this is tantamount to blaming the victim. Instead, it is critical that the root causes of resource disparities be illuminated, because only with attention to these causes will lasting solutions to entrenched health problems of the poor be possible. As Richard Wilkinson (1996) has demonstrated, it is also the case that in populations that are highly stratified, with large resource differentials within them, not only do the poor suffer more, but also everyone's health suffers compared with populations with more egalitarian resource distributions (see Chapter 10).

CULTURAL APPROACHES IN MEDICAL ANTHROPOLOGY

A biocultural perspective attempts to integrate both biological and cultural factors in the holistic study of health. However, some medical anthropologists employ approaches that are specifically cultural in focus. This reflects not only a pragmatic but also a theoretical orientation: the body, its biology, and evolution are considered of secondary importance to the social and cultural factors that more immediately influence health, healing, and well-being. But how does culture influence health? Culture is a set of shared meanings (i.e., it exists at the group level), embedded in social institutions, and an implicit shaper of individual beliefs and behavior. Indeed, when individual beliefs or behavior is at odds with a set of shared meanings, health may be compromised. William Dressler has pioneered "cultural consonance" analysis and demonstrated in several contexts that individuals who do not conform to or participate in some core cultural components (i.e., their experience does not match expectations about how the world works) tend to have worse health than those who do conform or participate (Dressler 1995). Several of these cultural approaches are outlined next.

Political Economy of Health

Sometimes also called **critical medical anthropology**, this perspective examines power differentials and their impact on health (Singer and Baer 1995). This perspective traces its origins to Rudolf Virchow (1821–1902), the pioneering German pathologist who was also a crusader for social reform in the service of public health. As demonstrated previously, one of the most obvious sources of variation in health across the globe is economic status. Wealthy groups within and across countries tend to have overall better nutrition, fewer infectious diseases, and longer life spans than poor groups. This difference in wealth can be traced to historical processes that have resulted in differential access to important economic resources such as land, other forms of capital, credit, political power, and so on, which mostly stem from the capitalist world system. Individuals with fewer resources are doubly at risk of poor health: they are more likely to be exposed to hazardous conditions that increase their risk of disease (through occupational hazards, contaminated domestic environments, unclean water or food, violence, etc.) and they have access to fewer health-care resources. This is what the physician-anthropologist Paul Farmer refers to as "structural violence": how the social machinery of oppression is embodied in adverse health outcomes and needless suffering among the poor or victims of racism, sexism, or all of the above (Farmer 2004).

From this perspective, the only lasting solution to health differentials lies in changes to the social, cultural, economic, and political structures that support or maintain differential access to resources within and between populations. Any other kind of specific health intervention will address only one or at best a few of the problems and usually only temporarily, leaving underlying structures unchanged.

Power differentials can exist in many social domains. They are easily seen in cross-country comparisons. As Table 2.1 indicates, there is a clear positive correlation between life expectancy and per capita wealth. Within countries there are differences that reflect local levels of economic or social stratification, political systems and ideologies, cultural heterogeneity, and ecology. In the United States, there are substantial differences among subpopulations with regard to health indexes, and they tend to track along with racial identity and economic status (see Chapter 10). Racial disparities in health are profound and well-documented, and largely result from the pernicious effects of racism. Gender differences in health are likely to be pronounced in societies with strong gender hierarchies. For biological reasons that are not well understood, women live longer than men, but this biological advantage can be undercut by social factors that serve to reduce female survival. On the one hand, across societies, females are more likely to have lower incomes, less representation in governments, and less power within a household context to make decisions about resource allocations. As a result, female health is often compromised relative to that of males. On the other hand, men may be subjected to other kinds of occupational hazards more often than women (coal mining, high-stress white-collar jobs, factory work). Likewise, children are vulnerable to such inequities because they rarely have access to their own economic resources and lack the skills to manage their own health and health care. They are subject to household decision making that may privilege the health of economically productive adults over that of children, sons over daughters, or older children over younger children.

Ethnomedical Systems

Some of the earliest work in medical anthropology was on indigenous healing systems (**ethnomedical systems**) and how they vary cross-culturally (Foster and Anderson 1978). Although the practice of healing may appear to be strikingly different across cultures (from chanting shamans to surgeons wielding scalpels), healing traditions have elements in common: all have theories of etiology (disease causation), diagnostic criteria, therapeutic measures, formalized interactions between patients and healers, and mechanisms for training new healers (see Chapter 3; Fabrega Jr 1997). The complexities of healing systems tend to track along with social complexity in general. In highly structured, large-scale societies (such as India or China), the practice of medicine is likely to be institutionalized, with formal mechanisms for training, authoritative medical texts, professional organizations of healers, and a complex pharmacopoeia for treatment. In smaller-scale societies, there may be no textual tradition and more informal mechanisms for training and transmission of knowledge. Thus, healing traditions and institutions are cultural products and "make sense" within their cultural context. To individuals within a culture, local healing traditions produce explanatory models of health and disease. Arthur Kleinman pioneered the concept of *explanatory models* in his research on doctor–patient clinical interactions, which revealed that physicians and patients (especially when they are from different cultural backgrounds) often have different explanatory models for the cause, appropriate treatment, and definition of an ailment (Kleinman et al. 1978; see also Anthropologist in Action: Arthur Kleinman box). This goes for highly complex systems such as Western biomedicine, Chinese medicine, Āyurveda (practiced in South Asia), or "folk healers" or shamanism.

One of the major distinctions among medical traditions is the extent to which the cause of a given ailment is located within or beyond the patient. In biomedicine, clinicians look for evidence of some disruption in function at the cellular level (a proximate cause), which may involve an infectious agent or replication of abnormal cells or other organic disturbances. Likewise, in Āyurveda, practitioners search for evidence of an imbalance in the body's humors (wind, bile, phlegm). Other traditions consider the possibility that religious or moral transgressions have resulted in divine punishment or that other individuals can "send" sickness out of spite or jealousy. These etiological differences in turn lead to the use of different types of therapies to restore health. In biomedicine these tend to be individual focused because interventions are focused on the body of the sick individual. In other contexts in which the cause of disease is supraindividual, social, or supernatural, appropriate interventions may include prayer, sacrifice, social reconciliation, and other types of group-level therapies, sometimes in conjunction with therapies that treat the immediate physiological cause.

In practice, healing traditions have come to be *pluralistic*, meaning that elements of one may be incorporated into another or that individuals in a society may seek out healers from various traditions in their quest for health. In India, Āyurvedic practitioners dispense antibiotics or give vaccinations or other injections; biomedical practitioners may recommend massage or acupuncture for pain (Leslie 1992). Thus, although people may profess a belief in one particular medical paradigm, in fact many are willing to try others, especially when a particular illness proves resistant to one therapeutic approach. This kind of permeability seems to be at odds with the idea that medical systems are embedded within one particular cultural context, but it may well be that when individuals are suffering, they become more open to alternative approaches in their search for relief. A drug store in the U.S. might have biomedical, homeopathic, Āyurvedic, herbal, and other remedies available. Furthermore, as biomedical therapies have become widely available around the globe and their clear success at treating or preventing some ailments such as bacterial infections or vitamin deficiencies has been demonstrated, these therapies have become widely acceptable and desirable for some types of symptoms.

People may understand or subscribe to only bits and pieces of the explanatory model of biomedicine (or any other medical system) but will still make use of its therapies.

As people encounter members of other populations or alter their subsistence or habitation patterns, their patterns of disease may likewise change. In response, new explanations of disease or therapies may be adopted. Across cultures individuals may try numerous healing methods that derive from widely varying cultural traditions in their efforts to cure themselves of seemingly intractable health problems. In the United States, surveys show that more than one-third of all American adults use some form of complementary or alternative medicine in addition to biomedicine (Clarke et al. 2015). Most common were dietary supplements, relaxation techniques, and yoga. Individuals make use of these healing traditions even though they are derived from cultures with very different concepts of the body or understandings of the causes of ill health. This openness to other forms of medicine suggests that beliefs and behaviors related to health and disease are aspects of culture that are especially open to change or, at the very least, experimentation. It may also reflect a pragmatic approach in which there is evaluation of different therapies for different ailments.

Although it may be tempting to see biomedicine as "superior" to other healing traditions, because of its widespread success at treating many ailments, it can also be viewed as an ethnomedical system of Western societies (Rhodes 1990). Biomedicine reflects the values of these societies as much as other medical systems reflect the beliefs and values of non-Western groups. For example, biomedicine focuses on purely natural causes of disease and sees the supernatural as irrelevant to disease causation. Furthermore, metaphors of the body as a machine with functional or malfunctioning parts are common. Medical anthropologists have argued that the rise of this common metaphor coincides with a transition to a factory-based production system in industrialized societies (Martin 1994). Political metaphors also pervade biomedicine, as in the immune system's capacity to "defend" the body against harmful "invaders," with which it is "at war" (E. Cohen 2009).

Interpretive Approaches to Illness and Suffering

Many anthropologists interpret medical systems, health, and disease strictly within their cultural contexts. This **interpretive approach** was strongly influenced by Clifford Geertz's notion of ethnography as "thick description." That is, the anthropologist must fully understand (through the process of long-term, in-depth ethnographic fieldwork) the role that various behaviors play within their cultural context and how the behaviors make sense within that milieu. Thus, the analysis of illness requires that these behaviors be considered in the context of the worldview of individuals, which is itself related to historical, ecological, political, economic, and myriad other factors. It becomes possible to see illness as the embodiment of an individual's role within that culture. For example, Nichter (1981) has described illness as an "idiom of distress," a culturally sanctioned way of expressing dissatisfaction with one's position or role at a given time.

Such idioms of distress are culture specific and referred to as **cultural syndromes**: clusters of symptoms that are recognized as illness in one society but not necessarily within another. Examples included *pibloktoq*, a syndrome recognized by Arctic peoples as a set of psychological symptoms that made afflicted individuals behave in ways at odds with their normal roles (see Chapter 11), or *tensan* in India, which shares symptoms with both clinical depression and anxiety but does not correspond exactly to either diagnosis and is frequently associated with difficult family relationships (Weaver 2017).

Likewise, among the Hmong of Laos, including those who have migrated to the United States, a syndrome known as *tsog tsuam* (nightmare attack) attributed to the *dab tsog* (nightmare spirit) is described (see further discussion of *pibloktoq* and *tsog tsuam* in Chapter 11). This was given the biomedical label sudden unexplained nocturnal death syndrome (SUNDS) because it often results in sudden death during sleep, but no proximate cause has been uncovered by biomedical researchers. The Hmong describe this syndrome as being caused by failure to perform traditional religious obligations, and it is characterized by intense psychological stress, especially in relation to their displacement and trauma subsequent to political persecution in Laos (Adler 1995).

The WHO **International Classification of Disease** (ICD) provides standardized definitions of all known human diseases. It was originally developed in 1900 by a group of representatives from the International Statistical Institute, and the WHO took over responsibility for it in 1948. The ICD represented a concentrated effort to create a universal classification of diseases that could be applied in any cultural setting. Nonetheless, anthropologists have found that even these standardized categories are subject to interpretation because they intersect with locally defined disease categories. For example, infant diarrhea may be recognized across cultures, but its causes and appropriate treatment vary widely. Similarly, in Ladakh, India, where average birth weight is around 2,700 grams, the WHO definition of 2,500 grams for low birth weight (below which babies are seen to be at greater risk of death) is relatively meaningless because almost 50% of newborns fall into this category (Wiley 2004a).

The **cultural construction of disease** refers to how disease categories, **nosologies** (systems of disease classification), symptomatologies, and treatments are subject to cultural influence. This is a major theme in culturally focused medical anthropology. This perspective links to the political economic approach by considering not only how disease is interpreted culturally but also how it is produced by social structures, cultural beliefs, values, and behaviors. For example, how do social conditions such as occupation, housing, and social stratification act to produce infant diarrhea? What historical processes produced these conditions and ultimately contributed to this outcome? How do culturally prescribed beliefs and behaviors shape the risk of this health outcome? In this case, disease is seen as a reflection of socially and culturally created conditions and, in turn, is interpreted within that cultural context.

An important component of this interpretive approach is analysis of language. As humans express culture through language, the particular words and expressions that individuals use in talking about health and disease are revealing. It is common in medical traditions with Greek and Arabic roots to talk about diseases as "hot" or "cold," reflecting a conception of the body as being made up of humors. Linguistic analysis can illustrate how worldviews are manifest in the classification of disease etiology. For example, Joseph Bastien (1985) described how the Qollahuaya Indians of Bolivia have a similar conceptualization of their bodies as they do of their surrounding mountain environment. Sickness and ecological problems derive from the same source, and both must be healed to reestablish wholeness and health (see also Adelson 2000).

Linguistic interactions between healers and patients likewise provide insights into social relationships. How do patients and healers describe the patients' symptoms and their causes differently? Is there mutual understanding and clear communication, or does each seem to be speaking a different language? How does their interaction illuminate social distinctions between patients and healers? Analyses of these "illness narratives" provide rich insight into divergence between a clinician's perspective and that of the patient, which in turn has implications for the likely success or failure of the prescribed treatment regimen. John Heritage and Douglas Maynard (2006) note that there are opportunities at every stage of the doctor–patient interaction during clinic visits (which they describe as having six stages: opening, presenting complaint, examination, diagnosis, treatment, and closing) for power differentials, lay versus biomedical misunderstandings, contesting diagnoses and treatment regimens, and so on to play out. The extent to which there are differences between patient and clinician understandings, priorities, and authority can have important effects on the success of the interaction and ultimately the resolution of the complaint.

Applied Medical Anthropology

A large number of medical anthropologists are engaged in applying the principles and ethnographic knowledge derived from anthropological scholarship to the design or implementation of health policies and interventions and, hence, are doing **applied medical anthropology**. They may work in a clinical setting by, for example, mediating between a patient's understanding of their condition and that of the clinician. Often patients and healers are from different social, cultural, and economic contexts, leading to a mutual lack of understanding. Anthropological "culture brokers" can play a vital role in facilitating communication between clinicians and patients, thereby increasing the likelihood of a positive outcome. This goes beyond simple language translation to ensure compliance by the patient with the treatment regimen. Instead, medical anthropologists in clinical settings help both patient and clinician to understand each other's perspectives and explanatory models so as to facilitate communication and ultimately enhance the likelihood of therapeutic success. In such a context, the medical anthropologist works as a kind of patient advocate. Most clinics do not have medical anthropologists on staff, and social workers often play this advocacy role. It is important that whoever is filling this role have some basic training in medical anthropology, especially in a multicultural society.

Applied medical anthropologists also work in institutions where health policies are designed to target specific populations or health problems. Here they bring their ethnographic knowledge and experience to bear on the development of health policy or interventions. They try to bring a user's perspective to the table, helping to ensure that any health intervention programs are culturally appropriate, do not violate social norms, or do not require resources that are simply not available. Organizations that employ medical anthropologists include various nongovernmental organizations; the WHO; federal, state, and local public health bureaus; and in the United States, the Centers for Disease Control and Prevention (CDC), among many others. In such contexts, medical anthropologists also act as community advocates by ensuring that members' voices are heard in the design of health programs and policies. Barry and Bonnie Hewlett served this role in investigation of early Ebola epidemics in central Africa

(Hewlett and Hewlett 2007). Applied medical anthropologists may also be hired to conduct short-term ethnographic research to assess the feasibility and likely success of a particular health-related intervention. Arthur Kleinman is a particular kind of "applied anthropologist" insofar as he brought his anthropological insights into his clinical practice (and vice versa); others will be featured throughout the book.

More broadly, medical anthropologists have much to contribute to the field of global health, a field that aims to improve health and reduce health disparities across the globe. In their review, Craig Janes and Kitty Corbett suggest four main ways in which medical anthropologists contribute to this field: "(a) ethnographic studies of health inequities in political and economic contexts; (b) analysis of the impact on local worlds of the assemblages of science and technology that circulate globally; (c) interrogation, analysis, and critique of international health programs and policies; and (d) analysis of the health consequences of the reconfiguration of the social relations of international health development" (Janes and Corbett 2009).

EPIDEMIOLOGY

Before delving further into medical anthropological topics, it is important to become familiar with some of the terminology used in the study of health at the population level. Many of these terms come from a discipline closely related to medical anthropology: **epidemiology**, which is the study of the distribution of disease in a population. Epidemiology is a key part of public health, a branch of health studies that is concerned with the health of the population (i.e., the public) as opposed to the individual (referred to as clinical health, or clinical medicine). Although epidemiology originated as the study of infectious diseases and how they spread, epidemiology is concerned with the distribution of all diseases, infectious or not. It is concerned with the factors that influence the distribution of disease and thereby affect the risk of disease. The following terms are used to describe patterns of disease in epidemiological work:

1. **Prevalence**—The total number of individuals with the disease in a particular time period.
2. **Incidence**—The number of new cases in a particular time period.
3. **Endemic**—A disease that has a long history in the population, with little change in either prevalence or incidence over time.
4. **Epidemic**—A disease that dramatically increases its incidence and prevalence in a short period of time. In the context of an infectious disease, epidemics result when an infection spreads rapidly through the population. Infectious disease epidemics often have a cycle, with rapid increases in incidence, followed by a decrease in incidence (see Figure 8.3 for an example of an influenza epidemic). The decrease results from the fact that most individuals will have been exposed (or are dead) and hence are no longer susceptible to contracting the infection. There can also be epidemics of noninfectious diseases. It is not uncommon to hear about epidemics of childhood obesity or hypertension in the United States.
5. **Pandemic**—An epidemic that occurs on a global scale. A current example that we are all too familiar with is COVID-19, which has had a stunningly rapid increase in incidence and prevalence in populations throughout the world.

Two other relevant terms are **morbidity** and **mortality**. Morbidity refers to disease; mortality refers to death. The mortality rate is the number of deaths in a given time period divided by the total population size. **Infant mortality**, which we refer to in many places in this text, refers to death in the first year of life. In the United States, the CDC publishes the *Morbidity and Mortality Weekly Report* (MMWR; http://www.cdc.gov/mmwr). Its ominous name aside, the MMWR lists the number of cases of notifiable infectious diseases[1] that occurred that week and for the previous year; this is the "morbidity" part of the MMWR. It also provides tables listing the number of deaths from those diseases (i.e., the mortality from those diseases) that occurred during those same time periods.

Medical anthropologists often work with epidemiologists or seek additional training in epidemiology to complement their anthropological skills. A sampling of their work can be found in *Anthropology and Public Health*, edited by Robert Hahn and Marcia Inhorn (2009). Many medical anthropologists bring to bear their ethnographic skills, which can be profitably combined with larger-scale (but necessarily less "rich") epidemiological surveys, thereby melding qualitative and quantitative methods. Their work can also help make sense of epidemiological patterns in ways that help better design culturally appropriate interventions. Anthropologists who use epidemiological data have much in common with social epidemiologists, who focus on the social factors that influence disease risk in a given population. In that way, there is overlap between critical medical anthropology and social epidemiology because it is routinely evident that marginalized or impoverished populations or those living in countries with high income inequality have poorer health (including dramatically increased risk of COVID-19 mortality) than those in the mainstream, with higher incomes, or living in more equitable societies (Krieger 2011; see also Chapter 10).

CONCLUSION

Medical anthropologists employ a variety of perspectives in their attempts to understand health within its local cultural context, variation in health between populations, or the ways in which health conditions have changed as a function of evolutionary or historical processes. There are important differences among the approaches with respect to the level of analysis. Some are concerned with individuals—their unique life histories that have made them vulnerable to a particular disease, how their maladies are interpreted and made sense of within their cultural context, or how to improve their well-being within the realm of a clinical encounter. Others are concerned with group-level trends in health. Typically, biocultural analyses are less concerned with the determinants of individual health and more concerned with why one population or group has a higher or lower incidence or prevalence of a given disease. From our perspective, these are complementary approaches, although our emphasis in this book is on health at the population level and the relationships between disease frequency and the social, natural, and historical contexts in which it occurs.

---

[1] The CDC has a list of notifiable infectious diseases that must be reported to them. Local health officials compile these data and send them to the CDC on a weekly basis.

STUDY QUESTIONS

1. Compare and contrast disease, illness, and sickness.
2. What are the basic causes of disease?
3. What is the "sick role"? How is it defined? How does a sick role become "legitimated"?
4. What does it mean to say that there are three bodies to be considered in the analysis of health?
5. How do the proximate and ultimate determinants of disease differ?
6. What are some of the problems encountered in trying to define biological normalcy?
7. What are stressors? What are some of the most critical stressors that influence health status?
8. What is adaptability and how is it related to adaptation? What are some examples of these responses and how are they related to health?
9. What roles do political and economic factors play in producing global patterns of variation in health?
10. What is the focus of critical medical anthropology? How does it differ from the biocultural approach or the interpretive approach?
11. How can biomedicine be viewed as the ethnomedical system of Western cultures?
12. Define these key concepts in epidemiology: prevalence, incidence, endemic, epidemic, pandemic, morbidity, and mortality.

CRITICAL THINKING AND DISCUSSION

1. What are three conditions that currently appear to be undergoing the process of medicalization? What are the costs and benefits for society of the medicalization of these conditions?
2. Why is it impossible to understand biological adaptation without reference to the environment in which an organism lives?
3. Identify ways in which our biologies seem to be mismatched for the contemporary environment. How do these mismatches negatively influence our health?
4. Think about your own health history. Where would you locate the causes (bodily, social, evolutionary, etc.) of your most significant instances of ill health?

CHAPTER 3

Healers and Healing

Chapter Goals
- To review healing systems, including Western biomedicine, as cultural traditions
- To establish the special role of healer and review how healers are recruited in different cultures
- To review alternative and complementary medicines and their growing popularity in Western cultures
- To discuss examples in different cultural settings in which biomedicine is the alternative medicine
- To introduce the placebo–nocebo concepts and how they may influence healing
- To understand the role of efficacy in healing decision making

Healing simply means "to restore to health." For example, when a person breaks a bone, a series of physiological steps is initiated to return the bone to health. First, the body works to stop bleeding at the site of the fracture, activates the immune system to prevent pathogens from invading the wound, and stimulates the formation of small blood vessels to supply the regrowth of tissue. Next, cells that lay down cartilage and bony tissue that join and stabilize the broken ends of bone are stimulated to do their jobs. A fracture callus eventually forms over the break, which is composed of a type of bone that is not quite as strong as normal compact bone. The final phase of bone healing (which can take months or years) involves replacing the fracture callus with stronger compact bone, remodeled to match the original structure of the broken bone.

The physiology of bone healing is not mediated by culture. It reflects an adaptive response that has been honed by millions of years of vertebrate evolution because all organisms with bony skeletons are vulnerable to bone injuries. Of course, humans are different from other vertebrates. We do not simply rely on the body's own healing abilities to fix a wound; we often intervene, or at least think we do. For a broken bone, putting on a splint or cast serves to reduce pain and protect the wound; it corrects the position of the bone to increase the chances of optimal healing. In some cases, surgery is undertaken and the healing process is enhanced by metal pins and plates (Figure 3.1).

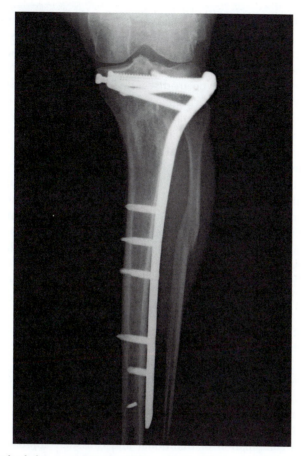

FIGURE 3.1 The body has a remarkable ability to heal on its own. However, in some cases, such as with a severely broken bone, medical intervention may be necessary. *Credit:* Fotosearch.

In most cases, the person who suffers the bone injury does not put on the cast or perform the surgery himself or herself; this task is done by someone else who takes on the role of "healer."

Like other interpersonal relationships in human societies, the relationship between the healer and the healed is a product of prevailing cultural norms and values. Medical anthropologists focus on understanding the broader contexts in which the healing relationship takes place. Religion, economics, colonial history, competing healing traditions, and a host of other factors influence how people are healed.

CULTURE AND HEALING SYSTEMS

There are several ways in which culture influences healing. First, almost all cultures specify healing roles that are recognized and legitimized by their members. Anthropologists and other observers have referred to people occupying these roles variously as witch doctors, medicine men or women, shamans, folk medical practitioners, and healers. In Western biomedicine, the healing roles are filled by doctors, nurses, and therapists, among others. Healing may also be mediated by others, such as parents and other kin, spouses, and friends. However, the distinction between those who may offer general care to individuals who are diseased or suffering and those who are recognized as specialists in the healing arts appears to be widespread cross-culturally.

Although healing roles may be culturally prescribed, it is also the case that within cultures there may be multiple healing systems; this is referred to as **medical pluralism**. In many Western countries various "alternative medicines" have been promoted in recent years, which compete with, or complement, standard biomedical practice. Competition with standard biomedicine is nothing new, and healing movements such as chiropractic and osteopathic medicine have thrived since the nineteenth century, establishing themselves as viable alternatives operating loosely within the biomedical sphere. Others retain popularity among consumers but remain more peripheral to biomedicine, such as homeopathy. The survival of alternative or complementary medicines in societies where biomedicine is dominant depends on a host of factors: the efficacy or effectiveness of treatment, the ability to complement standard biomedical treatments, their linkage to other cultural trends, or the persistence of cultural traditions that predate the dominance of biomedicine.

In most state-level societies, there have long been multiple healing traditions that have arisen from historical exchanges with other societies. In the colonial period in particular, local healing traditions encountered new forms derived from European sources (including rudimentary biomedicine, religious institutions, etc.). In these transitional contexts, new or hybridized healing modes can also arise. For example, among contemporary Navajo healers, there are those who subscribe to more traditional methods (traditional Navajo) and those who follow the Native American Church (NAC), which employs a combination of traditional and Christian approaches (Milne and Howard 2000). The Navajo healing situation (discussed in detail below) makes clear that "traditional" medical systems are not static relics of a lost age. Many forms of traditional medicine survive and thrive today because of their ability to adapt and change in a health-care environment increasingly dominated by forms of Western biomedicine.

Medical pluralism does not always lead to development of hybrid forms of traditional medicine or to the convergence of alternative Western medical traditions on the prevailing biomedical model (as has happened to some extent with both chiropractic and osteopathic medicine). Based on his long-term field research on South African forms of traditional healing, Robert Thornton (2015) suggests that the term "medical parallelism" may be more accurate in describing healing in the District of Umjindi in Eastern Mpumalanga. The area, which leads the world in HIV prevalence and has high rates of tuberculosis, is home to some 200 traditional healers (*sangoma*), 20 biomedical physicians, and a wide range of other medical practitioners (e.g., New Age, traditional Chinese, and so on).

Thornton points out that treatment, whether traditional or medical, magical or scientific, sometimes works and sometimes does not. To maintain a client base, all practitioners require an audience to view their successes. The intensity of audience involvement is much greater in traditional versus biomedical healing, which helps to maintain traditional healing in parallel with science-based medicine, despite the presumably greater (but far from universal) efficacy of the latter. There is a fundamental difference in the healer–client relationship between scientific and traditional medicine. As Thornton writes, "[The] public-as-population is the idealized client of biomedicine . . . [while] the 'client' of the healer is not the patient at all, but rather the set of relations—some broken, some dangerous, some healthy, some ambiguous—that tie healer, patient, and many others in a complex universe" (Thornton 2015, 364). Ideally, the biomedical physician is socially isolated from his or her client, dispensing treatment that has been verified in population-level studies, which minimize the importance of individual experiences and differences. In contrast, the *sangoma* is highly engaged with the client, sharing not only social relationships but, to some extent, the actual experience of illness.

Another example of parallel medical pluralism can be found among evangelical Christians in Samoa suffering from metabolic disorders (the majority of Samoans have obesity and they also have high rates of diabetes and hypertension) (Hardin 2016). Medical practitioners inevitably prescribe changes in lifestyle (activity) and diet to these chronic metabolic patients, which are difficult for them to comply with in the absence of cultural support or for economic reasons. Instead, as Jessica Hardin (2016) found when she spoke with these patients, many devout Samoans address their illness in the context of evangelical healing practices, which overlap with an ongoing commitment to practicing the Christian faith on a daily basis and engagement with others in the evangelical community. These patients find comfort and wellness in this process, which is linked to an ultimate reward provided by God. In contrast, biomedical care—diagnosis, prognosis, surgery, dialysis, medicines—is seen as more acute and intermittent, and not supportive of making long-term lifestyle changes. Some patients try to use Christian healing to help them follow biomedical recommendations, but among those who do not, wellness is created by the sense of agency conferred by a commitment to divine healing to address their chronic suffering.

Ideas about causation also play a fundamental role in the cultural construction of healing systems. Since the beginning of the nineteenth century, an explicitly scientific approach to determining the *biological* causes of ill health has been embraced in Western biomedicine (Foucault [1963] 1994); the development of disease is to be understood in the context of a comprehensive, empirically based view of natural phenomena. Such a perspective has older roots, but it competed with a host of others, including the far-reaching legacy of Greco-Roman medicine (long on description, short on explanation) and a variety of supernatural explanations, such as disease being a punishment from God or the result of witchcraft (Porter 1996). One of the ways in which contemporary biomedicine differs from traditional medical systems is that the latter often rely on supernatural causation of ill health rather than biological causation. The prototypical witch doctor or shaman intervenes between the ill person and the supernatural agency—a spirit or a curse or another shaman—that is the cause of the disease. In intervening, a shaman may put himself or herself at risk because the disease may be the result of a malignant force that also poses a risk to the healer.

The "biological versus supernatural" dividing line between biomedicine and traditional medicine is obviously simplistic (Scheper-Hughes and Lock 1987). It has some validity if we consider biomedicine a cultural system that has derived from a particular way of knowing (a positivist scientific biology based on the observable and verifiable) that developed in a particular place (Europe) at a particular time (the end of the eighteenth century). In contrast, traditional medical systems encompass a wide range of practices that have developed in multiple diverse cultural settings and ecological contexts. Many do emphasize supernatural causality, but that does not mean that they do not rely on the accumulation of scientific knowledge and experience over generations.

The Indian medical system Āyurveda (literally "life knowledge" in Sanskrit) dates back thousands of years. Although it is rooted in Hindu cosmology and Buddhist principles, it also incorporates sophisticated observations of the body and the effects of various forms of treatment (Lad 2002). The organizing principles of the body employed in Āyurvedic medicine (centered on the five elements of ether, air, fire, water, and earth) differ from those used in biomedicine, but over the past 200 years, Āyurvedic practitioners have become adept at combining the two forms of medicine in diagnosis and treatment. One example can be seen in how Āyurvedic practitioners incorporate the biopsychiatric concept of depression into their practice. Based on fieldwork in the south Indian state of Kerala, Claudia Lang and Eva Jansen have shown that biomedical concepts of depression are recognized and have been adopted by local medical practitioners, but that they are "adapted and transformed . . . to fit local medical and religious concepts" (Lang and Jansen 2013, 39). Although a more global concept of depression is recognized and treatments such as antidepressants may be widely used, traditional Āyurvedic categories are used to classify particular forms of depression. These categories do not always overlap precisely with formal biomedical diagnostic criteria.

One way in which biomedicine is not so different from traditional medicines is in the approach to treatment of conditions that have an "obvious" cause. As Virgil Vogel (1970, 13–14) points out, much attention has been paid historically to the supernatural or "irrational" aspects of Native American healing practices, but in the treatment of "fractures, dislocations, wounds of all kinds, including snake and insect bites, skin irritations, bruises, and the like" they took a wholly "rational" approach. Early observers of Native Americans commented that their approach was often more effective than the methods employed by Europeans in the treatment of these ailments. This kind of division is also found in the history of Western medicine, where for centuries a distinction was made between physicians, who received some measure of institutional or academic training, and surgeons, who did not. Organized in trade guilds, surgery traditionally carried little status. It could be portrayed as demeaning and defiling; unlike the clean-handed, bewigged, and perfumed physician, surgeons were habitually dealing with diseased and decaying flesh—tumors, wens (cysts), fractures, gangrene, syphilitic chancres, and such like. Their instruments were terrifying—the knife, cauterizing irons, the amputating saw (Porter 1996, 217).

The surgeon trade was degraded for the obvious nature of their interventions, whereas the physicians took on a more shamanistic role to deal with internal problems with causes and cures that were hidden from view (similarly, midwifery was also seen as a lower-status profession). The physician–surgeon distinction is maintained today in the British medical system, where physicians are addressed as "Dr." but surgeons, following their specialized training, revert back to "Mr." or "Ms." At the beginning of the nineteenth century, surgical training became more formal and credentialing was established; surgery became a high-status and lucrative profession. At that point, it served the surgeons to retain the Mr. title to distinguish themselves from other kinds of doctors (Loudon 2000).

Across cultures, the great variety of human practices and experiences related to healing emerges when causation is less than obvious. The act of assigning the ultimate cause of a disease or ill health places the condition in a wider cultural context. For example, the ongoing fascination in the U.S. popular media about whether the cause of one disease or another is "genetics" or "lifestyle habits" likely reflects a more basic underlying concern with the relative importance of personal responsibility in all aspects of American culture.

Sarah Castle's (1994) analysis of child death in Fulani communities in Mali provides a powerful example of how the assignment of a cause of death can reflect broader cultural issues. In the Mopti region where Castle worked, child mortality rates were extraordinarily high, with about half of all children dying before the age of 5 years. Early childhood death was thus an important and ongoing factor in shaping relationships among the women in these communities. About half of the child deaths were ascribed to a range of biomedical and other causes, but two folk illnesses, *foondu* ("bird"—recognized by the child's clenching of fists and seizures during illness) and *heendu* ("wind"—a prolonged illness, accompanied by body rigidity and staring eyes), accounted for the remaining half. These illnesses were not diagnosed by the mothers but by experienced elders or traditional healers, usually older women. In many cases, the diagnosis of these conditions was retrospective, occurring only after the child had died. Foondu in particular is a public diagnosis, which has the effect of publicly absolving the mother of responsibility for a child's death. At the same time, in accepting this diagnosis, the mother's subordinate position (relative to those making the diagnosis) is reinforced. Thus, the cause of a child's illness and death becomes an important factor in defining power relationships among women.

Another framework for understanding the cultural basis of medical systems is provided by a consideration of the *body*. As we discussed in Chapter 2, Scheper-Hughes and Lock (1987) argued that the mechanistic view of the body promoted by Western biomedicine imposes a series of false dichotomies (mind–body, natural–supernatural, rational–irrational) that have had a strong influence in anthropological interpretations of health systems. They propose that the body can be viewed from three perspectives. First, there is the individual body-self. This is the individual as we typically think of it—the body separate from other individuals—which experiences health and illness over the course of a lifetime. The second perspective encompasses the social body. In this sense, the body becomes a symbol modeling the relationship between a society or culture and the natural world. Disharmony in society becomes a model for ill health in the individual; conversely, disease itself may serve as a means to understand social conflict and disintegration. Third, there is the body politic. Bodies and their actions (reproduction, work, leisure, etc.) are controlled by the power apparatuses of the cultures in which they live. Individual bodies are subservient to the "collective body" of the culture as a whole, and there are a variety of means to enforce this subservience. It is in this realm that the body, as a sociocultural entity, is constructed.

Views of the body and disease causation directly influence the diagnosis of health conditions. Diagnosis is in itself an important part of therapy, and the arrival at an acceptable diagnosis is an essential part of a successful healer–patient relationship, in both biomedical and traditional contexts. Diagnosis not only initiates the treatment process but also gives the patient and other group members a benchmark by which to assess the performance of the healer. For example, in a biomedical setting, a person who presents with severe persistent headaches is not really fully treated (say with pain killers) until a proper diagnosis is made. The headaches could be caused by migraines (requiring treatment from a neurologist), a sinus infection (ear, nose, and throat specialist), or even a brain tumor (oncologist). Misdiagnosis is the basis of malpractice because by definition it prevents the patient from being properly treated for his or her condition. In Navajo traditional medicine, diagnosis plays a similarly critical role (Milne and Howard 2000). Self-diagnosis is almost impossible given the complex Navajo model of disease causality. People with illness consult with diagnosticians who point them toward the proper healer who can conduct the appropriate ceremony (*chant* or *chantway*). An incorrect diagnosis can lead to having an inappropriate chantway performed, which may be not only detrimental to health but also a waste of time and money.

Appropriate treatment initiates or facilitates the process of healing, which leads us back to the individual body (and mind) and its own intrinsic capacity for healing. Treatment does not always lead to wellness, of course, because a condition may be beyond treatment or the result of forces working beyond the healer–patient dynamic (i.e., an affliction of the social body or the body politic). Even incomplete treatment, however, incorporating diagnosis and the taking of some sort of action against the disease, can provide reassurance or an increased sense of well-being. At the end of this chapter, we discuss the placebo effect, which reflects the psychological effects that the process of healing itself has on enhancing well-being in a treatment setting.

From the perspective of biomedicine, many traditional or alternative forms of treatment appear to offer mainly *palliative* effects (Csordas and Lewton 1998). In other words, the proximate biological cause of the disease itself is not addressed but the patient is made to feel more comfortable physically, psychologically, or both. Biomedicine has achieved its prominence in part because of its real successes in ameliorating ill health based on a biologically based, positivist, scientific worldview, although it has historically paid little attention to the more global well-being of patients or to the ultimate causes of illnesses (e.g., economic conditions, nutrition). Nonetheless, even within scientific biomedicine there is still recognition that there is an "art of healing." Some physicians are better than others, as are some centers of treatment.

The **evidence-based medicine** (EBM) movement was initiated in the 1990s as an explicit program to improve patient care (Figure 3.2). Some of its advocates (Sackett et al. 1996, 71) describe it this way: "Evidence-based medicine is the conscientious, explicit and judicious use of current best evidence in making decisions about the care of individual patients . . . [it recognizes] individual patients' predicaments, rights, and preferences in making clinical decisions about their care." In response to critics who say this is the way biomedicine already works, advocates of evidence-based medicine respond that there are ample studies that show significant variation among treatment centers in the application of the clinically based scientific research and in terms of their respect for patient values. The EBM movement discounts the individual physician's clinical experience in favor of practices that have shown demonstrable statistical validity at the population level, preferably in double-blind and randomized studies.

Although the EBM movement has the laudable goal of providing consistent, trustworthy care for all patients, biomedical scientists, at every stage of their research, make choices about how evidence is constructed and validated, which are embedded in

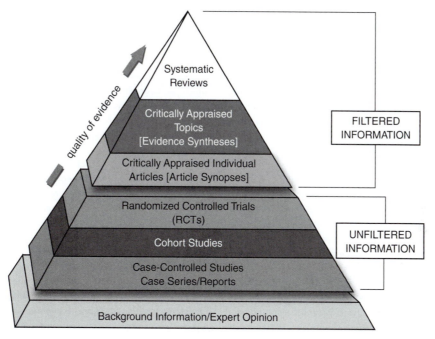

FIGURE 3.2   The evidence-based medicine pyramid illustrates the foundation of experience, systematic research, and peer review on which biomedical clinical practice should be based. *Source:* EBM Pyramid and EBM Page Generator ©2006 Trustees of Dartmouth College and Yale University. All Rights Reserved. Produced by Jan Glover, David Izzo, Karen Odato and Lei Wang.

cultural, political, historical, and economic contexts. Charlotte Brives, Frédéric Le Marcis, and Emilia Sanabria (2016) point out that EBM constructs narratives that are internally logical but that cannot be assessed outside their own frames of reference. Conflicts arise when EBM-based medical practices are introduced globally because too often the mono-lithic, positivist-scientific context in which these practices are developed does not align with the cultural contexts and experiences of the individuals who are supposed to benefit from them. Brives and her colleagues do not suggest that EBM is inherently hegemonic and colonial, but they note that we need to better understand and make explicit the con-texts in which EBM knowledge is created and subsequently dispensed.

The perceived need for an evidence-based medicine movement demonstrates that even within the confines of biomedicine, the healing experience can vary according to local physician "cultures." Economic, social, and political forces shape this experience, as well. If we look more broadly across cultures, we see that the patient–healer relation-ship is influenced by several factors: the nature of the specialist healer role in a given culture, cultural models of disease causality, cultural perceptions of the body, available treatment options, the extent of patient empowerment in the patient–healer relation-ship, the patient's social support, the severity of illness, and the individual's own psy-chological and biological capacity for healing. We explore some of these multiple dimensions of healing in the following sections.

Living Longer with Cystic Fibrosis

Cystic fibrosis (CF) is the most common autosomal recessive genetic disorder in northern European–derived populations (Ratjen and Doring 2003; see also Chapter 9). CF is a disease of the mucus- and sweat-producing glands characterized by symptoms such as excessive sweating (leading to mineral imbalances in the blood, which can in turn lead to heart problems) and the accumulation of thick mucus in the lungs and intestine. Lung disease is the most common cause of death in CF.

In the late 1950s, the average life span of a CF sufferer was around 3 years, and the mortality rate in the CF population was about 20% per year (Gawande 2004). At that time, a pulmonary specialist named LeRoy Matthews working at a hospital in Cleveland began treating CF aggressively as a chronic disease. He made his patients sleep in a tent at night filled with aerosolized water mist, which helped to loosen the mucus in the lungs, making it easier to cough up. Matthews also followed the lead of British physicians in having family members clap on the children's chest and back daily, which also helped loosen the mucus. Within a few years, Matthews demonstrated the extraordinary effectiveness of his methods (for example, it was shown in 1964 that no CF patients under the age of 6 years were dying with Matthews's treatment, a huge improvement over the 3-year life expectancy), which were widely adopted as standard practice in the United States. By 1972, the life expectancy for a CF sufferer was 18 years, and in 2003, it was 33 years.

In the 1960s, the Cystic Fibrosis Foundation initiated a program to keep detailed records on patient survival at each of the CF treatment centers around the country (there were 31 in the 1960s and there are now more than 100). In the early 2000s, data from this program showed that the average life expectancy of a CF sufferer was 33 years. However, there was substantial variation in the life expectancies of CF sufferers who were treated at different centers. Many centers regularly exceeded the mean, and at the best, the life expectancy was 47 years. But this meant that survival at many centers was below the mean.

In the late 1990s, the CF center in Cincinnati was producing results that were at best average, and for many indicators such as lung function in children, they were performing well below average. Caregivers there initiated a program of openness, sharing their results with parents of CF children, and developed a variety of committees that included parent representatives to explore means to improve the performance of the center. The medical writer and surgeon Atul Gawande (2004) visited the center and found that there was no questioning the knowledge, dedication,

or expertise of the staff—the standard of care was high and professional. The patients were being treated according to the latest recommendations of the CF Foundation, some of which had been written by physicians working there.

Gawande then visited one of the best centers, located in Minneapolis. The Minneapolis center was headed by Warren Warwick, a pediatrician who had helped establish that LeRoy Matthews's treatment methods were indeed valid. Like Matthews, Warwick treated CF aggressively. Not surprisingly, many patients, especially in their teenage years, experiment with their treatment regimes. They often find that if they cut back or stop treatment (which can be time-consuming or inconvenient), they do not necessarily feel any worse. But when Warwick found even a slight decline in lung function, he would ask the patients why they think it was happening. He made compliance with treatment a priority. Warwick was also always exploring new methods of treatment and assessment: he developed a special stethoscope for listening to lung function; he invented a new cough that was better for expelling mucus; and most far-reaching, he designed a special pneumatic vest that through quick compressions and deflations replaced the labor-intensive clapping on the trunk by family members.

After visiting the Minneapolis center, Gawande found that there was no mystery about why they were doing better than other centers: the combination of unusual diligence and a willingness to innovate kept them ahead of the curve. Centers such as the one in Cincinnati began to adopt the aggressive tactics of the better centers, and performance improved. However, the best centers also keep improving. This has been to the benefit of CF patients. One recent epidemiological study found that that the median survival age at birth is now well over 40 years of age, and that if current rates of improvement continue (as observed between 2006 and 2015), projected median expected survival ages should exceed 50 years (Keogh et al. 2018). Further extensions in CF life span may also result from the introduction of the first drug treatment that directly addresses the underlying genetic cause of CF, which was approved by the U.S. FDA in December 2019 (Voelker 2019).

Cystic fibrosis treatment demonstrates the vagaries of the healing experience: even with an explicit program of standardized care, significant variation arises among CF centers. Gawande points out that the "bell curve" is a fact of life; some doctors will be better than others even if the playing field is completely level. Most doctors provide average care, but why should patients accept "average" care if better is available elsewhere?

RECRUITMENT: HOW HEALERS BECOME HEALERS

Most cultures recognize healers as belonging to a special vocational or spiritual class (Figure 3.3). How someone becomes a healer varies both within and across cultures. A common theme, given the spiritualist nature of the healer role in many cultures, is that some sort of divination is involved. Evidence of enhanced spiritual qualities reinforces the healer as belonging to a class apart from the general population.

Among the Mayan Zinacanteco of the State of Chiapas in southwest Mexico, there are three different routes by which a person may become a *h'iloletik* (shamanistic healer, Fabrega and Silver 1973). Although the Zinacanteco are nominally Catholic, they retain a wide variety of Mayan cultural and religious traditions, and the h'iloletik maintain an important role in the community. The most widespread account of becoming a h'iloletik involves the most private form of selection—visitation during a dream. A potential healer has three dreams of being summoned before the ancestral gods (*Totilme'iletik*), who inform him that he (or occasionally she; the majority are male) has been selected to be a h'iloletik and give the healer a list of patients he or she must cure. Over the course of the dreams, the potential h'iloletik is instructed in forms of prayer, diagnostic knowledge, and ritual procedure. The new h'iloletik may also subsequently receive instruction from a more experienced healer.

FIGURE 3.3 Two healers: (left) A Crow Indian shaman in a photograph taken by Edward Curtis in 1908 and (right) a Kung San healer in a trance laying on hands. Kung San photo by Marjorie Shostak, AnthroPhoto.

The other two avenues of recruitment are more social. In one form, a potential h'iloletik is identified as such by an experienced h'iloletik who is treating him or her for an illness. The experienced h'iloletik is actually identifying a latent capacity in the potential healer: this person was predestined before birth to become a h'iloletik. The experienced h'iloletik informs the patient of this and tells the patient that he or she must also become a healer to be healed at this time. The experienced healer may instruct the novice healer, or the novice may have to depend on divine revelation to develop his or her skills. The third recruitment form occurs when a person has seizures or epilepsy, which may identify him or her as being predisposed to becoming a h'iloletik. Confrontation with Totilme'iletik is said to occur during the seizure, with the possibility of receiving instruction to be a h'iloletik at that time. It is important to note that not all people who have seizures become h'iloletik and that not all h'iloletik have had seizures.

Fabrega and Silver (1973) point out that similar forms of recruitment are found in groups neighboring the Zinacanteco; in addition, many other cultures also look for healers among those who suffer from epilepsy or seizures. The Hmong people, a tribal group who have lived in a number of areas throughout East and Southeast Asia (and who have established several communities in the United States following the Vietnam War), also regard people who suffer from seizures and epilepsy to be predisposed toward the healer role (Fadiman 1997). In Hmong, epilepsy is referred to as *qaug dab peg*, which literally means "the spirit catches you and you fall down." Although Hmong recognize that it is a serious condition, it is also seen positively as a sign that the sufferer, even a child, may have the qualities to be a shaman, or *txiv neeb* (person with a healing spirit). As Anne Fadiman (1997, 21) writes, "Their seizures are thought to be evidence that they have the power to perceive things other people cannot see, as well as facilitating their entry into trances, a prerequisite for their journeys into the realm of the unseen." In addition, their own illness is seen as a sign that they will have greater insight into the suffering of others. Similar to the Zinacantecan situation, a txiv neeb identifies the potential healer when called to perform a healing ritual, and the person who is ill has little choice but to accept the calling because to reject it means death. However, most people would not reject the offer to be a txiv neeb, despite the extensive training involved. It is a high-status role in the community, and being selected to be a txiv neeb is thought to be a sign of good moral character.

Traditional spiritualist healers have for centuries played an important role in African American communities (Snow 1993). These traditions started in the American South but were carried to other regions during the great northward internal migration of African Americans during the first half of the twentieth century. Healers can discover that they "have the power" or can hear "the call" in a variety of different ways. In some cases, the power is regarded as being fully inborn; in other cases, a single intense religious or spiritual experience can be a transformative event. Knowledge about specific healing practices can be passed on to others, although there may be limitations; for example, some believe that knowledge should only be passed on to members of the opposite sex who are not kin. For those who are born with the power, the key factor is identifying them. Birth order and birth circumstances can play a critical role. For birth order, being the seventh son or daughter of a seventh son or daughter is thought to be indicative of special healing powers. This old European belief was adopted by the

African American community by the mid-nineteenth century (Snow 1993); it was also considered a sign of special powers in some Native American communities, such as among the Mohawk (Bonaporte 2005).

Another critical birth circumstance indicative of special powers is being "born with the veil." This refers to a baby being born with an intact amniotic sac (or caul), which occurs when the sac is not broken (i.e., "water broken") before birth. The belief that babies born in the caul possess special powers is found throughout the world. In Britain, there is a saying that a baby born in the caul will never drown. Among African American healers, multiple birth signs may be considered better than one. Loudell Snow (1993) reports a healer who said that she was not only a seventh daughter but also that all of her siblings had been born under the veil. Other healers claim not to have been born with just one veil but more than one—seven in the case of one seventh-son healer. As Snow points out, multiple veils are not known to biomedicine.

For many African American healers, the process of becoming a healer occurs during the therapeutic process. Snow (1993) describes healers who reported hearing the word of God during a difficult time in their lives and were simultaneously healed. For others, becoming a healer is the outcome of a bargain made with God to get them through a low point in their lives, as in this example from Weidman and colleagues: "One day I was drunk; my mouth swelled up, and I could not talk. I asked God for his help and healing. I promised that if I were healed, I would change my way of life and serve Him. From that day I was able to heal bodies" (Snow 1993, 57). Stephen Childs (1991) interviewed an elderly African American woman whose path toward becoming a healer involved a series of dreams and visions that occurred to her at different points in her life, including as an anxious 11-year-old and a physically abused teenage bride. Childs suggests that the dreams and visions served as a coping mechanism for her during periods of personal crisis. Following one of these episodes, the woman visited a traditional "root doctor" who revealed to her that her husband had put a hex on her by placing a "rattlesnake root" in a pot containing a plant she watered regularly. He also told her, "you cut out to do the work I'm doing" (Childs 1991, 27). In combination with her visions and with the empowering words of the root doctor, the woman was able to take greater control of her life, healing herself as she became a healer.

Not all traditional healers achieve their status through mystical experiences or divine preordination. The Luo are one of the largest ethnic groups in Kenya; even in contemporary Kenya where many Luo live in cities, they still maintain connections with their traditional clans and rural communities (Prince and Geissler 2001). Although a wide range of medical services are available to the Luo today, many still look to *yadh nyaluo* (herbal medicine) for treatment. Most (but not all) traditional Luo *jothieth* (healers) are women "because they give birth," according to many informants. General knowledge about herbal healing is shared freely, and because children often help healers collect materials for treatment, they learn about them at a young age. However, there are also specialized healers who do not share their knowledge so freely. A woman who gains a reputation as a powerful and charismatic healer is sought by people outside of her own kin group and receives food in exchange for treatment (Prince and Geissler 2001).

Among the Luo, grandmothers and grandchildren often have a special relation-ship. Once older women pass menopause, they focus their attention on educating their grandchildren; older men, who can have multiple wives, are still involved in reproductive and economic activities as they get older. Ruth Prince and Wenzel Geissler (2001) describe how one traditional healer (Maria) chose her grandson (Ochieng') to succeed her as a healer. Although there is a spiritual element in Luo healing, especially in terms of maintaining a strong spiritual connection to ancestral healers (e.g., the grandmother who trained the healer), training as a healer depends on developing a strong base of knowledge about using herbal medicines to treat a wide range of conditions, both physiological and spiritual. Maria choose Ochieng' to succeed her not because she had received a sign that he was meant to be a healer but because at a young age he exhibited characteristics that made him a good candidate to be trained as such: intelligence, a good memory, not too stubborn, possessing of a "pure heart," selflessness, and, most important of all, a willingness to listen and learn. Ochieng' himself said that his grandmother chose him because she loved him, and he was old enough to start learning.

Biomedical physicians are chosen to be healers based on their abilities to get good grades, perform well on standardized tests, accumulate good letters of reference, be impressive in personal interviews, and write convincing personal statements on medical school applications. As biomedicine has become more scientific and treatment choices are more and more shaped by economic forces (e.g., managed health care by insurance companies), some concern has arisen that doctors are losing touch with their role as healers and their obligation to provide compassionate care for their patients.

Reciting the Hippocratic or another oath at some point during training has long been a part of the medical school experience in the United States (Dossabhoy et al. 2018), but some medical educators have felt that this was an insufficient reminder of future doctors' obligations to their patients. To address this shortcoming, the Arnold P. Gold Foundation was established in 1988 with a mission to foster humanism in American medicine. Professor Gold was a pediatric neurologist at Columbia University who was concerned that as technology increased in medicine, physicians were losing touch with their patients. One of the foundation's initiatives has been the promotion of the **White Coat Ceremony** (Figure 3.4). The ceremony is a self-conscious rite of passage that occurs when new medical students begin their training. It involves recitation of an oath (such as the Hippocratic Oath), in the presence of family, friends, and other medical professionals, reaffirming the students' dedication to fulfilling the personal responsibilities of the medical profession. The ceremony includes an address by a distinguished physician, after which the students are cloaked in their first white coat and directed to take the oath. The Arnold P. Gold Foundation has promoted this ceremony by providing grants to subsidize the purchase of white coats and covering the expenses of the distinguished guest speaker. More than 90% of U.S. medical schools have adopted the White Coat Ceremony or a similar event, suggesting that Professor Gold was not the only medical educator concerned about depersonalization in modern medicine.

The White Coat Ceremony conveys a dual message: it reminds physicians-in-training of their duties to patients and the community, at the same time reinforcing their unique status within their communities. The ceremony itself is not without controversy, with some critics arguing that it fosters a sense of entitlement, and its impact on medical education has yet to be adequately studied (Ellaway et al. 2014). Its popularity has spread, however, beyond medical schools to pharmacy, dental, veterinary, and other

FIGURE 3.4 American medical students about to begin their training participate in a White Coat Ceremony.
Credit: Photo by David L Ryan/The Boston Globe via Getty Images.

schools in health-related fields. There are even White Coat Ceremonies for high school students who have completed introductory courses in health topics. The spread of the White Coat Ceremony shows that healers are perceived to have a unique status—a perception shared by almost all cultures. Part of the effectiveness of healers rests on the perception that they are unusually spiritual, selfless, or knowledgeable and in possession of a power not available to regular people.

ALTERNATIVE AND COMPLEMENTARY MEDICINES

"Alternative medicine" refers to medical practices that are undertaken to replace standard biomedical practice, as when a cancer patient elects to change specific aspects of his or her diet to fight the disease rather than undergo chemotherapy. "Complementary medicines" are used in conjunction with standard biomedical practice; an example would be some kind of massage-based therapy used along with medication or surgery to treat back pain. Between 1990 and 2002, the use of alternative or complementary therapies, including herbal medicines, chiropractic, yoga, homeopathy, self-help groups, megavitamins, and so on, increased from about 33% to more than 40% of the population, and in 2002 about one in three Americans reported using complementary therapy in the past year (Eisenberg et al. 1993; Tindle et al. 2005). In 2012, a large-scale survey by the U.S. National Center for Health Statistics showed that at least 59 million Americans aged 4 and over had some health expenditure dedicated to alternative or complementary medicines, including $14.7 billion for visits to complementary practitioners, $12.8 billion for natural product supplements, and $2.7 billion for other self-care approaches (Nahin et al. 2016).

The status of these therapies in the medical establishment was codified by an act of Congress in October 1998 when approval was given to form the National Center for Complementary and Alternative Medicine—renamed the National Center for Complementary and Integrative Health in 2014—as one of the National Institutes of Health. In 1998 an entire issue of the widely read *Journal of the American Medical Association* was devoted to alternative medicine. The issue contained several randomized controlled studies looking at the efficacy of commonly used alternative treatments. Although many showed no positive effect, a yoga regime was found to be helpful for treating carpal tunnel syndrome (Garfinkel et al. 1998), an acupuncture-based therapy was found to stimulate fetal movement during breech presentation in late pregnancy (Cardini and Weixin 1998), and a Chinese herbal medicine treatment was found to be effective in lessening symptoms associated with irritable bowel syndrome (Bensoussan et al. 1998). The medical surveys show that alternative and complementary medicines are a growing part of the mainstream of American life. This is somewhat misleading because for much of American history, alternatives to standard biomedicine, both spiritual and mechanistic, have been available and used.

Consider what is actually meant by the term "alternative medicine." First, it reveals an implicit ethnocentric, or "ethnomedicocentric," bias because it gives biomedicine a privileged place. However, it could be argued that biomedicine has earned this privileged place by the success it has had in combating disease and ill health and because it—or many elements of it—has been adopted widely across cultures. Alternative medicine is often used to identify treatments that fall on the nonscientific side of the natural-supernatural divide. Fred Frohock (1992) points out that the line between the secular and the spiritual has been a shifting one over the course of human cultural history. In many cases, the spiritual is defined as anything that is in opposition to the secular and vice versa. In this sense, alternative medicines are simply those that are not biomedicine. Of course, some of these do explicitly invoke a spiritual connection, as in the variety of treatments advocated by New Age healers or many forms of traditional medicine. However, many alternative medicines are not particularly spiritual. They earn their place among alternative treatments because of the absence of clinical, scientific proof of the efficacy of their treatments; despite this, these treatments are widely used because they have anecdotal histories of effectiveness. Part of the mission of the National Center for Complementary and Integrative Health is to test these kinds of therapies using the same standards applied to biomedical therapies (e.g., controlled double-blind clinical trials).

Traditional forms of medicine are based not only on spirituality but also on the accumulation of practical knowledge about healing. Such indigenous knowledge concerning herbal treatments, massage therapy, or forms of specialized exercise or movement are of great interest to many people, including biomedical researchers. **Ethnopharmacology** is the study of indigenous medicines (almost always plant derived, hence the close relation of the field to ethnobotany), their use in their cultural contexts, and their possible applications in biomedicine. The scope of this field is potentially enormous. Daniel Moerman (1989) identified 15,843 medicinal uses of 2,143 species of plants in Native

American cultures alone! Traditional cures and treatments of conditions ranging from cancer to diabetes are being tested in laboratories throughout the world.

Let us consider an example of the interplay between indigenous knowledge and biomedical investigation. The infectious disease malaria (see Chapter 8) is endemic in parts of Peru where the Quechua people live. In the Quechua ethnomedical system, malaria is not a unitary illness but reflects multiple potential causal forces and is classified into two distinct disease entities (Roumy et al. 2007). In cases of the disease where the patient does not die, malaria is called *chukchu unkuy* (shaking illness) and is ascribed to a natural cause, namely an excess of "cold" elements affecting the individual's breath *samay* (referring to a vital principle). In contrast, malaria that kills or causes agony is seen to be the result of *wiritu*, which is "related to the ritual and shamanistic manipulation of power in order to harm" and indicates a "predatory intention (an external cause) to the problem" (Roumy et al. 2007, 484). The milder form of illness is typically treated by the use of medicinal plants, whereas the more severe form requires the intervention of a shaman and may subsequently also require social action.

Biomedical researchers are more interested in the efficacy of the medicinal plants than in the shamanistic or political interventions. However, a thorough understanding of the complete ethnopharmacological context is necessary to accurately identify potential treatments. A researcher who does not understand the classification of malaria by the Quechua could misinterpret the ritual or political responses to severe cases as being the only ones available. Quechua informants identified 14 different plant species as being useful for the treatment of chukchu unkuy; Roumy and his colleagues found that extracts from 7 of these demonstrated significant activity against the malarial parasite in the laboratory.

The ethnopharmacological approach may provide a "powerful tool to select plants from among countless possibilities" (Roumy et al. 2007, 487), but it is a tool that raises some important ethical issues. Indigenous peoples today are looking to be partners with researchers and not simply the subjects of research (e.g., Barnes 2000). Of more specific importance for medical treatment is the issue of ownership of indigenous knowledge: if a commercial pharmaceutical treatment is developed that is derived from an indigenous treatment, how should the ethnic group from which the treatment derived be compensated? Intellectual property rights are a complex issue even within developed, capitalist societies, and extending those rights to indigenous peoples, where the ownership of knowledge may be traditional and collective, is fraught with difficulty (Brush 1993). For example, indigenous groups are rarely neatly defined, so even if a treatment can be shown to have originated in one ethnic group, what if it is used by a neighboring and related group? Do they also deserve compensation even if they were not directly involved with developing a product for widespread use? As Stephen Brush (1993) points out, the introduction of intellectual property rights is often used as a means to prevent capitalist forces from exploiting indigenous peoples, but it is in itself a fundamental tool of capitalism.

In practical terms, alternative medicine encompasses all forms of medicine that are not represented by standard biomedicine. Many developed countries, in which biomedicine is the mainstream, credentialed form of treatment, also support multiple alternative and complementary healing systems. Indeed, while it was once feared that the globalization of health would lead to the decline of ethnomedical practices and knowledge, this does not seem to be borne out by research during the first decades of the twenty-first century (Forsyth 2018). In some populations, ethnomedical treatments persist due to simple economics (it's cheaper) or availability (e.g., if traditional healers are more accessible than medical practitioners). In others, traditional medicine is maintained as an option by consumer choice in a pluralistic medical environment.

We next consider in more detail three forms of alternative medicine, all of which have important places in shaping the environment of medical pluralism in the United States today: acupuncture, chiropractic, and Navajo healing. Acupuncture represents the introduction of a medical technique from a non-Western culture. Chiropractic is an alternative medicine whose long history and success in Euro-American society has earned it a place close to the medical mainstream. Navajo healing today represents an indigenous form of healing that is evolving to accommodate Western influences, both medical and nonmedical.

Acupuncture

From a Western perspective, **acupuncture** is one of the most well-known hallmarks of Chinese civilization. The development of acupuncture dates back at least 2,000 years (Kaptchuk 2002; Melzack and Wall 1988). It was first described in the Western world by a Dutch physician in 1683 and has been "rediscovered" periodically. Acupuncture involves the insertion of fine needles through prescribed points in the skin, which are then rotated at specific rates (Figure 3.5). It is part of a complex theory of medicine,

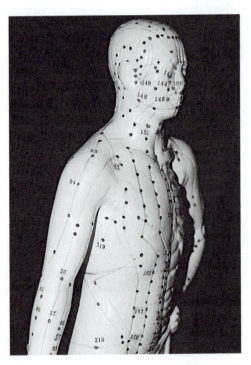

FIGURE 3.5 Acupuncture points and meridians indicated.
Credit: J. S. Allen.

honed over centuries of practice, based on the concept of disharmony between *yin* (cold, darkness, passivity) and *yang* (heat, light, assertiveness). The relationship between yin and yang is mediated by *qi* (pronounced "chee"). Qi can be considered something akin to a "vital force" or simply as a metaphorical way of expressing the interconnections between yin and yang (Kaptchuk 2002).

Classic acupuncture identifies about 365 points on the body distributed along 14 main channels (or "meridians"), through which qi flows; a typical acupuncturist uses only about 150 of these points. Although the insertion of needles is classic acupuncture treatment, manual pressure may also be applied at these points as a form of treatment. In addition, heat stimulation with burned herbs, known as "moxibustion," is common. The study of breech presentation (when the fetus's feet, instead of the head, are in the birth canal) mentioned earlier used moxibustion rather than needles (Cardini and Weixin 1998). Again, the goal of acupuncture treatment is to alleviate disharmonies between yin and yang in the context of an individual's own unique bodily environment.

On its widespread reintroduction to the West in the early 1970s, the effectiveness of acupuncture treatment for some conditions was readily apparent, but there were many, including the American Medical Association (AMA), who were troubled by the "metaphysical explanations and the necessity for mystical rituals" (Ulett et al. 1998). Researchers in the West and in China began looking for the scientific basis of acupuncture. They discovered that acupuncture points were often located near major nerve pathways and that only about 80 of the 365 classically defined points were really useful clinically. It was also discovered that the addition of electrical stimulation to the needle, a practice already commonly used by Chinese physicians, doubled the pain-relieving efficacy of acupuncture (Ulett et al. 1998).

The central nervous system effects of acupuncture have been demonstrated in a number of ways (Ulett et al. 1998). Studies on animals indicate that acupuncture causes the release of analgesic (pain-killing) substances that can be transferred from animal to animal via the cerebral spinal fluid and whose effects can be lessened by the administration of drugs that block receptors for the body's natural opiates. In terms of clinical treatment, the use of acupuncture for a variety of chronic pain conditions is reasonably well established (Kaptchuk 2002; Musial 2019; Ulett et al. 1998), and functional brain imaging shows that acupuncture stimulates patterns of brain activation in pain-modulating areas that are not activated under control conditions mimicking acupuncture (Pariente et al. 2005). There is also evidence that acupuncture may be effective in the treatment of several other conditions, including addiction, depression, anxiety, nausea, and gastrointestinal problems. For example, a recent double-blind study has shown that acupuncture (electrical acupoint stimulation) was as effective as a commonly used drug (tropisetron) in reducing postoperative vomiting and nausea in patients who had undergone gynecological surgery with general anesthesia (Yang et al. 2015).

Acupuncture has achieved somewhat mainstream status in American culture and in other Western countries. Comprehensive studies conducted in Germany in the 2000s showed that acupuncture compared to no treatment while on a waiting list, reduced the amount of pain associated with migraine, arthritis in the knee, and other conditions (Linde et al. 2005; Witt et al. 2005); these results prompted many German insurance companies to start paying for acupuncture for a variety of conditions

(Musial 2019). In the United States, more than 40 states license acupuncturists as independent health-care professionals, and there are approximately 30,000 licensed acupuncturists in the United States (Kaptchuk 2002; see also the Council of Colleges of Acupuncture and Oriental Medicine, http://www.ccaom.org). An acupuncturist's education typically consists of 2,000 to 3,000 hours of training at an accredited school, leading to the awarding of a master's degree. In some states, physicians may practice acupuncture with no training requirement, although most require 200 to 300 hours of special training. In 2004, nearly half of all employer health insurance programs covered acupuncture, an increase of 14% from 2002 (Devitt 2005).

The integration of acupuncture into Western medicine poses a host of issues for its advocates, issues that will be faced by any complementary healing system attempting to find a place in standard medical practice. Hannah Flesch (2013) conducted ethnographic research during the 2006–2007 school year at a university dedicated to training in complementary and alternative medicine. She focused on the program in acupuncture and Oriental medicine, which had grown from only 2 students in 1989 to more than 200 in 2006. This growth was accompanied by an increasing concern with positioning acupuncture as a partner to mainstream medicine. Flesch identified three ways in which the university shaped the curriculum to facilitate this partnership: (1) There was a careful *delineation of boundaries*. The acupuncture students were taught not only what they were capable of doing but also, important for maintaining a productive relationship with mainstream medicine, what they were *not* capable of doing. Thus, they were trained to recognize their limits and when to refer patients to physicians; (2) Despite the holistic orientation of traditional Chinese medicine, *specialization* was both encouraged and sought by students as a way of finding a place on the medical landscape. Specialization was seen as facilitating "integrative settings" among different kinds of health-care providers; and (3) The *science* in the curriculum was increased at the expense of Chinese terms and explanatory models. Although this could be seen as an abandonment of their roots, an increasing science orientation was encouraged to foster professionalization in the wider community and communication with other practitioners. For example, students were taught that pain around "acupuncture point GB 30" is the same as "sciatic pain" in Western medicine.

These moves to present acupuncture as a working partner with mainstream medicine come with some risks for students. As one of them told Flesch (2013, 16):

> I think, yes, it's good to integrate, but at the same time, we have a specific goal . . . as graduate students. And we don't want to come out and say, "I'm so well-rounded that I can't do acupuncture well or Western medicine well."

Not all "alternative" medicines aspire to partnership with mainstream medicine, but those that seek a "complementary" role do so by definition. For any of them, maintaining an identity separate from biomedicine can lead to a delicate balancing act.

Chiropractic

If health insurance coverage is the ultimate measure of acceptance of an alternative or complementary medical practice, then **chiropractic** is by far the most accepted. Virtually all insurance providers cover chiropractic care for some conditions, and about three-quarters of all spending on chiropractic comes from insurance coverage of various kinds (Cleary-Guida et al. 2001; Goertz 1996). The current state of affairs regarding chiropractic medicine is nothing short of remarkable. It was only in 1990 that a group of chiropractors won an antitrust lawsuit against several medical associations, including the AMA, for systematically preventing medical doctors from any professional association with chiropractors (Moore 1993). Beginning in the 1960s, the AMA actively discouraged medical practitioners from associating with chiropractors in any way, arguing that chiropractic is cultish and unscientific. During this period, physicians actually wrote to the AMA asking whether they had to resign from community service groups, such as Rotary Clubs, if they also allowed chiropractors to be members (Moore 1993). In the end, it was ruled that several major medical associations, including the AMA, had conspired against chiropractic medicine. One damning piece of evidence against the medical associations was that although they justified their opposition to chiropractic on scientific grounds, they changed and implemented antichiropractic policy without reference to any scientific research.

What is chiropractic? According to the American Chiropractic Association (www.acatoday.org), it is "a health care profession that focuses on disorders of the musculo-skeletal system and the nervous system, and the effects of these disorders on general health." Chiropractic treatment is literally hands-on (and generally drug free), based on a procedure known as "spinal manipulation" or "chiropractic adjustment." The focus of chiropractic treatment is impaired mobility of joints, which may result from a traumatic injury or repetitive strain. By manually manipulating these joints and surrounding structures, chiropractors seek to restore mobility and thereby reduce pain and discomfort.

Unlike acupuncture, which has its origins lost in deep historical time, the origins of chiropractic are much less mysterious: It was invented in 1895 by Daniel David (D. D.) Palmer (1845–1913), a Canadian-born healer working in Davenport, Iowa. The first patient to receive a spinal adjustment was a deaf African American janitor named Harvey Lillard, who was treated by Palmer on September 18, 1895 (Moore 1993). Chiropractic was born during a time of heightened medical pluralism in the United States as different kinds of medicine were competing with each other for patients and prestige. A practice known as "magnetic" healing combined vitalist notions of the universal power of magnetism with certain strains of faith healing and spiritualism. In chiropractic, Palmer combined some of the underlying principles of magnetic healing with manual manipulation to create a novel form of treatment (Moore 1993).

Eventually, in chiropractic, Palmer came to emphasize manual manipulation over magnetic healing, stressing the importance of communicative flow within the nervous system. Palmer also championed the importance of "innate intelligence," a vital force linked to the "All Wise," as an essential ally in the healing process; some followers of Palmer linked innate intelligence directly to Christian theology, helping to earn chiropractic its "cult" designation by the AMA (Moore 1993). Palmer was jailed briefly in 1906 for practicing medicine without a license. Interestingly, his defense at the time was that chiropractic was not medicine.

Chiropractic may not be medicine, but is there any evidence that it works in a biomedical sense? The claims for its influence on "general health" remain controversial, but what about evidence of success in its core area, the treatment of back pain? The UCLA Low Back Pain Study (e.g., Goldstein et al. 2002; Hurwitz et al. 2002; Hurwitz et al. 2005; Hurwitz et al. 2006) was a randomized clinical trial in which 681 patients with low back pain were assigned to four different treatment groups: medical care with and without physical therapy and chiropractic care with and without physical therapy. At a 6-month follow-up, treatment outcomes for the medical and chiropractic patients were comparable; however, at the 18-month follow-up, the chiropractic patients were significantly more likely to perceive an improvement, even if the actual change in status between medical and chiropractic patients was not clinically detectable. Overall, only 20% of all patients were without pain after 18 months, demonstrating that lower back pain is relatively resistant to treatment.

Studies like the one conducted at UCLA, which show little difference between medical and chiropractic care, create a potential conflict in identity for chiropractors (Villanueva-Russell 2011). On the one hand, the empirical validation of their treatment in a biomedical sense is no doubt welcome, contributing to a growing perception of "professionalism" for the field. On the other hand, these results can be used to restrict the scope of chiropractic care to only those areas in which its treatment is biomedically validated. This would undermine its status as an alternative to conventional treatment. Alternative forms of medicine need not match or exceed standard medical practice to justify their existence. Their appeal rests not only on clinical efficacy but also on the satisfaction derived from the treatment experience or from circumventing the biomedical establishment.

Navajo Medicine

The third example of alternative medicine in the United States involves a situation in which biomedicine has been introduced to a culture as part of the general process of Western colonialism. Among the approximately 200,000 Navajo, or Diné, who live around or maintain close ties with their traditional southwestern homeland, medical pluralism has long been a fact of life (Csordas 2000). Four primary avenues of medical treatment are present within the Navajo community, recognized not only by outside observers, such as anthropologists, but also by the people themselves. They include biomedicine, traditional Navajo healing, Navajo NAC healing, and Navajo Christian healing. Thomas Csordas (see also Begay and Maryboy 2000) suggests that these four treatment options can be conceptualized following the traditional quadripartite orientation of Navajo thinking based on the four cardinal directions (Figure 3.6). The three Navajo healing traditions are recognized as religious traditions as well.

Most Navajo are familiar with biomedicine via hospitals and clinics run by the Indian Health Service or by private organizations. Traditional Navajo healing is practiced by a *hataalii*, who performs sand painting and chants, and a diagnostician, who uses methods such as hand-trembling and crystal-gazing (Csordas 2000). Earlier, we discussed how the complex causal models of ill health in Navajo traditional medicine require the work of a diagnostician. The healer of the NAC is known as the "road man." Unlike traditional Navajo religion, the NAC is monotheistic and melds traditional and Christian beliefs (Milne and Howard 2000). Central to the NAC healing ceremony is the use of peyote, which is taken during lengthy prayer sessions that are conducted around a central fireplace in a tipi or hogan. Participants often sing accompanied by a drum. Unlike traditional Navajo medical healing, NAC healing ceremonies tend to be similar no matter what the diagnosis. Finally, there are the forms of Navajo Christian healing. These ceremonies are similar to Christian healing ceremonies observed

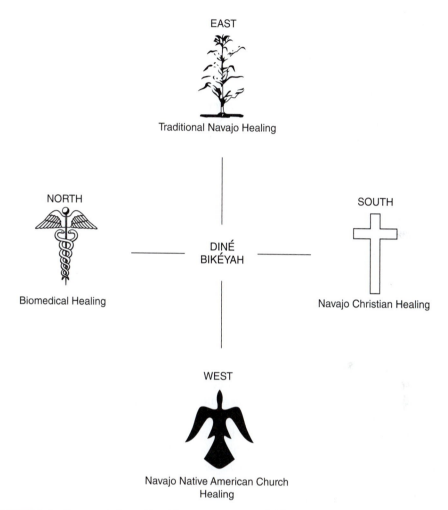

FIGURE 3.6 Representation of health-care systems available in contemporary Navajo society. *Source:* Thomas Csordas, University of California, San Diego and Case Western Reserve University, Navajo Healing Project.

elsewhere featuring revival meetings and laying on of hands (for Pentecostals) or group prayer (for Charismatic Catholics, Csordas 2000).

David Begay and Nancy Maryboy (2000) have provided a biographical account of a Navajo/Choctaw Catholic nun named Sister Grace. Over the course of her life, Sister Grace not only worked within the Catholic Church but also eventually became a healer incorporating all three of the Navajo-based approaches. She grew up on the reservation, the daughter of a NAC road man. During various periods of illness in the latter part of her life, Sister Grace underwent traditional Navajo healing. As Begay and Maryboy (2000, 515) state, "Sister Grace was born into synthesis." Like many other healers, Sister Grace moved toward the healing profession in the wake of several personal health crises (including car accidents, heart disease, and depression). She is recognized in the community as a spiritual leader and healer who "shares her spiritual life with many native people who are now experiencing conflicting beliefs and looking for balance and healing in their lives" (Begay and Maryboy 2000, 519).

Sister Grace is extraordinary in the level of her commitment and exposure to different healing traditions, including that of the Catholic Church. However, at a more basic level, she exemplifies the conflicts that many indigenous peoples face in the pursuit of wellness: they do not reject biomedicine, but they find that there is something missing in the healing experience it offers. In general, the "something missing" is what all alternative medicines try to provide, and it is quite clear today that it is not only indigenous people who seek a broader healing experience than that offered by biomedicine.

WHEN BIOMEDICINE IS ALTERNATIVE MEDICINE

Navajo medical pluralism provides one example of a kind of reconciliation between traditional and Western systems. The Navajo people came into contact with biomedicine as a result of their subjugation by the U.S. government in the latter half of the nineteenth century. Other cultural groups encountered biomedicine during the colonial period (see Chapter 9), and some encounter biomedicine when their members immigrate into Western countries. Still others have imported biomedicine into their cultures, maintaining many of its practices and institutions, but modifying them in certain key ways. Let us consider two more examples of when biomedical practice forms a direct conflict with cultural values or traditions.

A poignant cultural clash focused around biomedicine has been chronicled by the journalist Anne Fadiman (1997) in her account of encounters between Hmong immigrants and health professionals in the central valley of California. The Hmong came most recently from Laos following the Vietnam War, where they had collaborated for years with the U.S. government in the battle against communism. Laos is only their most recent homeland, however. Fadiman describes them as a fiercely independent group, who have maintained their ethnic identity as they have moved and been moved across East and Southeast Asia over the centuries. Their cultural cohesion results from a vigorous adherence to their traditional ways and a skeptical attitude toward the ways of the dominant cultures they have encountered. Fadiman's description of the Hmong has been criticized by the anthropologist Janelle Taylor (2003) as being rather simplistic and essentialist in nature, incorporating age-old Chinese stereotypes represented in the descriptive literature available about the Hmong from their traditional homeland. Taylor acknowledges that whereas the Chinese saw these "essential" traits of the Hmong as a negative, explaining their ongoing status as a "barbarian" people, Fadiman regards them positively, as an explanation for their cultural resilience in the face of much more politically powerful dominant cultures.

Whether positive or negative, such cultural stereotyping can obscure the importance of other factors in assessing the outcomes of interpersonal relationships in a cross-cultural context. It is important to note also that Fadiman's account reflects the earliest stages of Hmong settlement in the United States. A large number have made their way in American culture, albeit with many of them still focused on traditional Hmong occupations. For example, about 20% of the registered farmers in the Fresno, California, area are Hmong (Nguyen 2007). Fadiman describes how in their dealings with Western culture, the Hmong seem—to well-meaning health-care workers—to focus an inordinate amount of attention on the potential or imagined harm that doctors can do. Perhaps this should not be a surprise: the Hmong are suspicious of those in power, and healers possess a special kind of power. When a Hmong woman who had lived in the United States for several years was sent by the United Nations to talk to a large group of Hmong refugees about life in America, she was asked questions of this sort (Fadiman 1997, 32): "Why do American doctors take so much blood from their patients? After you die, why do American doctors try to open up your head and take out your brains? Do American doctors eat the livers, kidneys, and brains of Hmong patients? When Hmong people die in the United States, is it true that they are cut into pieces and put in tin cans and sold as food?" It was apparent that the health-care system was not getting good reviews from the Hmong who had already immigrated to the United States.

Not surprisingly, Hmong patients did not receive good reviews from American health-care workers. They were often seen as difficult and uncooperative patients, above and beyond the language barrier that was an inevitable part of their encounters with health workers. As Fadiman quotes one particularly negative physician,

> According to Dr. Small, the Hmong are highly uncooperative patients. "They don't do a damn thing you tell them," he said. "They just come in late and drop it out. In fact they wouldn't come at all if they didn't need to get a birth certificate to get more welfare. You or I, we can't conceive of the degree of ignorance. They're almost a Stone Age people. Hell, they never went to a doctor before. They just had a baby in the camp or the mountains or wherever the hell they came from." (1997, 73)

In contrast, clinical workers, members of a supposedly more enlightened non–"Stone Age" culture, often proved incapable of deviating from Western biomedical models to deliver care to the Hmong and ensure their "compliance" with medical directions. Indeed, the one physician in the community who was generally well liked by the Hmong, because he was more willing to accommodate their views in his practice, was widely regarded by other physicians as a barely adequate medical practitioner (Fadiman 1997, 76). Besides the cultural and linguistic differences that fueled these divergent viewpoints, the basic healer–patient relationship in the United States was nothing like what the Hmong were used to. Their traditional healer, the txiv neeb, spent hours with each patient and came to the patient's home, not expecting a sick person to make a journey to the hospital. Txiv neebs were able to render diagnoses quickly and did not rely on blood draws or x-rays and diagnostic tests that might take days to generate a result. They did not undress their patients. Most important, they did not neglect the soul, something never mentioned by doctors. Fadiman describes in detail the fate of a Hmong girl, Lia Lee, who suffered from epilepsy, and the sad, downward spiral of the relationship between her loving parents and the concerned doctors who tried to care for her. Lia's doctors found her parents to be uncooperative, willfully ignorant, and ultimately a danger to the life of their daughter. In contrast, the doctors appeared rigid to the parents, making demands about adhering to medication schedules and other interventions that were wholly foreign to the Hmong.

At 4 years of age, Lia suffered a massive infection that led to irreversible brain damage, placing her in an unresponsive persistent vegetative state. Although Fadiman characterizes her ruined life as being the result of "cross-cultural misunderstanding"

(Fadiman 1997, 262), more proximate factors, such as the competence of the physicians attending her, should not be discounted (Taylor 2003). Taylor is a great admirer of Fadiman's account, but she faults her for shaping Lia's story in such a way as to make her demise inevitable, consistent with the classic tragic narrative form. Rather than saying that Lia's condition was the result of a cross-cultural misunderstanding, it may be more accurate to say that the cross-cultural context made a story like hers possible, as did the personalities of her caregivers and parents, the competence and inflexibility of her doctors, her own body's biology, disruptions to the spiritual underpinnings of her own culture, and a host of other potential factors.

The immigrant Hmong must have regarded biomedicine as a powerful social institution (for further discussion, see Chapter 11). For Lia's family, this notion was reinforced when her physicians arranged for her to be removed from the family and placed in foster care for issues related to noncompliance with her treatment. There are, of course, limits to the power of biomedicine, such as when it comes into conflict with other social institutions or deeply ingrained cultural beliefs or belief systems. For example, ethical concerns and historical violations of basic ethical standards have led to the strict regulation of biomedical research on human (and animal) subjects in most developed countries. Biomedicine is constrained in what it can do by other, more powerful social forces.

ALTERNATIVE BIOMEDICINES

It is easy to look on biomedicine as a monolithic cultural entity, derived from some sort of generalized Euro-American culture. However, within Western biomedicine, there are multiple distinct cultural medical traditions that manifest themselves in a variety of ways. For example, going back to the nineteenth century when biomedicine was being sanctioned by governing bodies as "the" official form of medicine, different countries took different paths toward this outcome (Pickstone 1996). In the 1980s, the medical journalist Lynn Payer (1996) investigated and compared medical practice in the United States, France, Great Britain, and what was at the time West Germany. She found significant differences in the ways physicians in these countries, all supposedly trained and working under the same medical paradigm, approached both clinical practice and medical research.

Payer understood that there are dangers in national personality typing, but her analysis of medical practices in these four countries showed that they were in many ways a direct reflection of broader national characteristics. French medical practice was heavily theoretical, following their generally Cartesian view of the world (derived from the philosopher Descartes, who prized thought and the process of investigation over mere data collection). Payer characterizes the German physicians as embodying both a Romantic philosophical ideal and a tendency toward valuing authority and efficiency. German physicians are widely regarded as authoritarian, but the Romantic side is evident in a willingness to embrace more naturalistic and holistic approaches, such as homeopathy and mud spas. Compared with the other three national medical cultures, British medicine seems to be one of restraint. Their physicians spend less time with each patient, doing less complete examinations; they order fewer tests and prescribe fewer drugs. In contrast to Britain, Payer sums up the U.S. medical approach with one word: "aggressive." In the United States, doctors are much more likely to pursue surgery and other invasive and involved procedures over less active measures. They prescribe higher doses of medication and are more likely to approve of new therapies based on more limited results than the British would. Payer reports that medical observers from other countries suggest that Americans believe that their bodies, like their cars, should always work. Hence, the American invention of the annual checkup, sort of like a tune-up for the body, which is generally not part of medical practice in other countries. Payer's portraits of the national medical cultures do sometimes seem close to caricature, but they are supported by both qualitative observations and quantitative statistics.

Anthropologist in Action: Joan Cassell

The anthropologist Joan Cassell (Figure 3.7) has conducted extensive fieldwork in a variety of hospital settings, both in the United States and in other countries (Cassell 2005). Although the healing and treatment that occurred in all of these settings could be classified as biomedical, Cassell found that there was much variation in what constituted standard medical practice, even within a unit in a single hospital. For example, in an American intensive care unit (ICU), Cassell analyzed the conflict that arises between the intensivists (physicians responsible for the treatment and support of the critical-care patient) and the surgeons, who operate on patients with the immediate goal of fixing whatever problem is immediately at hand. The intensivists have as their goal the alleviation of the patient's suffering. In the

critical care setting, where many patients are on the brink of death, the alleviation of suffering may in fact be the withholding of medical care, heroic or otherwise. Ideally, the intensivists address the issue of quality of life with the patient's family or other supporters and come up with a plan that is in the patient's best interest. They are often charged with identifying when there is no hope for the patient and then informing the family of the unfortunate situation.

In contrast to the intensivists, surgeons have as their goal the avoidance of death. As Cassell writes (Cassell 2005, 73), "Surgeons define their relationship to the patient as a promise to battle death on that person's behalf." This "covenant" permeates the internal culture of surgeons, where losing a patient can become the stuff of a humiliating peer review during weekly meetings of the surgical staff. A successful outcome for a surgical patient is leaving the ICU alive, even if that means going to a convalescent facility for the rest of his or her life or dying in a regular hospital room a few days later. One of the intensivists in the ICU that Cassell studied was comfortable discussing end-of-life issues with the family of patients, reviewing options and the patient's wishes in a forthright way. The surgeons saw this doctor as too willing, even too enthusiastic, to engage in this discussion with families. They referred to him as "Doctor Death."

Alleviating suffering and avoiding/confronting death entail a range of complex issues. At the surface level, the ICU appears to be an environment of clinical efficiency, where different kinds of doctors and another critical group, the nurses, all work together to save grievously sick and injured patients. But looking below the surface, Cassell found that the ICU also encompassed some of the basic conflicts fostered by modern, technological biomedical care. Issues of status, control, economy, ideology, and autonomy (for patients often in no condition to make decisions about their own care) in the ICU all contribute to the variation in care a patient might receive. For all its quantifiable successes in the treatment of illness, biomedicine cannot cure death, and in the ICU, this inevitable failing fosters inevitable conflicts.

FIGURE 3.7 The anthropologist Joan Cassell. *Credit:* Joan Cassell.

DEATH AS A BIOCULTURAL CONCEPT

Cultures vary tremendously in their attitudes about death, with some known for exhibiting notably "hardened" attitudes toward it. For example, there is the stereotype of the "morbid Mexican," scorning and laughing in the face of death. This view of death has been incorporated into the national identity of Mexicans and is especially evident during the national Day of the Dead holiday. However, the historical genesis of this Mexican view of death is complex, and as Stanley Brandes (2003) notes, the attitudes displayed during Day of the Dead celebrations do not match the solemn emotional texture of funerals conducted throughout Mexico's diverse subcultures. Several circumpolar cultures are also notable for apparently having a callous or calculated view of death, especially for elderly people who are deemed to be no longer contributing members of society. In many of these cultures, "voluntary death," where one person (typically elderly or sick) requests another to kill him or her, was once relatively common and even persisted, albeit covertly for legal reasons, until recently. Among the Siberian Chukchi, the more recent occurrences of voluntary deaths are not linked to scarcity of resources (although they may be spurred for economic reasons) but, according to Rane Willerslev (2009), are a form of ritual sacrifice, intrinsically linked to traditional Chukchi notions of the interactions between the worlds of the living and the dead.

It is no surprise that attitudes toward death and ideas about how illness causes death vary from culture to culture. However, cross-cultural perspectives on the definition of death might be expected to converge. Immobility, unresponsiveness, the cessation of heartbeat and breathing—these signs would probably be recognized across cultures as being consistent with no longer being alive or among the living (cultural ideas about what happens next are another matter). For millennia, humans have recognized these signs of death and acted accordingly.

Starting in the 1960s, however, with advances in both transplant and life-prolonging technologies, biomedicine was forced to deal with the issue of defining death in a new way. For the first time, one person's dead body became an integral part of someone else's medical treatment. Transplant surgery is biomedicine writ large—expensive, technologically sophisticated, unprecedented in the annals of medical treatment, an option only for the relatively privileged—it has the power to provide new life to people who are gravely ill and otherwise untreatable. As Lesley Sharp (2006, 1) writes, "Transplantation simultaneously epitomizes technical genius and medical hubris." The focus in the media and the popular culture has been on the apparently heroic life-saving aspect of transplantation surgery. But as Sharp notes, transplantation encompasses three overlapping domains: surgery along with organ procurement and donation.

For the patient, the decision to have transplant surgery is not always an easy one. The surgery itself can be difficult, the recovery time long, including lifelong dependence on immunosuppressive and other drugs, and the chances for restoration of health in many cases limited. Many potential transplant patients decide it is not worth the effort. Laura Lynn Heinemann's (2014) ethnographic research among transplant patients demonstrates a perhaps surprising incentive for potential patients to undergo the surgery: their roles as caregivers in their family and social networks. Transplant patients require an extensive amount of postoperative care; in fact, the lack of a support network can make a patient ineligible for surgery. Heinemann points out that social obligations cut both ways; she writes (Heinemann 2014, 67) "the very pursuit of a transplant can become an act of care in itself." Many transplant patients decide to undergo the procedure because they feel they have obligations to their family and friends to do their best to stay alive and active. Healing, in this case, has a social imperative.

At a broader social level, gaining access to organs for transplantation is both a moral and a practical issue. To become a source of donor organs, a body must be sustaining those organs until they are "harvested"—it must be alive. Biomedical science addresses the morality of removing vital, life-sustaining organs (heart, lungs, liver) from one person to transplant to another by equating **brain death** with the "usual" kind of death. The first clinical description of brain death was published by French physicians in 1957. In the United States, publication of "The Report of the Ad Hoc Committee of the Harvard Medical School to Examine the Definition of Brain Death" in 1968, one year following the first heart transplant operation (conducted in South Africa), laid out the institutional guidelines for identifying brain death (Greenburg 2001; Hammer and Crippen 2006). In the U.S., and in many other countries, a person's organs are available for harvesting once brain death has occurred and if there is approval for the procedure indicated by the individual before becoming brain dead (e.g., via a donor card) or by the family (Figure 3.8).

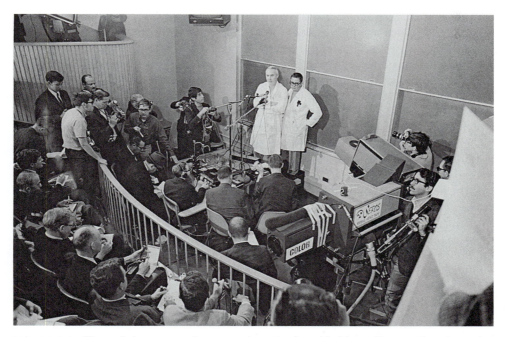

FIGURE 3.8 The early heart transplant surgeries gained worldwide media attention. Around 150 reporters gathered after Stanford University's Norman Shumway performed the first heart transplant in the United States in 1968.
Credit: Charles Painter/Stanford News Service.

The neurological definition of brain death is based on several criteria (Rowland 2000). The individual must be in a coma (persistently unresponsive to stimuli) and unable to breathe on his or her own (i.e., is on a ventilator). There is no response to stimuli in the head—pupils unresponsive, no sign of gagging, suckling, or swallowing, and so on. Spinal reflexes may be present in the limbs. Blood circulation may be intact and the body temperature should be normal (i.e., if someone's condition involves being exceptionally cold, body temperature must return to normal before he or she can be declared brain dead). Acute drug intoxication must be ruled out (i.e., a negative drug screen should be obtained). There are various time requirements for the absence of vital signs depending on the age of the individual (ranging from 6 to 48 hours). There should be no electrical activity in the brain. Brain death should be differentiated from *vegetative state*, in which a person (usually following massive cerebral injury leaving the brain stem intact) maintains cardiorespiratory function, sleep–wake cycles, and some responses to external stimuli, but in the absence of consciousness or any sign of voluntary activity. In contrast to vegetative state, *locked-in syndrome* occurs with certain kinds of strokes in the brain stem, which results in paralysis of the entire body, while retaining cardiorespiratory function and some control of eye movements and blinking. Individuals with locked-in syndrome are fully conscious and can communicate by blinking or moving their eyes.

Although the practice of recovering organs from brain-dead individuals for transplantation is widely accepted in most industrialized countries where biomedicine is dominant, there are some cultures that have not embraced this practice. Among Jews, especially orthodox Jews, it is thought to be essential that the body of the deceased is buried intact, hence the great efforts seen in Israel following terrorist attacks to recover all bodily remains no matter how miniscule. However, among some Jewish congregations, the prohibition against desecration of the body after death can be balanced against the benefit gained for saving a life. Organ donation has been approved by both reform and conservative Judaism in the United States, although it is widely thought among American Jews that organ donation is not allowed by Jewish law (Konig 2003). It is important to note that the orthodox proscription against organ donation is based not only on issues pertaining to desecration of the body but also to the equation of brain death with death itself.

The development of biomedicine in Japan closely followed European models, and Japanese biomedicine today is of a standard on par with that of Western medicine. Nonetheless, Japanese medical practice reflects and adheres to Japanese cultural traditions in some critical ways. One of these is that Japan has been remarkably resistant, in the eyes of outside observers, to embracing organ transplantation from cadavers, although kidney transplantation from living donors is allowed and frequently performed (LaFleur 2002; Lock 1996; McConnell 1999). Indeed, the first attempt to do a heart transplant in Japan (in 1968) resulted in the surgeon being tried for the murder of both the donor and the patient (he was not convicted), although there was an additional problem in the case because the surgeon, Toshiro Wada, had neglected to get another physician to confirm that his heart donor was actually brain dead (Hindell 1999). It was not until 1999 that a heart transplant operation was again conducted in Japan. The Wada case had a chilling effect on developing transplant surgery, and the Japanese news media has for years emphasized the risks associated with the assessment of brain death over the benefits of transplant surgery (Lock 1996). There were also far more deep-seated cultural and religious factors against transplant surgery in Japan.

Japanese views of death are shaped by the state religion, Shinto, and also by Taoist, Confucian, and Buddhist principles and practices. Shintoism places a primacy on the preservation of life. However, the beating heart is taken to be the primary sign of life; hence, to remove it or other vital organs would be precipitating death unnaturally. Taoist beliefs, which have been imported from China, also shape Japanese attitudes toward death. Taoism places a premium on maintaining the integrity of the body to ensure that immortality is achieved by providing a resting place for the soul (McConnell 1999). Although Buddhism has no general proscription against organ donation, Buddhist-derived funerary rituals in Japan often last a lengthy period before the soul or consciousness is thought to have passed on. Desecration of the body during this period is discouraged, precluding removal of organs for transplant (Hughes and Keown 1995). These beliefs and practices, among others, combined with a suspicion of the medical community derived from the Wada case, fostered a general bias in the Japanese population against the concept of brain death and the practice of organ donation.

In her analysis of Japanese attitudes toward brain death, Margaret Lock emphasizes that death in Japan belongs not just to the individual: "Death remains above all as a social event, and as such is best evaluated intuitively and through social consensus. Curtailing the reaching of this consensus in order to vivisect the dying is unthinkable for many people, including clinicians" (Lock 1996, 595). An example of the violation of this consensus is that the declaration of brain death is a wholly medical decision that is made without consultation with the family (although, of course, the family would be consulted concerning the donor status of the patient). Some Japanese commentators have also emphasized that the brain has not traditionally been considered the center of the body (only one-third of Lock's 50 informants did so) and that mind–brain dualism has not been a dominant ideology there. Resistance to the concept of brain death is therefore widespread in Japanese culture, based on several different cultural tenets.

There can be no doubt that thousands of Japanese people died earlier than they might have given the restrictions on transplantation (although wealthy Japanese have always been able to travel overseas for transplant surgery); even the liberalization of laws about transplantation in the late 1990s, promoted by the Japanese medical community, has not made transplantation widely available because the Japanese are restrictive in terms of having brain death legally declared (McConnell 1999). The transplant situation in Japan serves to illustrate the nature of cultural choice in healing and how culture produces alternative biomedicines.

The new medical technologies produced by biomedicine engender new debates about which healing practices are acceptable and which exact too high a cost. Cultures vary as to which new technologies they find problematic. In Japan, stem cell research, including therapeutic cloning, can be pursued quite freely, whereas in the United States it is restricted relative to international standards. If stem cell treatment turns out to be as beneficial as its proponents claim it might be (which remains to be seen), then any impediment to their development will affect thousands or even millions of lives.

Gender and Living Organ Donation

Surveys in Europe, China, India, and North America all indicate that there is a robust and consistent gender disparity in living organ donation: woman are substantially more likely to donate than men (Bal and Saikia 2007; Ge et al. 2013; Steinman 2006). In a fascinating comparative study, anthropologists Megan Crowley-Matoka and Sherine Hamdy (2016) looked at why living kidney donation is a gendered experience in Mexico and Egypt. Through independently conducted long-term ethnographic research in both countries, the authors determined that kidney donations overwhelmingly come from living donors rather than from cadavers. In the United States and other countries, cadaver donation programs have been encouraged in part to minimize coercion of family members to donate to relatives. In Mexico and Egypt, however, the absence or ineffectiveness of cadaver donation programs leaves living donation as the only choice. Women in both countries assume the responsibility for social and biological reproduction, with ideas about motherhood, fertility, and purity influencing choices and actions surrounding the act of organ donation.

In both Mexico and Egypt, mothers are considered to be the most "iconic" and "natural" living kidney donors. It is thought that mothers should want to donate to their children as an extension of their maternal duties. In Mexico, the perceived maternal desire to donate becomes an expectation that she will donate. In Egypt, some patients expressed the opinion that they would not consider a donation from anyone other than a parent—especially the mother—in order to avoid incurring a debt too great to repay.

In both countries, organ donation is seen as a logical extension of the birth process, suggesting an ongoing relationship between the mother's body and those of her children. This "fleshy continuity" supports the notion that maternal donation is more natural than donation from the father or other relatives. In Mexico, where the self-sacrificing Virgin Mary is an iconic figure and powerful symbol, organ donation to a child is seen as a sacrifice a mother should want to make. In Egypt, in the face of hostility towards organ transplantation in general, donation to a child is seen as a natural choice a mother should be allowed to make.

The gendered relationship between husband and wife also influences organ donation patterns. It comes as no surprise perhaps, in both Mexico and Egypt, that wives donate their kidneys much more often to their husbands than vice versa. In many cases this is dictated by conventional roles in the family: the husband must be well to go out and earn money to support the family; therefore, maintaining his health is critically important. In contrast, the economic "value" of the wife is relatively lower, and the husband is not dependent on her work to maintain himself or the family. He even has the option of withdrawing support, which she, practically speaking, does not.

Crawley-Matoka and Hamdy emphasize that this is a far from universal pattern. Both Egyptian and Mexican male patients sometimes refuse to "take" kidneys from their wives because they are concerned that the process could compromise the wives' abilities to care for their children. In Egypt, uncertainty about the outcome of kidney transplant surgery can lead husbands to decline to subject their wives to the risks of giving up a kidney. In addition, the parents of wives with sick husbands often work hard to dissuade or prevent their daughters from donating to their husbands. Should the ailing husband not recover, the parents are worried that their daughters' future marriage prospects will be compromised following donation. Families can also interfere with husbands' decisions to donate to wives, especially when younger husbands are involved. The donation of a kidney can be seen as too great a sacrifice—a sentiment that may be shared by the wife as well.

Gendered notions of purity and fertility also interact with living organ donation in both Mexico and Egypt but in somewhat different ways. In Mexico, "the bodily invasion required by living donation was sometimes likened to sexual penetration" (Crowley-Matoka and Hamdy 2016, 38). For example, one young woman waiting for a donor kidney was told that her sister—who wanted to donate—could not because that would be akin to her losing her virginity and she would no longer able to take Orders to be a nun. This attitude can work against men becoming donors, because if organ donation is analogous to being sexually penetrated, that would make them "less of a man." In Egypt, the preservation of young women's fertility as a family goal can lead to these women being shielded from the risks of donation. In addition, young unmarried women were more likely than young unmarried men to receive a transplant from either parent, again with the goal of preserving her chances for a good marriage. In contrast, in Mexico, economic factors figured more strongly in the family-based decision making surrounding donation involving young adult children.

Crowley-Matoka and Hamdy make it abundantly clear that in Mexico and Egypt decisions about living organ donor donation are entwined with ideas about gender. Surprisingly perhaps, in both of their field sites, the net result is that about equal numbers of men and women become donors. They point out that this is not the case in the United States, which shares with many other countries a strong bias (about 60/40) towards women being donors over men. They argue that more research is need on this issue: if, as biomedical ethics tends to frame it, organ donation is a "gift," why is it a gift that women are giving much more than men?

PLACEBO AND NOCEBO

At the beginning of this chapter, we discussed how a bone heals itself. Complex biological organisms have evolved the capacity to heal themselves when injured or to fight off the attacks of infectious agents and parasites. Although all organisms eventually die, they often manage to recover from any number of health challenges over the course of their lifetimes. Thus, healers are bound to have some success, if their timing is right, because in many cases patients will get better on their own. Biomedical clinicians have long noted a specific kind of self-healing, which occurs following the administration of a **placebo** to a patient. A medical dictionary (http://www.merriam-webster.com/medlineplus/placebo) defines placebo as "a usually pharmacologically inert preparation prescribed more for the mental relief of the patient than for its actual effect on a disorder." The **placebo effect** is defined as "improvement in the condition of a patient that occurs in response to treatment but cannot be considered due to the specific treatment used."

These definitions reflect the self-limiting perspective of biomedicine. Placebos are defined in terms of pharmacology, or the lack of pharmacological activity; mere "psychological" effects are considered a by-product of treatment, not an integral part of that treatment. A contradiction arises in that a patient can "respond" to treatment even when the effect is not "due to" the treatment itself. Placebo effects are critical in clinical studies of the efficacy of treatment of all kinds because their goal is to determine the efficacy of specific treatments and not the treatment setting itself. The use of inert substances or sham treatment is critical as an experimental control. For example, researchers have looked at brain function in response to acupuncture or sham acupuncture (the placebo condition). One of the primary experimental variables in any study of the placebo effect is "expectancy"—to what extent does the patient expect to get better as a result of treatment? In terms of the treatment of pain, where the placebo effect is most profoundly observed, acupuncture does stimulate neural pathways that are distinct from placebo treatment, and acupuncture may promote more long-lasting analgesic effects than the placebo (Dhond et al. 2007). Curiously, the sham-acupuncture conditions used in acupuncture pain studies, while not superior to actual acupuncture treatment, can also show a statistically positive effect compared to other physical and pharmacological placebos (Musial 2019).

The limited time course of placebo effectiveness is indicated by an old piece of medical advice to doctors, which states that they should not prescribe a placebo for too long a period to a patient. It may seem odd to think that a doctor would actually prescribe a placebo, but think of the millions of prescriptions of antibiotics that are handed out every year in the United States for the treatment of colds and sore throats that are known to be caused by a virus. "Mental relief" is worth something, and because most colds run their course in 10 days or so, antibiotic treatment, given after the cold virus has already been active for some time, will give the impression of effectiveness.

The placebo phenomenon is broader than simply describing when inert substances have treatment effects. The medical anthropologist Daniel Moerman (2002, 14) puts the placebo effect in the context of a more general *meaning response*, which he defines as the "psychological and physiological effects of *meaning* in the treatment of illness." Such effects can be positive, which result in what we usually think of as the placebo effect. When they are negative, then there is a **nocebo effect**. The nocebo effect is an

Harnessing the Power of the Placebo

Translational research in biomedicine is dedicated to taking basic knowledge from the lab or based on animal models and applying it in the clinical realm. As the biological, psychological, and cultural underpinnings of placebo and nocebo become better understood, it should be possible to use this basic knowledge to improve clinical care. Everyone knows that placebos can work, but how can they be made to work in a more clinically controlled and useful way?

Luana Colloca and Franklin Miller (2011) have looked at how translational research might apply to placebo and nocebo. They note that the placebo effect is real and is particularly effective for conditions such as pain, nausea, asthma, and phobia. The context in which the placebo is given is of critical importance. For pain treatment, placebos are more effective if patients are told how effective they are when they are given the substance, rather than simply handed them in a neutral way (as is often the case in clinical trials for analgesics). The flip side of this psychological phenomenon is that when patients are told about the side effects of a drug, their rates tend to increase—a clear nocebo effect. For example, when male patients are told that erectile dysfunction may be a side effect of a heart disease medicine, they have significantly higher rates of erectile dysfunction than if they are not told about it.

Colloca and Miller suggest there are at least two ways that basic knowledge about the placebo effect can be translated into clinical practice. First, studies show that certain drugs (e.g., immunosuppressive drugs) can retain effectiveness in progressively lower doses if they are linked to a conditioned stimulus. For example, patients can be given a drug along with a sweet-flavored syrup. Over time, the drug's effects can sometimes be maintained on the syrup alone, once the patient or the patient's body has made an association between the two. Some studies suggest that this sort of strategy might be useful in reducing the amount of drugs given to children with conditions such as ADHD.

The physician–patient relationship provides another potential vehicle for translating the placebo effect into clinical practice. The nocebo effect related to side effects demonstrates the power of suggestion coming from the physician to the patient. Colloca and Miller (2011) suggest that this power can also be used in a positive way. For example, pregnant women given an epidural injection during labor reported lower pain and discomfort from the procedure if the physician emphasized the positive aspects of relief from the procedure rather than warning them of the pain from the injection itself. In a more general sense, how physicians educate patients about their conditions and treatments clearly can play a positive or negative role on outcomes, independent of the material efficacy of the treatments.

How can physicians become better at using communication to harness the healing or analgesic powers of placebo? One way is by recognizing that their interactions with patients are influenced by the wider cultural and symbolic contexts. According to Ted Kaptchuk (2002), the physician–patient relationship in biomedicine, like healer–subject interactions in Navajo medicine or acupuncture, forms part of a healing ritual. Kaptchuk argues that the ritual component in biomedicine has clinically significant effects (i.e., placebo effects with neurobiological correlates) and that these effects vary according to both the individual biomedical practitioner and the medical treatment being used. Kaptchuk (2002, 1856) writes, "Both placebo and ritual effects are examples of how environmental cues and learning processes activate psychobiological mechanisms of healing." Insightful physicians probably recognize this implicitly, but translational research is necessary in this area to turn these insights into effective clinical practice.

---

interesting phenomenon in its own right. Robert Hahn (1998, 139) defines it as "the causation of sickness (or death) by expectations of sickness (or death) and by associated emotional states" (see the discussion in Chapter 10 of "voodoo death"). Hahn differentiates the nocebo effect from negative side effects that sometimes arise when people are given a placebo. Instead, nocebo illnesses occur in several different social contexts. For example, there are many historical instances of "epidemic hysteria" or "mass hysteria" in which a large group of people develop a similar illness, usually in response to shared exposure to some potentially malevolent substance. Such *sociogenic outbreaks* are probably more common than reported, as in cases where a large number of workers in an office become ill after smelling a strange odor. In all these cases, there is no known medical link between the illness and the putative causal agent. Social psychologists have also shown that it is not hard to manipulate subjects to have negative responses to inert substances if they are previously encouraged to have negative expectations about the substances. Hahn suggests that the nocebo effect is a "side-effect of human culture" (Hahn 1998, 142).

Returning to the placebo, its effects have been observed in a wide range of clinical studies and not only for pain, which has a significant emotional and subjective component. Placebo effects are present in studies of heart disease, knee surgery, and many other conditions. Great numbers of clinical studies show that patients in control groups who receive inert or sham treatment often show improvement, making it that much harder to demonstrate statistically the efficacy of a new treatment.

As Daniel Moerman notes, the placebo effect is part of the background of clinical research. Moerman (1983) demonstrated this in an analysis of 31 double-blind clinical trials for the ulcer drug cimetidine (Tagamet). Taken as a whole, as though all patients were in one supertrial, the drug showed highly statistically significant positive effects: 76% of those treated with the cimetidine were healed compared with 48% in the placebo group. However, taken separately, only 13 of the studies showed that the drug was more effective than the placebo, whereas 18 did not. Moerman analyzed the results from the separate studies and found that the variation in the placebo response was far greater than the variation in the drug response. For the 13 studies that showed a significant cimetidine effect, the mean response rate to the drug was 75% compared with only 37% for placebo; in the 18 studies where there was not a significant drug effect, the drug response rate was 77%, but the placebo rate was 58%. Thus, drug effectiveness was relatively uniform, but higher placebo response rates prevented the drug from showing a significant effect in the "unsuccessful" trials. Across all the studies, the placebo response rate varied from 10% to 90%. Moerman identified one cultural factor in producing this spread: the 6 studies done in Germany showed a significantly higher placebo response rate than the other 25 studies conducted elsewhere. He did not suggest a reason for this discrepancy but pointed out that such cultural variation would be useful knowledge when doing clinical studies of this kind. If clinical trials had only been done in Germany, then cimetidine would have looked like it was ineffective in the treatment of ulcer, but the overall picture clearly shows the opposite.

Efficacy

The placebo effect often comes to mind when addressing a basic question about traditional spiritual and religious healing methods: "Do they work?" Thomas Csordas and Elizabeth Lewton (1998) make the point that it is important to distinguish between *efficacy* and *effect*. Clinical biomedical research attempts to measure the efficacy of a treatment in the context of a scientific model of disease causation. Efficacy can be expressed in quantitative terms, such as how a treatment increases the percentage of patients who recover, reduces the number of patients with symptoms (e.g., for depression), decreases the number of side effects compared with another treatment, or allows people to live three years instead of one year. Healing in traditional contexts is about more than recovery from disease or illness. It is about "emotion, symbols, meaning, order, self, biology . . . about the meaning of being human" (Csordas and Lewton 1998, 496).

These issues also arise in a biomedical context, especially when a person faces a life-threatening disease, but a person in this situation does not necessarily look to doctors for ways to address them. Measuring the efficacy of traditional religious healing using standard biomedical outcomes does not make sense; however, as Csordas and Lewton (1998) point out, these treatments can have observable effects on well-being that may be quite profound. Rather than seeing the placebo effect as one that gives traditional healing its power, it may be more balanced to say that meaning responses (Moerman 2002) are a universal aspect of human cultural behavior, manifest in biomedicine as something called the placebo effect.

Although it might be inappropriate to assess indigenous healing methods with reference to biomedicine, it is reasonable to consider their efficacy in terms of what their consumers are seeking. James Waldram (2013) identifies two categories for examining the efficacy of indigenous treatments. "Transformative healing" is not concerned with returning an individual to a presickness state, but rather with changing the individual in some biological, cognitive, spiritual, or other way. Transformative healing is often an ongoing process, requiring a long-term relationship between the healer and the healed. In contrast, "restorative healing" has as its benchmark for efficacy a return to the presickness state. This can involve the elimination of pathology or, short of that, returning the patient to a functioning social condition. Although there may be an assumption that transformative healing will predominate in indigenous systems, this may in part be the result of a postcolonial context in which biomedicine is dominant for restorative healing. As Waldram (2013, 2015) has shown with his research among the Q'eqchi Maya healers of Belize (in a region where biomedicine is not easily accessible), their healing system is focused on identifying and curing specific pathological conditions. The stereotypical view that the indigenous healer and patient must share a significant relationship or symbolic language is not supported. As Waldram states (2015, 293), "like biomedicine, Q'eqchi healing seems focused on the treatment of the disorder more so than the patient." Q'eqchi patients accept this and see an efficacious treatment as one that restores them to their previous health and not simply transformed into a new state of being.

Vaccination and Anti-Vaxx Movements

One of the most efficacious biomedical practices ever developed is vaccination (see Chapter 8 for more details on how it works). Because of vaccinations, diseases that used to kill, disfigure, or maim a large percentage of the human population are now no longer a large public health threat. These diseases include smallpox, measles, mumps, rubella, chicken pox, polio, bacterial encephalitis, diphtheria, and whooping cough. Our best hope for eventually controlling diseases such as HIV/AIDS, Ebola, and severe acute respiratory syndrome associated with corona viruses rests with the development of effective vaccines. Yet despite multiple demonstrations of overwhelming efficacy with minimal risk, resistance to vaccination remains, and in some sub-cultures, is growing (Kinch 2018). The (semi-) organized opposition to vaccination has been termed the "anti-vaxx movement."

Opposition to vaccination has arisen in different cultural settings, for a variety of reasons. In a carefully constructed, comparative ethnographic study, Svea Closser and colleagues (Closser et al. 2016) looked at vaccine refusal in seven different countries (Nepal, India, Pakistan, Ethiopia, Nigeria, Rwanda, and Angola) in response to the multi-billion dollar Global Polio Eradication Initiative (GPEI). At sites where refusal is high, distrust of the government and nervousness about its goals are prevalent. Distrust of the government was fostered by the perceived (and real) mismatch between the high levels of funding the polio eradication program obviously enjoyed compared to the low levels given to support health systems in general. People expressed suspicion about why polio was receiving more attention than other, more pressing health issues. In the ultra-Orthodox Jewish community of New York City, low rates of vaccination are fueled by suspicion of outsiders and vaccination itself, as well as by the fatalistic religious view that illness is under the "control of God" (Silverberg et al. 2019). And in Samoa, vaccination rates for measles (MMR vaccine) for infants in the first year of life plummeted from 60%–70% to 31% after an incident in 2018 in which nurses mistakenly mixed the vaccine with a muscle relaxant instead of water, resulting in the deaths of two infants. The nurses were convicted of manslaughter, but a direct result of the decline in vaccination rates following this instance of medical malpractice was a measles outbreak that, as of late 2019, had sickened 4,900 people (out of a total population of about 200,000), killing 71, mostly under the age of 5 years (Sun 2019).

While there were local or cultural reasons for their low vaccination rates, ultra-Orthodox Jews in New York City and Samoans have also been subject to anti-vaxx campaigns from outside their communities. In fact, a Samoan activist influenced by outsiders was arrested for incitement in the midst of the epidemic for claiming that the government's vaccine would result in mass fatalities (Sun 2019). The anti-vaxx movement has been characterized in the United States as being led by "many of the nation's elite, wealthy, and progressive minds [who] suffer from a false sense of believing they have special insight into the truth" (Kinch 2018, x). This "truth," for which there is no scientific basis, is that some vaccines pose a substantial risk for developing conditions such as autism or other neurological and psychiatric impairments. Although in the U.S. vaccination rates for poor and uninsured children are substantially lower than for wealthier and insured children, the recent decline in vaccination rates among insured children is higher, reflecting the anti-vaxx movement's support among the relatively better-off (Hill 2016; Kinch 2018). The vast majority of children receive their vaccinations; however, among children aged 19–35 months, 1.3% of those born in 2015 had not received any vaccinations compared to 0.3% in 2001.

Anthropologist Elisa Sobo and her colleagues have conducted numerous surveys and interviews with parents who choose not to vaccinate their children and compared their attitudes with those who do (Brunson and Sobo 2017; Sobo 2015, 2016a, 2016b; Sobo et al. 2016). Sobo's anthropology of refusal and resistance reveals that a range of cultural and personal factors underlie the anti-vaccinator movement. Her research on the attitudes of parents at a Waldorf school—part of an alternative education movement emphasizing experiential learning and the arts—demonstrates that while they are suspicious of the potential toxicity of vaccines and the profit-driven motives of drug companies, these are not the most critical factors in adopting an anti-vaccination stance. Rather, in-group identification may play the most significant role. Sobo (2016b, 348) writes,

> To refuse vaccine-preventable diseases—to engage in or endorse vaccination—is to proclaim one's social communion with the mainstream. Similarly, to refuse a vaccination is to proclaim one's affiliation with significant others from beyond the mainstream . . .

vaccine refusal entails an act of identification—of opting in—of proclaiming "I belong" and "I share your values." Through vaccine refusal and related expressions of vaccine caution, parents make their commitment to the in-group norms clear, thereby ensuring continued good relations with socially valued others.

Sobo (2016a) has found that ideas about herd immunity (see Chapter 8) have little to do with parents' anti-vaccination stance. Many parents do not understand the concept, and even if they do, they generally do not perceive anti-vaccination as a selfish stance, even as other parents' children take on the risks of vaccination to the benefit of their own. She and her colleagues (Sobo et al. 2016) have also found that non-vaccinating parents also exhibit more "self-informed engagement" with the health-care system. That is, they are more likely than parents who routinely accept vaccination to do Internet research, leading to skepticism about vaccination but not a cohesive view of its risks and benefits. Sobo argues that these results suggest (1) that public health authorities cannot appeal to altruism to change anti-vaccination parents' minds because those parents do not think they are acting selfishly, and (2) that any narrative constructed to promote the benefits of vaccination should keep in mind the interactive nature of anti-vaccination parents' engagement with the health system and its self-defined experts.

CONCLUSION

Knowledge about healing is a form of power. As Horacio Fabrega (1997) points out, the power acquired in the healing realm can be translated into power in other realms. How healing power is converted into other forms of power differs in simple and complex societies, but in both, there are opportunities for abuse. Healers develop a better reputation when they have successful outcomes, but once they have achieved power and prestige, it may be in their interest to perpetuate illness or to expand the scope of their activities. The "medicalization of pregnancy" during the twentieth century and the expansion of psychiatric services to the "worried well" may be considered examples of the expansionist tendencies of biomedicine, which have occurred since it became the dominant and institutionalized healing force throughout the developed world. Of course, biomedicine, including practitioners and pharmaceutical manufacturers, also responds to consumer demands and broad political and economic forces. However, in recent years, concern has arisen over the power of the pharmaceutical industry to shape, as well as respond to, consumer demand. "Big Pharma," as it is sometimes called, spends billions of dollars in the United States on media advertising ($5 billion in 2016) and its sales force every year, along with hundreds of millions of dollars dedicated towards lobbying Congress; the nine largest pharmaceutical firms spend 2.5 times as much on marketing as on research and development (Hoffer 2019; Manchanda et al. 2005).

Medical systems in most multicultural societies rarely deliver the same quality of health care to all members of the society: the best care goes to the most powerful. In the 1990s, indigenous Maori health workers in New Zealand developed the concept of "cultural safety" to address inherent power imbalances in biomedical treatment (Curtis et al. 2019). Their goal was to lessen inequities in the health-care system related to ethnicity. It was apparent that even well-meaning physicians could be complicit in perpetuating inequities, if they themselves did recognize their role in the power asymmetry inherent in the medical system. Elana Curtis and colleagues have recently reviewed three decades worth of discussion about cultural safety and the closely related issue of cultural competency. They suggest that the following definition of cultural safety should be adopted by healthcare organizations (Curtis et al. 2019, 14):

> Cultural safety requires healthcare professionals and their associated healthcare organizations to examine themselves and the potential impact of their own culture on clinical interactions and healthcare delivery. This requires individual healthcare professionals and healthcare organizations to acknowledge and address their own biases, attitudes, assumptions, stereotypes, prejudices, structures and characteristics that may affect the quality of care provided. In doing so, cultural safety encompasses a critical consciousness where healthcare professionals and healthcare organizations engage in ongoing self-reflection and self-awareness and hold themselves accountable for providing culturally safe care, as defined by the patient and their communities, and as measured through progress towards achieving health equity. . . .

Although the framers of the statement are most concerned with inequities related to ethnicity, cultural safety could clearly address inequities based on gender, age, or economic status.

The rise in popularity of alternative and complementary forms of medicine in recent years may have been in part fueled by a suspicion of the power of biomedicine. If patients feel that health-care practitioners are not acting in their best interest, then it is natural for them to seek care elsewhere. It is a truism of the modern age that those in power are largely interested in expanding and consolidating that power, usually at the expense of others, but there is another factor that may also underlie the appeal of alternative forms of medicine. Medical practitioners these days often seem more like "body technicians" or "body mechanics" than healers (Watts 1996). Technology improves the efficacy of a wide range of treatments but also introduces barriers in the development of a strong relationship between the patient and primary caregiver. "Going to the doctor" can now seem more like a series of visits to stations and machines, where technicians make measurements or collect bodily fluids in assembly-line style. Many physicians are as uncomfortable with this situation as the patients, and they seek to maintain a strong relationship with their patients. We should keep in mind that the new physicians who are being recruited today may be people who are more comfortable working in a highly technological setting than in the past. In many ways, from the perspective of medical consumers, this may be desirable if it delivers more effective treatments of illness and injury. However, as we have seen, healing goes beyond the body returning to a healthy state—it is about engaging in a fundamental human social relationship that results in the patient feeling better.

STUDY QUESTIONS

1. How do cultural ideas about disease causation influence healing practices? Why is diagnosis so critical in all healing systems?
2. Are the boundaries between Western biomedicine and traditional medical systems always clearly demarcated? Discuss using three examples.

3. Why are English surgeons called "Mr." or "Ms." instead of "Dr.?" How does this relate to basic divisions seen in healing systems cross-culturally?

4. What is evidence-based medicine?

5. Compare and contrast three forms of healer recruitment. How do healers become socially validated to fill their role?

6. What are alternative and complementary medicines? Why is this an ethnocentric designation?

7. How do acupuncture and chiropractic differ from conventional biomedicine?

8. Describe the various forms of Navajo healing. What are their different cultural sources?

9. What is death? How do concepts of death influence medical treatment?

10. What are placebo and nocebo?

11. Compare and contrast restorative and transformative healing.

12. What role does efficacy play in shaping anti-vaccination attitudes?

CRITICAL THINKING QUESTIONS

1. How should the rights of indigenous peoples be protected when medications are developed based on traditional practices?

2. How legally regulated should alternative and complementary medicines be? What role should biomedical practitioners play in recognizing the validity of alternative practices? What role should insurance companies play?

3. What nonbiomedical healing practices were employed in your home while you were growing up? What were the sources of these practices?

4. Is cross-cultural misunderstanding a major problem in delivering health care in the United States? Or is it a convenient label that actually hides more fundamental problems of socioeconomic status and health care?

5. What does it mean to say you "trust" your medical practitioner in the 2020s?

SUGGESTED ETHNOGRAPHIES TO READ WITH THIS CHAPTER

Anne Fadiman. 1997. *The Spirit Catches You and You Fall Down: A Hmong Child, Her American Doctors, and the Collision of Two Cultures.* New York: Farrar, Straus, and Giroux.

Michel Foucault. 1994. *The Birth of the Clinic.* New York: Vintage.

Michael Kinch. 2018. *Between Hope and Fear. A History of Vaccines and Human Immunity.* New York: Pegasus Books.

Margaret Lock. 2002. *Twice Dead: Organ Transplants and the Reinvention of Death.* Berkeley: University of California Press.

Daniel Moerman. 2002. *Meaning, Medicine, and the "Placebo Effect."* Cambridge, UK: Cambridge University Press.

Lynn Payer. 1996. *Medicine and Culture.* New York: Holt.

Lesley Sharp. 2006. *Strange Harvest: Organ Transplants, Denatured Bodies, and the Transformed Self.* Berkeley: University of California Press.

Loudell F. Snow. 1993. *Walkin' over Medicine.* Boulder, CO: Westview Press.

CHAPTER 4

Diet and Nutrition in Health and Disease

Chapter Goals

- To understand some key concerns in human nutrition
- To understand how an evolutionary perspective on diet and nutrition helps clarify some contemporary diet-related diseases
- To see how diet changed with the transition from hunting-gathering to agriculture and the effects on human health
- To understand the role of biological variation in response to milk and wheat and its relationship with current dietary policies and patterns
- To understand more recent transitions in diet and how they are related to obesity and diabetes trends
- To consider the long-term consequences of dietary changes in light of climate change and sustainability concerns

The Paleo diet. Gluten free. Vegan. Low fat. Low carb. MyPlate. These are all contemporary types of dietary advice. They also recommend very different foods, but each purports to improve your health. In addition to these diets are frequent media reports about nutrition studies that may seem contradictory. Amid this chaotic array of dietary guidance, what should you eat? This is a decision that individuals make every day. The effect of diet on the body is the topic that interests scientists in nutrition and public health because a population's dietary patterns contribute to their disease patterns, whether they are rates of cardiovascular disease or child stunting from protein-energy malnutrition. What constitutes the "ideal" or "healthiest" diet for humans is the subject of a great deal of ongoing research. Many countries develop their own dietary guidelines, which are supposed to be authoritative statements about the best diet to enhance health, given food availability and local culinary traditions, but these guidelines are also controversial because they may be shaped by the interests of powerful food industries (Nestle 2018a). Understanding the links between diet and health is an especially pertinent issue given both the variability in human diets across the world and the globalization of food, which is generating greater homogeneity in dietary practices.

There's no question that diet plays a major role in health and disease. Specific nutrient deficiencies or surpluses can result in discrete syndromes, whereas more generalized shortages or excess can result in dysfunction across many physiological systems. Diet is a major contributor to cardiovascular and metabolic disease as well as some forms of cancer (Willett 2017). All humans require roughly the same nutrients, although the absolute amount varies depending on age, size, activity patterns, and unspecified individual factors. However, the range of possible diets that provides these nutrients is wide, as is the variation in the types of diets humans consume. Consider, for example, traditional Inuit diets, which were composed mainly of fatty meat because plant foods were available in the Arctic only during the brief summer. Contrast those with the heavily plant-based diets of populations living in tropical forests, where large game animals are scarce and plant life is highly diversified. Then there are typical American diets, in which refined grains and ultra-processed foods are staples, along with meat and dairy products.

In this chapter we present a brief overview of human nutrition and its relationship to human diets and biology. We then explore the links between nutrition and health and examine how anthropology provides a unique perspective on these relationships. Human biological characteristics evolved in the context of specific dietary environments, yet most contemporary humans consume foods different from those of our ancestors in the distant past. This dietary "mismatch" is likely to result in health problems of dietary origin because our bodies evolved to process a diet that little resembles those that are common today (Cordain et al. 2005; Eaton et al. 1999). Many of the foods that are relatively cheap and ubiquitous in markets around the world are dense in calories, fat, or salt; such foods would have been rare in human diets of the past. As human populations experienced different diets in their unique pasts, genetic adaptations emerged in some human groups during the major subsistence transition from foraging to food production around 10,000 years ago. In this new dietary context, new modes of food processing also enabled human populations to extract nutrients from what became a much less diverse diet. Within the past few hundred years, transport and trade have exposed people to new foods, and industrialization yielded new forms of processing that have transformed the foods we eat. New concerns about sustainability have come to the fore in dietary guidance in the twenty-first century.

HUMAN NUTRITION

Nutrition is a relatively young science, having been developed in the 1910s and 1920s. Much remains to be learned about how specific components of the diet affect human health and well-being, but most of the basic knowledge about human nutritional requirements was worked out by the mid-twentieth century. Importantly, the idea that nutrient deficiencies could cause disease was initially not considered likely because medicine was dominated by enthusiasm over Koch and Pasteur's germ theory of disease at the turn of the century (see Chapter 8;

Carter 1977). For example, beriberi was known as a widespread disease in Southeast Asia in the late nineteenth century, and efforts to demonstrate its infectious cause were fruitless. Christiaan Eijkman and Frederick Gowland Hodgkins were able to show that it was caused by a deficiency of thiamine (now also known as vitamin B1), a discovery consistent with growing evidence that other syndromes such as scurvy or pellagra were also caused by vitamin deficiencies (vitamin C and niacin [vitamin B3], respectively).

In light of this, it is interesting to note that training in nutrition remains marginal to medical education; until the mid- to late-twentieth century, nutrition was often folded into departments of home economics (which mainly trained women) rather than in schools of medicine or public health (which were dominated by men). A recent survey of the medical schools in the United States (Adams et al. 2015) found that although the National Research Council recommends 25–30 hours of nutrition education, the average number of hours reported in the survey was 19. More than one-third of schools required less than 12 hours and 9% required none. Furthermore, less than 20% provided a dedicated nutrition course, with most integrating nutrition into other preclinical classes and few providing nutrition training in the context of clinical practice. What is even more discouraging is the downward trend in requirements for the number of hours of nutrition education in medical schools, and fewer schools are providing a dedicated nutrition course. As Devries and colleagues recently lamented, "Nutrition education in medical school is rudimentary, at best, and limited for the duration of graduate medical education for many specialties. Requirements for meaningful nutrition education in all phases of medical training are long overdue" (Devries et al. 2019, 1351). They argued that there is good evidence for the effectiveness of dietary interventions for many chronic diseases (especially cardiovascular disease) yet physicians lack the training to adequately advise their patients.

Organisms eat primarily to get energy to fuel their metabolic and activity requirements. A certain number of calories is required each day just to stay alive, a number that varies by age, sex, and body size and composition.[1] For humans, up to 20% of that goes to fuel our large brain! Energy is derived from two main sources: carbohydrates in plant foods (which provide glucose) and fat in animal and some plant foods (especially nuts and seeds). Although these comprise the largest component of the diet, other nutrients are needed in smaller quantities. Protein can also be used for energy, but it is required in the diet as a source of amino acids; among the 20 known amino acids, 9 are considered essential for humans, meaning they must come from food. The remaining 11 can be synthesized from the essential amino acids. These are used to make the body's own proteins, which serve a variety of purposes, from the structure of muscle and bone to carrier proteins that transport

---

[1] A calorie is actually more accurately referred to as a kilocalorie, which is equivalent to the amount of energy needed to raise one liter of water 1 degree centigrade (a calorie itself is the amount of energy needed to raise 1 gram of water 1 degree centigrade, but this "small" calorie designation is rarely used). The standard international unit for energy is the kilojoule. One kilocalorie is equivalent to 4.18 kilojoules.

oxygen to tissues or molecules across the membranes of cells. Amino acids also serve as the sole source of metabolizable nitrogen for the synthesis of the genetic material deoxyribonucleic acid (DNA) and related molecules. Although animals can synthesize fat from excess calories, one fatty acid (linoleic acid), which is found in seeds and dark-green leafy vegetables, is considered essential because humans cannot make it themselves. This "essential" fat is used for making other fat-based biochemicals, such as steroid hormones.

Carbohydrates, protein, and fat are collectively referred to as macronutrients because they are needed in relatively large quantities, supply energy (calories), and are used to make fundamental body structures. In addition, there are many micronutrients required for various functions. Some are vitamins, which are divided into those that are water soluble and cannot be stored (the B vitamins and vitamin C) and those that are fat soluble and can be stored in the body (A, D, E, and K). Many of the B vitamins are involved in energy metabolism, a complex set of cycles requiring numerous enzymes and cofactors that include these vitamins. Vitamin B12 is of particular interest because it is found only in animal foods and requires a special mechanism, the intrinsic factor, for absorption in the stomach. Vitamin C is an antioxidant but is also involved in the synthesis of collagen, the protein in muscle and connective tissue. Many of the water-soluble vitamins act as antioxidants, protecting cells from sustaining damage from oxygen-**free radicals**, which are common highly reactive molecules that are known to cause cellular damage. Among the fat-soluble vitamins, vitamin A is found exclusively in animal foods, but can be synthesized from plant-based β-carotenes. Vitamin E is broadly distributed in plants, and vitamin K, which is involved in blood clotting, can be synthesized by specialized bacteria in the colon.

Vitamin D is found primarily in fish oils and is involved in calcium absorption and deposition of calcium in bone. It can also be synthesized; specialized skin cells convert a vitamin D precursor into active vitamin D in the presence of ultraviolet light. At high latitudes it is not possible to synthesize sufficient vitamin D during the winter months because the sun's rays are not sufficiently powerful to induce the conversion, and covering up most of the skin or having darker skin also reduces vitamin D synthesis. In some countries, such as the United States, milk is fortified with vitamin D because of its connections to calcium utilization.

The other group of micronutrients is the minerals. Calcium forms the inorganic matrix of bone and also regulates neuron activity, muscle contraction, and blood clotting. Sodium is required for maintaining fluid balance in the body and, in conjunction with potassium, for the conduction of nerve impulses. Among the trace minerals (those needed in minute quantities), iron is a component of hemoglobin, the protein in red blood cells that carries oxygen throughout the body, and it plays other roles in energy generation and the synthesis of collagen and various neurotransmitters. Zinc is an important cofactor for more than 300 enzymes and hence is involved in numerous functions throughout the body. Last, iodine is a key component of thyroid hormones, which regulate metabolic rate and promote growth and development.

What Is Hunger?

Everyone knows the feeling of being hungry, although it is hard to describe in words. Hunger pangs result from contractions in the stomach, possibly stimulated by the hormone ghrelin, which is associated with appetite for food. Prolonged hunger can stem from crop failures and famine, economic inability to procure food, or purposeful dieting, and can result in starvation, characterized by fatigue, weakness, or irritability, and ultimately the catabolism of the body's own energy and protein resources and death. Yet hunger is hard to quantify, and in 2006 in the United States, the problem of hunger was recast as varying levels of food security, with four categories:

Food Security:
- High food security (old label: Food security): no reported indications of food-access problems or limitations.
- Marginal food security (old label: Food security): one or two reported indications—typically of anxiety over food sufficiency or shortage of food in the house. Little or no indication of changes in diets or food intake.

Food Insecurity:
- Low food security (old label: Food insecurity without hunger): reports of reduced quality, variety, or desirability of diet. Little or no indication of reduced food intake.
- Very low food security (old label: Food insecurity with hunger): Reports of multiple indications of disrupted eating patterns and reduced food intake.

It did not escape notice that the new terminology removed the emotional impact of the word "hunger," replacing it with the more neutral term "food insecurity." The panel recommending this change distinguished hunger from food insecurity, noting that hunger is an individual-level physiological condition that may result from food insecurity and would require collection of more detailed and extensive information on physiological experiences of individual household members than could be reasonably accomplished in national surveys. Food insecurity is a household-level economic and social condition of limited or uncertain access to adequate food that can be assessed through national household surveys (Coleman-Jensen et al. 2019).

In 2018 about 11% of all households in the United States were categorized as "food insecure," which was down from the high of almost 15% in 2011, but 14% of all households with children and over 35% of households below the poverty line were classified as "food insecure" (Coleman-Jensen et al. 2019). For comparative purposes, about 8% of all households in Canada are food insecure, with much higher rates among households living in the northern and northwestern territories (Roshanafshar and Hawkins 2018). At the global level, the Global Hunger Index is calculated for countries based on the number of individuals with insufficient access to calories, along with rates of stunting (low height), wasting (low weight for height) and mortality among children under five years (https://www.globalhungerindex.org/results). Over 12% of the world's population (800 million people) is undernourished, and almost 28% of all children under five years are stunted and/or wasted. At present, countries in sub-Saharan Africa and South Asia have some of the highest levels of the hunger index.

Ending hunger has been a part of international food and health agencies for the past few decades. One of the UN's Millennium Development Goals was to halve the number of people suffering from hunger by 2015, which was close to being reached (prevalence went from 23% in 1990 to 13% in 2015). Among the UN Sustainable Development Goals for 2030, adopted in September 2015, is Sustainable Development Goal 2: End hunger, achieve food security and improved nutrition and promote sustainable agriculture (United Nations 2020). There is widespread agreement that hunger or food insecurity is not simply attributable to a lack of food production but rather to problems in distribution and economic access, but there is also a great deal of current concern about climate change's impacts on food production and sustainability (Watts et al. 2018a, b).

Undernutrition is well known to impair survival and contribute to numerous health problems, from chronic disease to infection (Black et al. 2013; Martins et al. 2011), and medical anthropologists Leslie Jo Weaver and Craig Hadley have considered the ways in which food insecurity also has negative effects on mental health: "Whether expressed as acute feelings of anguish and despair; as anxiety, resignation, hopelessness, and shame; or as embodied symptoms, qualitative analysis of this group of studies suggests that food insecurity compromises mental health" (Weaver and Hadley 2009, 275). Furthermore, food insecurity may be overshadowed by more visible health concerns such as HIV/AIDS, yet sufficient food is essential to effective treatment (Kalofonos 2010).

HOW MANY NUTRIENTS DO YOU NEED?

For any given individual, exactly how many macro- or micronutrients are required is not known. Instead, standards for nutrient needs are assessed at the population level and take the form of **Dietary Reference Intakes** (DRIs), which are a diverse set of standards that are not always straightforward to interpret. In the U.S. and Canada they are developed by the Food and Nutrition Board of the Institute of Medicine, which is part of the National Academies of Science; at present there is no global standard for these (see Allen et al. 2020 for a proposal to do so). They are the basis for the Dietary Guidelines for Americans (DGAs), which translate nutrient requirements into dietary recommendations and set the standards for food and nutrition programs.

The DRIs include the following:

- Estimated Average Requirements (EARs): This amount should satisfy the needs of 50% of the population.
- Recommended Dietary Allowances (RDAs): This amount should meet the requirements of nearly all healthy individuals in particular age/sex groups.
- Adequate Intake (AI): When no RDA is established, this is the amount that is believed to be adequate for a demographic group. It is used when firm scientific evidence does not exist for a given nutrient.
- Tolerable Upper Intake Levels (UL): For nutrients whose overconsumption can be dangerous (such as sodium or vitamin A), the UL is the maximum intake that does not appear to be associated with deleterious effects.
- Acceptable Macronutrient Distribution Range (AMDR): Provides a range of intake for macronutrients that is associated with protection from chronic disease while maintaining essential nutrient intake.

Adding to the confusion are Daily Values (DVs), which are used in food labeling, and regulated by the Food and Drug Administration in the United States. DVs are reported as percentages of the Recommended Daily Intakes (RDIs), based on the highest levels of the 1968 RDAs for adults and older children, standardized to a 2,000-kilocalorie intake. However, given that some are ULs and some are RDAs, the meaning of the percentage varies by nutrient.

DRIs have fluctuated over time as a function of new scientific evidence but also as a result of changing health concerns. For example, when the RDAs were established in 1941, they were used to assess the sufficiency of the American diet during wartime. However, current concerns about chronic diseases have resulted in changes in recommendations as linkages between nutrient intakes and cardiovascular disease, stroke, or cancer are demonstrated. Importantly, DRIs are based on the assessment of overall scientific evidence, but in fact most of the data come from the United States or Europe, so it is not known with any certainty whether there are meaningful population differences in nutrient requirements beyond those reported for different age or sex groups (King and Garza 2007). See Nestle (2013) for a critical history of the development of nutrient recommendations and the DGAs.

When people consume the nutrients they need in the appropriate amounts, they are said to be in nutrient balance, or to have good nutritional status. If they receive too few nutrients, they suffer from **undernutrition**. If they receive too many it is called **overnutrition**. A word that can cover both conditions is **malnutrition**—which simply means "bad nutrition." In practice, malnutrition is most often used as a synonym for undernutrition. **Protein-energy malnutrition** occurs when there are shortages of these macronutrients. Deficiencies in the macronutrients usually lead to weight loss or, in children, deficits in growth in weight or height, as we will see in Chapter 5.

It is often difficult to diagnose nutrient deficiencies except in their extreme forms. Symptoms take time to manifest, and a few days of nutrient deficiencies are not likely to have any serious or long-lasting consequences. However, chronic deficiencies can. In response to low intake of nutrients, there are several adaptive physiological responses: more efficient absorption, conservation, mobilization of fat stores, or breakdown of active body tissues (e.g., muscle for protein) and prioritization of nutrient flow to more critical organs such as the brain. In the case of energy deficiency (as in food shortages or deliberate dieting), fat stores are mobilized first because they can be used to fuel muscle activity. Organs such as the brain cannot use fat, but they can use ketones, which are a product of fat breakdown in the liver (and the source of energy recommended for those following a high fat "keto" diet). When these energy resources are exhausted, muscle protein, as well as that from the heart, liver, kidneys, and other organs, can be used to synthesize glucose, which is the preferred energy source, especially for the brain. Fatigue is common to low-energy diets and probably acts to reduce energy expenditure. Deficiencies of protein and energy are associated with reduced fat deposits and muscle wasting, as well as impaired growth among children.

Just as there are nutrient deficiency syndromes, there are also potential negative health effects of nutrient surpluses, although most vitamin and mineral excesses are

Anthropologist in Action: Ellen Messer

Ellen Messer is biocultural anthropologist who has worked extensively on hunger, food and conflict, and the human right to food. She is currently a visiting faculty member at Tufts University's Friedman School of Nutrition Science and Policy and has long been involved in bringing anthropological sensitivities to understanding both the roots of hunger and the policies designed to alleviate it.

As an "activist-scholar," Dr. Messer has spent the past decades investigating how hunger and inadequate access to safe, sufficient, and nutritious food (i.e., food insecurity) are involved in conflicts throughout the developing world. She and her colleagues coined the phrase "food wars" in the 1980s to describe how conflicts may stem from lack of food, how conflicts may result in widespread hunger or lack of access to food, and how food is used as a tool in wars and other smaller-scale conflicts. She has helped bring these complex issues (which are sadly on display in multiple sites in the world today including Syria and Yemen) to international food policy makers. Dr. Messer notes that domestic and global food and nutrition programs are not motivated primarily by the goal of ending hunger, but by other economic and political rationales that help proponents obtain continued funding.

Along with nutritional anthropologist Barrett Brenton, Dr. Messer produced "Talking Points on the Human Right to Food" for the office that advises the Holy See, which in turn informed Pope Francis's initiatives on hunger and environmental issues. These points were brought up at the UN General Assembly statement in September 2016. Working with other advocates and activists, her work brings the discourse and discussions on food-security and UN Millennium/Sustainable Development Goals back to the goals of ending hunger and respecting, protecting, and fulfilling human rights, while making the connections to food sovereignty frameworks advanced by Frances Moore Lappe, co-founder and co-principal of Food First! Institute for Food and Development Policy and the Small Planet Institute.

While working with policy makers at multiple levels, Dr. Messer emphasizes the importance of developing networks of colleagues to advance changes in policy, and as a scholar, she also sees her primary contribution as teaching and mentoring students at all levels and in a diverse array of disciplines, from anthropology to legal studies.

likely to come from nutrient supplements rather than from food. One food-related (if unusual) example is that it is possible to overconsume vitamin A if the liver of carnivorous animals such as polar bears is eaten because that is where vitamin A is concentrated. Overconsumption of fat, carbohydrates, and sodium is quite possible when the diet is based on energy-dense or ultra-processed foods. Excesses of sodium may contribute to **hypertension**. Overconsumption of the macronutrients can contribute to weight gain, which in turn is associated with increased risk of various chronic diseases such as heart disease, diabetes, and various cancers.

DIET AND DIGESTION

Humans have a generalized digestive system, which seems well adapted for a high-quality omnivorous diet that includes both plant and animal foods and is rich in nutrients relative to undigestible fiber. Other organisms, such as cows and leaf-eating monkeys, have big specialized stomachs that house colonies of bacteria to ferment the substantial quantities of fiber they consume from grass or leaves. An enlarged cecum, the pouch between the small and large intestine, fills the same role in other plant-eating organisms. Humans lack these gut specializations, as shown in Figure 4.1.

Digestion starts in the mouth, where the teeth break up large food particles and the salivary enzyme amylase begins to break down starches (complex carbohydrates). After swallowing, food goes through the esophagus into the stomach, where it is subjected to strong acids that kill potential pathogens and enzymes that begin the process of digesting proteins. After two to three hours there, the resulting material (chyme) is sent into the small intestine. Most of the work of digestion and absorption is done within the small intestine. Here digestive enzymes (many coming from the pancreas) interact with food particles to break down starches, sugars, fats, proteins, and micronutrient complexes into their component parts, which can then be absorbed by the cells that line the small intestine. The remaining undigestible material continues on to the large intestine (colon), where water is absorbed.

The colon also has large colonies of bacteria known as the gut microbiota, most of which can ferment fibrous material that humans cannot break down with their own digestive enzymes. The role that gut microbiota play in human health and disease has become a major new area of research because some bacteria are associated with greater risk of obesity or metabolic disorders, whereas others protect the integrity of the gut itself, modulate the immune system, alter drug activity, or influence mood, among other things (Collen 2016). "Healthy" microbiota help maintain the gut's barrier (so foreign substances don't leak through and get into circulation), prevent colonization of the gut by pathogenic bacteria, and also control inflammation (Collen 2016). Gut microbiota vary across human populations and diets that are higher in fiber and minimally processed plant foods appears to be associated with "healthier" and more diverse gut microbial profiles compared to the high fat/low fiber that are typical of many Western diets (Xu and Knight 2015). Routine use of antibiotics is also detrimental to gut microbiota in the long term (Ianiro et al. 2016). However, knowledge of the microbiota's relationship to health is in its initial stages, and what constitutes a "healthy" microbiome has yet to be established (McBurney et al. 2019).

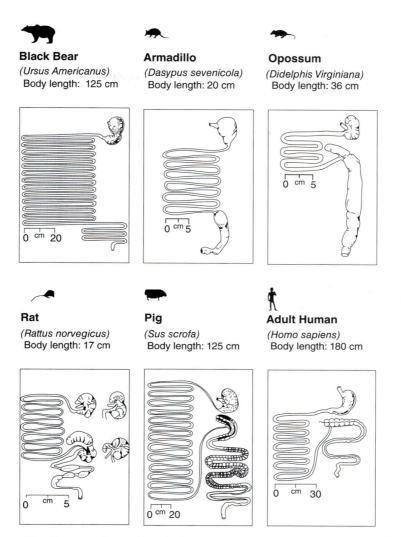

Black Bear
(Ursus Americanus)
Body length: 125 cm

Armadillo
(Dasypus sevenicola)
Body length: 20 cm

Opossum
(Didelphis Virginiana)
Body length: 36 cm

Rat
(Rattus norvegicus)
Body length: 17 cm

Pig
(Sus scrofa)
Body length: 125 cm

Adult Human
(Homo sapiens)
Body length: 180 cm

FIGURE 4.1   The diversity of gastrointestinal systems across mammals. Compared with other mammals, humans have a simple digestive tract, with no elaborated specialized digestive organs. This likely reflects an adaptation to a high-quality omnivorous diet.
Source: Stevens, C. Edward, and Ian D. Hume 1998. "Contributions of microbes in vertebrate gastrointestinal tract to production and conservation of nutrients." *Physiological Reviews* 78 (2):393–427. Reprinted with permission from The American Physiological Society.

Nutrients that have been absorbed are transported via the lymph system to the bloodstream or they are sent via the portal vein to the liver for further processing. Ultimately, nutrients go to tissues that need to utilize them immediately. Excess fats are stored, and excess sugar and amino acid skeletons can be converted to adipose tissue (fat) as well. In contrast, the body has a limited capacity to store protein, minerals, or water-soluble vitamins, so surpluses of these are excreted in urine.

Food Allergies

Food allergies are immunologically mediated reactions to foods that are not dangerous for the vast majority of individuals, with symptoms ranging from mild tingling of the mouth and tongue or hives (rash) to anaphylaxis, which can be fatal. A global survey of food allergies found rates varying from 1% to 2% in Thailand to 10% in Australia (Ashley et al. 2015). In high-income countries the prevalence of food allergies is between 5% and 8% (Dunlop and Keet 2018) and is generally understood to have increased dramatically over the past decade. Rates are higher among young children, who often outgrow them as they age. The most common food allergies are to peanut, milk, and shellfish. Children born in the winter in northern U.S. cities have higher allergy rates than those born in the summer, and it has been suggested that vitamin D (recall that vitamin D is synthesized in the presence of ultraviolet light, which is insufficient during winter months in such areas) may play a role in this finding (Vassallo et al. 2010).

In a systematic review of the literature, Chafen and colleagues (2010) found that there was no uniform definition, diagnostic standard, therapeutic course, or strategy for prevention of food allergies. They argued that food allergies are likely overreported and that individuals unnecessarily restrict their diets as a result; at the same time, the ambiguity surrounding their diagnosis "obscures the substantial morbidity caused in patients truly affected by immune-mediated food allergy and serves to perpetuate some public misperceptions that food allergy is a trivial medical condition" (Chafen et al. 2010, 1854). Individuals with allergies or their caretakers suffer from a variety of psychosocial stresses that negatively impact their quality of life, especially when the condition is trivialized or challenged by peers (Cummings et al. 2010).

A common theme emerges in the discussion of food allergies (or intolerances such as to lactose or gluten; see below): clinicians—and often peers—are skeptical of individuals' needs for dietary restriction. Why should this group of syndromes be singled out? In some ways they are not—other illnesses such as chronic fatigue syndrome, irritable bowel syndrome, or fibromyalgia are often treated with similar disdain, and individuals' suffering is not legitimated (that is, they are not allowed to take on the sick role). All have diverse symptoms, including chronic malaise, that overlap with multiple other disease states. There is a lack of clear diagnostic procedures and/or treatments, and these syndromes are often attributed to psychological stress by clinicians (Nelson and Ogden 2008). What makes food-related syndromes even more complicated is the social nature of eating. To reject food is to reject conviviality and engagement with others in routine social activity, and ostracism or outright challenges with the contested foods can result (Lieberman et al. 2010).

But food-related disorders also offer an option not available to those suffering from other kinds of diseases: the ability to self-treat by modifying one's own diet. Such treatment does not require medical authorization. That said, to be eligible for insurance, special government-funded meal plans, or exemptions from work, a medical diagnosis is usually required, and general practitioners find themselves having to negotiate their skepticism with patients' perceptions of food intolerance. As Mia Nelson and Jane Ogden report from their interviews with general practitioners, the negotiation and arrival at common ground did not involve the GPs' acceptance of the whole of the patients' belief systems or of food intolerance itself, but rather acceptance of the reality of the patients' distress and desire for relief, and acceptance that food intolerance is an uncertain diagnosis rather that an illegitimate one. This "accepting approach" was reported as being reinforced by the GPs' impression that, for whatever reason—placebo effect, secondary gain, or direct biophysical mechanism—many patients felt better for acting on their belief in food intolerance and for excluding foods from their diet (Nelson and Ogden 2008, 1044).

NUTRITION TRANSITIONS IN HUMAN PREHISTORY AND HISTORY

In a series of influential articles, Barry Popkin, a nutritionist at University of North Carolina, described five key dietary transitions in human history (Popkin 1993, 2002, 2006), which are outlined in Figure 4.2. Popkin was particularly concerned with the fourth pattern of transition as a major contributor to a global rise in obesity and chronic diseases, first in wealthy countries but rapidly followed by similar trends in poorer countries. Below we use a somewhat modified version of Popkin's patterns to illustrate the major transitions in human diets and their associations with health outcomes.

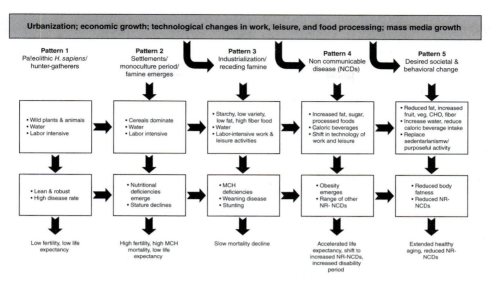

FIGURE 4.2 Barry Popkin's five transitions in human diet and nutrition in history and prehistory. MCH= maternal-child health; NR-NCDs = nutrition-related non-communicable diseases *Source:* Author provided; based on Popkin (2002, 2006).

Evolutionary History: Hunter Gatherer and "Paleo" Diets

As discussed in Chapter 2, the biology of contemporary organisms has been shaped by their evolutionary history. Some of the traits that organisms now possess reflect the advantages that accrued to individuals with those traits in a past environment, what is referred to as the **environment of evolutionary adaptation** (EEA). What constitutes the relevant EEA depends on what trait is being considered because traits evolved at different times. For example, having flexible fingers, including an opposable thumb, first evolved among early primates some 50 million to 60 million years ago. Bipedalism, on the other hand, evolved in our lineage sometime around 6 million to 8 million years ago, and the large brain of humans began to emerge around 2 million years ago.

With respect to general dietary trends, the most relevant EEA for humans is considered to be the Upper Paleolithic, when humans were biologically "modern" (meaning indistinguishable from contemporary humans in their anatomy) and lived as hunter-gatherers. This period is roughly between 200,000 and 10,000 years ago, with the latter date signaling a broad transition away from foraging to food production (i.e., agriculture). There was a great deal of geographic variation among these Upper Paleolithic hunter-gatherers that resulted in differences in diet, with some relying more heavily on animal foods (e.g., high-latitude populations), whereas others had access to more plant foods. Populations foraged for wild foods and ate a broad diversity of plants and animals, and tool technologies evolved to increase the efficiency of wild food acquisition and processing (Ungar 2006). Although historically this was considered a "hand-to-mouth" existence, where populations were constantly faced with the threat of starvation, ethnographic research among contemporary hunter-gatherers suggests that although they move around to sites with foods available, their diet is rich in nutrients and they do not need to spend the majority of their time searching for food

Scurvy in Evolutionary Perspective

A good example to illustrate an evolutionary perspective on a nutritional disease is scurvy. Scurvy is caused by a deficiency of vitamin C, and symptoms stem from the breakdown of connective tissues—bleeding gums, pinpoint hemorrhages, and opening up of old wounds, among others. It was recognized in the sixteenth century primarily as a disease of sailors, who were often at sea for long periods of time without fresh fruits or vegetables. In Europe there were more than 100 scurvy epidemics between 1550 and 1857, and ships often lost up to half of their crews to mortality from this deficiency. With the eighteenth century discovery that citrus fruits such as oranges, lemons, and limes prevented scurvy, cases among sailors plummeted (this is also how British sailors came to be called "limeys") (Magiorkinis et al. 2011).

Interestingly, most mammals are not vulnerable to scurvy, with the exception of fruit-eating bats, guinea pigs, monkeys, apes, and humans. What do these organisms have in common and how do they differ from other mammals? All have lost the ability to synthesize vitamin C. Vitamin C is similar in structure to the sugar glucose, and most other animals can synthesize it from glucose or other sugars. All mammals that require vitamin C lack the enzyme L-gulano-γ-lactone oxidase, which is needed for the final step in the synthesis of ascorbic acid from glucose.

To understand why humans lack this enzyme, it is necessary to trace its loss in the anthropoid primate lineage, some 30 million to 40 million years ago. The most compelling hypothesis for why this would have occurred is that the diets of these primates tend to be high in fruit and other plant materials, which contribute large amounts of vitamin C to the diet. There would have been no need to produce vitamin C under these conditions, and the glucose used for its synthesis could be used for energy or other functions.

(Howell 2010; Lee 1968). Furthermore, across hunter-gatherer groups, energy expenditure has been described as "moderate" rather than "high" (Raichlen et al. 2017).

In 1985, S. Boyd Eaton and Melvin Konner wrote a groundbreaking article in the *New England Journal of Medicine* outlining the ways that diets of populations in wealthy countries such as the United States deviate substantially from the diets of contemporary hunter-gatherers. The former tend to have a high prevalence of chronic diseases such as cardiovascular disease or cancer, whereas hunter-gatherers have notably lower risks of these diseases (Eaton and Konner 1985). These ideas and data have been updated and refined since (Cordain et al. 2005; Konner and Eaton 2010; Lindeberg 2012), and there is a difference of opinion about the foods that constitute Paleolithic diets (also dubbed the "Paleo diet"), but the general principles are the same. Most of the data on the Paleolithic diet come from studies of modern hunter-gatherers because it is difficult to accurately assess diet from the fossil record. Plant materials degrade rapidly, whereas animal bones are larger and contain inorganic material, making them more durable and evident in the fossil record. It is also important to emphasize that contemporary hunter-gatherers are neither "premodern" nor our ancestors; they are using a subsistence strategy that was, however, common among pre-agricultural populations.

Hunter-gatherer diets are high in fiber, micronutrients, and protein, and low in sodium, as shown in Table 4.1. In addition, hunter-gatherers consume almost no grains, have no dairy foods, and have limited access to saturated fat and salt. With the exception of high-latitude groups, most of the diet derives from a diverse array of plants and includes meat as a source of animal protein; wild animals rarely have the opportunity to accumulate rich fat deposits. Tobacco and alcohol historically were not available, although contemporary hunter-gatherers may use such products.

Hunter-gatherer diets contain a broad diversity of plant foods that provide a wide array of **phytochemicals**, which are nonnutritive but biologically active compounds

TABLE 4.1   **Widely Agreed-on Qualitative Differences between Average Ancestral (Hunter-Gatherer) Diets and Contemporary Western Diets**

	Ancestral/Hunter-Gatherer	Contemporary Western
Total energy intake	More	Less
Caloric density	Very low	High
Total carbohydrate intake	Less	More
Added sugars/refined carbohydrates	Very little	Much more
Fruits and vegetables	Twice as high	Half as much
Fiber	More	Less
Protein intake	More	Less
Total fat intake	Equal	Equal
Polyunsaturated fat	More	Less
ω-6:ω-3	Roughly equal	Far more ω-6
Long-chain essential fatty acids	More	Less
Micronutrient intake	More	Less
Milk products	Breastmilk only	High, lifelong
Cereal grains	Minimal	Substantial

Source: Based on data in Konner, Melvin, and S. Boyd Eaton. 2010. "Paleolithic nutrition twenty-five years later." *Nutrition in Clinical Practice* 25 (6), 594–602.

present in plants. Although these are not like vitamins in that they are not considered "essential" to life, more attention is being paid to them as important modulators of physiological function (Rodriguez-Casado 2016). They are broadly distributed in fruit and vegetables, but with plant domestication these often-bitter substances are frequently bred out in favor of more palatable varieties. Although some of these are potentially toxic (in fact many are produced by plants as defenses against being eaten or parasitized), their chemical properties may render them beneficial to health in both specific and generalized ways (Xiao 2016). Many phytochemicals have benefits via their actions as antioxidants, which reduce cell damage from oxygen-free radicals. Others have anti-inflammatory properties, important for cardiovascular health and potentially of significance in hampering tumor growth. Isoflavones, common in soy products, act as weak estrogenic compounds and appear to influence sex hormone activity, cell proliferation, and differentiation. Any given phytochemical may not be especially important when it comes to chronic disease, but diets containing an abundance and diversity of plant foods have a mix of phytochemicals that act synergistically in the reduction of chronic disease risk, and most hunter-gatherer diets fall into this category.

Because *Homo sapiens* evolved primarily under hunter-gatherer conditions, a diet characterized by a great diversity of wild plant and animal foods and limited in sugars, fats, and salt is likely to be the one to which our bodies are well adapted. Given that the latter nutrients are important to physiological function and energy storage and yet they are rare in nature, it is not surprising that consumption of foods with sugars, fat, and salt is experienced as pleasurable and that many mammals perceive these as "tasty" and seek them out preferentially (Bachmanov et al. 2011). However, in an environment characterized by cheap and widely available foods high in these nutrients, they are more likely to be consumed in large quantities.

The dietary patterns common in many countries (and the wealth on which they are predicated) represent an *evolutionarily novel* set of environmental conditions, and they contribute to an increased risk of chronic diseases. Dietary changes, along with the fact that many forms of contemporary work offer little opportunity for physical exertion and more or less confine people to their desks for hours a day, and prolonged sitting itself may increase the risk of many chronic diseases and mortality (Biswas et al. 2015).

The take-home message from the evolutionary approach to nutrition and chronic disease is that eating more like our hunter-gatherer ancestors and engaging in at least a moderate level of physical activity on an ongoing basis should result in a reduced risk of diseases such as CVD, diabetes, and stroke, and there is some evidence that individuals on a Paleolithic diet have better outcomes (in terms of chronic disease risk factors) than those on diets based on traditional dietary guidance (de Menezes et al. 2019; Manheimer et al. 2015). However, given that most contemporary humans cannot return to a hunter-gatherer lifestyle and live in agricultural or industrial societies, how is this supposed to occur? Most contemporary dietary guidelines—including the official "MyPlate," the visual representation of the Dietary Guidelines for Americans—emphasizes fruits and vegetables and protein sources, but also recommend grains and dairy, which would not have been part of a hunter-gatherer diet.

It is worth noting the proliferation of evolution-based diet books that advocate a hunter-gatherer-type diet, such as *The Paleolithic Prescription*, *The Paleo Diet*, *The New Evolution Diet*, and *The Primal Blueprint*. All of these are predicated on certain assumptions about human ancestral diets, often that they were rich in meat and light in seeds/grains or legumes and dairy beyond weaning. There are groups of people who attempt to recreate this lifeway by eating large quantities of meat, fruits, and vegetables, but no bread or dairy products, fasting for lengthy periods, and engaging in physical activities such as sprinting and jumping, and some eschew foods native to the New World or donate blood regularly to simulate blood loss from accidents (Goldstein 2010). Whether these types of diets actually benefit long-term health or lengthen life remains to be seen; suffice it to say that there probably is some benefit to consuming a diet more similar to that of our ancestors, but it is wise to keep in mind that we have no firm evidence for exactly what that diet entailed and how much it varied.

Hunter-Gatherer Life Expectancy

If hunter-gatherers had such a good diet, one that protected them from chronic disease such as cardiovascular disease or cancer, why was their life expectancy only around 35 years? If they had been able to live as long as most contemporary humans, would they too experience these diseases? In other words, is chronic disease the inevitable outcome of living longer? The answer to that question is no. Life expectancy is calculated as the average at which individuals in a population die, and hence is dramatically impacted by high levels of early life (infant and child) mortality. If large numbers of very young individuals die, the average life span will appear to be quite short, which is the case among hunter-gatherers (Howell 2010). When deaths of the very young are not included in calculations, or life expectancy is calculated at age 5, for example, life expectancies are much less variable across populations (Blurton Jones et al. 2002). Furthermore, mortality risk goes up with increasing age independent of chronic disease, so reducing death from chronic disease is likely to have only a modest effect on life expectancy, with some estimates of four to five years if all of the major known risk factors for the leading chronic diseases were eliminated (Danaei et al. 2010).

Agricultural Transition

Around 10,000 years ago a major transition in diet occurred with the domestication of plants and animals, which often coincided with more permanent settlements. Diet was altered in a number of ways. First, the types and diversity of plant foods that lent themselves to domestication and large-scale production were different from the foods consumed by hunter-gatherers. As noted above, hunter-gatherers consumed a diverse array of fruits, leafy vegetables, tubers, nuts, and multiple wild animal taxa. With food production, it is not efficient to try to replicate this diet because each organism has unique ecological requirements, so larger quantities of a smaller number of plant and/or animal species were domesticated. Grains such as wheat, barley, rice, or corn were more easily manipulated by early farmers, although the wild progenitors of these crops were tiny compared with their modern highly domesticated forms. Likewise, tubers such as potatoes or cassava (also known as manioc or yuca) are highly productive sources of carbohydrates, although they are not rich in micronutrients or protein. At the same time, plots of a single plant crop (or herd of animals) were vulnerable to random droughts or other weather problems and also to predation and pathogens, which could spread rapidly among a densely planted or housed single species. The net effect was a decline in dietary diversity, increased vulnerability to food shortages, and greater potential for nutrient deficits (Cohen 1989). Furthermore, energy expenditure was likely increased by this transition and would have been more intensive during particular seasons (planting, weeding, harvesting) (see also Dufour and Piperata 2008).

Jared Diamond once argued that agriculture was the "worst mistake in the history of the human race" (Diamond 1987). Although he can be critiqued for hyperbole, several studies of the fossil and archaeological record have shown that health generally declined among early food producers compared with earlier hunter-gatherers (M. Cohen 2009; Mummert et al. 2011). Before considering these studies, however, it is important to note that the reasons most hunter-gatherer populations took up food production are not entirely clear. The most likely scenario is that Paleolithic hunter-gatherers were successful at acquiring food, which led to population growth. Over time, sufficient food became more difficult to access, resulting in intensification of resource usage. This may have included greater protection of favored foods (plants and animals), enhancing environmental conditions that supported the growth of foods, or consumption of less preferred foods, among others (Cohen 1989). Ultimately, this could have created settlements around sites of food production and further "domestication" of plant and animal foods. Once these were in place, returning to hunting and gathering became increasingly untenable, especially because this transition appears to have stimulated further population growth along with multiple new challenges to health (Bocquet-Appel et al. 2008).

Ascertaining Diet and Nutritional Status from Ancient Bones

Ancient skeletons can provide insights into health and nutrition of past populations. The study of health and disease using ancient skeletal materials is called **paleopathology**. **Bioarchaeology** is another related field that focuses on the biological remains to provide insight into past lifeways (such as diet and activity patterns). Several conditions can be ascertained from skeletal remains, as shown in Figures 4.3a–c.

(continued)

(continued)

Harris Lines

Harris lines are horizontal bands visible on the long bones. They indicate periods of growth stoppage and an approximation of the age at which growth was disrupted. Multiple bands on a bone are evidence of multiple periods during which growth was interrupted during childhood. Growth may have been disrupted because of undernutrition, infection, or another form of stress.

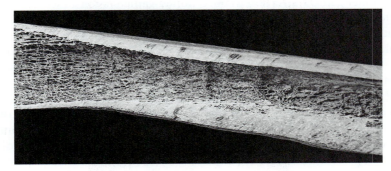

FIGURE 4.3A Harris Lines, visible as darkened bands on the outer (cortical) bone.
Credit: Photo courtesy of Della Cook and Jenny Raff, Bioanthropology Collections, Indiana University

Enamel Hypoplasia

Enamel hypoplasia is also an indicator of growth disruption. Bands of thin enamel in teeth indicate periods of growth disruption. The width of these bands can be used to ascertain the relative duration of the growth stoppage, with wider bands indicating a longer duration of growth disruption. The placement of these bands also provides insight into the age at which the growth disruption occurred. Growth may have been disrupted because of undernutrition, infection, or other forms of stress.

FIGURE 4.3B Enamel hypoplasia, visible as bands in the tooth enamel. Adult male with linear enamel hypoplasia. From the Mississippian period, Schild Cemetery, Illinois.
Credit: Photo courtesy of Della Cook, Bioanthropology Collections, Indiana University

Porotic Hyperostosis

Porotic hyperostosis is an indicator of anemia (reduced oxygen-carrying capacity of blood). Iron deficiency is a common cause of anemia, although there are many other causes. In response to anemia, red blood cell production increases, resulting in expansion of the bone marrow relative to the outer layer of bone. Porotic hyperostosis is visible when the outer bone is so thin or nonexistent that the porous inner bone is exposed.

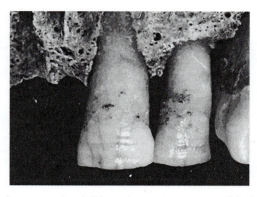

FIGURE 4.3C Porotic hyperostosis, visible as the porous texture of the back of the cranium. Early nineteenth-century Euro-American young adult male, Petersburg, Illinois. *Credit:* Photo courtesy of Della Cook, Bioanthropology Collections, Indiana University

Cavities

Cavities most often occur in the context of a diet made up of sugary or high-carbohydrate foods. Corn, for example, is high in sugar and is sticky, leading to the buildup of bacteria in the teeth, which ultimately can result in tooth decay.

C_3 versus C_4 in Bones

Plants have different carbon "signatures" that, when eaten by humans, leave a distinct chemical trace in ancient bones. Corn is a common C_4 plant, and fruits, wheat, and nuts tend to be C_3 plants. This method is thus useful to get a sense of the components and quality of the diet of past populations, although it is impossible to distinguish whether the C_3 or C_4 plants were consumed directly or indirectly through consumption of herbivores eating them.

Nitrogen Isotopes

Different isotopic forms of nitrogen are found in marine and terrestrial plants and the animals that consumed these plants. Thus, the balance of these nitrogen forms can provide insight into the relative importance of marine versus terrestrial sources of food.

The health consequences of this transition are evident from a variety of studies (see review in Mummert et al. 2011, with a focus on height as a measure of nutritional status). Claire Cassidy's classic work on the skeletons from two sites in Kentucky—one from a prehistoric hunting-and-gathering Native American group and one from an agricultural Native American group during the early colonial period (although they do not seem to have had contact with any Europeans prior to the site being abandoned)—provides an example (Cassidy 1980). The two sites were ecologically similar, but subsistence patterns and diet were different. The hunter-gatherers at the site called Indian Knoll appear to have eaten shellfish, fish, deer, other small mammals, and turkey, as well as a variety of wild plant foods. Members of the agricultural village (Hardin Village) ate corn, beans, and squash. Wild plants and some animals were supplementary to these staple plants. Table 4.2 shows some important differences in growth and nutrition between the two

TABLE 4.2   Differences in Health between Agricultural and Hunter-Gatherer Groups in Kentucky

	Indian Knoll (Hunter-Gatherers) 3350 BC to 2015 BC Skeletons(n = 285)	Hardin Village (Agricultural) AD 1500 to AD 1675 Skeletons(n = 296)
Porotic hyperostosis (iron deficiency anemia)	0.00%	8.20%
Harris lines (growth disruption)	11.30% (regular; mild)	4.10% (random; severe)
Tooth decay (number of cavities)	0.73, men 0.91, women	6.74, men 8.51, women

Source: Table based on data from Cassidy (1980).

groups. Growth was disrupted in a more irregular fashion among the agriculturalists than it was among the hunter-gatherers and was generally of longer duration. Rates of anemia were also higher, and there were more cavities, most likely from the corn-based diet.

Other archaeological evidence suggests that changes in social organization also occurred and contributed to disparities in health within agricultural populations. For example, some sites show that women became more likely to have evidence of nutritional deficiencies relative to men. With agriculture, surpluses of food are produced and must feed larger populations throughout the year, including seasons with little production. Those who could control land or food surpluses gained in economic and political power and were able to maintain better health than those with fewer resources (Vercellotti et al. 2014).

The Osteological Paradox

In an influential article from 1992, James Wood and colleagues (Wood et al. 1992) pointed out that increases in the number of individuals with nutritional pathologies in agricultural populations do not necessarily mean that health was getting worse. It may instead indicate underlying population growth. If populations are larger in the agricultural sites than in the hunter-gatherer sites, which is likely, the increased number of individuals with anemia, for example, could just be a reflection of there being more people, and the prevalence of disease could have actually decreased—hence the "osteological paradox." Without knowledge of population size, increases in skeletal pathologies cannot necessarily be attributed to worsening health overall. Furthermore, because skeletal samples are by definition from dead individuals, it may be that they overestimate the true extent of disease in the population. That is, if a skeleton is estimated at 20 years of age at death, it is probably more likely to show evidence of pathology than a representative sample of living 20-year-olds in the population. The sample of skeletons is likely biased toward higher rates of disease. One last problem is that those with evidence of pathology could in fact be healthier than others because the bony response develops when there is chronic exposure or as the problem heals. Thus, individuals with bony lesions may be the ones who survived because those who died of the disease may not have had time to develop the osteological traces. Thus, estimates of population health from skeletal pathologies must take these considerations into account (see updated discussion of this issue in Vercellotti et al. 2014).

POST-AGRICULTURAL DIETARY ADAPTATIONS AND CHALLENGES

Lactase Persistence/Non-persistence and Lactose Intolerance

Prior to the transition to plant and animal domestication, humans would not have been exposed to milk beyond the breastmilk they consumed prior to weaning. Milk contains the unique sugar, lactose, which in turn requires the intestinal enzyme lactase to be broken down into its two component sugars, glucose and galactose, so they can be absorbed. Most mammals—and most humans—produce lactase early in life when they are nursing, but then lactase production shut off, usually around the time of weaning. In some populations that domesticated animals for dairying, the genetic trait of lactase persistence, wherein this digestive enzyme continues to be produced through-out life, was selected for and achieved high frequencies. Importantly, the regulation of lactase production appears to be genetic; an area of DNA just upstream from the lactase gene itself appears to be the "switch" that maintains or shuts off lactase production. The cessation or continuation of lactase production occurs independent of the presence of milk in the diet; that is, it cannot be kept on simply by continuing to consume milk, nor does it decline when milk is not consumed (Sahi 1994).

One attribute of all populations with high rates of lactase persistence is a deep history of keeping domestic animals such as cows, water buffalo, goats, or sheep for their milk. This would suggest that they have adapted to exploit this new dietary resource by keeping the lactase gene "on" throughout life. Individuals who could make use of milk would have access to a rich new source of nutrients. Thus, those with a mutation that kept lactase on (e.g., lactase persistence) would have had a nutritional advantage and the mutation would have spread. However, this is not the whole story because it appears that some populations that keep dairy animals do *not* have high frequencies of lactase persistence. It turns out that these groups tend to use processed dairy products exclusively and do not consume fresh milk. Importantly, lactose is found in the highest quantities in fresh milk; the conversion of milk into yogurt or cheese removes much if not all of the lactose, depending on the preparation method. If only these dairy products are consumed, individuals are not being exposed to lactose, yet they can access the other nutrients in milk.

Although it would appear that there would have been nutritional advantages of being able to consume and digest milk throughout life in dairying populations, there is little evidence that populations that kept dairy animals were better nourished than those who didn't, and, as noted above, it is easy to convert milk into lactose-reduced products that obviate the need for lactase. The are several other hypotheses for the spread of lactase persistence alleles in some dairying populations. First, it provides lifelong access to an important carbohydrate and fluid source, which may be critical to pastoralist populations living in hot, arid environments. Fresh milk would have been useful as a source of water in arid environments and a way to include sugar (lactose) in a diet that is high in animal products but low in plant foods. Second, lactose can aid in calcium absorption, which may be compromised by low vitamin D synthesis in high latitude environments such as Europe. Recall that vitamin D can be produced by expo-sure of the skin to ultraviolet light, but this exposure is dramatically limited among high-latitude populations, where it is also cold (and so people cover up their skin to stay warm) and often cloudy. Drinking fresh milk in this context would have been advantageous as a way of avoiding vitamin D deficiency and its manifestation as rickets—weight-bearing bones that are soft and breakable because of the lack of calcium being deposited in them by vitamin D. Third, the consumption of other mammalian milk (e.g., from cows, goats, water buffalo, etc.) may have life history effects on humans including accelerated reproductive maturation or physical growth, or growth to larger adult size, likely due to milk consumption's contributions to higher levels of circulating insulin-like growth factor I (IGF-I); importantly, other dairy products do not show this effect consistently (see Chapter 5 for more discussion of the question of whether milk consumption affects child growth) (Wiley 2018).

Most humans (~60%–70%) retain the ancestral mammalian condition of lactase non-persistence, especially sub-Saharan African or Southeast and East Asian origin, Native Americans, South Pacific Islanders, and Native Australian populations. It is relatively rare among Europeans, some populations of Central or South Asia, and some herding populations of sub-Saharan Africa such as the Fulani, Hausa, Turkana, and Maasai, among others, where lactase persistence alleles predominate (Itan et al. 2010). When individuals who are lactase non-persistent consume milk or lactose-containing dairy products, they are likely to suffer from the symptoms of **lactose intolerance,** which include nausea, gas, bloating, and diarrhea. These stem from incomplete digestion of the milk sugar lactose in the small intestine, leaving it to be fermented by microbes in the colon.

Although most humans are lactase non-persistent and are at high risk of lactose intolerance if they consume milk, milk is included as a component of dietary guidelines in countries such as the United States, those in Europe, Australia, and New Zealand, and increasingly others throughout the world (Herforth et al. 2019). In the United States, two to three servings of milk or other dairy products are considered necessary parts of a healthy diet. But what about the 30 million to 50 million Americans who are lactase non-persistent? If they follow these guidelines, they may suffer from lactose intolerance. This begs the question as to the rationale for including dairy products in the dietary guidelines (Wiley 2004b, 2016). Most frequently, the calcium in milk is invoked as the primary reason for this, and Americans have been found to consume well less than the recommended daily allowance. Given the importance of milk production to the American agricultural economy, it comes as no surprise that its consumption should be encouraged (Nestle 2018a). Some researchers have gone as far as to suggest that the higher rates of many chronic diseases found among minority populations are attributable to their low rates of milk intake (Bailey et al. 2013; Jarvis and Miller 2002). Their high rates of "perceived" lactose intolerance contribute to low milk consumption and are thus considered an important "barrier" to good health. Suffice it to say that health disparities cannot be explained away as a consequence of low rates of milk consumption.

Most important, this example illustrates the dangers inherent to ideas about what constitutes medical or biological "normalcy." Until the 1960s, most European and American scientists assumed that lactase persistence was the norm for *H. sapiens* and that those who developed gastrointestinal symptoms when they drank milk had some sort of pathology. After all, the populations that these scientists came from were largely lactase persistent, and milk and dairy products were important parts of the diet.

Although it is now widely recognized that lactase non-persistence is the norm among humans, it is still labeled "abnormal" (Bailey et al. 2013). For example, the American Academy of Pediatrics uses the language "lactose malabsorption," but in the discussion of prevalence, it refers to "lactase deficiency":

> Approximately 70% of the world's population has primary lactase *deficiency*. The percentage varies according to ethnicity and is related to the use of dairy products in the diet, resulting in genetic selection of individuals with the ability to digest lactose. In populations with a predominance of dairy foods in the diet, particularly northern European people, as few as 2% of the population has primary lactase deficiency. In contrast, the prevalence of primary lactase deficiency is 50% to 80% in Hispanic people, 60% to 80% in black and Ashkenazi Jewish people, and almost 100% in Asian and American Indian people. (Heyman and the Committee on Nutrition 2006, emphasis added)

Likewise, lactose intolerance is described by the American Gastroenterological Association as "a *shortage* of the enzyme lactase, which is *normally* made by the cells that line the small gut …" (American Gastroenterology Association 2019, emphasis added). Writing in the American Academy of Family Physicians' journal, Swagerty, Walling, and Klein state that "lactose *malabsorption* is a normal physiologic pattern" and that there is "speculation that *lactase deficiency* is the 'normal' or 'natural' state, and the persistence of significant lactase activity into adult life in northern European populations is an 'abnormal' mutation" (Swagerty et al. 2002, 1845–1846, emphasis added). Thus, although it is generally acknowledged that lactase non-persistence is common, it is still seen as a medical condition characterized by a "lack" of lactase production. The assumption that European physiology is the healthy norm for the species remains widespread. This also plays out in donations of milk to populations experiencing food scarcity. The anthropologist Marvin Harris described his experience in Brazil in the early 1960s when the United States sent some 88 million pounds of powdered milk to Brazil as part of the Food for Peace program. Many Brazilians complained that the milk gave them upset stomachs and diarrhea, much to the disbelief of American officials, who suggested that they must have been preparing it improperly. Within the United States, surplus powdered milk was distributed to impoverished citizens as part of poverty-relief programs. Native Americans and African Americans were primary recipients, and frequent gastrointestinal complaints were noted to local clinicians (Harris 1985).

Celiac Disease

Another example of human biological variation that is related to dietary changes of the post-agricultural period is the condition known as **celiac disease** (CD). Unlike lactose intolerance, which is related to lactase production, CD is an immunologically mediated sensitivity to gluten, a protein found in wheat, rye, and barley, crops that were widely domesticated in the Middle East, Western Asia, and Europe. When individuals with CD consume these foods, their immune system responds by damaging or destroying the villi that line the small intestine and that are responsible for the absorption of nutrients. CD is considered an autoimmune disorder, meaning that gluten stimulates the immune system to attack the body's own cells. The resulting symptoms include those associated with malnutrition, as the villi become inefficient at absorbing nutrients, but also gastrointestinal pain and discomfort, dermatitis, and irritability. In addition to CD, individuals may have an allergic reaction to gluten or other wheat proteins, and there is another category of "gluten sensitivity" that has no clear biomarkers, but that is used when individuals suffer a variety of symptoms that resolve when gluten or cereals containing gluten are removed from the diet (Fasano et al. 2015).

The prevalence of CD varies among the world's populations, with the highest prevalence in North Africa and northern Europe and an overall prevalence of just under 1% (Lionetti et al. 2015). In the United States, the prevalence has doubled every 15 years since 1974 for reasons that are not understood (Catassi et al. 2010). Global estimates are not available, but CD is—not surprisingly—more common in populations that consume wheat (those in Europe, North and South America, and the Middle East) (Lionetti et al. 2015). Of course, CD, like lactose intolerance and milk, will not manifest unless gluten is in the diet—that is, if the diet does not contain wheat, rye, or barley. Thus, it was unlikely to occur in populations relying on traditional staple foods such as rice (such as in Southeast or East Asia) or corn (among Native North and South American populations). It was also unlikely to have been a problem for hunter-gatherer *H. sapiens*. However, in what has been dubbed the "evolutionary paradox of CD," CD prevalence and the underlying genetic correlates of the disease are more common among populations with longstanding histories of wheat production and consumption. It is unclear why the alleles associated with CD have not been eliminated from populations with long term usage of wheat. Furthermore, the consumption wheat in its various preparations such as bread, pasta, and other baked goods has increased markedly throughout the world, and rates of CD are escalating (Malekzadeh et al. 2005).

In a paper published well before CD and wheat consumption gained broader public health and medical attention, anthropologist Shirley Lindenbaum has described how wheat became an important part of the diet in Bangladesh, where rice had traditionally been the staple food. Indeed, the question "Have you had a meal?" translates as "Have you eaten rice?" (Lindenbaum 1987). Wheat production escalated in the 1970s and as foreign countries provided wheat as part of their foreign aid to Bangladesh. The United States in particular became a source of wheat, which became a part of a complex "gastropolitics," with the United States cutting off aid during the 1974 famine until Bangladesh agreed to stop exporting jute to Cuba. The net effect was that Bangladeshis were importing, producing, and consuming more wheat. However, wheat grows best there in the winter and has replaced the more proteinaceous crop of lentils, thus increasing rates of malnutrition. It also requires more work and during the hottest months of the year (unlike rice, which is harvested during the cooler months). Wheat has worked its way into the Bangladeshi diet, particularly among the urban middle classes, who see it as a more "progressive" or "Western" food. Although it is not clear whether rates of CD have risen in Bangladesh as a result, the disease is now widely recognized in South Asia, and in all likelihood rates will rise in populations now including more wheat or processed foods containing gluten in their diets.

Because the symptoms of CD or gluten sensitivity are similar to those of other gastrointestinal tract disorders such as irritable bowel syndrome or may present with more generalized symptoms, individuals who suffer from CD may find the path to official diagnosis long and difficult (Copelton and Valle 2009) and the disease is considered widely underdiagnosed (Lionetti et al. 2015). Thus, they often turn to self-diagnosis by either eliminating gluten from their diets and/or paying for stool testing via direct-access testing (when patients send samples for a laboratory to analyze, without a clinician's orders). As Copelton and Valle note,

> Celiac's permissive symptomology, its non-medical remedy, and the difficulty patients experience when trying to gain a medical diagnosis, support self-diagnosis. Self-diagnosed celiacs adopt their own subjective diagnostic standard in place of the biopsy, the objective medical gold standard.... Given the ubiquity of gluten in the average American diet, the social nature of meals, and the close scrutiny of ingredients and preparation techniques necessary to maintain a gluten-free diet, some self-diagnosed persons continue to seek medical legitimation for their diagnosis to garner social support from friends, family, and coworkers. (Copelton and Valle 2009, 629)

The difficulty of adhering to a gluten-free diet (GFD) in the United States or Europe should not be underestimated given how widespread wheat is in typical foods and the high cost of gluten-free products, and individuals following a gluten-free diet are often met with skepticism that such restrictive measures are necessary. That said, the number of individuals without a diagnosis of CD who state that they are following a gluten-free diet has risen markedly, and the market for gluten-free products has grown as well over the past 10 years (Koidis 2016). According to marketing reports, about 30% of Americans say they are attempting to restrict or avoid gluten intake for health or weight loss purposes, even if not adhering fully to a GFD (Gaesser and Angadi 2015). In a survey of the general U.S. population, the prevalence of individuals actually adopting a GFD without a CD diagnosis was low but had more than tripled from 0.5% in 2009–2010 to 1.7% in 2013–2014 (Choung et al. 2017). At present there is no evidence that a gluten-free diet offers health benefits to those without CD or other gastrointestinal conditions (Rej et al. 2018).

BARRY POPKIN'S NUTRITION TRANSITION: GLOBALIZATION AND ULTRA-PROCESSING

Subsistence agriculture was the basis for most human diets until the colonial period (roughly 1650 through the early twentieth century), when colonial enterprises established large plantations producing vast quantities of crops for export began to create new forms of wage labor and increased reliance on the market for basic foods. During this time, further global differentiation in nutritional status emerged, with some receiving the benefits of agricultural surpluses, even as others toiled to produce them for export (Ochoa 2012). This trend has continued in the postcolonial period with the rise of multinational corporations that control vast areas of farmland and produce single crops such as wheat, corn, rice, sugar, fruits (such as bananas or pineapples), cows and pigs, or nonnutritive crops (such as tobacco, coffee, or tea). The result is a surfeit of inexpensive carbohydrate, fat, and protein sources marketed primarily in wealthy countries and overconsumption of these foods. Among those who produce them, increased reliance on market foods due to subsistence land being used for export crops may lead to malnutrition and food insecurity.

A net effect of these changes was that contemporary dietary patterns are at odds with those that typified most of our evolution as a species. In other words, we are biologically adapted to a diet and lifestyle that no longer prevails, and our bodies are now being asked to function in different ways with different resources. Remember that genetic evolution is slow, with changes in gene frequencies accumulating slowly across generations. In contrast, cultural changes (e.g., in technologies and dietary patterns) can be rapid, with radical changes occurring within just one or two generations. It is no surprise that many chronic diseases such as cardiovascular disease, diabetes, obesity, stroke, and cancers that are prevalent in wealthy countries and increasing rapidly in nations with emergent middle classes are the outcomes of these diet changes. It is not only that access to cheap sources of energy, fat, and protein has increased (and these products dominate grocery stores and food advertisements), but also that other micronutrients and dietary components that were commonly consumed by our hunter-gatherer ancestors are missing from the diet. As a result, despite advances in prevention and treatment of disease, overconsumption combined with less physical activity contributes to obesity and diabetes, which in turn are also risk factors for cardiovascular disease and premature mortality. These are the essential nutritional trends that Popkin described in his fourth pattern, but this is the one most commonly referred to simply as "the nutrition transition."

Of particular note in this transition is a shift in food processing, with an increase in what are now known as "ultra-processed" foods. Recently Brazilian nutritionist Carlos Monteira formalized a categorization scheme for food processing (NOVA), in light of concerns that ultra-processed foods are a major contributor to diet-related chronic diseases and obesity (Monteiro et al. 2018a). The NOVA scale includes four food groups:

- Group 1: whole or minimally processed foods—the edible parts of plants or animals (also fungi, algae and water)—that are processed only for consumption or storage, and would have been the sole type of processing used in hunter-gatherer societies;
- Group 2: processed culinary ingredients such as oils, butter, sugar, and salt, which are combined with Group 1 foods in cooking or for greater palatability;
- Group 3: Processed foods, such as canned fruit, vegetables, or fish, cheeses, and fresh breads, which are made by adding Group 2 items to Group 1 foods or that are fermented and that contain very few ingredients (these would have come into use in the post-agricultural period, and were elaborated with the rise of industrialization in the 19th century);
- Group 4: ultra-processed foods: formulations of cheap industrial sources of nutrients, calories, and additives, derived from multiple processing stages. Typically, energy-dense, high in unhealthy fats, refined starches, added sugars and salt, and poor sources of protein, dietary fiber and micronutrients (often added through fortification). Ultra-processed products are made to be hyper-palatable, attractive, shelf-stable, and portable, and include items such as soft drinks, packaged sweet or savory snacks, reconstituted meat products, and frozen meals.

Well over half of the U.S. food supply (and just about half in Canada) is comprised of ultra-processed foods. Percentages in lower-income countries (typically around 20%–30%) are growing rapidly (Monteiro et al. 2018a). In Europe, household purchases of ultra-processed foods make up over 25% of food budgets but range from 10% in Portugal to over 50% in the United Kingdom (Monteiro et al. 2018b). These are the major sources of sodium, sugar, additives, and preservatives in post-transition diets, and their consumption has been associated with obesity, hypertension, metabolic disease, and various cancers (Fiolet et al. 2018; Monteiro et al. 2018a,2018b).

Below, we consider obesity and diabetes, two conditions that are currently frequently described as global epidemics and are associated with nutrition transition, and the propensity for these outcomes may be related in part to our evolutionary history.

Obesity

As of 2016, the World Health Organization (WHO) estimates that 39% of the world's adult population has overweight and 13% has obesity, although this percentage ranges from 2% in Vietnam to over 50% in many Pacific Island countries (see Figure 4.4). The obesity epidemic is an issue of global proportions (see also Brewis et al. 2011). Obesity prevalence is rising in many developing countries, where it often coexists with undernutrition, the so-called "double burden" of malnutrition (Abdullah 2015). Obesity has been defined in different ways over the years, and currently the most common measure used is the **body mass index** (BMI). BMI is calculated as weight (kg)/height (m)^2 or, to calculate it in pounds, weight (lbs)/height (in)^2 × 703. Currently a BMI between 18.5 and 24.9 is considered "normal" or "healthy;" 25 to 29.9 is considered **overweight**; and 30 or greater is defined as **obese**. A BMI less than 18.5 is considered underweight. Because of their different body proportions, children's BMI categories are constructed differently, with those over the 85th or 95th percentile for their age and sex considered in overweight or obese categories, respectively. When Ancel Keys proposed that BMI could be a good proxy for body fatness in 1972, he intended it to be used only for population studies; it was never meant to be used to ascertain an individual's risk of health problems (Gutin 2018). A high or low BMI is not, in and of itself, a diagnosis of ill health.

Mammals store excess energy as fat and appear to have virtually unlimited ability to do so. The function of this storage mechanism is to have a source of energy available for times when food is rare or difficult to find, or when an animal hibernates. However, most likely for the first time in evolutionary history, a large number of humans are able to store a large quantity of fat that becomes a more or less permanent part of their anatomy. A question is whether obesity is a problem in and of itself or whether its health significance results from other factors, such as increased risk for impairments in physiological function, individuals' ability to carry out daily activities, or social valuation of obesity (e.g., stigma) contributing to its associated health outcomes (Brewis et al. 2011; Tomiyama et al. 2018). It used to be thought that fat was metabolically inert, but research indicates that fat, especially that stored in the abdomen, is metabolically active and has the potential to influence the amount of fat in circulation or inflammation, both risk factors for metabolic and cardiovascular disease (Patel and Abate 2013). Thus, fat patterning is emerging as a more important risk factor for metabolic disease, but overall, having more fat tends to correlate with a greater risk of metabolic, cardiovascular, and cancer morbidity, even with a BMI in the normal range (Romero-Corral et al. 2010). Some individuals with obesity are metabolically healthy but may nonetheless have some subclinical health risk factors (Roberson et al. 2014), and there is a growing "fat activism" movement (Matacin and Simone 2019).

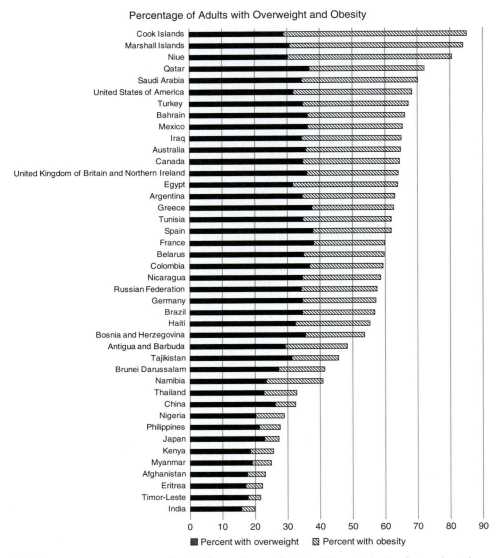

FIGURE 4.4   Current age-standardized prevalence of overweight and obesity from selected countries across the globe.
Source: World Health Organization 2016 data, https://www.who.int/gho/ncd/risk_factors/overweight_obesity/obesity_adults/en/

At the same time, it is worth questioning some of the causes of this epidemic. Over 30 years ago Cheryl Ritenbaugh described how standards for "ideal weights" have declined over the latter part of the twentieth century, especially for females, as shown in Figure 4.5. This alone could account for a sudden "rise" in rates of overweight and obesity evident in the 1970s and 1980s. Ritenbaugh (1982) suggested that changing ideals for appropriate weight are more reflective of shifting cultural ideas of the ideal body

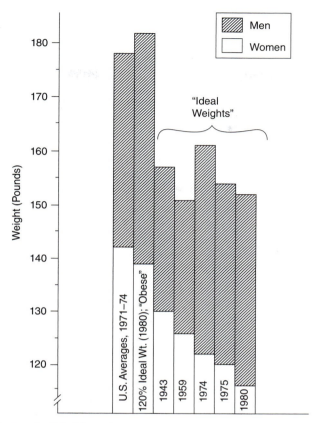

FIGURE 4.5 Changes in "ideal" weights over time.
Source: From Cheryl Ritenbaugh. 1982. "Obesity as a culture bound syndrome." *Culture, Medicine, and Psychiatry* 6 (4):355. Reprinted with kind permission from Springer Science and Business Media.

than based on strong scientific evidence that lower weights are associated with reduced morbidity and mortality. Starting in the 1980s, BMI replaced weight as a standard, so it is difficult to see whether this trend has continued and is evident in current recommendations. During the 1980s and 1990s, BMI standards for overweight tended to hover around 27 or 28 and allowed for increases with age and differences between males and females (males had slightly higher cutoffs for overweight). In 1997, the WHO established a standard of 25.0 for overweight for all adults, and the subsequent year the U.S. standard was aligned with it. This effectively redefined 35 million people previously considered of normal weight as overweight!

What is the relationship between BMI and mortality risk? Studies have shown a U-shape relationship between body weight and mortality (see Figure 4.6). That is, both high and low BMIs are associated with higher mortality than BMIs in between. The high mortality at the low end can occur because individuals who are very thin may be those who are already sick or who substitute smoking for eating, but thinness remains a risk for mortality even when these other factors are controlled for statistically.

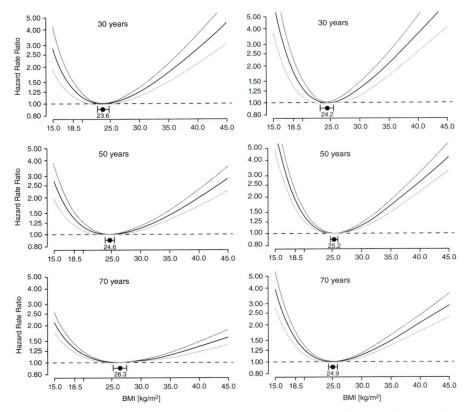

FIGURE 4.6 The relationship between body mass index (BMI) at different adult ages and mortality for women (left) and men (right) at different ages. Lines represent the risk relative to the optimum BMI and 95% confidence intervals. The black dot represents the BMI associated with minimum mortality. Mortality rises at both low and high BMIs, although the difference in risk associated with higher or lower BMI varies by gender and age.
Source: Reprinted by permission from Macmillan Publishers Ltd: Peter, R. S., B. Mayer, H. Concin, and G. Nagel. 2015. "The effect of age on the shape of the BMI–mortality relation and BMI associated with minimum all-cause mortality in a large Austrian cohort." *International Journal of Obesity* (2015)39, 530–534; doi:10.1038/ijo.2014.168.

Furthermore, the mortality risk associated with a given BMI changes with age; higher BMIs early in life (age 30 years) are associated with higher mortality than they are at age 70 years, and it differs by gender. Thus, the message should not be that thinness is, by definition, healthier than fatness, but rather that the behaviors that contribute to a given weight (such as age, eating patterns, physical activity, or smoking) are associated with different health consequences.

Moreover, it appears that the relationship between body size and health has itself changed over time and that it may be variable across populations. Barry Popkin has argued that Asians, Hispanics, and Africans experience more negative health outcomes at lower BMIs than do whites, suggesting that there is population variation in the meaning of BMI (Popkin 2002). Moreover, the association between BMI and fatness may also differ; in India, higher levels of fatness are seen at lower BMIs, resulting in what has been termed the "thin-fat" phenotype (Yajnik 2004). As a result, different countries and regional bodies set the cutoffs for normal, overweight, and obesity at different points. In Asians, for example, the cutoff for overweight and obesity is lower than the WHO standards (WHO Expert Consultation 2004). Max Henderson's historical work on BMI in the United States also shows that although BMIs have increased since the nineteenth century and obesity rates have increased 10-fold, the range of BMIs for men associated with lower mortality risk has shifted upward, from 20–26 to 22–28. There are a variety of reasons for this, including changing height, patterns of disease, dietary components, and infectious disease exposure, all of which affect the height-for-weight measure as well as health risks more generally (Henderson 2005). In sum, standards for body size change over time as a function of cultural trends and scientific understandings, and associations between a given body size and health are neither static nor universal.

What else has contributed to this rise in obesity, especially in children? Generally, it is assumed that increased consumption of more energy-dense, nutrient-poor foods with high levels of sugar and saturated fats combined with reduced physical activity are responsible, but the evidence supporting these claims is less strong than one would think, and there are myriad other factors that may also play a role, such as reduced sleep duration, some infections, gut bacteria, and positive assortative mating (Dhurandhar and Keith 2014). Increasing numbers of studies are pointing to the influence of advertising, especially that of high-calorie foods marketed to children in television programming, as one of the nonproximate causes (Powell, Schermbeck, and Chaloupka 2013); "pouring" contracts in schools whereby soft drink companies have been allowed to put vending machines in schools in exchange for financial support or educational materials; reduction in physical activity programs in school or safe places for children to engage in such activities outside of school; the decline in home-prepared foods and "family dinners" concurrent with the spread of fast-food restaurants in which calorie-dense foods predominate on the menu; large serving sizes of home meals and those served at restaurants; and the disproportionate amount of space in grocery stores devoted to foods that dietary guidelines suggest should be consumed "sparingly" (Brownell 2004; Cheyne et al. 2014). In other words, there are strong political, economic, and social interests at work that conspire against a healthy diet (Lobstein et al. 2015; Nestle 2013, 2018a). These are especially relevant for individuals living in working-class urban areas where caretakers work long hours and there is limited access to fresh foods and large grocery stores and a high density of fast-food restaurants.

In addition, a widely cited study in the *New England Journal of Medicine* found that obesity seems to "spread" through social networks (Christakis and Fowler 2007). The researchers found that if one person in a social network had obesity, there was an increased probability that others in the network would also have obesity in the future even if members of the network were not geographically close. The likelihood was higher still among close friends and siblings, especially those of the same sex. The authors of the study suggested that these trends could be a result of changing perceptions of the social norms regarding the acceptability of obesity. They noted,

> To the extent that obesity is a product of voluntary choices or behaviors, the fact that people are embedded in social networks and are influenced by the evident appearance and behaviors of those around them suggests that weight gain in one person might influence weight gain in others. Having obese social contacts might change a person's tolerance for being obese or might influence his or her adoption of specific behaviors (e.g., smoking, eating, and exercising). In addition to such social mechanisms, it is plausible that physiological imitation might occur; areas of the brain that correspond to actions such as eating food may be stimulated if these actions are observed in others. (Christakis and Fowler 2007, 370)

Thus, obesity has social roots that must be addressed as part of any sort of "treatment" program.

In the past, and among contemporary hunter-gatherers or subsistence agriculturalists, only individuals with ample resources would have been able to achieve overweight or obesity. In a study in Samoa, where obesity rates are very high, it was found that weight was positively associated with social status. Large-bodied men were considered to look more regal and commanded more respect, and high-status men and women could acquire more fat because they could order others to work for them (Brewis et al. 1998). Anthropologists have noted that as traditional societies transition to urban, industrial societies with greater exposure and access to Western goods and ideals, perceptions of weight tend to reverse, and fatness is no longer associated with wealth or health, especially among women, and becomes highly stigmatized (Becker et al. 2007; Brewis 2011). It is notable that obesity in the United States is more common among groups of lower socioeconomic status and minorities (the two categories often go together in the United States) such as African Americans, Native Americans, Hispanics, and Mexican Americans (Hales et al. 2017). As noted earlier, access to fresh produce and grocery stores is more limited in lower-income areas, fast-food restaurants have a much higher density in such areas, and access to safe parks or sports facilities is much lower than in middle-class neighborhoods (Engler-Stringer et al. 2014).

The reversal of a positive association of socioeconomic status and weight reveals an important evolutionary change. Historically and in the prehistoric period, weight would have been a symbol of resource accumulation and hence wealth: it reflects storage of energy that could be mobilized in seasons of hunger or food scarcity. The current negative relationship between socioeconomic status and weight in industrialized countries is therefore an evolutionary and historical anomaly. It seems likely that only in the context of unprecedented food security could the lack of excess fat be socially valued. This trend is spreading, however, with the global presence of Western celebrities and cultural values that emphasize slimness, and there is also evidence of a global spread of fat stigma, especially among middle-income and developing countries (Brewis et al. 2011).

Rising rates of overweight and obesity across the globe poses a challenge to public health, and interventions of various kinds designed to promote weight loss have been notoriously ineffective and unsustainable. As Brewis notes, "Obesity is a complex, multifaceted, deep-rooted part of the contemporary human condition that resists simple, singular, quick, or easy fixes. Because it has stemmed from fundamental social, economic, and ecological changes our species has faced over the past few decades, only sustained and fundamental examination of those conditions is likely to do much about it" (Brewis et al. 2011, 128–129). How fatness ultimately impacts human health on a local and global scale will be a critical issue for the twenty-first century.

Diabetes

Diabetes is a disease often found along with obesity, in which levels of sugar (glucose) in the blood are elevated and pose risks to health. The healthy range for blood glucose levels is considered to be between 70 and 100 milligrams per 100 milliliters in the fasting state. If they exceed the upper limit, glucose begins to be excreted in urine, and the person feels hunger and thirst. **Insulin**, a hormone produced in the pancreas, is released as soon as glucose enters the bloodstream after a meal, and it stimulates the uptake of glucose by muscle, fat, and other cells and the conversion of glucose into glycogen (the only form in which glucose is stored) in the liver. With diabetes, blood glucose levels are continually high because of problems with either insulin production or cellular responses to insulin.

There are two major types of diabetes. In diabetes mellitus type 1 (also called insulin-dependent diabetes, IDDM), the problem derives from reduced insulin production and release by the pancreas. This type of diabetes typically starts during childhood and requires insulin therapy. Much more common is type 2 diabetes mellitus, or non–insulin dependent diabetes mellitus (NIDDM). NIDDM results when the cells that are the target of insulin (such as fat or muscle cells) become resistant to it and more and more insulin is required to stimulate those cells to take up glucose. This can happen as a consequence of repeated insulin stimulation, as in a high-glucose diet, or as a consequence of reduced cellular need, as in a lack of activity. This type of diabetes is generally manageable or reversible. Reduced intake of sugars or other foods that increase blood sugar or insulin levels, combined with increases in physical activity, can reverse insulin resistance. Globally the age-standardized prevalence of diabetes among adults is 8% for women and 9% for men, which represents a doubling since 1980 (B. Zhou et al. 2016). Rates are highest in Oceanian populations (~25%) and lowest in Western Europe (~5%).

In 1962 the geneticist James Neel proposed an evolutionary hypothesis in an attempt to explain the relatively high frequency of diabetes (he initially did not make a distinction between NIDDM and IDDM) in many populations. In what became known as the "thrifty genotype" hypothesis, Neel (1962) posited that our hunter-gatherer ancestors would have experienced alternating periods of food abundance and food scarcity. Those with a "quick insulin trigger," who quickly released a large quantity of insulin in the presence of glucose in the bloodstream, would have had a fitness advantage. This is because they would be able to more efficiently store energy as fat by rapidly converting glucose into storable fat. During times of relative scarcity, such individuals would have had more energy reserves in the form of fat to use than those with a less-efficient energy storage mechanism. This would have served our ancestors well. However, in the context of continual access to abundant quantities of food, especially glucose-rich carbohydrates, this quick trigger is now highly detrimental because individuals continually produce high levels of insulin, leading to insulin resistance among target cells.

Subsequent to Neel's proposal, it became evident that not everyone eating a calorie-rich diet was equally likely to develop NIDDM. Instead, certain populations seemed to be more susceptible than others, even when eating similar kinds of diets. In particular, Native North Americans have high rates of both NIDDM and obesity. The Akimel O'odham, a Native American group living in the southwestern United States formerly referred to by anthropologists and other researchers as the Pima, have been singled out as having the highest rates of any population, with 38% of U.S. Akimel O'odham adults having NIDDM (Schulz et al. 2006). Among Akimel O'odham living in Mexico, however, the rate was much lower, at 7%, which was not significantly different from the rate found among nearby other Mexicans. For those 55 years of age and older, the rate for U.S. Akimel O'odham is 77%, compared with 9% among the those living in Mexico. Similarly, obesity rates were 3 to 10 times higher among those in the U.S. group compared to those living in Mexico (Schulz et al. 2006). Much research has focused on genetic characteristics of the Akimel O'odham, Native Americans in general, or Oceanian populations as predisposing them to higher rates of NIDDM and obesity, but it remains an open question as to whether and, if so, why there is a genetic predisposition among these groups that puts them at higher risk of NIDDM.

Variation among the Akimel O'odham stems, in part, from differences in activity patterns. Those living in Mexico have much higher activity levels because they have been able to maintain their farming tradition, whereas in the U.S. they rely on wage labor and have become more sedentary. Their traditional farming system was undermined in the nineteenth century by the usurping of their water supply by growth in the Anglo population in Arizona and increased competition from mechanized farming in the region (Smith-Morris 2006). In the wake of these trends, the Akimel O'odham became more reliant on government commodities and other processed foods, including eggs, bacon, potatoes, lard, cheese, beans, canned meat, dry cereals, and dried or canned milk, along with some fruits and vegetables. Frybread became an important food, with religious and social significance; it, along with other fried or sweet foods, is central to culturally valued forms of generosity and hospitality.

Carolyn Smith-Morris, who conducted extensive ethnographic work on diabetes among the Akimel O'odham, argues that effective prevention and treatment of diabetes must incorporate political–economic, cultural, and genetic and biological factors; they must "fit" the current conditions of life but also address the structural problems that underlie these conditions and give rise to high rates of diabetes and its negative health consequences (Smith-Morris 2004). Although genetic factors may indeed contribute to greater vulnerability to diabetes among the Akimel O'odham, it must be emphasized that the major proximate contributors to NIDDM risk derive from their diet and activity patterns. As Schulz and colleagues concluded,

> The low prevalence of type 2 diabetes and obesity in the Pima Indians (in Mexico in a more traditional rural environment contrasts sharply with that in the U.S. Pima population living in a Westernized environment. The difference in diabetes prevalence in these populations is mirrored by the differences in physical activity and obesity. The findings indicate that, even in a genetically highly susceptible population, type 2 diabetes is not inevitable and is preventable in environments that promote low levels of obesity and high levels of physical activity (Schulz et al. [1870] 2006).

Thrifty genes have been similarly implicated in the high prevalence of obesity and type 2 diabetes in many Pacific Islanders. Bindon and Baker (1997) posited that long sea voyages between islands would have selected for both thrifty use of scarce food resources and fat storage to maintain body temperature. However, the archaeological, historical, and anthropological record provide no support for such voyages for food shortage in the founding of these populations and genetic evidence indicates high levels of variability among Pacific Island populations and does not indicate unique thrifty genes showing signals of selection and associated with obesity or diabetes there (Gosling et al., 2015, although see Minster et al. 2016). Gosling and colleagues (2015) argued that the population genetics of Pacific Islanders has been strongly shaped by the founder effect (genetic drift) and selective pressures from infectious disease. The latter may, in fact, be related to metabolic outcomes as well.

In contrast, Europeans appear to have lower rates than other populations. John Allen and Susan Cheer have argued that the abundance of milk in the diets of northern Europeans made "thrifty genes" deleterious (Allen and Cheer 1996). This is because milk stimulates a larger than expected rise in blood insulin levels after it is consumed. Thus, individuals who had a thrifty genotype and who drank a lot of milk would have been likely to develop diabetes early in life and likely suffered higher rates of mortality at an earlier age as well. As a consequence, thrifty genes may have been eliminated from the population. Allen and Cheer also pointed out that Neel's assumption that hunter-gatherers were markedly more prone to food scarcity than agriculturalists was difficult to support. Others have similarly argued that famines are unlikely to have been a major selective force in human evolution or particular to specific human populations (Speakman 2013).

More recently, the "thrifty phenotype" hypothesis has been put forth to explain the high frequency of diabetes among populations transitioning from more traditional diets to a more "Western-style" diet, and rates of diabetes are now rising most rapidly among populations in transitional economies such as India (B. Zhou et al. 2016). Also known as the "developmental origins of health and disease" (DOHaD) hypothesis, it posits that exposure to nutrient scarcity during the fetal and infant stages of development results in metabolic programming for thriftiness (Barker and Thornburg 2013; Benyshek 2013; Gluckman et al. 2019; see Figure 4.7). Development gets channeled in different directions depending on the environment in which it occurs as a form of developmental adaptation. If the environment is characterized by nutrient scarcity, the developing body makes a "prediction" that future conditions will be similar and alters its trajectory accordingly by developing more thrifty mechanisms for nutrient uptake, retention, and metabolism. However, if during childhood or adulthood resources become abundant for a sustained period of time, those efficient metabolic adaptations serve to increase the risk of diabetes. Numerous studies show that low birth weight, as a measure of poor fetal growth, is a strong predictor of later life (including later childhood) risk of developing CVD, obesity, and diabetes in populations where children and adults have ample access to calories (Barker and Thornburg 2013; Yajnik 2014). Both the thrifty genotype and the thrifty phenotype models make use of the same concept of mismatch or discordance between the environment the body was "expecting" (resource scarcity) and that in which the individual lives (resource abundance) (Gluckman et al. 2019).

Although there appears to be population variation in susceptibility to NIDDM that may be genetically or developmentally based (keeping in mind that no gene associated

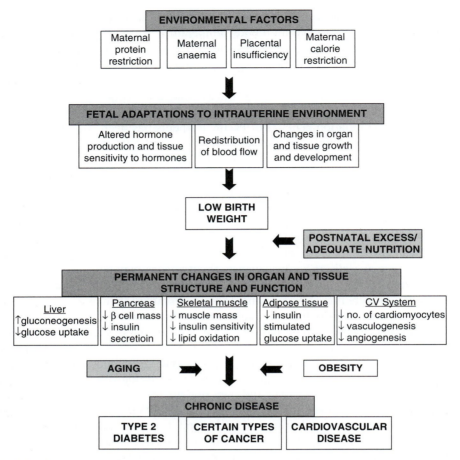

FIGURE 4.7   A schematic representation of the relationship between prenatal environments and later-life chronic disease.
Source: From M. S. Martin-Gronert and S. E. Ozanne. 2010. Mechanisms linking suboptimal early nutrition and increased risk of type 2 diabetes and obesity. *J. Nutr.* 140: 662–666. Reprinted with permission from American Society for Nutrition.

with vulnerability to type 2 diabetes has been identified that is variable across populations in ways that correlate with diabetes prevalence), the disease itself will not manifest except in the context of exposure to a hyperabundance of energy-rich foods and dramatic reductions in energy expenditure. The Akimel O'odham study and the dramatic rise of diabetes in India are clear demonstrations of this. Thus, any attempt to reduce the risk of diabetes must first concentrate on the environmental conditions that trigger it and the obesity that is often correlated with it. This is a difficult situation because currently a biological predisposition for sweet, fatty foods is aligned with ubiquitous, heavily advertised, and relatively cheap sweet fatty foods supported by political and economic interests (lobbying groups, industry involvement in setting dietary guidelines, reduced federal and state funding for educational programs that force schools into alliances with food corporations, etc.) and the rise of a sedentary lifestyle with few safe, accessible opportunities for routine vigorous activity. These contribute to the high rates of chronic disease in general and NIDDM in particular. These conditions are not evenly distributed across societies, with poor and minority groups disproportionately vulnerable.

FUTURE NUTRITION TRANSITIONS AND SUSTAINABILITY CONCERNS

Barry Popkin envisioned a fifth nutrition transition, in which dietary patterns would change to those that support a healthier body weight and protect against many chronic diseases, leading to higher quality and quantity of life. Whether or not that will come to pass at the global scale remains to be seen. But a new concern has been added to the list and is also linked to the aspirations that Popkin had for this stage: the sustainability of global dietary patterns, particularly in light of current and predicted changes in climate.

A current trend in dietary policy is to consider sustainability as an additional criterion in recommending specific diets. This is related to scientific and social concerns about climate change and the ways in which food production and consumption contribute to it. It is estimated that food production contributes to up to ~30% of global greenhouse gas emissions (Vermeulen et al. 2012). In the main, such dietary guidance encourages a move to a more plant-based diet; this is considered to have benefits in terms of mitigating climate change and in terms of reducing chronic disease and obesity, and thus enhancing human health. The acronym "SHARP" has been suggested as laying out a series of criteria that describe a sustainable diet: environmentally Sustainable, Healthy, Affordable (accessible to consumers and supporting the agriculture food sector), Reliable (stable and safe food supply), and Preferable (meets cultural norms and food preferences) (Mertens et al. 2017).

The global EAT-Lancet Commission aimed to align sustainability diet concerns with the UN Sustainable Development Goals, and made universal recommendations for a diet rich in vegetables, fruits, whole grains, legumes, nuts, and unsaturated oils, low to moderate amounts of seafood and poultry, and no or very little red or processed meat, added sugar, refined grains, and starchy vegetables such as potatoes (Willett et al. 2019). In other words, this would be a diet focused on plant foods and rich in fiber, and low in animal and ultra-processed foods, and which is known to reduce the risk of chronic disease. Commission members argued that these broad guidelines would also mitigate climate and land-system change, water use, biodiversity loss, and interference with nitrogen and phosphorus cycles while supporting a growing global population. A recent systematic review of the impact of different types of diets concluded that a plant-based, or largely-plant based (i.e., much reduced in consumption of meat or dairy) diet had the lowest negative environmental impact (Chai et al. 2019), and the so-called "Mediterranean diet" is often held up as a model of a diet that has both health and environmental benefits (Dernini et al. 2017).

There have been various critiques made against these recommendations, especially as shifts and substitutions in food production may not have the expected impacts on reduced greenhouse gas emissions or on reducing obesity or chronic disease rates. Concerns have also been raised that it would be too expensive for many in low- or middle-income countries, exceeding the average daily income in some, and would increase daily food costs by 60%, on average (Hirvonen et al. 2019), ironically due to the increase in animal source foods. On the other hand, potential negative impacts on nutrition have also been suggested, particularly among growing children and pregnant/nursing women or among populations experiencing undernutrition due to lower intake of animal source foods (Magkos et al. 2019). Not surprisingly, there has also been pushback from the meat and dairy industries on such guidance; in the United States, the 2015 U.S. Dietary Guidelines Advisory Committee (DGAC) included sustainability as one of their key themes (Millen et al. 2016). These were ultimately removed from the final Dietary Guidelines for Americans (DGAs) by the U.S. Departments of Agriculture and Health and Human Services, on the basis that sustainability concerns are outside of the scope of the DGAs. This restriction was then encoded in legislation to restrict future DGACs from considering environmental impacts. In 2019 the Trump administration further restricted the range of issues and type of evidence that the DGAC could consider in revising the DGAs for 2020. These government-mandated limitations have been viewed widely as reflecting the meat industry's lobbying influence on the U.S. government's dietary policy (Nestle 2018b).

CONCLUSION

This chapter has focused on basic nutritional requirements, as well as the links between nutrition and health and how diet has changed over the course of human prehistory and history. It has also outlined the ways in which there is population variation in the risk of these diseases and how an evolutionary perspective can inform the understanding of why these differences occur. Although a wide range of diets can be used to meet our nutritional needs, some are clearly healthier than others. An abundance of calories combined with reduced activity are evolutionarily anomalous, but with increasing globalization of Western diets, occupations, and lifestyles, this package is becoming more common. Along with it comes a rise in chronic disease, especially CVD, stroke, and diabetes. It is notable that as of 2016, CVD and stroke were the most common causes of death in the world, accounting for more than 26% of all deaths. Diabetes is now the seventh most common cause of death, although it also contributes to CVD deaths (World Health Organization 2018). All of these diseases have increased as a percentage of all deaths since 2000.

It is also important to recognize that the health consequences of a particular diet occur over the long term; especially when considering chronic disease, it is the cumulative effects of years of consumption and activity patterns, in combination with genetic inheritance and the conditions in utero, that ultimately impact disease risk. Thus, the links between diet and chronic disease are necessarily indirect and complicated by numerous other factors. Making healthy "choices" about what to eat is not simple. Our evolved biology, with its preference for energy- and salt-rich foods, in combination with a dietary environment characterized by the ubiquitous presence and low price of these foods in supermarkets, restaurants, and government surplus commodity programs, along with advertisements on television among myriad other places, makes it virtually impossible to do so. It is this dietary environment that has attained a global presence, and the negative health consequences of it have also achieved a global distribution. It also has negative environmental impacts. Whether this ultimately reverses a recent history of increases in life expectancy remains to be seen, but it is also the case that these chronic diseases are on the rise in the same places where undernutrition and infectious disease are also still common. The latter two conditions are particularly potent sources of child ill health and poor growth, which will be considered in greater detail in the next chapter.

STUDY QUESTIONS

1. Why do we say that there is a mismatch between our bodies and our contemporary environments, at least in terms of diet and nutrition?
2. What are the basic macronutrient and micronutrient requirements of the human diet?
3. How does the human digestive system reflect the fact that humans are omnivorous?
4. In general terms, how do the diets of agriculturalists differ from those of hunter-gatherers?
5. What are some of the problems associated with the assessment of the nutritional health of past populations based on bioarchaeological data?
6. What is lactase persistence? How does the biocultural distribution of lactase persistence inform biomedical conceptions of biological normalcy?
7. Why are food intolerances often greeted with skepticism? What factors might be responsible for these?
8. Why do people consuming hunter-gatherer-type diets have less risk of developing chronic disease than those who have a more "modern" diet?
9. What are some of the underlying biocultural causes of the worldwide obesity epidemic? In what ways does the epidemic vary among the world's populations? How does obesity affect mortality?
10. What are the two primary types of diabetes? What are some of the hypotheses offered to explain the population distribution of NIDDM?

CRITICAL THINKING QUESTIONS

1. Consider a cheeseburger and its component parts. Evaluate them in a biocultural and evolutionary context regarding their real and potential impact on human health and disease.
2. All studies indicate that obesity is a public health problem that will only increase in severity in the coming decades. What should we, as a society, do about this? Do you agree that it really is a problem that must be fixed?
3. What are the most important factors in your own food choices? Do you feel that you could make healthier food choices? Does the biocultural perspective help you understand the food choices you make?

SUGGESTED ETHNOGRAPHIES TO READ WITH THIS CHAPTER

Alexandra A. Brewis. 2011. *Obesity: Cultural and Biocultural Perspectives*. New Brunswick, NJ: Rutgers University Press.

Frederick Errington, Deborah Gewertz, and Tatsuro Fujikura. 2013. *The Noodle Narratives: The Global Rise of an Industrial Food into the Twenty-first Century*. Berkeley: University of California Press.

Deborah B. Gewertz and Frederick Karl Errington. 2010. *Cheap Meat: Flap Food Nations in the Pacific Islands*. Berkeley: University of California Press.

Jessica Hardin. 2019. *Faith and the Pursuit of Health: Cardiometabolic Disorders in Samoa*. 2019. New Brunswick, NJ: Rutgers University Press.

Seth Holmes. 2013. *Fresh Fruit, Broken Bodies: Migrant Farmworkers in the United States*. Berkeley: University of California Press.

Megan B. McCullough and Jessica A. Hardin. 2013. *Reconstructing Obesity: The Meaning of Measures and the Measure of Meanings*. New York: Berghahn Books.

Marion Nestle. 2018. *Unsavory Truth: How Food Companies Skew the Science of What We Eat*. New York: Basic Books.

Janet Poppendieck. 1999. *Sweet Charity?: Emergency Food and the End of Entitlement*. New York: Penguin.

Abigail C. Saguy. 2012. *What's Wrong with Fat?* New York: Oxford University Press.

Carolyn Smith-Morris. 2006. *Diabetes among the Pima: Stories of Survival*. Tucson: University of Arizona Press.

Andrea S. Wiley. 2016. *Re-Imagining Milk*, 2nd ed. New York: Routledge.

CHAPTER 5

Child Growth and Health

Chapter Goals
- To understand the basics of the human life history and life history theory
- To understand how each early life stage is characterized by unique health challenges
- To understand the environmental conditions that shape growth from gestation through adolescence
- To understand the multiple meanings of birth weight as an index of health across and within populations
- To understand the health significance of different growth trajectories and how they are related to the social environment

The very young and the very old are at greatest risk of health problems across organisms, and in this chapter we consider the factors that make the young vulnerable. Children are not only particularly sensitive to threats to their health, but the ways in which they respond to these threats also can have lifelong health effects. Children can respond to stressors in ways that are not available to adults because their physiology is more malleable and they are still growing, and their growth patterns can be altered by the environmental conditions to which they are exposed. These include local ecological, social, and cultural factors, and hence child growth is of great interest to medical anthropologists as well as public health policy makers because child growth reflects environmental challenges. In fact, Franz Boas, who was introduced in Chapter 1, was interested in cultural change and how it might also affect human biology; he demonstrated that the growth of child migrants to the United States was more similar to that of other U.S. children and less similar to that of children in their populations of origin (Boas 1912).

As Phyllis Eveleth and James Tanner wrote, "Better than any other single index, the average values of children's heights and weights reflect accurately the state of a nation's public health and the average nutritional status of its citizens. . . . This is especially so in developing or disintegrating countries. Thus, a well-designed growth study is a powerful tool with which to monitor the health of a population, or to pinpoint subgroups of a population whose share in economic and social benefits is less than it might be" (Eveleth and Tanner 1990, 1). Furthermore, Angus Deaton, who won the Nobel Prize for Economics in 2015, and his colleagues have analyzed the positive associations among height, income, and happiness across and within countries (Deaton 2007; Deaton and Arora 2009). In infancy and early childhood, health is primarily assessed through growth indices, which provide a window into the overall environmental conditions that impact the health of whole populations. Furthermore, growth trajectories have the ability to influence adult health parameters. To understand the unique health aspects of childhood and how they may contribute to health problems later in life, it is necessary to consider childhood within the context of the human life history.

LIFE HISTORY THEORY

Life history theory is a branch of evolutionary theory that attempts to account for the ways in which the stages of the life cycle and the behaviors associated with them are organized. All organisms experience physiological changes across the life span, but the timing and duration of these stages is highly variable across, and to some extent within, species. For mammals the basic life stages include gestation, infancy, a juvenile stage, sexual maturation, and then adulthood. Most organisms do not experience "old age" because they are likely to die before the aging process is well underway. Whereas many mammals move quickly from infancy to sexual maturity, for humans (and other ape species) this process is extended and the juvenile period continues for a longer period of time. What are children doing during this time? Most anthropologists agree that with such a large brain, humans need a long period of learning. In large part this learning is directed toward becoming a successful adult, with the requisite skills for subsistence and negotiating a complex social world. However, there are some unique features of human growth that require further explication.

In general, life history theory takes the perspective that organisms are faced with two fundamental constraints: time and energy. They have two main "tasks:" (1) growth and maturation and (2) reproduction. The former must precede the latter. Time and energy spent on growth and maturation or, in adulthood, bodily maintenance, cannot simultaneously be spent on reproduction. In other words, life histories are characterized by trade-offs and the key question is this: How should organisms best allocate their limited time and energy to these processes? That depends first on how much time and energy they are likely to have. Time is dependent on the likelihood of dying at a given age (Promislow and Harvey 1990). Is there a high or low risk of early (juvenile) mortality or adult mortality? If adult mortality is high, it is better to grow quickly and reproduce early. If juvenile mortality is high, it is better to have a large quantity of offspring to ensure that some survive. Conversely, if adult mortality is low, organisms can "afford" to grow for a longer period of time and to a larger size before devoting their time and energy to reproduction, and presumably they will be more successful in doing so. If juvenile mortality is low, parents can "afford" to have fewer offspring but invest more resources in each one to ensure their survival and future fitness. These are the basic predictions of life history theory.

TABLE 5.1   Key Stages in Human Life History

Gestation (first ~38 weeks): Prenatal life, rapid growth and tissue differentiation

Infancy (birth through weaning): Rapid growth, high nutrient needs, relative helplessness, breastfeeding and transition to community foods

Childhood/juvenile period: ~3 years to 10–12; moderate growth, dental maturation

Adolescence: Sexual maturity and final growth spurt

Adulthood: Maturity is reached; relative homeostasis

Old age/senescence: Decline in function in physiological systems, including reproductive system

The constraints of time and energy shape life history evolution in all organisms. Among humans, sociocultural phenomena influence human life history process in a number of ways. First, economic conditions are key predictors of the amount of resources individuals can access. Wealthy individuals may be able to both grow to a larger size and have more children; poorer individuals may have their own growth constrained and the health of their children may also be impaired. Poorer individuals may have restricted access to health-care resources or live in environments characterized by a high risk of morbidity or mortality. In addition, norms about childhood feeding, food taboos or restrictions placed on pregnant women, gender biases, the appropriate time for marriage and reproduction to begin and end, birth spacing, and contraceptive use are among the important contributors to life history variation across societies.

What kind of life history do humans have, and what health risks are particularly relevant to each stage? It is useful to consider some of the main life history stages laid out in Table 5.1. Each of these stages is characterized by unique biological transformations and health challenges. Especially during the early parts of the life cycle, there are critical periods during which environmental cues can alter the course of growth. Global public health researchers identify the "first 1,000 days"—corresponding to the period from conception to age 2 years—as the most critical window for growth and health, with problems arising in this age range having the potential for both short- and long-term health consequences (Black et al. 2013). Challenges to growth and health across the early stages of life are outlined in Figure 5.1.

GESTATION: THE FIRST 38 WEEKS OF GROWTH AND DEVELOPMENT

Among humans, a full-term pregnancy lasts about 38 weeks from conception. In practice, a pregnancy is divided into three trimesters, each of which exhibits a unique pattern of growth and development. The first trimester is when the **zygote** (the fertilized egg) grows and transforms into an embryo, with millions of cells differentiated into functionally distinct tissues. It is estimated that 10% of recognized pregnancies end in spontaneous abortion during the first trimester. Up to 75% of all fertilizations end very early, and these are most often a result of genetic abnormalities of the zygote (Gaskins et al. 2015). Any genetic mutations that disrupt the process of growth and maturation are likely to have the most severe effects during this phase and result in an

embryo whose further growth cannot be sustained. The frequency of genetic mutations increases with maternal age (Maconochie et al. 2007). When gestation occurs in
environments where severe infections are common, the embryo's survival may be
threatened. For example, early infection with malaria is frequently associated with
spontaneous abortion because the parasite is able to infect the placenta, disrupting

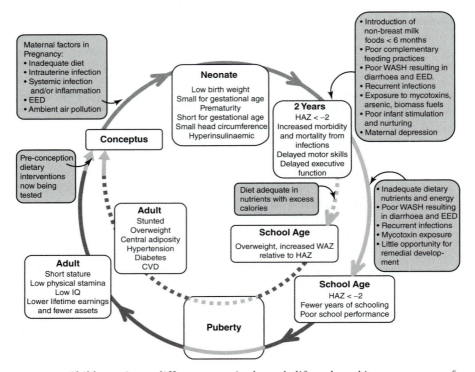

FIGURE 5.1 Child stunting at different stages in the early life cycle and its consequences for
health. The medium gray pathway denotes the period between conception and 2 years (the first
1,000 days), when stunting and probably all associated pathology are most responsive to, or
preventable by, interventions. The light gray pathway denotes periods between age 2 years and
mid-childhood and during the adolescent growth spurt when some catch-up in linear growth
may occur, although effects during these periods on other components of the stunting syndrome (e.g., cognition and immune function) are less clear. The short light gray pathway before
Conceptus reflects evidence that dietary interventions targeting stunted women during the pre-
conception period improve birth outcomes. The black pathway denotes periods when the
stunting syndrome appears unresponsive to interventions. The gray shaded boxes list
age-specific causative or aggravating factors. White boxes describe common age-specific
outcomes. Between 2 years and adulthood, the pathways diverge to denote the following:
dashed line, a stunted child whose environment becomes more affluent with abundant access
to food, causing excessive weight gain; solid line: a stunted child whose environment remains
resource-constrained/food insecure.
Source: Andrew J. Prendergast and Jean H. Humphrey. "The stunting syndrome in developing
countries." *Paediatrics and International Child Health* 2014; 34(4), 250–265. © W. S. Maney & Son
Ltd 2014.

oxygen and nutrient flow to the embryo (Espinoza et al. 2005). Although the embryo has few energetic needs because of its small size, it does require some specific micronutrients to develop properly. Folate (vitamin B9), which is found in whole grains, legumes, and dark-green leafy vegetables, is essential to embryological development, especially the enclosure of the spinal cord (Gaskins et al. 2015). Folate deficiency is responsible for most cases of the congenital disease spina bifida, a condition characterized by incomplete enclosure of the spinal column, which leaves the spinal cord exposed. A recent review found that countries with mandated folic acid fortification of major cereal grains had a prevalence of spina bifida that was over 30% lower than countries without such policies (Atta et al. 2016).

By the start of second trimester, tissue differentiation is largely complete, and the embryo is now considered a fetus. During these three months, the fetus experiences rapid growth of the skeleton. The mother's nutrient needs (for energy and also for calcium) increase to support this growth, and when maternal undernutrition exists, fetal linear growth may be slowed. The third trimester is characterized by rapid growth in weight and deposition of fat. It is also during this time that further maturation of the respiratory, gastrointestinal, and circulatory systems occurs, in preparation for the many changes the baby will experience after birth. Energy requirements for the mother are particularly high during this time (estimated to be an additional 466 kilocalories/day, Butte and King 2005) because about 80% of the newborn's weight is accumulated during the third trimester. Restriction of caloric intake during this time will likely reduce the weight of the newborn.

Because the fetus is entirely dependent on nutrient flow from the mother, if a mother's health is compromised in some way—because of undernutrition, infection, or stress—during pregnancy, there are likely to be consequences to birth outcome. The fetus is neither a "perfect parasite," able to extract whatever resources it needs from the mother regardless of the cost to her health, nor is its health perfectly correlated with that of the mother. The fetus is both vulnerable to the mother's own health problems and to some extent buffered from them. Furthermore, as described in more detail in Chapter 6, there may also be means by which the fetus can manipulate the flow of resources from the mother.

Birth weight is a commonly used measure of a newborn's health status. It is a measure of the resources that an infant is born with and a predictor of its survival chances, with both very small and very large babies having higher rates of death than babies weighing around the average, as shown in Figure 5.2. In evolutionary terms, birth weight is considered under *stabilizing selection*—that is, weights around the average have higher survival probabilities than those that are well above or below the mean. Small babies, even those who are born at full term, have few energetic resources to confront the challenges of the postnatal environment, and large babies are vulnerable to more complications with the birth process itself. Birth weight is influenced by maternal age, parity (how many previous births she has had), nutritional status (both current dietary behavior and weight, height, or fatness), infectious disease, smoking, altitude of residence, and sex and gestational age of the newborn (Chen 1983). Average birth weight in the United States (and other European countries) increased over the twentieth century but declined in the early twenty-first century, with a steeper decline among African American newborns (Catov et al. 2016). Low birth weights among African Americans

Fetal Alcohol Spectrum Disorders

Prenatal exposure to alcohol can cause a range of fetal alcohol spectrum disorders (FASDs), and the most severe end of that spectrum is **fetal alcohol syndrome** (FAS), a leading preventable cause of mental retardation and birth defects. FAS is a lifelong condition that causes physical and mental disabilities and is characterized by abnormal facial features, growth deficiencies, and central nervous system problems. Specific outcomes for individuals with FAS can include the following:

Small size for gestational age or small stature in relation to peers
Facial abnormalities such as small eye openings
Poor coordination
Hyperactive behavior
Learning disabilities
Developmental disabilities (e.g., speech and language delays)
Mental retardation or low IQ
Problems with daily living
Poor reasoning and judgment skills
Sleep and sucking disturbances in infancy

The exact mechanism by which alcohol (ethanol) impacts embryological and fetal development is not well known. Experimental studies have found that alcohol exposure has a variety of toxic effects on brain cell tissue and reduces intrauterine growth rates. These effects can occur very early in embryological development, as well as during the fetal period, and are dose dependent, meaning higher blood alcohol levels are associated with more deleterious outcomes (https://www.cdc.gov/ncbddd/fasd).

Worldwide rates of FAS range from a low of 0.5–2 per 1,000 births in the United States to a high of 39–46 per 1,000 births in South Africa. FAS is also well described among Native American populations, where the rate is 1–9 per 1,000 births. In some rural communities in South Africa, rates may reach 9%–13% of all children (May et al. 2017). Philip May, who has worked extensively on this topic in South Africa found that the highest rates in Africa occur primarily in the wine-growing areas of the country. Heavy, episodic drinking has been the norm among laborers in these areas, and historically alcohol was provided daily to farm workers as partial payment for work (the "dop" system, based on the Afrikaans word for drink). Although this system of payment has been outlawed, local laborers are low paid, have limited occupation opportunities, experience poor living conditions, and view alcohol as a valued commodity. Binge drinking is common. Weekend binge drinking and membership in a family with a history of drinking appear to be risk factors for FAS in these communities. It may also be related to women's relatively small body size, indicative of a lower threshold for metabolizing alcohol (May et al. 2013).

Although the prevalence in the United States is low, it is much higher than that of European countries, despite lower overall levels of alcohol consumption in the United States. As in South Africa, it is suspected that binge drinking may contribute more to FAS in the United States. The social conditions and norms that encourage or discourage alcohol consumption are implicated in the risk of FAS, and these are highly variable across cultures, although it is important to keep in mind that the primary link among FAS cases, regardless of their locale, is low socioeconomic status.

likely reflect ongoing structural violence and racism that are embodied via maternal stress and other pathways (Chambers et al. 2018; Mustillo et al. 2004).

Babies may be born small because they are premature or small-for-gestational age (SGA), and those underlying causes are associated with different health outcomes. On average, females are lighter than males, and firstborn babies are lighter than higher-birth-order babies. If a baby is born prematurely, it is likely to be small as well as relatively immature. If it has a congenital disease, it may also be small if proper development has not occurred. Smoking is also known to reduce birth weight, as is gestation at high altitude. If the baby is short, it is also likely to be light, and if there were constraints on growth in the third trimester, it is also likely to be of lower weight. There are also genetic inputs to birth weight. Many of these factors work together and their independent effects are difficult to assess. From a comparative perspective, the birth-weight

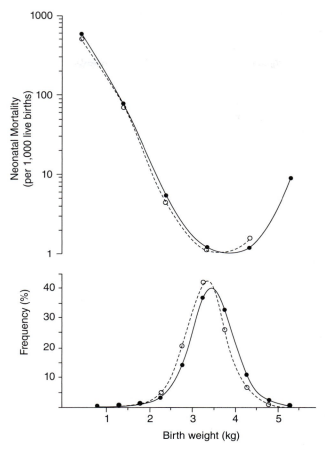

FIGURE 5.2   The relationship between birth weight and infant mortality. The dotted lines are from a high-altitude population (Colorado) and the solid lines are from sea-level populations. Note that the birth-weight distribution has the same shape at high and low altitude, but that the former is shifted to the left, with a lower mean weight. The birth-weight-specific mortality curve is also shifted to the left. This indicates that a given lower birth weight is associated with a different risk of mortality depending on where the infant was born. It also shows that the relationship between birth weight and mortality depends more on where the birth weight is relative to the average birth weight of the population (high or low altitude in this case).
Source: From Allen J. Wilcox, Birthweight and perinatal mortality: The effect of maternal smoking, *American Journal of Epidemiology*, 1993, Vol. 137(10):1098–1104, by permission of Oxford University Press.

distribution that characterizes any given population is likely to differ from that of other populations as a function of a unique combination of these variables.

Populations with the highest average birth weights reported are in wealthy countries and the lowest are in South Asian countries. Across the world, more than 30 million babies are SGA each year, representing about 27% of all births in low- and middle-income countries (Black et al. 2013). Almost half of all births in India and

Pakistan are SGA, and the vast majority of them are full term. Among the factors contributing to the high frequency of low-birth-weight babies are young maternal ages (because girls are frequently married during adolescence), maternal stunting, undernutrition, including high rates of anemia, continued subsistence work during pregnancy, and constraints on prenatal care usage (Black et al. 2013; Gururaj et al. 2015; Mistry et al. 2009).

Traditionally the World Health Organization (WHO) has used 2500 grams as the cut off for low birth weight, but there is an alternative global standard for assessing fetal growth based on data from 24 countries, which can be easily customized for use in any country (Mikolajczyk et al. 2011). Importantly, the health and mortality consequences of a given birth weight vary by population and environment. For example, although girls are smaller than boys at birth, they do not have correspondingly higher rates of mortality. Also, in some high-altitude populations, where average birth weight is diminished compared with that in low-altitude populations, the mortality associated with the lower weights is not elevated, as evident in Figure 5.2. Allen Wilcox (2001) has demonstrated that a more important determinant of an infant's mortality risk is where it falls relative to the average birth weight in his or her population. Thus, although the basic relationship between the birth weight distribution and mortality does appear to be universal, with high mortality at both the low and the high ends of the birth weight spectrum, any particular birth weight may be associated with different survival probabilities across populations. This nonintuitive finding challenges our ideas about "biological normalcy;" that is, the absolute measure (in this case, birth weight) may matter less than the relative measure (where an individual falls relative to the population mean).

Infants who are SGA have twice the risk of dying in the first year of life compared with infants who are appropriate size for gestational age in a given population (Katz et al. 2013). In addition, there is growing evidence that the negative consequences of SGA may be experienced well beyond infancy. Epidemiological data indicate that smaller newborns are more likely to die from coronary heart disease and develop type 2 diabetes than those of higher weights, as shown in Table 5.2 (Barker 1995). This seemingly unlikely association has been well documented across populations and appears to be especially evident when poor growth in utero is followed by rapid growth during childhood. Birth weight itself does not play the causal role in this relationship; it is a summary outcome measure of intrauterine growth processes. When lower birth weight derives from maternal undernutrition during pregnancy or high levels of maternal stress, alterations in fetal growth and development occur. These are adaptive in the sense that they represent a programming of fetal metabolism for conditions of scarcity, stress, or both, which should enhance survival during childhood (see the discussion of the developmental origins of health and disease in Chapter 4; Benyshek 2013; Gluckman et al. 2019). If, however, an overabundance of food rather than food scarcity is the norm during childhood or adulthood, this efficient programming can have the effect of increasing fat storage, resulting in overweight or obesity or insulin resistance and diabetes (Gluckman et al. 2019). In other words, there is a "mismatch" between the environment under which the fetus grew (and the adaptations it made to it) and the environment in which the adult lives, which results in an increased risk of chronic disease.

TABLE 5.2   Odds Ratios for Dying from Cardiovascular Disease or Developing Glucose Intolerance Based on Birth Weight of Men in the United Kingdom

Birth Weight (Pounds)	OR: Dying of CVD before 65 Years	OR: Dying of CVD All Ages	% with Glucose Intolerance	OR: Dying of CVD, adjusted for BMI
≤5.5	1.50	1.37	40	6.6
−6.5	1.27	1.29	35	4.8
−7.5	1.17	1.14	31	4.6
−8.5	1.07	1.12	22	2.6
−9.5	0.96	0.97	13	1.4
≥10	1.00	1.00	14	1.0
p for trend	0.001	0.005	<0.001	

Note: An odds ratio (OR) above 1.00 means an increased risk compared with the standard (defined here at those with the highest birth weights). Odds ratios below 1.00 signify a reduced risk compared with the standard. BMI, body mass index; CVD, cardiovascular disease.

Source: Adapted from Barker, David J.P. 2004. "The developmental origins of adult disease." *Journal of the American College of Nutrition* 23:588S–595S. Reprinted with permission from the American College of Nutrition.

INFANCY

Infancy is typically defined as the period from birth until the first birthday. One year does not correspond to a biologically meaningful period, although the first birthday may be a culturally salient event associated with changes in expectations about appropriate infant behavior, feeding, or treatment. Instead of relying on age, it is useful to think about the changes that occur in the earliest part of life that are likely to be meaningfully related to health. The period after birth is a time of rapid growth and changes, as the infant adapts to extrauterine life. The greatest challenges are to respiratory and gastrointestinal functions, as the infant switches from liquid breathing to air breathing and from direct nutrient delivery via the umbilical cord to oral feeding. In the first weeks and months following birth, the newborn is completely dependent. Because of its vulnerability, it requires full-time active care to keep it warm, safe from environmental dangers, and well fed. The latter is particularly important because human infants grow rapidly but are now entirely dependent on what caretakers feed them rather than having direct access to maternal resources. The brain in particular grows very rapidly and reaches more or less adult size by about five years of age. It requires between 40% and 85% of a young child's metabolic needs, and therefore the diet of infants and young children must be energy dense (Barker 2004). Human infants are exceptionally fat compared with other primate infants, and this fat may be used to support brain growth (Kuzawa 1998).

Most infants start out postnatal life consuming breast milk. Human breast milk is specifically tailored to the growth and maturation needs of human infants and contains not only nutrients such as sugar, fat, protein, and required micronutrients but also hormones and other biologically active chemicals that promote the growth of different tissues. Breast milk also contains secretory antibodies (IgA) that help protect the nursing infant from infections that the mother has already been exposed to and that are likely to be found in the local environment. Human milk oligosaccharides (carbohydrates unique to breast milk) provide energy to support the development of the infant's microbiota, and microbiota in breast milk further help "seed" the infant's own gut microbiota (Pannaraj et al. 2017; Wang et al. 2015). Thus, breast milk is more than just "food"; it is a whole package of biologically active constituents that help shape the health, growth, and development of the nursing child. Human milk is not rich in energy; it has about 70 kcal/100 ml. While this is not, for example, that different from cow's milk, human infants have very high energy needs. Across mammals, those species with energy-rich milk tend to be those that nurse relatively infrequently or that live in very cold climates. In contrast, human milk seems to be designed to be consumed frequently—numerous times per day. Careful observations of !Kung hunter-gatherers indicate that an infant nurses every 20 to 30 minutes (Konner and Worthman 1980) and Virginia Vitzthum (1989) found that highland Bolivian women nursed their infants every 45 minutes to one hour during the day, with reduced frequency at night.

Although breastfeeding is the norm among most societies and often continues well into the second or third year, in many it is truncated to a few weeks after birth or never initiated (Victora et al. 2016). As of 2016, 84% of women in the United States breastfed their infants, but only 57% were still nursing when their infants reached six months of age (http://www.cdc.gov/breastfeeding/data/NIS_data/index.htm). This initiation rate is low compared with that of other industrialized and non-industrialized countries, although the continuation rate is higher than what is found in other places. In the U.S. survey, 48% were nursing exclusively at three months and 25% at six months, and these numbers have increased steadily since 2009. The WHO recommends exclusive breastfeeding to six months. The reasons for early weaning, supplementation, or non-initiation of breastfeeding include maternal return to the workforce, lack of information on how to breastfeed successfully, lack of social support for breastfeeding, and easy availability and widespread promotion of infant formula (World Health Organization and UNICEF 2014). The issue of breastfeeding from the maternal perspective is considered in greater detail in the next chapter, but here it is worth noting how breastfeeding affects infant growth and health.

An interesting issue in the study of growth of breastfed infants is the standards that are used to assess their growth. You may remember having your height and weight measured and plotted on a growth chart when you were a child or adolescent. Growth charts consist of established growth "curves," which represent height or weight achieved by a given age, as shown in Figures 5.3a and 5.3b. The multiple curves represent different percentiles—ranging from the 5th to the 95th percentile for girls and boys. If you are at the 10th percentile for weight, that means that 10% of the population of children of the same age and sex weigh less than you; if you are at the 90th percentile, then 90% of children your age and sex weigh less than you. A child's weight or height is plotted against his or her age and matched up with a particular percentile. As you can see, the range of heights and weights in the normal range is wide. As a child ages and its size is plotted on the growth curve, it is easy to see whether he or she maintains the same percentile or whether it increases or decreases. Persistent rising above or dropping below an established percentile can be a cause for concern for overweight or growth faltering, respectively.

What are the data on which these curves are based? Currently, growth curves for children age 0–5 years typically are based on the multicountry growth study conducted by the WHO, whereas those used for 5- to 19-year-olds come from 1977 U.S. National Center for Health Statistics (NCHS) data, a large national sample of children in the United States from 1929 to 1975. Some countries either use the WHO charts or

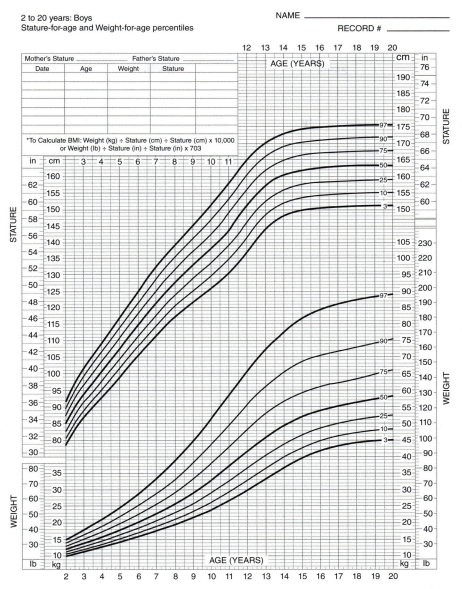

2 to 20 years: Boys
Stature-for-age and Weight-for-age percentiles

NAME _____

RECORD # _____

FIGURE 5.3A The 2000 Centers for Disease Control and Prevention Growth Chart for Girls, Weight and Height.
Source: http://www.cdc.gov/growthcharts

construct their own from local population studies. A key difference between the 0- to 5-year and the 5- to 19-year data is that the former is a standard for growth, whereas the latter is a reference. The difference between these terms is important: a *standard* reflects our understanding of healthy growth (i.e., how a child *should* grow), whereas a *reference* is simply a population against which one can compare data (i.e., a *description*

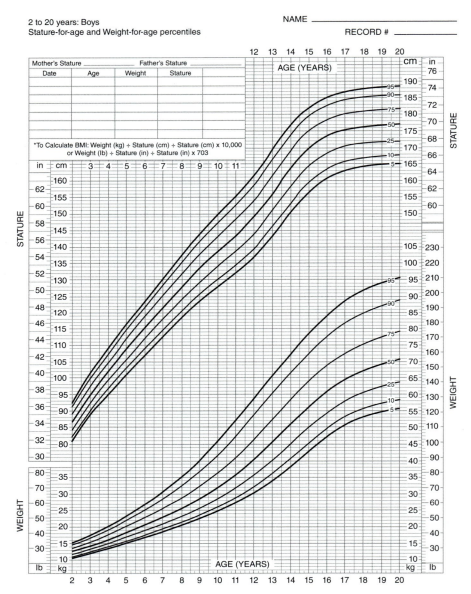

2 to 20 years: Boys
Stature-for-age and Weight-for-age percentiles

FIGURE 5.3B The 2000 Centers for Disease Control and Prevention Growth Chart for Boys, Weight and Height.
Source: http://www.cdc.gov/growthcharts

of growth in a population). Currently, there is no universal standard for the growth of older children (see http://www.who.int/childgrowth/en).

The WHO growth standard debuted in 2006. Prior to that time, infant growth was assessed in relation to U.S. samples. However, most of the infants in these samples were not breastfed and, in effect, the growth of a population composed of mostly formula-fed infants became the growth standard for *all* infants. Breastfed babies are known to grow more slowly and are leaner than formula-fed babies (Dewey 1998). As shown in Figure 5.4, when the growth of a sample of healthy breastfed babies was assessed relative to the 2000 U.S. Centers for Disease Control and Prevention (CDC) standard, they appeared to gain weight faster in the first months, but then they slowed down and exhibited a persistent downward trend in their percentile (plotted as a z-score; the 50th percentile is equivalent to a z-score of 0). The slower growth among breastfed babies was sufficient to lead pediatricians to warn breastfeeding mothers that their infant was "falling behind" on the growth curve; mothers were encouraged to stop nursing or add supplementary formula. However, when these same babies' growth was assessed in relation to the 2006 WHO standard based on healthy breastfed babies, they tracked right along the median, as expected (de Onis et al. 2007).

The WHO infant growth standard is based on a sample of breastfed babies living under optimal health conditions in six countries (Brazil, Ghana, India, Norway, Oman, and the United States) and establishes the breastfed infant as the biological norm for growth (http://www.who.int/childgrowth/en). What is also interesting about this standard is that the growth curves (weight-for-age, height-for-age) are similar in each of the participating countries, indicating that under "optimal" health conditions (i.e., breastfeeding, control of infection, adequate nutrition, nonsmoking mothers), environmental, rather than genetic factors, are much more important determinants of variation in early growth across populations. There was variation among the six countries, and the WHO opted to consider all measures within 0.5 SD above or below the mean to be consistent

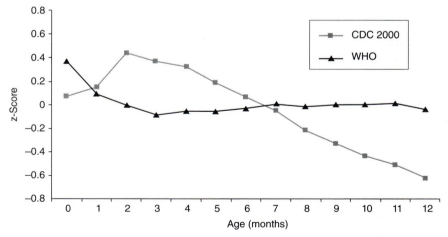

FIGURE 5.4   Both lines represent the growth of a sample of healthy breastfed babies. One line shows how their growth looks if judged against the NCHS/CDC 2000 standard, and the other (flatter) line hovering around the z-score of zero shows their growth compared with the WHO standard. Compared with the NCHS/CDC standard, these healthy infants appear to experience growth faltering; compared with the WHO standard, they are growing normally.
Source: de Onis, Mercedes et al. 2007. Comparison of the WHO child growth standards and the CDC 2000 growth charts. *Journal of Nutrition* 137:144–148. Reprinted with permission from American Society for Nutrition.

with the standard. There have been critiques of the standard, and a recent analysis of growth in 55 populations found that while most children had heights within 0.5 SD from the WHO standard, weight varied more markedly, with over 30% of populations having age-specific weights that were above 0.5 SD of the WHO standard (Natale and Rajagopalan 2014). The authors emphasized that the samples used to construct the WHO standard are reflective of advantaged populations living at a particular historical moment.

As an infant ages, his or her nutrient needs begin to outstrip that provided by breast milk alone. This happens by around six months of age. Because infants of this age have few or no teeth, they need foods that are soft and easily digestible and also free of contaminants. The introduction of "solid" foods is a feature of infant and young child feeding that is unique to humans (Sellen 2007). Other mammals, including primates, do not receive supplementary foods from their caretakers while they are also still nursing. The initiation of complementary feeding essentially begins the process of weaning, although nursing may continue as new foods are introduced. Although technically weaning refers to the complete cessation of nursing, it is better to view it as a process that starts with supplementation and ends with the child's complete independence from breast milk. The duration of this process can be very short to several years, although it tends to cluster around two and a half years in nonindustrialized societies (Sellen 2007).

Weaning is often a critical time for the health and growth of young children (Jones et al. 2003). It is not unusual to see growth disruptions around the time at which supplementary foods are introduced or weaning occurs, but this is largely dependent on the quality of foods weanlings receive. Those who receive nutrient-dense foods, animal source foods, or a more diverse diet tend to continue to grow well. However, many weanling diets around the world are mainly composed of cooked cereals, which are high in energy but low in other macro- and micronutrients (Onyango et al. 2014). Complicating weaning is the child's need to rely on his or her own immune system, as opposed to receiving the mother's antibodies from breast milk, which occurs along with increased exposure to food- or waterborne infections. Collectively, undernutrition and infection, especially diarrheal infections, contribute to growth faltering in weanlings (Onyango et al. 2014).

Assessing the relationship between breastfeeding and infant health requires understanding the cultural logic of local breastfeeding practices. In a study of Peruvian infants who suffered from stunting in growth, diarrheal disease, and low intake of supplementary foods, researchers found that infants who were breastfed were shorter in length than those who were not breastfed. However, they also reported that the mother's concern about the infant's ill health led them to breastfeed their infant more (Marquis et al. 1997). A similar result was found in Senegal, where mothers reported weaning children who were perceived as healthy and growing well earlier than children who were perceived as sickly (Simondon et al. 2001). Thus, although it appeared that breastfeeding was contributing to poor health, in fact, poor health precipitated an increase in nursing. These studies show how local cultural practices shape the relationships between nursing and infant health. They also demonstrate how associations between nursing and child health must be carefully disentangled to avoid attributing ill health to the practice of breastfeeding.

There is a wealth of evidence supporting the benefits of breastfeeding over bottle feeding on acute and chronic and health indices (Kramer and Kakuma 2012; Robinson and Fall 2012; Sankar et al. 2015). In the 1960s and 1970s there were global declines in breastfeeding rates that were attributed, in part, to aggressive marketing of formula to pregnant women and new mothers (World Health Organization 1981). In developing countries in particular, where water supplies were often contaminated, formula powders rehydrated and/or diluted with water and fed to infants led to diarrheal disease, or what Derek Jelliffe famously referred to as "commerciogenic malnutrition" (Jelliffe 1972). Furthermore, the formula often came with instructions in English, rather than local languages, and doctors and nurses were frequently provided with incentives for encouraging bottle feeding. In 1977 a boycott began of the Nestlé Corporation, the Swiss-based maker of infant formula for such promotional practices, especially in developing countries. As a result, in 1981 at the 34th World Health Assembly, an international code of marketing of breast milk substitutes was adopted. Among its provisions was the requirement that

> Informational and educational materials, whether written, audio, or visual, dealing with the feeding of infants and intended to reach pregnant women and mothers of infants and young children, should include clear information on all the following points: (a) the benefits and superiority of breast-feeding; (b) maternal nutrition, and the preparation for and maintenance of breast- feeding; (c) the negative effect on breast-feeding of introducing partial bottle-feeding; (d) the difficulty of reversing the decision not to breastfeed; and (e) where needed, the proper use of infant formula, whether manufactured industrially or home-prepared. When such materials contain information about the use of infant formula, they should include the social and financial implications of its use; the health hazards of inappropriate foods or feeding methods; and, in particular, the health hazards of unnecessary or improper use of infant formula and other breast-milk substitutes. Such materials should not use any pictures or text which may idealize the use of breast-milk substitutes. (World Health Organization 1981, 10)

There have been ongoing complaints that Nestlé remains out of compliance with the International Code. Formula continues to be promoted in various ways and there have been numerous cases of formal contamination (Kent 2015). Global data on the WHO infant and young child feeding indicators are provided in Figure 5.5. These mask substantial variation across and within countries. A recent UNICEF report found that while almost all (95%) of infants across the globe receive some breast milk, prevalence is lower in wealthy countries (the lowest are Ireland: 55%, France: 63%, U.S. 74%), while in poorer countries, the prevalence of ever-breastfeeding is almost 100%. Furthermore, in wealthy countries, poorer women breastfeed less, while in poor countries, it is wealthier women who breastfeed less (United Nations Children's Fund [UNICEF] 2018). It is important to note that the health benefits of breastfeeding are not unique to infants in developing countries. Even in wealthy countries, breastfeeding is associated with both short-term and long-term health benefits for both the mother and the infant (Stuebe 2009). Despite these known benefits, most women do not breastfeed to six months and few practice exclusive breastfeeding even to three months. As Dan Sellen notes, this appears to be a legacy of human evolutionary flexibility in infant feeding, which uniquely includes complementary foods:

> An evolutionary perspective provides insight into why contemporary patterns of IYCF [infant and young child feeding] often deviate from the optimal pattern indicated by clinical and epidemiological evidence. Human mothers are physiologically and behaviorally adapted to exercise more choice in the patterns and duration of full and partial breastfeeding than do other primates (Sellen 2007, 134)

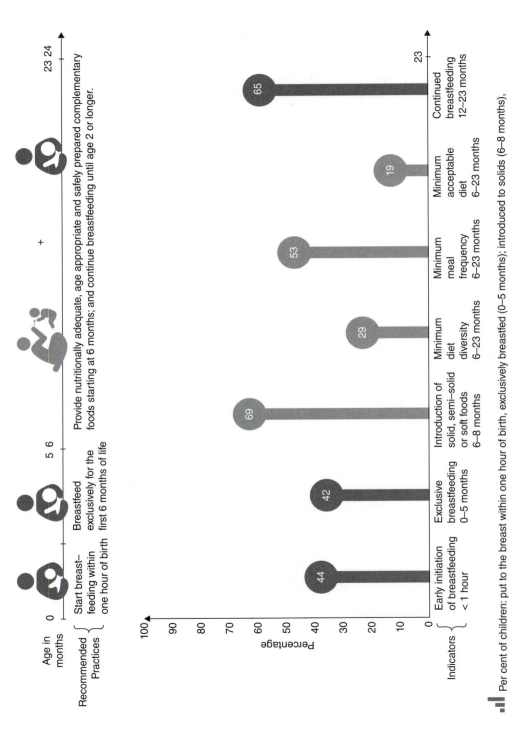

■ Per cent of children: put to the breast within one hour of birth; exclusively breastfed (0–5 months); introduced to solids (6–8 months); with a minimum meal frequency, minimum diet diversity and minimum acceptable diet (6–23 months) and continued breastfeeding (12–23 months), 2018.

FIGURE 5.5 Global indicators for the World Health Organization Infant and Young Child Feeding Indicators.
Source: https://data.unicef.org/topic/nutrition/infant-and-young-child-feeding

Development of the Gut Microbiome

As infants and children grow and develop physically, they also acquire a distinctive set of gut microbiota. The array of microbes that individuals acquire depends very much on the environmental context in which they grow up, and there is increasing evidence that the composition of the microbiota has consequences for a variety of health conditions,

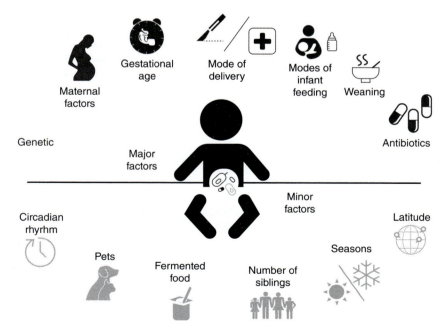

a Gut microbiota composition during the first years of life

- Euterobacteriaceae
- Clostridiaceae
- Bifidobacteriaceae
- Lachnospiraceae
- Lactobacillaceae
- Veillonellaceae
- Ruminococcaceae
- Bacteroidaceae
- Prevotellaceae

0 Months   1–2 Months   6–8 Months   1 Year   3 Years

b Prenatal, perinatal and postnatal factors affecting microbiome composition

Maternal factors

Gestational age

Mode of delivery

Modes of infant feeding

Weaning

Antibiotics

Genetic

Major factors

Minor factors

Latitude

Circadian rhyrhm

Pets

Fermented food

Number of siblings

Seasons

FIGURE 5.6 Infant microbiota composition (a) and the known factors affecting analysis and results in microbiota studies (b).
Source: Drago, L.; Panelli, S.; Bandi, C.; Zuccotti, G.; Perini, M.; D'Auria, E. What pediatricians should know before studying gut microbiota. *J. Clin. Med.* 2019, 8, 1206. https://doi.org/10.3390/jcm8081206

(continued)

(continued)

including cardiovascular and metabolic diseases, weight gain, allergies and autoimmune disease risk, and possibly mental health conditions as well (Boulangé et al. 2016). More immediately, microbes that colonize the gut influence the development of gut function, help maintain the intestinal barrier, provide protection against infection, and promote tolerance of foods by "educating" the immune system through exposure to microbes (Goulet 2015). Through the process of fermentation microbes produce short-chain fatty acids, which provide energy for the gut or other tissues and regulate metabolism (Boulangé et al. 2016).

The gastrointestinal system of a fetus traditionally has been thought to be sterile, although recent evidence suggests the presence of microbiota in the placenta, umbilical cord, amniotic fluid, and fetal membranes (Willyard 2018). During the birth process the infant begins to acquire a gut microbiome, and as Figure 5.6 indicates, over the course of infancy and childhood, a more populous and diverse microbiome develops. A recent paper that analyzed microbiota in a very large dataset of children age 3–46 months of age described three main phases in the development of the microbiota, all of which mark changes in both numbers and diversity of: a developmental phase (3–14 months), a transitional stage (15–30 months), and a stable phase (31–46 months) (Stewart et al. 2018). The authors ascertained that breastfeeding—whether alone or in combination with formula or solid foods—was the most important determinant of variation in gut microbiota during the developmental stage, likely because breast milk both contains and supports the growth of specific bacteria that ferment the oligosaccharides in breast milk (such as Bifidobacterium).

Mode of delivery (vaginal birth vs C-section) has a major impact on the initial establishment of gut microbes; newborns from a vaginal birth acquire microbes from the mother's vagina and greater microbial diversity overall, while those born by C-section have gut microbes that are less diverse and that derive from the mother's skin (Dominguez-Bello et al. 2010). Some studies (but not all) have shown that these differences persist into childhood. Interestingly, during pregnancy a woman's vaginal microbiota change and come to be populated by Lactobacillus species, the bacteria that a newborn will use to help digest milk (Mueller et al. 2015).

As the infant transitions from milk as a primary food to a more diverse, adult-like diet, their microbiota simultaneously mature. Their gut microbes transition to being largely from the Firmicutes and Bacteroidetes phyla, reflecting the distribution in their local households and communities. Between the 3rd and 4th year of life, the microbiome becomes relatively stable, although it can be disrupted by antibiotic usage, changes in diet and other factors that are not well described. While most of the work on the human microbiota has come from European or U.S. populations, differences have been found when investigating other populations. For example, a study in Papua New Guinea found that gut microbial diversity was much greater and exhibited novel strains compared to that found among U.S. samples, but also that there was less inter-individual variation and more community-level sharing of microbiota in Papua New Guinea (Martínez et al. 2015). Thus individual and community behaviors that are more individualistic or communal have implications for gut microbial composition and health.

CHILDHOOD

Once a child has successfully weathered the transition to adult foods, he or she enters childhood, a period of relatively slow growth. From a health perspective, this is a quiescent time. Generally, no new health challenges emerge, dietary and immunological capabilities have matured to an extent that most routine infections are not life threatening, and nutrient needs are lower per unit of body weight than during infancy. This is not to say that this life history stage is unproblematic for all children. Earlier or ongoing undernutrition and infection can contribute to continued growth deficits. In contrast, one of the greatest emerging threats to child health is the escalating rate of childhood obesity associated with high caloric intake and reduced energy expenditure among children.

Barry Bogin and colleagues' studies of growth among Mayan Guatemalan children in Guatemala and those in the United States illustrate just how responsive child growth is to changes in social conditions (Bogin and Loucky 1997). Although both groups were of relatively low socioeconomic status, conditions for the U.S. sample (many of whom had been born in Guatemala) were markedly better, with greater access to a wider variety of food, health care, food supplementation programs, and clean drinking water, among other things. In Guatemala, children were living in a village with an irregular and unsafe water supply, no effective means of waste disposal, limited access to health care, and a history of political repression and food scarcity from the civil wars of the 1970s and 1980s. The Guatemalan immigrant children in the United States were significantly taller (by 5.5 centimeters; more than 2 inches) and heavier than those in Guatemala. This growth differential occurred within only one generation of migration to the United States. Later studies found the same effect: Mayan American children 5–12 years old were 11.5 centimeters taller than those living in Guatemala (Bogin et al. 2002). Many other studies show the same pattern of increased growth in weight and height among immigrants to the United States and other wealthy countries, indicating that growth is extremely sensitive to social conditions (Danubio et al. 2005; Pawloski 2006). As noted, this trend was also observed early in the twentieth century by Franz Boas (1912) so it is not unique to the social conditions of the late twentieth century.

This effect is also evident in historical trends in body size. Changes such as those in height or weight that accumulate from one generation to the subsequent generation are referred to as **secular trends**. From the nineteenth century through the 1930s, American men of European descent were the tallest in the world at ~174 centimeters (5 feet 8 inches), whereas Dutch men were 165 centimeters (5 feet 5 inches) at that time, among the shortest in Europe. Currently, however, Dutch men are the tallest in the world at 184 centimeters (just over 6 feet), and European American men are about 179 centimeters (5 feet 10 inches). The same trend occurred in women's height as well, with average height 5.7 inches lower than men (Komlos and Lauderdale 2007). To what factors can this overall increase in height be attributed, and why did the Dutch grow much more than European Americans after the early twentieth century?

From 1850 to the present, enormous improvements in hygiene (especially a system to separate drinking water from contaminated waste water) and dramatic increases in the food supply in wealthier countries have reduced undernutrition and infectious disease, two main contributors to poor growth. It is worth pointing out that these improvements were made possible by greater wealth, which in part was a result of colonial enterprises, cheap or free labor (e.g., slavery), increased agricultural productivity, and trade. Thus, these were experienced primarily by those in wealthier countries, while there was little increase in height across the twentieth century in poor countries (Perkins et al. 2016; see Figure 5.7).

But why did the Dutch experience a much greater increase in height than the average American? As Figure 5.8 indicates, they are currently 5-6 inches taller than other populations. Differences in social inequality likely play a role, as efforts to decrease income inequality increase average height since gains are disproportionately achieved by those whose growth has been stunted (i.e., the poor) (Perkins et al. 2016). Richard Steckel (1995) famously referred to height as the "biological standard of living," and variation in that standard of living is clear in the global variation in height represented in Figure 5.8. The fact that one in five children in the world experience stunting (when their growth in height is more than two standard deviations below average), is stark evidence of inequality in environmental conditions that children experience, as stunting stems from poor nutrition, infectious disease, foodborne

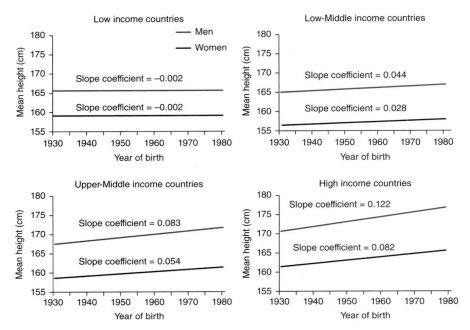

FIGURE 5.7 Predicted association between height and year of birth by sex and World Bank income classification. Note differences in changes in average height between low and high income countries.
Source: Perkins, J. M., S. V. Subramanian, G. Davey Smith, and E. Özaltin. 2016. Adult height, nutrition, and population health. *Nutrition Reviews*, 74:149–165. https://doi.org/10.1093/nutrit/nuv105 © The Author(s) 2016.

mycotoxins, and exposure to smoke from solid fuels (wood or dung), as indicated in Figure 5.9 (Vilcins et al. 2018).

SMALL BUT HEALTHY?

In 1980 the economist David Seckler proposed that high rates of mild to moderate malnutrition, which contributed to reduced growth among children, were not problematic (Seckler 1980). In fact, he went on to argue that such children, who grew up to be relatively small adults, were "small but healthy." The health of individuals who grew slowly because of moderate or mild food scarcity was not compromised in any way; their growth had simply been reduced to "fit" their resource-scarce environment. These individuals were stunted in height (defined as a *z*-score less than –2, or below the 2nd percentile), but not wasted, meaning not of low weight for their height. Smallness could therefore be considered adaptive. The political implications of such a perspective are wide ranging because it basically redefined malnutrition to be only that which could be considered acute or serious, and only individuals with severe malnutrition should be the priority of food or health policy makers. Therefore, millions of children and adults were no longer seen as malnourished and hence in no need of better access

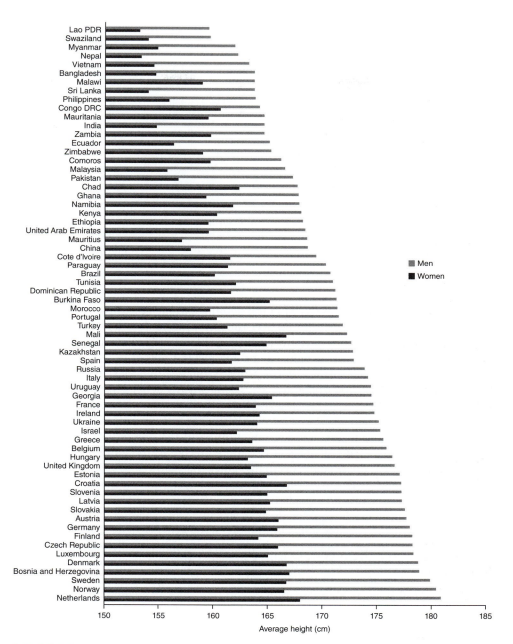

FIGURE 5.8
Source: Global variation in average adult female and male height.
Perkins, J. M., S. V. Subramanian, G. Davey Smith, and E. Özaltin. 2016. Adult height, nutrition, and population health. *Nutrition Reviews*, 74:149–165. https://doi.org/10.1093/nutrit/nuv105 © The Author(s) 2016.

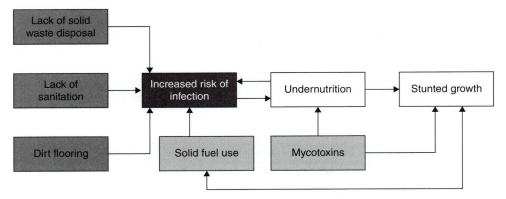

FIGURE 5.9 Environmental risk factors and child stunting.
Source: Vilcins, D., Sly, P.D. and Jagals, P., 2018. Environmental Risk Factors Associated with Child Stunting: A Systematic Review of the Literature. *Annals of Global Health*, 84(4), pp.551–562. DOI: http://doi.org/10.29024/aogh.2361

to food (recall the oddly analogous situation described in the previous chapter of ideal weights in the United States declining over time, resulting in more and more people being defined as overweight). Resources put toward food or agricultural assistance to such populations could thus be reduced and redirected to other uses. Seckler's ideas were roundly criticized by a wide range of scholars and health policy analysts, in large part because he ignored the underlying causes of growth deficits and their negative health consequences (Beaton 1989; Martorell 1989).

There are three points worth considering here. One is the concept of adaptation. It is perfectly appropriate to consider growth stunting in the presence of food scarcity adaptive, in the sense that scarce resources are redirected to the growth and maintenance of more critical physiological systems rather than growth in height. This is developmental adaptation. From a life history perspective, the body is making a trade-off between size and survival and a prediction that in the future food is likely to be scarce as it is during childhood. It would make no sense to devote energy to building a large body that would need more resources to support, at the expense of more critical organs such as the brain. However, to say that a biological outcome is adaptive is not the same as saying that it is "good" or "optimal" (Schell and Magnus 2007; Wiley 1992). In this case, stunted growth represents the "least deleterious" or a "good enough" outcome for the short and longer term. No adaptation is "cost free," and all adaptations are likely to be compromises among physiological systems and to a variety of environmental stressors.

Second is that the small but healthy hypothesis assumes that stunting is solely the effect of moderate food shortage. In fact, growth disruption most often occurs in the context of infectious disease, especially diarrheal disease, and undernutrition, with each exacerbating the other. Undernutrition may compromise immune function, an immune response to a pathogen requires energetic and nutritional resources, and diarrheal disease results in loss of appetite and nutrients from the gastrointestinal tract (Martorell 1980; Rytter et al. 2014). Even among well-nourished populations, sick children can experience transient disruption of growth, although they experience rapid catch-up growth after the infection disappears. Furthermore, deficiencies in micronutrients such as iron that result in specific health problems generally correlate with food scarcity, and these will manifest in myriad ways beyond stunting (Black et al. 2013). Prolonged psychosocial stress and growth disruptions are also reported (Prendergast and Humphrey 2014), and coexist with economic stress and food scarcity. Thus, growth is a marker of overall good health, and growth faltering is an index of overall poor health (Prendergast and Humphrey 2014). With regard to the longer-term consequences of stunting, stunted adults have less muscle mass and diminished work capacity or physical endurance, reduced immune function, cognitive shortcomings, and, among women, poorer birth outcomes (Black et al. 2013; Prendergast and Humphrey 2014). Stunted women have lower birth weight babies with a higher risk of infant mortality. Because of stunting's effect on birth weight, poor growth of girls can have intergenerational effects, persisting in their children.

Last, by considering stunting an adaptation to environments characterized by chronic food shortage, the question of why many populations live under such conditions is not

Anthropologist in Action: Gretel Pelto

Gretel Pelto received her Ph.D. in anthropology from the University of Minnesota, having studied literature and dance as an undergraduate. She was one of the pioneers of biocultural work in anthropology, particularly in medical and nutritional anthropology. Although her training was in anthropology, she held two academic appointments in departments of nutrition (at the University of Connecticut and Cornell University). Furthermore, in the 1990s she was in charge of behavioral research in the Division of Child Health at the WHO in Geneva, Switzerland, and she has continued to consult for the WHO and other health nongovernmental organizations. Her field research has primarily been in Mexico, and she has also been involved with studies in Latin America, China, Vietnam, the Philippines, Pakistan, Cameroon, South Africa, and Tanzania.

Dr. Pelto's work has focused on infant and young child feeding and household management of illness in infants and children. Her theoretical and social focus is on the interface between programs (including intervention design and evaluation) and families and communities. In her work with the WHO, she has been able to craft interventions to promote breastfeeding and safe complementary feeding that are sensitive to social and cultural context, especially women's roles, household economics, and cultural values. She has also been instrumental in developing methods for policy makers and evaluators that use "focused ethnographic studies," results of which were incorporated into health-care worker-training manuals and educational materials (see

Pelto and Armar-Klemesu 2015 for a recent example of this type of study on infant and child feeding in Kenya). Individuals involved with health interventions were encouraged to use emic concepts with the public and encourage beneficial traditional practices designed to improve relationships between health-care workers and clients and to provide a means by which communities could take action to improve child health or the treatment of child illness.

Throughout her career, Dr. Pelto has been involved in designing and evaluating health interventions to improve child nutrition while ensuring that anthropological perspectives are taken into account (cf. her involvement with the Sanitation Hygiene Infant Nutrition Efficacy Trial Team 2015). One major contribution was the incorporation of child social, emotional, and physical development into child nutrition and health issues. In particular, she has elaborated the concept of "responsive infant feeding"—that is, how caretakers and infants interact in the context of supplementary feeding. Moving beyond the question of "what" infants are given to eat, she considers how, when, and where feeding occurs and by whom, which she believes are equally important insofar as they "define the character of daily life experience . . . [and] are the key behavioral components of caregiving, specifics that will affect how well a child will grow, develop, and resist infection" (Pelto 2008, 241). In 2007 Dr. Pelto was awarded the Malinowski Award by the Society for Applied Anthropology in recognition of her work advancing the uses of anthropology in health policy and interventions.

addressed. Yet it is these conditions, largely attributable to social inequality, poverty, unemployment, war, and population dislocation, among many others, that are the ultimate causes of poor growth (Floud et al. 1990). Suffice it to say that child growth is a good measure of not only an individual's health but also that of a society. Although the historical circumstances that produced such conditions vary, there is a dismal uniformity to the experience of food shortage, infectious disease, and stress that characterizes impoverished communities throughout the globe.

IS BIGGER BETTER?
If growth is reduced under conditions of food scarcity, infectious disease, or stress, what about the opposite scenario, where high-quality food is available in large quantities? Food excess is a signal to the body that resources are abundant. It allows energy to be put toward growth, growth to occur at a faster rate, and excess energy to be stored as fat. If smallness incurs costs to health however, is it reasonable to ask, "Is bigger better?" If growth and a larger body size represent the relative absence of those factors, then the answer is most certainly yes. If it includes overnutrition, then the answer is no. Overnutrition is generally defined as chronic intake of excess calories from macronutrients (but not necessarily excess or even adequate micronutrients) in the diet, which can contribute to growth in height and in weight. It had been thought that some populations had reached their biological maximum for height, but recent evidence suggests that even the tallest populations, such as those in Nordic countries, are still gaining in height (Holmgren et al. 2019). Not only can excess energy support growth to a higher weight, but it also generates more rapid growth, such that both larger size and maturation occur earlier.

As of 2016, almost 8% of boys and 6% of girls age 5–17 years in the global population had obesity, compared to less than 1% in both sexes in 1975 (Abarca-Gómez et al. 2017). In the United States, data from 2016 indicate that the overall prevalence of child obesity is 18.5%, having risen quickly from just under 14% in 2000 and leveling off after 2003–2004. The prevalence of obesity rises with childhood age: 13.9% of children aged 2 to 5 years have obesity, while the percentage is 18.4 among those aged 6 to 11 years and 20.6 among 12- to 19-year-olds (Hales et al. 2017). In Western Europe, about 1.6% of children age 6–11 years have obesity, whereas in Eastern Europe the prevalence is 6.5% (Olaya et al. 2015). In South Asia (India, Pakistan, and Bangladesh), studies of child obesity find prevalence ranges between 1.2% and 14.5% (Mistry and Puthussery 2015). In the latter countries, obesity was associated with higher socioeconomic status, whereas in Western Europe and the United States the reverse is true (Ogden et al. 2014; Olaya et al. 2015). Obesity in children has been linked to both overconsumption of high-calorie foods and reduced physical activity around the world. It appears to be difficult to reverse and is associated with increased risk of diabetes and markers for CVD at an earlier age.

In her review of the social science and biomedical literature on child obesity, Tina Moffat (2010) noted a disconnect: on the one hand, social scientists have tended to portray the "child obesity epidemic" as a socially constructed problem, unnecessarily provoking alarm without a strong empirical base. On the other hand, biomedical health professionals are concerned that it is not being given sufficient medical or public health attention and that there is a "growing societal 'normalization' of childhood overweight and obesity," as average childhood weight increases (Moffat 2010, 9). While noting that the term "epidemic" signals a crisis and the need for immediate action and is not helpful in a context where there are no clear effective interventions, Moffat argues that medical anthropologists should be involved in dialogue and cross-disciplinary research that seeks to understand and address the underlying social roots of childhood obesity.

The anthropologist Deborah Crooks investigated child obesity in a poor rural community in eastern Kentucky and found that more than one-third of primary school children had overweight, and 13% had obesity (Crooks 1999, 2000). Overweight was associated with high fat and sugar intakes, related to local dietary patterns and low levels of physical activity. In the same sample, there was a high frequency of stunting in height; 20% of the children were of low height (<15th percentile for height of U.S. children) and more than 9% were less than the 5th percentile for height. Girls were more likely to be stunted and boys were more likely to have obesity. How can stunting and overweight exist simultaneously? Crooks found that stunting was more common among poorer households, suggesting poor-quality diets, but also that the larger community had few opportunities for children's activities, both in and outside of school. These results suggest that although urban poverty is often considered a more trenchant problem, rural poverty in the United States is often overlooked and also generates negative outcomes for child growth. However, the combination of stunting and overweight is surprising and suggests that poor-quality food available at the household level and little community investment in accessible physical activities combine to impair the current and future health of children in poor rural communities. Similarly, working in the Galapagos Islands, Amanda Thompson and colleagues found that over 3% of children, but almost 18% of adults were both overweight and stunted in height; over half of all households were made up of stunted and overweight individuals. Using a more inclusive set of markers of undernutrition (underweight and evidence of infection) and overnutrition (overweight and a chronic disease marker), the dual burden was evident among 16% of children and 33% of adults, and 90% of all households (Thompson et al. 2019). They linked these outcomes to food and water insecurity, also noting ways in which infectious disease exposure along with high fat food consumption can contribute to both stunting and obesity through low level inflammation. The coexistence of these outcomes poses a major challenge to the health of economically vulnerable households as well as policy making.

There is growing evidence that rapid growth in childhood has a number of other negative health consequences. Rapid growth is associated with an increased rate of cell turnover, and any factor that contributes to this increases the risk of the replication of malignant cells. Rapid growth is facilitated by a protein called **insulin-like growth factor I** (IGF-I), which promotes cell division and inhibits cell destruction (apoptosis). IGF-I production can be stimulated by components of the diet, especially milk. IGF-I levels are higher in individuals growing rapidly and those who are tall and lower in those suffering from undernutrition, suggesting that it plays an important role in modulating growth. IGF-I has been linked to proliferation of cancerous cells, especially in the breast and colon. Furthermore, height itself is positively associated with cancer risk, perhaps via the IGF-I mechanism (Giovannucci 2019).

Does Milk Make Children Grow?

In a growing number of countries around the world, cow's milk is provided for children at school, and milk is widely promoted as a food that enhances or is even necessary for adequate child growth. The link between cow's milk consumption and growth in height is widely used in milk advertisements. In the United States, older milk promotions announced, "Got Milk? Get Tall." In another advertisement, images of professional basketball players are coupled with milk and statements such as "Hey everybody! Want to grow? About 15% of your height is added during your teen years and milk can help make the most of it." Similar claims are found in China and India, countries recently experiencing tremendous growth in milk consumption (Wiley 2016).

These ideas are closely related to assertions that the well-documented increases in average height over the twentieth century can be attributed to greater milk consumption. For example, Stuart Patton, a well-known physiologist of mammalian lactation, writes,

> While many factors have contributed to this increase [in height] it is obvious that calcium in the diet would be essential, and that products of the expanding American dairy industry would be the logical source of the calcium enabling this growth. . . . Of course calcium, while essential to increased bone growth and stature, is not the only contribution that milk would be making in this situation. High quality protein and growth-promoting B vitamins and vitamin D from milk would be other contributing factors. (Patton 2004, 115).

The connection between milk consumption and child growth seems intuitive. Because milk is produced by mammalian mothers and is the only food consumed by their infants for some length of time, and because infants are defined as those of small size who undergo very rapid growth, it makes sense that milk should contribute to growth. Of course, some humans continue to consume milk long after the weaning period and throughout adulthood, and the milk they consume is that of another species. So the question is whether continued consumption of milk, especially that derived from large bovine species (i.e. cows), enhances growth throughout childhood. Milk contains calories, vitamins, minerals (such as calcium), and specific biochemicals (such as IGF-I) that may promote growth above and beyond its nutrient and energetic components. It would seem likely that these should collectively support the growth of older children, albeit possibly in an attenuated way compared with nursing infants.

Studies from the 1920s in Britain looked at growth in children age 5, 8, and 13 years from urban working-class areas who were provided with up to one pint of milk, a biscuit of equal caloric value, or no supplement over a seven-month period. The milk groups grew modestly more than those getting biscuits or no supplement, on the order of 0.2 to 0.4 inches over the seven-month period (Leighton and Clark 1929; Orr 1928). Thus, milk seemed to have "special" effects on growth above and beyond its caloric value. A study from Beijing (Du et al. 2004) indicated significantly positive effects from a milk intervention on growth in height over a two-year period among 10- to 12-year-old Chinese girls. Some girls were given 330 milliliters of calcium-fortified milk five days a week and these girls grew more (0.7 centimeters) than girls who did not receive any milk. Unfortunately, in this study the girls in the control group received no supplement, so it is impossible to assess what it was about milk that led to the increased growth. It could have been calories, protein, minerals, or some other factor. Furthermore, the difference between the groups was no longer evident three years after the study ended (Zhu et al. 2006). In a study in Kenya, where comparisons were carried out between children supplemented with calorically similar amounts of milk, meat, or fat, Grillenberger and colleagues (2003) found that among a large sample of primary-school children, those who were given daily milk for two years did not grow significantly more than those given meat or fat or those who received no supplemental food. Only children with a low baseline height for age grew more (1.3 centimeters) than children in the control group, although among this group milk did not produce greater gains in height than the energy supplement.

Overall, research on the relationship between milk and growth, especially in height, reveals mixed results (de Beer 2012; Wiley 2012) with stronger associations between milk consumption and height among preschool children and adolescents than among primary school-age children. Milk may have its most significant effects among children with existing undernutrition, but few studies have compared milk consumption with supplements of other nutrient-rich foods to ascertain whether milk has "special" growth-enhancing properties. This is not to say that milk is not a valuable food in the diet of children—it may have other positive effects, such as increasing bone density, or it may simply contribute valuable nutrients to the diet. But at present we do not know how much childhood milk consumption contributes to variation in adult height, and it certainly is not essential to growth.

SEX, GENDER, GROWTH, AND HEALTH

Males and females have somewhat different growth trajectories. They may also face different kinds of environmental conditions growing up, including variation in food quality or quantity, protection, responsibilities, and emotional care. The way they respond biologically to these conditions also varies. Differences between males and females in growth are evident at birth, with males being, on average, larger in body size than females, a difference that persists until adolescence. For a brief period in early adolescence the pattern reverses because girls experience an earlier growth spurt than boys. By about age 14, boys' growth exceeds that of girls, and boys generally become taller and heavier than girls by adulthood. These are average differences, however, and there is a great deal of overlap in body size among males and females at every age.

This description of sex differences in child growth is considered normative; that is, this is the standard pattern of growth. However, alterations in this pattern occur for a variety of reasons. First, evidence exists that boys are more vulnerable to undernutrition, infection, and environmental stressors than girls, and that they suffer more from fetal growth restriction if their mother is undernourished during pregnancy (Stinson 1985; Wells 2000). These may be biologically based sex differences, but postnatally, differences in growth between boys and girls are more likely to be attributable to differential treatment of each gender. Gender is distinguished from sex in that it indexes cultural norms about appropriate behaviors, expectations, roles, and attitudes related to sex. It is often the case that boys and girls within a family or community are treated differently because they are valued differently or there are different expectations about what they contribute to a family, and birth order and the sex of older siblings may be important influences. This is best illustrated in South Asia, the world region with the highest overall rates of child stunting. UNICEF estimates that almost 50% of all children under 5 years are stunted, representing one-third of all stunted children in the world (UNICEF 2019). Child mortality rates are also higher among girls (Guilmoto et al. 2018), especially in the northern regions, and strong ideologies of son preference may shape gender differences in child nutrition and growth.

In northern India, substantial bias against females exists at all points in the life cycle, and Monica Das Gupta's work (1995), as well as that of Patricia Jeffery and Roger Jeffery (Jeffery et al. 1988; Jeffery and Jeffery 1997) illustrates how this bias takes a toll on the health of girls and women. The society of this region of North India, as in other areas of South Asia and East Asia, can be considered strongly patriarchal, with patrilineage as the key social group. Girls marry outside of the village, and hence their contributions to their natal family are terminated at marriage. They also have little authority or autonomy within their husband's households. Sons are responsible for lighting the parents' funeral pyres and ensuring their afterlife. Furthermore, females require dowries to be married to a suitable family and hence incur large costs, whereas males are a net economic benefit because they bring in a dowry and wife, provide labor or wages for the household, and perpetuate the patrilineage. As a result, resources tend to flow to sons rather than daughters, especially in families with an existing daughter, and those resources support better growth and ultimately higher rates of survival among sons. Importantly, this effect is not more pronounced among the poor, among whom resources are more constrained. Rather, it is often more common among wealthier or high-caste families among whom the economic contributions of females are seen as minimal, and it is seen as inappropriate for women to work outside the household. Dowry costs for higher status families are very high to ensure a marriage into a family of sufficient status, whereas among poorer or low-caste families, females make greater economic contributions to the household and bride-price is more common than dowry. Discrimination against females that results in higher rates of morbidity and mortality is less pronounced in south India, where kinship systems are less strongly patrilineal (and in some cases are matrilineal, although they may still be patriarchal).

While there is a strong son-preference ideology in South Asia, evidence for substantial differences in growth or evidence of preferential feeding of males relative to females has been mixed (Fenske et al. 2013; Mishra et al. 2004; Munro and McIntyre 2014). Working with very poor mothers in Bangladesh, Munro and McIntyre provide evidence that mothers resisted any notion of sex-biased child feeding: "I divide the food equally between them [children]. Not more or less to anybody" (Munro and McIntyre 2014, 5). In national-level Indian data, Mishra and colleagues found that among children age three years and younger, stunting and underweight rates were similar among males and females, although they were higher in North India (Mishra et al. 2004). When analyzed by birth order, they found that boys were less likely than girls to be stunted when all older living siblings were girls and more likely than girls to be stunted when all older siblings were boys. Thus, the child's gender, as well as the number and gender mix of older siblings, contributes to differences in nutritional status. However, differential feeding patterns did not appear to explain these differences; there was strong evidence for gender discrimination with respect to immunization and treatment for diarrheal or respiratory disease, and infectious disease experiences may be a stronger contributor to gender differentials in growth than nutrition per se. Regardless, males and females continue to have different health experiences that may impact their growth in India, reflecting underlying gender ideologies and cultural practices, but it is also worth keeping in mind that poverty underlies the overall very high levels of growth stunting in India (Khera et al. 2014).

The Exposome

In 2005 Christopher Wild coined the term "exposome," which he defined as encompassing all environmental exposures that an individual has from conception on throughout their life span (Wild 2005). Wild imagined the exposome as the environmental parallel to an individual's genome. He argued that while much funding, research, and public attention has been directed toward characterization of the genome and its relationship to disease outcomes, genes actually contribute relatively little to the variation in disease risk or epidemiological patterns. Instead, the environment is made up of a wide array of "exposures" that need to be identified, characterized, measured, and considered for their additive and interactive impacts on human health. Exposures are grouped into three main categories: general external factors (such as social capital, neighborhood/residence and climate factors); specific external factors such as diet, activity, occupation, and individual pollutant exposure; and internal factors, which include metabolism, circulating hormones, gut microbes, oxidative stress, and inflammation, which all interact with the genome (Kim and Hong 2017; see Figure 5.10). These can be assessed using geographic information systems or social media networks, personal monitoring using different types of sensor technologies, and various biomarkers, respectively.

The exposome concept has its roots in environmental toxicology, and it emphasizes pollutants as major components of the exposome. These likely have particularly important impacts during critical periods, especially during development, and thus characterizing the exposome impacts on children is particularly important. As Martine Vrijheid noted, "There are large challenges in developing the concept of measuring every environmental exposure

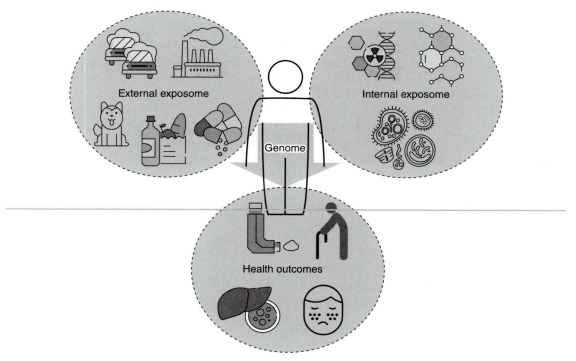

FIGURE 5.10 The exposome.
Source: Zhang, P.; Arora, M.; Chaleckis, R.; Isobe, T.; Jain, M.; Meister, I.; Melén, E.; Perzanowski, M.; Torta, F.; Wenk, M.R.; Wheelock, C.E. Tackling the Complexity of the Exposome: Considerations from the Gunma University Initiative for Advanced Research (GIAR) Exposome Symposium. *Metabolites* 2019, 9, 106. DOI: 10.3390/metabo9060106

over a lifetime into a workable approach: a successful exposome would have to integrate many external and internal exposures from different sources continuously over the life course" (Vrijheid 2014, 876). Unlike the genome, the exposome is dynamic, with hundreds (if not more!) of different exposures acting at different times across the lifespan, although they may act through some common biological pathways; a number of birth cohort studies aim to investigate the exposome's impact on individual health as it unfolds over the life span (Siroux et al. 2016).

ENVIRONMENTAL TOXINS AND GROWTH

Contemporary and historical environments in which humans have lived contain a variety of pollutants that are known to be harmful to health. Many of these have been shown to affect child growth, and insofar as they have the potential to alter developmental pathways, they can have lifelong deleterious consequences. They most often have a dose–response relationship, with increasing exposure leading to more extreme biological disruptions. Populations exposed to such pollutants are those that live in or around areas where they are produced, and such areas are more likely to be poor, often urban or periurban industrial zones near manufacturing plants that make use of toxic substances or produce them as a byproduct of industrial production. Recently pollution's impact on global health has been recognized by a Lancet Commission (Landrigan et al. 2018), which emphasized the ways in which the burden is greatest among the world's poor, who are also likely to bear the brunt of negative health impacts due to climate change. It may have particularly dire consequences for children's health (Perera 2017). Three pollutants are considered here, specifically with regard to their impacts on child health: air pollution, polychlorinated biphenyls, and lead.

Air pollution is caused by a large and heterogeneous array of toxins, including particulate matter and chemical gases. In terms of its effects on child growth, a reduction in fetal growth is most apparent. Indoor air pollution from using coal, kerosene, or biomass for fuel is also associated with reduced birth weight in India (Epstein et al. 2013). In Los Angeles, a city known for its poor air quality, a study of birth outcomes among women who were exposed to varying amounts of air pollution based on their area of residence found that newborns were smaller in areas with more pollution, an effect that remained even after other factors such as socioeconomic status had been controlled for statistically (Parker et al. 2005). The aspect of air quality that was most significantly associated with reduced birth weight was the amount of particulate matter that a pregnant woman was exposed to over the entire course of the pregnancy. In Pakistan, greenhouse gas exposure was associated with reduced birth weight (Parker et al. 2005). As demonstrated in Figure 5.9, biomass fuel usage also contributes to child stunting.

The effects of ambient pollution are likely to work via mechanisms similar to maternal smoking, but importantly, air pollution is a community-level phenomenon to which individuals are passively exposed simply by virtue of living in a given area. This is a particularly crucial issue because more and more people are living in megacities, especially in Latin America and Asia, where air quality is particularly poor (especially in Beijing and New Delhi). It should also be noted that although effects on growth have been seen prenatally, there is ample evidence of an association between urban air pollution and compromised lung function in children, manifesting most often as asthma; individuals of lower socioeconomic status are more likely to live in areas with very poor air quality (Goldizen et al. 2016).

Polychlorinated biphenyls (PCBs) are a heterogeneous group of organic compounds with a similar chemical structure that are used and produced in industrial manufacture. Many PCBs are fat soluble and can be retained in fat cells for long periods of time. They are therefore also found in fat-containing animal foods, including fish, meat, dairy products, and human breast milk. They are known **endocrine disruptors**, meaning they alter hormonal function in ways that affect growth, maturation, and cognitive-behavioral development (Mouritsen et al. 2010; Roy et al. 2009). In their collaborative work with the Akwesasne Task Force on the Environment, representing Akwesasne Mohawk populations living in upstate New York and along the Canadian border, the anthropologist Lawrence Schell and colleagues have found that local consumption of fish, an important component of the traditional diet, was a main source of PCB exposure (Ravenscroft et al. 2015). The St. Lawrence River had been contaminated by industrial waste containing PCBs since the 1950s, and they had been absorbed by the fish. Girls exposed to the highest amounts of PCBs had a much greater likelihood of reaching menarche before age 12 than did girls who were exposed to fewer PCBs, and the relationship was dose dependent (Denham et al.

2005; Schell and Gallo 2010). Women living in areas with high PCB exposure also had babies with lower birth weight and smaller head circumferences, an effect seen in other PCB-exposed populations (reviewed in Schell et al. 2006). PCBs are also transmitted in breast milk. Hence, Akwesasne women are caught in a double bind vis-à-vis advice to breastfeed their infants because their breast milk is likely to be a source of PCB exposure for their infants. Likewise, nutritional advice to eat more fatty fish to protect against heart disease runs up against the risk of PCB exposure with its negative impacts on reproductive outcomes, growth, and development (Schell and Gallo 2010).

Lead poisoning, most often from lead-based paint or gasoline, but also from water (as in the recent water crisis in Flint, Michigan), clusters in poor children living in urban areas in old dwellings with peeling paint, near heavily traveled roads, or whose water supply is contaminated by lead from corroded pipes. In other words, conditions of poverty conspire to expose children through multiple routes. Lead is a potent neurotoxin, and exposure in childhood compromises several aspects of biological and cognitive development. Like PCBs and air pollution, high maternal lead levels are associated with reductions in birth weight and newborn head circumference (Schell et al. 2006). There is also clear evidence that lead exposure is associated with reduced growth in height. Lead levels negatively correlate with growth hormone levels, indicating a pathway by which lead is associated with reduced birth weight, growth in height and weight, and head circumference. In contrast to the effects of PCBs on sexual maturity, high lead levels seem to delay sexual maturation (Denham et al. 2005; Schell and Gallo 2010). Lead levels tend to increase in early childhood but taper off unless there is continued exposure during adulthood, and lead is stored throughout the body, mostly in the skeleton (Schell et al. 2006). Chelation therapy, which reduces blood lead levels, can result in dramatic improvements in growth. In sum, the sources of lead exposure and abatement measures are well established; continued exposure of children to lead stems from failure of policies at all levels of government, as the Flint crisis starkly revealed (Bellinger 2016).

These environmental pollutants are important to understanding variation in growth among some communities, but it is difficult to tease out their effects among the myriad other factors that influence growth. Nonetheless, they illustrate a mechanism by which poverty and social, economic, and political marginalization (i.e., structural violence) generates another source of variation in growth among otherwise well-nourished populations.

PUBERTY AND THE ONSET OF ADOLESCENCE

Puberty signals the beginning of the transition between growth and sexual maturity (or, in life history theory terms, a transition from somatic to reproductive investment). Menarche (the onset of menses) is a well-defined marker of this transition for girls, but puberty is a longer process for both girls and boys, lasting from approximately age 9–14 for girls and 11–16 for boys. Puberty begins with breast development in girls and testes and penis development in boys. Because of the relative ease of collecting data on menarche, it is the most commonly reported assessment of sexual maturity, and more research has focused on female than male sexual maturation.

Age at menarche varies around the world, from 12 years to more than 18 years in highland New Guinea and Nepal (Eveleth and Tanner 1990). The average age in the United States, Canada, and European countries varies between 12.5 and 13.5 years, having declined from ~16 years in the mid-nineteenth century. Although the Bundi of highland New Guinea had the highest reported age at menarche in the past (18 years), it has declined rapidly since that estimate was reported. Twenty years later it was 15.8 years among Bundi living in urban areas and 17.2 years among those remaining in rural areas, reflecting a rate of decline of 0.5 (rural) to 1.3 (urban) years per decade (Zemel and Jenkins 1989). The faster rate of decline was attributed to increased access to energy-rich foods and health care in both areas, but especially in the urban areas.

Earlier ages for the onset of puberty have been reported in northern European and U.S. populations over the past decades although the age at menarche has not changed markedly (Toppari and Juul 2010). Rapid growth can accelerate the process of reproductive development, leading to earlier puberty and an earlier age at menarche among girls (Lee et al. 2007). In fact, IGF-I levels peak around puberty, when growth is most rapid (Bidlingmaier et al. 2014). Age at menarche is negatively correlated with BMI (Currie et al. 2012), and increases in BMI may contribute to lower age at menarche but also complicate the assessment of puberty in girls (e.g., breast development) due to increased body fat. The possibility that sexual maturation is occurring at earlier ages has received a great deal of attention among pediatricians, parents, and educators because it signals an early onset of reproductive maturity and the potential for early sexual activity and pregnancy (Cesario and Hughes 2007). There is mixed evidence for recent declines in age of onset of puberty in the U.S. and Europe, and there is variation by race/ethnicity and income groups (Abreu and Kaiser 2016; Krieger et al. 2015). Environmental endocrine disruptors have been implicated, but data are inconclusive, in part because different compounds can accelerate or delay puberty.

Declining ages of puberty reflects hormone-mediated alterations to life history patterns. Health consequences occur in at least two domains and have been most studied among girls: (1) higher rates of sexual activity and unintended pregnancy among adolescents and (2) higher lifetime exposures to the reproductive hormone estrogen, which is linked to increased risk of reproductive cancers (see Chapter 6).

With regard to the first domain, declines in the age of biological reproductive maturity have not been matched by declines in the age of social maturity. Indeed, the opposite is more often the case because jobs paying a subsistence wage usually cannot be acquired until the completion of increasing amounts of education, often well beyond secondary schooling. This disconnect between social and biological maturity has resulted in a variety of somewhat novel health problems among adolescents. High rates of sexually transmitted infections, teenage pregnancy, and psychological problems that derive from this dissonance are evidence of this disconnect. As Carol Worthman points out, "[C]linicians and the public alike are continually amazed at the psychological and behavioral precocities of contemporary youth and remained conditioned by schedules of childhood and youth that are dissonant with current patterns of maturation" (Worthman 1999, 152). Their expectations of how children and adolescents should look and act are out of date, usually based on their own experiences growing up in past generations. Furthermore, these current patterns of maturation are evolutionarily novel, made possible by the historically unimaginable abundance of food and the possibility and desirability of a wholly sedentary existence.

Humans appear to be unique in that they experience substantial growth after puberty (Bogin 1999). Other nonhuman primates exhibit surges in growth in association with sexual maturity, but humans continue to grow long after reaching sexual maturity, and a secondary peak in growth velocity occurs during adolescence. Sex differences in fat patterning also emerge during adolescence, as females accumulate more fat in general and more on their limbs (especially the hips and legs), whereas males gain it disproportionately on their trunk. This difference remains fairly stable across adulthood and is associated with different disease risk later in life (Palmer and Clegg 2015). Abdominal fat is involved in the regulation of energy metabolism and is more closely associated with CVD or diabetes risk than is peripheral fat. It is generally thought that the higher body fat percentage of females is related to energy stores needed to support pregnancy and nursing (Lassek and Gaulin 2006).

The reasons for this postpuberty growth are not entirely clear. Bogin (1999) posited that girls have learned much about infant and child care during childhood, but they need to learn more about adult sexuality before they actively begin reproduction themselves. Usually menarche is followed by a few years of subfertile menstrual cycles that are associated with a relatively low risk of pregnancy and, hence, although girls appear physically and sexually mature, they are not in fact fully capable of childbearing. In contrast, because the adolescent growth spurt is later for boys, they continue to appear boyish after puberty is initiated. Bogin hypothesizes that they must learn their adult male role while still appearing to be young, such that expectations for maturity are low. Thus, in both cases, the prolonged growth of adolescence offers unique opportunities for learning the complexities of adult roles.

Adolescent health has emerged as a global public health concern, in recognition of adolescence as a unique life stage (rather than just a transitional one), characterized by physical growth, sexual maturation, and neurological development ("the teenage brain") (Patton et al. 2016). It is often a period of exploration, experimentation, and increased risk taking. Health risks include drug and tobacco use, sexual activity and the risk of both pregnancy and sexually transmitted infections, injury, violence, mental health, and nutrition. In 2016 the leading causes of death for adolescents across the globe were HIV/AIDS, suicide, respiratory disease, road injury, and interpersonal violence, with the latter two more common among boys, who have higher mortality rates than girls during this period (World Health Organization, 2020a). Although adolescents are in some ways at their physical peak, there are many psychosocial challenges of this transition to adulthood, especially given current political instability and dire predictions about climate change (Patton et al. 2016).

TEENAGE PREGNANCY IN THE UNITED STATES

In the United States, teenage pregnancy is very much considered a social and public health "problem," present disproportionately among poor, particularly Black teenagers in inner-city contexts. Arline Geronimus and colleagues have investigated the correlates of high rates of early childbearing in impoverished urban centers populated largely by Blacks and applied insights of both sociology and life history theory to their research (Geronimus et al. 1999). They looked at age at first birth among Whites and Blacks in the United States at large and then focused on four inner-city areas characterized by intense poverty, violence, and poor life opportunities (Harlem, Chicago, Detroit, and Watts in Los Angeles). First, early childbearing was much more common among Blacks than among Whites in general and more common in the four cities. The researchers then considered age at childbearing in relation to the probability that the parents would be alive at the child's 20th birthday. First, as shown in Table 5.3, rates of adult mortality in these contexts were startlingly high. The probability that a mother would be alive at her child's 20th birthday ranged from 85% to 97% in these urban areas, compared with 94% to 99% among the larger U.S. population. For fathers, the probabilities of surviving were even lower, from 68% to 90%. These astonishingly low rates of adult survival are attributed to numerous causes: chronic diseases (heart disease or stroke), HIV, homicide, and cancer. What Table 5.3 reveals is that if a child was born when the parents were age 15, the probability of the parents being alive at the child's 20th birthday was much greater than if they waited until age 30 to have a child (96% vs. about 88% for mothers; 87% vs. 75% for fathers). This pattern is consistent with predictions from life history theory: if adult mortality is high, the more adaptive strategy is to reproduce early; if your survival in mid-adulthood is reasonably secure, you can afford to wait to begin childbearing.

Somewhat surprisingly, Geronimus and co-workers also found that birth outcomes are much better for young mothers in these contexts than for older mothers. Birth weights were higher for the firstborn children of younger mothers than for those of older mothers, and rates of infant mortality were, in some cases, half that of infants born to older mothers (Geronimus 1996). They referred to this differential as a

TABLE 5.3   The Probability of Being Alive at a Child's 20th Birthday, Based on the Age of the Mother or Father at Birth

	United States		Local Populations			
Age at Birth	Whites	Blacks	Harlem	Detroit	Chicago	Watts
Mothers						
15	0.99	0.98	0.95	0.97	0.95	0.96
20	0.99	0.97	0.91	0.95	0.93	0.95
25	0.98	0.96	0.88	0.93	0.90	0.92
30	0.97	0.94	0.85	0.90	0.87	0.90
Fathers						
15	0.97	0.94	0.89	0.90	0.86	0.87
20	0.96	0.92	0.82	0.88	0.82	0.85
25	0.96	0.90	0.74	0.85	0.78	0.83
30	0.94	0.88	0.68	0.80	0.71	0.80

Note: Parents who have children at younger ages (15 or 20) are much more likely to be alive at their children's 20th birthday.

Source: Geronimus et al. [1630] 1999. Reprinted with permission from Elsevier.

consequence of maternal "weathering," the rapid deterioration of a woman's health during early adulthood:

> The findings document important disparities in the levels and trajectories of mortality and functional limitation among young through middle-aged adults in the United States. For the typical white American, health considerations need not be a factor in the decision of whether to become a teenage parent or to postpone childbearing into or through the 20s. Urban, African American adolescents, on the other hand, face more dismal health prospects. Their likelihood of surviving, able-bodied to see their children grow up is not only lower on average than for their black or white counterparts nationwide, but also noticeably decreases as they increase their childbearing age.
>
> Peak maternal health and access to social support for childbearing and rearing might converge at a young age in this population. . . . The findings suggest alternatives to interpreting high rates of teen childbearing among African American residents of impoverished urban areas as signifying values that set them apart from the mainstream and harm children. For example, early fertility in this population may express the attempt to embrace the widely shared value that responsible parents strive to bring children into the world when they are most prepared to provide for their children's well-being (Geronimus et al. [1634] 1999).

For urban Blacks living in poverty, such attempts are made under adverse circumstances that constrain and qualitatively alter the routes available for achieving this ideal.

Note that although early childbearing may represent an adaptive life history strategy under these conditions, it in no way implies that these are acceptable conditions under which anyone should have to live. Faced with poor educational or occupational opportunities, violence, racism, and economic deprivation that preclude secure life situations, these urban populations adjust their life history strategies accordingly because they do not have the luxury of assured survival throughout adulthood. Furthermore, although teenage childbearing is largely considered deviant or inappropriate behavior in the larger cultural context of the United States, if such disparities in life chances continue to exist, it is necessary to acknowledge the benefits to early childbearing under those conditions. Therefore, instead of enacting policies that discourage or even punish early childbearing, health policies should be aimed at understanding and mitigating the causes of high rates of adult mortality in these areas.

CONCLUSION

In this chapter we have seen how the social and ecological contexts in which childhood unfolds present some unique challenges to health, which often manifest in altered growth patterns. Thus, child growth can be considered in some ways "the canary in the coal mine," meaning that it is a particularly sensitive marker of overall population health and the quality of the environment in which a population lives. Because children are literally encoding their environments into their bodies, the ways that growth and development are altered can have longer-term effects on adult health.

From a biological viewpoint, the transition from childhood to adulthood is reasonably straightforward. When linear growth stops and organ systems are fully functional (mature), the life stage of adulthood has been reached. From a health perspective, the risk of most health problems is low in early and middle adulthood and continues to be so until the aging process begins (see Chapter 7). From a sociocultural perspective, however, the transition is not as clear and adulthood may bring about new health challenges, such as childbirth for women or occupational hazards for men. Tremendous variation exists across cultures in terms of when children become socially recognized adults. Marriage, which may occur early in adolescence, may mark the transition although growth and maturation are not complete. Likewise, successful childbearing may be the important marker, although it can also take place before linear growth is finished. Other criteria include demonstration of cultural or economic competence (i.e., getting a job). In the United States, there are different legal ages that mark adulthood. Full participation in the electoral process can begin at age 18, but purchasing of alcohol is not possible until age 21. Marriage cannot occur before age 18 without parental consent in most states, and many states have similar laws regarding access to abortion.

What is interesting from a health perspective is the discrepancy between social and biological maturity. As noted earlier, teenage pregnancy represents one such disjunction, but overall, earlier biological maturation generates a series of potential mental and physical health consequences, many of which are only beginning to be understood. A different but equally problematic disjunction occurs when children grow slowly because of a lack of resources or infectious disease but find themselves in environments of abundance in adulthood. The metabolic efficiencies representing adaptations to scarcity are risk factors for later life diseases such as cardiovascular disease and diabetes because of their metabolic efficiency. Thus, the conditions under which children grow and mature are crucial not only to their health during childhood but also to their lifelong health.

STUDY QUESTIONS

1. What is life history theory? What are some of the important trade-offs in the evolution of mammalian life history stages? What are some uniquely human factors that affect life history patterns?
2. How is birth weight used as an indicator of a newborn's health status? What are the important factors that influence birth weight?
3. Compare and contrast health and growth in infants who are primarily breastfed compared with infants who are formula fed.
4. How do secular trends in growth observed in many populations and immigrant groups illustrate the impact of environmental conditions on childhood growth?
5. The small but healthy model of childhood growth seems compelling on the surface but neglects some critical issues. What are some of these issues?
6. What are some of the risks of overnutrition and rapid growth in childhood and adolescence? How are childhood obesity frequencies changing around the world?

7. What are some of the biocultural consequences in developed countries of lowering ages of menarche coupled with an increase in the age at which children are socially accepted as adults?

8. In what ways may early maturation lead to increased risks of cardiovascular disease and some cancers?

9. How do patterns of teenage pregnancy in urban, Black populations "make sense" in light of life history theory?

10. Why might humans have evolved an adolescent growth period that is not seen in even our closest primate relatives?

11. How do cultural factors lead to substantial variation in growth between boys and girls in some groups?

12. How does lead pollution affect childhood growth and development? Are environmental toxins evenly distributed throughout well-nourished populations?

CRITICAL THINKING QUESTIONS

1. In this chapter we discussed how the teenage pregnancy "problem" is in part a result of a disjunction between biological and social maturation in American culture. Can you think of any other examples of biological and social disjunction that are associated with social problems or the perception of problems?

2. Is it ethical or efficient for governments to "promote" growth? From a biocultural perspective, what would be the most sensible policy to pursue if a government wanted to ensure that its population achieved its maximal potential for growth?

3. What is your exposome? Is this a useful framework for thinking about health risks or population variation in health?

SUGGESTED ETHNOGRAPHIES AND OTHER BOOKS TO READ WITH THIS CHAPTER

Susan Cohen and Christine Cosgrove. 2009. *Normal at Any Cost: Tall Girls, Short Boys, and the Medical Industry's Quest to Manipulate Height.* New York: Penguin.

Katherine Dettwyler. 1994. *Dancing Skeletons: Life and Death in West Africa.* Prospect Heights, IL: Waveland Press.

Roderick Floud, Kenneth Wachter, and Annabel Gregory. 1990. *Height, Health and History: Nutritional Status in the United Kingdom, 1750–1980* (Cambridge University Press).

Roderick Floud, Robert W. Fogel, Bernard Harris, and Sok Chul Hong. 2011. *The Changing Body: Health, Nutrition, and Human Development in the Western World since 1700.* New York: Cambridge University Press.

Patricia Jeffery, Roger Jeffery, and Andrew Lyon. 1988. *Labour Pains and Labour Power: Women and Childbearing in India.* London: Zed Books, Ltd.

Roger Jeffery and Patricia Jeffery. 1997. *Population, Gender, and Politics.* New York: Cambridge University Press.

David Lancy. 2015. *The Anthropology of Childhood: Cherubs, Chattel, Changelings,* 2nd edition. New York: Cambridge University Press.

Margaret Mead. 1928. *Coming of Age in Samoa.* New York: William Morrow and Co.

Andrea S. Wiley. 2004. *An Ecology of High-Altitude Infancy.* New York: Cambridge University Press.

Andrea S. Wiley. 2016. *Reimagining Milk,* Second Edition *(Revised).* New York: Routledge.

CHAPTER 6

Reproductive Health in Biocultural Context

Chapter Goals

- To understand the evolutionary and social significance of the menstrual cycle and menarche
- To become familiar with the basic biology of fertility and infertility and their consequences
- To understand the issues surrounding the topic of female genital cutting
- To understand the complex biocultural nature of pregnancy and birth
- To understand the concept of "mothering" and how it is influenced by evolutionary and cultural forces

The previous chapter was concerned with child growth, the environmental conditions that shape it, and its association with various health issues. Child health is one aspect of reproductive health, which encompasses the factors that influence conception to the child becoming a fully mature adult, ready to embark on his or her own reproductive life. The health of children is intimately tied to that of their mothers, especially during pregnancy, and gradually that dependence dissolves as the child ages. This chapter focuses on the maternal part of this process, starting with conception and ending with issues pertaining to the concept of "mothering." We do not mean to neglect the paternal contribution to this process, but the overwhelming amount of medical anthropological research (indeed most medical research) on reproductive health has focused on women. We touch on two issues related to men's reproductive health: the global decline in sperm counts and the current proliferation of pharmacological treatments to enhance male sexual function (e.g., Viagra, Cialis).

MEDICALIZATION OF WOMEN'S HEALTH AND REPRODUCTIVE HEALTH

Women's health has long been defined in Western cultures by reproductive health. That is, women's health and reproductive health were viewed as largely synonymous (Ehrenreich and English 1978; Martin 1987). The predominant view of women's "other" health issues was that they were similar to men's, and few studies on cardiovascular disease (CVD), for example, were conducted on women. Heart disease is the most common cause of death for women, and it is now recognized that some of the risk factors and symptoms of heart disease are different in women (Maas et al. 2011). It was not until 1993 that the National Institutes of Health in the United States was required by Congress to ensure that women were included in clinical trials and other types of medical research, and the institute only reluctantly conformed (Hamilton 1996).

In contrast, reproductive health issues have dominated women's health research since the nineteenth century; in fact, one of the reasons why women were often excluded from clinical trials was because of their "complicated" reproductive physiology. The net effect has been that female reproductive processes came under biomedical scrutiny and our view of these processes has been largely through a biomedical lens. In other words, women's reproductive lives have become medicalized. As noted in Chapter 2, "medicalization" refers to a process by which some condition (physiological, behavioral, or emotional) becomes seen as a medical problem, a pathology necessitating treatment or intervention by a health-care professional. This can occur in any cultural context, but most commonly medicalization refers specifically to how biomedicine has extended its purview to various conditions that were not previously considered diseases or in need of biomedical oversight in Western culture (Conrad 2008).

The female life cycle is subject to much more medical oversight (or is seen as in need of such oversight) compared with the relatively "uncomplicated" male life cycle. Thus, the literature on menarche is increasingly concerned with the negative biosocial consequences of early menarche, and menstruation is described by the problems sometimes associated with it; pregnancy is overseen by biomedical practitioners under the guise of "prenatal care," which often involves extensive testing of the mother and the fetus; birth most often takes place in hospitals, with surgical births (e.g., cesarean births) becoming the norm in many countries; and menopause is treated as a pathology of female aging, characterized by hot flashes brought on by "estrogen deficiency." Much of the language used to describe these processes is likewise negative and often reflects cultural valuation of women. For example, in her classic work, Emily Martin analyzed historical and contemporary medical texts on reproduction for descriptions of fertilization and noted the high frequency of words describing the egg's passivity, whereas sperm were described as active, strong, and "on a mission" (Martin 1991). Thus, a great deal of work in medical anthropology is concerned with reproductive health, particularly as local traditions of reproductive health and life cycle concerns intersect with biomedical authority and technology (Browner and Sargent 2011).

In this chapter we outline the processes of reproduction, highlighting some associated health issues. We do not intend to replicate a medicalized view; indeed, an evolutionary understanding of reproduction also allows reproductive processes to be recast as adaptive rather than inherently pathological and thereby offers a corrective to a medicalized understanding of reproductive health. An evolutionary perspective asks why the reproductive process unfolds as it does, what is the functional significance of its components, and what fitness (including health) consequences are associated with them.

MENSTRUATION

The reproductive process in women is initiated by the onset of menarche, when menstrual cycles begin. Data gathered between the 1960s to 2010s from 89 countries indicate average ages at menarche ranges from 12 to 16 years (Šaffa et al. 2019). Menarche signals the onset of **ovulation** (the release of a fertilizable egg), but regular patterns of ovulation take some time to get established. In addition, the pelvis continues to grow after menarche, and thus full reproductive maturity tends to occur when the pelvis reaches its adult size and regular ovulatory cycles are established.

Females in our species are unusual, although not unique, among female mammals in that they menstruate and that ovulation, the time when they are most fertile, is not visible. Why do human females menstruate? Menstruation is the last phase of an ovulatory cycle and only occurs if conception has not taken place during that cycle. The full cycle, which lasts around 28 days (although this varies across women), includes two other stages and is illustrated in Figure 6.1 along with the two hormones produced by the ovaries: estrogen and progesterone. The first is the follicular stage, which occurs prior to ovulation. During this phase **estrogen** levels rise and cause the lining of the uterus (the endometrium) to become thicker. The egg follicle also enlarges and then releases the ovum at ovulation. Ovulation initiates the luteal phase, when progesterone supports further growth and enrichment of the endometrium in preparation for implantation of a fertilized egg. However, if implantation does not occur, progesterone levels fall, and the endometrial tissue is broken down. In most mammals the tissue and vasculature that supported it are resorbed without external bleeding. However, among humans, about one-third of the endometrial tissue and blood is shed during menses.

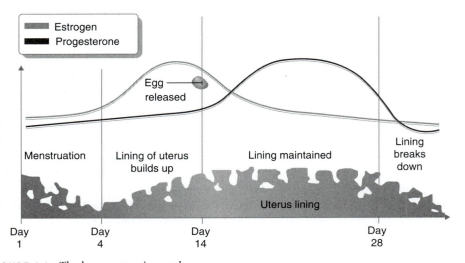

FIGURE 6.1   The human ovarian cycle.

So, why menstruate? As a biological phenomenon it is worth asking whether menstruation has a particular function—that is, whether it is adaptive. There are at least three hypotheses informed by evolutionary theory. Margie Profet (1993) argued that menstruation is itself an adaptation. She hypothesized that menstruation evolved as a defense against pathogens carried by sperm, citing evidence that menstrual blood is rich in immune cells. Furthermore, humans have no visible signs of ovulation and engage in sexual activity throughout the ovulatory cycle. This is in contrast to most other primate species in which females have a visually distinct estrus that marks ovulation. For example, in chimpanzees, females exhibit large "sexual swellings" during estrus, and they are only sexually receptive during this time. From Profet's perspective, the human female pattern of ovulatory and sexual activity would have increased the potential for sexually transmitted infections, and hence menstruation evolved to protect women from infections carried by sperm.

In contrast, Finn (1994) proposed that menstruation is a byproduct of the way that the thinning of the endometrium occurs in humans. In many other species that do not menstruate, the last part of endometrial development occurs only if implantation occurs. In humans this occurs regardless of whether there is a fertilized egg to implant and therefore there is more endometrial material to be shed if implantation does not occur. This results in a menstrual period.

Beverly Strassmann (1996) maintained that it is not menstruation itself that must be explained so much as it is the very nature of ovulatory *cycling*. In other words, why not simply leave the endometrium in place until conception occurs? Why build it up and then break it down in a monthly pattern? Strassmann found that cycling is more energy efficient than maintaining the endometrium for an extended period of time. During the luteal phase, a woman's metabolic rate increases by at least 7% relative to the follicular phase, indicating a greater need for energy resources. Thus, it is much more energetically efficient for the endometrium to be shed if no implantation occurs rather than for it to be maintained until it does. Strassmann estimated that the energy savings across one year of cycling would be on the order of 18 days' worth of food! There would be even greater economy during times of amenorrhea (i.e., when there is no ovulation and hence no growth of the endometrium), which occurs in women experiencing profound negative energy balance. Then why not resorb the endometrium as most other mammals do? Strassmann contends that this is a byproduct of the fact that human females have a large uterus relative to their body size, and hence the endometrium is too voluminous to be fully resorbed, resulting in external bleeding.

The question of whether menstruation or cycling has an adaptive function is important in relation to how the menstrual cycle is treated biomedically. If menstruation is indeed part of an immune response to ward off sexually transmitted infections, then suppressing menstruation, as is done by some hormonal birth control methods, is potentially deleterious for sexually active women. If it is a byproduct, then its suppression of the menstrual cycle is less problematic, and for women with marginal nutritional status, it may result in significant energy savings. Whichever hypothesis is correct, menstruation is neither deleterious nor wasteful; it is an important part of human female–evolved reproductive biology (see Emera et al. 2012 for a review of evolutionary hypotheses for menstruation).

There are now oral contraceptives that provide continuous hormones (levonorgestrel and ethinyl estradiol, the same hormones in traditional oral contraceptives) for 11 weeks, followed by 1 week of placebo pills to stimulate bleeding. Global surveys suggest that although many women are interested in suppressing their menstrual periods or having them less frequently, many are distrustful of contraceptives that do away with periods entirely (DeMaria et al. 2019). Manipulation of the cycle to reduce the frequency of menstrual bleeding simply delays the placebo week. Worries about the total absence of periods include lack of confidence that a woman is not pregnant, a sense that menstrual blood might be building up to unhealthy levels, and a belief that menstruation is needed to cleanse the uterus and expel "waste" (DeMaria et al. 2019). Embedded in such concerns is a sense that menstruation is normal or "healthy" despite whatever discomfort or inconvenience it may entail at times (Hillard 2014).

Lara Freidenfelds has traced the emergence of the "modern period" in the United States, describing how the creation of new technologies (pads, tampons, contraceptive pills, pain relievers), sex and hygiene educational materials, and changing beliefs about the health consequences of menstruation (e.g., taboos against bathing or sexual relations during menses) altered how women thought about their periods over the twentieth century. Collectively, these made periods more "manageable," and in line with new conceptualizations of the body, "one that was ideally always efficient, predictable, and presentable" (Freidenfelds 2009, 3). As she describes the experiences of women she interviewed,

> managing menstruation in a modern way relieved the same anxiety and discomfort of older methods, and usually allowed women to pursue their work and play as they and others had come to expect. A new mode of bodily management that enabled these activities perhaps felt especially liberatory to women, who otherwise often experienced menstruation as something that kept them from competing and participating effectively in schools and workplaces with male peers." (Freidenfelds 2009, 196–197)

It is important to note that although many contemporary women experience menstrual cycling as a routine part of adulthood, interrupted only by a few pregnancies, this pattern of cycling is not, and has not historically been, the norm. Indeed, because cycling is interrupted by pregnancy and long lactation and would have begun later in adolescence, the experience of menses would have been the exception, rather than the rule for many women. This also has implications for the risk of breast cancer, as discussed in detail later in this chapter.

A girl's first menstruation marks not only her biological reproductive maturation but also her social transformation to a new status—that of a woman. Menarche is an important life cycle rite across cultures, some very public, others more private in nature. Although ostensibly celebratory of a girl's emergence as a woman, the onset of menses is not without ambivalent emotions. In India, menarche often symbolizes new restrictions on a girl's movements and activities, as she is now considered marriageable and vulnerable to sexual overtures (Jeffery et al. 1988). Further, it may set into motion the search for an appropriate husband, to settle the girl into marriage before anything untoward such as a sexual relationship or pregnancy can occur, which would seriously compromise her marriageability and the family's status. In other cultural contexts, such as some in Africa, menarche signals the time for surgical alteration of the girl's genitalia, a culturally significant step in the process of becoming a marriageable woman (see the discussion of female genital cutting later in this chapter). In yet others, such as the Apache of Arizona, rituals following the achievement of menarche are celebratory and symbolically rich and complex. The girl is thought to take on some of the powers of the deity known as the Changing Woman, who has powers to enhance fertility, health, and material abundance. Thus, menarche is an opportunity to celebrate a girl's transition to womanhood, her health, and her productive value to the group (Bonvillain 2007).

Across cultures menstruation is subject to varying valuation. In some it is considered a time when women are polluted from menstrual blood. This is particularly true in India, where women cannot prepare food for others or engage in other domestic activities during their periods. In other societies women must go to separate menstrual huts and have no contact with men until menses is complete. Some anthropologists have interpreted this as evidence of patriarchy, a fear of women's biological powers, and women's relative powerlessness because they are banished from the community until menses has stopped. Others have argued instead that women may savor this time away from responsibilities and enjoy relaxed company with other menstruating women (see selections in Buckley and Gottlieb 1988). When a woman goes to a menstrual hut or it is otherwise clear that she is menstruating, it is a sign that she is not pregnant, and as Beverly Strassmann has argued for the Dogon of Mali, community members can make use of a woman's presence or absence at the menstrual hut as evidence of marital fidelity (Strassmann 1999). If a woman does not go to the menstrual hut and her husband is known to have been away for some time prior to her expected stay there, this may indicate that she is pregnant by someone other than her husband.

Addressing menstrual needs, particularly for school-age girls, has emerged as a global health priority, especially in relation to concerns about gender equity. A recent review of adolescent girls' and women's experiences of menstruation and expressed needs in low- and middle-income countries (Hennegan et al. 2019) found that women and girls reported that their menstrual experiences impaired their physical and psychological health, education, employment, and social participation. Menstrual stigma, internalized as shame, distress, and worry, and gender norms such as expectations of femininity and cleanliness, as well as taboos imposed on menstruating women and girls that limit their full participation in social life, contributed to poor mental and physical health outcomes. Additionally, women and girls reported a lack of knowledge and resources to adequately cope with menstruation, including access to materials to absorb menses, privacy and safety in changing and disposing of them, pain relief, and facilities to wash hands, genitals, and materials. Given that on any given day some 300 million girls and women are menstruating, this constitutes a major public health need that has, until relatively recently, been largely ignored and left un-addressed (Sommer et al. 2016).

The meanings of menstruation change over a woman's lifetime and with her varying experience of sexual relationships. In most contexts, on the one hand, menstruation is an indicator of a woman's health and fertility, even if menstrual blood itself is viewed with distaste or menses is experienced as painful. As such, the appearance of menstrual blood is greeted with relief. On the other hand, menstruation signals the absence of a pregnancy, and monthly bleeding may elicit sadness or despair as a sign of

Oral Contraceptives and Biological Normalcy

Oral contraceptives are widely used in Western countries but are less frequently adopted by women in developing countries. One reason for the difference in contraceptive use could be differences in circulating levels of the reproductive hormones estrogen and progesterone. In relatively wealthy countries such as the United States and Poland, women have levels of progesterone that are up to twice as high as those from rural subsistence populations such as in Zaire, Nepal, and Bolivia (Figure 6.2). Although the factors underlying it and the significance of this population variation with respect to fertility are unclear, women can and do ovulate and conceive with lower levels of estrogen and progesterone. From the perspective of fertility suppression through oral contraceptives, women with lower hormone levels metabolize estrogen and progesterone in oral contraceptives differently than women with higher levels. As a result, women with lower hormonal levels tend to experience greater suppression of reproductive function than do women with higher levels when given the same dosage of oral contraceptives. This suggests that standard dosages of oral contraceptives (currently 30 to 35 micrograms of ethinyl estradiol and a progestin) may be inappropriate for women with lower baseline levels of estrogen and progesterone and are likely also associated with increased rates of troublesome side effects from oral contraception. Side effects such as breakthrough bleeding, nausea, headaches, mood changes, libido changes, and breast tenderness often lead women to discontinue oral contraceptive usage, although family planning policy analysts often trivialize these concerns.

Virginia Vitzthum and Karen Ringheim (2005) argued that these may be much more common among women in less developed countries, in part because their hormone profiles are lower than those in Western populations, yet the dosage of oral contraceptives that they are given is the same. In Bolivia, where Vitzthum has conducted long-term fieldwork on reproductive ecology, there is a 59% discontinuation rate for oral contraceptives, of which more than 60% was attributed to side effects. Doctors often discount the severity of these side effects, yet they likely stem from

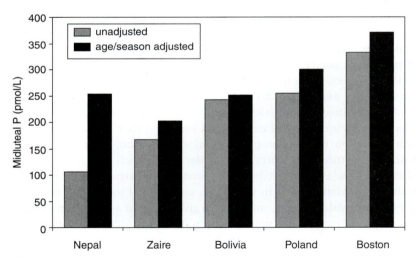

FIGURE 6.2 Population variation in midluteal progesterone (P). Unadjusted samples comprise all individuals observed in each study. Adjusted samples comprise only those women 25 to 35 years old and in Bolivia, Nepal, and Poland are restricted to the seasons of least work and greatest food availability; Zaire and Boston samples are not adjusted for season.
Source: Data from V. J. Vitzthum et al. 2000. Does hypoxia impair ovarian function in Bolivian women indigenous to high altitude? *High Altitude Medicine & Biology* 1 (1):39–49. Figure from V. J. Vitzthum. 2006. *Evolution and Endocrinology: The Regulation of Pregnancy Outcomes.* Symposium of the Society for the Study of Human Biology, York, United Kingdom. Reprinted with permission from V. J. Vitzthum.

the relative "overdose" of hormones in oral contraceptives given to women with lower circulating levels of these hormones.

Oral contraceptives have been developed based on hormonal data from well-nourished Western women and appear to be best tolerated by those same women, but the assumption that there is a universal, species-wide hormonal standard (i.e. that of Western women) is incorrect. Tailoring oral contraceptives that have lower dosages for women with lower levels of circulating estrogen and progesterone should enhance their tolerability and presumably reduce rates of discontinuation and unwanted pregnancies. Dosages of 20 micrograms of ethinyl estradiol appear to be sufficient to inhibit ovulation with substantially fewer side effects than the standard 30- to 35-microgram dosages. This issue provides another clear example of the problem of assuming that biological norms derived from Western populations should be considered norms for the species or a universal standard for health. As Vitzthum and Ringheim (2005, 23) note, "the assumption generally is made that species-wide minimal levels of reproductive steroids are necessary for conception to occur and that all fecund women have levels of endogenous hormones above this minimum." As the cross-population data indicate, conception can occur at much lower levels of reproductive hormones, and lower levels of hormonal contraceptives can effectively suppress ovulation with fewer side effects among women with lower levels of endogenous hormones.

potential infertility. Efforts to regulate menstruation are made use of in all cultures, and irregular or missed menses are often seen as problematic. Remedies used to bring on menses may in fact have abortifacient properties and are used if a woman suspects a late period is because of an unwelcome pregnancy (such "remedies" were widely advertised in American newspapers of the nineteenth century as cures for "menstrual blockage"). Oral contraceptives are often prescribed for irregular periods because they are frequently used in a pattern of three weeks of estrogen/progestin followed by one week of "placebo" (nonhormonal) pills that cause hormone levels to drop and the endometrial lining to be shed. Oral contraceptives generate a synthetic "regularized" menstrual cycle, although as noted earlier, the regular monthly appearance of menses is a relatively recent historical phenomenon and is linked to declines in fertility and breastfeeding.

PREMENSTRUAL SYNDROME

For some women menstruation is painless, but for others it is accompanied by severe pain and discomfort. **Dysmenorrhea**, or having painful periods, is characterized by cramping, backache, bloating, or any combination of these and is fairly universally recognized, if not experienced with every period. In addition, some women experience a range of negative emotional symptoms just prior to the onset of menses, which now has a recognized medical term—**premenstrual syndrome** (PMS). PMS became formally recognized in the medical literature in the 1980s as a cluster of psychological symptoms including mood swings, irritability, depression, anxiety, and feeling "out of control," among others, that were sufficiently severe in some women to disrupt their normal functioning. In 1987 PMS was first listed in the *Diagnostic and Statistical Manual of Mental Disorders–III–R* as "late luteal phase dysphoric disorder," although the exact criteria for describing the disorder remained ambiguous and encompassed a wide array of poorly defined symptoms. It remains unclear why women vary so much in their experience of their menstrual cycles, and thus far no specific biological marker has been found that correlates with reported PMS symptoms.

Anthropologists have been interested in PMS from the perspective of whether it is actually a culture-bound syndrome unique to some Western cultures or whether it is found universally and closely tied to the hormonal shifts associated with the menstrual cycle. It appears that although menstrual symptoms are widely recognized, PMS historically was not universally recognized as a medical syndrome and was much less frequently noted in subsistence societies, where menstruation is more often perceived as a sign of health, youth, fertility, and femininity than in the United States or in European countries (Johnson 1987). However, a review of studies of PMS from countries around the world found an average prevalence of 48% of women reporting symptoms, but the range was wide, from 10% in Switzerland to 98% in Iran, with some evidence of higher rates in Asia overall compared with Europe (Direkvand-Moghadam et al. 2014). Thus, recognition of the symptomatology does not necessarily map neatly onto its prevalence in a society.

What then explains PMS's appearance as a syndrome in Western societies? "Women's complaints" have long been privileged as mental health problems purportedly unique to the female sex, which render women inherently weaker than men. In the nineteenth century, hysteria and neurasthenia were two common medical diagnoses for women's mood disorders. PMS can be considered a twentieth century version of these; that is, a medical label for a disease found only among females, which contributes to a view of women as "naturally abnormal" or with more troublesome biologies than men. It may also be a reflection of a more general tendency to medicalize mental and reproductive health and to attribute feelings of stress or discomfort to a woman's reproductive biology. Some have argued that as a culture-bound syndrome it reflects the current Western ambivalence about women's roles as productive workers and reproductive homemakers, as a multivalent symbol of both fertility and nonpregnant status (Davis 1996; Johnson 1987). Emily Martin proposed that the "disciplining of work," with its emphasis on productivity in and out of the home, left women with latent anger, which could seep through and find expression during the hormonal changes of the late luteal phase. Although there is little evidence that women's performance at any task is significantly altered prior to their period, Martin notes many women clearly sense that they "function differently during certain days, in ways that make it harder for them to tolerate the discipline required by work in our society. We could then perhaps hear these statements not as warnings of biological flaws inside women that need to be fixed but insights into flaws in society that need to be addressed" (Martin 1988, 170).

It is interesting to note that recognition of PMS becomes more likely with exposure to and adoption of Western societal norms and practices. Maureen Fitzgerald's study of Samoan women living in contexts along the traditional–Western continuum showed that those living more traditionally were much less likely to recognize PMS symptoms than those living in Hawaii, who offered elaborate descriptions of PMS's symptomatology and reported experiencing those symptoms much more frequently (Fitzgerald 1990). She argued that as Samoan women become familiar with and embedded in American culture, they make use of dominant ideologies about women's reproductive cycles to interpret their own bodily states. Similarly, Corey Pilver and colleagues found that reports of PMS and any premenstrual symptoms increased among immigrants to the United States with duration of residence, suggesting that acculturation contributed to an increased likelihood of reporting premenstrual symptoms, regardless of the country of origin (Pilver et al. 2011).

DETERMINANTS OF FERTILITY

Successful reproduction is central to every society; thus, it comes as no surprise that much attention is paid to a woman's ability to have children. From a health perspective, this becomes most evident when the desired outcome of a healthy infant is not achieved due to problems with either conceiving or maintaining a pregnancy. It is useful to consider factors that influence fertility by organizing them into a set of proximate determinants, which are the mechanisms by which fertility can be affected by a variety of biological, environmental, behavioral, and cultural factors. Table 6.1 provides a list of the proximate determinants of fertility, from the perspective of a woman's life cycle. (A note on terminology: **fertility** refers to having a live birth; **fecundity** refers to the ability to sustain a pregnancy; **fecundability** is the ability to conceive).

For females, age is a crucial determinant of fertility. Menarche signals the onset of the possibility of fertility, but across societies the age at marriage is a better index of when fertility truly begins. Sexual activity and reproduction among females are generally sanctioned only after marriage, and marriage most often occurs after menarche has occurred. A woman's fertile years end with menopause, which is less a defined event than a process of decreasing ovulatory cycles that eventually end altogether. Menopause typically occurs around 50 years of age. If marriage ends from divorce or spousal death prior to this, it can truncate fertility earlier, unless a subsequent marriage or sexual union occurs.

Within this set of reproductive years, the likelihood of conception is not constant. Fertility generally peaks between 20 and 30 years and then declines until menopause. Age variation may be the result of changes in any of the proximate determinants. It is not clear whether there are meaningful changes in ovarian function between the ages of 20 and 40, and there is a paucity of evidence regarding how age differences in ovarian function might vary across populations (Vitzthum 2009). There is also variation in reproductive hormone levels, such as progesterone, as shown in Figure 6.2, some of which may be

TABLE 6.1   Proximate Determinants of Fertility

Determinants of fertility "possibility"

 Age at menarche

 Age at menopause

 Rates of marriage and marriage dissolution or sanctioned sexual relationships

Determinants of fertility "probability"

 Frequency of intercourse

 Ovarian cycle length; proportion of cycles that are ovulatory, duration of fertile period given ovulation has occurred, probability of conception from a single insemination during fertile period

 Duration of lactational infecundability (resulting from suppression of ovulation while nursing)

 Probability of pathological sterility (usually from sexually transmitted infections)

 Frequency of spontaneous abortion or fetal death

 Length of gestation (invariant)

 Use of contraception and induced abortion

Source: Adapted from Campbell and Wood (1988).

attributable to variation in nutritional status, although there are numerous factors that could contribute to reproductive hormone differences (Vitzthum 2009). Very thin women and women engaging in strenuous physical activity often become amenorrheic and stop ovulating until positive energy balance is achieved. It was once thought that there was a critical amount of fat that a woman needed to maintain ovulatory function (Frisch 1994), but that does not seem to be the case, and the signals relating nutritional status to fertility are not well understood. In any event, how these individual-level processes play out in terms of population variation is not clear, nor is the significance of variation in hormone levels in terms of their effects on fertility because populations with lower levels of ovarian hormones are able to maintain high fertility rates (Vitzthum 2009).

A woman's likelihood of conceiving also depends on the frequency of sexual intercourse. This varies cross-culturally within sexually sanctioned relationships, and varies by age of both partners and marriage duration, among other factors (Brewis and Meyer 2005). Sexual intercourse may be forbidden during particular religious rituals or after birth, as in postpartum taboos against sexual intercourse among many sub-Saharan African populations.

Across populations, especially those that do not make extensive use of contraceptives, the most important factor that influences a woman's likelihood of getting pregnant again after a birth is the duration of **lactational infecundability**, which is associated with lactational amenorrhea (lack of periods). Women are infertile for a few weeks after birth until ovulation can be reestablished, but this period of time can be greatly lengthened by nursing. Both the duration of the breastfeeding period and the frequency with which a woman nurses her child strongly influence the length of time that she will be infertile after birth. Every nursing episode is associated with a burst of the hormone **prolactin**, and more frequent nursing prevents prolactin levels from declining. Women who experienced longer duration of lactational amenorrhea have been shown to have greater prolactin levels after nursing bouts and maintain higher prolactin levels than those who return to cycling earlier. In addition, suckling inhibits gonadotropin-releasing hormone and luteinizing hormone, which in turn are necessary for estrogen to stimulate ovulation. Thus, it is not simply a matter of how long nursing occurs; the frequency with which infants are nursed is much more important to the suppression of postpartum fertility (Neville 2013). Women who nurse infrequently, as is common in Western societies where infants are encouraged to be on scheduled feedings, are more likely to resume ovulation earlier than women who nurse on a more frequent, opportunistic basis. Nursing frequency tends to decline with the introduction of supplementary foods, and the likelihood of ovulation increases as a result.

The other main factor that influences conception is **sexually transmitted infection** (STI). The two most common sexually transmitted bacteria known to infect the reproductive tract and cause fertility problems are gonorrhea (*Neisseria gonorrhoeae*) and chlamydia (*Chlamydia trachomatis*), and they contribute to a syndrome called **pelvic inflammatory disease** (PID). PID can be asymptomatic or characterized by severe pelvic pain. These bacteria can infect the fallopian tubes, where the immune response to the infection causes inflammation, and, if untreated, scar tissue forms in the tube. Consequently, fertilization and implantation may become more difficult to achieve. Or, if fertilization occurs and the zygote cannot move to the uterus for implantation, a tubal (also called ectopic) pregnancy can result, in some cases causing the rupture of the fallopian tube itself. In men, these STIs can cause similar scarring and blockage of the seminal tract. STIs are more likely to be asymptomatic among women than among men, thus increasing the risk for reproductive problems for women. Gonorrhea and chlamydia are both easily treated with antibiotics, although *N. gonorrhoeae* has developed resistance to multiple antibiotics (Rowley et al. 2019).

Data from 2016 analyzed by the World Health Organization (WHO) indicate a global prevalence of 3.8% and 0.9% for chlamydia and gonorrhea, respectively, among women age 15–49 years, with slightly lower rates for men (2.7% and 0.7%, respectively, Rowley et al. 2019). There were more than 200 million new chlamydia or gonorrhea infections as well as 156 million cases of trichomoniasis and 6.3 million cases of syphilis (all of these STIs are treatable with antibiotics). Figure 6.3 shows the global variation in STI prevalence

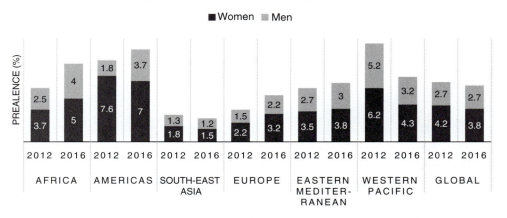

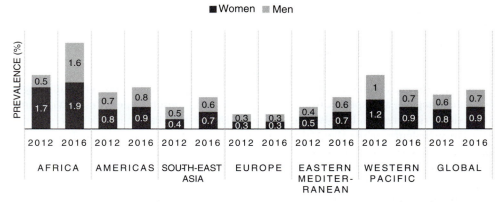

FIGURE 6.3 Estimated prevalence (%) of the sexually transmitted infections chlamydia, gonorrhea, trichomoniasis, and syphilis in women and men aged 15–49 by World Health Organization region, based on 2012–2016 data.
Source: Rowley, J., S. Vander Hoorn, E. Korenromp, N. Low, M. Unemo, L. J. Abu-Raddad, R. M. Chico, A. Smolak, L. Newman, and S. Gottlieb. 2019. Chlamydia, gonorrhoea, trichomoniasis and syphilis: global prevalence and incidence estimates, 2016. *Bulletin of the World Health Organization*, 97:548.

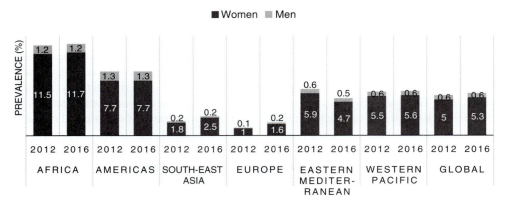

TRICHOMONIASIS PREVALENCE IN 2012 & 2016

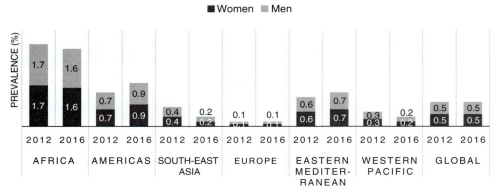

SYPHILIS PREVALENCE IN 2012 & 2016

FIGURE 6.3 (*continued*)

in 2012–2016; overall rates remained fairly constant across the globe, but with differences by gender, region, and specific infection. Some of the highest prevalence estimates come from the African region, but also the Americas. The western Pacific is experiencing a decline in prevalence, while the African region shows increasing prevalence. Europe and Southeast Asia tend to have the lowest prevalence. Overall, the key point is that STIs remain a major health burden for reproductive-age adults, particularly women, and in some regions, such as Africa, prevalence is increasing rather than declining.

The risk of infertility caused by such STIs increases with years of sexual activity, and repeated infections, even those treated successfully with antibiotics, contribute to an increase in tube-blocking scar tissue. As a result, these "silent" infections can be a major cause of infertility, especially among women who attempt to become pregnant later in their reproductive years. It is estimated that the risk of tubal infertility among women with PID is about 15% overall, with multiple infections dramatically increasing the risk (Tsevat et al. 2017). Globally it is estimated that about one-third of female infertility is attributable to tubal factor infertility (TFI), usually resulting from PID, but the rate may be as high as 85% in sub-Saharan Africa (Inhorn and Patrizio 2015).

INFERTILITY

The inability to get pregnant or sustain a pregnancy is a cause of significant distress for women around the world. Although males contribute to more than half of the cases of infertility, interventions to improve a couple's fertility more frequently target women. When it is not possible to ascertain the source, because it is females who do or do not get pregnant, women are most often blamed for a couple's inability to produce a child. Although from a physical standpoint infertility is not a disease per se, it is frequently treated like other health problems across societies, insofar as traditional and biomedical treatments are rapidly sought, and it can be an impairment to a couple's social and emotional well-being (i.e., it may be considered an illness) (see Figure 6.4).

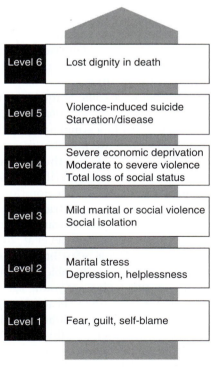

FIGURE 6.4 Psychological, social, and physical consequences of infertility. In developed countries, the consequences of infertility rarely extend beyond level 2; in developing countries (especially Asia and Africa) the consequences are infrequently as mild as level 3.
Source: Ombelet, Willem, Ian Cooke, Silke Dyer, Gamal Serour, and Paul Devroey. 2008. "Infertility and the provision of infertility medical services in developing countries." *Human Reproduction Update* 14 (6):605–621. doi:10.1093/humupd/dmn042. Reprinted with permission of Oxford University Press.

The WHO definition of **infertility** is the absence of conception after 24 months of regular, unprotected intercourse. Infertility is considered either primary, if a woman has never conceived, or secondary, if a woman has conceived at least once. On a population level, **primary infertility** is often measured as the percentage of women who have not conceived after five years of marriage without contraceptive use, and **secondary infertility** is measured as the proportion of women with at least one child who do not go on to have another despite taking steps to do so. One analysis found that almost 2% of all couples desiring children experience primary infertility (defined here as inability to have a live birth after five years of "exposure"), and more than 10% had secondary infertility (Mascarenhas et al. 2012). By this criterion, infertility affects almost 50 million couples worldwide, with a wide variation across populations, and rates would be more than 2.5 times higher if the standard WHO definition was used. Figures 6.5a and 6.5b illustrate global variation in rates of primary and secondary infertility.

The determinants of fertility (Table 6.1) are relevant to a discussion of infertility, and they constitute pathways through which any number of diseases, dietary and environmental toxins, nutrient deficiencies, and medical treatments (such as chemotherapy, unsafe abortions) can seriously impair fertility among men and women. Additionally, many cases of infertility are described as **idiopathic**, meaning of unknown origin or cause. The Global Burden of Disease (GBD) project demonstrated that rates of infertility have been increasing overall for both males and females, for reasons that are not well understood (Sun et al. 2019).

Sub-Saharan African countries have some of the highest rates of infertility in the world. In many countries in this region, strongly pronatalist ideologies are ubiquitous (i.e., there is a high value placed on childbearing) and population rates of fertility are high, yet many couples find that they are not able to achieve their fertility goals. Infertility rates range from 10% to 30%, although there is evidence that rates have been declining (Mascarenhas et al. 2012). Secondary sterility rates, however, are particularly high—more than 30% in many countries in the region (Rutstein and Johnson 2004). The highest rates are in southern and western Africa, with much lower rates in East Africa, suggesting that there is not some "pan-African" pattern of behavior or environment that puts people at risk of infertility (Ombelet et al. 2008).

Studies have reported that tubal factor infertility accounts for 42% to 77% of all infertility in sub-Saharan Africa, most attributable to an infection (Ombelet et al. 2008). Among the risk factors in this region are young age at first sexual experience, which exposes girls to the risk of contracting STIs at a younger age and heightens the risk of primary infertility from tubal scarring; not being married or in a steady sexual relationship; and urban residence (Ericksen and Brunette 1996). Given the infectious origin of much of the observed infertility, more aggressive testing and treatment of bacterial STIs should provide at least a partial solution to problems of infertility. However, it fails to address patterns of sexual activity and the context that gives rise to them, which ultimately must be understood before any preventive mechanisms can succeed.

HIV is associated with infertility as well, and HIV and other STIs tend to be correlated: HIV infection increases the likelihood of subsequent STI infection and vice versa. Importantly, the epidemic of HIV in sub-Saharan Africa has led to more

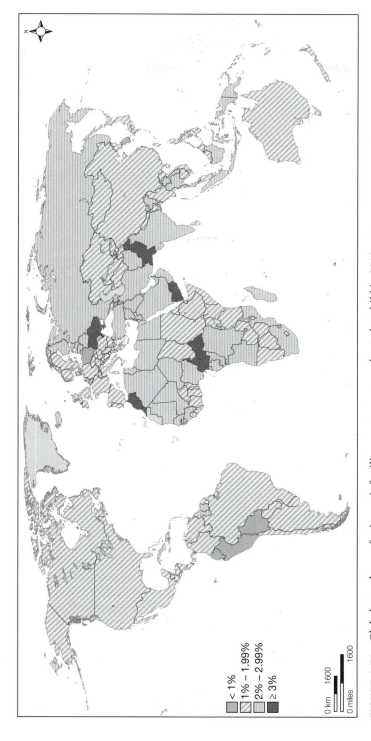

FIGURE 6.5A Global prevalence of primary infertility among women who seek a child in 2010.
Source: Mascarenhas, Maya N., Seth R. Flaxman, Ties Boerma, Sheryl Vanderpoel, and Gretchen A. Stevens. 2012. "National, Regional, and Global Trends in Infertility Prevalence Since 1990: A Systematic Analysis of 277 Health Surveys." *PLoS Med* 9 (12):e1001356. doi: 10.1371/journal.pmed.1001356.

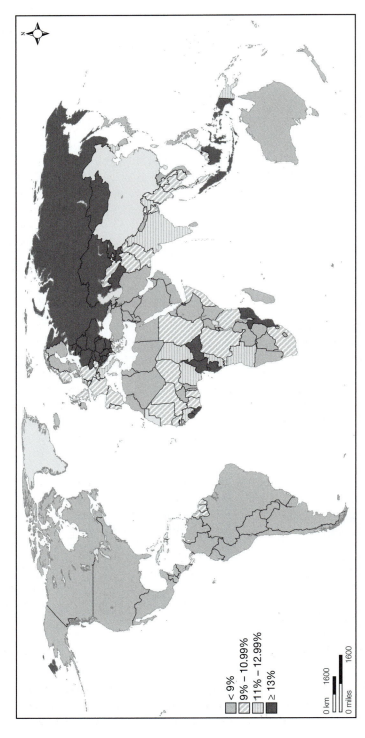

FIGURE 6.5B Global prevalence of secondary infertility among women who have had a live birth and seek another in 2010.
Source: Mascarenhas, Maya N., Seth R. Flaxman, Ties Boerma, Sheryl Vanderpoel, and Gretchen A. Stevens. 2012. "National, regional, and global trends in infertility prevalence since 1990: A systematic analysis of 277 health surveys." *PLoS Med* 9 (12):e1001356. doi:10.1371/journal.pmed.1001356.

sophisticated anthropological understandings of sexual behavior, which is at the heart of the spread of STIs and deeply embedded within cultural, political, and economic networks (Leclerc-Madlala 2009; Mah and Halperin 2010). As Ezekiel Kalipeni noted with respect to educational programs to counter HIV in southern Africa,

> The general ineffectiveness of AIDS prevention programs in Africa does not just stem from lack of funding, but from an unwillingness to look beyond simplistic approaches that focus on the peculiarities of individual sexual behavior rather than the social, economic, and political contingencies which make certain social groups such as commercial sex workers vulnerable.... Poverty is one factor that limits the number and amount of resources available and gender is another ... for women in particular, jobs are scarce, resources such as government training projects or agricultural extension services are directed toward men, and local income-earning opportunities are generally unavailable. Scarce job opportunities for men mean that migrancy is high among many sub-Saharan countries as jobs are sought in neighboring countries or in far away regions from the home country. The result is that prostitution is the only income-earning occupation open to many women who must find a way to feed not just themselves but their children in the absence of their husband's or any other means of support. (Kalipeni 2000, 967)

One clear problem is that older men seek young girls for sex, recognizing the higher risk of HIV transmission by their older sexual partners. Young girls in turn may be economically vulnerable to "agreeing" to this arrangement, hoping that an older man can provide them with economic support and security. Gendered economic imbalances further reduce the ability of a woman or girl to insist on condom use by a man, and labor migration contributes to wider sexual networks and transactional and/or commercial sex (Mojola and Wamoyi 2019). Thus, individual sexual behavior and having multiple concurrent sexual partners is intrinsically tied to larger regional political and economic realities, and poverty is always a "risk factor" for infection and, in the case of STIs, for infertility (Mah and Halperin 2010).

Women's relative powerlessness is likely to make their experiences with infertility especially difficult. This is particularly true in strongly patriarchal societies, where a woman's role is intimately tied to her ability to produce a child. As Marcia Inhorn (Figure 6.6) writes of her foundational work on infertility in Egypt,

> If fertility is recognized as perhaps the most potent (if uncontrollable) source of women's power, then infertility, which serves to strip women of this power, can only be seen as unusually threatening. Not only does infertility pose a threat to women—whose fundamental value in the eyes of their husbands, relatives, communities, and themselves may be closely bound to their reproductive abilities—infertility threatens men as well, for it effectively nullifies proof of their virility and masculine procreativity, as well as their ability to perpetuate the patrilineage, its name, and its patrimony. (Inhorn 1996, 12)

Furthermore, infertile women not only are a threat to the continuation of patrilineage and the larger community, but also are dangerous to other individuals by virtue of their "uncontrollable envy." They may be subject to ostracism, divorce, and

FIGURE 6.6   The medical anthropologist Marcia Inhorn at Conceive, an in vitro fertilization clinic in Dubai and Sharjah, United Arab Emirates. Dr. Inhorn has worked on issues related to infertility and infertility treatments in both men and women in multiple countries in the Middle East. Her work considers how infertility and decisions to seek treatment must be understood within a cultural context and how cultural contexts may themselves give rise to infertility or adverse birth outcomes.
Credit: Photo courtesy of Marcia Inhorn and Kirk Hooks.

harassment in addition to their personal anguish and uncertain personal and social identity as a childless female (Sembuya 2010). It is no surprise that women eagerly seek out fertility assistance, from both traditional sources and biomedical fertility clinics. As Inhorn notes, they often endanger their reproductive health further through some of these procedures. That said, Inhorn's recent research indicates that as couples make use of biomedical fertility services, gender relations may change in a positive way as both male and female causes of infertility are acknowledged and understood as medical conditions that can be treated, and stigma, blame, and social suffering are diminished for both men and women (Inhorn and Patrizio 2015).

The number of biomedical fertility clinics, which used to be only accessible to the wealthy in developed countries, has grown enormously over the past 20 years, especially in Asia, the Middle East, and Latin America. Importantly, however, the services offered by such clinics are expensive, rarely covered by private or state insurance, and as such are accessible only to elites. Thus, they are a last resort and only for a select few, when ethnomedical treatments or other biomedical care have proven fruitless. Fertility clinics offer **assisted reproductive technologies** (ARTs), including in vitro fertilization (IVF), the only possibility for women with tubal blockage from PID. IVF is notoriously expensive; even in a wealthy country such as the United States, the average cost is about 20% of the national median income. In developing countries, the relative cost is even greater—the cost of one IVF cycle is often more than half of the national average annual income (Nachtigall 2006) and its success rate is low. Furthermore, although sub-Saharan Africa has some of the highest rates of tubal infertility (which IVF can address) and strong pronatalist ideals, this region has the poorest coverage of ART services (Inhorn and Patrizio 2015). See Figure 6.7 for the global distribution of ART clinics in Asia, Africa, and Latin America in relation to the prevalence of infertility, which shows a similar imbalance in central Asia, where rates of secondary infertility are also high but ART facilities are lacking. Thus, practically speaking, this technology is well beyond the means of most couples. There have been recent efforts to subsidize ART for couples (e.g., in Turkey) or to provide lower-tech and lower-cost options (e.g., the "Walking Egg" project—see Ombelet 2014), and transnational travel to seek out ART services in areas where costs are low has also exploded (Inhorn and Patrizio 2015).

It is important to note that IVF is based on biomedical ideas about male and female reproductive biology that may not be widely shared across cultures. In her work in Egypt, Marcia Inhorn described how only males are thought to contribute the "biogenetic" material for conception, whereas females provide only its nurturing medium. Thus, having women provide the "egg" while men provide "sperm" in a nonintercourse context is at odds with these understandings of reproduction (Inhorn 2003). There are also religious injunctions against assisted reproduction in Catholicism, and in Islam IVF is not forbidden but any kind of third-party egg or sperm donation is, leading to anxiety about "mix-up" in IVF laboratories. A country's political commitment to encouraging high fertility or population growth, stabilization, or decline also impacts its likelihood of offering subsidized access to ARTs, as do views of who appropriate "parents" are or are not.

Infertility has wide-ranging negative impacts on the well-being of a couple, as Figure 6.4 shows. Couples with infertility living in developing countries or those with high fertility ideals are likely to experience suffering in numerous ways. But infertility is also painful for couples in societies with low fertility rates and high levels of contraceptive usage. Although the outward manifestations of devaluation are not as transparent, childless couples are subject to various forms of social stigma, marital instability, uncertain personal and social identity, and personal anguish as their desires to become parents are unfulfilled. They are often unable to afford ARTs, which are made use of disproportionately by white, older, affluent, urban couples. Tubal infertility is not uncommon in such contexts, and the delay of childbearing while career goals are fulfilled is most often the cause of infertility in this group. It becomes an unpleasant irony at best for couples trying to conceive in their thirties and forties who had been avidly trying to avoid conception for so much of their adult life.

THE MEDICALIZATION OF MALE SEXUAL DYSFUNCTION

Erectile dysfunction (ED; the inability to achieve or maintain an erection) emerged into American popular culture with television commercials featuring the former senator and presidential candidate Robert Dole describing the syndrome and advertising a

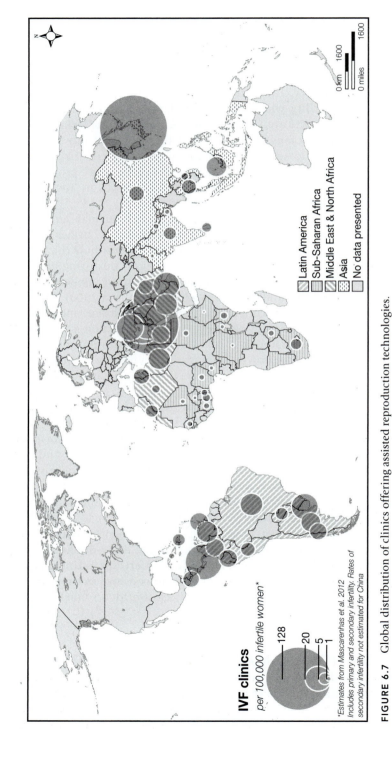

FIGURE 6.7 Global distribution of clinics offering assisted reproduction technologies.

Source: Inhorn, Marcia C., and Pasquale Patrizio. 2015. "Infertility around the globe: New thinking on gender, reproductive technologies and global movements in the 21st century." *Human Reproduction Update* 21 (4):411–426. doi:10.1093/humupd/dmv016. Reprinted with permission from Oxford University Press.

Falling Sperm Counts: Environmental Causes of Potential Male Reproductive Health Issues

In 1992 a study was published in the *British Medical Journal* (Carlsen et al. 1992) that revealed a global downward trend in sperm counts. The report suggested that sperm counts in populations throughout the world had declined by almost 50% since the 1930s. Not surprisingly, this finding was met with alarm and stimulated a large number of studies on various aspects of sperm quantity and quality in populations across the globe, which to date have not yielded consistent results (Ravanos et al. 2018). When the original finding was published, researchers working on diverse species were also reporting high rates of unusual reproductive abnormalities: bald eagles in Florida were sterile; mink herds in the Midwest and Great Lakes area were suffering reproductive failures; alligators in Lake Apopka, Florida, were not hatching, and those that did died early and many males had abnormally small penises; and in Southern California, there appeared to be a shortage of males among gull populations. Danish reproductive physiologists were finding increases in rates of testicular cancer among men; in the 1970s a cluster of women with a rare form of vaginal cancer were described; and breast cancer researchers found their cancerous cells were proliferating even without the administration of estrogen (Colborn et al. 1997).

Do these observations have anything in common? Many scientists have argued that they are all the outcome of exposure to endocrine disrupting chemicals (EDCs) in the environment. Some of these take the form of synthetic estrogens are compounds that are structurally and functionally similar to the female reproductive hormone estrogen and include pesticides such as DDT, PCBs, dioxins, furans, diethylstilbestrol (which was given to women in the 1940s and 1950s to reduce the symptoms of pregnancy sickness and the risk of miscarriage, along with other conditions), and many others that are ubiquitous in common household products, including many forms of plastics, canned foods, detergents, and personal care products.

When incorporated into animal tissues, these compounds can act as estrogens and have the potential to inhibit the body's own estrogen or act more or less potently than it. Estrogen stimulates mitosis (cell division) among cells with estrogen receptors; when these are exposed to synthetic estrogens continuously, they multiply. For example, breast cells have estrogen receptors, and synthetic estrogens, which can be stored in fatty breast tissue, can cause these cells to divide more rapidly, increasing the risk of breast cancer. Estrogen-dependent breast cancers have been on the rise, perhaps in part because of increased exposure to environmental estrogens. The focus of research in this area has branched out to consider a broader range of environmental endocrine disruptors that affect other endocrine systems beyond those acting through estrogenic pathways (Schug et al. 2016).

One such product is bisphenol A (BPA), widely used in plastic beverage and heating containers as well as in the lining of metal cans used for food storage. In the United States, exposure to BPA is common (as are products such as water bottles now advertised as "BPA-free"). Almost all individuals tested in multiple sites around the world have BPA in their bodies; it has also been found in breast milk and fetal tissues and is biologically active (see review in Schug et al. 2016). Thus, BPA is an important potential modulator of contemporary human biology and health. It has effects equivalent to estrogen and can disrupt a number of hormonal and cellular signaling pathways, even at very low doses. Furthermore, it acts in an epigenetic fashion, such that early life exposure is associated with increased risks of prostate and breast cancer, urogenital abnormalities in male infants, a decline in semen quality, early onset of puberty, metabolic disorders including insulin resistance, diabetes, and obesity, among others (Peretz et al. 2014).

In males, exposure to environmental estrogens, especially in utero when organs are being formed, appears to inhibit normal male reproductive development, resulting in a range of reproductive system outcomes including undescended testicles, small penises, abnormal sperm, and reduced fertility (Peretz et al. 2014). Thus, these largely invisible and unreported industrial compounds are ubiquitous in the environment, and substantial evidence now points to their ability to generate significant alterations to reproductive function. Whether these are in fact the cause of the drop in male sperm counts remains unclear, as is their contribution to infertility rates, but it seems likely that high levels of pesticides or industrial compounds can account for a substantial portion of male infertility in some areas.

new drug—Viagra (sildenafil citrate; produced by Pfizer, which received the patent for it in 1996; on the market as a prescription drug since 1998). Viagra was originally developed as a medication to treat heart disease (and is now used for that purpose under the prescription name Revatio), but quickly became known for its ability to enhance erectile function in men. According to Pfizer, 63 million men worldwide are taking Viagra, making it one of the most successful drugs of all time. Other pharmaceutical companies have launched, and widely marketed, similar drugs, such as Levitra and Cialis. Collectively, more than $400 million has been spent on advertising these products, although advertising is diminishing as the generic versions of these drugs have come on the market.

About 18% of men over the age of 20 years have ED (about 18 million men), and ED is estimated to affect more than 150 million men worldwide, a number that is expected to exceed 300 million men by the year 2025 because of population aging. The prevalence of ED ranges from 7% in men aged 18 to 29 years to 85% in men aged 76 to 85 years (Jackson et al. 2005). ED can be caused by any number of factors, from stress, anxiety, and depression (or taking the medications that are used to treat these disorders) to cardiac disease and prostate cancer, among others. ED can be a contributing factor to a couple's infertility, and Viagra may help overcome this issue, but effects on sperm quality are not well established.

Why this recent interest in ED, a syndrome hardly talked about publicly across cultures? Viagra and related drugs are not generally marketed as fertility-enhancing drugs, but rather as means to improve male sexual performance and a couple's sexual satisfaction. With the septuagenarian Bob Dole advertising them initially, it spoke to the high frequency of ED in elderly men, but later advertisements featured sports figures such as the baseball player Rafael Palmeiro or NASCAR drivers in cars at a race as the announcer says, "Gentlemen, start your engines." One advertisement, which was subsequently withdrawn, showed a man with V-shape horns taking Viagra to "get back to mischief." The association of young men with ED drugs became clear with evidence of recreational use of such drugs among college-age males. It is worth noting that the surge of interest in Viagra has led to both inappropriate prescriptions and a lack of close attention to the health risks associated with taking the drug. Older couples, and now attractive women alone, are used in ED drug advertisements, presumably as an attempt to pair these drugs with couples and women's sexual pleasure.

Studies of the effectiveness of ED drugs such as Viagra have been conducted in several countries throughout the world. With their proliferation, and with the enormous profits to be made by global sales of such pharmaceuticals, important questions are raised. In the United States, for example, it has been argued that ED drug promotion is consistent with an emphasis on "performance" in general and that it creates new standards for what constitutes normal male sexual function across the life cycle (Loe 2006). In doing so, ED was created as a "problem" in need of a pharmacological "solution." Furthermore, it serves to emphasize male sexuality, whereas drug advertisements related to female sexuality tended to emphasize their reproductive health (e.g., contraceptives).

In 2012 the U.S. Food and Drug Administration (FDA) identified female sexual dysfunction as one of 20 disease areas of high priority. In 2015 it approved flibanserin (sold under the brand name Addyi) to treat "hypoactive sexual desire disorder," a move that has been seen by some as medicalization of female sexuality in the service of selling more drugs. Unlike Viagra, Addyi must be taken daily and was originally approved as an antidepressant, and it also has a relatively low effectiveness rate of 8%–13%, compared to over 70% for Viagra (Lue 2000; Moynihan and Mintzes 2010). In 2019 the

FDA required a label on Addyi warning that it should not be taken with alcohol due to the risk of hypotension, and in the same year approved another drug, bremelanotide, marketed under the name Vylessi, which is injected under the skin before sex. Only about 8% more women reported an increase in sexual desire after taking Vylessi compared to those taking a placebo and about 40% experienced nausea (U.S. Food and Drug Administration (2019). Suffice it to say that sexual desire (to be treated with Addyi or Vylessi) and sexual function (to be treated with Viagra) are two different aspects of sexuality, with the latter being more tractable to pharmaceutical treatment. See more on ED and aging in the next chapter.

FEMALE GENITAL CUTTING

A practice that has relevance for female reproductive health is **female genital cutting** (FGC), also referred to as female circumcision or female genital mutilation. Genital cutting encompasses a range of procedures that vary in the extent to which parts of the female genitalia are removed. It often occurs as part of initiation rites around the time of menarche, but it may occur earlier or after a woman's first birth. In its simplest forms, only the clitoris or clitoral hood is removed (**clitoridectomy**). More extensive is **excision**, in which the clitoris and part or all of the labia minora are removed. The most radical form is **infibulation**, which involves the removal of the clitoris, the labia minora, and most or all of the labia majora. The remaining skin is stitched together, leaving a small opening for the passage of urine and menstrual blood. These stitches must be removed for intercourse and birth and are usually resutured after birth. Excision and clitoridectomy are the most common forms, with infibulation restricted to Sudan, Somalia, northeastern Kenya, Eritrea, and parts of Mali and northern Nigeria. As Figure 6.8 shows, some countries, particularly in Northeast and West Africa, have a high prevalence, whereas FGC is virtually nonexistent in other African countries. There is also substantial variation by ethnic group within countries. FGC is also found in areas of the Middle East, Malaysia, and Indonesia, but it is not an Islamist practice. In its most recent report, UNICEF notes that the practice is becoming less common in many African countries, and there is less support for it among younger women (United Nations Children's Fund [UNICEF] 2013).

Local explanations for the practice of FGC include preparing a girl for marriage and increasing her marriageability, emphasizing a woman's femininity by reducing the likeness of her genitals to those of males, enhancing fertility, maintaining female purity and virginity, solidifying a girl's identity and membership within the group, or establishing the appropriate bounds of female sexuality. The pain associated with the genital cutting is widely acknowledged, yet that too is often an important aspect of its meaning: to demonstrate that a woman can bear pain, especially that of childbirth, which thereby confirms her womanhood. These are all crucial aspects of culture and women's participation in that culture, yet they are often challenged by groups working to eradicate FGC in the interest of protecting women's health. Ellen Gruenbaum noted that this medical view of FGC "implies not only that the practice is 'pathological,' but its solution might lie in a sort of campaign-style attack on the problem. Social customs, however, are not 'pathologies;' and such a view is a poor starting point for change since it is not one necessarily shared by the people whose customs are under attack" (Gruenbaum 1982,6).

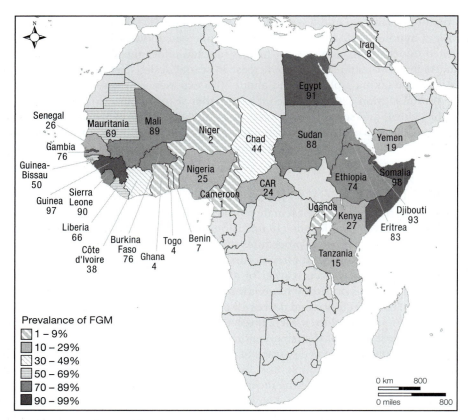

FIGURE 6.8   Prevalence of female genital cutting (FGC) across Africa.
Source: https://data.unicef.org/resources/fgm-statistical-overview-and-dynamics-of-change.
UNICEF.

The health consequences of these procedures are generally considered negative and extensive, although data supporting this conclusion are surprisingly rare. There is in all likelihood tremendous variation in these outcomes based on the conditions under which the procedure is performed, including instruments and hygiene, the skill of the practitioner, access to health facilities, the extensiveness of tissue removal, and social support. The WHO classifies the potential effects into short-term consequences, such as pain, infection, or hemorrhage, and long-term complications, such as difficulty in urination, urinary tract infections, menstrual difficulties, scarring, cysts, painful sex or sexual dysfunction, problems with pregnancy and birth, and emotional and sexual suffering. Existing data suggest that these complications occur, although at highly variable rates, and complications are more likely with more extensive FGC (Klein et al. 2018). It would seem that reduced sexual pleasure would result from any form of genital cutting, yet surveys routinely find that although some women report diminished sexual pleasure, others report either no difference or heightened sensations after such procedures. There are some older data indicating that infibulated women have lower fertility and are more likely to be divorced, perhaps because of higher rates of infertility, including tubal infertility possibly caused by PID (Balk 2000). A study in Sudan found that women who had experienced more extensive FGC had a higher prevalence of tubal factor infertility than did those with less extensive cutting (Almroth et al. 2005).

Much less attention has been paid to traditions of male circumcision, which may take place just after birth or around the time of puberty (Silverman 2004). **Circumcision** itself usually involves removal of the foreskin of the penis, although in some cultural contexts more extensive incisions are made. In the United States and Europe there is debate about the necessity of routine circumcision of infant boys (see the range of medical association policies at http://www.cirp.org/library/statements). Some see it as a surgical procedure conducted with neither informed consent by the child nor medical indication. Others emphasize the health benefits of the procedure in terms of reduced risk of STIs including HIV, urinary tract infections, and penile cancer, among others (see Kim et al. 2010 for a review). In contrast to female circumcision, which may be practiced to diminish sexual desire and promote fidelity (Anis et al. 2012), male circumcision is not practiced with the intention of, and does not appear to decrease sexual satisfaction (Morris and Krieger 2013). As anthropologist Eric Silverman notes, opponents of male circumcision have often used the same moral, legal, and human rights arguments that are deployed against FGC, yet it has not generated the same level of anthropological or international interest (Silverman 2004).

FGC has spawned an enormous and disparate literature. One end of the spectrum of writing is characterized by outrage at this practice, citing the "unnecessary" pain, suffering, and physiological damage incurred. This perspective is common among feminists, public health officials, international aid organizations, and Westerners in general. At the other end of the spectrum is a cultural relativist approach that maintains that this practice can only be fully understood within its cultural context, and it is viewed by women as desirable (Gruenbaum and Wirtz 2015). Thus, to adopt the position that FGC is uniformly unacceptable is ethnocentric and tantamount to undermining the integrity of cultural norms. A middle-of-the-road approach has emerged that focuses on reducing the short- and long-term harm associated with the practice— that is, reducing any harm associated with it—and providing alternative models for womanhood, status, sexuality, and marital relationships (Gruenbaum 2005; Shell-Duncan and Hernlund 2000). The very term female genital cutting is reflective of this attempt to create middle ground, rather than using the more value-laden older term genital mutilation or the term female circumcision, because the procedure is in many cases not analogous to male circumcision.

The debate surrounding FGC is unlikely to resolve soon. It has become entrenched in discussions of human rights, including the rights of women and children, the right to health and bodily integrity, freedom from torture, and the legal ramifications of these rights. It reveals an important paradox within the definition of well-being. If it is accepted that there are universal standards for well-being and that freedom from physical pain and suffering is part of that, but well-being also encompasses social and mental attributes, how is FGC to be evaluated? If it inflicts pain, suffering, and a nontrivial risk of physical dysfunction, yet also establishes social status, marriageability, and a crucial part of being a woman in a given society, is it a healthy or an unhealthy practice? In other words, if health is shaped and defined by culture, is FGC healthy? Is a Western standard appropriate, especially given widespread circumcision of infant boys (which has not always been done with anesthetic) and various forms of cosmetic surgeries that involve pain and at least temporary disfigurement, but are done to enhance conformity with social standards of beauty? Is it appropriate to focus so much attention on this one practice when so many other important health concerns face individuals in societies that practice FGC? The debate over FGC thus highlights the ethical dimensions of health and interventions that run counter to local beliefs and practices.

Anthropologist in Action: Ellen Gruenbaum

The medical anthropologist Ellen Gruenbaum (Figure 6.9) has spent many years studying the issue of female genital cutting in Sudan and Sierra Leone. In the many, often acrimonious, debates about this practice, she has maintained a steadfast commitment to understanding the meaning and importance of FGC in African cultures while simultaneously urging those who value the practice to take "harm reduction" measures to reduce the pain or risk of complications from the procedure.

As Dr. Gruenbaum has noted, "What ultimately is at stake [in the debate over FGC] is not only the improvement of children's and women's rights and health, but also the empowerment of the people affected by FGC, to develop their own approaches, setting their own priorities and mitigating the risks they face for abandoning the practices" (Gruenbaum 2005, 437). In some cases, girls have run away to safe houses run by anti-FGC groups, thereby displacing children from their families and

FIGURE 6.9 Ellen Gruenbaum (middle) studies female genital cutting in the Sudan and Sierra Leone. *Credit:* Photo courtesy of Ellen Gruenbaum.

undermining the family as a social institution. Thus, efforts to eradicate FGC can have unintended social consequences.

Dr. Gruenbaum has consulted for UNICEF on the topic of female genital cutting in both Sudan and Sierra Leone, noting the similarities and differences in the practice in the two regions. UNICEF has been involved because the FGC is most often done when girls are still defined as children. The reports she has produced for UNICEF are used to guide their efforts to protect child health, although UNICEF has changed its emphasis to female genital cutting as a human rights violation rather than specifically a child health issue, and as such continues to use the term female genital mutilation rather than "cutting."

PREGNANCY

In humans, the duration of pregnancy is around 38 weeks from conception (although a recent study suggested that rising temperatures may shorten this, as evidence shows that extreme heat accelerated some births in the United States by as much as two weeks over a 20-year period) (Barreca and Schaller 2020). For most women the course of pregnancy is "routine," although the experience is subject to individual and cultural variation ranging from intensive medical oversight involving numerous clinical appointments to little public notice of the woman's pregnant state or modification of behavior. In a medicalized context, pregnancy may be described with medical terminology—e.g., a "diagnosis" or "symptoms" of pregnancy—and medical care for all stages as well as birth is deemed essential. Pregnancy is a complex process to be sure, and it involves a variety of compromises between the well-being of the mother and that of the fetus. Aside from the obvious parameters of growing a baby (outlined in Chapter 5), pregnancy is characterized by some physiological and behavioral adaptations that serve to enhance birth outcome, but there are also cases where these pose some health challenges. These compromises are to be expected because the mother's body is now supporting a fetus that has different physiological requirements (and different genes) than she does.

One example is the experience of nausea and vomiting in early pregnancy (**NVP**). Rates of NVP vary across populations, with 35% to 90% of women reporting it, but with averages clustered around 65%–70% (McKerracher et al. 2015). For most women who experience it, NVP lasts only through the first trimester. In Western cultures it is sufficiently ubiquitous that literary or film references to a woman vomiting can be interpreted as a sign of pregnancy. Several authors have argued that the experience of NVP (sometimes also called "morning sickness," although it is not confined to the morning hours), which is characterized by food aversions, nausea, and vomiting, is related to the high sensitivity of the embryo to toxins (Pepper and Roberts 2006; Profet 1992). Flaxman and Sherman (2000) and Profet (1992) have argued that NVP has evolved as a mechanism to protect the embryo from toxins that the mother might ingest during early pregnancy. The mother has fully functioning detoxification mechanisms such that these toxins are not deleterious to her, but the embryo does not, and is therefore more vulnerable to their teratogenic (toxic) effects. If the mother avoids them because their odors offend her or she becomes nauseous and vomits after she eats them, the embryo is not exposed to them. Food aversions, nausea, or vomiting may appear to be problematic insofar as they reduce food consumption or nutrient intake, but the nutrient needs of early pregnancy are not markedly greater than the nonpregnant state. Evidence supporting the NVP–toxin hypothesis is that women who experience NVP have lower rates of miscarriage and premature birth, and their infants show lower rates of congenital malformations and better fetal growth (Koren et al. 2014). Thus, although NVP is hardly enjoyable, it may be a sign of healthy embryological development and attempts to stop it through medical interventions (e.g., antinausea drugs) may undermine its adaptive attributes.

Food aversions of early pregnancy may also stem from the fact that the mother's immune system is suppressed during pregnancy. This must occur because the developing embryo produces antigens that are not the same as those the mother herself produces. These "foreign" proteins derive from the father's genes. For gestation to proceed, the mother's immune system must be suppressed to some extent to prevent her from generating a response to the foreign proteins expressed by the embryo. However, immune suppression carries the risk of maternal infection, which itself can be detrimental to embryological development. Thus, it is interesting to note that across cultures, the focus of most food aversions of early pregnancy tends to be animal products, which would be more likely sources of infectious pathogens than plants (Fessler 2002). Restricted iron intake deriving from meat aversion may also reduce infection because many pathogens require iron to proliferate.

Along with food aversions and NVP, a dietary phenomenon widely recognized across societies is the craving of specific foods, or in many cases, nonfood items such as clay. Daniel Fessler (2002) has argued that many foods craved by pregnant women may in fact enhance immune function. Cravings for fruit are especially common, and many fruits are rich in vitamin C, which can play an important role in modulating immune function. Women may consider cravings manifestations of the fetus's desires or needs; if they are not satisfied, the infant may be born "marked" in some way.

Cravings for and consumption of specific kinds of clay during the first trimester of pregnancy may also be beneficial. Clay consumption is surprisingly widespread, occurring in cultures throughout the world (Young 2011). Most of the research done on clay consumption in pregnancy has focused on the practice in sub-Saharan African societies and among African Americans in the United States. Because clay particles have a large surface area, they have the ability to bind foodborne toxins, thereby preventing them from being absorbed into maternal circulation (Johns and Duquette 1991). If a woman ate clay during the first trimester of pregnancy, the embryo could thus also be protected from foodborne toxins. Clay is also reported to quell the unpleasant gastrointestinal symptoms of NVP, which may provide a proximate motivating factor supporting its consumption. Because they have these properties, kaolinic clays are important components of many over-the-counter antidiarrheal and antinausea medications. Clay consumption may play another role in pregnancy as a dietary supplement—many clays that women report craving have relatively high calcium concentrations. Wiley and Katz (1998) found that women in African cultures who did not consume dairy products were much more likely to consume clay than women in cultures that made extensive use of dairy products. This suggests that in addition to the benefits associated with clay consumption in the first trimester, clay may also provide minerals such as calcium that are valuable to fetal growth in the second trimester.

Rules about appropriate dietary behavior during pregnancy are common to most cultures. These include food restrictions and taboos, as well as recommendations to consume certain foods. Tabooed foods are those considered dangerous to fetal physical or psychological health, whereas prescribed foods may enhance fetal health and growth or facilitate delivery. These dietary rules are consistent with ethnomedical understandings of the reproductive process and the role that food plays in maintaining health. A theme common to populations with ethnomedical systems based on a humoral conceptualization of the body is the consumption or avoidance of foods considered "heating" or "cooling" to a pregnant woman's body. In Latin America and India, pregnancy is considered heating to the body, whereas in Southeast Asia, pregnancy is a period in which a woman is cooler, although the body becomes hotter as the pregnancy progresses. Food avoidances are in sync with these conceptions of the body as hot or cold; in Southeast Asia strongly heating foods are to be avoided, in part because they are also thought to induce a miscarriage (Laderman 1983). Diet can also affect the characteristics of the child—if lighter skin is desired, as is often the case in southern India, for example, white or yellowish foods are preferred over darker-colored foods. Many women also prefer to have smaller babies, fearing the difficulty and pain of birthing a large baby, and choose to eat less (Nichter and Nichter 1983). The cultural logic of this practice must be understood by biomedical practitioners and public health workers concerned about the high prevalence of low birth weight in India.

Humoral Medicine: Concepts of Hot and Cold

In ancient Greek medicine, the body was conceptualized as having four humors, or fluids: blood, phlegm, yellow bile, and black bile. Each had its own qualities: blood was hot and moist, phlegm was cold and moist, yellow bile was hot and dry, and black bile was cold and dry. A balance of these humors was considered essential to health and disease stemmed from the body being too hot, dry, cold, or moist. Rebalancing the humors could be done through dietary modifications, among other interventions. Foods themselves were perceived as having humoral qualities; hence, if one's body was too hot, cooling foods would be prescribed and vice versa.

Humoral medicine was elaborated in European, Arabic (Middle East), Ayurvedic (South Asia), and Chinese (East Asia) medical practices. Hence, conceptualizations of health based on humoral balance are widespread. The humoral concept spread to the Americas during the colonial period and remains common in Latin America. Although each system has its own classification of humors and foods that affect them, basic ideas of hot and cold, dry and moist appear to be common to all of them. Importantly, hot and cold do not necessarily index actual temperature, but rather the qualities of "cooling" or "heating" in the body that have both physiological and psychological correlates.

In Western cultures humoral ideas about health remain, although less in formal medical practice than in linguistic forms and common disease-related practices. The common "cold," for example, gets its name from its association with

winter and cold weather, although it may be associated with a fever. Cucumbers are "cool" and linguistically marked by phrases such as "she's cool as a cucumber," meaning imperturbable and calm in demeanor. In contrast, people who are quick to anger are "hot tempered."

As noted earlier, different life stages can have different humoral qualities. Mark and Mimi Nichter (1983) have described how pregnancy is viewed as a hot condition in southern India. Foods that are considered heating, such as papaya, pineapple, pumpkin, bitter gourd, and wheat, are to be avoided by pregnant women. Too much heat can result in the loss of the pregnancy. Instead, women are advised to eat cooling foods—although not so many that the body becomes too cool. Rice, which is the staple food of the diet, is neutral in its qualities. Indeed, staple foods are rarely associated with strong humoral properties. Of particular importance in Nichter and Nichter's study in southern India was that pregnant women were often prescribed iron tablets to prevent or treat anemia, which were considered very heating to the body. Furthermore, the tablets were thought to interfere with digestion (although liquid supplements or "tonics" were acceptable) and women avoided taking them for fear of their deleterious effects on the pregnancy (Nichter and Nichter 1983). They were further avoided because they were advertised as producing a big baby, something many women wished to avoid because of the difficulties it might pose for birth.

Another physiological change that occurs during pregnancy is insulin resistance. Recall from Chapter 4 that insulin resistance occurs when cells become less responsive to the effects of insulin, which stimulates the uptake of glucose. In most pregnancies, insulin resistance begins near mid-pregnancy and progresses through the third trimester to levels seen in individuals with type 2 diabetes. When blood glucose levels rise to a higher level, **gestational diabetes** is diagnosed. Gestational diabetes occurs in about 7% of pregnancies and is more common among women who are older, obese, have a family history of type 2 diabetes, have a history of delivering large babies, or who are of non-European ancestry (Setji et al. 2005). Gestational diabetes appears to result from a combination of increased maternal fat stores and the effects of hormonal products of the placenta.

This form of diabetes is unique to pregnancy and resolves on its own after birth. But why might women who otherwise have no risk factors for diabetes develop it during pregnancy, and why does insulin resistance occur during healthy pregnancies? David Haig (1993) suggested that it might result from a kind of resource conflict between the mother and the fetus. That is, although the mother and the fetus can be said to have the same "goal"—that of a healthy birth outcome—their genetic interests are not exactly the same because they share only half of their genes. The fetus may "demand" more resources than the woman "wants" to give; this may result from fetal genes derived from the father that attempt to manipulate the mother's resources. In fact, it appears that fetal genes derived from the father play a larger role than those of the mother in the growth of the placenta, through which the fetus receives nutrients from the mother. The placenta can also secrete hormones into maternal circulation, and alterations in placenta function may result from maternal–fetal conflict (Fowden and Moore 2012). In this case, the fetus may be able to increase maternal blood glucose levels by stimulating the release of hormones that increase maternal insulin resistance. This keeps maternal blood glucose levels higher longer, thereby increasing the flow of glucose to the fetus. The mother counteracts this process by increasing her own insulin production, which in turn exacerbates insulin resistance among her cells. In other words, there is a fetal attempt to increase glucose flow across the placenta and a maternal counter attempt to redirect glucose into her own cells. If this process escalates, gestational diabetes can result. Thus, rather than seeing gestational diabetes as only a pathology of pregnancy, it can be viewed as one of the compromises between fetal and maternal health that play out during pregnancy.

A similar model may help explain **pregnancy-induced hypertension** (PIH). PIH is diagnosed when a pregnant woman's blood pressure remains elevated (usually >140/90 mm Hg) for a sustained period of time, and it usually occurs during the second half of pregnancy. If left uncontrolled, PIH can progress to preeclampsia, a potentially life-threatening condition characterized by hypertension and protein excretion in the urine, or full eclampsia, which can result in death. Because the rate of nutrient flow to the fetus is in part caused by maternal blood pressure forcing blood through the arteries, if the fetus could increase that pressure it could divert more resources to itself. The mother, in turn, may try to restrict resource flow to the fetus by reducing blood pressure. Haig has argued that if resource flow to the fetus is constrained by maternal undernutrition, a viable fetal response is to try to manipulate maternal blood pressure to capture more of the mother's resources. The mechanism by which this could occur is not well described. As Haig notes, "The conflict hypothesis suggests that mothers reduce vascular resistance during early pregnancy to ration fetal nutrients, and that the subsequent increase in vascular resistance represents the changing 'balance of power' as the fetus grows larger. A corollary is that placental factors contribute to the increase in maternal cardiac output" (Haig 1993, 515). Adding support for this hypothesis is evidence showing that PIH is associated with higher birth weights (Xiong and Fraser 2004), especially among women with low prepregnancy weight or low weight gain during pregnancy. Although PIH can be deleterious if it develops into preeclampsia or eclampsia, in most cases it may simply represent one of the many compromises of pregnancy.

BIRTH

Birth represents the literal and figurative emergence of a new individual into a community of siblings, kin, and neighbors and the biological transition from complete physiological symbiosis with the mother to a more fluid, yet still dependent relationship on her and other caregivers. The birth process for humans is unusual compared with that of other mammals, or even other primates, and may have given rise to the need for social support during the birth event (Rosenberg and Trevathan 2002; Trevathan 2015). For most quadrupedal animals, the pelvis is relatively flat, so the baby's exit is constrained only by the dimensions of the pelvic outlet. However, humans are bipedal, and to accommodate this form of locomotion the pelvis has a distinctive narrow bowl shape that supports upper body weight while walking. The fact that humans also have wide shoulders (a legacy of our ape past) and very large brains complicates the birth process further. The human pelvis cannot widen substantially to accommodate a baby with these characteristics without compromising locomotion; this has been referred to as the "obstetric dilemma." The net outcome of these changes has been that human babies are born at an earlier stage of maturity, such that much of their brain growth occurs postnatally. It may also be that there are energetic constraints that contribute to this because maternal metabolism may be taxed to its limits by the growth of a large fetus (Dunsworth et al. 2012). Compared with ape newborns, human infants are helpless at birth; chimpanzee babies can cling to their mother's fur from birth, but it takes several months for a human infant to be able to hold on to its mother securely without support.

As Figure 6.10 illustrates, there is a much tighter fit between the fetus's head and the pelvic bones of humans during birth compared with that of chimpanzees, which makes for a more difficult birthing process for humans. Furthermore, during the process of human birth, the baby descends into the birth canal head first, but because the pelvis is bowl shaped, midway through the birth canal it must make a 90-degree turn and face the back. At this point the shoulders are sideways, and before the final exit out of the birth canal the head is turned to the side so that the shoulders are oriented front to back to fit the widest dimension of the birth canal, as shown in Figure 6.11. The baby is generally born facing backward. It is important to recognize that the shape and size of the birth canal varies greatly among women. African women's pelvises show the most variability (similar to other traits), and genetic drift and migration seem to have shaped the current distribution of variation in birth canal dimensions (Betti and

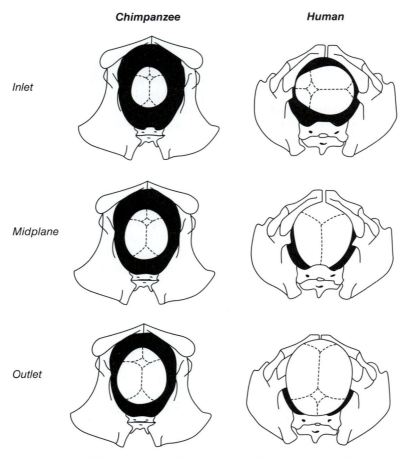

FIGURE 6.10   Pelvises of chimpanzee and human in relation to the size of the fetus's head. Black areas represent empty space between the head and pelvic structures.
Source: From W. Trevathan. 1999. Evolutionary obstetrics. In *Evolutionary Medicine*, ed. W. Trevathan, E. O. Smith, and J. J. McKenna, 183–207. New York: Oxford University Press. By permission of Oxford University Press.

Manica 2018). As Betti and Manica (2018, 7) conclude, "Given the geographical differences in canal shape among modern populations showed by this study, a wider range of variation in childbirth might be expected in modern multi-ethnic societies, and should be taken into account in obstetric training and practice."

The anthropologist Wenda Trevathan (2015) has argued that a laboring woman is in need of assistance during birth to guide the baby out, clear the baby's breathing passage, untwist the umbilical cord, or lift the baby to the mother's breast. Unlike most female mammals that give birth alone and often seek solitude for the event, humans may be predisposed to seek help during the birth process, and Trevathan suggests that midwifery may have appeared as early as 5 million years ago with the evolution of

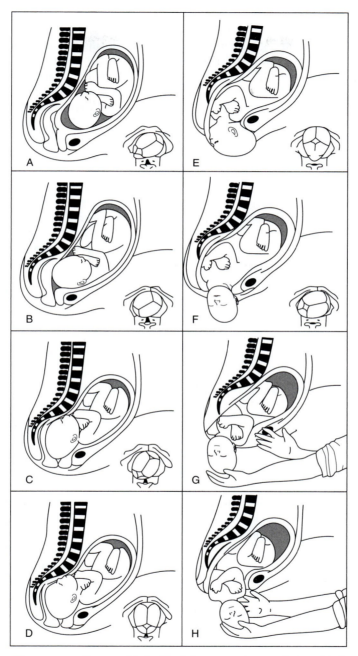

FIGURE 6.11   The process of human birth. The baby must rotate and turn as it descends the birth canal. As a result, it is born facing backward.
Source: From W. Trevathan. 1999. "Evolutionary obstetrics." In *Evolutionary Medicine*, ed. W. Trevathan, E. O. Smith, and J. J. McKenna, 183–207. New York: Oxford University Press. By permission of Oxford University Press

bipedalism. Importantly, birth assistants provide not only physical support for the birthing woman but also emotional support to allay the increased pain and anxiety associated with birth among humans. Social support during the pregnancy itself also enhances the outcome of the birth (Pike 2005).

The obstetric dilemma likely contributes to relatively high maternal or fetal mortality rates in humans. In 2017 there were ~295,000 maternal deaths from pregnancy and birth-related causes across the globe, including postpartum bleeding, infection, delivery complications, and preeclampsia (see data at: https://www.who.int/gho/), although the maternal mortality ratio (maternal deaths per 100,000 births) has declined by 35% since 2000. Most of these occurred in resource-poor countries, but it is worth noting that the United States has the highest rate among wealthy countries (19/100,000 vs. 4/100,000 in Denmark). Although the human legacy for birth may make the process more complicated than it is for other mammals and increases the need for companionship and assistance at birth, many contemporary birthing practices work against, not in support of, these considerations. Around the world, about 80% of all births are estimated to occur with a "skilled professional," regardless of whether they occur in a health facility or at home. This percentage has increased from 60% in the early 2000s and the World Health Organization attributes some of the decline in maternal mortality to this increase (data available here: https://www.who.int/gho/). Although having skilled attendants enhances birth outcomes in many ways, the conditions imposed by more medicalized births may contribute to other kinds of problems. For example, most hospital births have women lying down during labor and delivery, whereas a more upright or squatting position would allow for an easier passage down the birth canal with the assistance of gravity. A woman may be separated from her partner or supportive kin or friends, increasing her fear and anxiety and heightening the experience of pain. The fetus's condition is frequently monitored during labor, and this often results in a woman being confined to her bed rather than up and about. These all contribute to increased pain, which in turn results in greater administration of anesthesia. Deliveries taking "too long" rapidly transition to intravenous synthetic hormones to speed up and strengthen contractions or surgical interventions. In sum, many women come to fear birth as a process in which things can "go wrong" and are reticent to even imagine a delivery outside of a hospital context in which technological backup is readily available. As anthropologists Davis-Floyd and Cheyney note, "Once birth becomes viewed as inherently risky, then it appears as if all measures *must* be taken to keep it safe. Yet birth, especially among healthy, well-nourished women, is not necessarily or generally risky business—most babies are born healthy to healthy mothers, no matter what impediments we throw at the birth process" (Davis-Floyd and Cheyney 2019, 6).

In the United States, almost one-third of births currently occur by cesarean section ("C-section"), where the baby is surgically extracted from the uterus. Among other countries, Brazil has the highest rate, with more than half of all births done this way (Molina et al. 2015). In a letter to the journal *Birth*, the prominent birth advocate Sheila Kitzinger noted that obstetricians in London consider elective cesarean the safest method of delivery for modern mothers and babies, and some women, including obstetric staff and obstetricians' wives, are booking cesareans as soon as they know they are pregnant. As one obstetrician noted, "There are great advantages to having a cesarean. You can choose who is going to do the delivery. And it is marvelous for people who want the social convenience of knowing exactly when they are delivering. It is a good option for women who are worried about pain and about possible bladder damage or sexual dysfunction." He went on to claim that if a woman "is older or it is to be her last pregnancy, an elective caesarean is a better option and less risk to the baby." Kitzinger further writes,

> There is an argument for caesareans when a doctor wants to protect himself against being sued by a patient, particularly in cases where there has been a difficult delivery before. There are also financial considerations. With a normal pregnancy and normal delivery, you can't claim off your health insurance policy unless it is a European or American one with higher premiums and less exclusions. But there is an inducement for the patient to opt for a caesarean if the insurance company will pay, because the whole process is then cheaper for the patient. (Kitzinger 1998, 5)

Although Kitzinger's letter referenced practices in the United Kingdom, similar factors boost C-section rates in many other countries, including China and Brazil. In private hospitals in Brazil, more than 80% of births are cesarean, which are more convenient for doctors and more can be scheduled (and billed) per day, so women may be "encouraged" to deliver this way, whereas women may prefer them to reduce the risk of pelvic floor problems or to reduce the pain associated with labor and childbirth (Barros et al. 2015). C-sections are, in many cases, non-evidence based interventions (along with routine episiotomies for first births) (Sadler et al. 2016). A recent analysis of global C-section rates found that national cesarean delivery rates of up to ~19 per 100 live births were associated with lower maternal or neonatal mortality at the national level (Molina et al. 2015), suggesting that countries should aim for this rate because there was no further reduction (or increase) in maternal or neonatal mortality with C-section rates higher than 19%.

In June 2015 the Brazilian government announced a new policy to reduce the C-section rate by requiring doctors to explain the risks, obtain a woman's consent, and provide a rationale for it. But concern over high C-section rates, particularly in Latin America, also raised the visibility of the larger issue of "obstetric violence." This includes abuse, mistreatment, or neglect of pregnant and birthing women, and, in part, reflects gender inequalities that are particularly acute among poor or marginalized populations (Rutherford et al. 2019; Sadler et al. 2016). It includes performing procedures—many unnecessary—without informed consent, abuse (physical, sexual, verbal), stigma, discrimination, failure to meet professional standards of care, poor rapport between women and providers, and health system conditions and constraints (Bohren et al. 2015). Obstetric violence is considered by the WHO to be a violation of human rights, and in 2014 it issued a statement on the prevention and elimination of disrespect and abuse during facility-based childbirth, asserting that every woman had the right to access dignified and respectful health care.

How do medicalized birth practices compare with birth in societies with low rates of C-sections or hospital births? Most cultures have some tradition of midwifery. Some midwives are trained through apprenticeships or have biomedical training; others are simply those recognized for their experience in handling deliveries. Some 50%–90% of births in low-income countries are overseen by traditional birth attendants (TBAs) (Wilson et al. 2011), who are almost always women who have had experience in birthing their own children. Descriptions of births attended by such women inevitably focus on the atmosphere of social and emotional support for the laboring woman, encouragement of her active participation in the process, and the use of nontechnological means to facilitate the delivery and relieve pain, such as trying different positions, massage, breathing techniques, and so on (Davis-Floyd et al. 2009).

In her classic ethnographic work, the late anthropologist Brigitte Jordan provides an illuminating description of Doña Juana, a 60-year-old Mayan midwife from the Yucatan, Mexico (Figure 6.12). Doña Juana received her training as a midwife from a local physician and also a midwifery course given by the Mexican government in Mexico City. Her mother was also a midwife, but it was not clear how much of her craft Doña Juana learned from her. Doña Juana offers prenatal care to pregnant women in the area, which is conducted at the pregnant woman's house. Throughout each visit there is casual discussion intermixed with exchanges of information relevant to the birth. Doña Juana gains an appreciation for who in the household can be counted on to help with the birth, a woman's pain sensitivity, issues of modesty, importance of traditional rituals to the woman, and so on. These conversations occur while Doña Juana massages the woman's abdomen (to assess the position of the fetus) and back. All of this is done in the presence of household members. Births take place at home, and Doña Juana describes how labor is likely to proceed. As Jordan explained,

> Whenever possible her teaching is demonstrative rather than verbal. She not only *tells* the woman that she will have to push with all her strength but *shows* her, and so realistic is her performance that invariably somebody will make a joke about Doña Juana being the one who is having the baby. Often the woman's attendants join in too, each one of them demonstrating her own favorite method of giving birth. Doña Juana says that every woman must *buscar la forma* (find her own style). For her, the midwife's function is to assist with whatever method the woman comes to find best. (Jordan 1993, 33)

Births most often take place in a chair or hammock, with attendants centrally involved in assisting the woman during the birth, "urging, encouraging, scolding, demanding that she get back to work" (Jordan 1993, 38). Doña Juana uses sterilized instruments such as tongs, a rubber bulb to clear mucus from the baby's breathing passages, and scissors to cut the umbilical cord. The baby is then bathed, swaddled, and given to the mother. After everything is cleaned up and the mother and baby are settled, a meal is served, and Doña Juana's fee is negotiated. Doña Juana also follows up with postpartum care.

Doña Juana blends traditional and biomedical practices, and she is a well respected midwife, who also has a good working relationship with the local obstetrician, whom she will call on if there are complications. This situation contrasts with other traditions of midwifery, however. In South Asia, the *dai*, or midwife, is a woman of low caste, whose job is mainly to deal with the pollution associated with the birth and its products. She is not accorded any particular authority over the birth process, which is directed by female relatives (Jeffery et al. 1988). In this case, it is older women in the household who have authority over the birth, and they may themselves have extensive experience in delivering babies.

Throughout the world a biomedical perspective on birth is becoming routine. As occurred in Europe and the United States, traditional midwives are being replaced by

FIGURE 6.12 Brigitte Jordan interviewing midwife Doña Juana in the Yucatan.
Credit: Photo courtesy of Brigitte Jordan.

medical birth "authorities" with professional degrees, specialized knowledge, use of intensive and expensive interventionist technologies, and a set of expectations about what constitutes a normal or "appropriate" birth. Indeed, these expectations often involve arbitrary standards for the timing of the progression of labor, cervical dilation, and assessment of fetal distress (Rutherford et al. 2019). The more informal knowledge and experience of midwives are discounted as "old fashioned" and, more damningly, "dangerous." Lucia Guerra-Reyes describes how traditional birth attendants (*parteras*) in Peru have been replaced by biomedically trained midwives and births in health centers have been deemed the only "safe" form of childbirth (Guerra-Reyes 2019). Although Peru's Intercultural Birth Program (IBP) ostensibly values the beliefs, practices, and knowledge of indigenous women, it has largely marginalized TBAs and asserted biomedical authority over birthing. As Guerra-Reyes writes, "The experience of giving birth under the IBP, like most other medical encounters, still serves to assert that all the knowledge that really counts comes from biomedicine, that 'culture' is a temporary barrier to progress, and the only people who have 'culture' are the backward, pre-modern, indigenous Peruvians, whose overarching need is to be modernized" (Guerra-Reyes 2019, 212–213).

With the ascendancy and professionalization of obstetrics in the late nineteenth and early twentieth centuries, midwifery was outlawed in many states in the United States, and home deliveries by midwives continue to be illegal in some areas. Yet evidence suggests that labor is shorter, C-section and other intervention rates are lower, and maternal outcomes are better with midwife-attended births, which Rutherford and colleagues maintain are more in keeping with the evolutionary model for human birth as described earlier by Wenda Trevathan (Rutherford et al. 2019). Interestingly, in the United States, there is currently a trend toward more midwife-assisted home births, with an increase of 41% from 2004 to 2012. Home births still represent less than 2% of all births, however (American College of Nurse-Midwives 2015). A review indicated that planned home births were associated with lower rates of prematurity, low birth weight, and neonatal complications and had perinatal mortality rates similar to hospital births. But, for reasons that are not clear, planned home births had higher neonatal mortality rates than planned hospital births, although the absolute rate was very low (Wax et al. 2010). Ironically, as midwifery and home births enjoy a resurgence in wealthy countries as alternatives to a highly medicalized (and expensive) birth, home-based births attended by local midwives have been disparaged in poorer countries, where rhetoric about unhygienic conditions and unsafe practices is common (Guerra-Reyes 2019).

The management of birth in low- and high-income countries is in flux, with movement toward and away from biomedical interventions (Davis-Floyd and Cheyney 2019). It is worth noting that in their 2005 World Health Report, the WHO reported that training programs for traditional birth attendants, which they had advocated in the 1970s, had largely failed to have any positive impact on improved birth outcomes (World Health Organization 2005). They noted, "the strategy is now increasingly seen as a failure," but also recognized that part of the problem was the lack of understanding of the important social (as opposed to medical) roles that traditional birth attendants played. Instead, the WHO advocates that births be attended by skilled health professionals and occur in the hospital if at all possible. However, studies of TBAs found that programs that providing them with training and support significantly reduced perinatal and neonatal deaths (Sibley et al. 2012; Wilson et al. 2011). It remains unclear what types of training are particularly effective.

MOTHERING

After birth, the relationship between the mother and baby enters a new period of negotiated care. Mothers are not the only individuals who can be involved in infant care, and their care strategies are very much influenced by their kin, neighbors, husbands, work obligations, economic constraints, and cultural expectations of what constitutes appropriate "mothering" (Hrdy 2009). Mothering is generally taken to mean nurturing behavior; a concern with the care, feeding, and protection of children; and sometimes the subsuming of a woman's individual interests to those of her child. There has been much debate over how much of this is instinctive to women and how much is the result of sociocultural influence. As Sarah Blaffer Hrdy asserts, however, mothering across mammals encompasses a wide range of behaviors that include not only those just listed, but also the purposeful neglect or outright killing of babies born at importune times or with undesirable characteristics (Hrdy 1999). What is "natural" about nurturing behavior varies considerably and all mammalian mothers face various challenges to raising offspring, and sometimes it is not in their best interests to invest in some or all offspring at a given moment.

The discussion of mothering and the idea that there was an "instinctive" bond between mothers and infants is related to attachment, a core concept in modern psychology. **Attachment theory**, first proposed by the British psychiatrist John Bowlby in the 1950s, posited that infants are born with a drive to "attach" to one caregiver, most often the mother (Bowlby 1969). This, Bowlby argued, would be adaptive because infants who did not engage in behaviors to elicit the attention of a caregiver (crying, smiling, reaching) would have been at risk of predation in the environment of evolutionary adaptedness, a phrase that Bowlby coined. Mothers who respond reliably to such cues foster a sense of *secure attachment* among their infants, which then grows into a strong emotional tie and provides infants with a sense that the world is a safe and reliable place. As this process unfolds, the emotional connection between mothers and infants grows and they can be said to be attached to each other. Bowlby proposed that this relationship is established within the first year of life. Infants whose mothers (or other primary caretaker) do not respond reliably and reasonably to them may develop an emotional insecurity, a sense that the world is precarious, unsafe, and unpredictable. Thus, infants' attachment experiences give them important clues about the nature of their environment, and some anthropologists and psychologists argue that different forms of attachment (secure vs. insecure) can be considered adaptations to different environmental conditions, remembering that adaptation does not equate with overall mental or physical health (Chisholm 1993).

Bowlby's model has the infant as the initiator of the attachment process, but two American pediatricians, Marshall Klaus and John Kennell, proposed that the mother, too, "bonds" with her infant and that there is a critical period shortly after birth during which the mother must have close contact with the infant for her "mothering instincts" to be stimulated (Klaus and Kennell 1976). Although such critical periods for maternal bonding and newborn imprinting on the mother have been observed in some organisms, the consensus seems to be that they are of limited relevance to humans. Nonetheless, popular notions of mothering and maternal–infant attachment tend to conflate Bowlby's and Klaus and Kennell's ideas, interpreting mother–infant "bonding" as a natural, universal phenomenon in which mothers and infants are biologically driven to carry out an attachment script.

Perhaps the most compelling illustration of the constraints on maternal nurturing comes from Nancy Scheper-Hughes's book *Death without Weeping* (1992), which describes her research with mothers in a terribly impoverished shantytown of northeast Brazil. In her fieldwork, Scheper-Hughes was struck by the apparent lack of "maternal sentiment" displayed by the mothers. This was particularly evident in their attitudes toward ill and dying infants, which she described as characterized by pity, but not the expected painful emotions of sadness or grief. This apparent indifference led Scheper-Hughes to question the "naturalness" of nurturing and to uncover the forces that led to this "other" maternal script. Living in extreme poverty, where life is precarious for all but the hardiest, strong emotional attachment to infants whose likelihood of survival was slim would be unwise at best, and at worst, could potentially destroy a woman's own will to survive. Only infants who exhibited signs of spunk—a "will to live" (e.g., attachment-eliciting behaviors)—were worth the emotional investment. The devaluation of life fostered by wretched economic realities is internalized by women, whose sense of self-esteem and value was deeply eroded. They said they have "nothing to give" to their fragile babies. Their breast milk, the lifeblood of young infants, was considered of little worth, leading them to abandon nursing in favor of highly diluted powdered milk, often mixed with contaminated water. Ideally, powdered milk would be provisioned by the infant's father, a sign of his interest in and commitment to the mother and child, even if it came erratically. The net result contributed to the alarmingly high rate of infant mortality to which mothers appeared to respond with only minimal emotion.

Scheper-Hughes's work powerfully illuminates the ways in which maternal nurturing is shaped by economic exigencies and the disenfranchisement of women from the larger society, internalized as an inability to give anything of value to their infants (see also Chin and Solomonik 2009 for a description of this phenomenon in the United States). It might be tempting to blame mothers for the neglect of their children, but it is important to understand the ways in which their ability to nurture is radically limited. That said, Scheper-Hughes's interpretation that selective neglect, enabled maternal detachment in the face of infant death, has been challenged by another anthropologist, Marilyn Nations, and her colleagues who also work in northeast Brazil (Nations et al. 2015). They argued that "the selective maternal neglect theory fails to peel away each of the contextual constraints of the ultimate and intermediate tiers of causes of infant death to unmask the stifled bereavement that our informants claim to abide daily … our mothers' stories epitomize the fruits of real maternal investment in each of their children" (Nations et al. 2015, 615). In Nations and colleagues' work, the complex historical, political, economic, ecological, biological, social, and spiritual conditions of northeast Brazilian life that contribute to infant death and restrict public displays of maternal grief are described. Based on mothers' stories of profound grief over a child's death, "we found an elaborate local moral world that sculpts the maternal responses to child illness and death. And according to one of our interviewees, Pipiu, 'The scar of an infant death remains etched into the face of each grieving mother'" (Nations et al. 2015, 626).

What constitutes "appropriate" maternal behavior in relation to infant health takes different forms across cultures, and a reasonable prediction is that when women have both economic resources and some degree of decision-making autonomy, they generally act in ways that foster infant health. Indeed, the several UN agencies concerned with reproductive health emphasize the clear connection between women's empowerment and maternal and child health (United Nations 2012) but there are so many contexts that conspire against this ideal. In South Asia, a new mother has little authority to act on her or her child's behalf but must bend to the will of her husband or mother-in-law, who may not have her or her child's interests at heart (Jeffery et al. 1988). Instead, the interests of the patrilineage or household prevail and support for a given child is withdrawn. Additionally, it is not appropriate for women to travel alone to a clinic, further restricting their ability to seek care for a child. In the United States, the abandonment of babies reported in grizzly detail by the media is often done by women in desperate straits—those too young or too scared, those who hide their pregnancy from their families and friends, or those who have no support for child-rearing.

In another example that highlights the cultural and public health context for mothering, Aaron Denham and colleagues (2010) investigated the death of "spirit children" in northern Ghana. Spirit children are considered bush spirits born in human form; as such they are not considered "human." Furthermore, they are dangerous: "Once born, they will take over the house and destroy the family, through conflict, sickness, and death, only returning to the bush when satisfied" (Denham et al. 2010, 611). Although spirit children are heterogeneous in their characteristics, many had physical disabilities, acute or chronic illnesses, or behavioral tendencies such as excessive crying, indicative of their desire to destroy the family. After extensive diagnostic procedures, if the spirit child label is confirmed, the child is killed; since they are not considered human, it is not considered killing per se, but rather saving the lives of family members. The authors did not report maternal indifference, but concluded that

> because most spirit children are sick or disabled, elements of the spirit child phenomenon are connected to and exemplify the root public health issues confronting Nankani life: poverty, food insecurity, limited health care options, no support for disabled children, and the omnipresent need for more infant and maternal care and education. (Denham et al. 2010, 614)

On a final note, like the issue of FGC, this type of research calls into question anthropological ethics and cultural relativism. Should anthropologists intervene when a mother has clearly given up hope on a child? Should they take the child to a clinic? Scheper-Hughes faced this dilemma during her early Peace Corps work in Brazil. She took Zé, a lifeless toddler whose mother had just given birth to a "robust little tyke" and who was wasting away while his mother's attention was focused on the newborn, from his mother. Using the local expression, "Give me that child, for he'll never escape death in your house," she took the child to the local crèche for care. The women at the crèche advised her against this, saying they had seen many babies like Zé: "There was no sense in frustrating him so, for here was a child who was completely 'lifeless,' without any 'fight' at all" (Scheper-Hughes 1992, 343–344). Yet Scheper-Hughes persisted in her efforts and the little boy eventually began to eat and grow. He was returned to his mother, whose interest in her son resurfaced at his improved appearance. But Scheper-Hughes wondered if she had done the right thing:

> Could Zé ever be "right" again? Could he develop normally after the traumas he had been through? Worse, perhaps, were the traumas yet to come, as I would soon be returning him to Lordes in her miserable lean-to on the trash-littered Vultures' Path. Would he have been better off dead after all that I had put him through? And what of Lordes? Was this fair to her? She barely had enough to sustain herself and her newborn. (Scheper-Hughes 1992, 345)

BED-SHARING AND SUDDEN INFANT DEATH SYNDROME

Parenting an infant is a 24-hour responsibility, and part of parenting thus occurs at night, or while sleeping. Most parents (usually mothers) around the world accommodate this by sharing a bed with their infants. However, in countries such as the United States and those in Europe, parent-infant bed-sharing is not the norm; indeed, it may be viewed as downright dangerous, deleterious, or distasteful. Bed-sharing parents may be judged as "bad," acting in ways that violate cultural norms and medical recommendations. Estimates from 2010 suggest that ~13.5% of U.S. parents of young infants routinely slept with them in bed, and bed-sharing is more common among ethnic minorities and lower income families (Colson et al. 2013). A different pattern exists in the United Kingdom, where bed-sharers are more likely to be well educated and have higher incomes (Ball and Volpe 2013).

The anthropologist James McKenna has argued that the global norm of parent–infant bed-sharing is associated with healthier outcomes for babies than is solitary sleeping, although at present there are no studies confirming a reduced risk of **sudden infant death syndrome** (SIDS) with bed-sharing. In 1986 McKenna published a lead article in *Medical Anthropology* that outlined a possible relationship between infant solo sleeping and the risk of SIDS. SIDS is a mysterious disease in which infants, mostly between the ages of two months and six months, simply stop breathing and die in their sleep. Sometimes SIDS cases cluster in families, and there are a variety of genetic mutations that are found among some babies who die of SIDS, which may act by increasing an infant's vulnerability to SIDS (Moon 2011). The known genetic mutations under study account for only a small percentage of SIDS cases. What makes the disease so intractable to research is that it is impossible to establish it in experimental animals, and thus all information on this disease comes from children who have died from SIDS. McKenna maintained that the fact that SIDS is (apparently) unique to humans and occurs during a relatively narrow window of time in infancy constitutes an important clue to its underlying cause(s). During this period, infants' breathing undergoes a transition from a pattern of reflexive breathing to one under greater control by higher brain centers. This seems to be related to the development of a breathing pattern necessary to produce speech (unique to humans), the sounds of which are mainly produced during exhalation. Some infants experience disordered breathing during this transition, leading to an increased risk of SIDS.

What does this have to do with where an infant sleeps? According to McKenna, infants who sleep alone during this period have no rhythmic stimulus against which they can pattern their breathing. As his research has demonstrated, in a solitary sleeping environment, infants are more likely to go into deeper layers of sleep, from which it is more difficult to be aroused (McKenna and Mosko 1993). It is during deep sleep that the risk of SIDS increases. Sleep apnea, the cessation of breathing during sleep, is more likely to occur at this time and, in infants with disordered breathing patterns, can lead to SIDS. In contrast, when bed-sharing, infants are exposed to the parent's rhythmic breathing and their presence in bed produces a lighter sleep, during which the infant is more easily aroused. Therefore, infants are less likely to go into the deeper layers of sleep, less likely to suffer from sleep apnea, and more likely to have more organized, regular breathing patterns.

As noted, infant–parent (usually mother) bed-sharing is the norm in most societies, and those places where it is not common are those that also have the highest rates of SIDS (the United States, European countries, Australia, New Zealand). It is a reasonable assumption that during the environment of evolutionary adaptedness human infants co-slept, and co-sleeping is routine in our primate relatives. A solitary sleeping infant would be an easy target for a predator, not to mention that nursing a baby at night is less convenient if the parent has to awaken and walk to get the baby. Bed-sharing babies are also better able to maintain their core temperature, resulting in more effective thermoregulation.

The American Academy of Pediatrics (AAP) is opposed to bed-sharing because their task force on SIDS concluded that sufficient evidence exists to indicate that it is associated with an *increased* risk of SIDS (there is no evidence that it directly *causes* or *prevents* SIDS), although the AAP is also opposed to solitary sleep environments, where the baby is not in close proximity (Moon 2011). The AAP makes a distinction between co-sleeping (sleeping in close proximity but not necessarily in the same bed—also called "room sharing") and bed-sharing (when parent and child sleep on the same surface) and recommends room sharing as a means to reduce SIDS risk. Pediatricians' concerns stem from the dangers of an adult bed—bedding may be too soft, with pillows and quilts that can suffocate a baby, or a baby may fall or get trapped between the mattress and headboard. Parents may smoke in bed or have taken medications, drugs, or alcohol. In other words, it is the potential dangers of the adult sleeping environment that make pediatricians nervous about parent–infant bed-sharing. Sleeping together on a couch or armchair appears to be particularly risky for the infant (Fleming and Blair 2015). There are additional cultural issues such as the parental bed as a site of sexual activity and hence a place unsuitable for children, fear of the infant not being able to "self-soothe" or becoming "dependent" on the parent, and an emphasis on a long period of uninterrupted sleep for both parents and children (McKenna and McDade 2005). These are not often issues of concern in other societies, where bed-sharing and breastfeeding are normative, there may not be such an emphasis on individual autonomy, and daytime rest is possible and work schedules allow for it.

There are certainly ways to make the adult bed a safe environment, and it is worth further investigating the health outcomes associated with different kinds of sleeping arrangements (Fleming and Blair 2015; McKenna and McDade 2005). Breastfeeding, for example, is more common among bed-sharing mother–infant pairs, and bed-sharing is associated with longer breastfeeding duration, which exerts a protective effect against SIDS (Blair et al. 2010; Moon 2011). McKenna and his anthropology colleague Lee Gettler proposed the term "breastsleeping" to describe the inseparability of bed-sharing and breastfeeding:

> Breastfeeding is so physiologically and behaviourally entwined and functionally inter-dependent with forms of cosleeping that we propose the use of the term breastsleeping to acknowledge the following: (i) the critical role that immediate and sustained maternal contact plays in helping to establish optimal breastfeeding; (ii) the fact that normal, human (species wide) infant sleep can only be derived from studies of breastsleeping dyads because of the ways maternal–infant contact affects the delivery of breastmilk, the milk's ingestion, the infant's concomitant and subsequent metabolism and other

physiological processes, maternal and infant sleep architecture, including arousal patterns, as well as breastfeeding frequency and prolongation; and (iii) that breastsleeping by mother–infant pairs comprises such vastly different behavioural and physiological characteristics compared with nonbreastfeeding mothers and infants, this dyadic context must be distinguished and given its own epidemiological category and benefits to risk assessment. (McKenna and Gettler 2016, 17)

Helen Ball, an anthropologist who has conducted extensive research on bed-sharing in the United Kingdom, notes how pediatric recommendations for infant sleep can be at cross-purposes: prevention of infant death/injury and safety awareness versus promotion of breastfeeding, bonding, and infant mental development. Recommendations to achieve each of these ends may be contradictory, and interventions addressing one agenda may have a detrimental impact on the other (Ball and Volpe 2013). Furthermore, given that bed-sharing can co-occur (or not) with any number of other risk factors for SIDS across ethnic groups, a single "don't bed-share" message is likely to be ineffective in reducing SIDS rates or changing parental behavior that may have its roots in strong cultural traditions and ideologies about parenting. Ball has been instrumental in shaping policy about bed-sharing and breastfeeding in the United Kingdom (and maintains the Baby Sleep Info Source [https://www.basisonline.org.uk] that provides parents with up to date information on what constitutes biologically "normal" sleep and infant feeding). In 2018 she was awarded the Queen's Anniversary Prize for Higher Education for leading influential research on parent-infant sleep with a widely-used public information service.

MENOPAUSE

As a woman enters her forties, her chances of becoming pregnant diminish substantially and ultimately her menstrual periods stop, indicating the cessation of her reproductive abilities. This is a normal part of the female aging process. Menopause is defined biomedically as having occurred when a woman has not menstruated for one year, and typically occurs around the age of 50 years. The underlying physiology of menopause derives from a process that begins early in fetal development, when some 7 million oocytes form by the fifth month. These immediately begin to dwindle in number: 2 million remain at birth and 400 thousand are left at menarche. Over the course of the reproductive years, only a few hundred at most will go through meiotic division during ovulation, and the rest gradually disappear as the follicle, the oocyte itself, or both, shrink and cease to be viable. When so few follicles remain to produce sufficient estrogen to induce ovulation, the menstrual cycles stop and menopause ensues. The fact that so many oocytes are produced when only a tiny proportion have any chance of becoming zygotes seems to be a relic of an evolutionary ancestry of organisms that produced millions of eggs continually throughout life for external fertilization.

What is unusual about human menopause is that it occurs in the middle of the life course, and women typically experience long postreproductive lives. In other words, the life expectancy of oocytes (germ cells) is much shorter than that for other physiological systems (somatic cells). There are a variety of evolutionary hypotheses to explain the evolution of menopause. The most common is the "grandmother hypothesis," which posits that natural selection favored truncating a woman's reproductive span to reduce competition between her offspring and her grandchildren and allow for increased grandmaternal care of grandchildren (Hawkes 2003). Given that human babies are born in such a dependent state compared with those of other apes and grow rapidly, they require large amounts of resources that may exceed the ability of a mother, father, or both parents to procure. Furthermore, because oocytes become more vulnerable to chromosomal dislocation mutations with age, a woman's fitness would be better served by investing in existing children and grandchildren rather than in more offspring with a greater chance of damaging mutations. Therefore, the package of cessation of a woman's own reproduction and extension of postreproductive life became advantageous. Other hypotheses focus on the loss of viable eggs itself; menopause may be a byproduct of atretic follicles, which produce the progesterone required to support pregnancy. Or, as some have suggested, menopause is of recent origin, occurring only when it was "uncovered" by the lengthening human lifespan (see Leidy Sievert 2006 for a review of these hypotheses). Because human ancestors did not live as long as contemporary humans, they never would have experienced menopause. As discussed earlier, this hypothesis fails to consider that low life expectancies in the past, as in the present, disproportionately reflect high levels of infant and child mortality rather than old age mortality, and many women would have lived into their postreproductive years.

In contrast to evolutionary-based hypotheses that view menopause as adaptive or as an evolutionary byproduct, biomedical views of menopause tend to pathologize the cessation of ovulation. Menopause has become an "estrogen deficiency disease" caused by "ovarian failure" and "treated" with **hormone replacement therapy** (HRT) (Leidy Sievert 2006). Initially only estrogen was used, but it was associated with an increased risk of endometrial cancer, and in the 1980s a new form of HRT was developed in which estrogen was combined with progestin, which appeared to be protective against endometrial cancer. The transformation of a normal life cycle event to a deficiency disease occurred in the middle part of the twentieth century, based on cases of women experiencing a variety of negative symptoms: hot flashes, palpitations, headaches, melancholy, and so on (the association of these symptoms with menopause is highly variable cross-culturally and is considered in more detail below). At the start, HRT was prescribed only to women suffering from these symptoms, but by the 1990s menopausal women were encouraged to consider HRT regardless of whether they experienced any negative consequences of menopause, so they could remain "feminine forever" (Leidy 1999). The rationale for this approach came from studies indicating that the withdrawal of estrogen was associated with an increased risk of CVD and osteoporosis, and women taking HRT appeared to have a lower risk of these two syndromes. Thus, the definition of menopause as a disease state, or risk factor for disease, became solidified with the standard treatment of HRT. Indeed, analogies were drawn between the treatment of menopause with HRT and the treatment of diabetes with the hormone insulin (Leidy 1999).

The association of menopause with CVD or osteoporosis is highly variable. In many non-Western populations postmenopausal women do not experience the same increased risk of osteoporosis or CVD as they do in the United States and Europe (Leidy 1999). What could account for this variability? CVD and osteoporosis are two chronic diseases with complex, multifactorial etiologies. Osteoporosis risk varies with diet (animal protein consumption increases the risk) and activity patterns (weight-bearing activity reduces the risk of bone demineralization or bone fracture). As described in Chapter 4, CVD risk stems from diet (high saturated fat, high-salt, and high-sugar diets), smoking, stress, poor physical fitness, and myriad other factors. With so many contributing factors that vary across populations, the role of estrogen may be critical or minimal in any given population. There remains some controversy over whether HRT lowers the risk of CVD. The Women's Health Initiative (WHI) study found that women taking HRT had higher risks of breast cancer, heart attacks, and stroke (Writing Group for the Women's Health Initiative Investigators 2002). The high level of media coverage of that finding contributed to a 70% decline in HRT usage (Ettinger et al. 2012). Several studies and a re-analysis of the WHI data suggest that HRT (particularly estrogen alone, rather than combined with progesterone) in the early postmenopausal years (ages 50–60) may confer some benefits with respect to cardiovascular health, overall survival, and symptom relief (Lobo 2017). The relationship between HRT and breast cancer risk remains somewhat more controversial (Rymer et al. 2019). Collectively, these recent findings have altered the medical recommendations for HRT, such that only women for whom menopausal symptoms seriously diminish their quality of life are recommended HRT, and then only at the lowest effective dose for the shortest period of time.

The anthropologist Margaret Lock and others have studied menopause in a variety of non-Western cultural settings, finding that menopause does not always follow the same course, with the same symptoms, as seen in North America and Europe. For example, in Japan, women are much less likely to report trouble sleeping, hot flashes, and cold or night sweats (Lock 1998). About 27% of Japanese women report no symptoms of menopause (in contrast to about 15% of Canadian and U.S. women), and only 10% report having five or more symptoms, compared to 26%–34% of their counterparts in Canada and the United States. A study of 14,906 women (aged 40–55 years) from five different ethnic backgrounds in the United States supports the finding of significant variation in menopausal symptoms, as shown in Table 6.2 (Avis et al. 2001). Across all ethnic groups, statistical analyses showed that menopausal symptoms clearly cluster into two distinct categories: vasomotor symptoms (e.g., hot flashes and night sweats) and psychological and psychosomatic symptoms (e.g., depression, irritability, nervousness).

Variability in menopausal symptoms has several possible sources. Linguistic factors are a source of variability in symptom reporting and may also reflect fundamental cultural differences in attitudes toward menopause. In Japan, there is no term that corresponds precisely to menopause (Lock 1998). Instead the term *kōnenki* is used to describe a female climacteric—a long, gradual process of change in middle-age women, of which the end of menstrual cycles is just one part. In her interviews with Japanese women, Lock found that the end of menstruation is not seen as a distressing event to them, and the absence of a specific term for menopause may reflect this underlying cultural attitude.

TABLE 6.2   Prevalence Percentages of Menopause Symptoms in Five Racial/Ethnic Groups in the United States

Symptom	Whole Sample	Racial/Ethnic Group				
		African American	Hispanic	Chinese	Japanese	Caucasian
Tense	51.9	46.2	60.1	39.2	34.4	56.1
Depressed	40.5	40.8	51.8	32.0	22.2	40.2
Irritable	51.6	50.6	43.9	43.4	40.0	56.1
Headache	47.7	44.4	53.2	38.9	37.9	50.0
Stiffness	54.3	56.3	47.6	48.0	49.8	55.9
Hot flashes	27.5	38.8	26.0	15.5	11.8	24.2
Night sweats	23.6	32.4	24.7	10.9	9.3	20.9

Source: From Avis et al. 2001; population labels as used in the study.

The language of hot flashes in Japanese also reflects a fundamental difference in symptom reporting between Japanese- and English-speaking women (Melby 2005). Japanese women have a more nuanced linguistic approach to hot flashes, employing five different terms, in addition to the English, borrowing *hotto furasshu*. Anthropologist Melissa Melby found a somewhat higher prevalence of hot flash symptoms (adding together all of the hot flash terms) in Japanese women compared with that from Lock's study done 20 years before, but the rates she found were still substantially lower than for women in the United States. She suggests that the increase in hot flash symptoms could be a sign of changing diet in Japan between the 1980s and the 2000s. More generally, Melby found that hot flash symptoms do not correspond to menopausal status (as indicated by irregular periods or the end of menstruation); instead, they were associated with self-reported *kōnenki* status. In many cases, hot flash symptoms were reported in women who were clearly premenopausal, but in no women who were pre-*kōnenki*. Melby writes, "Japanese women's language, including their self-assessment of *kōnenki* stage and the linguistic demarcation of symptoms, seems to be more fine-grained than the Western biomedical terms of menopause status and hot flash, and may offer insight into subtle differences in the experience and underlying physiology of menopause" (Melby 2005, 257).

REPRODUCTIVE EVENTS AND BREAST CANCER RISK

A woman's reproductive career not only has implications for her reproductive health but also extends to the risk of breast cancer. Because women's reproductive lives vary tremendously across cultures, there is likewise variation in the risk of breast cancer. Among Western women, a common pattern consists of early menarche, a long period of time between menarche and first birth, short or absent breastfeeding, and few births overall, and these are each linked to a higher risk of breast cancer (Kobayashi et al. 2012). S. Boyd Eaton and colleagues (1994) compared the reproductive parameters of contemporary American women with those that prevail among hunter-gatherers, which more closely match our evolutionary history, and found a remarkable discrepancy. Whereas American women average 450 menstrual (ovulatory) cycles in their lifetimes, hunter-gatherer women experience only 160. This difference is attributable to the later age at menarche, earlier first birth and higher fertility, ubiquitous and longer breastfeeding, and earlier menopause among hunter-gatherer women. Beverly Strassmann (1999) found that Dogon women of Mali, who have about eight births each on average, experienced even fewer menses—only about 109 over the course of their entire life span. In contrast, for women in countries such as the United States, fertility is low and delayed, breastfeeding is rare and brief, menarche is early, menopause is late, and they are well nourished.

An increased risk of breast cancer is one result of the large number of ovulatory cycles, as there is compelling evidence of a link between the total number of ovulations and postmenopausal breast cancer, likely through exposure to estrogen (Chavez-MacGregor et al. 2005). Most breast cancers are estrogen dependent; that is, they are more likely to occur and grow more rapidly in the context of high levels of estrogen. Breast tissue cells have estrogen receptors and are sensitive to the estrogen milieu. Estrogen is produced by the ovaries starting at menarche, and each ovulatory cycle is associated with a burst of estrogen (see Figure 6.1). If ovulatory cycles (menstrual periods) are more or less continuous for a long period of time after menarche, a woman is exposed to continual spikes of estrogen. Pregnancy and breastfeeding both interrupt this cycle and allow breast tissue to differentiate into mature milk-producing glands. This differentiation appears to be protective against the growth-promoting effects of estrogen on breast cells. Estrogen production declines with menopause, as ovulation ceases, but when menopause is late in life or "treated" with HRT, estrogen exposure continues.

Figure 6.13 shows age-standardized breast cancer rates from several countries plotted against the total fertility rate, used here as a proxy for the number of lifetime ovulations, with higher fertility indicating fewer ovulations caused by more interruptions by pregnancy and lactation. Higher fertility is associated with lower breast cancer incidence across countries (Kaiser and Bouskill 2013). Furthermore, these authors found that average adult height and rates of overweight were positively associated with breast cancer risk, and in a multivariate model the effects of both the total fertility rate and height remained significant. This research indicates that the reductions in fertility and access to more food during childhood—both characteristics of wealthy countries—serve to increase the risk of breast cancer. Thus, both increased exposure to estrogen through recurrent ovulatory cycles and ample and consistent calories represents an evolutionarily novel condition for women in many Western societies, whose bodies are not well adapted to this endocrinological environment. At the same time, this represents a life history trade-off in the sense that estrogen is positively associated with fertility and the negative effects of estrogen are experienced only later in life. This trade-off is referred to as antagonistic pleiotropy and is considered in more detail in the next chapter on aging.

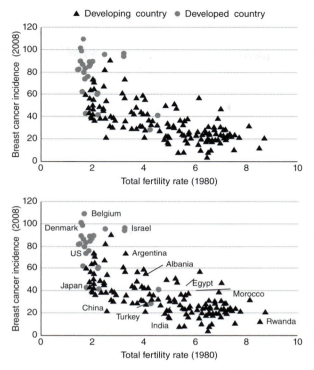

FIGURE 6.13 Breast cancer incidence rates in relation to total fertility rates across countries. *Source: Journal of Population Research.* "What predicts breast cancer rates? Testing hypotheses of the demographic and nutrition transitions." Vol. 30 (1), pages 67–85. doi:10.1007/s12546-012-9090-9. Kaiser, Bonnie, and Kathryn Bouskill. Copyright 2013. With permission of Springer.

CONCLUSION

The phrase "reproductive health" almost inevitably references women's health, as opposed to men's health, and obscures the fact that women suffer from other health problems that have little to do with reproduction per se. That said, reproductive health encompasses a wide range of factors that permeate a woman's life cycle. These stretch back to her own experience in utero to later life and thus are not confined to her reproductive years. Given the centrality of reproduction to all societies, it comes as no surprise that there is tremendous interest in reproductive health and how it is subject to culturally specific management to achieve culturally specific ideals. The biomedical view of reproductive health is becoming more widespread and, in many cases, is at odds with traditional understandings and practices. Examples include ART, hospital or surgical births, or hormonal contraceptives. In some cases, biomedical interventions may provide options for achieving fertility goals (by avoiding childbearing or enhancing fertility), but in other cases they may undermine the cultural integrity of local reproductive health traditions or contribute to reproductive health problems (e.g., inappropriate birthing technologies or high levels of hormones in oral contraceptives).

Reproductive behavior and its health consequences are always entrenched within a cultural context, but political and economic forces continually shift the terrain within which reproduction occurs. This can give rise to an increase in STIs and infertility or make childbearing compete with other occupation-related goals, such that low fertility and short (if any) breastfeeding durations put women at increased risk of breast cancer. Suffice it to say that reproduction has always been risky at some level or another and that social forces can mitigate or increase the risk.

STUDY QUESTIONS

1. In what ways are the reproductive lives of women more medicalized than those of men?
2. What are three evolutionary hypotheses for why women menstruate? How does the evolutionary perspective inform how menstruation is treated biomedically?
3. How do different cultures address the onset of menstruation in girls?
4. How do statistics concerning the adoption of oral contraceptives in developed versus developing countries support the claim that there is no universal human profile for hormones important in female reproductive health?
5. What is the biocultural history of PMS in Western countries? Why might it be less of a problem in non-Western groups?
6. What are the most critical factors in determining a woman's level of fertility? What is lactational infecundability? How do STIs affect fertility?
7. How do cultural attitudes shape perspectives on acceptable infertility treatment?
8. What is FGC? Describe the perspectives expressed in cross-cultural debate concerning this group of traditional practices.
9. What biological and cultural factors influence eating behavior in pregnant women? What are the possible advantages of being nauseous and vomiting during early pregnancy? Why do some women crave specific foods during pregnancy?
10. How can gestational diabetes and PIH be seen as arising from a conflict between the mother and fetus?
11. What is a midwife and what does she do? What is an evolutionary explanation for the existence of assisted births in humans?
12. Is nurturing behavior natural for human mothers? What is adaptive behavior in the context of the mother–infant relationship?
13. How might bed-sharing be related to the risk of SIDS?
14. How does the conceptualization and experience of menopause in Japan differ from that in Western countries?
15. How many menses do women in developed countries experience compared with women living traditional lives? How might this affect rates of breast cancer of women living under those different cultural settings?

CRITICAL THINKING QUESTIONS

1. In many cultures (including Western societies), infertility is typically gendered as a woman's problem, although there is frequently not a biological basis for this. Why do you think this is the case?
2. Are pregnancy and childbirth overmedicalized in Western cultures? How do we reach a balance between taking advantage of the most modern medical technology and not marginalizing the role of the parents, kin, and nonmedical practitioners in pregnancy and birth? Is the concept of a natural pregnancy and birth justifiable in a cross-cultural perspective?

SUGGESTED ETHNOGRAPHIES AND OTHER BOOKS TO READ WITH THIS CHAPTER

Dána-Ain Davis. 2019. *Reproductive Injustice: Racism, Pregnancy, and Premature Birth New York University Press.*

Robbie Davis-Floyd and Melissa Cheyney. 2019. *Birth in Eight Cultures.* Waveland Press.

Lucia Guerra-Reyes. 2019. *Changing Birth in the Andes: Culture, Policy, and Safe Motherhood in Peru.* Nashville, TN: Vanderbilt University Press.

Marcia C. Inhorn. 2003. *Local Babies, Global Science: Gender, Religion and In Vitro Fertilization in Egypt.* London: Routledge.

Marcia C. Inhorn. 2015. *Cosmopolitan Conceptions: IVF Sojourns in Global Dubai.* Durham, NC: Duke University Press.

Grazyna Jasienska. 2013. *The Fragile Wisdom: An Evolutionary View on Women's Biology and Health:* Cambridge, MA: Harvard University Press.

Brigitte Jordan. 1993. *Birth in Four Cultures.* Prospect Heights, IL: Waveland Press.

Ray Moynihan and Barbara Mintzes. 2010. *Sex, Lies, and Pharmaceuticals: How Drug Companies Plan to Profit from Female Sexual Dysfunction.* Vancouver, BC, Canada: Greystone Books.

Elizabeth F.S. Roberts. 2012. *God's Laboratory: Assisted Reproduction in the Andes.* Berkeley: University of California Press.

Nancy Scheper-Hughes. 1992. *Death without Weeping.* Berkeley: University of California Press.

Lynnette Leidy Sievert. 2006. *Menopause: A Biocultural Perspective.* New Brunswick, NJ: Rutgers University Press.

Wenda Trevathan. 2010. *Ancient Bodies, Modern Lives: How Evolution Has Shaped Women's Health.* New York: Oxford University Press.

CHAPTER 7

Aging

Chapter Goals
- To understand the biology of human senescence
- To understand cultural and environmental factors important in extending longevity and achieving successful aging
- To review theories of the evolution of human aging patterns
- To examine the relationship between increasing age and health with an emphasis on conditions such as osteoporosis and Alzheimer's disease

Although we may not like to think about it, there is nothing more natural than aging. As we age, we are all subject to the effects of physiological decline, or **senescence**. The effects of senescence are highly variable. Not only do different systems of the body age at different rates and following different courses, but also individuals age at different overall rates. One thing is clear, however: the only "cure" we have for old age is death. Medical and public health advances over the past century have helped extend the average life span but have had little influence on the maximum life span. Living 100 years is still extraordinarily unusual, and living to 120 years, the oft-cited maximum for human beings, has been achieved less than a handful of times (Figure 7.1). Why should this be the case? In other words, why has medical science not been able to have as much success in extending the maximum life span as in extending the average life span?

Increases in the average life span have resulted primarily from preventing infectious disease and reducing infant mortality. To a lesser extent, advances in the treatment of heart disease and cancer, two conditions associated with increasing age, have also contributed to extending the life span. However, even a healthy, "super-elderly" person over the age of 85 years has a much greater chance of dying within a year than a middle-age individual, even one who is not particularly healthy. A healthy older person may not have any signs of disease, but what constitutes normal in an 80-year-old would be cause for alarm in a 40-year-old. There is much talk about healthy aging and how to achieve it—how to extend the "healthspan," as it is called, if not the life span, but it is a mistake to equate healthy aging with turning back the clock.

FIGURE 7.1   Jeanne Calment (1875–1997) of France is the only person who has indisputably lived at least 120 years.
Credit: Wikimedia Commons.

Why we age can only be addressed in the context of our evolutionary biology. All complex organisms age. From a zoological perspective, there is nothing unique about human aging, other than the fact that a relatively high percentage of people today now have the opportunity to age. Most organisms die long before they reach reproductive age, much less old age. However, it should be recognized that as far as mammals go, we are among the most long-lived (although short of the 200 years that the arctic bow-head whale can live), and certainly we are the longevity champions of the primates. So there are two distinct evolutionary issues related to human aging. First, why does aging exist in the first place? Second, has natural selection favored longevity in human evolution? Finally, we must ask whether understanding the evolutionary history of senescence helps us evaluate claims about postponing, slowing, or even circumventing the aging process.

How we age is influenced not only by our evolutionary past but also, and more critically, by the biocultural present. The evolutionary perspective complements an understanding of aging as a cross-cultural phenomenon. Which cultural practices promote long life and aging well? There can be no doubt that "lifestyle" has a tremendous influence on mortality in old age and whether a person can achieve healthy aging. Although there are individual genetic differences that influence how people age, cultural or economic factors also have tremendous influences on the average longevity of entire populations. For example, in Russia in the 1990s, male life expectancy was lower than in it had been the 1960s, falling to 59 years in 1993 (Tulchinsky and Varavikova 1996). This was despite the fact that deaths from infectious diseases declined significantly over the same period. There are many reasons for this decline in longevity. Some of the increased mortality is attributable to non-aging-related factors (homicide, accidents, poisonings), but the long-term effects of high alcohol consumption and the neglect of cardiovascular health in men have also made a significant contribution. Few public health measures have been taken to encourage individual changes in diet or activity to combat heart disease. Government action to prevent alcoholism is complicated by the fact that the government earns a large income from the sale of alcohol. If healthy aging is an ideal, then Russian men are not living in a cultural environment that would promote its achievement.

It is not only Russian men (and to a lesser extent, Russian women) who are at risk for reduced life expectancy. An analysis of U.S. mortality data by the economists Anne Case and Angus Deaton (2015) suggests that non-Hispanic White Americans between the ages of 45 and 54 years showed an increased rate of mortality, in some ways reminiscent of the Russian situation. Case and Deaton found that between 1999 and 2013, the mortality rate in this age group increased by 33.9 to 415.4/100,000 per year. This increase ran counter to substantial reductions in mortality rates in this age group for U.S. Blacks and Hispanics over the same period and steady but more moderate reductions in middle-age groups in other rich countries. Case and Deaton found that the increase was almost wholly among those without a college education, who were dying at increased rates from drug and alcohol poisoning, suicide, and chronic liver disease. They suggest that the rise in economic insecurity in this group was a potential underlying cause for the increased death rate. Although Case and Deaton identified a decrease in life expectancy for non-Hispanic Whites only, a subsequent analysis, based on census data extending through 2016, has shown that the trend for increased mortality can be seen across all major U.S. ethnic categories (Hispanics, non-Hispanic American Indians/ Native Alaskans and Asians, Pacific Islanders, non-Hispanic African-Americans) (Woolf et al. 2018). This trend was most pronounced in rural areas, although for certain groups and certain causes of death, suburban/urban populations showed the greatest increases in mortality. As the authors of this study point out, the increases in mortality for some of these groups are particularly worrisome given the already substantially higher baseline morality levels (compared to non-Hispanic Whites).

As also noted in Chapter 4, one group of distinguished aging researchers has predicted that life expectancy in the United States will decline in the future because of increasing rates of obesity (Olshansky et al. 2005). Obesity is directly associated with increased risk of type 2 diabetes, coronary heart disease, cancer, and other conditions. All of these diseases primarily affect older individuals, not only increasing the chance of dying at any given time but also substantially reducing quality of life. As Jay Olshansky and his colleagues point out, the decrease in life expectancy linked to obesity is not trivial: it exceeds the total negative impact of all deaths from accidents (including homicide and suicide) and may even exceed those from heart disease or cancer. An analysis of mortality and obesity data from 26 European countries has also demonstrated the potential impact of increasing obesity rates on life expectancy (Vidra et al. 2019). Although mortality and obesity rates among the countries is quite variable, Vidra and colleagues estimate that without obesity, life expectancy would be from 0.86 to 1.67 years greater for men and from 0.66 to 1.54 years greater for women.

There is tremendous heterogeneity in the healthfulness of older individuals (Lowsky et al. 2013). Although obesity and other problems may lead to premature aging in some groups, as measured by the frequency of chronic disability, older people today are healthier than they have ever been (Manton et al. 2006). Of course, it is difficult to predict how long and how well people will live in the future, but if older people in the future are less healthy, that will have tremendous economic and cultural ramifications. Unhealthy older people stop working at a younger age and accrue ever-increasing medical expenses.

These examples demonstrate the complexity of human aging. **Gerontologists**, the scientists who study aging, must examine a myriad of evolutionary, physiological, economic, and cultural factors that influence how people get older. As in medical anthropology, there are some gerontologists who focus on biological factors, whereas others are more concerned with psychological or social issues. As we will see, the biocultural perspective of medical anthropology provides a fitting approach to the topic of human aging, a biological phenomenon with ancient evolutionary underpinnings, the expression of which is strongly influenced by the cultural environment.

THE AGING BODY

Before moving on to the medical anthropology of human aging, let us consider some of the basic changes that happen to a body starting from around the age of 40 years. Many of these changes are pretty obvious to all of us. Facial wrinkling develops from the age of 30 years, a result of several different age-related processes: lines form along the frequently used facial muscles; the amount of collagen, a long fibrous protein that contributes to skin elasticity, declines, making the skin stiffer; the skin itself becomes thinner, leading to the development of wrinkling bags of skin under the eyes or in the neck. After the age of 40 years, scalp hair becomes thinner, both in the diameter of each hair itself and in its distribution. *Male pattern baldness*, in which hair loss begins at the crown of the head and ultimately leaves only a fringe of hair on the sides and back of the head, is an age-dependent condition seen in about 20% of men in their twenties, two-thirds of men in their sixties, and 90% of those in their nineties (figures for European-derived populations). Male pattern baldness is under strong genetic control and is quite variable, both within and between populations (Lolli et al. 2017). It is a health (and not just beauty) concern because it is associated with a greater risk (with increasing age) of conditions such as an enlarged prostate and coronary heart disease. Women also exhibit hair loss as they age in a similar, but less pronounced, form, and the underlying physiology and genetics of hair loss in men and women are probably different (Redler et al. 2017). Other sex differences in health issues associated with age are found in Figure 7.2.

As people get older, they get shorter as well. This is in part because of the long-term effects of gravity, which leads to compression of the vertebral column. Height loss is typically about 0.4 centimeters per decade beginning at age 40, with the rate accelerating after the age of 70. Women tend to lose a greater relative amount of stature than men. This is in part because of a greater loss of bone mass in women resulting from a decrease in mineralization (calcium and phosphate) of bone. The disease **osteoporosis** is indicated by a thinning of bone tissue and loss of bone density, leading to an increased risk of bone breakage (Figure 7.3). The decreases of estrogen in postmenopausal women and of testosterone in aging men are directly related to the development of osteoporosis, although the effects are much more pronounced in women. Hormone replacement treatment (HRT) with estrogen is often recommended to help maintain

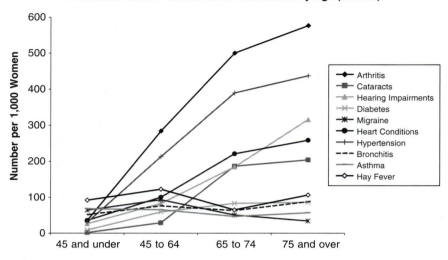

Prevalence Rate of Various Health Conditions by Age (women)

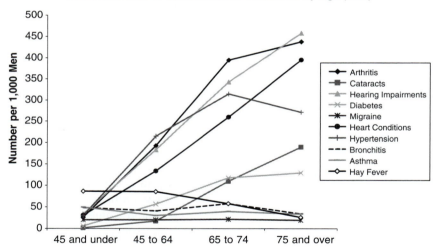

Prevalence Rate of Various Health Conditions by Age (men)

FIGURE 7.2 Prevalence rates by age for various medical conditions for women and men. *Source:* Created by author/OUP with data from U.S. Census Bureau 2006.

bone tissue in older women. Vitamin D and calcium supplements are also recommended. Weight-bearing exercise helps to increase bone density because of the effects of muscle pulling on bone. There are also drugs used to treat osteoporosis, such as selective estrogen receptor modulators, which enhance the beneficial effects of estrogen in maintaining bone density.

People in all populations are susceptible to developing osteoporosis and low bone mass (LBM), although prevalence rates vary. An analysis of National Health and Nutrition Examination Survey Data 2005–2010 by Nicole Wright and colleagues (2014)

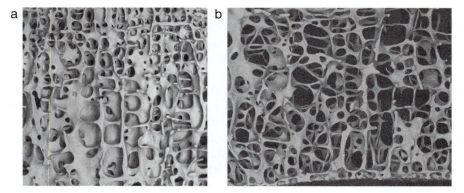

FIGURE 7.3   Two scanning electron micrographs of bone. Left, normal healthy bone; right, osteoporotic bone. Note the substantial loss in bone density in osteoporosis. *Credit:* Wellcome Images.

TABLE 7.1   Prevalence Rate Estimates of Osteoporosis and Low Bone Mass in the United States for Individuals 50 Years and Older (National Health and Nutrition Examination Survey Data 2005–2010)

	Group	OP prevalence % (SE)	LBM prevalence % (SE)
Both sexes			
	Total	10.3 (0.37)	43.9 (0.72)
	NH White	10.2 (0.47)	44.9 (0.89)
	NH Black	4.9 (0.65)	29.7 (1.51)
	Mexican American	13.4 (1.10)	43.2 (1.41)
Women			
	Total	15.4 (0.63)	51.4 (0.93)
	NH White	15.8 (0.81)	52.6 (1.17)
	NH Black	7.7 (1.10)	36.2 (2.03)
	Mexican American	20.4 (1.70)	47.8 (2.33)
Men			
	Total	4.3 (0.40)	35.2 (0.93)
	NH White	3.9 (0.39)	36.0 (1.13)
	NH Black	1.3 (0.40)	21.3 (1.75)
	Mexican American	5.9 (1.08)	38.3 (2.55)

Source: Wright et al. (2014); OP, osteoporosis; LBM, low bone mass; NH, non-Hispanic; SE, standard error.

gives a sense of the variation within the U.S. population (Table 7.1). For all racial/ethnic groups, osteoporosis and LBM rates are substantially higher in women than in men; in addition, rates for osteoporosis steadily increase with increasing age (data not shown). Compared with non-Hispanic Whites and Mexican Americans, non-Hispanic Blacks have substantially lower rates for both osteoporosis and LBM. This does not mean that there are not substantial numbers of non-Hispanic Blacks who have osteoporosis and LBM: Wright and colleagues estimate that about half a million non-Hispanic Blacks suffer from osteoporosis and nearly 3 million have LBM, indicating that they are at risk for developing the disease. Studies of clinical records show, however, that at-risk African American women are significantly less likely than at-risk European American women to be referred by their physicians for clinical screening for osteoporosis (via a bone density scan, Miller et al. 2005). This is despite the fact that risk factors for developing osteoporosis (age, low body weight, smoking, family history of osteoporosis, personal history of fracture) are the same for women in both groups.

Recommendations for increases in calcium in the diet are also complicated by population factors. African Americans have substantially higher rates of lactase impersistence than European Americans (see Chapter 4), and dairy products are a common (and widely advertised) source of calcium in the U.S. diet. Recommendations to African Americans for increased dairy consumption should include information on how and in what form dairy products can be consumed while minimizing the effects of lactase impersistence (Byers and Savaiano 2005). The use of vitamin D supplements to prevent osteoporosis also has an ethnic component: African Americans are less likely to be recommended to take vitamin D, despite the fact that darker-skinned people in temperate climates have lower vitamin D concentrations than lighter-skinned people. Controlled studies suggest that it is likely that African Americans would also benefit from vitamin D supplements, but that their recommended level of dosage (to reach a given blood plasma target level) may be higher than that for European Americans (Dawson-Hughes 2004; Ng et al. 2014). It is interesting to note that across populations there is a "calcium paradox:" fracture rates (an index of osteoporosis) are highest in countries with the highest calcium and dairy product intakes and lowest in countries with low intakes (Food and Agriculture Organization 2000; Frassetto et al. 2000; Hegsted 2001). The lower concentrations of vitamin D in African Americans, combined with lower rates of osteoporosis, signify a more general osteoporosis paradox (Aloia 2008). The effects of calcium and vitamin supplementation on osteoporosis are small at best. Instead, other lifestyle factors such as weight-bearing exercise, animal protein consumption, and smoking, among others, are likely to play more important roles in mediating the risk of osteoporosis and fractures among aging individuals. Further, biological and genetic factors relating to bone density, vitamin retention, and obesity (which may actually be a protective factor) complicate cross-cultural comparisons of osteoporosis.

People may become shorter as they age, but at the same time they also become heavier, at least in Western countries where the vast majority of research on aging has been conducted. The reason is that basal metabolic rate declines at a rate of about 3% every 10 years as we age (Schulz and Salthouse 1999), which means that we need fewer and fewer calories with each passing year to maintain body weight. The "middle-age spread" is not a myth of aging. Weight increases actually stop with the passing of middle age as gains in fat are offset by loss of musculature and other tissues with increasing age. The loss of muscle and strength is a hallmark of aging, although why this should occur is not well understood. Reduced levels of activity and exercise play a role. Hormone-mediated changes in protein synthesis may make it more difficult for older individuals to develop muscle tissue; older muscle tissue may thus be particularly sensitive to short-term inactivity. Maintaining activity levels and taking nutritional supplements (e.g., certain amino acids) to promote protein synthesis may be keys to maintaining strength and physical vitality in old age (Fujita and Volpi 2006).

The effects of physiological aging are not seen only in the musculoskeletal system. Almost all vital systems of the body undergo decline with increasing age, even in aging in the absence of pathology. The magnitude and rate of decline are not the same for all systems, but the general pattern is shared by all of them.

The load of diseases borne by older people is illustrated in Figure 7.2. Prevalence rates for some conditions, such as asthma, hay fever, and migraines, do not rise with increasing age. In contrast to this, however, we see skyrocketing rates for conditions such as arthritis and heart disease. In addition, the rate of falls and fractures in individuals over the age of 65 years is at least double that for the rest of the population (U.S. Census Bureau 2006), with about one-third of adults older than 65 suffering a fall each year (Hausdorff et al. 2001; Nazrun et al. 2014).

The devastating effects of hip fractures (i.e., fractures at or below the neck of the femur) in older individuals are generally underappreciated: about 20% of people who fracture their hips die within the following year and a large proportion of the rest require assistance for the remainder of their lives. A study conducted among older women living in Australia showed that 80% of respondents would rather be dead than have a bad hip fracture followed by admission to a nursing home (Salkeld et al. 2000). Rates of hip fractures in the elderly vary greatly across populations. A phylogenetic analysis of genomic data and hip fracture rates from 28 countries showed that there was little covariance between the two, implicating environmental rather than genetic factors in producing variation among populations (Wallace et al. 2016). Hip fracture rates are generally higher in developed countries, suggesting that decreased activity levels may play a role in elevating the risk of hip fracture.

Older people are much more likely to develop cancer than younger people (U.S. Cancer Statistics Working Group 2005). Figure 7.4 shows how the incidence rate (new cases per year) of all cancers increases dramatically with age. For example, the incidence rate for 50- to 54-year-olds exceeds that for all those under 45 years old, and the rate for 75- to 79-year-olds is six times that of the 50- to 54-year-olds. There are several potential underlying causes for the increased risk of cancer in old age (Ricklefs and Finch 1995). Cancer is basically a disease of cell growth and proliferation. Cell growth can be affected by mutations to specific genes, and mutations in general increase with increasing age. Hormones also influence gene expression, and cancers such as breast cancer are the result of the interplay of genetic, hormonal, and environmental factors. Proliferation of cells in the prostate gland, which can lead to an enlarged prostate and, in about 10% to 15% of all men in the United States, prostate cancer is influenced by the hormone testosterone. Skin cancer rates in light-skinned individuals are influenced by exposure to sunlight, which has an additive effect over the course of the lifetime. Similarly, cancers caused by cigarette smoking increase in frequency with exposure to the carcinogens and are therefore age related.

In sum, the body's physiological systems show a functional decline beginning in the decade of the forties and accelerating in the sixties and seventies. Declines in physiological capacity are mirrored by increases in the risk of developing a wide range of diseases and other debilitating conditions. There is variation at many different levels in the rate of physiological aging: there is no single marker of "old age." Menopause (see

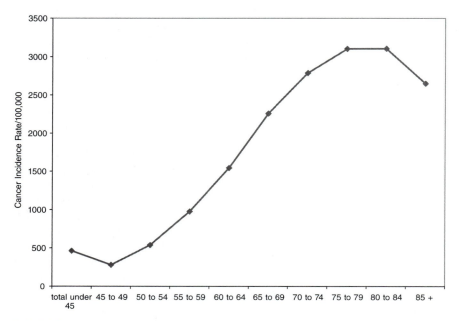

FIGURE 7.4 Incidence rate for various cancers by age.
Source: Created by author/OUP with data from U.S. Cancer Statistics Working Group 2005.

Chapter 6 and later in this chapter) in some cultures is seen as just such a marker, and there is no denying that the loss of the ability to conceive is a discrete loss in function that can be used to demarcate one life phase from another. However, menopause actually follows a period of declining fertility that begins in the thirties and accelerates through the forties. Male fertility and libido also decrease over this same period, although in the absence of disease, male fertility can be maintained until an advanced age. From a physiological standpoint, there is no such thing as "male menopause" or an "andropause," except in conditions that directly affect the testes (Morales 2004; Morales et al. 2000). Testosterone function typically (although not always) decreases with age, and some urologists recognize a condition known as *symptomatic androgen deficiency of the aging male.*

Testosterone therapy should not simply be viewed as the male equivalent of HRT for older women. However, in the contemporary context in which more attention is being given to the sexuality of aging males (e.g., the ubiquitous advertisements for the treatment of erectile dysfunction [ED]), testosterone replacement therapy is becoming more common. Between 2000 and 2011, a time period during which no new clinical indications for the use of testosterone were adopted, global sales of testosterone increased 12-fold, from $150 million to $1.8 billion (Handelsman 2013). Testosterone therapy has been shown to be effective in the treatment of a variety of specific sexual symptoms in older men, although not necessarily as a promoter of general health or vitality (Morgentaler et al. 2014). There has been some alarm expressed about the extraordinary rise in the use of testosterone to treat old age (*New York Times* editorial, February 4, 2014, http://www.nytimes.com/2014/02/05/opinion/overselling-testosterone-dangerously. html). Some of these concerns were driven by studies purporting to show that testosterone therapy may be associated with increased cardiovascular risk, although other studies have shown the opposite (Morgentaler et al. 2014). Recent research does show an elevated risk of blood clot formation with testosterone therapy (Walker et al. 2019). Whatever the risks or benefits of testosterone therapy, the increase in its use certainly shows that there is a consumer-driven market for it.

PHYSIOLOGICAL THEORIES OF AGING

Over the years, many theories have been offered to explain why the body ages over time (Ricklefs and Finch 1995). Although the systems of the body may age at different rates, the distressing cumulative effect is of a mechanism gradually running down and ultimately ceasing to function. Investigators looking to "cure" aging have tried to identify a single critical causal factor for aging because that would make a cure that much easier to find. However, the evidence points to aging as the result of multiple processes, which in concert produce the changes to the body we associate with senescence. Let us consider some of these theories.

Somatic Mutations

Mutations are errors in DNA replication that can lead to changes in the structure of a protein or the regulation of gene expression. In sex cells, mutations that are passed on to the next generation are the ultimate source of variation and provide the raw material for natural selection to act on. However, mutations also occur in the cells of the body. These **somatic mutations** clearly have the potential to undermine the body's physiological processes and thereby influence the way that aging will occur. Early studies of the effects of radiation (which causes mutations) on mice showed that even with sublethal doses, irradiated mice appeared to show a generalized wasting that could be interpreted as premature aging, resulting in the hypothesis that aging was simply a result of the accumulated effects of increasing numbers of somatic mutations. As a general theory of aging, this has not been well supported. The very existence of species-specific life history stages indicates that aging is not simply a matter of the accumulation of mutations (although certain age-related diseases, such as cancer, may be mutation related).

Free Radicals

Free radicals are highly reactive molecules that contain at least one unpaired electron. They can be formed when atoms collide with one another and are also formed by the impact of x-rays and ultraviolet radiation. Given their reactivity, free radicals promote the creation of more free radicals. Through a process known as oxidation, they can react with other molecules, including DNA, proteins, and lipids. The oxidative damage sustained by these important biomolecules in aging can affect many physiological processes. Oxidized proteins disrupt enzymatic reactions in the body and oxidized lipids may promote thickening of the arteries, contributing to the development of vascular disease. Antioxidants such as vitamins E and C can neutralize the effects of free radicals and are thus occasionally touted as aging cures. The body also produces endogenous enzymes such as superoxide dismutase (SOD), which clean up free radicals. People who do not produce SOD develop a familial form of *amyotrophic lateral sclerosis* (Lou Gehrig's disease), a degenerative nerve disease (Renton et al. 2014). It is important to keep in mind that free radicals are also a normal part of many metabolic processes and are even produced by cells of the immune system to help fight infection.

In addition to the diseases that result when we do not produce endogenous antioxidants (such as SOD), evidence for the free radical theory of aging is supported by the observation that animals with higher metabolic rates—and higher rates of producing endogenous free radicals—also tend to have shorter lives (Finkel and Holbrook 2000). There are exceptions to this pattern, however. Birds and primates tend to live longer than their metabolic rates would predict. Studies have shown that they actually produce fewer reactive oxygen radicals than other high-metabolism species. This highlights the central role of free radicals in aging, rather than metabolic rate in general. The relationship between free radicals and aging is embedded in a complex web of biochemical reactions affecting a wide range of physiological processes. Because of these multiple actions, simple antioxidant "treatments" for aging do not seem to have much of a positive effect and, in fact, may introduce a host of other problems (Adomaityte et al. 2014). The action of free radicals in our bodies may be a classic case of natural selection acting more forcefully during the prime reproductive phase of life than in the later, senescent phase (see discussion later)—the benefits of free radicals to the young outweigh their negative, cumulative effects in the old.

Wear and Degeneration

As anyone over the age of about 35 can attest, things do not work as well as they used to. One reason for this is that the long-term effects of wear on the body start to be felt. This is obvious for structures like the adult teeth, which have no regenerative or healing capacity once damaged or lost. For other parts of the body, such as muscles or joints, however, which do have some regenerative capacity to bounce back from overuse or injury, at some point the accumulated wear on these parts cannot be overcome, and there is a net loss in functional capacity. Heavy use of certain parts of the body, such as the leg joints of athletes or dancers, can actually accelerate age-related degeneration, but damage to joints is typical of aging in general. An almost universal example of age-related functional decline is *presbyopia*, the eye condition that makes focusing on near objects (e.g., reading) more difficult. This is caused by a thickening of the lens of the eye and also probably by a gradual loss of strength in the muscles that bend the lens for focusing. It strikes most people beginning around the age of 40 years.

In a sense the effects of age resulting from general wear and tear are obvious. However, if we consider the issue more broadly, we see that obvious does not necessarily mean inevitable. Although our adult teeth cannot change once they are grown, beavers have teeth that grow and regenerate over the course of their entire adult life. Most female mammals maintain the ability to reproduce throughout their entire lives, no matter how senescent they become. Human females maintain eggs from birth for decades before there is a loss in their vitality. Peak performance in certain endurance- and strength-based sports is not reached until the age of 30 years or more, indicating that our ability to add muscle is not simply an extension of the initial phases of growth and development. It is physiologically possible to counter many of the effects of wear and degeneration, but at some point, the body loses the ability to make the physiological investment necessary to do so. This suggests that there are trade-offs in the allocation of resources that occur over the life of an animal, which are directly relevant to the overall changes in the body related to aging.

Other factors are also involved in governing how the body ages. Hormones play a critical role in determining the timing of menopause and changes in male libido. Other hormone-mediated changes likely contribute to overall physical frailty and loss of muscle strength (Lamberts et al. 1997). The immune system also shows sign of aging. T- and B-cells become less responsive, increasing the susceptibility to infectious disease in older individuals; in contrast, some immune cells (macrophages) become overactivated, leading to an increased risk of autoimmune conditions, such as rheumatoid arthritis. Although neither could be considered the "cause" of aging, the endocrine and immune systems contribute to the overall decline of the aging human body.

Telomeres

Telomeres are the ends of chromosomes, which consist of thousands of pairs of a repeating sequence of six bases (see Figure 7.5; Gomes et al. 2011). Although telomeres may help protect genes against the loss of nucleotides during cell proliferation, they shorten with each cell division, ultimately leading to cell senescence and the end of cell replication in most tissues of the body. Telomere-based cellular aging seems to be related to aging and mortality in general: several studies have shown that elderly people with shorter telomeres have increased mortality, perhaps due to impaired immune and cardiovascular function (Eisenberg et al. 2012; Eisenberg and Kuzawa 2018). This suggests a strong association between telomere length and aging, although whether telomere shortening is a cause or effect of aging remains to be determined (Simons 2015). There is substantial variation in telomere biology among different mammal lineages; for example, telomeres are much longer in rodents than in humans, and telomere length does not appear to be associated with aging (Gomes et al. 2011). The human-type pattern of telomere biology may have evolved as a protection against developing malignancy (cancerous growth). The cellular transformation to malignancy typically requires multiple mutations, and shutting down cell replication is one way to prevent the accumulation of mutations in a cell lineage.

Not all tissues of the body are subject to telomere shortening with cell replication. An enzyme called *telomerase* works to add telomere repeats to the ends of chromosomes, thereby allowing for continued cell division. This occurs in certain germline and stem cell lines. In addition, telomerase is active in the testes, and the sperm telomeres are longer in older men than in younger men (telomere length is basically steady in eggs, because the formation of all eggs is initiated early in development). Dan Eisenberg and colleagues (Eisenberg et al. 2012; Eisenberg and Kuzawa 2013, 2018) have investigated the possibility that older fathers may be able to pass on longevity to their children in an **epigenetic** way—that is, via changes to gene function without changes to the genes themselves (telomeres are not genes).

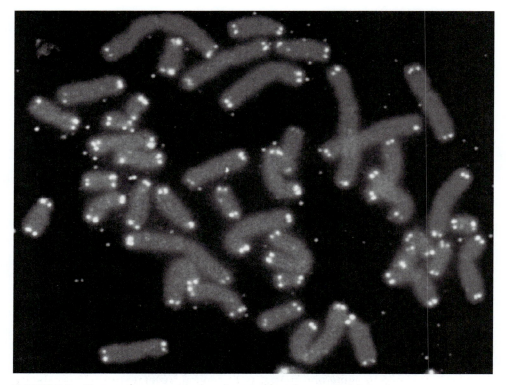

FIGURE 7.5   Human chromosomes (gray) capped by telomeres (white).
Credit: U.S. Department of Energy Human Genome Program.

For such an older father effect to be possible, it must first be shown that longer telomeres can be passed on to subsequent generations. Eisenberg and colleagues (2012) investigated this in a large, mutigenerational sample from Cebu in the Philippines. They found that children with older paternal grandfathers at the time of their fathers' births had relatively longer telomeres, independent of and additive to the age of their own fathers' when they were born. In other words, a grandfather who was an old father established a long-telomere lineage that was still observable even in a child with a relatively young father. The health ramifications of these long telomeres have yet to be measured, and an explanation has not been determined for why there was no maternal grandfather effect observed.

Eisenberg and Kuzawa (2013, 463) have hypothesized that paternally variable telomere length contributes to "adaptive intergenerational phenotypic plasticity." This is clearly a complex issue, involving not only a plastic response to different environments (i.e., those that are more or less supportive of increased longevity) but also the potential for variable inheritance among the younger and older offspring of a single individual. In addition, these plastic or epigenetic responses will interact with some of the basic factors underlying the evolution of aging, which are discussed in the next section. We are still in the early days of telomere research, and the consequences for variably inherited telomere length in human evolution are only beginning to be explored.

EVOLUTIONARY THEORIES OF AGING

In the 100 years after Darwin published his argument for evolution by natural selection in 1859, the evolution of senescence garnered relatively little attention. The prevailing view was generally some variant on the wear-and-tear model: organisms would wear out over time and, when they became weak enough, natural selection in the form of predators or disease would take care of them. The somatic mutation model of aging, which was introduced in the 1930s, is a variant on the wear-and-tear model, except the wear is occurring at the genetic rather than at the organismal level. A more refined, group-selectionist view of this position held that there were intrinsic mechanisms working within species whereby older and infirm members made way for younger members for the good of the group. In this way, there would be a counterforce to natural selection working to extend longevity as a means to increase survival. Actual biological mechanisms underlying such a group-benefit model were difficult to come by, however.

In the 1950s, evolutionary biologists such as Peter Medawar (Medawar 1952) pointed out that selection for aging per se in wild animal populations would be difficult because only a small proportion of all animals born live until they undergo senescence. Even if there were a plausible explanation for why older individuals were able to achieve higher fitness, the effects of selection would be limited by the fact that there would be very few senescent individuals for selection to act on. Medawar suggested that genes that cause negative effects later in life would simply accumulate in a species, but the negative effects would only be seen in the relatively small proportion that live to an advanced age.

Building on the ideas of Medawar and others, George C. Williams (1957) published what is now recognized as the foundation paper in the study of the evolution of senescence. Williams based his model on the fundamental observation that for any organism, the probability of reproduction peaks at maturity and declines thereafter. This is true even in the absence of senescence because death reduces the opportunities for reproduction to zero. As an animal increases in age, so also does its probability of dying from an accident, predation, or disease (extrinsic mortality). Thus, once an organism reaches sexual maturity, at a given age, reproductive potential is greater than at any subsequent age. The implication of this for longevity evolution is straightforward and profound: natural selection will have a greater impact on an organism during the earlier rather than the later parts of its reproductive life, making direct selection for increased longevity unlikely. The implication for this view is that the fact that some species might live longer than others is not a result of selection for longer life spans, but a cumulative secondary effect of other aspects of their evolved physiology.

G.C. Williams also suggested a potential genetic mechanism underlying senescence. The concept that individual genes have multiple effects is called **pleiotropy**. The kind of pleiotropic effects in which Williams was particularly interested involved genes whose effects were positive in the early life of an organism, but negative later in life, after the force of natural selection was greatly reduced. An example of this might be a gene for calcium metabolism that promotes bone healing and strength in early life but leads to increased arterial blockage in old age (Nesse and Williams 1994). The gene's bone-strengthening phenotypic effect would be subject to strong positive selection, but negative selection would have little opportunity to act on the senescent phenotype; thus, the gene could spread throughout the population despite its negative effects. Williams referred to this as "antagonistic pleiotropy," a term that emphasizes the potentially contradictory effects of a single gene during different life phases. The **antagonistic pleiotropy theory of aging** therefore attributes senescence to a combination of negative physiological effects that accumulate over a lifetime as a byproduct of selection acting during the reproductive phase of life. It is not difficult to see that this view, as Randolph Nesse and George Williams (1994, 212) put it, "discourages . . . hope that senescence is a disease that may someday be cured."

The theory of antagonistic pleiotropy still forms the framework for most investigations of the evolution of senescence, but alternative or complementary theories have been proposed. Notable among these is the **disposable soma theory of aging**, developed by Thomas Kirkwood in the 1970s (for discussions, see Kirkwood and Rose 1991; Kirkwood and Austad 2000). The disposable soma theory is essentially about resource allocation. It recognizes that there is a basic trade-off in an organism between resources devoted to maintaining the body and those devoted to reproduction. As discussed earlier, it is possible to maintain bodily structures over a long life, but there is a cost. On the one hand, an organism that devoted no energy to maintaining the body would rapidly age, so there is a fitness advantage to be gained by allocating some resources to maintenance. On the other hand, Kirkwood argues that devoting too many resources to maintaining the body is not optimal because that would be foregoing fitness gains that are to be had via reproduction. Thus, there will evolve a balancing point between somatic maintenance and reproductive investment. The body is "disposable" because it only needs to be in a good condition through the normal reproductive life of the organism—there is no need to maintain it after that.

The antagonistic pleiotropy and disposable soma theories of aging are not mutually exclusive, although they focus on different aspects of the evolutionary biology of organisms. Antagonistic pleiotropy identifies a basic constraint on selection for longevity; the disposable soma theory is more helpful in explaining the ecological trade-offs that underlie variability in longevity. Both of these theories of the evolution of aging have received support from numerous studies conducted on both wild and laboratory animals (Johnson et al. 2019). However, exceptions have been found that suggest the complex interplay among longevity, ecology, and physiology.

As we saw earlier, antagonistic pleiotropy suggests that aging cures will not be easily obtained, and the disposable part of the disposable soma theory also conveys a somewhat pessimistic message in this regard. Nonetheless, the search for the means to extend human life goes on, with particular attention being paid to certain "longevity hotspots" where people seem to live healthier and longer lives than the vast majority of humanity. Of course, we already know that avoiding obesity increases longevity, as does not smoking and maintaining an active lifestyle, along with other lifestyle habits.

But while these may promote healthy aging, they do not prevent or even postpone aging changes in the body.

THE AGING BRAIN

In the seventh century BC, the Greek physician Pythagoras wrote of the last stage of life: "The scene of moral existence closes, after a great length of time, to which, very fortunately, few of the human species arrives. The system returns to the imbecility of the first epoch of the infancy" (Berchtold and Cotman 1998, 173). He is referring here to a condition we now call **dementia**, which is characterized by memory impairment, loss of *executive function* (decision making, judgment), and speech difficulties, among other symptoms. As Pythagoras indicates, in his time relatively few people lived long enough to suffer from dementia. In our day and age, however, with a growing aged population, dementia is becoming an increasingly important public health issue.

The brain undergoes changes as it ages over the adult life span (Allen et al. 2005a, 2005b; Raz 1999). Let us consider changes visible in the gray and white matter. The *gray matter* of the brain consists of the cell bodies of neurons, which are distributed in a rim about 4 millimeters thick around the outside of the brain (the cerebral cortex) and in agglomerations (nuclei) found in the basal core of the brain. The *white matter* forms the core of the brain and consists of the cell processes that connect one neuron to another, constructing the neural networks that underlie coordinated brain function. These processes are white because they are sheathed in *myelin*, a white, fatty substance that facilitates electrical conduction along the cell processes. Diseases such as multiple sclerosis, which are characterized by disorders of movement, are caused by the loss of myelin in parts of the nervous system (brain and spinal cord).

Over the course of the adult life span, the gray matter declines in volume at a steady, linear rate. Compared with a 30-year-old, a 70-year-old has about 10% less gray matter and an 80-year-old only about 12% less (Allen et al. 2005b), so the loss of neurons during aging is not particularly profound. The white matter shows quite a different aging pattern. Throughout much of adulthood, white matter volumes hold steady or even increase, reaching a peak sometime in the forties or fifties. Thereafter, white matter declines, at first slowly and then more precipitously. Compared with a 30-year-old, a 70-year-old has about 6% less white matter volume, but by the age of 80, the decrease is more than 20%. It appears that throughout much of adulthood, the ability to form new or more complex connections among neurons outpaces the steady loss of the neurons themselves. However, after the age of 50 or 60, this ability is compromised; after the age of 70, we start to see the combined effects on white matter of the loss of neurons and of the reduction in the ability to maintain or grow new connections among neurons. It is the loss of white matter that causes the aged brain to have a relatively shrunken appearance, with expansion of the sulci as the gyri shrink (Figure 7.6).

The changes in the gross anatomy of the brain are matched by measurable changes in functional connectivity in brain networks (Damoiseaux 2017). The *default mode network* consists of an interconnected group of brain regions that show greater activation when an individual is at rest and not attending to a specific cognitive task. It is associated with mind-wandering and episodic memory, among other cognitive phenomena. The connections between default mode network regions are weaker in older

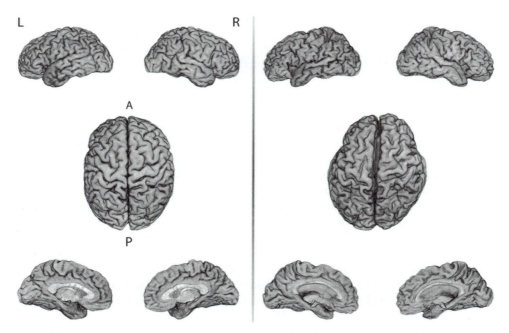

FIGURE 7.6   As the brain ages, there is a loss of gray and white matter tissue resulting in an expansion of the sulci on the brain's surface. The brain of a 28-year-old male (on the left) is compared with that of an 88-year-old male (on the right). L, left; R, right; A, anterior; P, posterior. *Credit:* Courtesy Joel Bruss, Laboratory of Computational Neuroimaging, Department of Neurology, University of Iowa.

individuals and may underlie poorer performance on tasks related to memory and executive function. Studies of white matter tracts that connect different brain regions also show a decline in integrity, which makes processing networks less efficient (Damoiseaux 2017).

What happens to cognitive function as the brain shrinks and connections between brain regions weaken with age? There is some controversy about this depending in part on the perspective of who is answering the question. On the one hand, from a normal performance perspective, there is strong evidence for a number of cognitive measures that cognitive decline begins in the twenties and extends through the life span (Salthouse 2009). On the other hand, despite the slowing of reaction time and declines in other specific abilities (e.g., memory), there are abundant examples of older people who clearly maintain their cognitive abilities while working in highly complex environments. In the absence of neurological disease, social and intellectual competence is typically maintained throughout most of the normal life span. So from a clinical perspective, although people over the age of 60 perform somewhat less well than younger adults on neuropsychological tests (Petersen 2003), most older people can cognitively and behaviorally maintain an active and socially engaged life.

This rather rosy picture of the maintenance of cognitive function in old age can be rudely and tragically disrupted by the appearance of dementia. Not just 2,700 years ago, but as recently as 30 or 40 years ago, *senile dementia* was widely considered an inevitable consequence of old age. Although it was recognized that not everyone became senile, it was considered part and parcel of the general aging process and therefore not worth devoting much effort to curing or even understanding it. In the medical community, this view started to change in the 1970s, when some medical researchers argued that senile dementia was a specific form of dementia, the cellular pathology of which had been identified in the 1890s by a physician named Alois Alzheimer. **Alzheimer's disease** is characterized anatomically by the accumulation of localized areas of neuronal cell death or damage (called plaques), which can only be seen microscopically. The primary component of these plaques is a protein called *amyloid*. The gene for the amyloid precursor protein is found on chromosome 21, and in Down syndrome (trisomy 21), nearly all individuals develop an Alzheimer-like dementia due to overexpression of this protein. In the earliest stages of the disease, these plaques are most commonly found in brain areas involved in memory, but they spread outward from there. Before 1976, only 150 medical articles had ever been published on Alzheimer's disease. A search on the PubMed database for "Alzheimer's disease" now yields more than 106,000 hits. This rechristening of senile dementia reflected not only a more nuanced picture of pathology in the aging brain, but also described a discrete illness for which funding for research and clinical treatment could be obtained (Drachman 2006; Lock 2013).

The prevalence of Alzheimer's disease is about 2% to 4% in the general population over the age of 65 years; the rate increases dramatically over the age of 75 years and at least 20% of all people over the age of 85 years have the condition (American Psychiatric Association 1994). In 2015, it was estimated that about 5.4 million Americans had Alzheimer's disease and that by 2050, the number will be 13.8 million; currently, about 700,000 people per year over the age of 65 years die with Alzheimer's disease (Alzheimer's Association 2016). In 2016, total health care payments for Alzheimer's disease was estimated to be $236 billion. It is important to note that Alzheimer's disease is not the only form of dementia that afflicts older people, but it does account for about 80% of all cases (the second most common form is vascular dementia associated with heart disease) (Hou et al. 2006). Although the risk of developing Alzheimer's disease increases with age, there are 100-year-old people who have no signs of Alzheimer's pathology. Thus, Alzheimer's disease should not be considered just another name for a universal form of senile dementia that affects anyone who lives long enough.

The increasing risk of Alzheimer's with age is probably the result of an interaction between normal brain aging (i.e., loss of tissue) and the accumulation of Alzheimer's pathology (Drachman 2006). Is dementia an inevitable consequence of brain aging, even in the absence of Alzheimer's disease? Robert Terry and Robert Katzman (2001) suggest that the rate of loss of synapses (connections between neurons) and the breakdown of neural networks with increasing age indicates that the average person living to 130 years of age would be demented from age effects alone. This would suggest that even if Alzheimer's disease is not an inevitable consequence of aging, developing some form of dementia is. There are no "average" 130-year-olds around right now, but if medical science succeeds in substantially extending the life span, the problem of maintaining brain health and function over an extended life will need to be addressed.

Alzheimer's disease undoubtedly results from a combination of genetic and environmental factors. One way researchers hope to gain insights into the causes of the disease is to look at ethnic variation in its prevalence and course. Within the United States, there are some differences in the expression of dementia in European American and African American communities: vascular dementia may be relatively more common in African Americans; genetic markers that predict increased susceptibility to Alzheimer's disease in European Americans have not yet been shown to be effective in African Americans; and the actual cognitive profiles of dementia differ somewhat in the two communities (Froehlich et al. 2001). A cultural difference between European and African American communities emerges in how individuals with cognitive impairments and their caregivers report the level of impairment (Ford et al. 1990; Hinrichsen and Ramirez 1992). African American patients and caregivers were more likely to describe cognitive impairments as more severe than clinical measures would indicate. This tendency could form the basis for a cultural bias that would lead to the overestimation of dementia prevalence in African Americans (Ford et al. 1990). We must be aware of the possibility that the tests used to assess cognitive impairments may be culturally biased and a source of the differences in the two communities.

Studies comparing Alzheimer's dementia rates in Japanese and Japanese Americans have shown that rates for Japanese Americans are about twice as high as those for Japanese and similar to those observed for European Americans (Shadlen et al. 2000). Although this could point to environmental factors such as differences in diet (the Japanese diet is typically lower in fat but higher in salt than the American diet), diagnostic differences across cultures could also play a role. Diagnostic practices are difficult to account for in comparative studies that make use of published data or clinical reports. A carefully controlled diagnostic study comparing Alzheimer's and other dementia rates in the African American population of Indianapolis, Indiana, and among Yorubas living in Ibadan, Nigeria, found higher rates for both dementia overall and Alzheimer's disease in particular in the U.S. sample (Hendrie et al. 1995). In the Ibadan sample, among adults aged 65 years and older, the prevalence rate for dementia was 2.29% and for Alzheimer's disease it was 1.41%. In Indianapolis, the rates were 4.82% and 3.69% in the community-based sample and 8.24% and 6.24% for the combined nursing home and community-based sample. The African American rates were similar to rates obtained in a large-scale Canadian study (predominantly European-derived population) using a similar methodology. It is important to note that the increased risk of developing Alzheimer's disease with increasing age was the same in both the African and the African American samples.

The lower rates of dementia in the Yoruba sample were accompanied by lower rates of diabetes and hypertension and lower levels of cholesterol (Hendrie 2006). These results and those derived from other studies indicate that there may be an interaction between vascular health and the expression of Alzheimer's disease. Compared with the African American diet, the Yoruba diet is lower in calories and fat. In addition, Hugh Hendrie also points out that the Yoruba elderly were much more likely to live in extended families and have larger and more active social networks than the African Americans. Although there is no such thing as a perfect "natural experiment" allowing the testing of environmental variables in genetically similar populations,

Alzheimer's Disease, Genes, and Evolution

One of the most exciting developments in Alzheimer's disease research in the 1990s was the discovery that different polymorphisms of the lipid transport protein apolipoprotein (apo) E conferred different risks for developing the disease. ApoE, which is produced in the brain and liver, plays an important role in the intracellular transport and metabolism of triglycerides and cholesterol. It has several important neurobiological functions, especially in myelinization and the formation of connections between neurons (Mahley and Rall 2000). The three forms of apoE (apoE2, apoE3, apoE4) are produced by three different alleles at a single locus. They differ from one another only by single amino acid substitutions.

ApoE4 is the critical allele for the development of Alzheimer's disease (Corder et al. 1993). In European Americans, possession of just one copy of apoE4 nearly triples the risk of developing Alzheimer's disease. Homozygote individuals for apoE4 are more than eight times more likely to develop the disease compared with people who possess only apoE2 or apoE3. The average age of onset also decreases in a dose-dependent fashion with possession of one or two apoE4 alleles. ApoE4 is also associated with increased risk of heart disease, stroke, slower recovery from head trauma, and poorer outcome for multiple sclerosis. The association of apoE4 with Alzheimer's disease in Africans and African Americans is weaker than that for European Americans, although apoE4 homozygotes are still about four times more likely to develop Alzheimer's disease (Sahota et al. 1997). In Japanese populations, the association between apoE4 and Alzheimer's disease is actually stronger than in European populations (Farrer et al. 1997). Despite this variation, it is safe to conclude, after thousands of studies have been conducted, that "apoE4 carriers are more prone to amyloid deposition and [Alzheimer's disease] than apoE3 carriers, who in turn are more prone than apoE2 carriers" (Belloy et al. 2019, 827). Indeed, the apoE polymorphism is one of only five that has been shown in large genomic scans to be associated with exceptional longevity, presumably due to the relatively negative effects of apoE4 compared to the other variants (Revelas et al. 2018).

ApoE4 clearly plays a critical role in the development of Alzheimer's disease, but the heterogeneous epidemiological data (both within and between populations) point to other genetic or environmental factors being involved; after all, a significant number of people (approximately 20%) develop the disease without possession of even a single copy of apoE4. General population variation in apoE4 frequency is difficult to explain simply in terms of its relationship to Alzheimer's disease, and some researchers speculate that its distribution may also be shaped by factors such as infectious disease load (Mahley and Rall 2000). Evolutionary modeling suggests that apoE4 alleles should be lost in human populations over time (i.e., it is selected against), in part because of relatively increased mortality over the entire life span and not just in old age (Drenos and Kirkwood 2010).

Caleb Finch and Robert Sapolsky (1999) hypothesized that the evolution of the apoE polymorphism may offer critical clues to understanding increased longevity in humans. They look at apoE in a broader zoological context and point out that phylogenetic analyses show that the apoE4 form of the protein is likely the oldest or ancestral form. They also note that in other long-lived mammals, aging brains tend to develop Alzheimer-like pathologies, which compromise cognitive function when the animals are older. Finch and Sapolsky propose that apoE2 and apoE3 were selected for with the increase in longevity over the course of human evolution. One context in which longevity selection could have occurred is if older women gain a fitness advantage by no longer reproducing themselves (hence the evolution of menopause) while still being able to contribute to the well-being of their grandchildren. This "grandmother hypothesis" (Hawkes 2003) is probably the best evolutionary explanation currently available for an extended postreproductive lifespan in humans. Finch and Sapolsky argue that women who did not possess the apoE4 allele would maintain better cognitive function as they aged and hence would be in a better position to assist in the upbringing of their grandchildren through the sharing of information and knowledge accumulated over the course of their lives.

One limitation of the Finch and Sapolsky model, which became known only after it was published, is that the apoE polymorphism probably only dates to about 200,000 to 300,000 years ago (Fullerton et al. 2000). This means that although it may have had a critical role in the emergence of modern *Homo sapiens*, it could not have played a role over the longer course of human evolution. A more recent analysis of apoE allele frequencies throughout the world shows that their frequencies vary according to absolute latitude and temperature, but not elevation (Eisenberg et al. 2010). ApoE4 frequencies were found to be lowest in areas with moderate temperatures—it was higher in both colder and hotter locales. This pattern goes along with that seen for latitude: apoE4 rates are highest in hot climates (low latitude), decrease in the moderate mid-latitudes, and increase again at high latitude. These patterns were independent of population structure and history, suggesting that they result from the effects of natural selection. Dan Eisenberg and his

(continued)

(continued)

colleagues hypothesize that given that metabolic rates are elevated in both colder and warmer climates, placing greater energetic demands on the body (including the need for more cholesterol), selection for apoE4 would protect against low cholesterol levels.

The evolution of the distribution of apoE alleles has undoubtedly been complex. The persistence of apoE4, the rise of apoE3 to become the most common allele in the polymorphism, and the relatively recent appearance and spread of apoE2 some populations have yet to be fully explained (Huebbe and Rimbach 2017). Several polymorphisms have been shown to be associated with preventing

cognitive decline in older age, apoE among them (Schwarz et al. 2016). This would support the idea that maintaining cognitive abilities in conjunction with enhanced longevity was important in human evolution, and that apoE3 in particular may have played a key role in that development.

The apoE alleles evolved in an evolutionary context that saw an unprecedented increase in brain size and cognitive ability (Allen et al. 2005a; Stern 2002) and the distribution of human populations into a wide range of environments. Factors relating to aging, cognition, diet, and disease resistance likely all played a role in the evolution of this polymorphism.

---

cross-cultural studies, such as those comparing dementia rates in Japanese and Japanese Americans and in Africans and African Americans, help to identify potentially important environmental factors that could increase the risk of developing Alzheimer's disease.

EXTENDING LIFE? CALORIC RESTRICTION AND AN OKINAWA CASE STUDY

Most Americans are aware of the most basic advice to achieve a healthy "three score and ten" years that the Bible cites as the human life span: don't smoke, drink a little alcohol but not too much, don't eat too much, exercise, wear your seat belts, and so on. Of course, many people do not follow these lifestyle recommendations; they depend more on medical science to make sure they live as long as they can. This leads us to the question of whether we can depend on medical science to extend our lives in a substantial way. Jay Olshansky and his colleagues (1990) looked at this issue using U.S. mortality statistics from the 1980s. In 1985, a 50-year-old woman had a life expectancy of 30.9 years and a 50-year-old man had another 25.5 years to live on average. If deaths from cancer, all circulatory disease, and diabetes were eliminated, that would reduce mortality by about 75%. Life expectancy for 50-year-old women would increase to 46.2 years and for men to 40.6 years. Thus, with the elimination of three-quarters of all causes of death in the elderly, life expectancy for both sexes could be more than 90 years of age. It goes without saying, but even 25 years later we are nowhere near achieving such improvements in health. Olshansky and his co-authors make it clear from other analyses that the substantial reductions in mortality rates in the elderly required to greatly increase the life span will be hard to come by. They suggest that public health expenditures be directed toward making sure more people reach a healthy old age rather than trying to extend the life span, especially because the physical frailty of most people over the age of 90 years usually precludes a high quality of life.

This sort of advice has had little appeal to *prolongevity* advocates, who seek the means to extend the normal healthy life span beyond 80 or 90 years or more. Decades of laboratory experimentation on rodents and nonhuman primates have identified one reliable way to extend the lives of these animals: *caloric restriction*, or undernutrition without malnutrition (Casadesus et al. 2004; Hursting et al. 2003). By reducing caloric intake 40% to 60% through a greatly reduced daily diet or alternate day feeding, the two-year survival rate of laboratory rats is doubled, and similar gains have been seen in a wide range of mammal species (Figure 7.7). One way caloric restriction appears to work is by both reducing cellular free radical sources and increasing the endogenous production of antioxidants. Studies of primates indicate that caloric restriction improves a host of cardiovascular indicators and the maintenance of insulin sensitivity and healthy blood sugar levels (Lane et al. 2001). Because it has effects on various cell growth factors, caloric restriction may also reduce the risk of cancer (Hursting et al. 2003).

Although the data are hard to come by given our long life spans, it is reasonable to expect that caloric restriction could have a positive effect on humans. Indeed, there have been many advocates for adopting a caloric-restriction lifestyle; there is even a Caloric Restriction Society (http://www.crsociety.org). However, the reality of a world where overeating and obesity are considered major health issues (and an evolved biology that biases us toward excess food consumption) makes it unlikely

FIGURE 7.7 A long-term research project at the National Primate Research Center at the University of Wisconsin has examined the effects of a calorie-restricted diet on rhesus monkeys. Both monkeys in the photo (taken in 2006) had been involved in the project since 1989—the one on the left on a calorie-restricted diet and the one on the right on an unrestricted diet.
Credit: Jeff Miller/University of Wisconsin–Madison.

that most people will want to subsist on such a low-calorie diet. In addition, to avoid malnutrition, careful attention must be paid to all aspects of such a diet, not just calories.

Most researchers do not actually advocate adopting a low-calorie diet but are instead using caloric restriction as a model for developing drugs that could mimic the effects of such a diet (Balasubramanian et al. 2017). Several different metabolic pathways in the body have been targeted as potential targets for prolongevity pharmaceutical intervention (Longo et al. 2015). For example, human growth hormone receptor polymorphisms are known to influence longevity, and it has been shown in dwarf mice that the longevity-enhancing effects of caloric restriction can be reversed by giving them growth hormone (Gesing et al. 2014). So although the absence of growth hormone is lethal, drugs that reduce the activity of growth hormones may promote longevity. Periodic or intermittent fasting may also provide a dietary intervention that is less of a burden than full caloric restriction (Longo et al. 2015).

Cross-cultural studies of aging are helping researchers identify environments that may be conducive to living a long, healthy life. Over the years, several populations have been claimed to be exceptionally long lived (e.g., in highland Ecuador and the Republic of Georgia), leading some to visit those sites to seek clues for the "secret" of long life. Unfortunately, these claims have been shown to be unsubstantiated and the product of exaggeration and dubious or nonexistent documentation. More recently, the island of Okinawa, a prefecture of Japan located within the Ryukyu Islands chain that extends southward from the main islands of Japan toward Taiwan, has gained much attention for having the longest-lived people in a country that has the highest life expectancy in the world (Arakawa et al. 2005; B.J. Willcox et al. 2006; D.C. Willcox et al. 2006;; Yamori et al. 2001). As of the year 2000, the overall life-expectancy rate for Japan was 81.2 years (compared with 76.8 years for the United States), but for Okinawa it was 81.8 years. Japanese females had a life expectancy of 84.0 years; for Okinawan females it was 85.1 years (Figure 7.8). More significant, perhaps, is the proportion of Okinawans who live to be more than 100 years old. In 2004, the Okinawan population was 1.35 million. Among these were approximately 1,800 centenarians, with women outnumbering men by about 5 to 1. The centenarian rate is 42.5/100,000 in Okinawa compared with 16.1/100,000 for the whole of Japan. It is interesting to note that Okinawans have the longest lifespans despite living in the poorest part of Japan. This flies in the face of the conventional wisdom that higher socioeconomic success is correlated with better health (Cockerham et al. 2000). Of course, Okinawans escape some of the stresses that accompany socioeconomic development, which may have a deleterious effect on longevity in other parts of Japan.

In a proximate sense, it is not difficult to figure out why the Okinawans live so long. Their mortality advantages are mostly attributable to lower rates of cardiovascular disease and cancer. In addition, medical histories and autopsy reports indicate that although they may eventually succumb to age-related diseases and impairment, very old Okinawans maintain good health for a remarkably long time. One autopsy report on a centenarian Okinawan woman, who had maintained an independent life until she was 97 years of age, showed that her heart, kidney, and stomach were "remarkably healthy" (Bernstein et al. 2004). Compared to other Japanese centenarians, Okinawan

FIGURE 7.8 A significant proportion of Okinawans maintain vital lives into advanced old age. The 99-year-old Harumi Ota (top) refuses to share the secret for her longevity. The 102-year-old Buddhist monk Tenryu Taba (bottom) sings and plays the sanshin, an Okinawan stringed instrument. *Credit:* Chiyomi Sumida/*Stars and Stripes*.

centenarians have higher bone density and lower rates of dementia, and their measured level of disability are more similar to individuals ten years younger (Willcox et al. 2017). There is likely a genetic component underlying the long survival of the oldest Okinawans. Genetic analyses of the siblings of centenarians show that sisters have a 2.6-fold greater likelihood of reaching 90 years of age and brothers have a 5.4-fold increased chance compared with others in their birth cohort (B.J. Willcox et al. 2006). What the genetic factors might be are as yet unknown.

Although genetics may account for why some Okinawans live an exceptionally long time, it is clear that the overall rates of longevity are in large part the result of an environmental factor: diet. Compared with the rest of Japan, where stomach cancer rates are among the highest in the world, Okinawans have a much lower rate, which some attribute to a much lower sodium intake (Yamori et al. 2001). The Okinawan diet differs from the diet of most of Japan in part because it developed under a wider range of cultural influences from China and Southeast Asia, and it also reflects the limitations of life on a very small island (Sho 2001). In the nineteenth century, the staple of the Okinawan diet was the sweet potato, and they consumed much more of it than in any other region of Japan. Sweet potato is much richer in vitamins, energy, and fiber than rice, the staple of most of the "mainland" of Japan. Sweet potato continues to be eaten, along with large quantities of seaweed, leafy vegetables and herbs, tofu (a source of soy protein), and fish; these foods are all rich in nutrients that may contribute to lifelong cardiovascular health. Okinawans prize pork, another source of protein, and consume it in many traditional dishes and in conjunction with traditional festivals. Because it was never abundant, great effort was made to use all parts of the pig, including the feet, ears, stomach, and intestine. Laboratory studies on rats show that consumption of these collagen-rich tissues actually lowered serum triglyceride levels, which would be consistent with better cardiovascular health (Sho 2001). Studies comparing the health of Okinawans living in Okinawa, Hawaii, and Brazil further demonstrate the importance of diet for Okinawan longevity: the Okinawans in Hawaii have maintained a diet and a health profile similar to that seen in Okinawans, whereas those living in Brazil have a diet much higher in salt and fat and subsequently have much higher rates of cardiovascular disease, obesity, and diabetes (Yamori et al. 2001).

The Chinese influence in Okinawan cuisine can be seen most clearly in the concept of *shingi gusui* ("infused medicine") in which the medicinal qualities of food in specific combinations were identified and exploited (Sho 2001). For example, *chimu* and *shinji*, pig's liver and vegetables, is believed to be curative of a wide range of illnesses, and broths made from them in combination are given to sick people (much like chicken soup is given to sick individuals in the United States). Another combination consisting of fish and bitter vegetables is still sold together in Okinawan markets and is used by people to ward off the effects of colds and flu. The practice of combining diverse foodstuffs in a broth is adaptive for life on a small island where food scarcity could be a periodic issue.

This returns us to the concept of undernutrition without malnutrition. Although the Okinawan diet was not traditionally abundant, it was diverse, and that diversity was reinforced through cultural beliefs that emphasized the beneficial qualities of eating different foods in combination. Researchers have also considered caloric restriction as an underlying cause of Okinawan longevity (D.C. Willcox et al. 2006). In the 1960s, surveys showed that Okinawan schoolchildren only consumed 62% of the calories of other Japanese children; in the 1970s, the adult Okinawan diet had only 83% of the calories of the adult Japanese diet. Craig Willcox and his colleagues analyzed dietary trends in the Okinawan population from 1949 until the late 1960s and found that during this period, Okinawan septuagenarians consumed 11% fewer calories than would normally be recommended for maintenance of body weight. Body mass indexes showed that Okinawans were very lean during this period and maintained this leanness throughout adulthood. Willcox and his colleagues argue that although definitive proof cannot be obtained, it is not unreasonable to suppose that caloric restriction has played some role in extending the longevity of Okinawans, although the restriction itself was much less drastic than the typical lab animal dietary regime. They emphasized again that although the Okinawan diet is limited in calories, it is rich in nutrients, antioxidants, and protein. If there is a secret to Okinawan longevity, it may be contained in this piece of advice traditionally given by Okinawan grandmothers: *hara hachibu*, or "eat until you are 80% full" (D.C. Willcox et al. 2006, 176; Willcox et al. 2014).

HEALTH, ILLNESS, AND THE CULTURAL CONSTRUCTION OF AGING

For most of this chapter, we have treated aging as a biological variable with evolutionary and health consequences. However, aging is a biological phenomenon embedded in a cultural context, and concepts of illness as they relate to age vary cross-culturally (Lock 1998). The basic biomedical model of aging and health sees age-related declines in health as being the result of several factors: increased susceptibility to disease resulting from a loss of vitality; extended exposure over a lifetime to stresses causing disease; and the accumulated effects of wear and overusage of various body parts. A cultural model of illness need not deny the relevance of these factors but seeks to explain why similar biological indicators (starting with age) in older people in different cultures can lead to markedly different experiences of age-related disease or illness. Or, how is it that biomedical definitions of impairment in older people do not match those traditionally identified in a wide range of cultures?

We have already seen how one biological aspect of aging, menopause, is constructed differently cross-culturally (Chapter 6); other age-associated conditions, such as Alzheimer's disease, also vary in terms of how they are recognized and expressed. Indeed, we have already discussed the cultural reconfiguring of senile dementia as Alzheimer's disease in the 1970s and 1980s. Given that Alzheimer's disease had been described decades prior, the change from regarding dementia as a normal outcome of aging ("senile dementia") to seeing it as a pathological process in the United States was undoubtedly the result of several cultural trends: an increase in optimism about what medical science can accomplish to fight disease; a growing economic affluence that allowed the public to look beyond simply maintaining and toward extending life; and an increased focus on youth and youthfulness as a cultural norm, which rendered many aspects of old age pathological.

The final assessment and interpretation of a woman's menopausal status rest ultimately with herself—it is a private condition. In contrast, senility in an older person is defined by others, and that definition depends on the normative relationships in a culture between older people and members of their family or the community in general. Alzheimer's disease or cerebrovascular dementia may have well-defined pathological signs, but their expression, even in Western cultures where the biomedical diagnosis has primary status, is variable. This intrinsic variability intersects with economic status, lifestyle histories, educational attainment, and so on.

Other cultures have categorized the experience of dementia in other ways. Lawrence Cohen (Cohen 1995, 1998) has done an extensive study of aging and senility in the city of Banaras in the northern Indian state Uttar Pradesh (Figure 7.9). He found that Western medical terminology did not match the ethnomedical model he encountered in northern India. He thus proposed a more general, heuristic definition of senility:

> The attribution of difference of discontinuity to an old person, or to old people as a group, when that difference is embodied in terms of organs or states of volition, affect, character, or cognition, when that difference is marked by others in terms of the behavior—actions or utterances—of an old person, and when that difference implies a deleterious change. (Cohen 1995, 317)

FIGURE 7.9 An elderly couple from Ladakh, India.
Credit: Andrea Wiley.

This definition accommodates a wide range of behavioral changes that occur in older people and acknowledges that different cultures may focus on different behavioral signs of aging. For example, in Western cultures, memory issues occupy a central role in the diagnosis of dementia. Changes in affect can even be interpreted as being a result of the "frustrations" of dealing with memory problems, although such changes (e.g., disinhibition resulting from frontal lobe pathology) can be a primary symptom of Alzheimer's disease as much as memory problems.

In northern India, Lawrence Cohen found that signs of *dimāg* (a "weak brain") in older people were categorized three ways: *kamzor hote hain* (emphasizing weakness), *saṭhiyā jāte hain* (becoming stubbornly "sixtyish"), or *inke dimāg garm ho jāte hain* (becoming angry and hot-brained). These categories emphasize affective (emotional) rather than cognitive changes that occur with age. A weak brain is typically defined in the context of overall weakening of the body; younger people link the development of brain weakness in aging to broader concerns about becoming dependent in old age as a result of weakness in both body and mind. An extreme form of weakness is madness, traditionally embodied in the figure of the old madwoman (*pagli*) of Hindi literature. Older women who are disconnected from the support of families through widowhood (especially at a young age), or even abandonment, become the object of ridicule and scorn—an embodied representation of what happens to women in a bad family.

The notion of becoming sixtyish comes closest to the concept of senility in English. In this context, the development of stubbornness and willfulness—developing a hot brain—leads to conflicts about authority within the family. In most accounts, it is exemplified by a refusal of older people to listen to younger people. Lawrence Cohen points out that being sixtyish is not necessarily the same thing as being physically old or weak, which complicates the intergenerational conflicts that accompany saṭhiyā. The outcome of such conflicts is not in question because the young will surely supplant the old, but conflicts arise nonetheless. As Cohen (1995, 326) writes, "The paradoxical thermodynamics of aging reflect the paradox that the accumulation of power and experience cannot be linear, that the foolishness of a will that must deny its body overwhelms the wisdom of years."

The introduction of the biomedical concept of Alzheimer's disease provides an interesting parallel to the traditional categorizations of senility in India. Cohen describes a case from Calcutta in which a daughter-in-law in a family was attempting to provide care for her mother-in-law, who was clearly demented. Through family connections, the daughter-in-law and son located an acceptable old-age facility where the mother could be cared for. After only a short time there, however, the mother was rejected by the facility on account of her "madness." Such madness (and potentially the deliberate deception of the authorities at the care facility) reflected badly on the family as a whole and on the daughter-in-law in particular. The family then took the mother to a psychiatrist; although psychiatry carries a stigma, it is not as terrible as being labeled a bad family. The mother was diagnosed as having Alzheimer's disease, which was a relief to all, because she could therefore be described as having a medical condition. When she eventually was placed in a care facility a year later, the fact that she had a medical condition provided a legitimate reason for providing her with care outside of the family home (i.e., she was not placed there simply because she was old).

Changing concepts of senility in India are an example that attitudes toward aging and health change along with other cultural currents. In contemporary Western cultures, as older people make up an increasingly larger proportion of the population, we are accustomed to hearing statements such as "you are as old as you feel" and "60 is the new 40"—statements that supposedly exemplify a more positive attitude toward old age. New models for living an active and vital old age are increasingly being sought. Elizabeth Whitaker (2005) describes a community of avid cyclists (all men) in northern Italy. These 22 men, ranging in age from 49 to 84 years, average three or four rides per week of three to four hours in duration; various anthropometric and physiological measures indicate that they are very healthy. Not everyone is going to become an avid cyclist in old age, but Whitaker's analysis shows that if a person wants to embrace a more active life, then it should be through an activity that provides satisfaction on multiple levels. These older Italian cyclists are not just riding bikes to put in the kilometers; rather, they find in cycling an "enjoyment of adventure, competition, natural beauty, and both company and solitude . . . they speak of fun, adventure, and the freedom to do more riding once one is retired" (Whitaker 2005, 31). Too often, biomedical prescriptions for increased activity are laid out with little concern for the context in which those activities take place.

Over the past 20 years, the sexual activity of older people, especially older men, has drawn much attention. The introduction, marketing, and widespread use of drugs to treat ED (discussed in Chapter 6) have changed perspectives on the maintenance of masculinity in old age. ED is definitely an age-related condition: prevalence studies conducted throughout the world show a marked increase in ED rates starting in the 50–59 age range, which then accelerate over the age of 60 years (Lewis et al. 2010). Implicit in much of the advertising about ED drugs is that they are necessary to maintain "real," phallocentric masculinity and that such masculinity is dependent on a man's ability to maintain an active, youthful sex life to satisfy his partner (Wentzell 2008).

Despite the widespread use of ED drugs following these advertising campaigns (directed at both doctors and men with ED), ethnographic research suggests that patients who use these drugs do not necessarily embrace the portrait of revived masculinity conveyed by them. In a New Zealand study, Annie Potts and colleagues (2004) interviewed dozens of men who had used Viagra, as well as the women partners of men who used the drug. They found a range of perspectives on ED and the use of Viagra; some men's views closely matched that portrayed in advertising linking ED treatment with restored masculinity. However, the range of responses from both the men and the women suggested that there was not a single view of ED as a "problem" and of Viagra as a "solution." As Potts and colleagues concluded, "There is no standard experience of a 'functional' erection, even less so of a 'dysfunctional' erection; there appears to be no necessary relationship between a particular kind of erection and a satisfying sexual relationship; and there is no definitive view of what constitutes 'normal' masculinity or 'being a man' in relation to erectile 'functionality'" (Potts et al. 2004, 497–498). Some men and women embraced the "different" kind of sexuality that reduced erectile function encourages.

A different ethnographic perspective on ED therapy use and nonuse comes from Emily Wentzell's (2013) research among older, working-class men, based in a hospital urology clinic in Cuernavaca, Mexico. Wentzell found that many men who might have been eligible for it did not elect to use ED treatment. There were financial considerations involved, but Wentzell points out that these men could address their decreasing erectile function in two ways: to acknowledge it as a sign of failure of masculinity requiring medical treatment or to see it as an "embodied marker of manly maturity." Although an abundance of penetrative sex might be an appropriate marker of masculinity for a younger man, Wentzell's interviews with both older men and women finds support for the idea that masculinity changes over time. Among these working-class Mexicans, mature masculinity means focusing on home and family rather than sexual conquests. Medicalizing natural bodily changes actually undermines the legitimacy of this transition.

If nothing else, the introduction and widespread use and discussion of ED treatments in developed countries is indicative of a change of perspective on one aspect of the lives of older individuals. However, changing attitudes toward aging is a separate issue from whether older people are living better and more fulfilled lives today compared with the past. Julie Livingston's (2003) research on aging in Botswana demonstrates that the status of older women in this developing country is changing, but not necessarily for the better. *Botsofe*, or old age, in Botswana was always seen as time of physical decline and increased frailty. However, *botsofe* was also regarded as a period of spiritual potency, and older people were granted power, respect, and status in accordance with their accumulated lifetime's worth of knowledge and experience. Livingston describes the relationship between a woman and her frail, somewhat confused, and mostly blind 94-year-old mother. Although the woman regarded her mother as almost childlike and treated her as such, she also appreciated her spiritual strength; she was a source of happiness for others in her family and community. The woman never referred to her mother as sick despite her infirmity.

With increasing development and the introduction of government social services, attitudes toward old age have changed in Botswana. The introduction of a pension at 65 years old imposed a strict boundary on the beginning of old age, where no such demarcation had existed before. Furthermore, advances in limiting infant mortality and controlling infectious disease have allowed people to live longer, which in turn has

The Anthropology of Disability

The anthropologists Faye Ginsburg and Rayna Rapp (2013, 2020) have been forceful advocates for a place for disability studies in the mainstream of anthropological inquiry. Disability is a universal component of human diversity. As Ginsburg and Rapp (2013, 55) write,

> Unlike the categories of race and gender from which one can only enter or exit very rarely and with enormous and conscious effort – "passing" or "transgendering," for example – disability has a distinctive quality: It is a category anyone might enter through aging or in a heartbeat, challenging lifelong presumptions of stable identities and normativity.

Disability cuts across all aspects of a culture or society. Although a critical anthropological focus on disability could be limited to the nature of medicalization on "embodied limitations and social discrimination" (Ginsburg and Rapp 2013, 54), a broader anthropological perspective could more fully illuminate the lives of people with disability and society in general. With aging, disability is not necessarily a given, but becoming less-abled certainly is.

As we have seen, the line between not-elderly and elderly is somewhat arbitrary, and dependent on cultural values and contexts. The same can be said for the line between abled and disabled. Indeed, in some cultures, there is not a single category of "disabled" but rather a

(continued)

(continued)

recognition of a number of disabling conditions. Some conditions that are disabling, such as epilepsy, may be seen as a blessing or a curse, depending on the culture. As Ginsburg and Rapp (2020, S5) write, "Disability is profoundly relational and radically contingent, (inter)dependent on specific social and material conditions that too often *exclude full participation in society*" [emphasis added].

Ginsburg and Rapp (2020) point out that disability intersects with and is shaped by many aspects of society that have been of core interest to anthropologists. For example, they have labeled the web of relationships that coalesce around disability as "new kinship imaginaries," reflecting the fact that while disabled people often rely on kin for support and care, these care relationships often become kin-like even when they do not originate in flesh-and-blood. Disability can also be studied from the perspective of biopolitics. The identification of new categories of disability is an issue for both medicine and the business of medicine. One of the main reasons health fields reclassified senile dementia as Alzheimer's disease—a chronic, disabling condition—was to make it easier to raise funds for research, both basic and clinical. The impact of technology, a favorite topic of contemporary anthropology in developed countries, can also be examined through the lens of disability. New digital technologies are "increasingly providing infrastructures of possibility for the creation of new disability imaginaries, virtual and otherwise." (Ginsburg and Rapp 2020, S12). What is the impact of people with disabilities becoming participants in worlds from which they were formerly excluded, or in which their disabilities are neutralized?

Changes in demographics—namely, the increasing aging of societies, the survival of people with chronic diseases, and the increasing survival rates of fragile infants—will alter the landscape of disability in the future. Ayo Wahlberg's term "chronic living" and Pam Block's notion of "unplanned survival" (in Ginsburg and Rapp 2020) are evocative of the origins of these new worlds, which will be characterized in part by a higher proportion of disabled individuals than traditional social institutions were designed to care for or support. These social institutions will have to change, or new ones will have to be invented. Ginsburg and Rapp write, "These emergent formations—both public and intimate—[will] require political will as well as recognition that disability worlds are projects of cultural creativity and reinvention that routinely intersect other biopolitical regimes"(Ginsburg and Rapp 2020, S6).

---

made the chronic age-associated diseases more common than ever before. The AIDS epidemic has further complicated the situation, with increasing numbers of younger people coming into competition for care with older people. The result of all these societal changes is that "chronic illness [is] increasingly seen as part of 'normal' old age and with the elderly now lacking much of the socio-economic and cultural power they once had" (Livingston 2003, 225). Development and modernization always seem to come with a price, and for the elderly women of Botswana today, that price is to live in a time of transition and uncertainty regarding their "biosocial" status.

THE FUTURE OF AGING

There are more older people than ever. Despite some of the upticks in middle-aged mortality in the first decade of the twenty-first century that we discussed at the beginning of the chapter, the overwhelming trend since 1900 has been that people are living longer and, with declines in birthrates, older people are forming a greater proportion of many populations. The decline in overall mortality has come in two separate phases: before 1920, improvements in infant survival and health fueled the increase in life expectancy, while after 1950, decreasing mortality among older individuals was the main contributor (Christensen et al. 2009). There are many statistics that serve to illustrate this trend. An analysis of data from 30 different developed countries showed that in 1950, an 80-year-old woman had about a 10% chance of dying in the coming year; in 2000, there was a less than 5% chance, and in Japan, home of the longest-lived peoples, it was less than 3%. In Germany, in the mid-1950s, only 10% of the population was over the age of 65 years and 1.3% were over the age of 85. By the early 2000s, 19% were over the age of 65 and 4.4% were over the age of 80. Given the current birth-rate in Germany, these proportions should all go up substantially in the coming decades (Christensen et al. 2009).

Based on her research among elderly people and their caregivers in northern Thailand, anthropologist Felicity Aulino has introduced the term "demographic imaginary" to describe "how population categories take hold and shape group identification and personal expectations.. . . Age and other demographic factors form the basis of identity and predictions about the future in a confluence of individual experience and social discourse" (Aulino 2017, 321). The demographic imaginary fuels policy debates about the future funding of social security in the United States, as well as individual concerns about retirement amongst the middle-aged. Aulino talked to Thai caregivers about their future retirements, eliciting narratives that were positive ("Condos! That is our dream!") but that reflected anxieties about an uncertain future (e.g., how to survive with little traditional extended family support or ensure access to healthcare).

Ideals about "successful aging" also arise out of the demographic imaginary. In the United States, the ideal is that older people should remain vital, healthy, and independent—in other words, they should not be old. Some critical scholars have argued that this is a function of biopolitical and biomedical hegemony, but Sarah Lamb (Lamb 2019, 268) suggests that "political, economic, and medical agendas to counter old age resonate with and are propelled by long-standing cultural values surrounding personhood and the life course, tightly woven together in mutually constitutive ways." In her interviews with older Americans (a total of 65, mostly White, from across the economic spectrum), Lamb found a range of attitudes expressed as aging reality caught up with imaginary ideals. One of her most striking findings was the extent to which her poorer subjects felt that they could not do the things necessary to age in the prescribed, American way—successful aging is expensive aging. They felt that they could not afford to exercise, buy the right foods, or get the health care necessary to age successfully. A poignant reflection of this could be seen in Lamb's open recruitment of subjects for her "aging study." Lower-income people in their 60s felt that they were qualified to participate, while wealthier people saw themselves as qualified when they were in their 70s or 80s. Low-income participants envisioned dying around 70, while high-income participants aimed to live into their 90s or even reach 100. The future of aging in the United States looks to be one that will be shaped by economic inequality.

The biocultural anthropology of aging and health is an exciting field that encompasses a critical part of the human experience. In the United States, in 1990 the proportion of the population 65 and older was 12.5%; in 2050 it is estimated that it will be more than 20%. The proportional changes will be greater in Japan and some European countries, which have lower birth rates than the United States and hence smaller numbers of younger individuals. The needs of these aging baby boomers will not only shape political discussions, as indicated by debates about how to pay for their care, but will also influence biomedical research funding, which will flow to projects relevant to this large and influential part of the population. Many developing countries will also see a rise in their populations of elderly. How the nations of the world deal economically, socially, and ethically with their aging populations will be fascinating to observe (for those of us around to see it).

The biocultural perspective will be essential to solving the aging problem—a problem born of success in so many other areas—at all of its manifest levels. Of course, aged individuals should not be seen as problematic on an individual basis. Cross-cultural observations and evolutionary theory support the view that they are as much a resource as a burden. As a species, humans are unique in that they are able to take advantage of the stored knowledge, wisdom, and experience of older members of their groups. This has shaped cultural development in myriad ways and may even have had an essential role in the biological evolution of our species.

STUDY QUESTIONS

1. Although average life span has generally increased over the past 100 years, what are some reasons to think that this pattern will not continue in the twenty-first century?

2. What are some of the ways that the human body typically changes after 40 years of age?

3. How does the frequency of osteoporosis vary by sex and population? What interventions (both public health and clinical) are taken against this common disease?

4. Which diseases show a clear pattern of increasing rate with increasing age? Which do not?

5. Compare and contrast three physiological theories of aging. Are they mutually exclusive?

6. Why in general is the reproductive success of older individuals less subject to the forces of natural selection than that of younger individuals?

7. What is the antagonistic pleiotropy theory of the evolution of aging? How does it relate to the disposable soma theory of aging?

8. What is Alzheimer's disease? Is it an inevitable consequence of aging?

9. How do dementia rates compare between African Americans and a West African population? What environmental factors might influence these rates?

10. What are the potential benefits for increasing the life span of a caloric-restricted diet?

11. What are the possible factors that contribute to the long lives of Okinawans? What is the concept of *shingi gusui* and how might it relate to the relationship between health and diet in Okinawa?

12. Compare and contrast Lawrence Cohen's more culturally focused definition of dementia with the biomedical definition.

13. What is the demographic imaginary?

CRITICAL THINKING QUESTIONS

1. Is aging a disease? Should the elimination of aging per se be a major public health priority?
2. Given what you have learned about aging as a biocultural phenomenon, how do you think the goal of "successful aging" is best achieved?
3. Cosmetic surgery is increasingly used to maintain the appearance of youth in older people. Do you think that avoiding the appearance of aging contributes to successful aging? Does Western mass-media culture make it harder or easier for people to confront the inevitability of aging?

SUGGESTED ETHNOGRAPHIES AND OTHER BOOKS TO READ WITH THIS CHAPTER

Felicity Aulino. 2019. *Rituals of Care: Karmic Politics in an Aging Thailand*. Ithaca: Cornell University Press.

Lawrence Cohen. 1998. *No Aging in India: Alzheimer's, The Bad Family, and Other Modern Things*. Berkeley: University of California Press.

Atul Gawande. 2014. *Being Mortal: Medicine and What Matters in the End*. New York: Metropolitan Books.

Margaret Lock. 1993. *Encounters with Aging: Mythologies of Menopause in Japan and North America*. Berkeley: University of California Press.

Margaret Lock. 2013. *The Alzheimer Conundrum: Entanglements of Dementia and Aging*. Princeton: Princeton University Press.

J. Sokolovsky, ed. 2009. *The Cultural Context of Aging: Worldwide Perspectives*. Westport, CT: Greenwood Press. Some chapters available online at http://www.usfsp .edu/~jsokolov.

CHAPTER 8

Infectious Diseases

Pathogens, Hosts, and Evolutionary Interplay

Chapter Goals

- To become familiar with the diverse set of microorganisms that cause disease in humans
- To know the basics of human defenses against pathogens, including immune system detection and destruction of pathogens
- To understand how and why pathogens change over time
- To know how infectious diseases such as malaria have affected human biological evolution
- To understand why pathogens vary in their virulence and the ways in which human behavior may affect virulence
- To understand how reductions in childhood exposure to infections contribute to the rise of allergies and asthma

As World War I was coming to a close in 1918, leaving about 15 million people dead, a new wave of death spread around the world. This "second wave" killed between 20 million and 100 million people, not by warfare but by a familiar source: influenza. This was the 1918 flu pandemic, the first recorded worldwide outbreak of a particularly virulent strain of the flu virus. About one-quarter of the entire world's population was sick with the flu that year, including 28% of people in the United States. As Gina Kolata notes, so many died in the United States that life expectancy dropped by *12 years* in 1918 (Kolata 1999). The current SARS-CoV-2 virus, which is causing the COVID-19 epidemic has sickened 20 million people across the globe so far, with almost 750,000 deaths at the time of this writing (August 2020). COVID-19 is currently the leading cause of death in the United States, with more deaths than cardiovascular disease and cancer. Its ultimate effects on life expectancy remain to be seen, in part because it is those over 60 years of age who are most vulnerable. Regardless, while it appears to be less dramatic than the 1918 flu pandemic, we are still very much in the first wave and there is no vaccine as yet on the horizon. How is it that these viruses - invisible to the naked eye (indeed, only visible with an electron microscope) - can wreak such havoc on so many human bodies in such a short period of time?

Influenza and COVID-19 are caused by viruses, and among a diverse category of **infectious diseases**. Infectious diseases are caused by microorganisms that make use of the resources of an individual to carry out their lifecycle, and in doing so they provoke an immune response or otherwise disrupt the functioning of that individual. Some infectious organisms are highly specialized and can only infect a particular species, whereas others can infect a broad array of species. The distribution of infectious diseases within species is not uniform but will vary according to environmental conditions and population characteristics.

Microorganisms that act in this way are part of a large category of organisms called **parasites**, defined by the fact that they live off the resources of other individuals, usually of a different, larger-bodied species. Not all parasites cause disease. In fact, most live unobtrusively in or on organisms without disrupting their health in any way. Others actually benefit the individual they inhabit, such as gut microbes that manufacture vitamin K or digest fiber in the diet. In fact, it is estimated that an individual provides a home for some 90 trillion microbes, most of which either have neutral or positive effects (Collen 2016; Knight 2015). Those that cause infectious disease (from the Latin *infectio*, meaning tainted) are caused by several different types of microbes; some are only minor nuisances, but others are deadly and range in size from truly microscopic to visible to the naked eye. Infectious microorganisms are also called **pathogens** (from the Greek *pathos*, meaning suffering, disease) or germs (from the Latin *germen*, seed or sprout).

To be evolutionarily successful, pathogens must be able to infect an individual (referred to as the **host**), go through the necessary maturation phases, reproduce, and then get to another susceptible host before they are destroyed by the immune system or the host dies (although as will become evident later in this chapter, some parasites are able to be transmitted to new hosts after thel host dies). The ways that pathogens carry out these processes are truly remarkable in their complexity and diversity, although from a human disease perspective, these strategies can also inflict a tremendous amount of pain, suffering, or death. From an evolutionary perspective, it comes as no surprise that hosts have equally complex means of avoiding infection or destroying the microbes once inside the body.

This chapter introduces the basic biology and epidemiology of infectious diseases of humans. First, we describe the major categories, along with the conditions that allow them to spread in a given population, and then outline the basics of the human immune response to different types of pathogens. Subsequently, we consider the more anthropological questions of how infectious diseases have shaped human evolutionary processes and how human behavior can in turn shape the evolution of microorganisms. The protozoan disease malaria will serve as a primary example. We will also review the ways in which human behavior affects pathogen virulence and how allergies and asthma may be related to a lack of exposure to infectious agents in industrialized societies.

KOCH'S POSTULATES

How do we know that a given set of symptoms experienced by a person is being caused by a pathogen? Robert Koch (1843–1910), a German scientist who discovered that anthrax symptoms were always associated with the presence of the anthrax bacterium, is responsible for the development of the **germ theory of disease**. In 1891 he published a series of postulates (**Koch's postulates**), which are still considered the benchmark for establishing the infectious cause of a disease. They are illustrated in Figure 8.1.

Koch's postulates are foundational to identifying a disease as infectious, but in practice these criteria may not always be met. One relatively common exception is when the pathogen is isolated from a sick person and introduced into another individual who then does not get sick. This may happen for a variety of reasons that have nothing to do with the pathogen itself—perhaps the second person has been exposed previously and readily mounts an immune response, or his or her immune system is especially adept at responding to that particular pathogen. Koch never stated that a germ must *always* cause disease in every individual. The focus on the microorganism as the main causative factor of disease contributed to a narrow emphasis on the "germ" to the exclusion of the environmental characteristics that might encourage the spread of the pathogen or characteristics of individuals that contribute to variation in

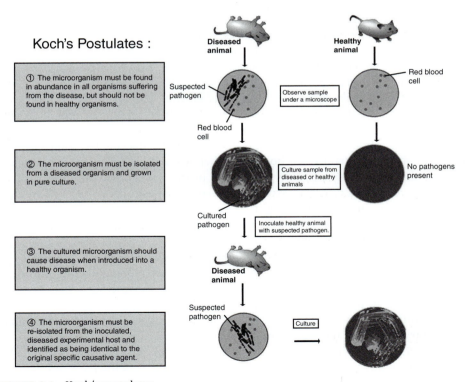

FIGURE 8.1 Koch's postulates.
Source: https://commons.wikimedia.org/wiki/File%3AKoch's_Postulates.svg.

susceptibility to infection. Indeed, Koch's specifications of infectious disease diagnosis can be said to typify the biomedical approach to disease, with its attempts to "reduce down" the complexity of disease processes to single causative factors and to rely on empirical evidence to establish disease causality (as discussed in Chapter 3). In contemporary epidemiology, the germ is viewed as only one of three important components that affect its distribution. The other two are the host and the environment in which they both exist. We will focus on each of these in turn.

TAXONOMY OF INFECTIOUS DISEASE

Table 8.1 shows the six different types of pathogens, arranged from smallest to largest, along with some of their features and examples of diseases caused by them. There are numerous forms within each category, only a few of which may cause disease in humans.

TABLE 8.1 The Major Groups of Pathogens Infecting Humans

I. Viruses
  – RNA or DNA, with a protein coat
  – Must get into host cell and use cellular machinery to replicate
  Examples: Poxvirus (smallpox)
       Herpesvirus (herpes simplex, varicella zoster, cytomegalo Epstein–Barr)
       Retrovirus (HIV)
       Sarbecovirus (SARS, coronavirus)
       Orthomyxovirus (influenza)
       Togavirus (rubella, yellow fever, dengue fever, encephalitis)

II. Unicellular (one-celled organisms)
  A. Prokaryotes (no cell nucleus)
    1. *Chlamydia spp.* (*trachomatis* and *psittaci*): obligate intracellular; cause trachoma, pelvic inflammatory disease
    2. *Mycoplasma sp.* (*pneumoniae*): smallest entities that can grow independent of host cells; no cell wall
    3. Rickettsia: small, obligate intracellular
       Examples: Rocky Mountain spotted fever, typhus, Q fever, trench fever
    4. Bacteria: highly variable based on shape, whether they are aerobic or anaerobic, their staining properties, motility, among others
       Examples: *Streptococcus, Staphyloccocus, Neisseria* (gonorrhea), *Clostridium, Bacillus, Escherichia, Shigella, Salmonella, Yersinia* (bubonic plague), *Vibrio* (cholera), *Brucella, Legionella* (Legionnaire's disease), *Mycobacterium* (tuberculosis), *Treponema,* etc.
  B. Eukaryotes (have cell nucleus)
    1. Fungi: molds and yeast
    2. Protozoa: *Trypanosoma* (sleeping sickness or Chagas's disease), *Giardia, Toxoplasma, Plasmodium* (malaria), etc.

III. Multicellular
  A. Helminths (worms)
    Platyhelminthes (flat worms): *Schistosoma, Echonococcus,* etc.
    Nematoda (round worms): *Trichinella, Ascaris, Onchocerca,* etc.
  B. Arthropods (insects)
    Mites
    Lice

Viruses

Viruses are among the simplest of pathogens, composed only of DNA or RNA surrounded by protein. They have distinct geometric shapes, the most common of which are the rods and the spheres (which actually have 20 sides), as shown in Figure 8.2a. Viruses are obligate parasites, meaning that they can only replicate in a host, and as a result there is debate about whether these are true "living" entities. In order to replicate, a virus must first get inside a host cell by attaching to receptors on the surface membrane. Every virus has a protein on its surface that matches receptors on the target cells, which allows viruses to infect specific cell types (e.g., red blood cells rather than kidney cells). The receptors that host cells display are not there to welcome in the virus, but serve as receptors for chemicals that initiate cellular activities (e.g., hormones, growth factors, immune cell proteins). Viruses have evolved mechanisms to exploit those receptors by creating proteins that mimic the shape of the host's own molecules.

Once the virus has replicated, it can either cause the host cells to burst (as the rhinovirus does), allowing it to spread, or encapsulate itself in a lipid (fat) envelope derived from the cell membrane. In this form, the virus can leave the cell without destroying it, a process called "budding," and because the original cell remains intact, it can continue to shed viruses indefinitely (as in influenza or hepatitis). Another option for the virus is to remain latent, causing no symptoms unless the host's immune function is suppressed for some reason (age, stress, chemotherapy, etc.), and then symptoms of infection may emerge. The herpes viruses, which include chicken pox (in the spinal cord) and herpes (in the skin especially around the mouth and genitals), use this strategy.

It is estimated that about 8% of the human genome is composed of old viral genomes (Horie et al. 2010). When some viruses integrate with the host's DNA, they activate cancer-causing genes (oncogenes) that initiate cellular transformations and growth and, in some cases, form cancerous tumors. One of the best known is human papilloma virus, a sexually transmitted virus associated with cervical cancer.

Bacteria

Bacteria are a group of single-celled prokaryotic organisms (these do not possess a nucleus) that were likely among the earliest life forms on earth. They have their own genetic material and reproduce by simply duplicating their DNA and dividing. There are some 400 recognized genera of bacteria, but fewer than 40 regularly cause disease in humans. Each of us has ~10 times as many bacterial cells as human cells in and on our bodies; those in our gastrointestinal tract make up about 500 species and collectively weigh 3.3 pounds (Knight 2015). They come in different shapes including spheres (the cocci), rods (the bacilli), and spirals (the spirochetes; see Figure 8.2b). The characteristics of bacterial cell walls affect their survival in and outside of the host. *Mycobacterium tuberculosis* (the cause of tuberculosis) has a thick, waxy cell wall that allows it to survive for long periods of time outside the host and under dry conditions. Others are unable to withstand prolonged exposure to the external environment but may be resistant to digestion in the gastrointestinal tract. Some have additional characteristics such as capsules (that prevent their destruction by immune cells), flagella (spiral-like tails that are used in propulsion), or pili (small hairs that allow bacteria to

(a)

VIRAL SHAPES

Polyhedral
(Adenovirus)

Spherical
(Influenza)

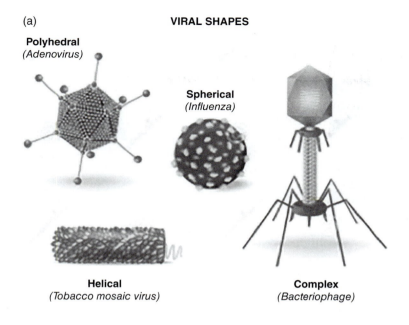

Helical
(Tobacco mosaic virus)

Complex
(Bacteriophage)

(b)   **COCCI**   **BACILLI**   **OTHERS**

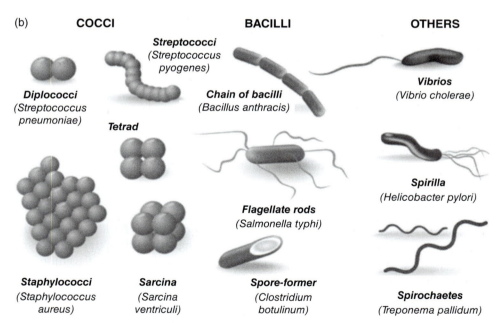

Streptococci
(Streptococcus pyogenes)

Diplococci
(Streptococcus pneumoniae)

Chain of bacilli
(Bacillus anthracis)

Vibrios
(Vibrio cholerae)

Tetrad

Flagellate rods
(Salmonella typhi)

Spirilla
(Helicobacter pylori)

Staphylococci
(Staphylococcus aureus)

Sarcina
(Sarcina ventriculi)

Spore-former
(Clostridium botulinum)

Spirochaetes
(Treponema pallidum)

FIGURE 8.2   (a) The main forms of viruses that affect humans.
Source: Dreamstime.com.
(b) Different types and shapes of bacteria.
Source: by Mariana Ruiz/LadyofHats via Wikipedia, public domain.

(c)

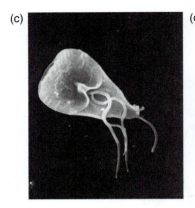

(d)

(e)

FIGURE 8.2   (*continued*)
(c) Giardia, a protozoan pathogen that causes diarrheal disease.
Credit: Image from CDC/Janice Carr.
(d) Candida, a common fungal "yeast" infection of the skin.
Credit: Image from CDC 1976.
(e) Helminths. An example is the trematode Schistosoma, shown as a pair; the smaller male is wrapped around the larger female worm.
Credit: Image from CDC.

adhere to other cells). There are bacteria that form spores such as *Bacillus anthracis*, the cause of anthrax; dormant spores can survive for prolonged periods of time outside the host. Others produce toxins (such as *Vibrio cholerae*, a bacterium with a flagellum that causes cholera) that are debilitating to the host. Some bacteria require oxygen and are likely to be found in well-oxygenated tissues such as the lungs, whereas others are anaerobic and sometimes infect deep wounds (such as the rod-shape *Clostridium*, the cause of tetanus, botulism, and gangrene). Then there are the virus-like bacteria, which must rely on the host's metabolic machinery to reproduce (such as *Chlamydia*).

Protozoa
Protozoa are single-celled eukaryotic organisms that have a cell nucleus. They may have elaborate life cycles, with growth and reproductive stages in different organs, or

in more than one species or insect vectors. Some are intracellular and others extracellular. In general, protozoan infections are difficult to treat and often generate chronic symptoms. As eukaryotes, their cellular structures are more similar to those of mammals, allowing them to more easily evade a host's immune defenses.

Among the most common protozoa are species of *Plasmodium*, which cause malaria. Others include *Giardia* (a waterborne gastrointestinal disease; see Figure 8.2c), *Entamoeba* (another gastrointestinal disease), *Trichomonas* (a sexually transmitted protozoal disease that infects the vagina or urethra), *Trypanosoma* (in Africa it causes sleeping sickness, carried by the tsetse fly; in South America it causes Chagas's disease, carried by the reduviid bug), *Leishmania* (carried by sand flies; causes damage to skin or the spleen and liver), and *Toxoplasma* (cats carry this and it can infect the eyes and brain and cross the placenta—hence, pregnant women should stay away from cat feces).

Fungi

Fungi are a diverse taxon of eukaryotic organisms, and of some 70,000 species, only a few are significant pathogens of humans. Generally fungal infections (also called mycoses) are not virulent and they are kept in check by the immune system, although in immunocompromised individuals they can be lethal. Some fungi cause skin diseases, including *Candida* (see Figure 8.2d), which is a normal part of the colon and moist skin areas, but can overgrow and become bothersome, causing common "yeast infections" or thrush. *Trichophyton* and *Microsporum* are molds that cause tinea (athlete's foot, ringworm, etc.). Several fungi species form spores that can be inhaled, causing symptoms of pneumonia. It should be noted that the mold fungus *Penicillium* was the original source of penicillin, one of the first antibacterial chemicals used to treat human infection. Some bacteria also produce antibiotics and tend to be soil dwelling and spore forming like the fungi, and both produce these chemicals for their own survival purposes or to ward off potential competitors for resources.

Worms

Worms (also called **helminths**) are a diverse taxon of multicellular organisms, with three groups causing disease in humans: the roundworms (nematodes), the tapeworms (cestodes), and the flukes (trematodes), as shown in Figure 8.2e. As multicellular forms, they have internal organs and tough outer coatings, making them difficult for the immune system to destroy. Helminth infections are very common, especially those that are from soil-borne worms (see http://www.thiswormyworld.org for maps and data on human helminth infections). Some are spread by intermediate hosts such as flies, mosquitoes, snails, or fish, and others are transmitted through contaminated water, soil, or food. *Onchocerca* causes blindness and is carried by the black fly, whereas *Wuchereria* infects the lymph system and causes the debilitating symptoms of elephantiasis. The Guinea worm *Dracunculus* lives under the skin and can grow to over 1 meter. *Ascaris*, the giant intestinal roundworm, is among the most common helminth infections. It can reach up to 30 centimeters long, and individuals may harbor up to 1,000 such worms! Tapeworms are large, segmented flat worms that can be up to 10 meters in length, although they cause only mild gastrointestinal symptoms.

Among the flukes, *Schistosoma* is responsible for most human disease, in the form of the chronic disease schistosomiasis.

Prions

The last group of pathogens is perhaps the oddest. **Prions** are infectious proteins that cause neurodegenerative diseases such as Creutzfeldt–Jakob disease, Kuru (known from New Guinea), and other nonhuman forms that cause bovine spongiform encephalopathy (or mad cow disease) and scrapie, a similar disease of sheep. Collectively, these are referred to as the *transmissible spongiform encephalopathies.* Prions remain mysterious; because they have no DNA or RNA to replicate, it is not clear how they are transmissible. It may be that some aspect of their tendency to form as masses of fibrils causes adjacent proteins to fold into similar shapes in a rippling effect.

HOW PATHOGENS SPREAD

For a pathogen to be evolutionarily successful, it must be able to access a host's resources and it (or its descendants) must also be able to get to new hosts. In general, microbes use the most permeable parts of a host's body to do so. The epithelial cells, which comprise the skin, reproductive tract, and respiratory and digestive systems, are the most common sites of entry because these are the parts of our anatomy designed to either take in molecules (e.g., water, oxygen, nutrients, sperm) or excrete them (e.g., water, sweat, carbon dioxide, waste, sperm, menstrual blood, breast milk). Pathogens can exploit these existing systems to enter and exit the host's body during eating, sex, skin-to-skin contact, nursing, sneezing, coughing, and other behaviors. These are all means of **direct transmission** from host to host. In addition, some pathogens use a **vector** to spread. A vector is any intermediate species or material that can take a pathogen from one host to the next. It can be a mosquito that takes a blood meal with parasites in it from one person and then bites another and injects them. Or, it can be water that carries parasites from fecal waste to a site where a person drinks or cooks with that water. It can be a caretaker who carries germs from a sick patient to a well person, or a needle used on one sick patient that is then used to inject another. There are lots of these kinds of vectors, and they are considered in more detail in the later section on virulence.

When a pathogen enters a human population, its initial spread can be very rapid. This is an **epidemic**, meaning an increase—sometimes dramatic, depending on transmission rates—in the incidence of the infection. At this stage there are many susceptible hosts around (assuming the population is not immunized against the pathogen) – such is the case with COVID-19. However, as the epidemic progresses, more and more of the population is (1) infected already; (2) immune because of successful resolution of the infection; or (3) dead. Hence, the number and density of susceptible hosts declines, and incidence rates likewise fall. This is called the **epidemic curve**, illustrated in Figure 8.3. Eventually the epidemic burns out and incidence drops to near zero and prevalence likewise remains low or at zero. An infectious disease is said to be **endemic** when its prevalence and incidence remain relatively constant over time.

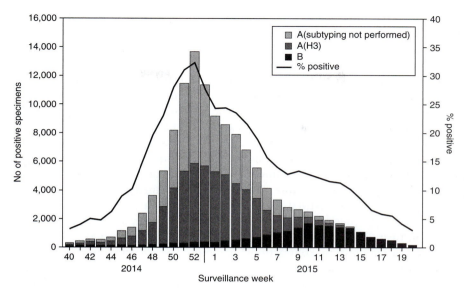

FIGURE 8.3 The shape of an epidemic curve, using data from the 2018–2019 influenza epidemic in the United States.
Source: Centers for Disease Control and Prevention. https://www.cdc.gov/flu/weekly/weeklyarchives2018-2019/Week39.htm.

HUMAN DEFENSES AGAINST PATHOGENS

Given the ubiquity of infectious agents, their diversity across environments, and the fact that all humans will contract a variety of infectious diseases during their lifetimes, in what ways has the body evolved responses to these threats? In other words, what defenses do humans and other organisms have against pathogens?

Air, water, and food are inevitably rich in microbes, and the cells lining the nose, lungs, and intestines are routinely exposed to potential pathogens. Thus the physical and chemical characteristics of these surfaces serve as initial barriers to infection. As the body's primary barrier, skin and immune cells in the skin produce antimicrobial proteins. However, if the skin is compromised or damaged, pathogens can gain ready access to the interior of the body, as when *Staphylococcus* spreads at the site of a wound or burn. Some can stick directly onto the skin, such as the pox viruses, Papova viruses (warts), some fungi, and helminths. Bites from insects or infected animals may allow pathogens direct access to the bloodstream.

Pathogens entering through the respiratory system are usually entrapped in mucus that is then pushed upward through the lungs by the means of tiny hairs (cilia) to be coughed out. Thus coughing, sneezing, and blowing the nose are all mechanisms to get rid of respiratory pathogens. To avoid this, some pathogens such as the rhinovirus or influenza firmly attach to the bronchial membranes, whereas others, such as *Bordetella* (the bacterium that causes whooping cough) or the measles virus, inhibit the action of the cilia. A secondary barrier defense between the mucus and epithelial layer in the lungs is a thin layer of fluid containing antimicrobial proteins.

A key defense against food- or waterborne pathogens is the very low pH of the stomach, caused by strong stomach acids that effectively kill many microbes, especially bacteria. An interesting note about this defense mechanism is that antacids taken against heartburn (which is caused by acid from the stomach getting up into the esophagus) often contain sodium bicarbonate, which neutralizes the acid and raises the pH of the stomach. However, this reduces the effectiveness of the acid defense against pathogens, resulting in increased risk of infection (DuPont 2018). As with the respiratory system, there are also immune proteins all along the gut to destroy pathogens that persist beyond the stomach.

The body has multiple ways of responding to pathogens. Many of these are often thought of as mere "symptoms" of infection but can be considered adaptive responses. For example, vomiting and diarrhea are symptoms associated with food- or waterborne infections of the gastrointestinal tract, and both function to expel the pathogen. In support of the hypothesis that these are adaptive responses are data indicating that people who treat *Shigella*-induced diarrhea with a medication such as Lomotil (which slows down gastrointestinal contractions) had more *Shigella* bacteria in their stools for a longer period of time than those who did not treat the diarrhea (Nesse and Williams 1994). In this case, treating the diarrhea as merely a symptom of disease actually undermines its effectiveness as an adaptive response to the infection. Coughing serves a similar function for respiratory infections, expelling pathogens in the airways.

The fever that often accompanies infection is usually viewed as an annoying, uncomfortable symptom of infection, but it too seems to be adaptive. Why should body temperature increase when a person has an infection (note that not all infections are associated with fever)? A hotter body milieu has the effect of inhibiting bacterial or

To Treat or Not to Treat

The preceding discussion about the adaptive significance of some "symptoms" of infection raises some important issues. One is whether this view of symptoms as adaptive is likely to be widely adopted, especially in cultures such as the United States where symptom-relief medicines are easily procured over the counter. Advertisements for these palliatives claim that we need not and should not suffer from such symptoms when relief is readily available. The over-the-counter pharmaceutical industry generates billions of dollars in profits, and it is unlikely that pharmaceutical companies, which often fund clinical trials, would offer money for research on when symptoms are adaptive and hence should not be treated! It could also be argued that the pharmaceutical industry generates a kind of "pain intolerance" in American society: Why should anyone suffer from symptoms that are nothing but annoying or disruptive? Furthermore, for patients who seek out medical care for relief from their symptoms, a response that they should rest and recover without intervention may seem like time and money poorly spent. Clinicians, in turn, want to alleviate the pain and suffering of their patients.

Another issue is that of cultural expectations about work (or school) attendance and performance. Employees are expected to show up for work; a cold or stomachache is not a sufficient excuse for missing work, and work schedules often demand participation on a specific date. There are expectations that such unpleasant symptoms should be ameliorated such that employees can continue working or return to work quickly after the most severe discomfort has abated. Employees generally have relatively few "sick days" and children's sicknesses can wreak havoc on parents' work schedules. Thus, the structure of U.S. social institutions and the easy availability and marketing of drugs for symptom relief makes symptom management much more likely than the extended rest and recovery advocated by a more evolutionary approach.

viral reproduction. Data once again show that individuals who treat the fever with various drugs (aspirin, acetaminophen, or ibuprofen) are sicker longer than those who do not treat it. Other similarly adaptive responses include iron sequestering. Because many pathogens such as bacteria need iron, a common physiological response is to bind iron to special proteins such as transferrin. Thus, during infection individuals may appear to be iron deficient, but providing them with iron supplements undermines this adaptive response (Nesse and Williams 1994).

Not all symptoms are adaptive. However, there has been little research on the significance of various symptoms associated with infectious diseases, and thus it is currently difficult to generate a list of those that are adaptive or nonadaptive. At the same time, it would be helpful to know when it is appropriate to intervene. Each of the responses already described is helpful in the short term; if prolonged or excessive, they can become deleterious. These are best thought of as short-term adaptability responses, as described in Chapter 2. Diarrhea that lasts for several days or is extreme can result in dehydration; fevers can destroy a person's own cells, which function best at lower temperatures.

It is also important to recognize that although these responses may be helpful to a sick individual, they are often exploited by pathogens to facilitate their spread—diarrhea expels gastrointestinal pathogens in fecal material, and coughing up mucus expels airborne pathogens out into the environment. What may be adaptive from an individual's perspective can be deleterious to the health of the larger group, and thus public health may be endangered by not suppressing these responses. Masking symptoms such as coughing does prevent the spread of disease within the school or workplace. Of course, if individuals are separated from others while symptomatic, by resting and recovering in relative solitude, pathogen spread should be reduced. In any event, considering symptoms from an evolutionary perspective provides some new insights that may ultimately enhance the way that we "treat" disease at the individual or population level. Unfortunately, medical school curricula rarely cover evolutionary principles (Hidaka et al. 2015).

THE IMMUNE RESPONSE: A BRIEF OVERVIEW

The aforementioned responses act as a first line of defense against infection. However, there is also a powerful second level of response: the immune system. The immune system has three important tasks: (1) it must recognize the presence of a microbe and learn which ones require a response and which do not; (2) it must have mechanisms for destroying or otherwise denaturing pathogenic threats; and (3) it must have a communication system that allows the diverse cells of the immune system to coordinate the first two tasks. The human immune system involves the coordination of a complex set of proteins and white blood cells, called **lymphocytes**, which both circulate throughout the body and congregate in the lymph nodes.

The human immune system is made up of two functionally interactive systems: the **innate immune system** and the **adaptive immune system**. The adaptive system is found only among vertebrates, whereas the innate system evolved much earlier and is found among most multicellular organisms. The adaptive system is especially useful for long-lived organisms that encounter a broad array of ever-changing pathogens over the course of their lifetime. Some of the differences in the two components of the human immune system are listed in Table 8.2. In general, the innate system involves

TABLE 8.2   The Innate and Adaptive Immune Systems Compared

	Innate Immunity	Adaptive Immunity
Evolutionary origin	Earliest animals all invertebrates and vertebrates	Vertebrates only
Principal cells	Phagocytes	Lymphocytes
Principal molecules	Complement and cytokines	Antibody and cytokines
Specificity of recognition	Broad	Very high[a]
Speed of action	Rapid (minutes, hours)	Slow (days)
Development of memory	No	Yes[a]

[a] High specificity and memory are the hallmarks of adaptive immunity.

Source: Playfair, J., and G. Bancroft. 2004. *Infection and Immunity*. New York: Oxford University Press.

recognition of some common patterns rather than specific characteristics of pathogens and is a much faster response. The innate system is also more involved in the destruction of pathogens, whereas the adaptive system is highly sophisticated at pathogen recognition. In reality, the two systems have interrelated functions and their specificity and modes of signaling are more similar than previously appreciated (Vivier and Malissen 2005).

The task of both the adaptive and the innate systems is to recognize a foreign entity (whether it is a speck of dust or a tapeworm) and to do this the immune system first must be able to identify material that is "self." The immune system must destroy foreign material before it can cause serious problems, but at the same time it must not indiscriminately destroy an individual's own cells. Each individual has a unique set of biochemical markers that are identified as self (such as the red blood cell surface proteins that determine blood type) and when an entity bearing different markers is found, it is identified as "non-self" and targeted for removal. It appears that during embryological development the embryo "learns" which molecules are self and destroys the immune cells that would target self cells for destruction.

This view of the immune system as protecting self cells from non-self is overly simplistic though. Organisms often harbor many more microbial cells than their own cells, which they clearly tolerate although the microbes have different DNA and surface proteins (Pradeu 2010). In other words, individuals are heterogenous rather than composed of only cells with a similar protein signature resulting from common DNA. Furthermore, the immune system must not only reject non-self elements, but also scan for and destroy an individual's own cells that are malignant, damaged, or dead. Thomas Pradeu and Edgardo D. Carosella propose the *criterion of continuity* as a replacement for the self/non-self distinction as the defining function of the immune system (Pradeu and Carosella 2006), which is summarized here:

> every strong molecular discontinuity in the antigenic patterns (whether endogenous or exogenous) with which immune receptors interact induces an immune response. There is a discontinuity if there is a strong modification of molecular patterns with which immune cells interact. To put it very simply, the immune system responds to strongly unusual patterns. The criterion is molecular difference, as stated in the self–nonself theory, but not the *origin* of the molecular pattern (i.e. endogenous or exogenous), contrary to what is stated in the self/nonself theory. (Pradeu 2010, 256)

The Language of Immunity

It is difficult to talk about the immune system without resorting to metaphors. After all, for most of us, our understanding of how the immune system works is abstract. People are familiar with the symptoms associated with inflammation (redness or swelling at the site of an infection), but most processes associated with the immune response are undetectable and produce no obvious symptoms. Of course, should they malfunction—generating an insufficient response or overreacting—other symptoms become apparent. Thus, metaphors are used in discussing the immune system to help conceptualize how it actually functions. As Emily Martin observed, such metaphors derive from the larger cultural context in which they are produced (Martin 1994). In Western culture, the predominant way in which the immune system is described is through the use of military metaphors. These work particularly well in a context in which the individual body is seen as autonomous and discrete, with boundaries clearly separating it from the outside world and from other bodies.

For example, when a body is infected with a pathogen, it is described as being "attacked" by a "foreign invader." It must therefore have a "defense system" ready to "target" the invader and "destroy" it. The immune cells are analogous to soldiers, working together to mount a "coordinated defense" against the "enemy." The body is "at war." In 1988, *Time* magazine featured the immune system in a cover article titled "The Battle Inside Your Body," and in 1990 *U.S News & World Report*'s cover described "The Body at War." Martin summarizes some popular published descriptions of the immune system, which reflect a common view of the immune system as patrolling the boundaries of the self:

The notion that the immune system maintains a clear boundary between self and nonself is often accompanied by a conception of the nonself world as foreign and hostile. . . . As a measure of the extent of this threat, popular publications depict the body as the scene of total war between ruthless invaders and determined defenders: "Besieged by a vast array of invisible enemies, the human body enlists a remarkably complex corps of internal bodyguards to battle the invaders." . . . A site of injury is "transformed into a battle field on which the body's armed forces, hurling themselves repeatedly at the encroaching microorganisms, crush and annihilate them." . . . Small white blood cells . . . are "kept permanently at the ready for a blitzkrieg against microorganisms" and constitute the "infantry" of the immune system. (Martin 1994, 53)

In his book *A Body Worth Defending*, Ed Cohen traces the history of this metaphor, which he sees as having roots in seventeenth-century conceptualizations of the body as property, with rights of self-ownership and self-defense (E. Cohen 2009). Moving forward to the era of HIV/AIDS, he argues that this view has generated fearful individuals who must defend themselves against the outside world and a pharmaceutical industry ready with medicines to do so, while at the same time this view deflects attention from the role of political, social, and economic factors in contributing to disease.

Elements of the innate system are good at recognizing generalized molecular patterns that are common among pathogens but not among hosts. These are often essential components of the microorganism, such as unusual sugars in membranes or cell walls, which cannot be modified to avoid immune system detection. Adaptive immunity involves recognition of specific **epitopes**, which are bits of a pathogen's proteins that are identifiable as non-self. Any large molecule or cell that contains epitopes on its surface is called an **antigen**; some may display hundreds of epitopes! In practice, the terms antigen and epitope are sometimes used interchangeably. A functioning human immune system can detect somewhere on the order of 100 million epitopes and remember which markers it has encountered previously.

The key cells of the adaptive system involved in pathogen recognition are the lymphocytes, which exist in two major groups: the **B-cells** and the **T-cells**. B-cells are made in the bone marrow, whereas T-cells come from the thymus. Both are concentrated in the tonsils, adenoids, lymph nodes, spleen, and the Peyer's patches around the

TABLE 8.3   B- and T-Cells, Compared

	B Lymphocytes	T Lymphocytes
Origin	Bone marrow (in fetal life the liver)	Thymus (stem cells from bone marrow)
Recognition molecules	Antibody (immunoglobulin)	T-cell receptor
Secreted product(s)	Antibody	Cytokines
Disposal mechanisms	Antibody (leading to phagocytosis, lysis)	Some T-cells are cytotoxic; others activate phagocytes
Mainly effective against	Extracellular infection	Intracellular infection

Source: Playfair, J., and G. Bancroft. 2004. *Infection and Immunity*. New York: Oxford University Press.

intestines, although they circulate more widely. Generally speaking, the B-cells monitor extracellular spaces (such as blood and other fluids), whereas T-cells monitor intracellular infections. Key differences are summarized in Table 8.3.

Each B- or T-lymphocyte derives from a unique combination of genes that allows it to display surface molecules that recognize or "fit" specific epitopes. When a lymphocyte encounters a pathogen that displays "its" epitope, it begins to proliferate, a process that can take days. Individuals experience this as the swelling of the lymph nodes. After the infection has resolved, some lymphocytes remain as memory cells and thus a subsequent infection with the same pathogen will result in more rapid detection and a more efficient immune response.

The primary function of B-cells is to manufacture **antibodies** (also called immunoglobulins; IgA, IgD, IgE, IgG, and IgM are the five classes of human antibodies), which are antigen-receptor proteins on the B-cell's surface. When the B-cell recognizes its antigen, it begins to make large quantities of its antibody, a Y-shape structure that binds to the antigen and "labels" the pathogen for destruction by other cells of the innate system. Antibodies are also involved in neutralizing bacterial toxins, such as those produced by tetanus and diphtheria, by preventing the toxin from binding to a cell receptor and damaging the cell.

T-cells are faced with the difficult problem of recognizing a cell that has a pathogen "hiding" inside it. This problem is solved by the action of another set of important immunological molecules of the **major histocompatibility complex** (MHC; also called the **human leukocyte antigens**). MHC molecules are present within cells, and move pieces of pathogenic proteins out to the surface of the cell where they can be recognized by T-cells, as shown in Figure 8.4. Once the epitope and MHC complex is presented on the surface of a cell, a T-cell with a matching receptor can bind to it and tag it for destruction by other immune cells.

The genes that give rise to MHC molecules (located on chromosome 6 in humans) are among the most highly variable sections of the human genome, which presumably arose in response to the vast array of intracellular pathogens faced by our species. Every individual has a unique combination of MHC genes, which results in variation in the way that this arm of the immune response functions. Some MHC variants are associated with increased likelihood of severe cases of leprosy, Lyme disease, malaria, herpes simplex, HIV, or severe responses to a pathogen, as in reactive arthritis in response to the plague bacterium or *Salmonella* infection. Small, isolated populations also have more limited variation in MHC genes from genetic drift, which can contribute to an increased severity of some infections.

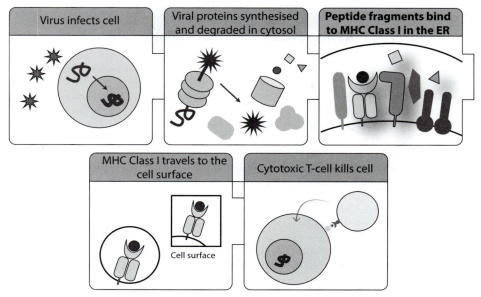

| Virus infects cell | Viral proteins synthesised and degraded in cytosol | **Peptide fragments bind to MHC Class I in the ER** |

| MHC Class I travels to the cell surface | Cytotoxic T-cell kills cell |

Cell surface

FIGURE 8.4 The action of MHC molecules.
Source: Bailey, Alistair (2014): MHC class I antigen processing & presentation overview. figshare figure. https://doi.org/10.6084/m9.figshare.1265139.v1

Once a pathogen has been recognized by the immune system, it must be destroyed. In the innate system a protein cascade called **complement** is initiated upon recognition of those general markers and pathogens labeled with antibody. Complement activates cells called **phagocytes**, the most common of which is the macrophage. These engulf the pathogen, bringing it into contact with powerful enzymes and toxins that destroy the pathogen in a process known as **phagocytosis**. In the process, phagocytes may also present epitopes from the pathogen on their surface for recognition and destruction by other immune cells. **Natural killer** cells can bind to the surface of recognized pathogens or infected host cells and "kill" them by poking holes in their membranes. Natural killer cells also produce **cytokines**, which are proteins involved in communication between immune cells.

Inflammation is another important part of the process of pathogen destruction and increases the blood supply to the site of infection. Specialized mast cells release granules of histamine and other molecules that increase blood vessel permeability so that various immune proteins, phagocytes, natural killer cells, and other immune cells can get to infected tissues. Individuals experience inflammation as redness, heat, pain, and swelling at the site of infection and, although uncomfortable, it is an essential component of the immune response.

T-cells also produce cytokines and toxic molecules that take action against an infected cell. There are two types of T-cells: **cytotoxic** and **helper T-cells**. Cytotoxic T-cells kill cells infected with intracellular pathogens such as viruses, whereas helper T-cells can stimulate B-cells, macrophages, and other forms of immune activity by binding to an epitope and MHC complex presented on the surface of B-cells or macrophages.

Vaccination: How Does It Work?

Vaccination, or immunization, makes use of the ability of the adaptive immune system to remember what pathogens or pathogen products it has encountered before. The earliest form of vaccination was practiced in China about 500 years ago, using material from lesions of people infected with smallpox (this process is actually called variolation, from Variola, the scientific name for the pox viruses). Although it offered some protection, it had a high mortality rate because some people receiving the "vaccine" developed full-blown smallpox. This technique was introduced into Europe in the eighteenth century and in 1796 the English physician Edward Jenner extended the principle by inoculating a child with material from a cowpox lesion on a local milkmaid's hand. It was recognized that milkmaids rarely got smallpox, and Jenner hypothesized that this was because they were routinely exposed to cowpox, a disease well known in cows with symptoms similar to smallpox. Jenner's experiment was a success, leading to routine administration of cowpox vaccine to prevent smallpox throughout Europe.

There are two forms of vaccination: passive and active. Passive immunization is transitory and does not generate memory cells to protect against future infections. It makes use of preformed antibodies from another individual, such as the fetus receiving maternal antibodies in the womb or an infant receiving IgA antibodies in breast milk. Antibodies or antitoxins from other species can also be used against pathogens or deadly insect or snake bites. In contrast, active vaccination provokes the immune system to generate memory cells and provide long-term protection. Many vaccines, such as those against tuberculosis, measles, mumps, and chickenpox, use an attenuated or inactivated form of the pathogen to stimulate this process. Attenuation occurs through a process of artificial selection, in which mutant forms are selected for that cannot grow under normal host conditions. However, in rare cases a virulent form is produced, which can cause disease and be passed on to other nonvaccinated individuals. The Sabin polio vaccine causes polio at the rate of 1 per 2.4 million doses; an alternative vaccine using inactivated polio (the Salk vaccine) is now the preferred vaccine as it is less risky.

Inactivated vaccines are created from pathogens killed by heat or some chemical means. Influenza, anthrax, rabies, and rubella vaccines are made in this way. Inactivated vaccines generate a pure antibody response (rather than a cell-mediated response) and often require multiple boosters to maintain protection. Other vaccines are made from only parts of pathogens, such as proteins, polysaccharides, or deactivated toxins.

While vaccinations provide protection for individuals, they also have public health benefits via **herd immunity**. If a sufficiently large portion of the population has been vaccinated, opportunities for a pathogen to spread are limited. In the United States, vaccination against several diseases is required for entrance into schools. Because students are clustered together in the same building, infections have the potential to spread rapidly, but if most students are immunized, schoolchildren (and, by extension, their families and the larger community) are protected. Indeed, the introduction of vaccines for polio, diphtheria, rubella, mumps, and measles caused a dramatic decline in reported cases of these infections and deaths from them. If there are lapses in vaccination because of intolerable side effects, failure of vaccines to provide long-term protection, lack of availability, worries about ill effects, or other reasons, new outbreaks of these diseases can easily occur (see discussion of the anti-vaxx movement in Chapter 3).

Immune function can be compromised by a variety of factors, including age, HIV infection, stress, and undernutrition, among others. Because the immune system requires energy, protein, and many micronutrients to function adequately, nutrient deficiencies can compromise its function. In turn, infectious disease can cause or exacerbate undernutrition by using up host nutrients. It has been said that "protein-calorie malnutrition is the underlying reason for the increased susceptibility to infections . . . [and] . . . certain infectious diseases also cause malnutrition, which can result in a vicious cycle" (Rodríguez et al. 2011, 1174). In other words, undernutrition and infection are synergistic in their effects and can lead to severe disease and death, especially among children whose nutrient needs are relatively high and whose immune systems are not as competent as those of adults.

Undernutrition impairs the integrity of cell-mediated defense mechanisms by causing the thymus and lymph tissue to atrophy, which in turn limits T-lymphocyte numbers and maturation. The antibody response is not as profoundly affected. Deficiencies of a number of micronutrients (vitamin A, vitamin C, zinc, etc.) impair the integrity of epithelial cells, making the body more vulnerable to infection.

Infection can precipitate undernutrition in several ways. Infections are often accompanied by a lack of appetite, and pathogens' nutrient needs compete with those of the host. The body may also break down its own tissues, such as muscle or digestive enzymes, to fuel an immune response or a pathogen may destroy host tissues. If the infection is in the gastrointestinal tract, digestion and absorption of nutrients may be impaired if the pathogen generates diarrhea or is sufficiently large that it both takes nutrients and blocks surface cells from absorbing nutrients. The persistence of food insecurity and undernutrition in poor populations throughout the world contributes importantly to their greater burden of infectious disease, as discussed further in Chapter 9.

Immune responses require a great deal of coordination and different types of bodily materials. It must be recognized, too, that immune suppression must also be involved so that immune cells act only when and where necessary. It is just as important to stop an immune response as it is to initiate one. When the antigen is disposed of, the immune response should cease because there is no longer any presentation of pathogen epitopes to immune cell receptors. Most lymphocytes self-destruct after they have acted, and helper T-cells mutually inhibit each other and thereby regulate immune activity. Inappropriate immune responses—either to self-antigens or to nonpathogenic molecules—can lead to autoimmune diseases or allergies, respectively.

HUMAN–PATHOGEN COEVOLUTION

Like other organisms large and small, humans have been exposed to infectious pathogens throughout our evolutionary history. They are part of our environment and serve as selective forces—that is, they affect our survival and reproduction. Here we outline what is known about human evolutionary history with pathogens and how one infectious disease in particular, malaria, has wrought biological changes in populations exposed to it. We then turn to how pathogens respond to our adaptations, including those involving our immune systems, how human behavior can select for changes in pathogen characteristics, making them more benign or virulent, and how early exposure to pathogens may be protective against allergic diseases.

Many human pathogens derive from ancestral species and also affect our primate relatives. Among the pathogens that likely afflicted our ancestors and that are known to infect many primates and other mammals are ectoparasites such as lice, fleas, and ticks, as well as helminths, protozoa (including many different types of malaria), fungi, bacteria, and a large variety of vector-borne viruses (arboviruses) (Cockburn 1971). In part, these diseases reflect the fact that for most of our evolutionary history we lived in the tropical woodlands, where the broadest diversity of organisms, including microorganisms, flourishes under the warm and moist conditions.

There is an important distinction to be made between the pathogens just listed and those that constitute the major infections affecting modern humans. The former are diseases endemic to the tropical forest (although some are more broadly distributed) and generally do not cause epidemics. This is not to say that our hunter-gatherer ancestors did not get sick or die from infection, but rather, by and large, these were chronic, mild pathogens that only rarely spread rapidly or caused life-threatening illness. The mobile, low-density, and small-scale groups that typified their social organization were unlikely candidates for epidemics. With the advent of meat-eating some 2.5 million years ago, new foodborne parasites and **zoonoses** (diseases acquired from other animals) were likely added to the mix, but when fire was domesticated and cooking of foods became common around 500,000 years ago (the exact date remains controversial), meat-borne pathogens presumably declined (Stahl 1984; Wrangham 2009).

The turning point in human prehistory that drastically altered the distribution of diseases was the transition from mobile foraging to settled cultivation, which began around 10,000 BP in several places in the Old and New Worlds (Cohen 1989). This changed the human–infectious disease relationship in several ways. For example, as humans stopped moving around in search of food and established permanent settlements, their population density increased, which allowed for greater contact between hosts and thus facilitated pathogen transmission. Second, the problem of waste arose with permanent villages. Instead of being able to leave fecal matter and other waste behind, humans now had to find a way of living with it. This increased exposure to pathogens, particularly from water and food. Third, agriculturalists also had to live with the surplus of food yielded by this new mode of production. Stores of grain or tubers are vulnerable to a variety of pests; several rodents and insects became unwelcome human commensals and brought along their own parasites. Fourth, the clearing of land for cultivation created new ecological conditions for pathogens or their vectors (such as irrigation ditches) and increased contact with soil and soil-dwelling microbes when cultivating crops. Furthermore, among some populations, domestication of animals generated prolonged intensive contact between humans and animals and gave rise to a large number of zoonotic diseases. Domesticated animals can serve as carriers of pathogens more widely distributed among wildlife (Pearce-Duvet 2006) and thus a new set of diseases was added to the existing infectious disease burden of ancestral populations. Many of these remain common among human populations today.

Among these new diseases are those that routinely cause epidemics, because with larger and denser populations, an infection can spread rapidly and sicken large numbers of people. Table 8.4 lists several important zoonotic diseases and the domesticated animal associated with them. Note that these are common epidemic infections today, and many of them are or were routine diseases of childhood. There are now effective vaccines against many of these zoonoses, but prior to the twentieth century, they would have been major causes of death, especially for children. Indeed, some, such as measles and tuberculosis, remain so in populations without access to vaccination. Tuberculosis is an interesting zoonotic disease because it appears that the form that causes most disease in humans (*Mycobacterium tuberculosis*) predated animal domestication (Brosch et al. 2002). The cattle disease *Mycobacterium bovis* can be transmitted to humans, but it is also the case that humans can transmit *M. tuberculosis* to cows and other mammals. Thus the close association between humans and domesticated animals that occurred during the agricultural transition resulted in disease transmission in multiple

TABLE 8.4 Some Important Diseases of Humans That Derive from Domesticated Animals

Human Disease	Pathogen	Zoonotic Source
Measles	Orthomyxovirus	Dogs or cattle
Cold	Rhinovirus	Horses
Pertussis	*Bordetella pertussis*	Pigs or sheep
Tuberculosis	*Mycobacterium tuberculosis*	Cattle
Diphtheria	*Corynebacterium diphtheriae*	Cattle
Smallpox	Poxvirus	Cattle
Plague	*Yersinia pestis*	Fleas are vectors; rats
Influenza	Myxovirus	Pigs, fowl
Typhus	*Rickettsia prowaszekii*	Lice are vectors; rats, mice
Brucellosis	*Brucella abortus*	Cattle
Sleeping sickness	*Trypanosoma spp.*	Tsetse fly is vector; cattle
Toxoplasmosis	*Toxoplasma gondii*	Cats, sheep, pigs
Chlamydia	*Chlamydia trachomatis*	Domestic birds

directions—from animals to humans, humans to their domesticates, and between different species of domesticates (Huard et al. 2006).

Analysis of skeletons from pre- and post-agricultural populations confirms the change in infectious diseases with agriculture. Like diseases of dietary origin, some infectious diseases leave a characteristic signature in bone. Others leave no such trace, although generalized markers of infection may be visible in remaining skeletal materials. These are **periosteal reactions**, characterized by a rough appearance of the outer layer of bone, and indicate inflammation, as shown in Figure 8.5. The bacteria *Staphylococcus* and *Streptococcus* are among the pathogens that leave such a mark. Dickson Mounds, a well-described archaeological site in the state of Illinois, is a particularly informative site for examining the infectious disease consequences of the transition to agriculture. There, a gradual shift from hunting and gathering to settled maize agriculture occurred between about 900 AD and 1200 AD. The number of individuals with periosteal reactions was more than three times as high in the later agricultural group compared with the earlier hunter-gatherer group (73% vs. 21%) (Goodman and Armelagos 1985), although it is wise to keep in mind the osteological paradox from Chapter 4 when interpreting these findings. These changes correlated with an increase in evidence of undernutrition and, given the synergistic effects between the two, it is likely that both morbidity and mortality from infectious disease and malnutrition increased notably. It is also significant that evidence of undernutrition and infection is most common among infants, children, and women. Importantly, the Dickson Mounds population did not domesticate animals, and so the rise in infections did not result from zoonoses. Similar patterns are found in studies of populations transitioning to agriculture in other parts of the Old and New Worlds, although one exception comes from Nubia in North Africa. There, the frequency of periosteal reactions was lower in the settled group, which George Armelagos attributed to their

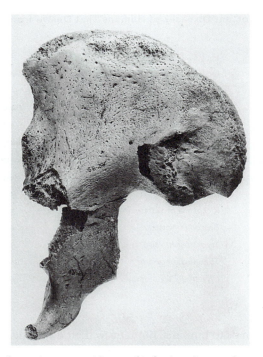

FIGURE 8.5 Periosteal reactions are evidence of infection that can be ascertained from the study of ancient skeletons. This pelvis of a young adult female shows evidence of tuberculosis infection. Mississippian period, Schild Cemetery, Illinois.
Credit: Photo provided courtesy of the Center for American Archeology.

consumption of grain contaminated by the mold-like bacterium *Treptomycetes*, which produces the broad-spectrum antibiotic tetracycline (Armelagos 1990).

MALARIA: A POST-AGRICULTURAL DISEASE

Malaria is an excellent example of a disease that has acted as a selective force in human populations in the post-agricultural period. It remains a major threat; in 2017 there were 219 million cases and 485,000 deaths, mostly in Africa and among children and pregnant women (http://www.cdc.gov/malaria). Four species of the genus *Plasmodium* cause disease in humans: *P. vivax*, *P. falciparum*, *P. ovale*, and *P. malariae*. The first two are responsible for most cases, with *P. falciparum* being the most lethal. The vectors of *Plasmodium* are mosquitoes of the genus *Anopheles*.

Protozoa often have complex life cycles and malaria is no exception. Briefly, the life cycle goes like this: a mosquito carrying the protozoan bites a human and injects microscopic threadlike sporozoites, which travel first to the liver, where they divide asexually into thousands of merozoites. The liver stage can last from weeks to years, and eventually the merozoites are released into the bloodstream, where they infect red blood cells. There they again divide asexually, and the red blood cell bursts, freeing the merozoites to infect other red blood cells. See Figure 8.6 for a diagram of the malaria life cycle.

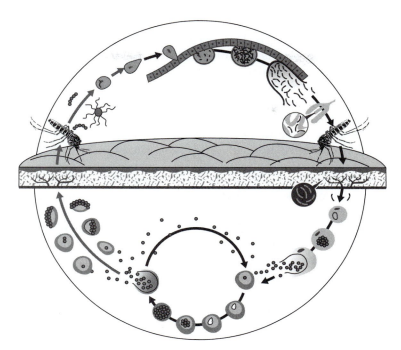

FIGURE 8.6 Life cycle of Plasmodium, the protozoan causing malaria in humans.

The bursting of the red blood cells is what causes the episodes of chills and fever that typify a malarial infection as the immune response is stimulated by the presence of free parasites. Several days after the initial infection of red blood cells, sexual forms of the parasite are formed—the gametocytes—and these can be taken up by a mosquito acquiring a blood meal. The time when the gametocytes are most infectious is synchronized with the nightly feeding cycle of the mosquito. In the female mosquito, fertilization occurs, and the fertilized ova form a cyst on the stomach wall. Within the cyst, thousands of sporozoites form over the course of one to two weeks, depending on the ambient temperature, among other factors. The cyst then bursts, releasing the sporozoites into the mosquito's saliva, which can then be injected into a human when the mosquito takes its next blood meal. Importantly, the parasite does not harm the mosquito.

Anopheline mosquitoes prefer to breed in warm, sunlit bodies of water and their geographical distribution is determined primarily by the availability of breeding sites, local temperatures, and mammals from which to attain blood meals. Malaria's range has fluctuated, shrinking and expanding primarily as a function of human activities affecting the breeding opportunities for the Anopheline vectors, and is now expanding because of global warming (see Chapter 9).

Malaria was undoubtedly around during the time of our hunter-gatherer ancestors and likely originated in the Old World, spreading to the New World during the colonial period. The combination of breeding grounds for *Anopheles* mosquitoes and sufficiently dense human host populations would have been rare in an intact tropical forest context populated by human foragers. This was not the case following the transition from hunting-gathering to horticulture. Frank Livingstone's (1958) work on the origins of malaria in West Africa traced malaria to this transition. Why should horticulture result in increased exposure to malaria? First, to convert forested land to make it suitable for plant production, the forest is cleared to allow sunlit spaces for plants to grow. In the tropics, soils generally harden when exposed to sunlight, resulting in standing pools of water during the rains. These are ideal breeding grounds for Anopheline mosquitoes. Furthermore, the transition to horticulture was associated with increasing human population density. Together these formed the ideal context into which malaria could emerge. With warm temperatures, ample breeding grounds, and food sources for the vector, the malarial parasite could easily be transmitted from human to human. This process is summarized in Figure 8.7.

Malaria is particularly dangerous to infants and children and to pregnant women. Children have immature immune systems that cannot mount an effective response to malaria infection. In pregnant women, malaria has the ability to be especially severe because during pregnancy the immune system is somewhat suppressed. Spontaneous abortion, fetal death, premature birth, and low birth weight are some of the outcomes of malarial infection during pregnancy. *P. falciparum* is the most troublesome form for pregnant women because the red blood cells infected with the protozoan accumulate

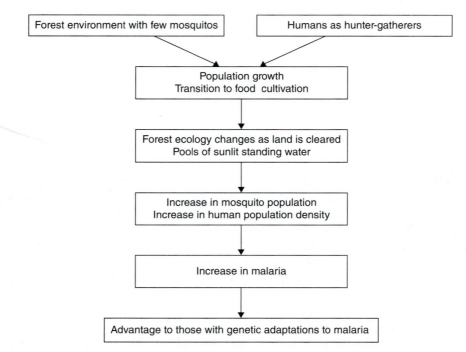

FIGURE 8.7   The process by which malaria came to be an important disease of humans with the spread of horticulture.

in placental blood vessels, yet it is often asymptomatic (Desai et al. 2007). Thus, malaria came to constitute an important selective force, and there is strong evidence that a variety of genetic adaptations to malaria have occurred in human populations exposed to malaria, especially *P. falciparum* and *P. vivax*. Repeated exposure to malaria during childhood does result in immunity in adulthood, but this immunity is rarely complete, and adults may suffer from recurrent milder cases of malaria. One of the ironies of malaria control efforts is that temporary respites from malaria (as opposed to sustained efforts to control the disease) can interrupt the process of acquired immunity, resulting in more adult sickness and death from the disease.

The best described of the human genetic adaptations to malaria is a mutation that creates an altered form of the red blood cell protein hemoglobin (Hb). There are actually more than 200 variant forms of hemoglobin found among contemporary human populations, with the A form being by far the most common. HbA is a globular protein made up of four component peptide chains held together in the center with an iron molecule. This structure gives red blood cells their characteristic spherical shape and ability to bind and transport oxygen. Another form of hemoglobin, the S form (HbS), is created by a single DNA base substitution mutation in the gene for one of the hemoglobin protein chains. This mutation substitutes the amino acid valine for glutamic acid and radically changes the function of the resulting hemoglobin protein. Instead of creating red blood cells with a spherical shape, sickle-shape cells result, as shown in Figure 8.8. These cells are not effective at taking up oxygen or releasing it to cells and they tend to get stuck in smaller blood vessels, resulting in local hemorrhaging. However, having one copy of the HbS allele seems to confer some resistance to malaria. In the 1950s, Anthony Allison, a British physician working in East Africa, observed that the geographic distribution of falciparum malaria overlapped with that of the sickle-cell allele and that individuals with some sickled red blood cells were rarely hospitalized with malaria (Allison 1954). More recently, this effect has been demonstrated in Kenyan children (Aidoo et al. 2002; Williams et al. 2005).

With Allison's observations, ideas about the link between **sickle-cell hemoglobin** and malaria began to take shape. There are three possible phenotypes created by these

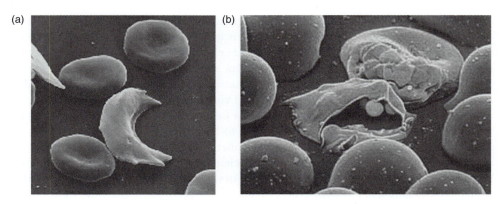

(a) (b)

FIGURE 8.8 (a) Red blood cells formed by HbS and HbA. (b) An HbA red blood cell parasitized by malaria.

two alleles: individuals with two HbA alleles, who are vulnerable to malaria; individuals with two HbS alleles, who have the deadly disease **sickle-cell anemia**; and heterozygous individuals with one of each allele, who have roughly half HbA red blood cells and half HbS red blood cells. These heterozygous individuals have some resistance to malaria without all of the negative effects of sickle-cell anemia. The fact that they can pass on both alleles keeps both the HbS and the HbA alleles in the population. HbS never reaches a frequency of 50%, however. In areas where its prevalence is greatest, the allele frequency is only about 15% because the negative effects of having two HbS alleles are much greater than those associated with two HbA alleles. A person with two HbA alleles may never contract malaria or may get only a mild case, whereas an individual with two HbS alleles is almost certain to die at a relatively young age from sickle-cell anemia. Hence, the HbA allele will get passed on more frequently than the HbS allele.

There are several other mutations that also confer some resistance to malaria. Most result in red blood cells with some form of functional impairment that inhibits malarial parasitism. In West Africa, modifications in the **Duffy blood group** protein gene confer resistance to the *vivax* form of malaria. The Duffy protein is one of several on the surface of the red blood cell, and *P. vivax* makes use of this protein to enter the cell. If the red blood cell does not have this protein on its surface, the parasite cannot get into the cell. In West Africa nearly 100% of individuals have the otherwise rare Duffy negative allele, which does not make a Duffy protein. In this region, *P. ovale*, which is not susceptible to the effects of the Duffy negative allele, has taken over the *P. vivax* niche (http://www.cdc.gov/malaria).

In the Mediterranean there is a common mutation in the gene for **glucose-6 phosphate dehydrogenase** (G-6PD for short). This protein is involved in a complex metabolic pathway that produces a compound called glutathione, which in turn is necessary for preventing the buildup of hydrogen peroxide in the cell. Hydrogen peroxide is a potent oxidant that is destructive to cells. The variant form of G-6PD (which is referred to as G-6PD deficiency, although there is a whole spectrum of reduced protein activity) does not carry out this function well, causing hydrogen peroxide to build up in cells, making them fragile and vulnerable to any further stressor. When a malarial parasite attempts to infect the cell, the cell bursts, and the plasmodium dies. Although G-6PD deficiency sounds deleterious, a person can generally survive well with this condition.

However, for individuals with G-6PD deficiency, consumption of any substance that exacerbates oxidative stress in a red blood cell can cause major destruction of red blood cells and possibly death (Katz 1987). One such example is the **fava bean** (*Vicia faba*). Fava beans are very large beans widely consumed among Mediterranean populations. They contain a powerful oxidant called vicine, which contributes to red blood cell fragility. Indeed, the consumption of fava beans itself confers some resistance to malaria because it causes the red blood cell to burst when the parasite attempts to infect it. Vicine is chemically similar to pyrimethamine, a well-known antimalarial drug. However, individuals with G-6PD deficiency who eat fava beans are at risk of having their red blood cells destruct, resulting in widespread hemolysis and potentially death. G-6PD deficiency is most common among males because the gene for it is carried on the 23rd chromosome—the X chromosome—of which males have only one copy. The allele for G-6PD deficiency is recessive, so if males have that copy, it will not be masked by the dominant allele for G-6PD functionality. Because females have two X chromosomes, they need two copies of the recessive allele instead of just one to display G-6PD deficiency. Not surprisingly, there is widespread lore in the Mediterranean about the dangers of boys consuming fava beans. Some are exquisitely sensitive to even just the pollen of fava bean plants; others can consume a few without ill effects. Thus, fava beans do confer resistance to malaria for the non-G-6PD deficient population, but for those with the recessive allele, they are already protected from malaria and eating fava beans can rapidly destroy their red blood cells.

These biological adaptations have evolved over thousands of generations and appear to be effective against malaria. The hemoglobin variants also generate their own problems—for persons who only produce sickled red blood cells, resistance to malaria was small comfort because their disease was (and still is for most people) fatal. There are also behavioral adaptations to malaria—fava bean consumption is one such adaptive dietary behavior, but other foods can also have such effects. Working with the Hausa of Nigeria, the late Nina Etkin and her colleague Paul Ross found a number of dietary behaviors that were protective against malaria (Etkin and Ross 1991). During peaks of malaria infection, usually corresponding to the onset of the rainy season, the Hausa consume many plants that are rich in oxidants—compounds that disrupt red blood cell integrity, much like fava beans. Some are specifically consumed for their antimalarial properties, whereas others are consumed as part of the normal diet. Wild plants tend to be especially high in oxidants, and these were more frequently consumed during the early rainy season, when stores of staple grains were running low. The net effect is that these dietary behaviors reduce some of the burden of malaria infection among this West African group. A wide variety of plants, some of which have been used as traditional medicines for malaria, have been found to inhibit the parasite, including those strains resistant to common biomedical drugs, such as chloroquine (Nondo et al. 2015).

It is interesting to also consider attempts to control malaria from an evolutionary perspective. Most of these efforts have attacked the Anopheline mosquito vector directly or eliminated its breeding grounds. In the late 1950s there was a massive global program to eradicate the *Anopheles* mosquito by spraying large quantities of the insecticide DDT, a pesticide with such ill effects on the environment that its use was subsequently banned in the United States and other countries. The initial results of this program were spectacular—malaria morbidity and mortality plummeted, especially in South Asia. However, these effects proved to be short lived because DDT-resistant mosquitoes became more common (i.e., they were selected for) as a consequence of incomplete or short-term insecticide use. With the resurgence of these mosquitoes, the number of malaria cases once again began to rise. In India, malaria all but disappeared in the 1960s, but by the 1980s it was an epidemic (Kumar et al. 2007). In contrast, in the 1930s when malaria was endemic to the southeastern areas of the United States, there were massive public works programs that drained swamps, screened buildings, and used larvicides to reduce the population of malaria-causing mosquitoes. These measures were highly successful, and malaria is no longer common in the United States.

Malaria remains a disease associated with agricultural practices. Rice agriculture, for example, which involves keeping fields flooded for extended periods of time, creates the ideal conditions for the spread of malaria because Anopheline mosquitoes can easily and rapidly breed in the still, sunlit waters of flooded fields. Unfortunately, peak transmission times for malaria co-occur with the time of rice planting, leading to farmers being debilitated by disease during a time when their labor is most crucial. In one example of a rice agriculture development project in Kenya, the land was originally home to mosquitoes that were not vectors of malaria; after rice fields were created, the majority of mosquitoes were *Anopheles gambiae*, a potent vector for malaria, and local malaria rates surged. Similar outcomes have occurred in other places where rice-farming initiatives have taken place (Venezuela, Tanzania, and India, among others) (Desowitz 1981). Deforestation associated with agricultural production or the extraction of forest resources also results in increases in malaria. Malaria is now endemic to the Amazonian basin, where logging and commercial agricultural enterprises have replaced the once-dense forest (Stefani et al. 2013). Workers are routinely infected with malaria, and widespread use of chloroquine contributes to the rise of chloroquine resistance among malaria parasites.

EVOLUTIONARY CHANGES IN PATHOGENS

Just as humans have evolved defenses against pathogens, the latter have evolved strategies to avoid them. Since microbes have a much shorter generation time than humans, counter adaptations can evolve relatively quickly because there are more opportunities for mutations to occur. Indeed, one of the most interesting and frustrating aspects of pathogens is their ability to change quickly over time and evade the various physiological and technological interventions humans impose to reduce their spread. This is easily demonstrated by the multiple drug-resistant forms of malaria and bacterial **antibiotic resistance**. Although most of the time mutations are deleterious to the microbe, sometimes they provide a new epitope that is not recognized by the immune system, or a protein variant that resists drug treatment. In addition, some bacteria and viruses have the ability to exchange genetic material, and they can acquire new, potentially advantageous (from their perspective) traits this way as well. Others, through various recombinations of hundreds of genes, can produce a huge array of possible antigens, preventing memory cells from mounting a rapid response. Still others produce different antigens at different life cycle stages.

The influenza virus is particularly adept at acquiring new antigens. It has two kinds of antigens on its surface, each of which is highly variable. Every year, mutations in the virus produce new antigens, in a process called **antigenic drift**. As a result, new vaccines must be made each year. In addition, influenza viruses can exchange RNA. Different types of influenza viruses circulate in humans and birds, and pigs are vulnerable to both of them, such that recombination of viral RNA from other species may occur in pig hosts. This process produces major changes in the virus and is called **antigenic shift**. The flu pandemic that began in 2009 (influenza A H1N1) resulted from this process; the virus contained a novel combination of genes from strains known to circulate in pigs, birds, and humans. Human domestication of these animal species and close habitation with them has facilitated this process.

Other strategies that pathogens have evolved to escape immune detection include concealment and immunosuppression. Some conceal their presence by hiding in host cells or enrobing themselves in host proteins. Pathogens are especially vulnerable when they attempt to spread beyond a cell, so those such as the bacterium *Listeria* cause

Antibiotic Resistance

The phenomenon of bacteria becoming resistant to existing antibiotic drugs is widely known. Antibiotics were first developed in the late 1940s from the naturally occurring products of molds and fungi, such as the penicillin family of antibiotics. Subsequently, these were synthesized and altered for specific properties that were effective against particular bacterial types. However, almost from the beginning, it was acknowledged that some bacteria were resistant to the various antibiotics in use at the time. Most relevant now is that the number of bacteria that are no longer susceptible to existing drugs has been increasing rapidly.

There are myriad means by which bacteria can become resistant to antibiotics. Bacteria have genes that encode membrane transport proteins that rid them of toxic compounds and enzymes that inactivate antibiotics, alter binding sites for antibiotics, or disrupt metabolic pathways. It appears that most bacterial genomes contain resistance genes or their precursors; thus far, a few bacterial species have been found to be resistant to all known natural and synthetic antibiotics (Wright 2007). In fact, resistance is likely to be an ancient phenomenon, not exclusively derived from antibiotic usage in the twentieth century. As Gerard Wright notes, "Environmental microorganisms are successful chemists that continue to evolve new biosynthetic pathways that produce complex bioactive natural products while maintaining evolutionary successful ones that arose millions of years ago" (Wright 2007, 187). Bacteria may acquire resistance genes through mutation or acquire DNA directly from other bacteria (transformation), viruses (transduction), interorganism DNA exchange (conjugation), and movement of genes within the genome (transposition). Variants that have resistance genes will proliferate in an environment characterized by antibiotic usage. In addition, there is some evidence that exposure to antibiotics may in fact increase the mutation rate of bacteria. It is important to note that antibiotic resistance is not exclusively a product of human behavior because bacteria infect other microorganisms that produce antibiotic chemicals in turn, and the mechanisms that generate resistance are very complex. On the other hand, some bacterial species cannot evolve resistance. *Trypanoma*, which causes syphilis, has a very small genome and cannot acquire genetic material from other bacteria.

There is no doubt that extensive use of antibiotics, especially when unwarranted, gives rise to new resistant forms through natural selection (regardless of how bacteria acquire resistance genes). How and why did antibiotics come into such wide usage? Most of the antibiotics used today are given to animals for the food market to prevent infection that would impede their growth or result in unsalable products. There is evidence that this practice has resulted in antibiotic-resistant bacterial strains that infect these animals and humans, and routine administration of some antibiotics to farm animals has been restricted. What about antibiotic usage among people? New guidelines have been issued by the Centers for Disease Control and Prevention that restrict usage to cases where there is an empirical basis for bacterial infection and the disease is considered non-self-limiting.

Many clinicians argue that their patients "demand" antibiotics even when their diagnosis does not fit the protocol for antibiotic administration. This appears to be especially true in pediatric clinics, where Rita Mangione-Smith and colleagues found that pediatricians prescribed an antibiotic 62% of the time for respiratory symptoms or ear pain when they thought that the parents wanted them versus 7% of the time when they thought the parents did not want them (Mangione-Smith et al. 1999). Even when it was ascertained that the child's condition was caused by a virus, doctors prescribed an antibiotic more than half of the time if they thought the parents expected it compared with less than 10% of the time if they thought the parents did not. Parents expected antibiotics for their child's respiratory symptoms the majority of the time, whereas the clinicians were much less likely to perceive these expectations (Mangione-Smith et al. 2006). Importantly, antibiotics were more likely to be given to patients of low socioeconomic status, although the reasons for this are unclear at this time.

Parents were more likely to question a treatment regime if the clinician specifically recommended against antibiotics. Mangione-Smith and colleagues noted,

> Parental questioning of the treatment plan was strongly associated with the physician communication practice of ruling out the need for antibiotics. Qualitative analyses of these exchanges suggested that these rule-out statements may motivate such questioning because they seem to delegitimize the parent's decision to seek medical help for the child's condition. These effects may be aggravated when attempts are made to reassure a parent by minimizing the significance of symptoms, or when recommendations for nonprescription medicines are vaguely described. (Mangione-Smith et al. 2006, 949–950)

A review of pediatric clinical encounters for acute respiratory tract infections found that clinicians anticipated parental requests for antibiotics and interpreted parental statements only intended to communicate concerns or to elicit further information as pressure to prescribe antibiotics

(continued)

(continued)

(Cabral et al. 2014). More recently, Mangione-Smith and colleagues (2015) reported that providing positive messages about ways to alleviate a child's symptoms in addition to negative messages about the lack of need for antibiotics increased parental satisfaction with the clinical encounter.

These studies of doctor–patient interactions suggest the ways in which cultural expectations about antibiotic usage play out in a clinical context and how they may lead to inappropriate prescribing of antibiotics. Given the problem of antibiotic resistance, understanding both cultural knowledge and expectations about antibiotics and how they influence both the prescribing and the actual use of antibiotics is critical (see Fleming-Dutra et al. 2016 for a review and current trends).

---

the cell membrane to protrude into a neighboring cell, thereby moving to the next cell without having to be outside of a cell. Others shed through the skin, the gut, or the lungs and exit the body. Some helminths form cysts, which are then covered with scar tissue, which is made from host material and is thus invisible to the immune system. Various viruses also produce proteins that mimic host cytokines and cytokine receptors.

Some infectious agents actually cause the immune system itself to be suppressed or prevent it from functioning properly. HIV makes surface antigens that bind to receptors found only on T-cells and antigen-presenting cells and allow the virus into these cells. HIV is a retrovirus and can integrate itself into host DNA, where it goes through a process of antigenic drift, producing many variants over the course of an individual's infection. This creates a moving target for immune response, but further, because immune cells are themselves infected, they are destroyed in the process of the response. As a result, HIV-infected individuals are highly susceptible to other pathogens that are able to proliferate without incurring an effective immune response.

VARIATION IN PATHOGEN VIRULENCE

Pathogens vary in terms of how sick they can make us. On the one hand, the rhinovirus that causes the common cold is perhaps reason for dismay, but it is not life threatening. On the other hand, anthrax is a likely death sentence without rapid treatment with antibiotics. Why are some microorganisms merely annoying, whereas others have the potential to kill us? The common answer to this question for much of the twentieth century was that pathogens tend to evolve into relatively benign forms the longer they are associated with their hosts. That is, pathogens should not "want" to kill their hosts because they need the resources provided by those hosts, and over time, hosts and pathogens should coevolve to mutually tolerate each other. This would imply that pathogens to which humans have been exposed for a long period of time should be benign, whereas those that are relatively new to us are **virulent** (that is, cause serious or life-threatening disease). The problem with this hypothesis is that although in some cases pathogens with long associations with humans are relatively benign, there are also many "old" pathogens that still cause terrible disease and death (such as malaria), and "new" pathogens are not always deadly.

In his book *Evolution of Infectious Disease*, Paul Ewald (1994) took the pathogen's view to demonstrate how both the mode of transmission and the host behavior can affect a pathogen's characteristics. To start, Ewald defined a pathogen's virulence to be a function of a faster reproductive rate (which should increase the likelihood of transmission) and production of toxins, both of which are "expensive" for the pathogen. Pathogens with these characteristics require more resources than those that reproduce more slowly or do not produce toxins. On the one hand, the costs associated with a more virulent strategy imply that there must be some sort of advantage to them, such as being able to spread to more susceptible hosts more quickly, thereby having higher fitness. On the other hand, reproducing slowly and causing only mild disease can also be an adaptive strategy. Thus, there are likely trade-offs that shape pathogen virulence (Alizon et al. 2009).

The mode of transmission is an important determinant of which strategy pathogens use, and there are two basic modes: direct and vector borne. Direct transmission can be skin-to-skin contact, airborne, or through sexual contact. Vector-borne transmission can include organisms that serve as vectors (often biting insects), as well as human made elements of the environment (e.g., needles or sewage systems). As a general rule, Ewald posited that pathogens that transmit directly from host to host will be more benign than those that use vectors, and this has been confirmed in other evolutionary models (Boldin and Kisdi 2012). Why? Because for the pathogen to get transmitted, the host must be having contact with other hosts; this will be less likely if the host is very ill or dead.

For a pathogen that uses direct transmission, its chances of getting to a new host are low if the infected person is not up and around and interacting with other susceptible individuals. Most likely, it will be destroyed by the immune system before it can get to another host, and its fitness will be severely limited. The rhinovirus, for example, uses direct transmission through airborne droplets. A person with a mild cold is likely to continue to go about his or her daily activities and interact with other people. As a result, the virus is likely to have its highest fitness by making the person only slightly ill. A highly virulent rhinovirus variant that made the person extremely sick such that he or she was home in bed would not have these opportunities to spread and, consequently, these "virulence genes" would not spread. Likewise, with sexually transmitted pathogens such as gonorrhea or chlamydia, the person must be feeling sufficiently well to engage in sexual activity or the pathogen cannot spread. This is true of HIV as well because there is an extended period of time before illness symptoms manifest, which increases its chances of spreading to new hosts.

Malaria is a good example of why vector-borne diseases are likely to be more virulent. An *Anopheles* mosquito takes a blood meal with malarial parasites from one individual and then bites another individual at a later date. For transmission to occur, all that is necessary is that the mosquito be able to access a person infected with malaria and then bite another person. If there is variation in virulence among a population of malarial parasites infecting a person, those parasites that are more virulent are more likely to be transmitted because they reproduce more rapidly and there are more of them available for uptake by the vector.

Water can also serve as a vector. Waterborne infections spread when contaminated material (e.g., fecal matter) gets into water that is subsequently consumed. In this case, the water serves as a vector, transporting the pathogen from one infected individual to others who consume the contaminated water. Imagine an individual sick with cholera, a gastrointestinal bacterium that generates watery diarrhea. That person's waste (which contains cholera bacteria) goes into a sewage system. If wastewater is not effectively treated and separated from water used for drinking, the pathogen can easily be ingested by many other individuals using that water source. The original host can be virulently ill and confined to bed, but if his or her waste can get into the water, the pathogen can spread readily, and pathogen variants that make the host very ill are more likely to be the ones getting transmitted because they reproduce more rapidly. However, if there is adequate separation of waste and drinking water, virulent forms of cholera have a more difficult time spreading to new hosts. Under these conditions the more benign forms are likely to succeed in being transmitted because if the pathogen makes the host only mildly ill, the host can be up and around, although perhaps spending more time in the bathroom. There, without scrupulous attention to hygiene, the pathogen can be taken up by new individuals.

People can also serve as vectors. Hospitals are often sites where virulent infections spread easily. These are referred to as **nosocomial infections**. Doctors and nurses who take care of multiple patients can act as vectors of pathogens by carrying pathogens from one patient to the next. This can happen if protective masks, gloves, and gowns are not used or if hands are not thoroughly washed before and after care of each patient. Surveys of hand-washing behavior in hospitals around the world find highly variable rates; on average, hand washing occurs less than 40% of the time when it is recommended (World Health Organization 2009). Doctors are much less likely to wash their hands than nurses, even in known high-risk contexts (Gawande 2008). In addition, because people who are patients in a hospital are sick and often immunocompromised for a variety of reasons, they are more vulnerable to severe infection.

There is another context in which pathogens can be extremely virulent, even if they are directly transmitted. These are what Ewald calls the **"sit-and-wait" pathogens**, which are able to exist somewhere in the environment for extended periods of time and can be transmitted even if the host has died of the disease. Table 8.5 provides a list of sit-and-wait pathogens, the length of their durability in the external environment, and the mortality associated with these diseases. Tuberculosis is an example of such a pathogen. The bacterium *M. tuberculosis* has a tough, waxy cell wall that protects it. An infected individual can spray out the bacilli in airborne droplets from the lungs, and these can land on surfaces and linger for several months. Thus, although the original infected person may eventually die, tuberculosis can still be transmitted. *M. tuberculosis* is destroyed by ultraviolet light, so it really flourishes as a domestic or hospital-based infection. Similarly, the virus that causes smallpox can persist for years in the external environment and be transmitted even when the host is ill or dead. Anthrax bacteria can form spores that can exist for decades in the soil and reactivate when in a host, and spore-forming pathogens can evolve toward high virulence (Day 2002). Sit-and-wait pathogens flourish best in places where numerous individuals congregate or pass through frequently, enhancing the likelihood that the pathogens can be picked up and activated in a new host.

Another disease that can be usefully understood using Ewald's ideas is **kuru**, which initially was described among the Fore of New Guinea in the early 1960s. Individuals were dying from a disease characterized by tremors, slurred speech, and problems with motor coordination (Lindenbaum 1979). The Fore attributed the

TABLE 8.5   Pathogens That Persist in the External Environment and the Mortality Associated with Them

Pathogen	Mortality (M/I) %	Rank	Survival in External Environment Days	Rank
Variola virus (DNA)	10	1	885.1	1
Mycobacterium tuberculosis	5	2	244.3	3
Corynebacterium diphtheriae	0.2	3	369.8	2
Bordetella pertussis	0.1	4	11.6	6
Streptococcus pneumoniae	0.036	5	28.6	4.5
Influenza virus (RNA)	0.010	6	13.7	4.5
Neisseria meningitidis	0.007	7.5	1.9	11.5
Rubeola virus (RNA)	0.007	7.5	4.4	11.5
Mumps virus (RNA)	0.005	9	0.9	11.5
Parainfluenza virus (RNA)	0.004	10	4.6	11.5
Mycoplasma pneumoniae	0.003	12.5	1.9	11.5
Respiratory syncytial virus (RNA)	0.003	12.5	1.1	11.5
Varicella-zoster virus (DNA)	0.003	12.5	0.9	11.5
Rubella virus (RNA)	0.003	12.5	0.9	11.5
Haemophilus influenzae	0.002	15	1.3	11.5
Rhinovirus (RNA)	0.000	16	2.3	11.5

Source: Walther and Ewald 2004. Reprinted with permission from John Wiley & Sons, Inc.

disease to malevolent sorcerers, whereas early medical researchers focused on it as a possible genetic disease. The biomedical proximate cause of kuru symptoms is now known to be a prion that infects the brain, transforming it into a sponge-like mass and causing a slow deterioration in body function over the course of years.

The anthropologist Shirley Lindenbaum and Robert Glasse suggested that the practice of cannibalism was the means by which kuru spread. Cannibalism appears to have been a relatively new practice for the Fore, having been adopted from neighboring groups in the twentieth century. After a person died, the body was cooked and consumed. The prion was able to withstand this processing and be transmitted to the person who ate infected tissue. Wives of the brothers of the deceased were given the brain to consume (a pattern that seemed to support the idea that it was a genetic disease), and rates of kuru were highest among women and children. Thus, to understand the epidemiology of kuru it was necessary to understand social and kin-based relationships. Because there was a means of transmission that occurred only after the host had died, the prion could generate a lethal disease that would facilitate its transmission. The Australian administration in New Guinea had attempted to end the practice of cannibalism in the 1950s, but it continued in a more covert manner, especially among the South Fore, among whom rates of kuru were highest. As one elderly man described, "We hid and ate people still. Then the *luluais* [government-appointed local leaders] and *tultuls* [their appointed assistants] tried to stop us, but we hid from them, too. We only stopped when the big road came through from Okapa to Purosa [1955]" (Lindenbaum 1979, 20).

It is now recognized that kuru is similar to variant Creutzfeldt–Jakob disease, which causes spongiform encephalopathy. An outbreak of this disease in England in the 1990s killed more than 100 people and was traced to eating beef from cows that were infected with bovine spongiform encephalopathy (or mad cow disease). The cows acquired the disease through feed containing bone meal from sheep who had scrapie (the sheep form of the disease). Here again, transmission occurred only after the infected organisms died and others fed on their body parts, which raises questions about the wisdom of using dead animals as part of animal feed.

This framework for understanding why some pathogens cause life-threatening disease whereas others only cause a stuffy nose and sneezing can be fruitfully applied to interventions designed to reduce the incidence of severe disease and death from infection. If the conditions that are likely to cause pathogens to evolve toward greater benignness are known, then interventions can be designed to create those conditions. For example, Ewald (1994) has shown that the more virulent forms of the waterborne *Shigella* bacteria circulated in the early part of the century in the United States, but with improvements in sewage systems and water treatment facilities, the virulent forms were replaced by those that do not cause serious disease, because only the benign forms could now be transmitted. Likewise, mosquito nets or window screening are effective at reducing mosquito access to individuals infected with malaria because the vector cannot access an infected individual. Only malarial forms that are sufficiently benign to allow infected individuals to be up and around will be transmitted. Scrupulous attention to hygiene can likewise reduce the incidence of virulent nosocomial infections.

Such interventions are aimed not at eliminating infectious microorganisms, but living with them in ways that do not cause life-threatening disease. Even populations that suffer only infrequently from waterborne infections are actually exposed to many microorganisms. However, the forms that dominate in the water are benign and cause little or no harm. Thus, taking into account the ways that human behavior can influence the spread of virulent or benign forms of pathogens is an important issue for public health policies to consider.

There are other hypotheses for why pathogens vary in their virulence, and the evolution of virulence is a complex process that involves multiple strains of pathogens, inter- and intrahost competition, infectivity, mode of transmission, host susceptibility, and recovery, among others (Hawlena and Ben-Ami 2015). Different levels of virulence may be selected for over the course of an epidemic, both in a population and within a given host. At the beginning, when there are many susceptible hosts, natural selection may favor pathogens with the ability to reproduce quickly. However, as the epidemic subsides, there are fewer susceptible hosts and so a pathogen's fitness might be enhanced by reducing its virulence and maintaining itself within a host for a longer period of time. Within a single host there can be selection for pathogens that can invade new habitats within the host (as they face competition in well-colonized tissues), yet over the longer term these new habitats prove deleterious for transmission. For example, the poliovirus usually lives in the mouth and gastrointestinal tract, but if there is intense competition among viral populations living there, selection may favor those that can proliferate in other tissues such as the central nervous system, although these viral strains have little chance of being transmitted. Thus, there are other ways of understanding the evolution of pathogen virulence, and this is an active area of research because it has tremendous implications for the management of infectious diseases.

ALLERGIES AND ASTHMA: RELATIONSHIP TO INFECTIOUS DISEASE EXPOSURE?

Some individuals exhibit symptoms of immune responses in the absence of an infectious disease, but in the presence of seemingly benign substances. These are **allergies** (also called **atopy**, or atopic disease) and **asthma**. Rates of allergies and asthma have skyrocketed over the past few decades, especially in industrialized countries. According to the American College of Allergy, Asthma, and Immunology(https://acaai.org/), currently over 20% of the U.S. population suffers from some type of allergy symptoms or asthma, a rate that reflects a doubling over the past 20 years. At the same time, allergies and asthma were virtually unknown among other populations, especially those of the Amazon and Africa, although globally rates are on the rise (Pawankar 2014). However, when migrants from countries with low rates of allergy and asthma come to industrialized countries, their children develop asthma and allergies at the same rate as local children. All of these data point to the role of environmental conditions as key to the rise in atopy. How can this variation over space and time be understood?

The symptoms of allergies result from immune responses to allergens. Allergens are foreign proteins (antigens) that are not pathogenic, but for some reason the immune system responds to them as if they were. The most common allergens are dust mites, pet dander, molds, pollens, and foods (especially shellfish, peanuts, milk, and eggs, among others). For most people, they do not stimulate any immune response, but for susceptible individuals, a debilitating or even life-threatening immune response can develop. The immune response that typifies allergies is characterized by a high level of production of the antibody **IgE**. When an allergic person is exposed to an allergen, IgE is released and binds to receptors on mast cells in the respiratory, gastrointestinal, and urinary tracts as well as the skin, which causes them to produce histamine, along with other chemicals, to damage and expel the antigen. The symptoms of allergies ensue: coughing, sneezing, congestion, wheezing, vomiting, or diarrhea, which mimic those of a respiratory or gastrointestinal infection.

Another part of the immune response to allergens involves helper T-cells, which are classified into two types: Th_1, which usually responds to intracellular pathogens and stimulates further T-cell activity, and Th_2, which upregulates IgE production. Importantly, Th_1 and Th_2 inhibit one another; a rise in Th_1 inhibits Th_2 and results in lower Th_2 production and vice versa. Therefore, any antigen that generates a large Th_1 immune response will reduce the production of IgE. It is also the case that if the Th_2 cells are already actively responding to antigens, IgE does not generate allergic symptoms. It turns out that IgE's primary role is to respond to helminth infections, and individuals with helminth infections have higher IgE but have a much lower risk of allergies.

At first it may seem odd that there is a link between helminth infections, intracellular pathogens such as viruses or bacteria, and the risk of being allergic to antigens from plants, dust mites, or foods such as peanuts. The connection is that many common allergens are in the same protein antigen families as those found in helminths, and both elicit an IgE response (Fitzsimmons et al. 2014). They tend to be very small proteins or protein particles. Note that because foreign proteins stimulate an immune response, food allergens tend to derive from proteinaceous sources. However, mammalian meats rarely stimulate allergic reactions because their protein signature tends to be similar, if not identical, to that of humans, such that these proteins are not recognized as "foreign."

With this background it becomes evident that exposure to pathogens, especially those that either generate a Th_1 response (any intracellular bacterium or virus) or a rise in IgE (helminths), is likely to inhibit an immune response to potential allergens. In addition to pathogens, the microbiota that inhabit an individual's skin, respiratory system, and gut also act to modulate immune responses to potential allergens. Overall then, it appears that changing exposure to microbes—both pathogenic and benign—is important for understanding the dramatic increase in allergies/asthma that has been primarily found in industrialized countries, but which is also now occurring throughout the globe. There have been two main hypotheses developed to explain this phenomenon: the hygiene and helminth hypotheses, which are outlined below. More recently a more synthetic model has been proposed that integrates these with the growing literature on the importance of human microbiota in shaping the immune system (see Figure 8.9).

Based on the observation that rates of allergy and asthma are highest in industrialized countries, in 1989 David Strachan proposed that hygienic practices within households in these countries were at least partially responsible (Strachan 1989). This became known as the **hygiene hypothesis**. If, for example, populations are rarely exposed to pathogens that generate the Th_1 response (such as tuberculosis), Th_2 levels are not inhibited, and IgE may be free to respond to benign antigens. In one study in Japan,

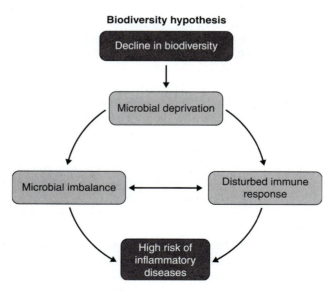

FIGURE 8.9 A schematic overview of how loss of exposure to microbes contributes to inflammatory diseases, including allergies, asthma, autoimmune disorders, and other chronic diseases. *Source:* Haahtela, T. 2019. A biodiversity hypothesis. *Allergy*, 74:1445–1456. Reprinted with permission.

children who had been exposed to tuberculosis had higher Th_1 levels, lower IgE levels, and lower rates of asthma and allergies than did children who had negative tuberculosis tests (Shirakawa et al. 1997). This exposure may be especially important during childhood, when the immune system is still naive and is being shaped by exposure to pathogens. Other evidence in support of this is that children with older siblings tend to have lower rates of atopy than do those who are the oldest or only children, and children with more older siblings have lower rates than those with fewer siblings. Younger children tend to be exposed to many more pathogens as a consequence of their older siblings' infections. Likewise, children in day-care settings tend to have lower rates of atopy compared with children who spend more time at home. Vaccination and frequent antibiotic use have also been associated with increased risk of allergies and asthma (Flöistrup et al. 2006). The latter two may prevent a complete immunological response to pathogens, thereby reducing the inhibition of Th_2 by Th_1 cells. Further evidence is that children who grow up on farms, where exposure to microorganisms in daily life is more extensive than in contemporary cities (at least in wealthy countries), have lower rates of atopy than children in suburban or urban contexts (Alfven et al. 2006).

The **helminth hypothesis** emphasizes the lack of helminthic infection (as opposed to intracellular pathogens) as the reason behind the high rates of atopy in contemporary industrialized societies. In the absence of a burden of worm infections, IgE may be free to respond to allergens similar in structure to the helminth antigens. Numerous studies have found an inverse relationship between helminthic infection and the risk of developing asthma and allergies. Under conditions of helminthic infections, IgE levels are consequently high, but worm antigens seem to stimulate production of anti-inflammatory cytokines such as interleukin-10 (McSorley and Maizels 2012). This appears to inhibit the airway inflammation typical of both asthma and allergy. Helminthic infections are widespread in human populations and most likely have had a continued presence throughout history and prehistory. It is only in wealthy industrialized societies where helminthic infections are no longer commonplace. It should be noted that in the United States, hookworm infection was common, especially in the South, well into the mid-twentieth century; allergies and asthma rates began to rise in the United States and other industrialized countries after this time (Schabussova and Wiedermann 2014).

There are other factors that also appear to predispose industrialized populations to atopy and asthma. Well-insulated homes furnished with carpets, drapes, and copious bedding allow dust mites to proliferate, thereby increasing exposure to their antigens. Transitions to more Western-style housing tend to be correlated with a rise in allergies. Even the simple addition of wool blankets to villages in Papua New Guinea precipitated a dramatic increase in asthma (Dowse et al. 1985). There are also genetic underpinnings to allergy risk. Individuals vary with respect to their IgE levels, and those with higher levels (independent of exposure to helminths) are more vulnerable to atopy. People from populations with higher helminth burdens may have been exposed to selection for high levels of IgE as a response. However, when individuals with alleles for high levels of IgE migrate to industrialized countries, they are at high risk of developing atopic disease from both genetic predisposition to higher IgE levels and increased exposure to allergens (Hagel et al. 2004).

As knowledge about the importance of the human microbiota (especially in the gut) to human health has grown rapidly over the past several years, more attention is now being paid to the impact of overall exposure to both pathogenic and beneficial microbes on allergy (Bloomfield et al. 2016). This is referred to as the **old friends hypothesis**, which recognizes that exposure to a diversity of microbes as the immune system is developing early in life stimulates regulatory T-cells (T_{reg}) (Rook et al. 2003). These "old friends" were the microbes (including helminths) that humans co-evolved with but that have been lost due to changes in diet, occupation, and living conditions (Bloomfield et al. 2016). These would have come from diet (breast milk, whole/minimally processed animal and plant foods), interactions with the natural world, and from other individuals in the community. T_{reg} cells reign in immune activity and promote immunological tolerance, thereby preventing the overreactive immune response to antigens. This model has been updated as the "biodiversity" hypothesis, which broadens the scope of exposure to biodiversity (including microbes) both within and outside of the body. In industrialized and/or highly urbanized contexts, human contact with biodiversity is reduced, resulting in reduced tolerance to harmless microbes or antigens and increased allergy and asthma (see Figure 8.10). Exposure to dietary antigens (such as eggs or peanuts) early in life may also generate T_{reg} cells (Kim et al.

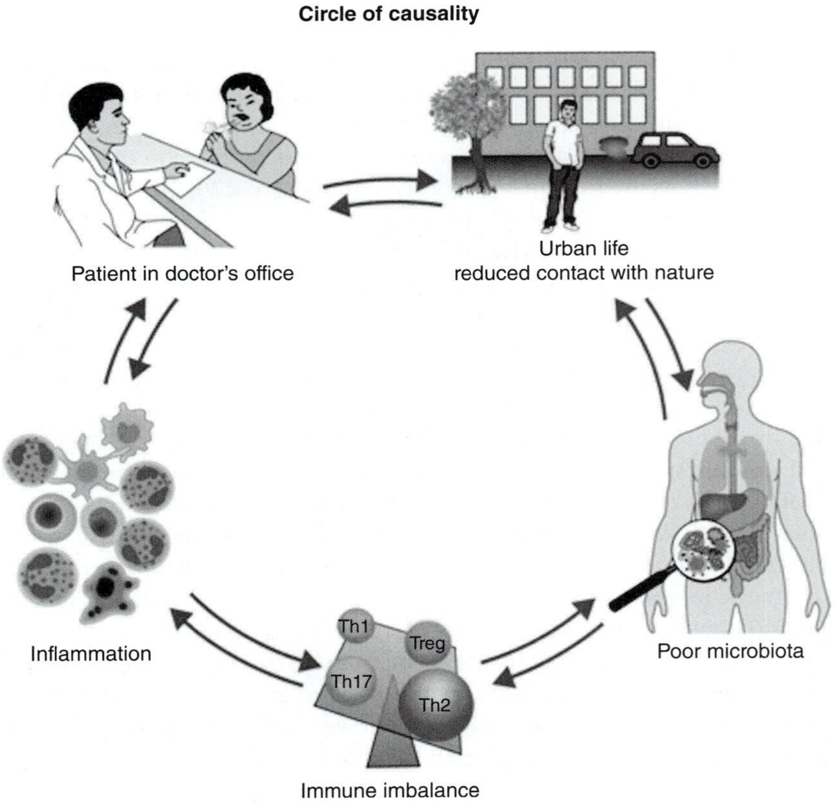

Circle of causality

Patient in doctor's office

Urban life
reduced contact with nature

Inflammation

Poor microbiota

Th1 · Treg · Th17 · Th2

Immune imbalance

FIGURE 8.10 Immunological consequences of loss of exposure to bio- and microbial diversity. *Source:* Haahtela, T. 2019. A biodiversity hypothesis. *Allergy,* 74:1445–1456. Reprinted with permission.

2016). Many other factors are known to reduce both microbial diversity as well as T_{reg} cells, and these typify conditions associated with increased wealth across countries or in urban areas. As Figure 8.11 indicates, antibiotic usage, cesarean section delivery, lack of exposure to farm animals, use of infant formula rather than breast milk, processed food, and smaller family sizes, among other factors, contribute to an increased risk of allergy (Aitoro et al. 2017).

At present there is no cure for allergies, only treatments that reduce their likelihood or provide relief from symptoms. The best strategy is avoidance of known allergens, which often proves difficult for individuals with multiple allergies. Gradual immunological exposure to allergens seems to confer some benefits, although it requires ongoing injections of antigens over the course of months or years. Anti-IgE treatment for asthma is effective (Stokes and Casale 2015), and while there was hope that **probiotics**, which are helpful microorganisms that colonize the gastrointestinal tract, could ameliorate allergies, at present there is little evidence supporting their effectiveness (Mennini et al. 2017). One interesting possibility is the treatment of autoimmune disorders with benign helminths. Autoimmune disorders are similar to allergies except they are characterized by overexpression of Th_1 cells, and an individual's own tissues

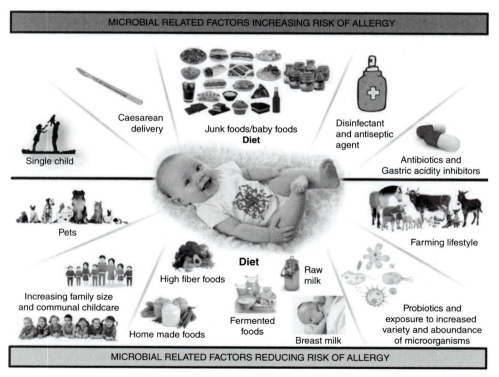

FIGURE 8.11   Risk factors for the development of allergies and asthma.
Source: Aitoro, R.; Paparo, L.; Amoroso, A.; Di Costanzo, M.; Cosenza, L.; Granata, V.; Di Scala, C.; Nocerino, R.; Trinchese, G.; Montella, M.; Ercolini, D.; Berni Canani, R. Gut Microbiota as a Target for Preventive and Therapeutic Intervention against Food Allergy. *Nutrients* 2017, 9, 672.

Anthropologist in Action: David Van Sickle and Managing Asthma

David Van Sickle received his Ph.D. in medical anthropology, conducting research on asthma among Navajo populations in the Southwest of the United States, and in India. After finishing his Ph.D. in 2004, he served as an epidemic intelligence officer at the Centers for Disease Control and Prevention in Atlanta, Georgia, where he provided epidemiological data on asthma to the National Asthma Control Program. During his time there he also worked on airborne illnesses stemming from Hurricane Katrina in communities along the Gulf Coast.

Van Sickle is the cofounder and chief executive officer of Propeller Health (bought by ResMed in 2019), which develops and markets sensors, mobile apps, and services to help track usage of medication such as inhalers for people who have chronic respiratory diseases (e.g. asthma or chronic obstructive pulmonary disease). The Propeller tracking tools involve putting small sensors onto inhalers used to treat asthma or chronic obstructive pulmonary disease symptoms, such as shortness of breath or wheezing, that send data on time and location to your phone and a remote server via Bluetooth. That way, individuals and practitioners can track usage of inhalers,

symptoms, triggers, and other relevant information. This information is stored and can then be used to ascertain patterns in triggers and symptoms and thereby better monitor and treat asthma sufferers within their community context.

His research on asthma in native populations in the Southwest and Alaska, as well as India, has documented barriers to effective treatment of asthma among these groups. In India, physicians may be reticent to give an asthma diagnosis for patients out of concern that it would be socially stigmatizing. In particular, there is concern among parents that it might make their child less eligible for a good marriage. Clinicians are sensitive to this fear, using aphorisms like "wheezy bronchitis" rather than asthma. Among the Navajo, because of cultural values related to individual autonomy, children are largely expected to manage their asthma treatment themselves. However, clinicians often focus on parents rather than children in prescribing a treatment plan, and Van Sickle suggests that children must be more central to this discussion so that they have adequate training and education to successfully treat their asthma (http://davidvansickle.com).

---

are the target of immune action. Such treatment can reduce the severity of gastrointestinal autoimmune disorders (remember that helminth infection stimulates anti-inflammatory cytokines) such as inflammatory bowel disease and may also reduce symptoms associated with allergy and asthma (Maizels 2016).

The use of helminths as treatment would never have been imagined except for an appreciation of how our evolutionary association with microbes of all kinds has profoundly shaped our biological responses, including the shaping of our immune systems. In the absence of the expected infections or commensal microbes, we are vulnerable to alterations in immune function that result in allergy symptoms, asthma, and autoimmune disorders. Thus, declines in infectious diseases and lack of broader exposure to a diversity of microbes have not been an unalloyed good for wealthy industrialized societies, and it can be predicted that rates of allergies and asthma will increase with economic development.

CONCLUSION

The biology of infectious disease and immune response is complex, with each pathogen, and in some cases each strain of a pathogen, presenting unique challenges to recognition by the immune system. Pathogens evolve and spread in environments shaped by human behavior, and this may have importance for the evolution of characteristics of both pathogens and hosts. Alterations in infectious disease exposure may also underlie the high rate of allergies and asthma in industrialized countries. All in all, it is important to understand the ways in which human behavior has influenced the course and distribution of microbes more generally, and infectious diseases in particular. Using an understanding of the basic biology of infection, in the next chapter we consider the relationship between infectious disease and human behavior over the course of human history and across societies in more detail.

STUDY QUESTIONS

1. What is an infectious disease? Compare and contrast pathogens and parasites.
2. What are Koch's postulates? In what ways do they foster a relatively narrow conception of infectious disease?
3. What are the six different kinds of pathogens? How are they distinguished from one another? How do they reproduce?
4. How do pathogens gain entry to hosts? What is the role of a vector?
5. What is the difference between epidemic and endemic? What is the epidemic curve?
6. Besides the immune system, what are the body's main defenses against pathogens? How can symptoms of infection actually be defenses against infection?
7. What are the three important tasks of the immune system? What are its basic components?
8. What are antigens, epitopes, and antibodies? What are B-cells and T-cells? What is the role of inflammation in the immune response?
9. How do pathogens try to "hide" from the immune system? Compare and contrast antigenic drift and antigenic shift.
10. Explain how exposure to malaria has shaped the genetic characteristics of some populations. How is diet related to malaria risk?
11. What factors are important in determining the virulence of a pathogen? How does direct versus vector-borne transmission influence virulence? What are sit-and-wait pathogens?
12. How can nosocomial infections be prevented?
13. What does IgE have to do with allergic responses? What seems to be its "real" function in nature?
14. Why have rates of asthma and allergies skyrocketed in developed countries during the twentieth and twenty-first centuries? What are three hypotheses that have been developed to account for these?

CRITICAL THINKING QUESTIONS

1. Is our body at war with disease? What other metaphors can you think of to describe the way the immune system works?
2. Are laws requiring universal vaccination ethically sound? Is it right to require people carrying dangerous infectious diseases to be quarantined?
3. Should every infectious disease be aggressively treated? Should Americans stay home and rest rather than go to work when they are ill with infectious conditions?

4. There is increasing interest in probiotics as beneficial to health, and at the same time, advertisements for antimicrobial products (e.g. hand sanitizer, household and personal cleaning products, etc.) are common. How can we reconcile these two phenomena?

SUGGESTED ETHNOGRAPHIES AND OTHER BOOKS TO READ WITH THIS CHAPTER

Ed Cohen. 2009. *A Body Worth Defending: Immunity, Biopolitics, and the Apotheosis of the Modern Body.* Durham, NC: Duke University Press.

Alanna Collen. 2016. *10% Human: How Your Body's Microbes Hold the Key to Health and Happiness.* New York: Harper Publishing.

Robert Desowitz. 1981. *New Guinea Tapeworms and Jewish Grandmothers.* New York: Norton.

Rob R. Dunn. 2011. *The Wild Life of Our Bodies: Predators, Parasites, and Partners That Shape Who We Are Today.* New York: Harper.

Emily Martin. 1994. *Flexible Bodies: Tracking Immunity in American Culture from the Days of Polio to the Age of AIDS.* Boston: Beacon Press.

Ed Yong. 2018. *I Contain Multitudes.* The Microbes Within Us and a Grander View of Life. New York: Ecco Press.

CHAPTER 9

Globalization, Poverty, and Infectious Disease

Chapter Goals

- To understand how infectious diseases "emerge" or "resurge" in populations as a result of changes in ecological, social, political, and economic forces
- To understand the historical factors influencing the global distribution of infectious diseases
- To understand how pathogens posed a problem for colonialism in some areas and how "tropical diseases" came to be framed
- To understand how colonialism contributed to the spread of disease
- To understand how climate change is impacting the distribution of infectious disease
- To understand how economic development projects such as construction of dams may contribute to the spread of disease
- To understand how HIV/AIDS and multi-drug-resistant tuberculosis have been able to "emerge"

The current COVID-19 pandemic has brought to the fore the immense challenges associated with confronting a new infectious disease that has no effective means of treatment or prevention (i.e. vaccination). It has laid bare the ways that new infectious diseases "emerge" into human populations through zoonotic pathways, and how risk of disease is not evenly distributed, with some populations at increased risk of both contracting and dying from the virus. Most of us are experiencing the chaos it has generated related to its highly infectious nature, yet uncertainty about many aspects of how it spreads; the fact that some people are infected but show no symptoms, while others end up on a ventilator or die; unclear and/or inconsistent government policies about how to prevent the spread; the severe impacts the pandemic has on the economy; how disease and responses to it are easily politicized; clashes between the caution articulated by public health officials and politicians, businesses, and citizens eager to resume "normal life;" the fragility of that "normal life" in an epidemic, including the erosion of social life as we knew it; and so much more.

The previous chapter covered some of the key biological processes involved in the human experience of infectious disease, and in this chapter we describe the global spread of infectious disease, considering the conditions that cause specific infectious diseases to emerge or resurge and cause harm among human populations. Although there is much current discussion about "emerging" diseases, especially in relation to the current pandemic, in fact there have been periods of emergence throughout the history of our species, beginning with the transition to agriculture, as the example of malaria illustrated. The conditions that cause diseases to spread in human populations are related to local ecologies and, more often than not, the ways in which humans create social environments out of their natural surroundings (Snowden 2019). We provide examples of how the different historical experiences of human societies have had direct impacts on the infectious diseases from which they have suffered. These experiences have shaped the variation in infectious disease distribution across the globe today, and they contribute to differential life expectancies and qualities of life. The core message is that social forces, which alter local and global ecologies, are the primary cause of changes in exposure to infectious disease.

EMERGENT AND RESURGENT DISEASES

We start with the concept of emergent and resurgent infectious diseases. According to the 1992 Institute of Medicine definition,

> **Emerging infectious diseases** [EIDs] are clinically distinct conditions whose incidence in humans has increased. . . . Emergence may be due to the introduction of a new agent, to the recognition of an existing disease that has gone undetected, or to a change in the environment that provides an epidemiologic "bridge." Emergence, or, more specifically, reemergence, may also be used to describe the reappearance of a known disease after a decline in incidence. (Lederberg et al. 1992, 34)

Emerging diseases may thus be "new" or "old," and are defined by an increase in incidence. Old diseases that show an increase in incidence are considered **resurgent infectious diseases**.

It was thought that the "era" of infectious disease would come to a close with the use of antimicrobial drugs, especially antibiotics, and widespread vaccination. By the mid-twentieth century a major **epidemiological transition** had occurred in many wealthy countries; infectious diseases appeared to no longer be a major threat to health (Omran 1971). Infant and child mortality had declined to unprecedented low levels, and older adults were instead dying of chronic diseases such as cancer, cardiovascular disease, or stroke. Less research was conducted on infectious diseases, as funds flowed toward the prevention and treatment of chronic diseases. In 1969 the U.S. Surgeon General announced to Congress that it was "time to close the book on infectious disease as a major health threat . . . it was only a matter of time before every plague that has ever struck fear into the heart of Americans would be a distant memory" (Ryan 1997, 6). Such statements reveal not only a hubris about the triumphs of Western medicine but also a lack of concern with the fact that for many of the world's citizens, infectious diseases had never lost their ability to cause tremendous suffering and death. As of 2016 the World Health Organization reported that lower respiratory tract infections, diarrheal disease, and tuberculosis (TB) were still among the top 10 most common causes of mortality across the globe, and infectious diseases cause about 25% of all deaths across the globe each year (See interactive data on causes of mortality by region and year at https://www.who.int/gho/mortality_burden_disease/causes_death/top_10/en). Furthermore, it is estimated that infectious disease continues to cause about 75% of all mortality in poorer countries (Lozano et al. 2013).

By the 1980s this view that infectious diseases were a thing of the past was becoming increasingly unsupportable, as the potential for new infectious diseases to cause serious harm to humans in the industrialized world was realized. Deaths from infectious diseases in the United States had been declining throughout the twentieth century at a rate of 3%–8% per year (except for 1918, the year of pandemic influenza), but that decline was interrupted in 1980, when it increased by 5% per year until 1996, when it began to decline again (Armstrong et al. 1999). Figure 9.1 shows the

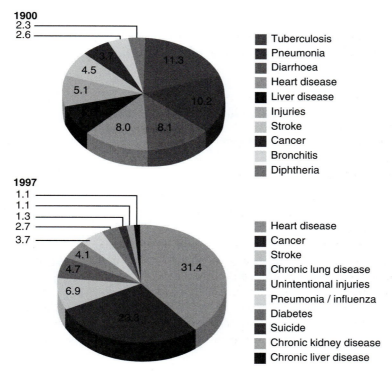

FIGURE 9.1 Changing pattern of causes of death in the United States, 1900–1997.
Source: Reprinted by permission from Macmillan Publishers Ltd: Cohen, Mitchell L. "Changing patterns of infectious disease." *Nature* 406 (6797):762–767, copyright 2000.

distribution of known causes of death in the United States at the beginning and end of the twentieth century. More than 30% of all deaths were caused by TB, diarrhea, or pneumonia in 1900; by the end of the twentieth century only pneumonia and influenza remained as major infectious causes of death, accounting for less than 4% of deaths (Cohen 2000); by 2017, those two respiratory diseases accounted for fewer than 2% of all deaths in the United States (U.S.Centers for Disease Control 2019),

The rise of infectious disease in the late twentieth century was a reminder to those living in wealthy countries that infectious diseases had neither died out nor lost the capacity to kill (remembering that this assumption had been erroneous for most of the world's populations). More than any other disease, HIV/AIDS, which accounted for much of the increase in infectious disease mortality in the 1980s, forced this acknowledgment, and COVID-19 is a powerful reminder. There had been other epidemics of new, virulent, and highly infectious diseases—Ebola, hantavirus, Lassa fever—all causing severe internal hemorrhaging and particularly ghastly deaths. Collectively, these diseases captured the public imagination, leading to fears that such lethal and mysterious pathogens could take hold in the United States.

Figure 9.2 provides a map of the geographical distribution of emerging and resurging infectious diseases. Some were thought to be under control but their incidence is increasing; others are spreading beyond their "traditional" areas; and still others are resistant to existing antimicrobial therapy (e.g., antibiotic-resistant bacteria, chloroquine-resistant malaria). The vast majority are viruses or bacteria, and non-vectorborne, but zoonotic infections are rising and increasingly novel in human populations

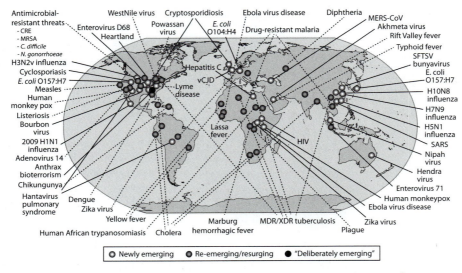

FIGURE 9.2   Geographic distribution of some recent emerging or reemerging infectious diseases.
Source: NIAID (niaid.nih.gov)

compared to known human diseases. It is estimated that more than 60% of EIDs are zoonotic, with most of those coming from wildlife (Atlas 2013). Given this trend, the interdisciplinary "One Health" initiative recognizes "the need to recognize the essential link between human, domestic animal and wildlife health and the threat disease poses to people, their food supplies and economies, and the biodiversity essential to maintain the healthy environments and functioning ecosystems we all require" (Atlas 2013, 8). One Health brings together clinicians, epidemiologists, microbiologists, veterinarians, wildlife ecologists, environmental scientists and anthropologists, among other specialists, to investigate, predict, and respond to EIDs. Medical anthropologists are engaging with human animal health, highlighting the ways in which animals and humans are drawn into complex ecological, economic, social, and affective relationships in ways that impact the health of both humans and domestic and wild animals (Brown and Nading 2019). As Brown and Nading note, in relation to zoonotic diseases, "Ethnographic approaches attuned to the multiple temporalities of multispecies relations are important for making sense of pathogenic entanglements and devising ways to live well with non-human others. Zoonotic events are not single moments in time or space; rather they reflect a recursive and ongoing set of interactions, mediated by the short-term management of acute outbreaks, the longue-durée of colonial and postcolonial biomedical practice, and the deep timescales of animal, insect, and microbial evolution" (Brown and Nading 2019, 11–12).

What is driving the emergence or resurgence of these infectious diseases? Environmental, biological, and social factors all contribute, but most scientists agree that human social behavior is a primary driver, affecting both environmental conditions and biological evolution in pathogens. Below is a list of those factors that have been identified as important in the current context of emergence and resurgence of infectious diseases.

- Sociodemographic factors such as increases in population density, including urbanization, falling living standards and rising poverty, which encourages incursions into forests in search of food, infrastructure declines, including investments in public health, international travel and trade, and conflicts and social instability
- Environmental factors including deforestation, expansion and industrialization of agricultural practices, and natural disasters such as floods, droughts, or other extreme climatic events
- Biological factors including pathogens developed as biological weapons for destruction or changes in pathogen genomes due to exposure to chemicals and antimicrobial agents (e.g., antibiotics) or gene exchange via other hosts (e.g., in the case of influenza viruses) may lead to emergence of drug-resistant pathogen variants that could cause new forms of infectious disease (Lederberg et al. 1992; Nii-Trebi 2017).

More specifically, the growth of cities, especially in low and middle income countries, has given rise to periurban slums and shantytowns with no public health infrastructure and abysmal living conditions. Urban migration is fueled by the lack of opportunities in rural areas, where land is used for export crops. Labor migration separates spouses and increases the likelihood of extramarital sex, which contributes to the spread of sexually transmitted infections (STIs) such as HIV/AIDS. Extractionist activities (logging, grazing of cows for the international beef or dairy market, hunting wild animals), and expansion of agricultural land along with expanding populations bring more people into previously uninhabited areas of the forest, where sylvatic diseases such as yellow fever and malaria can spread. As humans have increasing contact with their wild animal reservoirs, new zoonoses can spread. Civil wars give rise to massive population movements and relocation in refugee camps, where conditions promote the spread of infection. Airline travel transports hosts and pathogens efficiently over long distances, and airplanes themselves facilitate infection through the recirculation of air and the close quarters in which travelers are confined for long durations. In one case from 1977, 70% of people on an airplane became infected with influenza, and only one person on board had had an active infection. Global shipping traffic carries waterborne pathogens such as cholera in ship hulls, and global trade in food allows contaminated products to be distributed widely.

Then there is the waxing and waning of public and private investments in public health infrastructures. Clean water, adequate waste disposal, access to food, vaccination, and clinics all require political will and monetary resources to maintain. Something seemingly as simple as a shortage of syringes and inadequate means of sterilization in health clinics leads to the reuse of supplies and transmission of bloodborne infections, which contributed to the Ebola epidemic in central Africa. The breakdown of conditions often occurs in the context of political and economic instability, and the result is a rise in infectious disease and undernutrition, which collectively contribute to a downward spiral of health and often death.

Researchers such as Paul Farmer point out that many of the diseases classified as emergent or resurgent have long been "hidden" among the poor, and only when they capture media attention do they come into the larger public consciousness (Farmer 2001). Furthermore, it is also clear that attention is focused on them only insofar as they are perceived as a threat to those in power. As the original Institute of Medicine report bluntly acknowledged, "Diseases that appear not to threaten the United States directly rarely elicit the political support necessary to maintain control efforts" (Lederberg et al. 1992, 33). One could argue that almost 30 years later a disease that has threatened the United States has not been able to elicit such support in the current political climate.

SOCIAL TRANSFORMATIONS, COLONIALISM, AND GLOBALIZING INFECTIONS

It is tempting to see the problem of emergent diseases as only relevant to the current historical period, and there is evidence that we are in a period of especially rapid disease emergence, but the example of malaria from the previous chapter shows that the definition of emergent and resurgent diseases can fit even prehistoric situations. Thus, it is worth outlining the historical processes that have led to the current distribution of infectious diseases since there have been numerous episodes of disease emergence and resurgence across the globe.

To start, the transition to agriculture not only created ecological change but also ultimately wrought a whole series of social transformations that profoundly shaped global infectious disease patterns, although there was substantial variation in how these were experienced (Larsen et al. 2019; Milner 2019). First, cultivation places greater demands on labor, especially during periods of planting, weeding, and harvesting, and thereby places a strain on individual energy resources. Second, whereas contemporary hunter-gatherer bands are generally egalitarian, with little difference in economic status between group members (Boehm 1999), settled agriculture has been widely associated with the emergence of social stratification. Ownership of critical resources such as arable land and water and control over surplus became the means of amassing wealth, opportunities that were not available to hunter-gatherers. Control over these key resources enabled elites to establish political and economic power and extract labor from other population members. Not surprisingly, this was associated with the emergence of health differentials within populations. Furthermore, in efforts to expand the subsistence base to support the elites, expansionist activities into new areas and control over new populations also began on a large scale in the post-agricultural period. Infection and war go together, with injuries, poor diets, and crowded conditions all providing new opportunities for pathogens. With incursions into new territories also came exposure to new diseases that were also brought back to the homeland.

Trade is a more benign form of interaction between societies, but likewise led to new means by which disease could spread. By the Middle Ages, when long-distance trade networks from East Asia, South Asia, and Europe were established, a chain of populations of both humans and disease-carrying rodents connected populations across a vast space (McNeill 1976). With European exploration and colonization of the Americas, Australia, and New Zealand, as well as areas in Africa and South Asia, diseases that had been largely confined to Europe and Asia achieved global distribution. In the Americas, trade routes along roads and rivers became major means by which infection spread.

The rise of urban centers, supported by agricultural surpluses from the rural areas, provided new loci in which infectious diseases could take hold and expand. Crowded housing with scant means of waste disposal became a new kind of breeding ground for more "domesticated" pathogens, those that thrive indoors or in the water supply, such as TB or cholera, respectively. With large and dense populations, pathogens that spread by direct contact could easily become epidemic and incur widespread morbidity and mortality. Some infectious diseases such as measles require a large population (more than 250,000 to 500,000) to maintain themselves. Mosquitoes that transmit yellow fever, dengue fever, or the Zika virus prefer to breed in small enclosed pools of warm water such as cooking vessels or abandoned tires. The new urban ecology opened new niches for infectious diseases that were aided by low levels of immunological resistance among many poor urban dwellers worn down by poor nutrition, stress, violence, pollutants, and other pathogens. Epidemics of dengue fever in 2018 and 2019 in countries as disparate as Honduras, India, and the Philippines are evidence of these conditions (Hosangadi 2019).

Collectively, these conditions formed what William McNeill referred to as the "civilized pattern of disease." As he argues,

> Person to person, "civilized" types of infectious disease could not have established themselves much before 3000 BC. When they did get going, however, different infections established themselves among different civilized communities in Eurasia. Proof of this fact

is that when communications between previously isolated civilized communities became regular and organized, just before and after the Christian era, devastating infections soon spread from one civilization to another. (McNeill 1976, 55)

With long-distance trading routes and large urban centers, this pattern became particularly well established in the Old World. There, a common "disease pool" developed, with some regional differences based on climate, subsistence, and social organization. This disease pool began expanding into new areas (the "New Worlds" of the Americas, Australia, and New Zealand) when Europeans began more extensive global exploration and colonization. By around 1522, Europeans had a good sense of how to navigate the globe using the prevailing winds and, as Alfred Crosby put it in *Ecological Imperialism*, with this knowledge:

the seams of Pangaea were closing, drawn together by the sailmaker's needle. Chickens met kiwis, cattle met kangaroos, Irish met potatoes, Comanches met horses, Incas met smallpox—all for the first time. The countdown to the extinction of the passenger pigeon and the native peoples of Tasmania had begun. A vast expansion in the numbers of certain other species on this planet began, led off by pigs and cattle, by certain weeds and pathogens, and by the Old World peoples who first benefited from contact with lands on the other side of the seams of Pangaea. (Crosby 1986, 131)

Although all of these organisms played a role, perhaps the most significant to the indigenous human populations were the pathogens.

As noted earlier, peoples in the Old World had been exposed to a wide variety of pathogens through their intersecting histories. As a result, by the time of the exploratory period, Europeans had extensive historical experience with a diverse array of pathogens. Epidemics of plague, smallpox, TB, and many other respiratory and gastrointestinal diseases occurred regularly throughout the Middle Ages. Several infectious diseases had come to typify childhood, with the result that children either died from them or grew up to be adults with immunity. Less clear is whether any specific genetic adaptations to these pathogens evolved, besides those associated with resistance to malaria. Thus, Europeans and Asians had been exposed to more infections for a longer period of time than had many other populations, especially those of the Americas, Australia, or New Zealand. This familiarity with infectious disease would prove to be advantageous to Europeans in their efforts to colonize these regions and relentlessly lethal to indigenous populations.

One key reason behind this differential experience with pathogens was the long history of domestication of animals in the Old World and the relative lack of domesticated animals in the New World (Crosby 1986; McNeill 1976). European and Asian farmers had kept cattle, goats, sheep, pigs, and chickens, along with other assorted poultry, for food for thousands of years. Subsistence farmers lived in close association with their animals, often sharing housing with them. As a result of this close affiliation, some of the parasites of these animals "jumped" hosts and became human pathogens (zoonoses). The pathogens responsible for epidemics in Old World populations were largely derived from domesticated animals (see Table 8.4).

In the Americas, animal domestication played a much smaller role in the subsistence of indigenous populations, possibly because of the extinction of many large mammals prior to the adoption of agriculture. Native Americans had dogs and, in the Andes, llamas, alpacas, and guinea pigs, along with some poultry. Furthermore, although there were urban centers in the New World and contact and trade between them, population size and density were lower overall. Thus, the extensive array of zoonotic diseases known throughout the Old World was largely absent from the Americas, resulting in a lower number and narrower diversity of infectious pathogens.

This meant that when Native Americans (as well as indigenous populations of Australia and Oceania) encountered pathogens of Eurasian origin, their mortality rates were staggeringly high. **Virgin soil epidemics**, which occur when a new pathogen enters a new population, are akin to epidemics of emerging infectious diseases; they hit in successive waves and are associated with massive mortality. In a review of the impact of virgin soil epidemics on native New World populations, Henry Dobyns (1993) estimated that more than 90% of the population in Meso-America and the Andes died by the middle of the sixteenth century. Although accurate statistics are hard to come by and there is a vigorous scholarly debate about the exact numbers, it is estimated that in 1500 there were between 50 million and 100 million people in the Americas. One hundred fifty years later, indigenous populations in North and South America numbered less than 10 million and perhaps as low as 5 million (Hays 1998). Genetic evidence confirms a major population decline about 500 years ago (O'Fallon and Fehren-Schmitz 2011). Some groups were wiped out entirely and others rebounded slowly. Although there were numerous infectious diseases that played a role, none is better documented or more horrific in its symptoms than smallpox.

Before considering smallpox in detail, it is worth acknowledging that indigenous populations of the Americas were not living in some sort of infection-free paradise. There were established urban centers, especially in Mexico and the Andes, which were undoubtedly sites of localized epidemics, just as they were in the Old World. They most certainly had experience with the trepanomas (the bacteria that cause pinta, yaws, and the venereal form of syphilis), hepatitis, Chagas's disease (trypanosomiasis), encephalitis, polio, some nonpulmonary forms of TB, and intestinal parasites (Crosby 1986). By contrast, in Europe the following infectious diseases were common: smallpox, measles, influenza, diphtheria, whooping cough, scarlet fever, bubonic plague, malaria, typhoid, cholera, dengue fever, chicken pox, and trachoma, among others. These diseases have all become well established in the New World, whereas to date it appears that perhaps only syphilis had been unknown to Europeans prior to the Columbian voyages.

Increased vulnerability to new infectious diseases is still evident among populations that have been more or less isolated. Magdalena Hurtado and Kim Hill, anthropologists who have worked extensively with the Aché, a foraging group in Paraguay, have described how they seem to be exceptionally vulnerable to TB compared with other populations. Within 15 years after contact with the larger society (which often included settlement), almost 20% of the population had active cases of TB (Hurtado et al. 2003). Moreover, those who had more contact with non-Aché and who engaged in wage labor (i.e., those identified as "more acculturated") had significantly higher rates of TB than those who remained more isolated.

Smallpox

Smallpox is a zoonotic virus of the orthopox group of viruses that likely originally spread from domesticated cattle to humans. In cows it exists as a relatively benign disease (cowpox), as it does in other mammalian species (such as monkeys). In humans there appear to be at least three forms. *Variola major* is the most deadly, killing up to one-third of individuals infected with it. Smallpox is spread by any form of direct contact—primarily by breath, but also through skin-to-skin contact. As noted in Chapter 8, smallpox is a sit-and-wait pathogen, with the ability to persist for long periods of time outside of a host. After an incubation period of 10 to 14 days, fever, weakness, and headaches occur, followed in 2 to 3 days by a distinctive rash that evolves into raised pustules, as shown in Figure 9.3. When the pustules occur in the mucus membranes lining the respiratory passages, they release the virus into the air, spreading it to other hosts. A person is infectious from the time the rash begins to when it scabs over, which usually happens after 9 to 10 days. The healed pustules form "pock-marks," permanently scarring survivors. Pustules can form on any surface of the body, including the internal organs, eyes, lungs, heart, and liver, thereby causing other physiological problems. The rash of pustules is described as a feeling of being on fire (Giblin 1995). The only positive aspect of smallpox is that it generates permanent immunity, and thus individuals will not have the misfortune of recurrent episodes.

The mummified remains of the Egyptian pharaoh Ramses V (who died around 1150 BC) appear to be covered in pox, suggesting the disease's fairly deep history in the Old World (Giblin 1995). In India the smallpox goddess Sitala ("the cool one") is simultaneously worshipped and feared because she had the power to inflict smallpox when aggrieved, as well as cool the fevers of those afflicted (see also Figure 9.4). In China smallpox was known as early as AD 250 and was thought to have been introduced during the Hun invasion (hence the Chinese called it "Hunpox") (Giblin 1995). There, too, a smallpox goddess was worshipped in an attempt to prevent its appearance in a household. In Europe, smallpox appears to have been a relatively benign childhood disease until the sixteenth century. At that point there are reports of outbreaks of a more serious form that were responsible for up to 12% of all deaths (Hays 1998). It is an unfortunate coincidence that this was occurring simultaneously with the voyages of exploration out of Europe because it appears to be this virulent form (*V. major*) that was transported to the destinations of European explorers and colonists.

The first wave of smallpox in the Americas occurred on the island of Hispaniola (today shared by Haiti and the Dominican Republic) in 1519; within 20 years of Columbus's landing there, more than one-third of the native Taino people were dead, mostly from infectious disease. Smallpox subsequently moved quickly to Puerto Rico and then to Mexico, where it decimated the Aztecs prior to Cortes's military attacks. It moved into the Andes, killing many in the well-established and powerful Incan empire, and then spread along rivers east and south into the lowlands of South America. To the north, smallpox spread from Cuba into Florida and from there into the southeastern United States and along the Mississippi River. Within 10 years, it may have covered the Americas from the Great Lakes to Paraguay (Crosby 1986). Because of its long incubation period, smallpox could easily spread along established roads and rivers among unsuspecting individuals or those fleeing from epidemics. A similar story played out in Australia. With the arrival of the British in 1788, smallpox soon followed with its

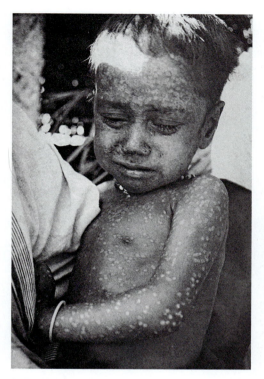

FIGURE 9.3   A smallpox victim.
Credit: Photograph from CDC/World Health Organization; Stanley O. Foster, 1975.

predictable destruction of Aboriginal populations. This first wave left about one-third of the native Australian population dead.

It is important to note that smallpox was the most disfiguring and hence most visible (and amenable to post hoc diagnosis), but it was only one of a large number of infectious diseases that decimated indigenous populations. Measles, typhus, influenza, plague, and later malaria and yellow fever were among other deadly diseases that came in the wake of smallpox. It was these *successive* waves of *new* diseases that collectively destroyed the populations and cultures of indigenous peoples. In addition to these, STIs seem to have taken an enormous toll on local populations, where they rendered local women sterile from infection of the fallopian tubes (see Chapter 6). This seems to have been particularly problematic in the islands of the Pacific.

Not surprisingly, the net effect of these waves of disease was widespread cultural and demographic collapse, for which there was, as far as we know, no historical precedent. It is difficult for us in the twenty-first century to imagine the scale of this calamity because smallpox was eradicated by a global vaccination effort by the WHO and the last case existed in the late 1970s (see Fenner 1988 for a description of the history of that project). A relentless onslaught of infection, the source of which is unknown and which seemed to target only native populations and not foreigners, was nothing short

FIGURE 9.4   Shapona, a smallpox goddess from West Africa.
Credit: Photo from James Gathany/CDC, 2005.

of disorienting and dispiriting. In virgin soil epidemics everyone is vulnerable, including adults who are responsible for subsistence, protection, and reproduction. Those dying of disease cannot grow food, hunt, or gather; they cannot reproduce the next generation, care for the young, or maintain cultural traditions. Those who survived were crowded into missionary settlements or used as plantation labor, which further disassembled their social and economic traditions and facilitated the spread of disease by creating conditions of malnutrition, hard labor, and crowding. Deities worshipped by local populations seemed to have let them down, sparing the seemingly invulnerable Europeans, thereby casting the latter as more powerful. This cultural dissolution made indigenous populations more tractable and assimilation all the more possible.

In the Northeast, British and French colonists commented on their good fortune at the demise of native populations. John Winthrop, the first governor of the Massachusetts

Bay Colony, noted in 1634, "for the natives, they are neere all dead of small Poxe, so as the Lord hathe cleared our title to what we possess" (Crosby 1986, 208). In the same spirit, a French colonist wrote, "Touching these savages, there is a thing that I cannot omit to remark to you, it is that it appears visibly that God wishes that they yield their place to new peoples" (Crosby 1986, 215). There is some evidence that smallpox may have even been intentionally "sent" to Native Americans by British soldiers in their quest to take North America. Sir Geoffrey Amherst, the British commander in chief in North America, inquired in 1763, "Could it not be contrived to send the smallpox among those disaffected tribes of Indians? We must, on this occasion, use every stratagem in our power to reduce them." To which the ranking officer replied, "I will try to inoculate the Indians with some blankets that may fall in their hands and take care not to get the disease myself" (Oldstone 1998, 33). If this did indeed happen, it represents an early case of biological warfare.

Colonialism and Disease in the Tropics

As Alfred Crosby demonstrated, the impact of diseases on native populations in the Americas, Australia, and the Pacific took the form of rapid depopulation and colonization of their lands by Europeans. However, Europeans were unsuccessful in colonizing other parts of Asia or in Africa. From a disease perspective, there are two reasons for this. First, Europeans shared a common disease pool with Asians for the most part, so they had no immunological advantage there. Second, in the southern parts of Asia and sub-Saharan Africa, Europeans ran into a "disease barrier." In the more tropical areas there existed a greater diversity of pathogens, including many with which Europeans had no experience, and these were devastating to them, as well as their plants and animals. Yellow fever, trypanosomiasis (sleeping sickness), and intestinal parasites, among others, posed a serious impediment to European efforts to establish colonies there. Malaria was known in Europe, but more virulent forms existed in the tropics and were more broadly distributed. In sub-Saharan Africa **sleeping sickness** was particularly problematic because the tsetse fly (genus *Glossina*) that is the vector of this protozoan (*Trypanosoma spp.*) feeds on cattle, preempting European attempts to establish their cattle herds. In the absence of other hosts, the tsetse fly will bite humans. In both cattle and humans, sleeping sickness is characterized by chronic lassitude and ultimately coma and death.

Europeans were not able to fully establish the large self-supporting colonies of North America or Australia in the tropics. People were loath to move there after hearing tales of ghastly diseases and descriptions of "the white man's grave." As a result, the European presence was dominated by military and government administrators whose job was to ensure that European economic and political interests were being served. They tended to segregate themselves in towns, away from native populations, constructing military cantonments and establishing "civil lines" to control the movement of peoples within towns. In the most extreme form of this, Afrikaner colonists in South Africa prevented black Africans from living in European towns. Hill towns were built to provide relief for the colonists from the oppressive heat and seasonal epidemics of the lowlands. The colonists established their own sanitation systems, assuring them safe water and waste disposal and hospitals to serve the military and civil service. Native populations were viewed with suspicion, as possible carriers of disease, and were to be avoided., and these views supported the widespread colonial sentiment that they were biologically inferior and in need of "civilizing" by Europeans.

All in all, efforts to understand and control disease in these situations were largely in the service of protecting colonists rather than improving the health of local populations. Even when interventions served the locals, they were seen as enhancing the productivity of the labor force needed to produce or extract the resources so valued by the colonists (Hays 1998). There were humanitarian efforts as well, although in many cases they were sponsored by religious groups rather than the civil governments. Missionaries became "the acceptable face of colonialism" but the care they provided sometimes came at the price of religious conversion and repudiation of traditional healing practices; their clinics often became loci for the transmission rather than cure of diseases (Porter 1997).

The nineteenth century was one of scientific advances in Europe, and one of the public justifications for colonialism was that benefits of scientific medicine could be made available to peoples across the globe. Civilization, empire building, and medicine went hand in hand. Diseases of the tropical colonies were viewed as an enemy of civilization, to be conquered in the name of progress and civilization. As Ronald Ross, a British Army surgeon, described malaria, "It strikes down not only the indigenous barbaric population but, with still greater certainty, the pioneers of civilization—the planter, the trader, the missionary and the soldier. It is therefore the principal and gigantic ally of Barbarism. . . . It has withheld an entire continent from humanity—the immense and fertile tracts of Africa" (Porter 1997, 465). New centers for the study of what came to be defined as "tropical medicine" were established, although these were constructed in European capitals (e.g., the London School of Hygiene and Tropical Medicine), not in the colonies, where their impact would have been more direct. The priorities of these centers were aligned with those of European colonists and scientists, and money was channeled toward high-profile research despite critics suggesting that the health problems of the colonies would be better addressed by more rudimentary interventions: safe drinking water, sanitation, and better nutrition. As Porter noted, "not least, tropical medicine was vulnerable to characterization as the tool of colonial powers . . . mopping up the mess created by the 'development' (or perhaps 'underdevelopment') which imperialism and capitalism produced" (Porter 1997, 480).

Furthermore, as Roy Porter has pointed out, what came to be defined as tropical diseases was a hodgepodge of diseases certainly not confined to the tropics. Indeed, many of them were well known in Europe: malaria, plague, cholera, TB, and smallpox, to name a few. European medicine had little to offer in terms of prevention or cure for this group of deadly diseases, with the exception of smallpox variolation and quinine, which was used to prevent and treat malaria. **Quinine** is a bitter substance derived from the bark of the cinchona tree, which is native to Ecuador (South America). Jesuit missionaries learned of this bark, which was used locally to treat fevers, and introduced it back to Europe by the 1630s (Desowitz 1991). A substantial trade in quinine grew but its quality was highly variable, and it only sometimes proved effective at preventing or treating malaria. Ultimately, the Dutch created a monopoly on the trade in quinine by establishing cinchona plantations in Java. It was their stocks that were used by colonists attempting to assert their domination in Africa and Southeast Asia. There is some suggestion that the "gin and tonic" so favored by British colonists may have had some antimalarial effects because tonic water is made bitter by the addition of quinine. It was not until World War II, when Java came under Japanese control, that an adequate synthetic quinine—chloroquine—was developed to prevent American troops from succumbing to malaria (Desowitz 1991).

European efforts to extract resources also had the major effect of spreading diseases that had previously been more localized. Plantation systems created new niches for pathogens and new groupings of often undernourished and overworked laborers. Clearing land for agriculture or for forest products disrupted local ecosystems; without animal hosts, some pathogens (e.g., *Trypanosoma* or *Plasmodium*) found new human hosts. New urban centers grew, bringing diverse peoples together in dense settlements and becoming focal points for disease, as did mines. Productive adults were taken out of subsistence activities and put to work in extractive enterprises, with negative health consequences for the families left behind. All of these—often involuntary—changes were accompanied by physical and psychological stress, which made individuals more vulnerable to infection and debility.

Among the most significant of these was the dislocation of local populations. This happened both within and between colonies. Railways and roads, built to move people and raw materials to production and distribution sites, allowed pathogens to penetrate new areas. One of the main achievements of British colonial rule in India was to establish the most extensive rail network in the world. Cholera, smallpox, TB, malaria, dysentery, and diarrhea traveled along these rail lines. Movements of the military to quell local uprisings or defend a border meant that pathogens went along, too, especially STIs. The British encouraged Indian laborers to migrate to South Africa to work in the sugar plantations; with the depopulation of the islands of Fiji by a measles epidemic that killed more than one-quarter of the population, Indian laborers were sent there, bringing with them more measles, smallpox, and cholera. Indians were also sent to Malaysia and as far west as Trinidad to supply labor in British colonies.

As the Fijian example illustrates, the demise of indigenous populations resulted in a severe labor shortage for colonists seeking to establish plantations to grow crops for export back to Europe. In the New World, the solution emerged in the form of African slavery. Slaves from West Africa were brought to the Americas to provide the labor for plantations, and the slave trade added another variable to an already complex epidemiological situation. Especially in the Caribbean, where sugar plantations were established to fuel the urban workers of Europe (Mintz 1985), slaves were considered biologically more adept at surviving than their European owners and the remaining local populations. They appeared to be somewhat more resistant to many of the diseases that Europeans succumbed to in the tropics, such as malaria and yellow fever, both introduced and reintroduced via the slave trade from Africa. This disease resistance encouraged the colonial rhetoric that Africans were well suited to the conditions of slavery (Krieger 2002). Yet Africans suffered unimaginably high mortality from the nightmarish conditions of slave ships and from malnutrition, pathogens, and trauma brought about by terrible living conditions. As a result, Europeans had only a minimal physical presence, whereas Africans predominated in the Caribbean, although Europeans maintained political and economic control of most of the islands until well into the twentieth century.

Colonialism's Health Legacy

In broad terms, the health legacy of the colonial era was twofold. One aspect was the global homogenization of infectious disease. Pathogens previously known only in Europe and Asia were now to be found anywhere and everywhere. Syphilis became well established in Europe. Yellow fever and malaria moved from Africa to the New World. Cholera moved to Europe from South Asia and then around the world, popping up in large port cities. Less dramatic, but probably more significant, was the establishment of the routine diseases of poverty in urban Europe and in colonial cities and towns. TB, smallpox, plague, measles, and dysentery, among others, came to be associated with poverty wherever they went. Simultaneously, Western medicine became "cosmopolitan medicine" as it was established in the colonies and subsequently retained and supported by local governments, nongovernmental organizations, international groups such as WHO and the United Nations, and the governments of wealthy countries in the postcolonial period.

The second was a striking divergence in the burden of infection, which began shifting in the eighteenth century and persists. The health of European populations in Europe, North America, Australia, and New Zealand improved markedly, whereas that of the colonized peoples got worse. The preceding paragraphs suggest the reasons for the latter, but why European health improved is more mysterious. The phenomenon has most often been attributed to the rise of biomedicine and the scientific advances associated with it. Biomedical practitioners, trained in the European scientific tradition, were considered responsible for declines in mortality and overall improvement in health. Yet the evidence seems to suggest otherwise. As Thomas McKeown (1979) described in *The Role of Medicine: Dream, Mirage, or Nemesis*, mortality from infectious disease in Britain began to decrease long before biomedicine had anything efficacious to offer. For example, as Figure 9.5 indicates, deaths from TB had already been declining in the mid-nineteenth century, but Robert Koch identified the bacillus in 1882 and an effective cure (streptomycin) only became available in 1947. The same pattern exists for other diseases such as whooping cough, diphtheria, scarlet fever, and measles. If effective interventions were not available until rates of these diseases were already diminishing, what can explain this phenomenon? McKeown proposed that dramatic improvements in nutrition and, secondary to that, improvements in public sanitation were responsible. That is, with improvements in nutritional status, individuals were better able to mount an effective immune response to infection, and at the same time new sanitation measures ensured that they were exposed less frequently. Better sanitation came not only from public health measures such as effective separation of waste from drinking water but also from changes in personal and household hygiene (Tomes 1998).

How was nutritional status improved, and where did the funding for municipal infrastructural improvements in sanitation come from? It is highly likely that the wealth flowing to Europe from the colonies provided the resources. Europe was the recipient of grains and other crops from its colonies abroad, and in England enclosure laws (which created individual property rights to land that was previously held in common) brought more land under cultivation. Larger food imports and domestic production led to lower prices and greater availability of staple foods. The profits from extractive enterprises in the tropics (minerals, textiles, and commodities such as coffee,

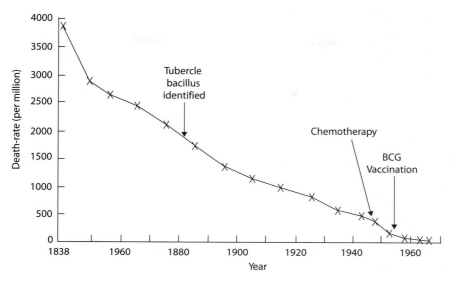

FIGURE 9.5   Mortality from respiratory tuberculosis over the course of the nineteenth and twentieth centuries. Mortality had already begun to fall markedly before any biomedical interventions were possible.
Source: From Thomas McKeown, *The Role of Medicine: Dream, Mirage, or Nemesis?* © 1979 Princeton University Press. Reprinted by permission of Princeton University Press.

tea, sugar, and tobacco) allowed governments to put funds toward improvements in health at home, especially by ensuring safe drinking water and effective waste removal. Thus, although infectious diseases spread to new vulnerable populations, Europeans were increasingly protected from them by the resources generated by colonial activities.

This raises a number of important points. One is that as wealth was extracted from the colonies and sent to Europe, the resources available to postcolonial nations (especially those in the tropics that had been targeted for extractionist activities) after independence were scant compared with those available to European countries. Thus, the improvements in health that occurred in Europe were unlikely to happen in the former colonies without some outside monies. Second, it suggests that although biomedical interventions can certainly be effective cures of existing diseases, the prevention of disease is more likely a function of investments in public health infrastructures and improving access to food. Third, it forces a different kind of perspective on human health. As McKeown (1978, 6) stated, "The role of individual medical care in preventing sickness and premature death is secondary to that of other influences (i.e. public health and nutrition); yet society's investment in health care is based on the premise that it is the major determinant. It is assumed that we are ill and made well, but it is nearer the truth to say that we are well and made ill." Health tends to be seen as the appropriate purview of medical authorities, rather than those concerned with the conditions of society as a whole. Yet those very conditions have the capacity to profoundly shape disease risk.

With this historical review in mind, we return to the concept of emerging and resurging diseases in contemporary populations. First, we will consider the role that contemporary environmental changes play in disease emergence and resurgence, focusing on climate change and the building of dams in relation to cholera, malaria, and helminthic diseases. Then multi-drug-resistant TB and HIV will be used as examples of contemporary emergent diseases. Throughout we will consider how these have been shaped by colonialism's legacies.

Climate Change and Emerging/Resurging Diseases

There is currently politically charged debate about global climate change, most especially the contributions of human behavior (e.g., greenhouse gas emissions, methane production from animals produced for meat), and its impacts on infectious diseases that affect humans, as well as other organisms in the ecosystem such as the plants and animals that humans rely on for food. There is widespread concern in the scientific and public health community that climate change, especially in the form of rising global temperatures and climate volatility (e.g., hot and/or drought conditions followed by torrential rains and flooding), might increase the spread, seasonal duration, and/or severity of infectious diseases (Altizer et al. 2013; McMichael 2013; Woodward et al. 2014; Wu et al. 2016). See Figure 9.6 for a diagram of the potential health impacts of climate change.

This could happen by enlarging the range for vectors, such as mosquitoes, or increasing their overall activity, including biting rates and reproductive rates, which are temperature sensitive (Campbell-Lendrum et al. 2015). For example, in the highlands of East Africa, malaria cases used to be few because of the cooler temperatures, but its long absence means that residents have no acquired immunity, making the disease now more severe for adults as well as children. This has in turn necessitated an expansion of malaria control efforts like insecticide spraying, disease surveillance, and drug treatments (Alonso et al. 2011).

Climate change is but one factor that interacts with a variety of ongoing processes that influence disease spread and population susceptibility, and disentangling the independent impact of climate change from these other factors is difficult (Lafferty and Mordecai 2016). For example, in the malaria example described above, there are simultaneous issues such as chloroquine resistance, changes in mosquito control efforts, and population increases also in play. Most researchers agree that health consequences of climate change will be, on balance, negative and, while infectious disease vulnerability is one of these, multiple other aspects of heath are also likely to be negatively impacted (see Watts et al. 2018b for a comprehensive review).

Although the exact ways in which current climate trends, including warming and weather volatility, will affect human infectious disease patterns are not yet fully understood, climatic changes have a long history of impacting human health (McMichael 2017). It is clear that some new patterns of infectious disease have already been established in the contemporary context (Watts et al. 2018a). Moreover, these phenomena likely will have a disproportionately negative effect on health among the poorest populations of the world, who contribute proportionately less to anthropogenic climate changes, through increased rates of diarrheal disease, vector-borne diseases, and undernutrition.

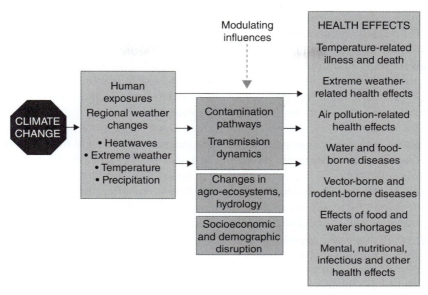

FIGURE 9.6   The potential health impacts of global climate change.
Source: Reprinted from International Consensus on the Science of Climate and Health: *The IPCC Third Assessment Report. Geneva: World Health Organization,* 2003.

Cholera

Cholera was one of the first infectious diseases considered in relation to climate change (Colwell 1996) and is caused by a bacterium (*Vibrio cholerae*) that is indigenous to the Bay of Bengal in South Asia. The disease appears to have a long history in that region and there are references to it in the ancient Sanskrit literature. Cholera passes from one individual to the next when an infected person's fecal matter becomes part of the water that others drink or otherwise have contact with. The bacillus produces a toxin that causes intestinal cells to pump out water and electrolytes, resulting in a voluminous, watery diarrhea that quickly dehydrates the victim. Other symptoms include vomiting, convulsions, fever, and skin color changes and deterioration. These can take only a few hours to several days to manifest. At present, cholera can be treated by rehydration (preferably through intravenous fluids) and antibiotics, and there is a vaccine that offers some protection. The best way to prevent cholera is to stop its spread through the water supply by adequate sanitation measures that keep wastewater away from sources of drinking water.

The first recorded cholera outbreak was in 1817 around Calcutta in eastern India, and there have been seven pandemics since. It appears to have spread to England by 1832, where it caused successive urban outbreaks. There, it primarily affected poor neighborhoods, where water was drawn from a common pump. In fact, the first demonstration of waterborne infection was done by John Snow, a London physician who was able to trace the source of one particularly virulent outbreak in 1854 to the now infamous Broad Street Pump. Snow persuaded the local authorities to disable the pump (although the epidemic had largely subsided by then), and ultimately a series of bills were passed to overhaul the water and sewage systems of London. As a result, cholera epidemics diminished and eventually disappeared altogether in England and in cities throughout Europe. Snow demonstrated that cholera was waterborne, but the bacterium itself was not identified as the causative agent until Robert Koch did so in 1883. It was called the "comma bacillus" because it has the standard rod shape with a flagellum that enables it to move about in the water.

Cholera thrives in contexts where large, dense populations make use of a single water source and hygienic measures are insufficient to assure the separation of wastewater from drinking water. As such, it historically was a disease of urban areas in proximity to rivers or along coasts. In India cholera tracks pilgrimages; as religious pilgrims congregate in holy cities (which, for Hindus, are often located on rivers) the risk of infection increases where there are inadequate infrastructures to maintain safe drinking water and waste disposal. It is also a major problem in refugee camps and among other displaced populations; after the 2010 earthquake in Haiti, which left 1.5 million people homeless, cholera became epidemic after 50 years with no cases. The epidemic spread throughout displaced persons camps, as well as rural Haiti, as those who lost their homes in Port-au-Prince sought refuge with rural relatives. Haiti ranks the lowest of all countries in water security according to the Water Poverty Index, and the lack of an adequate water and waste infrastructure surely contributed to the spread of cholera after the earthquake (Walton and Ivers 2011). But there has been controversy over whether the epidemic in Haiti stemmed from local climatic conditions (see below) or whether it was introduced by Nepalese soldiers deployed to Haiti as UN peacekeeping troops. It now appears that at least two different strains were circulating during the epidemic, including both foreign and indigenous forms of *V. cholerae* (Jutla et al. 2013). As Jutla and colleagues noted, conditions were ideal for a cholera epidemic in Haiti in 2010: a lack of safe water and sanitation infrastructure, elevated air temperatures, and above-average rainfall.

Cholera is considered a resurgent disease, and its spread is very much tied to human activities. New strains of cholera have emerged over the past 20 years, with varying degrees of virulence. Despite the fact that cholera is a curable and preventable disease, there have been several recent epidemics, some reaching pandemic proportions. It is among the infectious diseases considered resurgent. The factors underlying the continued spread of cholera mainly stem from three sources. One is the failure to produce or maintain an adequate system of water sanitation. Countries undergoing civil strife often let the public health infrastructures lapse, including those that maintain a safe water supply. Political conflict in Peru in the late 1980s and early 1990s had this very effect, and an epidemic of cholera followed. Second is global shipping traffic. The cholera bacillus can persist in the water contained in ship ballast and spread through port cities. Third, and most pertinent to the climate change discussion, is the related fact that cholera has the ability to maintain itself in a dormant state in warm saline waters, especially those of bays, where it tends to be concentrated in algal blooms—large congregations of floating plankton. Here *V. cholerae* can also exchange genetic material with other bacteria, picking up new genes, including those that can make it more virulent (Colwell 1996; Meibom et al. 2005). Algal blooms form when sea temperatures rise, a widely documented current symptom of overall global warming. They form in warm coastal waters where sewage and fertilizer runoff provides the nutrients for algae growth. Diverse communities of microorganisms thrive in the algal blooms, and their reproduction rate often rises as a function of warmer temperatures, which increases the frequency of mutations. The presence of *V. cholerae* in the algal blooms is directly correlated with sea temperatures, as shown in Figure 9.7. In inland areas, cholera outbreaks are associated with both higher air temperatures and heavy rainfall (Jutla et al. 2013).

Vibrio species are not unique to low-latitude regions. Starting in 1994, *Vibrio vulnificus* emerged as a cause of human wound infections among individuals who had been engaging in recreational activities in the Baltic Sea area of Northern Europe. *V. vulnificus* replication is highly temperature sensitive, and the Baltic Sea is demonstrably warming rapidly. The number of cases of *V. vulnificus* was found to be tightly positively correlated

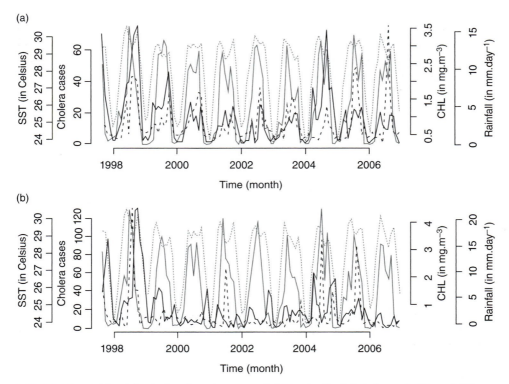

FIGURE 9.7 Epidemiological and environmental dynamics for (A) Kolkata, India, and (B) Matlab, Bangladesh. The cholera cases, the CHL (a measure of plankton density), the SST (surface sea temperature), and the rainfall are shown in black, dashed, dotted, and grey lines, respectively.

Source: Guillaume Constantin de Magny, Raghu Murtugudde, Mathew R. P. Sapiano, Azhar Nizam, Christopher W. Brown, Antonio J. Busalacchi, Mohammad Yunus, G. Balakrish Nair, Ana I. Gil, Claudio F. Lanata, John Calkins, Byomkesh Manna, Krishnan Rajendran, Mihir Kumar Bhattacharya, Anwar Huq, R. Bradley Sack, and Rita R. Colwell *PNAS* November 18, 2008 105 (46) 17676–17681. Copyright (2008) National Academy of Sciences.

with surface sea temperatures, and overall, the number of cases has increased over the past 20 years (Baker-Austin et al. 2013). *V. vulnificus* is also contracted by eating contaminated seafood, especially oysters; it does not cause the watery diarrhea of *V. cholerae*, but it can result in gastrointestinal illness, sepsis, or necrotizing wound infections and can be fatal. Overall, infections with various forms of *Vibrio* are on the rise, including in places with no previous incidence, and because they are so temperature sensitive, they likely act as good barometers of climate change, especially in marine contexts (Baker-Austin et al. 2017).

Most forms of *Vibrio* do not have the ability to make cholera toxin, and these forms are widespread in coastal waters. There are two forms that do: strains 01 and 0139. Classical cholera (or 01) appears to have been replaced by a new strain, 01 El Tor, by the seventh pandemic, which started in 1961. A more virulent form, the Bengal strain or Type 0139, possibly formed by exchanging genes with 01 El Tor, emerged in 1992, causing epidemics in several Indian cities (Lipp et al. 2002). Cholera is most chronically problematic in the low-lying areas of Bangladesh, where seasonal flooding and inadequate sanitation expose people to the bacteria. Researchers have found that because *V. cholerae* is attached to plankton, the use of material from local women's saris as a filter is sufficient to remove up to 99% of the bacteria from water (Huq et al. 2010). Thus, a relatively simple practice can have profound positive effects in a population chronically exposed to cholera because of ecological and social conditions.

Genetic Adaptation to Cholera

There may be genetic adaptations to cholera, although they are found only among populations of European descent. In the nineteenth century, it was a routine scourge of cities in Europe, where it spread rapidly through the water supply. In any given year, it could kill tens of thousands of people. There is some evidence that this source of mortality, along with other severe diarrheal diseases such as typhoid (caused by the bacterium *Salmonella typhi*), caused natural selection to favor certain genotypes that ameliorated the dehydration caused by diarrheal disease. Much like the example of sickle-cell hemoglobin and malaria, it has been hypothesized that the gene variant that causes cystic fibrosis (CF) may in fact have some protective effect against the diarrheal disease cholera (Bertranpetit and Calafell 1996). CF is the most common lethal genetic disease in populations of European descent. About 5% of all Europeans carry the variant gene associated with CF, and about 1 in every 2,500 European newborns has the disease. In other populations the rate of CF is about 1 in 100,000 individuals, which is approximately the rate of mutation.

CF results from a mutation in a gene that makes chloride channels in cell membranes. These channels allow chloride (a salt) to pass out of cells, which in turn draws water out of the cell by osmotic pressure. As a result, cells are bathed in a watery saline solution that washes away pathogens and debris. This is particularly important for the cells lining the lungs and gastrointestinal tract because these areas are routinely exposed to pathogenic substances. In the gastrointestinal system this saline solution also facilitates food digestion because most nutrients must go into solution to be absorbed. In sweat glands chloride channels recycle salt from sweat back into skin cells. With CF, these chloride channels do not function properly. As a result, instead of the cells being bathed in an aqueous solution, a thick, sticky mucus forms around them. This mucus obstructs both oxygen uptake and digestion and attracts, rather than repels, pathogens and debris. People with CF thus exhibit symptoms of both respiratory impairment and undernutrition. Respiratory symptoms are the most problematic, and CF victims ultimately die of suffocation. There is no cure for CF; treatments include frequent clapping on the back to loosen mucus obstructing the airways, inhaled medications to keep the airways as open as possible, and antibiotics to keep bacterial infections in check (see Chapter 3 for more discussion of treatments for CF).

At first glance it is hard to imagine what the connection between CF and cholera might be, but it stems from the ways that the cholera bacillus acts in the gastrointestinal tract. If an individual infected with cholera has malfunctioning chloride channels (i.e., CF), the toxin is relatively ineffective at causing cells to pump out water. Thus, dehydration and death from cholera are less likely. However, that is small comfort to an individual with CF, who suffers from the chronic debilitating and ultimately fatal effects of CF. Much like the malaria–sickle cell hemoglobin example, it is the individuals with only one copy of the CF allele who do best under conditions of cholera. About half of the chloride channels function in an individual who is heterozygous; half do not. Hence, they do not suffer the extensive symptoms of CF, but they are also not as vulnerable to the dehydration caused by cholera as are people with no CF allele. This evolutionary hypothesis helps explain why the CF allele—which is so very deleterious in individuals with two copies—could have spread in European populations exposed to cholera and other diarrheal diseases that result in rapid dehydration.

However, given that cholera is much more broadly distributed beyond Europe and originates in South Asia, why has the CF or a similar allele not spread in those populations that have been exposed to cholera for much longer than Europeans? The answer to that question may lie not only in the random nature of genetic mutations but also in the other function of the chloride channels: to recycle salt lost through sweat. In warmer climates where there is greater salt loss through sweat, a condition that reduced salt recycling (remember that salt is rare in nature) would have been even more deleterious. Thus, it may be that the problems associated with a CF or CF-like allele would have been greater than any benefit it conferred against cholera. In the temperate climates of Europe, greater loss of salt through sweat is much less deleterious. A recent review of the cholera-CF link can be found in (Mowat 2017), which also evaluates the relationship between CF alleles and typhoid (another diarrheal disease) and TB.

DAMS AND INFECTIOUS DISEASE

Another human-induced ecological transformation that has profound effects on pathogens that are sensitive to water dynamics is dam building. Dams are often constructed to generate hydroelectricity and control water for irrigation purposes. Just as often, they produce an increase in malaria prevalence. Still waters and eddies result as rivers are dammed, creating breeding grounds for mosquitoes. Furthermore, intensified agricultural activities around fields irrigated by such water increase human contact with mosquitoes (Rohr et al. 2019). Figure 9.8 shows how dams can be associated with malaria. For example, the Gilgel Gibe hydroelectric dam in southwestern Ethiopia, which began operations in 2004, is the largest generator of hydroelectricity in the country. Children living in villages within 3 kilometers (the maximum flight range for *Anopheles* mosquitoes) of the reservoir created by the dam were shown to have higher rates of malaria than those living in more distant but socioeconomically similar villages (Yewhalaw et al. 2009), presumably because the reservoir provides suitable breeding grounds for malaria's mosquito vector. A recent survey of the more than 1,200 existing dams in sub-Saharan Africa (where 90% of all malaria deaths occur) found that more than 1 million cases of malaria could be attributed to dams, and reservoirs associated with large dams contribute to almost half of the malaria cases in communities living within 5 kilometers of them (Kibret et al. 2015). Planned dams are likely to add another 56,000 malaria cases.

Dam building in other parts of Africa has also been associated with an increase in two other parasitic diseases: **schistosomiasis** (bilharzia) and **onchocerciasis** (river blindness) (Heyneman 1984), which are also likely to rise as a result of global warming and climate instability (Haines et al. 2006). Both are helminthic infections that cause chronic, debilitating disease. Schistosomiasis is broadly distributed in Africa and Asia,

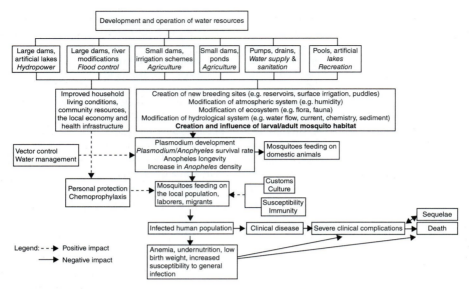

FIGURE 9.8 The pathways by which the construction of dams and other forms of water management affect human experiences with malaria.
Source: Reprinted from Jennifer Keiser et al. 2005. Effect of irrigation and large dams on the burden of malaria on a global and regional scale. Report prepared for the WHO commissioned study *Burden of Water-Related Vector-Borne Diseases: An Analysis of the Fraction Attributable to Components of Water Resources Development and Management.* Geneva: World Health Organization and Swiss Tropical Institute.

and onchocerciasis is more common in West Africa. Both diseases are also found in Latin America and probably derived from the slave trade and from African soldiers deployed there by the French in their attempt to control Mexico in 1862.

Onchocerciasis is caused by a filarial helminth called *Onchocerca volvulus*, which uses a vector, the black fly (*Simulium damnosum*), to be transmitted from host to host. *Onchocerca* only infects humans, which restricts research on this parasite in animal models. This worm has a threadlike form that lives just beneath the skin. The females hatch ~1,000 eggs (microfilariae) each day, and any given female can live up to 20 years. The microfilariae then migrate just underneath the skin to many parts of the body, including the eye, causing local inflammation, which over time leads to loss of sight and eventually complete blindness. In other areas, the skin becomes unbearably itchy and chronically inflamed, and gradually it becomes thickened and depigmented. It is estimated that 37 million people are infected, almost all in sub-Saharan Africa, with 2 million suffering visual impairment or blindness (Tanya et al. 2012). In the most severely affected communities it has been estimated that more than 40% of the population would be blind in their lifetime (Tanya et al. 2012).

The disease is transmitted when a black fly (genus *Simulium*) bites a human and ingests the microfilariae, which then go through a series of developmental stages over the course of about two weeks. The bites themselves are itchy and painful. After this, infective forms can be found in the fly's mouth. When the fly bites another human, it injects these forms (filariform larvae) into the skin. Given the longevity of the adult form and ongoing infection (one person might be infected with 50,000 larvae each year in endemic areas), onchocerciasis is a profoundly debilitating disease.

As with other vector-borne diseases, the ecology of the black fly vector is the key to the spread of onchocerciasis. In contrast to the *Anopheles* mosquito, the black fly prefers to breed in rapidly flowing, well-aerated waters rich in suspended organic matter. It thus tends to be found around rapidly flowing rivers and below dam spillways, but adults can disperse several miles from river breeding sites. In Ghana, when the Volta River was dammed in 1966 to provide hydroelectricity for aluminum smelting, Lake Volta was created above the spillway and effectively rid the previously riverine area of black fly and onchocerciasis. However, below the dam was another story. The spillway created the ideal, well-aerated water conditions for black flies to breed continually and resulted in perpetual infection of local populations. Because the river was continually fed with water from the spillway, it never went through its natural cycle of slower flow and reduced volume during the dry season, when black flies could not reproduce. The net effect was that the well-irrigated lands along rivers that had great agricultural potential could not be inhabited, and populations must move well into the savannah, where they are mercifully free of black flies but where water for cultivation is far more difficult to acquire.

Another helminthic infection that has spread after dam construction is schistosomiasis, which is caused by three species of the genus *Schistosoma*. This helminth is common throughout the warmer parts of the Old and New Worlds and also has a long history in human populations—there is some evidence of calcified eggs in 3,000-year-old mummies from North Africa. Schistosomiasis is a chronically debilitating and potentially fatal disease, although not as extreme in its symptoms as onchocerciasis. The pathogen has a complex life cycle that involves humans, the helminth (which in its adult size is around 1 inch in length), and an intermediate host, which can be a number of different freshwater snail species. The snail is the intermediate host rather than the vector because humans do not actually have to have any contact with the snail for the schistosome to be transmitted. In warm, still freshwater, free-swimming forms of the schistosome called miracidia are taken up by the snail and then develop and reproduce, to emerge from the snail as free-swimming cercariae, which are emitted in the morning. Humans washing clothes or bathing in the water are vulnerable to the cercariae penetrating their skin. The cercariae can also be ingested in contaminated drinking water. The worm then enters the bloodstream and is carried throughout the body, first in the liver, where it matures further and then leaves via the veinous system, and eventually hooks onto the veins of the bladder or those surrounding the intestines. There, the male and female remain together for as many as 30 years and produce more than 3,000 larvae each day. These larvae must penetrate through the vein wall and then are excreted in urine or fecal material. If this infected human waste (or that from other mammal hosts such as water buffalo) gets into water inhabited by the appropriate snails, transmission of the disease becomes likely.

There are several ways in which *Schistosoma* cause disease symptoms in humans. The site on the skin where the cercariae burrow in becomes intensely itchy and inflamed. As it matures there, it exhibits antigens that are recognized by the immune system, and in hosts with a history of schistosomiasis infection, most of the parasites are killed at this stage. In its adult form, the schistosome covers itself with human red blood cell antigens. This prevents the immune system from recognizing it as foreign and allows it to remain undetected for years. However, when the eggs are released, some escape into urine or feces (causing blood in the urine or feces as the eggs burrow through the wall of the bladder or intestine), but others become entrapped in local tissues. There, immune cells gather, building fibrous scar tissue around the eggs, which over time cause local tissues to lose their functionality.

It is fairly straightforward to see the ways in which dams and human activities can interact to spread schistosomiasis. First, the snails that form the intermediate host of the schistosome require large bodies of still water such as lakes or reservoirs. Second, in contexts where there is no access to indoor plumbing and no separation of wastewater and water used for washing, bathing, or drinking, schistosomiasis can spread easily (see Figure 9.9). Thus, schistosomiasis is a primarily rural disease found among poor populations without access to adequate sanitation systems. The dam on the Volta River in Ghana produced onchocerciasis below the spillway, whereas above it, the vast Lake Volta became a prime locus for a schistosomiasis epidemic. *Bulinus rholfsi* snails colonized the lake, especially when it was filled to capacity and small inlets and coves formed, providing ideal locations for the weeds among which snails live. Local populations used the lake for fishing and bathing and the areas around it for growing crops.

FIGURE 9.9 Children wading in a stream in Puerto Rico despite a sign on bank stating, "Danger—There is Bilharzia."
Credit: CDC Public Health Image Library, 1964.

Desowitz (1981) reports that within three years after the dam was completed, all children between the ages of five and nine living around the lake were infected with *Schistosoma*.

A similar scenario has played out in other dam construction projects. The prevalence of both urinary and gastrointestinal schistosomiasis increased in the wake of construction of the Diama Dam on the Senegal River (completed in 1986) (Sow et al. 2002). Construction of the Aswan Dam on the Nile River in Egypt (1971) controlled the flooding of the Nile and provided hydroelectricity for large cities downstream such as Cairo and Alexandria but had unintended consequences for the spread of schistosomiasis. The disease had long been known in the region but was largely confined to the delta; when the dam formed Lake Nasser, this large body of still water was rapidly populated by vegetation and *B. rholfsi* snails. As villages were inhabited along the lake, human contact with water increased and so did cases of schistosomiasis. Below the dam, the continuous irrigation meant chronic exposure to the disease. A recent analysis indicated that another means by which dams contribute to schistosomiasis is by blocking the migration of river prawns, which prey on the *Bulinus* snails (Sokolow et al. 2017). Thus the loss of native prawn species contributed to an increase in snails and schistosomiasis in areas where native prawn habitat had been altered through dams.

Historically, ridding lakes of snails was the primary method used to reduce the spread of schistosomiasis. China launched the "Peoples War against the Snail" in 1950, employing thousands of Chinese to dredge ponds and swamps, remove snails one by one if necessary, apply moluscicides, and enforce strict sanitation laws forbidding defecation in water sources. Simple sealed latrines were built to prevent transmission, which had the effect of reducing many gastrointestinal parasites besides schistosomiasis. Indeed, the focus on the snail generally put the health infrastructure, which is also a crucial aspect of schistosomiasis (or any other infectious disease), in the background (Sandbach 1975). As a result, schistosomiasis rates in China have decreased dramatically, although it remains an endemic chronic disease. There is evidence, however, that with warming temperatures, schistosomiasis is likely to spread into northern areas of China (Zhoui et al. 2010). Currently there is an effective drug (praziquantel) that paralyzes the adult forms of the schistosome and prevents their reproduction, and it has become the primary means of schistosomiasis control.

As Donald Heyneman argued almost 40 years ago, dam building, often viewed as essential to economic development by wealthy and poor governments alike, generates profound changes that alter the complex ecological relationships among humans, vectors, intermediate hosts, and microorganisms. Most often they have resulted in an increase in infectious diseases such as malaria, schistosomiasis, onchocerciasis, and others such as Guinea worm (dracunculiasis), filariasis, or trypanosomiasis, all debilitating chronic diseases (Heyneman 1984; Rohr et al. 2019). Failure to consider these unintended consequences results in widespread human suffering and the need for funding to treat the diseases that flourish under these altered conditions. As Kibret and colleagues note in their analysis of the impact of dams on malaria spread in Africa, "whilst recognizing the importance of dams for economic development, it is unethical that people living close to them pay the price of that development through increased suffering and, in extreme cases, loss of life due to disease" (Kibret et al. 2015, 339).

These consequences are now widely recognized, and it is recommended that disease abatement plans be part of dam projects. This is of current concern in China, where rates of infection with *Schistosoma japonicum* were predicted to increase in the lake area created above the Three Gorges Dam on the Yangtze River, the largest hydroelectric dam in the world (McManus et al. 2010). A review of studies on schistosomiasis in the dam region over the past 10 years indicated no evidence of increase in schistosomiasis; instead its prevalence has continued to decline (Y. Zhou et al. 2016). Both the unique ecology of the dam region and public health efforts to prevent infection likely have played major roles.

Ebola: A Highly Virulent Emerging Disease

The Ebola (*Ebola virus disease* [EVD]) epidemic of 2014–2015 captured the world's attention and had all of the attributes of an emerging disease. It seemingly burst mysteriously from the African forest, was associated with gruesome symptoms and very high mortality, created panic among local populations in West Africa (especially Sierra Leone, Guinea, and Liberia) and beyond, was highly stigmatizing for patients and their caretakers, and garnered much media attention in countries far removed from its epicenter, especially when isolated cases of travelers or health-care workers occurred within their borders. Ebola was not, however, new; there had been several previous epidemics dating back to 1976. Despite almost 30 years of awareness of the virus, the biomedical community had little new to offer when the epidemic began in 2014. This last epidemic was by far the largest in scope, with 15,000 confirmed cases (28,000 if probable and suspected cases are included) and more than 11,000 deaths. Unlike previous outbreaks that had been largely rural and localized, this one included cities and multiple countries and disrupted social, political, and economic life, with ramifications throughout the world.

EVD is caused by an RNA filovirus, a threadlike virus with four strains known to infect humans. It infects a wide array of tissue types and generates a strong inflammatory response, as well as hemorrhaging and organ failure. Its reservoir in nature is thought to be various species of bats (Shapiro et al. 2020). It spreads through contact with bodily fluids, either directly or indirectly through handling of infected materials such as clothing or bedding (the virus can persist for days—i.e., it is able to "sit and wait" for some period) and may be transmitted through semen after the virus is no longer detectable in blood (see Figure 9.10). Its spread has been attributed to a number of social factors. Bushmeat hunting may have exposed hunters to infected fluids of bats or primates, which are hunted for food and sold in cities. Much attention focused on funerals as a locus for contagion (up to two-thirds of all cases have been attributed to funerary practices) because they may bring hundreds of persons into close contact with infectious corpses that may be kept for days, and mourners wash their hands in water used to bathe corpses (Roca et al. 2015). Culturally defined proper burials are essential to usher a person safely into the afterlife. As Paul Farmer noted, "Preparing the dead for burial has turned hundreds of mourners into Ebola victims" (Farmer 2014, 38). Distrust of medical personnel, which in some cases led to their brutal murder, and well-founded fears of hospitals as the loci of contagion compounded the spread. This was also true of earlier Ebola epidemics, chronicled by anthropologists Barry Hewlett and Bonnie Hewlett, who worked with the WHO to understand the ways that cultural practices both protected people from, and put people at greater risk of Ebola disease (Hewlett and Hewlett 2007).

That said, the most fundamental contributor to the epidemic was the lack of a functioning public and clinical health infrastructure. In the three countries hardest hit, there was little public investment in surveillance, laboratories, health-care facilities, supportive treatments such as rehydration, and infection control mechanisms, which in turn diminished the number of health-care workers as they succumbed to EVD and caused people to fear coming to a hospital. As experience with EVD cases in wealthier countries demonstrates, survival rates can be dramatically increased and containment successful with well-funded and well-coordinated clinical care that includes aggressive supportive measures.

It has not escaped notice that EVD attracted substantial global media attention and containment efforts, but relative to more "mundane" or "routine" diseases such as malaria, TB, or HIV, it affected and killed many fewer, by several

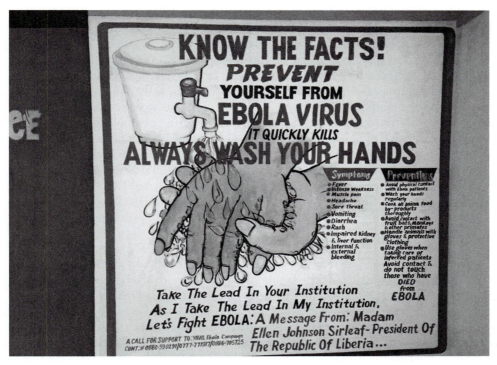

FIGURE 9.10   A public health education poster from Liberia during the outbreak in 2014, noting the dangers of the Ebola virus.
Credit: CDC/Sally Ezra, 2014.

orders of magnitude, and these diseases continued unabated and attracted little new attention. Furthermore, with attention diverted to EVD, health-care systems had even fewer resources to address these ongoing scourges. Although there was a great deal of cynicism regarding the likelihood of pharmaceutical investment in a vaccine, because there would be no financial payoff given that its users would be a relatively small population of poor Africans (the satirical magazine *The Onion* ran an article entitled "Experts: Ebola Vaccine at Least 50 White People Away"—see http://www.theonion.com/article/experts-ebola-vaccine-at-least-50-white-people-awa-36,580), the scope of the epidemic finally motivated a massive pharmaceutical effort to develop a vaccine, and in summer 2015 it was announced that Merck had licensed one with a very high level of effectiveness. But as Paul Farmer further observed, "the Ebola crisis should serve as an object lesson and rebuke to those who tolerate anaemic state funding of, or even cutbacks in, public health and healthcare delivery. Without staff, stuff, space and systems, nothing can be done" (Farmer 2014, 38).

TUBERCULOSIS: EMERGING AND RESURGING

Tuberculosis is a bacterial disease that is startlingly common among the world's populations. It is estimated that at least one-third of contemporary humans carry the bacteria; of them, 10% develop active infection with potentially devastating consequences, not only for individual sufferers but also for those who are in frequent contact with them, because a person with active infection can spread the disease to 10–15 people over the course of a year (World Health Organization 2020b).

TB is considered a resurgent disease, insofar as it was widely hailed as an infectious disease that had been all but vanquished in the 1960s. Recall from earlier in this chapter that its rates had been going down in industrialized countries since the nineteenth century (see Figure 9.5) and continued to fall with the discovery of streptomycin, one of the first drugs used to treat TB. Current concerns about TB stem not only from its intractability and refusal to disappear as a human scourge but also from the rise of multi-drug-resistant (MDR) and even extremely multi-drug-resistant (XMDR) forms. In 2018 there were 10 million new cases of TB and 1.5 million deaths, about 20% of which were among individuals co-infected with HIV. It is estimated that about 3.8% of all new cases of TB are MDRTB, and of those about 6.2% are extensively multi-drug resistant (XMDRTB) (World Health Organization 2020b). Half of the MDRTB cases are in India, China, and the Russia Federation.

As described in Chapter 8, *M. tuberculosis* is a bacillus with a waxy coating, which prevents its destruction by immune cells and allows it to remain viable outside of the host for prolonged periods of time (a sit-and-wait pathogen). The bacterium is sensitive to ultraviolet light and destroyed by the high temperatures used in cooking. *M. tuberculosis* also requires oxygen in large amounts and therefore is found in the lungs, skin, and the epiphyses of bones, which are all well-oxygenated. In the lungs, TB infects macrophages, which, if activated, stimulate a T-cell response and are destroyed. However, the bacteria may remain undetected, hidden in macrophages. In many cases the bacteria are walled off by the formation of a granuloma or tubercle. Activated macrophages congregate at the granuloma and release enzymes that destroy the pathogen but also inflict substantial damage on surrounding tissue. Ultimately, this results in caseous necrosis, lung tissue that has the appearance of cottage cheese (hence, the name caseous, from the milk protein casein). This liquefies over time, allowing TB to spread to new sites and to be exhaled in aerosolized droplets. This is what makes people with active TB highly infectious to others.

TB can spread rapidly in dwellings or other enclosed spaces inhabited by large numbers of people if there is one active TB case. Urban areas with crowded housing, public transportation, and factories are more likely to generate TB infections than are more rural areas, although the disease can easily move from urban to rural settings as people move between them.

There is a TB vaccine (the Bacille–Calmette–Guérin vaccine), but it is of unpredictable effectiveness. Furthermore, vaccination will result in a positive TB skin test, which assesses whether the body has anti-TB antibodies. In countries such as the United States that rely on TB testing to gauge exposure, vaccination would confound efforts to assess which individuals are at risk of developing the disease. If an active infection does occur, there are effective treatments, but because of its somewhat unusual biological characteristics, TB requires long-term courses of antibiotics such as isoniazid and rifampin. Treatment usually lasts at least six months, which is likely to result in missed doses and incomplete therapy. Patient noncompliance is usually blamed for "failure" to finish the full course of treatment (Farmer 2001). To counter this problem, directly observed therapy, short course, used when a health worker observes patients taking their medications, has been developed and resulted in improved outcomes, including total cures.

In the 1980s, "excess" cases of TB (i.e., more than were expected given the previous decline in cases) were reported in the United States. About one-third of these cases could be attributed to HIV because TB is one of the many opportunistic infections that plague AIDS patients with impaired immune function, and HIV/TB is a deadly combination. The rest were among immigrants from areas where TB had a high prevalence, racial and ethnic minorities, incarcerated populations (i.e., prisoners), and those in homeless shelters and nursing homes. Although the latter can be understood as a function of housing conditions or large numbers of people with impaired immune function, the use of racial and ethnic categories as "risk groups" implies that there is either some biological reason for increased prevalence or "cultural" factors that facilitate the spread of TB among minority populations. This has long been a theme in analyses of TB, with some populations (in Europe, the Irish; in the United States, African Americans, especially in the South) considered more susceptible to the disease than others. More likely, TB has long hidden among those living in poverty, including minority populations in wealthy countries.

What most TB patients have in common, regardless of their nationality, is poverty, and that goes for individuals co-infected with HIV. Despite the romanticized TB deaths among nineteenth-century European novelists, poets, and musicians (e.g., Keats, Shelley, the Brontë sisters, and Chopin, among others), TB has always been primarily a disease of the poor. The Industrial Revolution, with crowded dirty cities, air pollution, substandard housing, factory work in close quarters, compulsory schooling, stress, and poor nutrition, conspired to increase the incidence of TB, especially among the working poor (Hays 1998). Sanatoria, where well-off TB patients were sent to convalesce, were the antithesis of these conditions. Often situated in the mountains, with abundant fresh air and copious food, they also sought to reestablish the "good habits" that urban life eroded.

In *The White Plague*, René and Jean Dubos situated TB as "a social disease . . . [that] presents problems that transcend the conventional medical approach . . . its understanding demands that the impact of social and economic factors on the individual be considered as much as the mechanisms by which tubercle bacilli cause damage to the human body" (Dubos and Dubos 1952, i). Thus, claims made in the same decade that TB could be a disease of the past might suggest that these social conditions—namely poverty—had been ameliorated. In some respects they were; there were substantial improvements in housing and working conditions toward the end of the nineteenth century in Europe and the United States, but in the vast majority of the world this was hardly the case, and TB has remained the number one infectious disease cause of mortality for adults. This is despite the fact that TB is fully curable and has been for several decades. This can only be seen as a failure to provide both standards of living that reduce TB exposure and access to the drugs that can limit the destruction wrought by the bacterium. Drug companies seem indifferent to the prospect of developing new treatments for TB, a problem that is compounded by the fact that many current cases of the disease are resistant to the standard front-line drugs.

MDRTB and now XDRTB are the true emergent diseases here, and they derive from a number of factors. The prolonged treatment required to cure TB lends itself to the development of drug-resistant strains. When treatment is truncated or sporadic, bacteria that are not affected by the antibiotic in use are able to flourish. What is also important is the failure to adequately assess which antibiotics are actually useful for the given strain with which a person is infected. If a person with a form resistant to rifampin is given that drug simply because it is the standard first-line treatment, the drug-resistant pathogen will persist and can be spread to others.

Paul Farmer (2001, 190–193) relates the story of a Peruvian peasant woman living in the slums north of Lima who developed TB. Unable to get to a clinic because of her long working hours, she treated herself with herbal remedies to no avail. As her condition worsened, she went to the clinic, where her sputum tested positive for TB, and she began the standard treatment. When her condition did not improve, she visited a private clinic, where she was prescribed four drugs, only two of which she could afford. Finally, with her health deteriorating, she was referred to a private hospital but again was unable to afford the drugs prescribed for her. A health workers' strike intervened, and when she finally returned to get her medications, she was chastised for not taking her medications promptly. At some point her son also began coughing, and the standard regimen of antibiotics offered from the public health post had no effect. She returned yet again to the clinic and was informed that her TB strain was resistant to the drugs, but for some unknown reason they were prescribed for her once again. When she did not respond to treatment, she was advised to give up her "futile" efforts to treat her TB. She doggedly found additional drugs that cost more than eight times her husband's monthly salary when he was working regularly. Eventually, she was treated for free with a multidrug regimen, but adverse reactions caused her to have to terminate that treatment. Finally, she wound up again at the private hospital, where she was told, "We have nothing we can do for you; your case is too chronic." Shortly thereafter, she died.

This saga could be read as simply a case of medical mismanagement, but it was much more than that. While the woman was being treated with medications known to be ineffective, she was riding the bus to work and back—four hours round trip—likely infecting others with her drug-resistant strain. It certainly spread within her household to her son. For six years, she was infectious with a drug-resistant form. Why wasn't she, and thousands like her in developing countries such as Peru, treated appropriately from the start, given that other antibiotics suitable for her case were available? Farmer argues that health policy makers make a number of erroneous assumptions about MDRTB: that it is essentially untreatable in poor countries because of the expense of the drugs; the best public health strategy is to treat the drug-susceptible forms to prevent MDRTB; MDRTB is less infectious than drug-susceptible forms; and that because TB is a disease of poverty, it is best to focus efforts on economic development rather than treating cases of existing TB.

In 2018 the United Nations (UN) held its first ever high-level meeting on TB. Ending the TB epidemic by 2030 is part of the Sustainable Development Goals, with the aim of a 90% reduction in TB deaths and an 80% reduction in TB incidence. The strategy also includes a 2020 milestone that no TB patients and their households face catastrophic costs as a result of TB. Whether these goals will be achieved remains to be seen. It is undoubtedly the case that the "ultimate" solution to TB lies in social change to improve the living conditions of the poor and thereby prevent the disease altogether, but this is little comfort to those millions of people already suffering from the disease, who are also transmitting it to others in their environs. Furthermore, the cost-effectiveness argument fails to hold water because the long-term costs of confronting many cases of MDRTB that will result from inadequate treatment will grossly outweigh the costs of treating all new cases promptly and appropriately with multidrug regimens. To deny treatments that are known to be effective to someone suffering from a potentially fatal disease reflects nothing less than a blatant devaluation of the lives of the poor.

HIV/AIDS: A NEW(ISH) DISEASE

The diseases discussed above have long histories in human populations, although they have resurged because of ecological and social changes or, in the case of MDRTB/XMDRTB, antibiotic-resistant forms have emerged. In contrast, **HIV** is an example of a new disease, one that seemed to come out of nowhere in the 1980s. It had been preceded in the late 1970s by another seemingly new disease, which first gained public attention at a 1976 convention of American Legionnaires at the Bellevue–Stratford Hotel in Philadelphia. There, some of the conventioneers came down with a mysterious and deadly pneumonia-like disease, which was quickly dubbed Legionnaire's disease. It affected 182 people and resulted in 29 deaths. Shortly after its outbreak, the culprit was ascertained to be a bacterium (*Legionella pneumophila*). The bacterium was isolated from the biofilm scums lining the hotel's cooling tower and had been pumped out into room air via the air conditioning (Garrett 1994). *Legionella*, it turned out, is widespread in soil and many different kinds of water—from hot tubs to fountains, chlorinated and distilled water, cooling towers, creeks, and ponds, among others. Importantly, it is not transmissible from human to human, but if contracted it can be difficult to treat because it is resistant to many antibiotics. It has probably been the cause of numerous pneumonia-like deaths since the advent of indoor plumbing, and there continue to be outbreaks, most of which are associated with contamination within cooling towers.

The 1976 Legionnaire's disease outbreak came and went and never spread more broadly. In 1980, reports came out of young men in New York City suffering from some unusual diseases: pneumocystis, a fungal pneumonia usually kept in check by the immune system; Kaposi's sarcoma, which had previously been known almost exclusively in elderly Jewish and Italian men; and cytomegalovirus, one of the herpes viruses that is generally a "silent" infection causing no symptoms. These occurred in conjunction with low T-cell counts. This cluster of syndromes was then reported in San Francisco, Los Angeles, and other urban centers. The victims had one thing in common: they were gay men. Within a year, however, intravenous drug users were showing up in hospitals with the same symptoms; one had a newborn suffering from the same illness. Then an elderly man who was a hemophiliac died of pneumocystis, and he also appeared to have a depressed immune system. The syndrome was also found among urban immigrants, especially from Haiti, and a baby who had received multiple blood transfusions. Being gay, therefore, did not seem to be the sole risk factor, but the association of the disease with drug users, homosexuals, or other marginalized groups did little to endear researchers attempting to get funding from government agencies to study the disease. As late as 1987, when more than 20,000 Americans had already died of HIV, President Reagan finally publicly acknowledged the existence of the AIDS epidemic. In his speech to the American Foundation for AIDS Research he mentioned only the disease's "innocent victims"—those who had contracted HIV through blood transfusions or the spouses and children of intravenous drug users.

The human immunodeficiency virus (HIV) is an RNA retrovirus. Its RNA can be "reverse transcribed" into DNA, which is integrated into host DNA, and then used to make viral proteins. The first stage of infection is marked by a strong immune response to the virus, with high levels of HIV antibodies and cytotoxic T-cells. As a consequence, the density of the virus drops sharply, but small amounts of the virus remain embedded in T-cells, particularly the CD4 T-cells. Over the course of several years, these cells replicate, and because they contain viral DNA, the virus multiplies as the immune system is activated, and because it mutates at a rapid rate, it constitutes a moving target for antibodies and T-cells. Infected cells are destroyed by other immune cells, and the body's ability to mount an effective cell-mediated response to other pathogens diminishes. These multiplying opportunistic infections mark the onset of **AIDS**—acquired immunodeficiency syndrome. The patient's demise is characterized by a decline in CD4 T-cells and ultimately death from one or several opportunistic diseases.

HIV was formally recognized as the cause of AIDS in 1984. It is most commonly transmitted by three routes, all of which involve exchange of bodily fluids: sexual contact, blood-to-blood contact, or from mother to fetus because HIV can cross the placenta. It can be transmitted in breast milk, semen, and female genital secretions and by needles contaminated with infected blood. Compared with other viruses such as measles or smallpox, it is actually difficult to transmit—less than 5% of individuals get the infection during a single exposure through sexual contact. Coexisting STIs that form genital ulcers can facilitate transmission. Blood-to-blood transmission rates are much higher—one can be infected with HIV by just one unit (equivalent to one pint) of blood.

The history of how the discovery of HIV came about and the political context in which decisions were made about actions designed to stem the spread of the disease have been the subject of several reports, including the gripping documentary *And the Band Played On* (1987) by journalist Randy Shilts, who subsequently died of AIDS. A few key events are worth highlighting. First, the appearance of the disease among hemophiliacs and those receiving blood transfusions indicated that the blood supply might be a source of infection. However, despite clear evidence that the blood supply was contaminated with whatever was causing AIDS, the U.S. Food and Drug Administration, along with the American Red Cross, adopted a "wait and see" attitude toward screening the nation's blood supply. Because at that time the cause of AIDS was not known, the Centers for Disease Control and Prevention (CDC) recommended that blood be screened for antibodies to hepatitis B, a disease that most gay men and intravenous drug users seemed to have had at some point. Or, it was suggested that gay men, drug users, and subsequently Haitians be rejected as blood donors. These interventions met with resistance, and it was not until the HIV antibody test was available in 1985 that the blood supply was screened for HIV antibodies. In the interim thousands of individuals continued to be infected with HIV through blood transfusions. It is worth noting that the U.S. Food and Drug Administration had a policy in place since 1992 preventing men who have sex with men (along with other "high-risk" groups, including anyone with an HIV diagnosis) from ever donating blood. In December 2015 that policy was relaxed to a ban on blood donations among men who have sex with men until 12 months has lapsed since last sexual contact, a move both applauded and seen as continuing an overly restrictive practice for men who are not HIV positive.

Second, those thought to be carriers of the disease or even simply members of groups with high rates of infection became known as the 4-Hs, homosexuals, hemophiliacs, Haitians, and heroin addicts, and were subject to stigmatization and ostracism (Hays 1998). Gay men bore the brunt of this stigma. Just as sexuality in general was attaining greater public acknowledgment and acceptability and the gay community was becoming more socially recognized and politically active, the epidemic struck. Some of the public saw this as evidence of "God's wrath" striking down gay men as punishment for their immoral behavior. This view posed a dilemma for the male gay community, especially in the early years of the epidemic. Although wanting to protect themselves from the deadly disease, admission that it was transmitted through men who have sex with men, especially in urban bathhouses where a man might have multiple sex partners, was tantamount to acknowledging that there was something "unhealthy" about at least some aspect of male gay lifestyles. Worries about the erosion of civil rights and a resurgence of homophobia were as rife as worries about contracting a deadly disease. Ultimately the bathhouses were closed by public order and the rhetoric of "safe sex" through the use of condoms and fewer sex partners became normative among the gay male community.

Haitians suffered from stigmatization as a group as well, not because of their sexual practices so much as the public's imagination of bizarre cultural practices such as voodoo. In the American mind, voodoo was a secret ritual practice of animal sacrifice, drinking of blood, frenzied dancing, and sexual activity, with the purpose of creating powerful black magic. As Paul Farmer (2001) notes, the ethnographic and epidemiological data on voodoo and disease in Haiti in no way bear out accusations that voodoo is the cause of HIV infection among Haitians in the United States or in Haiti. Indeed, as detailed later, Haitians more likely contracted HIV from American men visiting the islands for cheap gay sex in the capital of Port au Prince. Haitian immigrants to the United States then brought HIV back with them, and HIV moved throughout Haiti through sexual contacts, mostly heterosexual.

Where did HIV come from? There have been equal amounts of research and speculation on its ultimate origins. The current consensus has settled on Africa as the locus of the precursors to HIV, with primates as the nonhuman reservoir of the disease. In African monkeys and apes there is a similar virus called simian immunodeficiency virus (SIV), and it may have "jumped hosts" early in the twentieth century. The mechanism by which this species transfer occurred has focused on bushmeat hunting. As noted earlier, many pathogens that become diseases of humans are zoonotic in origin; most EIDs are zoonotic, and of those, most are from wildlife (Atlas 2013). Nathan Wolfe and colleagues have been working in Cameroon, West Africa, where they have found that individuals who have been exposed to nonhuman primates via hunting and butchering show evidence of some unusual human T-lymphotropic viruses (Wolfe et al. 2005). These are closely related to the viruses that circulate in nonhuman primates and suggest that new human T-lymphotropic viruses can transfer easily from nonhuman primates to humans via bushmeat hunting and butchering. Bushmeat hunting and consumption is relatively common in Cameroon and throughout the Congo basin in West and Central Africa, especially among poorer households (Wolfe et al. 2005), and may serve as an important food or income buffer during periods of scarcity (Schulte-Herbrüggen et al. 2013) because it can be sold to meet demand in urban markets. Thus, people with different kinds of involvement in the bushmeat trade may be exposed to zoonotic pathogens through a variety of mechanisms from hunting, preparing the carcass, transporting the carcass, further preparation for selling the meat, and cooking it to consuming the meat. Expansion of the bushmeat trade has been facilitated by extractive logging, which opens up new areas via roads; it exposes more wildlife to human activities, makes access to wildlife habitat easier, and encourages the growth of villages in previously forested areas. Importantly, other zoonotic diseases have emerged in the Cameroon–Congo basin over the past 30 years, including Ebola, monkeypox, HIV, anthrax, and a variety of simian foamy viruses (Wolfe et al. 2005).

Bushmeat hunting—including of apes and monkeys—has a long been practiced in central Africa, so the question is why HIV emerged sometime between 1915 and 1930. Stephanie Rupp and colleagues (2016) have argued that the emphasis on a bushmeat hunter as the "index case" of HIV is misplaced, and that the larger context for colonial activities at the time are all implicated in the emergence of HIV. Based on archival data, oral histories, and ethnographic research, they propose that the expansion of agriculture and other extractionist activities, forced labor and labor migration, increased access to guns for hunting, domestication of primates by colonists, and colonial medical practices that included invasive procedures such as injections or surgery. In other words, there are multiple potential routes beyond bushmeat hunting that could have contributed to the emergence of HIV during the later colonial period in Africa.

In the United States, the incidence of HIV has declined, but it increasingly has become a disease of African Americans. According to the CDC, although African Americans represent approximately 12% of the U.S. population, 42% of new HIV infections in 2017 occurred in this group and 42% of all people living with HIV are African American (U.S Centers for Disease Control 2020). In 2017 African Americans are 8 times more likely to have an HIV diagnosis than Whites, and 10 times more likely to be diagnosed with AIDS. Among males, same-sex activity is the primary source of HIV infection; for females it is heterosexual sex with infected males. The CDC notes,

> Stigma, fear, discrimination, and homophobia may place many African Americans at higher risk for HIV. . . . The poverty rate is higher among African Americans than other racial/ethnic groups. The socioeconomic issues associated with poverty—including limited access to high-quality health care, housing, and HIV prevention education—directly and indirectly increase the risk for HIV infection and affect the health of people living with and at risk for HIV. These factors may explain why African Americans have worse outcomes on the HIV continuum of care, including lower rates of linkage to care and viral suppression. (U.S Centers for Disease Control 2020)

HIV remains pandemic. The most current estimates, from 2018, indicate that almost 38 million people are infected with HIV in the world, with cases in every country; 2.6 million are children under the age of 15. There were 1.7 million new cases in 2018 and 770,000 deaths (U.S Centers for Disease Control 2020). Although these numbers seem impossibly high, cases are declining: the number of new cases has dropped by 40% since peaking in 1997, and AIDS-related deaths have fallen by 56% since they peaked in 2004. Access to anti-retroviral treatment has accounted for the drop in AIDS-related deaths; over 60% of individuals living with HIV and over 80% of HIV+ pregnant women now have access to retroviral treatment, both dramatically increasing since 2010. There are also pre-exposure prophylaxis (PrEP) medications, which, when taken daily, are very effective in preventing HIV infection from sex or injection drug use (U.S Centers for Disease Control 2020) but they remain very expensive.

Table 9.1 shows the most current numbers of individuals living with HIV and new cases of infection in different regions of the world. Sub-Saharan African countries are the hardest hit and account for more than 70% of existing and new HIV infections. There, HIV is transmitted through heterosexual contact and from mothers to fetuses during pregnancy. In sub-Saharan Africa, the population dislocation initiated during the colonial period has continued, with rural–urban migration, refugee movements, transnational movement of labor, and outmigration of men searching for work. This leaves women and children to support themselves, and few opportunities for female labor results in prostitution or patronage relationships with men offering resources. Furthermore, inequality in gender relations makes it difficult for women to insist on condom usage. All of these social processes continue to contribute to the spread of HIV (Mojola 2014; Susser 2009).

TABLE 9.1   Global Regional Statistics for HIV, 2018

	Adults and Children With HIV	Adults and Children Newly Infected	Percentage of Adults Receiving Anti-viral Therapy (%)	Adult and Child Deaths from HIV
Sub-Saharan Africa	25,600,000	1,080,000	52–67	470,000
Middle East and North Africa	240,000	20,000	32	8,400
Asia and the Pacific	5,900,000	310,000	54	200,000
Latin America	1,900,000	100,000	63	35,000
Caribbean	340,000	16,000	56	6,700
Eastern Europe and Central Asia	1,700,000	150,000	37	38,000
Western and Central Europe, North America	2,200,000	68,000	79	13,000
Total	37,900,000	1,700,000	62	770,000

Source: Fact Sheet UNAIDS World AIDS day 2019 https://www.unaids.org/sites/default/files/media_asset/UNAIDS_FactSheet_en.pdf

---

Anthropologist in Action: Paul Farmer and HIV in Haiti

Haiti provides, for better or for worse, a useful example of the HIV epidemic. It illustrates many of the themes relevant to our discussion of emergent diseases, and there is also sensitive and wide-ranging work done there by the physician-anthropologist Paul Farmer. Farmer's work vividly documents the ways in which social inequality and globalization ultimately generated not only the epidemic of HIV but also the rise of drug-resistant tuberculosis and other infectious diseases in Haiti (Farmer 2001). As mentioned earlier, it is possible that HIV was introduced into Haiti by North American tourists coming to Haiti's capital, Port-au-Prince, for commercial sex or through other forms of commerce among the United States, Haiti, and other Caribbean countries. Haiti is the poorest country in the Caribbean, indeed in the Western Hemisphere; poverty drew many men and women into the tourist industry, which offered prostitution as a way to earn money. HIV became, as it were, an "occupational hazard" of this last-resort means of earning a living. From its original urban locus among bisexual men in the early 1980s, HIV spread throughout Haiti to its most rural villages and to women.

Farmer demonstrates how in one particular rural area, villagers had been displaced to higher ground by a large hydroelectric dam built in 1956. Many lost all of their land in this project and were not compensated, leading to high rates of rural poverty in what had previously been a lush agricultural area. With few economic opportunities at home, young adults—especially young women—moved to Port-au-Prince to seek out employment, frequently finding it in domestic work. Without sufficient money to provide for themselves and send money back home, many young women entered into long-term relationships with men, often soldiers or truck drivers, and received modest economic support from them. Given their economic dependency on men in these relationships, women were not in a position to demand condom use among their partners—and soldiers and truck drivers have very high rates of HIV infection in Haiti. With the demise of a relationship, harsh working conditions, and deteriorating health, women often returned home to their villages, already infected with HIV. In addition, a political coup in 1991 had the army enforcing brutal political repression in the slums of Port-au-Prince, resulting in a massive exodus to rural areas. Thus, neither voodoo nor promiscuous sexuality can account for Haiti's rural HIV epidemic, which can be best understood as a function of economic and political pressures.

The prognosis for HIV patients in Haiti is grim but cases of HIV are declining and antiviral therapy access has been expanding, mainly through nongovernmental organizations such as Partners in Health, which Paul Farmer helped establish. For additional inspiration from Farmer's work directed at students, see Farmer (2019).

CONCLUSION

Infectious diseases have largely spread as a function of human activities, particularly the movement and intermingling of peoples from different places and more extensive contact with wild and domesticated animals. For some populations, infectious disease smoothed their takeover of peoples and land; for others, infectious disease prevented their subjugation; and for many, infectious disease resulted in widespread suffering, death, and societal collapse. The situation becomes more complex for diseases spread by vectors because ecological changes wrought by human activities provide the means by which infection can spread. The past 500 years have been characterized by intensive population movements and ecological changes, which have resulted in both a globalization of infectious disease and a radical divergence in exposure to and suffering from infection. Europeans and their descendants in North America, Australia, and New Zealand came to enjoy unprecedented freedom from most deadly infections, and their life expectancies have surged as a result. That said, COVID-19 reminds us that infectious diseases can spread across all countries – rich and poor – quickly, and any smugness about "freedom" from infectious disease is ill-considered. The colonies and the newly independent countries that were formed at the end of the colonial period have had the opposite fate: a more extensive disease burden and a lack of resources needed to prevent or cure infections. Their life expectancies remain much lower than those of wealthy countries as a result.

STUDY QUESTIONS

1. What are emergent diseases? How do they belie the notion that infectious diseases have been "conquered" by biomedicine?
2. How do human–animal relationships contribute to emergent diseases? What factors shape these interactions?
3. What is the socioeconomic background in which new diseases emerge? Why do some researchers argue that they are better thought of as hidden rather than new?
4. Why are agricultural populations more at risk from infectious disease epidemics than hunter-gatherer populations?
5. Why did Crosby describe Europeans and Asians as being "immunologically sophisticated" compared with the peoples of the New World? What effect did this have on European expansion? What is a virgin soil epidemic?
6. What causes smallpox? How do its forms vary in the severity of disease they cause? Why has this one disease had such a huge impact on human history?
7. How did the introduction of new infectious diseases to the New World populations work to weaken and, in some cases, destroy their cultures?
8. What is the "disease barrier" that prevented European expansion into tropical Asia and Africa? How did European colonial powers deal with tropical diseases? Was there much concern for the health of "native" peoples?
9. What are some of the legacies of the colonial period on the distribution of infectious disease throughout the world?
10. What evidence is there that improved nutrition and hygiene played a significant role in reducing the impact of infectious disease in European countries?
11. Why are malaria and cholera considered resurgent diseases? How is global climate change playing a role? How might being a CF gene carrier confer some resistance to developing cholera, at least under certain environmental conditions?
12. How has dam building as a tool of development led to ecological transformations encouraging the spread or redistribution of infectious diseases? What are onchocerciasis and schistosomiasis and how has their transmission been influenced by dam building?
13. How did the cultural response to AIDS shape the spread of the disease itself, as well as the scientific mission to identify and attempt to control HIV?
14. What is the source of HIV in human populations? How is this similar to/different from the source and spread of Ebola?
15. Why is TB such an easily transmissible disease? What makes it primarily a disease of impoverished urban settings?
16. Outline the case for and against TB as a resurgent disease in the early twenty-first century.

CRITICAL THINKING QUESTIONS

1. The distribution of infectious diseases is a complex biocultural issue. What are the most essential facts about infectious diseases that the informed citizens and leaders of developed nations must understand to make sensible public health decisions?

2. Can we eliminate infectious diseases without eliminating poverty?

3. Defend or critique the following statement: European expansion has only been possible with the help of infectious disease.

4. Defend or critique the following statement: wealthy countries have an obligation to provide health resources to poor countries to help them deal with infectious diseases.

5. How can you use the information you learned in this and the previous chapter to analyze the COVID-19 pandemic from a medical anthropological perspective?

SUGGESTED ETHNOGRAPHIES AND OTHER READINGS FOR CHAPTER 9

Ron Barrett and George Armelagos. 2013. *An Unnatural History of Emerging Infections.* New York: Oxford University Press.

C.L. Briggs and C. Mantini-Briggs. 2004. *Stories in the Time of Cholera: Racial Profiling during a Medical Nightmare.* Berkeley: University of California Press.

Paul R. Epstein and Dan Ferber. 2011. *Changing Planet, Changing Health: How the Climate Crisis Threatens Our Health and What We Can Do about It.* Berkeley: University of California Press.

Paul Farmer, J.Y. Kim, A. Kleinman, and M. Basilico. 2013. *Reimagining Global Health: An Introduction*: University of California Press.

Ann Herring and Alan C. Swedlund, eds. 2010. *Plagues and Epidemics: Infected Spaces Past and Present.* New York: Berg.

Barry Hewlett and Bonnie Hewlett. 2008. *Ebola, Culture and Politics: The Anthropology of an Emerging Disease.* Boston: Cengage Learning.

Arthur Kleinman and James Watson. 2005. *SARS in China: Prelude to Pandemic?* Palo Alto, CA: Stanford University Press.

Shirley Lindenbaum. 1979. *Kuru Sorcery: Disease and Danger in the New Guinea Highlands.* Palo Alto, CA: Mayfield Press.

Sanyu A. Mojola. 2014. *Love, money, and HIV: Becoming a modern African woman in the age of AIDS*: Univ of California Press.

Alan Nading. 2014. *Mosquito Trails: Ecology, Health, and the Politics of Entanglement.* Berkeley: University of California Press.

Frank M. Snowden. 2019. *Epidemics and Society: From the Black Plague to the Present.* New Haven: Yale University Press.

Ida Susser. 2009. *AIDS, Sex, and Culture: Global Politics and Survival in Southern Africa.* New York: Wiley–Blackwell.

CHAPTER 10

Stress, Social Inequality, and Race and Ethnicity

Implications for Health Disparities

Chapter Goals

- To understand the basic biology of the stress response
- To understand the negative health consequences of chronic stress
- To understand the complex interactions between stress and immune function
- To understand how social inequality contributes to stress-related disease
- To understand the ways in which race/ethnicity and racism/discrimination affect health

People in industrialized societies often complain about the level of stress in their lives. They are "stressed out" in ways that are perceived as debilitating. This is not to say that people in nonindustrialized or more traditional societies do not experience stress or express feelings of stress. There is tremendous cross-cultural (as well as interindividual) variation in the perception of stress, identification of stressful situations, or means by which stress is expressed, discussed, or thought to have bodily manifestations.

What exactly is stress? It turns out that it is difficult to define the word. It is easier to define stressors and the physiological response to stressors than it is to pinpoint what any given person means by "stress." In this chapter we review the biology of the stress response and consider the ways in which stress worsens health, especially in the domains of immune and cardiovascular function. Attention will then shift to the source and nature of stressors. For humans (and the social primates as a whole), stress most often derives from social circumstances. From the fear of public speaking (surveys in the United States routinely find that respondents fear it more than death) to violence, discrimination, illness, and scarcity of material needs associated with poverty, our social worlds shape both our exposure to stressors and the resources we have to respond to them.

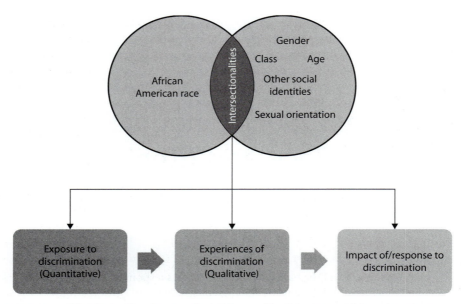

FIGURE 10.1 Discrimination, intersectionalities, and health among African Americans. A working framework for how African American race might interact with other social identities to shape exposure to discrimination; experiences of discrimination; and the physiological (or psychological) impact of or response to discrimination.
Source: Lewis, T. T., & Van Dyke, M. E. (2018). Discrimination and the Health of African Americans: The Potential Importance of Intersectionalities. *Current Directions in Psychological Science*, 27(3), 176–182. https://doi.org/10.1177/0963721418770442 Reprinted with permission, SAGE Publications.

We focus here on the ways that social stratification is associated with stress both within and across societies. In the U.S. context, social stratification occurs along economic, race/ethnicity, sex/gender, and regional lines, and multiple others, which are in turn associated with various forms of privilege, disempowerment, and discrimination. Black feminist scholars have advanced the concept of **intersectionality** to address the multiplicative, interacting effects of categories of identity such as sex/gender and race/ethnicity on individuals' lived experiences and life chances (Collins and Bilge 2016; Crenshaw 1989). The word "intersectionality" denotes the *intersections* of identity, social position, oppression or privilege, and policies or institutional practices, as illustrated in Figure 10.1. These most certainly have impacts on individual health in ways that are not simply additive but compounding, and that contribute to health disparities (Bauer 2014). They likely act, at least in part, through stress-related physiological pathways.

BIOLOGY OF THE STRESS RESPONSE

The **stress response**—that is, the way that your physiology is altered when you are exposed to a stressor—is a complex network of nerve signaling and hormonal messaging designed to activate certain processes and suppress others. Stressors are defined as anything that activates a stress response, and for most animals this includes all of the threats to survival or reproduction such as predators, competitors, extremes of cold or heat, treacherous landscapes, and food shortages. For humans, a large brain and consciousness allows us, for better or for worse, to activate a stress response by just imagining a stressful situation. Thus, *perception* of a stressor is an important determinant of whether a stress response will be activated. Some individuals perceive threats in situations where others do not. It is important to note that stress is a normal part of everyday life—or rather, activation of the stress response occurs routinely, starting with waking up in the morning. Thus, the stress response is best understood as a way by which individuals regulate their physiology in response to daily activities and a changing environmental milieu, rather than a "special" system that is activated only under acutely threatening conditions.

The stress response is a generic physiological reaction, meaning that is happens more or less the same way, regardless of the nature of the stressor itself. Given the diversity of stressors that an organism might be faced with, from the acute stress of being chased by a predator to chronic hypothermia, the main purpose of the stress response is to channel resources - most especially energy - to adapt to these challenges. The consistent nature of this set of responses was first described by one of the original stress researchers, Hans Selye, as the "general adaptation syndrome," which is characterized by physiological changes that increase energy availability, inhibit long-term growth or maintenance activities, blunt pain, and sharpen memory. The stress response can also be conceptualized as a means by which organisms can maintain their crucial physiological systems within functional limits under diverse conditions.

The term **allostasis** has been coined to acknowledge that the range of normal for different physiological systems varies by circumstances. For example, body temperature is considered "normal" at ~98.6°F (although this ranges across individuals), but when faced with a stressor such as a virus, body temperature rises to meet this challenge and is adaptive (see Chapter 8). The higher temperature reflects the upper range of tolerance under conditions of infection. Allostasis is different from homeostasis in that the normal range shifts in response to environmental stressors. The stress response can thus be conceptualized as a means by which the body attempts to maintain allostasis given some stressful condition. However, if a stressor is prolonged, the costs of maintaining a stress response mount and contribute to negative health outcomes, which the stress researcher Bruce McEwen referred to as **allostatic load** (McEwen 2002).

The Nervous System Stress Response

Starting with the nervous system, the network of neurons involved in physiological changes that are largely unconscious is referred to as the **autonomic nervous system**. As Figure 10.2 illustrates, there are two arms to it: the **sympathetic nervous system** is activated during a stress response, whereas the **parasympathetic nervous system** is suppressed. Both receive signals from the brain and send chemical messages along nerve pathways to organs throughout the body. In a threatening situation the sympathetic nervous system relies on two related chemicals: norepinephrine, which is secreted by nerve endings, and epinephrine, which is secreted by the **adrenal gland** (specifically the adrenal medulla), which sits just above the kidneys. Epinephrine circulates in the bloodstream to activate various elements of the stress response.

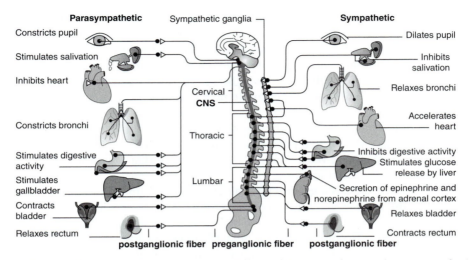

FIGURE 10.2   The autonomic nervous system: Effects of the sympathetic and parasympathetic systems.

Norepinephrine and epinephrine (also known as noradrenaline and adrenaline, respectively) cause a variety of rapid physiological changes including increased heart rate, blood pressure, sweating, pupil dilation, airway dilation, blood flow to the muscles, and muscle contraction (the "rush" of adrenaline). They also inhibit digestion and other nonessential functions for the duration of the threat. In contrast, the parasympathetic nervous system stimulates digestion, slows the heart rate, facilitates growth and repair, and constricts the pupils. The net effect of stimulation of the sympathetic system and suppression of the parasympathetic system during a stressful event is that energetic resources are made available and can get to the muscles quickly, and there is heightened acuity to make a rapid response (the classic "fight or flight" scenario). While being chased by a predator, an individual should not be putting energy toward digestion, reproduction, or growth. These functions can be put on hold as nonessential until the stressful situation has subsided. What this also suggests, however, is that chronic activation of the sympathetic nervous system can compromise these other important functions.

The Hormonal Stress Response

Activation of the sympathetic nervous system provides a mechanism for immediate action. There is another arm of the stress response that allows for a slower and more sustained response. It is activated by hormones, the most crucial of which is **cortisol**, a steroid hormone made from cholesterol and secreted by the cortex of the adrenal gland. Cortisol secretion is controlled by both the hypothalamus and the pituitary glands in the brain—hence, the hormonal stress response is said to be controlled by the hypothalamic–pituitary–adrenocortical (HPA) axis, as illustrated in Figure 10.3. The brain perceives a threat, which triggers the release of corticotropinreleasing hormone by the hypothalamus, which then stimulates the pituitary gland to secrete adrenocorticotropic hormone

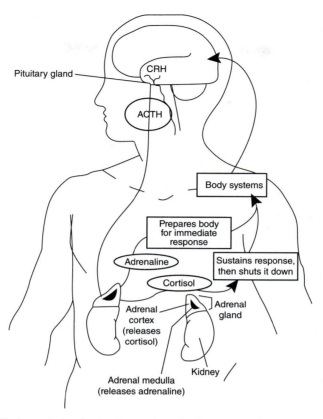

FIGURE 10.3 The hypothalamic–pituitary–adrenal axis. ACTH, adrenocorticotropic hormone; CRH, corticotropin-releasing hormone.

(also called corticotropin). Adrenocorticotropic hormone circulates in the bloodstream and triggers the release of cortisol by the adrenal gland. Various brain structures such as the hippocampus have receptors for cortisol and also can stimulate cortisol release; thus, the brain plays an important role with respect to the stress response, both up and down-regulating cortisol.

Cortisol not only forms part of the stress response but also is involved in the routine functions of many organs, including the kidneys, immune system, liver, muscle, and reproductive organs, all of which have cortisol receptors. When cortisol binds to these, it may suppress or stimulate the organ's activities. Because its secretion is relatively slow compared with that of epinephrine, cortisol is also involved in recovery from a stressful event. Cortisol directs energy stores used for the initial burst of energy to be replenished and facilitates the deposition of fat and the synthesis of glycogen, the stored form of glucose. It initially supports a burst of immune activity, making leukocytes stickier so that they can attach to sites where an injury might occur, but over the longer term cortisol suppresses immune function, as detailed later.

In sum, the sympathetic nervous system arm of the stress response can be activated rapidly during an acutely stressful event, releases norepinephrine and epinephrine, and functions to mobilize energy resources and deliver them efficiently to muscle cells. Increases in heart rate, blood pressure, respiration, and mental acuity enhance this response. The secondary response is via cortisol, which supplements the initial response and has wide-ranging effects throughout the body. Importantly, the stress response shuts down physiological functions that are nonessential during a stressful situation. Virtually all cells in the body have receptors for either epinephrine or cortisol (Dhabhar 2009), so it should come as no surprise that the effects of stress on health are wide ranging.

WHY IS STRESS DIFFERENT FOR HUMANS?

For most organisms, the stress response is activated episodically. That is, in the face of a predator, for example, the stress response is engaged for a brief period of time, and then (assuming the organism escapes) it resolves. As Robert Sapolsky (2004) notes in his acclaimed book, *Why Zebras Don't Get Ulcers*, zebras do not spend their time worrying about predators, upcoming presentations or tests, or a headache that just might be a brain tumor. As a result, the suppression of the "nonessential" physiological systems is short lived, and they are not compromised over the longer term.

In contrast, stress for contemporary humans is often more chronic. There are two key reasons for this. One is that humans have a very large brain that allows them consciousness, language, and extensive memory. These give rise to a number of possibilities that are not available to most other organisms. Perhaps the most salient of these is the ability to imagine the future. Because the future is inherently unknowable, we are free to construct multiple scenarios, regardless of their likelihood, and some are more frightening than others. Just imagining the future, especially one characterized by scary outcomes such as a life-threatening disease diagnosis, can generate a stress response (even writing about stress can be stressful!). We can then communicate these scenarios to others, causing them to activate their stress response as they listen to us describe our fears. We can call up stressful memories or rework an unpleasant memory over and over again (such as why a job interview did not go well). In other words, there are numerous means by which our large brains allow for increased perception of stress, even in the absence of actual stressful events. Chronic anxiety about the future requires persistent vigilance and ongoing activation of the stress response.

The second reason is that the social situations in which contemporary humans live are themselves often the source of stressors. Although predation in the traditional sense is not a threat for most humans, there are myriad other threats to our well-being: life-threatening interpersonal and intergroup violence, food scarcity, unemployment and ensuing monetary shortage, inadequate housing, jobs that are physically or psychologically debilitating, marital conflict, physical illness or being the caregiver for someone with a serious illness, and a lack of a strong network of social support or kin, among others. There is also reason to think that these can worsen in the context of economic development or other forms of social change. As people migrate from villages to urban centers or to other countries to seek employment, they often leave behind their traditional social networks. Their social lives change dramatically, and their traditional coping mechanisms may be either insufficient or absent (Baker et al. 1986; Y. Lu 2010). As they live among strangers with different social norms and where little is familiar, stress—or a need for the ongoing vigilance made possible by the stress response—is likely to ensue.

Thus, for many humans in the twenty-first century, life seems to be increasingly stressful. Wars, terrorism, international and urban migration, un- or underemployment, economic downturns, political instability, rapid social change with the emergence of new social institutions, and social stratification are all (among others) difficult to negotiate. It is worth taking an evolutionary perspective for a moment to consider this context in relation to that of our hunter-gatherer ancestors in the environment of evolutionary adaptedness. Was chronic stress typical of our Paleolithic ancestors, or is contemporary stress novel, and hence something to which we are not well adapted as a species? The answer to that question is most likely the latter. Although our Paleolithic ancestors had a fully modern brain size and well-developed linguistic capabilities, the social environments they lived in were different from those in which most twenty-first-century peoples live.

Prior to the 1960s, prehistoric hunter-gatherers were portrayed as living stressful lives, not knowing where their next meal was coming from and constantly on the verge of starvation, predation, and disease (Childe 1951). Their lives were, to quote the philosopher Thomas Hobbes, "nasty, brutish, and short." We now know this characterization to be false, based on studies of contemporary hunter-gatherers and the osteological record of Paleolithic peoples. The !Kung hunter-gatherers spend relatively little time actively engaged in subsistence work and have plenty of time for leisure and social gatherings (Lee 1968). Periods of food or water insecurity are considered stressful and often cause them to congregate in larger units around water holes, which sometimes generates social conflicts. There is most certainly interpersonal violence, often over mates (Howell 1979). In general, however, they live in relatively small, most likely kin-based groups, where individuals know most of the people they meet in their lives or are connected to other groups through kin relationships. Furthermore, hunter-gatherers are typically egalitarian in their socioeconomic structure. Without the ability to amass material goods because of their need for mobility and with strict social sanctions against those who try to establish power or status, the inequality in economic and social status that characterizes state-level societies is notably absent, as is full-scale war (Boehm 1999). Thus, one of the major contemporary sources of stress, social and economic inequality, was not likely to have been typical of the lives of our ancestors; hence, these are relatively novel environmental conditions that result in chronic activation of the stress response, which is associated with poor health outcomes.

STRESS AND BIOLOGICAL NORMALCY

As much medical research is done in countries such as the United States, physiological profiles standardized on such populations are likely to be biased toward those associated with higher levels of stress. Rarely is the question asked whether these are or should be indicative of the norms for our species. By way of historical example, in the nineteenth and early twentieth century when cadaver dissections were done in teaching anatomy, cadavers most often came from the unidentified poor. The sizes of various organs were duly noted, including the adrenal gland. The adrenal gland enlarges when it chronically secretes high levels of epinephrine and cortisol, and hence the perception of the normal adrenal was that of a large organ. It was often remarked on when a cadaver of a higher-class person was dissected that the adrenal gland was unusually small. They were thought to suffer from the syndrome "idiopathic adrenal atrophy" (Sapolsky 2004). What was defined as medically or biologically normal was derived from individuals who more likely than not experienced chronic stress. Similarly, in a more contemporary example, it is often assumed that blood pressure rises with age. Yet studies of other more traditional cultures or nuns living in secluded cloisters show that aging is not necessarily associated with increased blood pressure (Poulter et al. 1985; Timio et al. 1999). Thus, what is seen as a part of normal aging may be a byproduct of aging under stressful psychosocial conditions.

STRESS AND HEALTH

Chronic activation of the stress response can have negative effects on a wide variety of health parameters. Because the cardiovascular system is one of the main targets of epinephrine, it is compromised by continued stimulation. There are indirect effects on cardiovascular health via cortisol as well. The immune system is also affected by stress hormones in ways that can lead to both its suppression and its overactivation. In childhood, chronic stress can stunt growth. Although stress has other negative effects on health (especially neurological functions such as memory, cf. Lovallo 2016; McEwen 2013; Sapolsky 2004), we focus on these three domains here.

Cardiovascular Disease

There are a number of ways by which the cardiovascular system's function is undermined by chronic stress. First, repeated release of epinephrine means repeated spikes in blood pressure, which makes the heart work harder. In turn, high blood pressure puts more force on the blood vessels, especially the smaller ones, which respond by building more muscle around them. However, this makes them rigid and more resistant, so the blood returning to the heart is under greater pressure. In response, the heart also builds muscle around the left ventricle. The overgrowth of this side of the heart is a well-established risk for heart attacks. In addition, the junctures where large blood vessels branch into smaller ones are especially vulnerable to damage by increased blood pressure. Small tears or lesions form there and stimulate an inflammatory response. This localized inflammation, which is accompanied by an accumulation of fat-containing cells, and the thickening of blood resulting from the aggregation of platelets (which is caused by epinephrine so that blood can clot more easily in response to an injury) all contribute to the formation of plaques at these junctions. These plaques result in atherosclerosis, another risk factor for cardiovascular disease (CVD), because they obstruct the movement of blood through the blood vessels, both to the extremities and to the heart. Since blood is under more pressure as it moves through the vessels, there is an increased risk that a plaque will tear off and then get stuck in a smaller blood vessel, completely blocking blood flow to it and all of the "downstream" vessels (Hering et al. 2015; Steptoe and Kivimaki 2012). This can cause a heart attack, or, if it occurs in a blood vessel in the brain, a stroke.

A person who has experienced chronic activation of the stress response becomes ever more susceptible to blood vessel damage. Each new episode worsens the underlying damage, and damage in the arteries surrounding the heart is particularly dangerous. For a person with existing heart disease, another stressful event can cause the coronary arteries to constrict rather than dilate, as is typical in an acute stress response (Hering et al. 2015). This constriction further reduces blood flow to the heart and can cause chest pain, a condition that is referred to as myocardial ischemia. Even short-term stressors such as a brusque encounter with a co-worker or an unwelcome phone call can generate transitory ischemia. Chronic stimulation of the sympathetic nervous system also makes it more difficult to turn it off, which creates a positive feedback cycle that worsens the effects of stress on the cardiovascular system.

A particularly alarming example of the relationship between stress and heart attack is the phenomenon that was pejoratively termed "voodoo death" by Walter Cannon in his original description in 1957, or "psychophysiological death." During an extremely stressful event, sympathetic stimulation of the heart can become disorganized, resulting in cardiac ischemia and fibrillation and ultimately cardiac failure and death. Although this is not common, it is a well-described phenomenon, especially in non-Western societies, where a transgression results in a person being cursed or "sent" death. The prophecy is fulfilled as the person becomes so agitated that his or her heart gives out under acute sympathetic stimulation. Extreme negative emotions, accompanied by overwhelming feelings of helplessness and hopelessness, precede the death (Lovallo 2016). Interestingly, population studies (Steptoe and Kivimaki 2012) show increases in sudden cardiac deaths following extremely stressful circumstances, including earthquakes, missile attacks, death of a loved one, and even losses by beloved sports teams (the risk of cardiovascular events almost tripled compared with a control period in Munich, Germany, when the German team played in the World Cup Soccer matches in 2006, Wilbert-Lampen et al. 2008). Extreme stress may also be implicated in the sudden nocturnal death syndrome documented among Southeast Asian Hmong refugees (see Chapter 11). Nightmares of "supranormal" or spirit attacks may have generated a disorganized stress-related cardiac response (Adler 1995). It is not clear why some people might be more vulnerable to this than others. Although some undoubtedly have underlying CVD such as atherosclerosis, other victims of psychophysiological death have been young and otherwise healthy adults with no apparent underlying pathology (Hering et al. 2015).

Another means by which stress influences cardiovascular health is via energy metabolism. Epinephrine stimulates glucose synthesis and increased blood glucose levels, which are maintained by a reduction in insulin production (recall that insulin is involved in helping cells take up glucose from the bloodstream) to generate a rapid source of energy for emergency situations. If fat stores are used as an energy source, blood levels of fat also rise. Reduced insulin also prevents other cells not involved in critical processes (such as fat cells) from absorbing glucose. These cells become insulin resistant, so as not to take up energy resources desperately needed for other cells, such as those in muscle tissue. As a result, repeated acute stress results in increases in circulating fat and glucose and insulin resistance, risk factors for diabetes and heart disease (Black 2006).

Cortisol also promotes insulin resistance, but it is also involved in replenishing energy stores diminished by epinephrine. It stimulates appetite so that more energy is ingested. It also causes insulin levels to increase in an effort to have fat cells take up excess circulating glucose. Visceral fat cells are especially sensitive to cortisol, and thus fat gets preferentially stored in the abdominal region. Fat in this area is considered a major risk for diabetes and heart disease. With chronic elevation of cortisol, insulin levels remain high, and cells become insulin resistant, resulting in the need for yet more insulin to be released from the pancreas (Black 2006). Thus, chronic stress has effects on metabolic processes that themselves are risk factors for CVD. For most organisms a stress response is accompanied by physical exertion (e.g., running from a predator), and the energy loss associated with this activity is replenished by cortisol. However, among humans, if stress derives from social circumstances, it is likely not occurring in a context in which running away is the appropriate response. Hence, the flood of glucose, followed by increased appetite and fat storage, can result in increased adiposity and insulin resistance (Black 2006; McEwen 2002). In addition, individuals' coping behaviors for stress may include smoking, eating, or alcohol use, all of which increase the risk of CVD as well (Mainous et al. 2010).

Immune Function

One of the most potentially deleterious relationships between chronic stress and health involves alterations in immune function. The immune system and stress hormones are intricately interrelated, with epinephrine and cortisol playing a role in both the stimulation and the suppression of the immune system. Lymphocytes, for example, have receptors for both of these molecules, so their activities are modulated by a stress response. The immune system and the central nervous system signal each other via cytokines, which can cause the hypothalamus to initiate the HPA cascade.

Immunosuppression   Many of the immune system's functions are activated during a short-term crisis, whereas others are suppressed, and so the inhibition of the immune system by stress hormones is variable across its components. The best known effects on immune function derive from the actions of cortisol. In the early twentieth century, it was observed that adrenal enlargement (a symptom of chronically high cortisol release as described earlier) was found in association with an atrophied thymus. Recall from Chapter 8 that the thymus is responsible for maturation of T-cells. Cortisol causes the thymus to shrink, reduces levels of cytokines including those that stimulate inflammation, and inhibits antigen presentation. It lowers T-cell levels in circulation and actually kills off lymphocytes. Oddly, the lymphocytes themselves may stimulate cortisol production! Epinephrine can increase antibody synthesis, whereas cortisol inhibits it.

Cortisol and epinephrine help modulate immune activity over the duration of the stressor (Dhabhar 2009; see Figure 10.4). Given the potential need for immune cells to respond to an immediate stress (e.g., a wound from a predator or an acute infection), initially immune function is enhanced, and immune cells are increased in circulation. Subsequently, they diminish in circulation as they are routed to sites in the skin and lymph nodes, where their ability to survey and respond quickly is improved. Initially, pro-inflammatory cytokines may increase. As the stress subsides, cortisol's role then shifts to reining in immune activity in an effort to bring it back to baseline levels. However, if a stressor becomes chronic, the net effect of cortisol on the

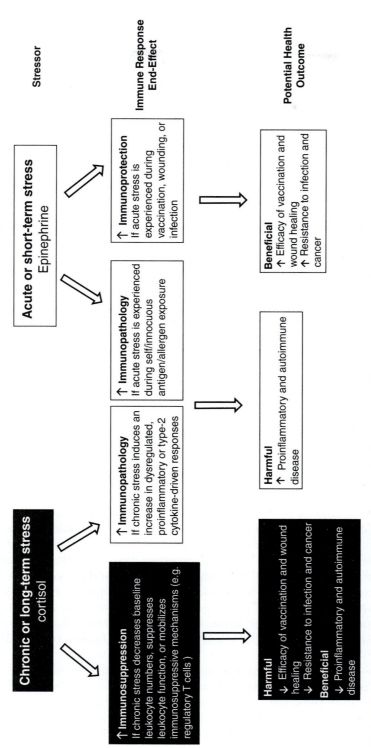

FIGURE 10.4 Potential pathways and health outcomes for short-term and long-term (chronic) stress.

Source: Redrawn from Firdaus S. Dhabhar. 2009. "Enhancing versus suppressive effects of stress on immune function: Implications for immunoprotection and immunopathology." *Neuroimmunomodulation* 16 (5):300–317.

immune system is suppressive, and immune activity stays below baseline levels. Why should cortisol do this? It is hypothesized that cortisol dampens the increased vigilance of the immune system that is adaptive in the early stages of a stress response. In fact, synthetic corticosteroids are used as treatments for diseases characterized by inflammation, such as allergies, asthma, or autoimmune disorders, precisely because of their demonstrated suppressive effects on inflammation and other aspects of the immune response.

There are numerous lines of evidence demonstrating a negative effect of chronic stress on immune function. In one of the most elegant studies of this, Sheldon Cohen and colleagues (Cohen et al. 1991) gave volunteers a nasal spray with cold viruses and monitored progression to symptomatic disease. Participants reporting more negative life events, poor coping strategies, or negative emotional states had higher rates of respiratory disease symptomatology. In a related study, Cohen and coworkers (Cohen et al. 2002) observed stress reactivity among a group of participants in the laboratory and then followed the participants for 12 weeks. Those with the highest cortisol response to a stressor or the largest number of life stressors had the highest incidence of respiratory infections over the course of follow-up. Among university students, examinations are associated with higher levels of catecholamines and cortisol and evidence of immunosuppression, including lower T-cell activity and cytokines (Lovallo 2016). Hence, the seemingly high rate of illness around exam times, which often troubles professors, may have a strong physiological basis.

In other analyses of life stresses, the effects of chronic stress on immunity are also apparent. Caregivers of spouses with Alzheimer's disease often report feelings of physical and mental fatigue, depression, and social isolation. These in turn are associated with low levels of T-cells and increased numbers of respiratory infections. Caregivers show slower rates of healing to superficial wounds, an index of reduced cytokine production and macrophage activity. Those who reported that they had fewer sources of social support were more dramatically impacted by these outcomes than individuals who reported greater social support (Glaser and Kiecolt-Glaser 1994).

Another example of the suppressive effect of stress on immunity comes from responses to vaccinations. Many studies have shown that chronic psychosocial stress reduces the antibody response to vaccines, resulting in incomplete immune protection (Yang and Glaser 2002). When U.S. troops were given vaccinations prior to being deployed to invade Kuwait during the 1991 Gulf War, tests showed that their antibody responses were lower than expected, an effect likely mediated by higher stress hormone levels (Lovallo 2016). Thus, the effectiveness of the vaccine was reduced in highly stressed individuals because it was less able to generate a sufficient antibody response. This has obvious public health and clinical implications vis-à-vis how, when, and to whom vaccines should be given to maximize their effectiveness or minimize the likelihood that they will confer insufficient protection against the disease.

If chronic stressors impair immune response, is there evidence that behavioral or cognitive modifications can reverse the relationship? Laughter seems to reduce secretion of both epinephrine and cortisol. Meditation has been associated with decreased cortisol levels (Matousek et al. 2010) and with improved antibody response to the influenza vaccine (Davidson et al. 2003). Having an outlet for the expression of trauma has also been shown to improve immune function (Lovallo 2016). Thus, the means by which stress is managed or the coping strategies individuals can use are crucial to how stress affects the function of their immune systems. Indeed, individual variation in coping strategies and responses to stress, whether they are biological (i.e., genetic) or behavioral, contributes greatly to the differential experience and health outcomes of stress. Some individuals are more reactive to stressors—their levels of epinephrine or cortisol are higher, they are quicker to rise in the face of a stressor, or they decline more slowly after a stressor. There are also sex differences in the relationship between stress and immunity. Estrogen, the sex hormone found in much higher levels in females than males, enhances immunity and thus in some ways offsets the risk of immunosuppression with chronic stress. Testosterone has the opposite effect—it is associated with suppression of immune activity (Daruna 2004). Not surprisingly, females are more likely to suffer from autoimmune disorders than are males, an outcome related to their more active immune systems.

Autoimmunity   Cortisol has a suppressive effect on immunity, yet it also appears that stress can increase the risk of autoimmune disorders or serve as a trigger for flare-ups. Autoimmunity is when the immune system targets self tissues as if they were foreign; one's own tissues are thus damaged or destroyed in the process. Depending on what tissues are affected, symptoms can range from mildly debilitating to life threatening. Some of the most common autoimmune disorders are rheumatoid arthritis (joint tissue), type I diabetes (insulin-producing cells in the pancreas), Graves's disease (thyroid), lupus (connective tissue), and multiple sclerosis (nerve tissue). How is it possible that cortisol is involved in both impaired immune response and immune hyperactivity?

Immune function is initially enhanced during an acute stressor and then is brought to baseline by cortisol. If acute stressors are repeated, however, it becomes more difficult to bring immune activity down to baseline. In fact, the baseline level itself may rise, as repeated episodes of acute stress ratchet up immune activity (Daruna 2004). Thus, there is an important distinction to be made between chronic stress and repeated acute stress because their effects on immune function take opposite directions (see Figure 10.4). This helps explain why corticosteroids are used to treat the inflammation and other symptoms associated with autoimmune disorders, but at the same time an acutely stressful event can cause a flare-up in symptoms among individuals with an underlying autoimmune disorder.

For example, the insulin-dependent form of diabetes (IDDM) is a disease in which the β-islet cells of the pancreas are damaged or destroyed and are unable to secrete sufficient amounts of insulin. Because insulin is required for cells to take up glucose, inadequate production of this hormone results in high blood glucose levels and cells that cannot access this sugar for energy. Individuals with IDDM must monitor their blood glucose levels several times each day and administer insulin in order to maintain normal blood glucose levels and ensure that their cells can get sufficient glucose. IDDM is different from non–insulin dependent diabetes mellitus (NIDDM) in that the problem is the lack of insulin production by the pancreatic cells, whereas NIDDM is generally caused by insulin resistance among target cells.

In many cases, IDDM is triggered by a viral infection of the β-islet cells, and there is also a strong genetic component to the risk of IDDM, via the human leukocyte antigen/major histocompatibility complex (MHC) genes. β-Islet cell damage can be induced by the action of lymphocytes, macrophages, and other cells of the immune system. Importantly, once IDDM is established and the β-islet cells are destroyed, the condition is permanent. There is some evidence that among genetically susceptible individuals, stress plays a role in the development of IDDM. In children, several studies show that severe emotional distress caused by war or the death of a parent precedes the initiation of IDDM (Thernlund et al. 1995; Zung et al. 2012).

Child Growth

Chronic stress can stunt child growth. This effect can even occur in utero; hence, maternal stress levels can influence very early growth. Cortisol can cross the placenta, and there is ample evidence from experimental studies with laboratory animals that stressing mothers during pregnancy generates offspring with altered HPA reactivity and cortisol levels (Glover et al. 2010). Just as mothers who are undernourished during pregnancy may have children who are metabolically efficient (see Chapter 5), the same is true of stress. If a mother is stressed during pregnancy, the fetus "interprets" the high levels of cortisol as evidence that the postnatal environment is stressful. Hence, the child is born well prepared with a robust stress response to meet the challenges of his or her environment. Altered HPA responses because of stress in utero can have lifelong and transgenerational effects on health, although outcomes depend on the timing and duration of stress in utero (Glover et al. 2010; Graignic-Philippe et al. 2014). One particularly relevant example of this was a study of women in New York who were pregnant during the time of the World Trade Center bombing in 2001. Infants born to women who experienced post–traumatic stress disorder (PTSD) after 9/11 during their last trimester of pregnancy had lower cortisol, and PTSD is associated with lower cortisol levels (Yehuda et al. 2005). A different study found a reduction in birth weight, length, and head circumference among babies born to women who were pregnant during 9/11 (Yehuda et al. 2005), and a meta-analysis confirmed a pattern of maternal stress was related to lower birth weight and higher risk of premature birth (Lederman et al. 2004).

In general, prenatal stress is associated with higher cortisol in infancy (although PTSD is associated with lower cortisol, see review in Glover et al. 2010). One mechanism by which this can occur involves reduced cortisol receptors in areas of the brain responsible for modulating the stress response (Van den Bergh et al. 2005). Fewer receptors mean less sensitivity to cortisol; more hormone is required to turn off the stress response. In other brain areas, such as the amygdala, there may be more cortisol receptors, resulting in heightened anxiety among the offspring of stressed mothers. Thus, chronic stress in utero can have negative health effects—not only in terms of mental health but also in terms of CVD and suppressed immunity, as discussed earlier. Such effects can, however, be somewhat ameliorated by nurturing behavior and emotionally sensitive child care (Grant et al. 2009).

Severe stress during childhood, taking the form of abuse, parental loss, or abandonment, is associated with increased cortisol levels, increased vulnerability to infection, and impaired growth due to both elevated cortisol and greater infectious disease burdens (Grant et al. 2009; Nyberg et al. 2012). There is a syndrome called "psychosocial dwarfism" in which severe stress slows growth dramatically and growth hormone levels are extremely low, but this is rare, and more commonly there are more subtle deficits in growth (Johnson et al. 2019; Money and Annecillo 1987). Recall that stress hormones suppress nonessential processes during a stressful event; if these are frequent or chronic, other processes are seriously compromised. Reduced digestive activity, growth hormone secretion and responsiveness to growth hormone, and more energy-draining infectious diseases come together to slow growth.[1] The fact that stress can impair growth adds to the challenge to the small but healthy hypothesis of David Seckler (discussed in Chapter 5). If smallness is the result not only of food scarcity but also of stress (and the two are likely to go together), this can hardly be considered a healthy outcome, either in the short or in the long term.

There have been a number of biocultural anthropological studies of childhood stress and growth. In an early work by Thomas Landauer and John Whiting (1964), the relative stressfulness of rites of passage for children 6 to 15 years of age was investigated in relation to growth in height. Stressful rituals might include piercing, genital modification, scarification, exposure to extreme environments, or isolation. The researchers attempted to control for other influences on height (i.e., they looked only at genetically related populations and those with similar diets) and discovered that cultures with more stressful childhood rituals had individuals with adult heights that were significantly lower (about 1.5 inches) than cultures with less stressful rites of passage.

Mark Flinn and colleagues investigated childhood stress in Dominica, a small island in the Caribbean, and found that the household environment was a strong predictor of cortisol levels in children (Flinn and England 1997). Children living with stepfathers, half-siblings, or distant relatives had higher cortisol levels than those living with nuclear kin including mothers, fathers, and grandparents. Stepchildren had higher cortisol levels than children who were the biological offspring of both parents, and episodes of parental conflict were associated with higher cortisol levels among children. In the area where Flinn and his colleagues worked, parental absences are common when adults leave to find work on other Caribbean islands, and children often find themselves living in households with more distant relatives or stepparents and stepsiblings, situations that appear to be more stressful to them than residence with close relatives. Higher cortisol levels were also associated with more frequent illness among children, usually from infection, suggesting the immunosuppressive effects of cortisol.

Household environments and parenting behavior are key modulators of stress for children. These have the potential to buffer the stressors from the larger social

---

[1] The relationship between stress and growth hormone is actually more complicated. Growth hormone stimulates bone growth and cell division, and it stimulates fat cells to release fat into circulation for energy. During the stress response, the former activities are suppressed and the latter are not, thus making energy available for stress-related activities. Thus, growth hormone levels do not always decline with stress and sometimes are enhanced, but growth hormone's activities are carefully parceled such that growth is suppressed whereas energy release is increased.

environment, or they can exacerbate stress for children. Nurturing parenting styles reduce stress levels for children, whereas parental absence, abuse, and neglect increase stress and cortisol levels. Exposure to these different types of environments has the potential to alter child health and growth. For example, Robin Nelson found that young children in Jamaica who lived in institutional care facilities due to neglect, abandonment, or parental death had, on average, worse growth outcomes than those who lived with family (Nelson 2016).

With attentive, responsive care, children develop emotional attachments that result in the sense that they are secure in the world, whereas those who experience indifferent or even abusive caretaking develop insecure attachments and internalize a sense that the world is unsafe and unpredictable (Bowlby 1969; Chisholm 1993; see also Chapter 6). Parenting styles that enhance or impede secure attachment are likely to correlate with the stresses experienced by adults; those who live in poverty or in dangerous environments or whose employment is uncertain and unpredictable (and these three often go together) and whose own childhood was stressful are more likely to foster insecure attachments among their children. Those with more secure life circumstances are able to pass on that sense of security to their children through their parenting behavior (Chisholm 1993). Gunnar and colleagues found that children with secure attachments show less of a cortisol surge when confronted with strange or frightening situations, and attachment security was related to greater maternal responsiveness and lower baseline cortisol levels (Gunnar et al. 1996). Insecure attachments are associated with higher cortisol levels among children (Johnson et al. 2018). Co-sleeping is also associated with lower cortisol levels than solo sleeping (Waynforth 2007). Adults who experienced abuse in childhood often show high cortisol levels, but blunted cortisol responses to stress, suggesting that early childhood stress can chronically activate the HPA axis (Danese et al. 2009).

Somewhat surprisingly, it appears that childhood stress simultaneously sends a signal for *delayed physical growth* (via cortisol) and *accelerated development*, especially sexual maturation. Jay Belsky and colleagues (1991) and anthropologist James Chisholm (1993) have argued that childhood stress (acting through attachment experiences) is associated with a lower age at sexual maturity and an earlier age at first birth. They hypothesized that when children internalize a sense that adult life is unpredictable, the optimal life history strategy is to reach sexual maturity earlier to maximize the chance of reproducing. A strategy of delayed reproduction would incur the risk that one might not survive to reproduce (see also the discussion of Arlene Geronimus's work on teenage childbearing in impoverished circumstances in Chapter 5). There is some evidence suggesting that childhood stress is associated with early menarche in the United States (Allsworth et al. 2005). High levels of allostatic load (i.e., biological measures of effects of chronic stress) were associated with an increased risk of early menarche (at age 10 years or earlier). Insecure attachment has also been associated with earlier menarche (Belsky et al. 2010). Given the association between early menarche and later-life reproductive cancers (see Chapter 6) and the link between childhood stress and adult cortisol activity, these studies provide more evidence for a link between childhood health parameters and late-life disease risk. They also provide a mechanism by which stressful conditions can have effects on health that persist across generations (see Thompson 2014 for a comprehensive overview of stress, attachment, caregiving, and health).

Anthropologist in Action: Dr. Brandon Kohrt

Brandon Kohrt is a medical anthropologist and psychiatrist (MD/Ph.D.) who directs the Global Mental Health Equity Lab at George Washington University. Among his goals is to improve access to mental health resources in low- and middle-income countries, and to reduce stigma often associated with mental illness.

His current project, funded by the National Institutes of Health, involves implementation and assessment of a stigma reduction training strategy called "REducing Stigma among HealthcAre ProvidErs" (RESHAPE) in Nepal. Pilot work for this study suggested that health-care providers who had RESHAPE training showed less stigma toward individuals with mental illness than those with the standard WHO training, which may improve detection of mental illness. This project aims to build research capacity and research networks, with a focus on gender equity among researchers in Nepal.

Dr. Kohrt has worked with children and families affected by war and political violence, disasters, and other forms of adversity in Africa, Nepal, Mongolia, Haiti, and Brazil. Since 2006, he has served as technical advisor to Transcultural Psychosocial Organization (TPO) Nepal, where he worked to develop and implement mental health and psychosocial support programs for former child soldiers and earthquake survivors. He has also worked with the Carter Center Mental Health Program in Liberia, where he designed anti-stigma programs to increase utilization of mental health services and helped establish the first Crisis Intervention Team training program for the Liberian National Police.

Dr. Kohrt has expertise in post-traumatic stress disorder (PTSD). According to the *Diagnostic and Statistical Manual of Mental Disorders*, Fifth Edition (DSM-5), PTSD is the "development of characteristic symptoms following exposure to one or more traumatic events" (American Psychiatric Association 2013, 274; see Chapter 11 for more on the DSM-5). This simple description hides variation in causes and effects of the condition. Common traumatic events underlying PTSD include (but are not limited to) exposure to war, either as combatant or civilian; threatened or actual physical assault; threatened or actual sexual assault; being kidnapped or taken hostage; terrorist attacks; torture; incarceration; natural or man-made disasters; and severe motor vehicle accidents. The signs and symptoms of PTSD include having recurrent and intrusive recollections and dreams of the event; experiencing dissociative states of various duration during which parts of the event are relived (i.e., flashbacks); experiencing intense psychological distress when exposed to events that are a reminder or symbolic of the event (i.e., triggering); and suffering from negative alterations in mood, expectations, or in a desire to participate in normal life activities. In children and adolescents, signs of PTSD include

having trouble with peer relationships; being irritable, reckless, or violent; harboring beliefs that the events they have endured have somehow changed them to make them unacceptable or estranged from peers; and harboring negative self-judgments (e.g., of being cowardly).

PTSD has been most closely associated with adult combat veterans, who were once characterized as suffering from "shell shock" or "battle fatigue." Very little has been known about the effects of combat on children. Brandon Kohrt and his colleagues examined the mental health of former child soldiers involved in the 10-year war between the Communist Party of Nepal-Maoists and the Nepalese government, which ended in 2006. Both sides recruited children under the age of 18 into their armies, to serve as "soldiers, sentries, spies, cooks, porters, and messengers" (Kohrt et al. 2008, 692). Kohrt and his colleagues interviewed a large sample of former child soldiers and a matched group of children who had not served. The groups included boys and girls who ranged in age from 5 to 16 years at the time they were conscripted. The children were interviewed, and their mental health was assessed with diagnostic instruments for depression, anxiety, PTSD, and general psychological difficulties.

It is important to keep in mind that during the war, Nepalese children experienced relatively high rates of trauma, whether or not they served as soldiers. The soldiers experienced significantly more exposure to bombing than the non-conscripted (56.0% vs. 20.6%), as well as torture (29.1% vs. 10.6%) and witnessing a violent death (28.7% vs. 17.0%). The child soldiers showed high rates of mental health impairment: 53.2% for depression, 46.1% for anxiety, 55.3% for PTSD, and 39.0% for psychological difficulties. After accounting for exposure to trauma, the girl child soldiers had significantly higher rates of depression and PTSD compared to the non-soldiers, and the boys soldiers had higher rates of PTSD. The association between child soldier status and PTSD was twice as high in girls as boys.

What is it about the experience of being a child soldier that contributes to the development of mental health issues? One possible explanation, which may contribute to the higher rates seen in girls, is exposure to sexual violence. Studies conducted in Africa have shown that child soldiers are at psychological risk due to sexual violence, but cultural norms precluded Kohrt and colleagues from asking study participants in Nepal about this. Another possible explanation is that communities may fear returning child soldiers, and association with the Maoist cause may have been seen as a violation of Hindu cultural norms. There may be a stigma associated with being a former soldier, especially among poorer and lower caste children. Such stigma and other forms of social rejection might lead to the development of PTSD in children at risk due to their wartime experiences.

INEQUALITY, STRESS, AND HEALTH

There is abundant evidence that stress has negative health consequences, and anthropologists have demonstrated that household and society-level phenomena mediate how stress influences health. Taking a broader view, a question that must be addressed is why so many people's lives are stressful to begin with, such that stress-related diseases are common. This requires that we consider the social contexts that give rise to routine stressors in contemporary human populations. The work of Richard Wilkinson, Michael Marmot, and their collaborators (Friel and Marmot 2011; Marmot 2004; Marmot and Wilkinson 2006; Marmot 2017a; Wilkinson 1996;; Wilkinson and Pickett 2009a; Wilkinson and Pickett 2009b) on the social determinants of health has been formative in this investigation. Marmot chaired the World Health Organization Global Commission on Social Determinants of Health, which was established in 2005, and has been a passionate advocate for the study of inequality in epidemiology and public health (Marmot 2017b).

Stress as a cause of ill health comes into greater relief when the material necessities of life such as access to clean water, sanitation, adequate food, and basic medical care are in place and not contributing to morbidity and mortality. Notably, many of the causes of mortality that affect people in very poor countries contribute only a small amount to the mortality in wealthy countries. Figure 10.5 shows how life expectancy is related to national indexes of wealth across countries. It indicates that below a certain per capita income (around U.S.$5,000), rising wealth is associated with higher

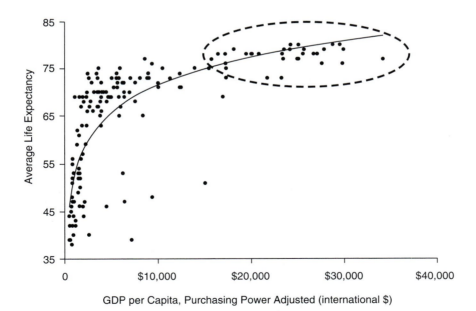

FIGURE 10.5   The relationship between life expectancy at birth and income across countries. *Source:* From J. Lynch et al. 2004. "Is income inequality a determinant of population health? Part 1. A systematic review." *Milbank Quarterly* 82 (1):5–99. Reprinted with permission from John Wiley & Sons, Inc.

life expectancy. Greater wealth equals greater health. However, once that threshold is reached, higher incomes are not associated with improvements in life expectancy (the same pattern is found if the data in Table 2.1 are graphed). Across wealthy countries, *average* income does not predict better health (Wilkinson and Pickett 2009a).

As Figure 10.5 also illustrates, there is substantial variation in life expectancy *between* countries above this income threshold that is not explained by differences in wealth. But *within* countries, there is a strong relationship between wealth and health. In the United States, for example, the average income of a postal (zip) code area is strongly negatively correlated with age-adjusted death rates. How can these two observations be explained? As Wilkinson and Pickett argue, "Health in rich nations is strongly graded by income within societies but is unrelated to the differences in average income between them. If individual income within societies is highly predictive of health but differences in the average incomes of whole populations are not, this implies that what matters may be social position, or income relative to others, rather than material living standards regardless of others" (Wilkinson and Pickett 2009b, 500).

Research has shown that variation in life expectancy among wealthy countries is closely related to how wealth is distributed within those countries. That is, *relative* income may matter more than *absolute* income. As Figure 10.6 shows, countries with greater income inequality tend to have lower average life expectancies than those in which income does not follow a steep gradient from rich to poor (Kawachi and

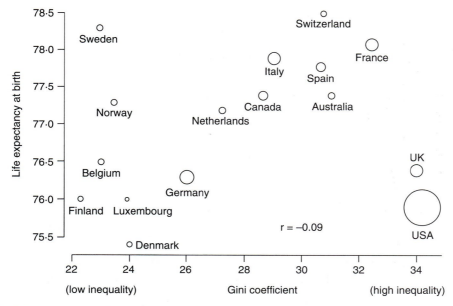

FIGURE 10.6 Income inequality in relation to life expectancy.
Source: Reprinted from J. Lynch, G. Davey Smith, M. Hillemeier, M. Shaw, T. Raghunathan, and G. Kaplan. 2001. "Income inequality, the psychosocial environment, and health: Comparisons of wealthy nations." *Lancet* 358:194–200. Copyright 2001. Reprinted with permission from Elsevier.

Subramanian 2014; Kondo et al. 2008). People living in countries where resources are distributed more evenly have better health regardless of their income than people living in countries in which there are substantial differences between rich and poor. Keep in mind that in these countries, poverty is not usually associated with contaminated water, inadequate calories, or the absence of basic health care as it is in poor countries. This suggests that within wealthy countries there are more often than not inequalities in access to other kinds of resources and other meanings of status differentials that are important to health.

The Whitehall studies are a set of well-known studies carried out among British civil servants since 1967, and these studies enabled researchers to tease out the relationships between social inequality and health. The British civil service is highly stratified, with distinct ranks assigned to different classes of employees. The hierarchy is unambiguous, with each grade subdivided further into higher and lower ranks. With ample data on health characteristics of individuals of all ranks, it provides a "natural experiment" for examining the relationship between hierarchy and health. The Whitehall studies show that there is a clear gradient in health, with the highest classes having the best health. This is illustrated in Figure 10.7 for adult males. As you move down the occupational hierarchy, health gradually worsens, such that overall death rates among the lowest classes are almost one and a half times those of the highest classes. This is astonishing, especially considering that these are all clerical jobs of some sort or another, so the lower classes are not exposed to more occupational hazards. Thus, the gradient in health observed among civil servants is likely to be *less* dramatic than that which is observable in entire populations. What is also significant is that the gradient in health is visible for virtually all forms of disease. Although Figure 10.7 illustrates the gradient in overall mortality, the same pattern exists for infant mortality, with the lower classes having infant mortality rates almost four times those of the higher classes (Leon et al. 1992).

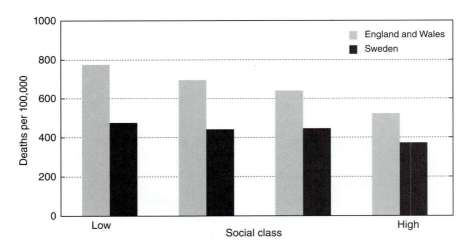

FIGURE 10.7 Differences in adult mortality between Britain and Sweden, across social classes.
Source: Reprinted from D. Vågerö and O. Lundberg. 1989. "Health inequalities in Britain and Sweden." *Lancet* 1, 2 (8653): 35–36. © 1989. Reprinted with permission from Elsevier.

Thus, whatever is driving the gradient has the ability to affect health in multiple ways. Comparing the United Kingdom with Sweden, which has a much more equitable distribution of wealth, indicates that there is much less of a gradient in mortality (both adult and child) across the social class spectrum in Sweden. This pattern is also observed with child height, across a wider diversity of countries with high (United States) to low (Sweden) inequality (Bird et al. 2019).

There are many potential causes of these differences. In his book, *The Status Syndrome*(2004), Michael Marmot reviews several hypotheses (see also the summary and review by Kawachi and Subramanian 2014). The first, which can be dismissed, is that those lower in the hierarchy have less access to quality health care. For the Whitehall studies at least, this is not a relevant variable because there is universal access to health care in Britain. Is it that people lower in the social hierarchy engage in more risky health behaviors such as smoking, drinking alcohol, eating fatty foods, and not exercising than those higher in the hierarchy? These behaviors were more common among the former group, but they explained less than one-third of the variation in health across the hierarchy. Another possibility is that those who are unhealthy are downwardly mobile (i.e., their income goes down), whereas healthy individuals are able to raise their socioeconomic status and income. This does occur, but the overall contribution to the gradient is small. Is it that the poor are somehow genetically predisposed to bad health such that their health could not be improved by bettering their social position? The evidence provides no support for this hypothesis. For one thing, over the course of the twentieth century, health statistics have improved for all groups in wealthy countries. If the poor were genetically predisposed to ill health, their health should not have changed in accordance with the improved infrastructure for health (i.e., cleaner water, safer and sufficient food, better preventive and curative medicine, etc.). It is also the case that individuals from impoverished backgrounds who rise in the hierarchy have better health than those who remained poor. Conversely, those who are downwardly mobile become less healthy as a function of their social status. Both observations indicate that health is not "fixed" by genes and that the differential healthiness of groups within a society is not caused by the poor having "less healthy genes" than the well-off.

If none of these hypotheses withstands scrutiny, then what are the relevant factors that create the gradient in health? Both Marmot and Wilkinson (among others) suggest that it is a combination of factors related to the lived experience of inequality and the extent to which a country's public policies elaborate or attenuate social hierarchies (e.g., Pickett and Wilkinson 2015). Relevant factors include: (1) one's relative wealth and status; (2) social cohesion and social participation; and (3) sources of social support. All of these are related to one another and to the experience of chronic stress and its negative health sequelae.[2]

---

[2] Humans are not the only ones to suffer from stress-related diseases that derive from their psychosocial conditions. Robert Sapolsky, whose work on stress was outlined earlier, has also conducted extensive fieldwork among wild olive baboon populations of East Africa. Baboons live in large, highly structured groups with distinct status hierarchies among males and females, although females are generally of lower status than males. Low-ranking males tend to have higher cortisol levels than higher-ranking males. They also tend to have higher blood pressure levels and other CVD risk factors associated with chronic stress (Sapolsky 2004).

Relative Status

If the basic materials of life that protect health are available to those living in wealthy societies, what is it about one's place in a social hierarchy that influences one's health? Part of the answer has to do with the experience of relative status, that is, the recognition that there are those above and below you in the status hierarchy. If you are higher up, there are fewer people above you; if you are lower down, there are many more people above you and fewer below you. Why does this matter? Hierarchies themselves generate stress and status anxiety (Wilkinson and Pickett 2017). Recall the research showing that greater inequality was associated with lower life expectancy across wealthy countries. Within countries with high inequality, individuals worry about their status—that they might lose it, how to enhance it, and what the consequences of these changes might be. Living in a hierarchical society means that evidence of lower-status or higher-status lives is visible on a daily basis. People are either cautioned about what might happen should they lose their job or wondering why they do not have access to the things that higher-status individuals take for granted (i.e., a nice car, house, interesting job, leisure time, etc.). This is especially burdensome for those with lower status, but the important point for the moment is that this generates stress for everyone. It is the subjective experience of hierarchy that is most salient in wealthy societies. Lack of control over one's life, worry about what the future might bring, anxiety over not being able to demonstrate prosperity and social status or worry about losing one's current status, and fears about one's children's safety and future all contribute to the erosion of health.

If resources were distributed more evenly across society, as they are in many Scandinavian countries (where there is a health gradient, although it is not as steep as it is in Britain—see Figure 10.7), how would health be impacted? Would it not diminish the health of the wealthy?[3] Wilkinson (1996) reports that overall health does improve with a redistribution of resources, and the effects are greatest among the lower classes. Importantly, the health of high-status individuals is not diminished (e.g., by higher taxation of the rich and the use of that money to improve the well-being of those lower in the social hierarchy). In contrast, their health is enhanced, although not as dramatically as is that of the poor, such that health disparities are reduced.

There is also evidence of the negative effects on health from increased disparity in wealth and status within a society. During the 1980s, when the British prime minister Margaret Thatcher undertook the dismantling of government support of various industries and encouraged privatization based on principles of competition in the market, unemployment tripled. When confronted by the higher rates of mortality among the unemployed, the government responded that individuals' illnesses caused their unemployment, rather than acknowledging that unemployment itself might contribute to worsening health. Studies at the time, however, showed that morbidity had occurred in

---

[3] It is also worth pointing out that redistribution of wealth through taxes is not the only means by which industrialized nations can be more egalitarian. In Japan, for example, greater equality across the social gradient is achieved by having a narrower range of incomes. That is, chief executive officers are not compensated with incomes that are wildly higher than those of regular workers as they are in other countries such as the United States (Wilkinson and Pickett 2009b).

the wake of unemployment, not prior to it (Marmot 2004). Furthermore, Wilkinson found that a multi-year downward trend in mortality slowed notably during the Thatcher years and that the poor suffered the most (Wilkinson 1996). A more recent study in Scotland found that in 1981 (the beginning of the Thatcher government) there was little variability in life expectancy between areas characterized by differing degrees of deprivation, but these quickly diverged and disparities grew. The authors noted that this trend was consistent with other studies showing that "the most deprived experience the lowest life expectancy and highest lifespan variation, a double burden of mortality inequality" (Seaman et al. 2019, 147). In other words, there was more variability in age at death among the most deprived groups, while there was more uniformity in age at death among least deprived. This mortality inequality was especially evident for men and resulted from deaths from cardiovascular diseases and external causes such as drug use, suicide, accidents or violence.

Social Cohesion

The extent to which societies are well integrated and individuals are embedded in meaningful social networks also contributes to the gradient in health. Social cohesion refers to shared values, goals, and distribution of resources within a society. It also allows for individual participation in social life, through involvement in meaningful social activities and organizations. Hierarchical societies tend to be less integrated and offer fewer opportunities for social participation and network formation, especially among the lower classes (Marmot 2004; Wilkinson and Pickett 2009b). An analysis of European countries found that several measures of social cohesion (trust, informal and formal social contacts, and social resources) were higher among the Scandinavian countries, all with universal welfare systems, and that these were in turn positively related to life expectancy (Rostila 2013). Almost all measures were lower in the postsocialist countries of Europe.

Japan provides an illustrative example of the health benefits of social cohesion. Japan has the highest life expectancy of any country in the world, at 83 years. It has also been characterized as a society with a strong group ethos, where individuals are secondary to the group, and the group's well-being is privileged such that selfish individual behavior is not tolerated. The income distribution in Japan is also much narrower than that of the United States, and the Japanese government remains committed to high employment levels, even during downturns in the economy. The workplace is characterized by loyalty and solidarity, with lifetime employment in one company being the norm. In addition, even factory work is made less mind-numbing by rotation among tasks and opportunities for workers to make suggestions for improvements (i.e., they have some control over their work). There are fewer status distinctions apparent between managers and employees in terms of dress and behavior; everyone eats together.

This is not to say that stress is not part of life in Japan; the pressures to succeed economically are strong. But a strong social ethos may ameliorate some of these pressures, such that there are not major differentials in health within the country. All in all, Japan presents a picture of a more cohesive society, and despite high rates of smoking and Westernization of the diet, Japan retains the highest life expectancy, and CVD and death rates are relatively low (Marmot 2004). William Cockerham and colleagues have argued that the social gradient model of health may not be relevant to Japan, based on evidence that Okinawans (who were described in Chapter 7) have the lowest socioeconomic ranking, yet the best health and highest life expectancy not only of any group in Japan, but also of any group in the world. The authors argue that the particularly healthy diets of Okinawans, along with high levels of social support, enhance their health and longevity despite their low relative socioeconomic status in Japan (Cockerham et al. 2000). Other researchers have found that relative status (independent of absolute income) was an important determinant of perceived health among Japanese men and women (Kondo et al. 2008), suggesting that despite Japan's social cohesion, perceptions of relative status are associated with health differentials.

At the other end of the economic scale is Kerala, a state in India. Kerala's per capita income is among the lowest in India, yet its health statistics are astonishingly positive. Much has been written about the apparent paradox that Kerala seems to present, but social cohesion, participation in the public and political spheres, high rates of female literacy, strong labor unions, accessible health care, and various forms of social security have been highlighted as contributors to good health there (Franke and Chasin 1992). From the perspective presented here, opportunities for social participation by both males and females (which is not common in many other Indian states) increase the control that people have over their lives and the satisfaction that they have with their lives. As a result, there is less stress and better health. Recent studies have shown variation in infant mortality in Kerala that correlates with inequality in ways that are similar to other Indian states (Thresia 2018), but importantly, the overall level of mortality is lower (Patel et al. 2015).

In contrast, the collapse of the Soviet Union is an example of how as countries become less cohesive and more unequal, the health of their citizens declines. In the aftermath of the breakup of the Soviet Union, adult health took an unexpected turn for the worse. From 1990 to 1994, mortality among Russian men soared. Their life expectancy dropped to 58 years, and the main contributor to the diminished life expectancy was high middle-age adult mortality. In 2008, the chance of a man dying before age 65 was 54%, a stark contrast to 16% in Western European countries (Zatonski and Bhala 2012). A more attenuated but similar pattern was found for females. As Perry Anderson notes,

> The starkness of the break in the early 1990s is not to be gainsaid. As AIDS, TB, and skyrocketing rates of suicide are added to the list of traditional killers—alcohol, nicotine, and the like—public health care has wasted away, on a share of the budget that is no more than 10 percent.. . . There are now 15 percent more women alive in this society than men. Virtually half of them are single. Such is the solitude of those who, relatively speaking, are the survivors. (Anderson 2007, 22)

Under communist rule few consumer goods were available, but basic social and health services were intact and there were not major divisions in income or material possessions among most of the population. After privatization of many enterprises previously run by the state, the income distribution widened and unemployment rose, generating an increasing gap between rich and poor. Open markets led to greater availability of material goods, yet many individuals had become unemployed and could not afford them. Formal governmental institutions had provided social services and support; when these disappeared, there were few community organizations to fill the gap. There were rising perceptions of greater inequality, fewer sources of social support, and a general lack of cohesion. Increases in accidental and violent deaths ensued, many attributable to alcohol consumption. Overall, many peoples' lives spun out of control, and their health suffered as a consequence.

Social Support

If one has access to networks of social support, this can ameliorate some of the negative effects of low status. Social support is a form of "social capital"—social resources that can be drawn on to support you in times of need. Spouses, kin, friends, neighbors, and community organizations are all sources of social support and social capital. The medical anthropologist William Dressler has conducted formative research on the relationship between social status and health in hierarchical societies by considering the concept of **lifestyle incongruity**. Lifestyle incongruity refers to inconsistency between one's real or desired lifestyle and one's education and occupation, such that the expectations associated with a particular lifestyle (i.e., accumulation of material possessions) are higher than what one's education or occupation can reasonably maintain. One's lifestyle aspirations derive from larger social, cultural, and economic processes that emphasize the accumulation of material goods or knowledge, yet local economies do not often offer opportunities to amass sufficient skills or wealth to achieve these lifestyle goals. Collecting data in both developing countries such as Brazil and wealthy countries, Dressler (1995) found that higher levels of lifestyle incongruity were associated with higher blood pressure. Having—or desiring—more material manifestations of high status while economic resources are insufficient generates higher blood pressure, an indicator of the stress response. Dressler (1992) also found that the stress associated with lifestyle incongruity can be attenuated by social support. That is, individuals who are parts of webs of kin, neighbors, churches, or other community groups have additional social resources to call on in times of need compared with individuals with fewer of these networks. Others working on cardiovascular disease have also found that social support systems are protective of health (see Figure 2.2; Berkman and Glass 2000).

Another example of the stressfulness of lifestyle incongruity comes from Thomas McDade's work with adolescents in Samoa (McDade 2001). Samoa has been undergoing rapid social and economic change, including increasing availability of material goods associated with Western lifestyles and greater access to Western-style education. McDade reported that adolescents living in households with greater lifestyle incongruity had higher levels of antibodies against Epstein–Barr virus (EBV). EBV antibodies are a marker of stress levels—increased cortisol levels reduce the immune system's ability to maintain pathogens such as herpes viruses or EBV (a virus to which most individuals have been exposed) in a latent state. High levels of EBV antibodies suggest a reduction in immunoprotection that keeps this virus in the latent state. Thus, living in households where accumulation of material goods exceeded economic resources was associated with higher stress levels among adolescents. However, in contrast to Dressler's work, McDade found that adolescents living in households with high levels of social support had higher levels of stress than those with fewer sources of social support or those who were less socially integrated. He suggests that in Samoan culture, social support is associated with the subsuming of the individual's interests to those of the family or community, a theme consistently noted by ethnographers working in Samoa. Thus, networks of kin impose substantial financial and social burdens on individuals. Individuals firmly embedded in such networks may experience heightened anxiety about not having sufficient economic resources to maintain their desired lifestyle because of the obligations these networks put on them.

Transgender Health

Minority status, particularly in relation to stigmatized groups, such as LGBTQ, is generally considered to be associated with higher levels of stress and to be a contributor to poorer mental and physical health outcomes among LGBTQ individuals (Fredriksen-Goldsen et al. 2014). In a classic paper on stress among lesbian, gay, or bisexual groups Ilan Meyer defined the concept of "minority stress" as "the excess stress to which individuals from stigmatized social categories are exposed as a result of their social, often a minority, position" (Meyer 2003, 3). Meyer considered two major sources of stress—proximal and distal—with the latter attributable to violence, victimization and discrimination resulting from stigma and prejudice (similar to structural discrimination, described below). Proximal stress stems from individual perceptions of their environments and interactions with other individuals, and can include expectations of rejection, the need for vigilance or to conceal one's sexual identity, and internalization of stigma (self-stigmatization) (see also Brewis and Wutich 2019).

The anthropologist L Zachary Dubois and colleagues (DuBois et al. 2017) investigated the experience of stress among trans men undergoing testosterone therapy during the transition from female to male, focusing on four salient domains of stress: (1) transitioning-identity stress; (2) coming out stress; (3) gender-specific public bathroom stress; and (4) general perceived stress. They found that morning cortisol levels were associated with the first three specific domains of stress. The fact that general perceived stress was not associated with higher cortisol suggests that this does not adequately capture the stress experience for transitioning men. In light of U.S. "bathroom bills" that criminalize the use of gender-specific bathrooms by those whose gender identity and expression is at odds with their assigned sex at birth, DuBois's work highlights the ways in which such social stigmatization and discrimination have biological impacts on well-being, likely through stress pathways.

DuBois's earlier work (2012) also showed that transitioning men experiencing coming out stress had elevated nocturnal blood pressure (when it should decline relative to daytime levels) and those who reported more stress with "passing" had higher levels of c-reactive protein (CRP). Both of these biomarkers are contributors to cardiovascular disease risk, with CRP measuring inflammation related to chronic stress. But he also documented a decline in stress over the course of testosterone therapy in the transition process, affirming that transitioning contributed to the well-being of trans men. That said, stress around being "out" remained among men who had been on testosterone therapy for over three years, suggesting the enduring stressfulness of having a non-normative gender identity in a context (i.e., the United States) in which norms about gender identity are entrenched and rigidly enforced.

DuBois's research also speaks to issues of gender identity, gender expression, and biological normalcy. Aside from normative views about sex (e.g., that there are only two distinct biological sexes) or gender norms (i.e., expectations of behavior and presentation for each sex), his work with transgender people also exposes the ways in which some methods used by medical anthropologists are based on these normative views. For example, in his work he used multiple biomarkers of health including measures of body composition from bioimpedance monitors to assess impacts of stress and stigma experience on health. But like many other health measures, interpretation of these data relies on population-based reference values derived from binary sex categories—male and female—based on self-report or by phenotypic assessment on the part of the person collecting the data. Despite the breadth of human variation, we currently lack data to interpret measures for people who fall outside of normative categories, in this case people who are medically transitioning (i.e., through surgeries and/or hormonal therapies) in order to align their bodies with their gender identities. The issue emerges—in the case of transgender (and also intersex people), which (if either) reference value should be used?

RACE/ETHNICITY, RACISM/DISCRIMINATION, AND HEALTH IN THE UNITED STATES

In multiethnic countries such as the United States, the question often arises as to whether health differentials within the population are attributable to differences between ethnic groups or races. Race is generally conceptualized as a group of people who share a set of biological characteristics that differ from those that characterize another group. In the nineteenth century and up through the mid-twentieth, race was the main lens through which human biological variation was interpreted. However, by the 1960s, interest in race as a biological category declined, as biological variation came to be understood as more or less continuous across human populations. That is, instead of groups having unique traits that differentiated them from others, traits were instead seen as having high frequencies in some places, with diminishing frequency as geographic distance increased (*clinal variation*). In other words, some populations may have a higher frequency of a given genetic trait (e.g., lactase persistence), whereas others have lower frequencies. The frequency of a given trait is thus continuous across geographic space. Richard Lewontin's famous study showing that little of human biological variation could be accounted for by racial affinity further undermined the use of race as an adequate descriptor of human variation (Lewontin 1972). Race is generally considered a social construct; its meaning is subject to cultural interpretation and varies across societies and through history. The fact that race is often conflated with ethnicity, which reflects cultural rather than fixed biological affiliation, further indicates the social character of the race concept.

Despite these understandings of race in anthropology, the use of race as a biological category remains very common in health research. The question is whether race is an appropriate variable to use in understanding population variation in disease risk. Can some health differentials be attributed to one's racial affinity (e.g., census categories in the U.S. are White, Black, Asian, American Indian/Alaskan Native, Hawaiian/Pacific Islander)? Are different races susceptible to different diseases or do some have higher or lower risk of developing a given disease such as hypertension? Is this because of racial genetic differences? Is the health gradient a result of the higher frequency of minority racial groups among the lower social classes? Or is race useful as a social category, as cultural anthropologists have argued? As Nancy Krieger writes, "Just because 'race' is not a meaningful biological construct does not mean that 'race,' per se, is a meaningless or 'unscientific' category. Instead, . . . 'race'—and more broadly 'race/ethnicity'—is a powerful *social* category, amenable to scientific analysis, that we daily produce and reproduce through the race relations of our society" (Krieger 2000, 212).

There is little evidence suggesting that races differ in their overall health in ways that can be directly traced to biological differences between groups (Cooper 1984; Krieger 2011). This should not be surprising given that all contemporary humans share a relatively recent common ancestry and that there is not a high level of genetic variability among our species. That said, analyses of health in the United States regularly use race as an important determinant of variation in health, and racial differences in health often emerge in such analyses. We can first ask this: Why is race so routinely used in analyses of health? Jones and colleagues (Jones et al. 1991) found that more than half of the studies published in *American Journal of Epidemiology* from 1921 to 1990 used race as a variable. The underlying assumption has been that race reflects some biological qualities that differ across groups, and this has been especially evident in comparisons of peoples of African descent (Blacks) with peoples of European descent (Whites) (Cooper et al. 2003; Whaley 2003). What is also notable is that the United States is alone among wealthy countries in not reporting social class in vital statistics records (i.e., records of birth and death). However, race, sex, and age are reported. In 2003, educational attainment was added as a summary measure of socioeconomic status, but it is an imperfect measure of economic well-being. It does not highlight economic differences between groups or contribute much to the understanding of the ways in which race might act through other social and economic variables to influence health.

Variation in health may be apparent across racial groups, not because there is some intrinsic biological difference that contributes to variation in risk, but rather because, as anthropologist Clarence Gravlee argues, race *becomes* biology:

> There are two senses in which race becomes biology. First, the sociocultural reality of race and racism has biological consequences for racially defined groups. Thus, ironically, biology may provide some of the strongest evidence for the persistence of race and racism as socio-cultural phenomena. Second, epidemiological evidence for racial inequalities in health reinforces public understanding of race as biology; this shared understanding, in turn, shapes the questions researchers ask and the ways they interpret their data— reinforcing a racial view of biology. It is a vicious cycle: Social inequalities shape the biology of racialized groups, and embodied inequalities perpetuate a racialized view of human biology. (Gravlee 2009, 47–48)

The term "embodiment," which was coined by epidemiologist Nancy Krieger is another way to conceptualize Gravlee's first point; it refers to how individuals "literally incorporate, biologically, the world in which we live, including our societal and ecological circumstances," (Krieger 2005, 351). If that world is characterized by differential treatment of people according to socially defined racial characteristics, then biologies are shaped accordingly. Privilege and discrimination can leave vastly different bodily signatures. Those with multiple identities subject to discrimination are likely to suffer the most, as noted in the earlier discussion of intersectionality, and in ways that might be unexpected. For example, discrimination among African Americans with higher education was associated with higher cortisol or C-reactive protein [a measure of inflammation] than among those with less education, or Whites at any educational level (see summary of these and additional studies in Lewis and Van Dyke 2018). Thus, group differences in particular health outcomes such as blood pressure are *consequences* of the embodiment of race, rather than race being the *cause* of them.

Krieger outlined three types of discrimination that can contribute to apparent racial/ethnic differences in health:

> **institutional discrimination** typically refers to discriminatory policies or practices carried out by state or nonstate institutions; **structural discrimination** refers to the totality of ways in which societies foster discrimination, via mutually reinforcing systems of discrimination (e.g., in housing, education, employment, earnings, benefits, credit, media, health care, criminal justice, etc.) that in turn reinforce discriminatory beliefs, values, and distribution of resources; and **interpersonal discrimination** refers to directly perceived discriminatory interactions between individuals—whether in their institutional roles (e.g., employer/employee) or as public or private individuals (e.g., shopkeeper/shopper). (Krieger 2014, 650)

While "race" or ethnic identity might account for variation in health outcomes in public health studies, the reasons why they do so are likely related to these three forms of discrimination. Bailey and colleagues (2017) note that most studies of discrimination and health have considered *interpersonal* discrimination, and acute and chronic stress associated with it as a likely pathway connecting it to negative health outcomes. As an example, a meta-analysis of studies on racism—measured as self-or group reported experiences, vicarious, or proxy reports, and internalized racism—found the strongest relationships with mental health, but also physical health and overall health (Paradies et al. 2015). The authors proposed chronic activation of the HPA axis and other stress-related physiological mechanisms as pathways linking self-reported experiences of racism to worse health outcomes. State-level structural and institutional discrimination are also connected to poor health; living in states with more extensive forms of discrimination is associated with higher rates of heart attack among Blacks but not Whites (Lukachko et al. 2014). All forms of discrimination are likely to act on individual health at least partially through stress-mediated pathways (Goosby et al. 2018).

The phenotype of skin color is a good example of how race and racism are conflated in studies of health, in large part because skin pigmentation has long been used as a key biological racial trait. Importantly, it is not skin color itself that is associated different health risks (aside from vitamin D status or skin cancer), but rather it is *cultural interpretations* of skin color variation that are driving associations between skin color and stress-related health outcomes. For example, African American individuals with darker skin color perceive and receive more discriminatory treatment than those with lighter skin (Klonoff and Landrine 2002), and in a large national interview survey among African Americans, variation in self-reported skin tone was a significant predictor of perceived discrimination, which in turn was a significant predictor of self-reported mental and physical health outcomes, after controlling for several other contributing factors (Monk Jr. 2015). In a Puerto Rican study, Clarence Gravlee and colleagues found that it was culturally defined categories of color assessed by participants along a continuum from *claro* (light) to *oscuro* (dark) that were associated with differences in blood pressure among middle and high socioeconomic status groups; level of skin pigmentation objectively measured through reflectometry was not associated with blood pressure (Gravlee et al. 2005). In Latin America, where categories of race/ethnicity and skin color are fluid and complex, research across four countries found a gradient in self-rated health by skin color, and that darker skin color influenced self-rated health primarily through class (rather than color) discrimination and low socioeconomic status (Perreira and Telles 2014, see Figure 10.8).

There is also racial discrimination in medical care. One experimental study had physicians make recommendations for treatment of patients describing identical symptoms of chest pain (Schulman et al. 1999). The patients were actually actors who were videotaped, and they ranged in age, sex, and race. Schulman and his colleagues reported that Black patients were much less likely to be referred for treatment than were White patients, and Black women were the least likely of all to be referred, although all patients were describing the same set of symptoms. This provides strong support for the existence of racial discrimination in treatment for cardiac disease and a proximate mechanism by which racism contributes to poor health outcomes and higher mortality

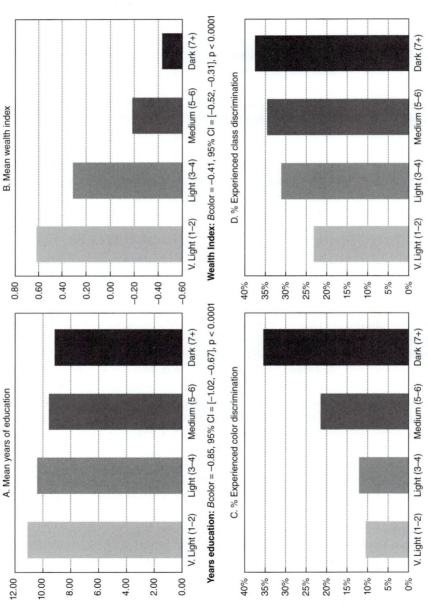

FIGURE 10.8 Skin color, socioeconomic status, and discrimination in Latin America.

Source: Perreira KM, Telles EE. The color of health: skin color, ethnoracial classification, and discrimination in the health of Latin Americans. *Soc Sci Med.* 2014;116:241–250. doi:10.1016/j.socscimed.2014.05.054

from CVD. Numerous other studies have found similar discriminatory practices in a wide range of clinical practices (Feagin and Bennefield 2014). In sum, Blacks are subject to structural violence in the United States through a variety of mechanisms that cumulate over time and contribute to health and life chance disparities.

Arline Geronimus (whose work on teenage pregnancy was discussed in Chapter 5) has developed the term "weathering" to describe the process that leads to group differences in health and longevity in the United States. She notes, "prolonged psychosocial or physical challenges to metabolic homeostasis in socially marginalized groups increase the risk of disease and early onset of chronic conditions, and ultimately, accelerate aging. . . . This view emphasizes that population differences in the early onset of chronic disease result from the qualitatively different life experiences, exposure to stressors, and access to coping resources associated with socially constructed categories, such as race, from conception onward" (Geronimus 2013, S57). Allostatic load and reduced telomere length (discussed in Chapter 7) are biomarkers of weathering and premature aging; in an early study of weathering she and co-workers found that African American women aged 49 to 55 had shorter telomeres—estimated as equivalent to ~ 7.5 years biologically older than White women with similar socioeconomic status (Geronimus et al. 2010). Recent studies have found similar results: shorter telomeres are routinely associated with various self-reported forms of discrimination, especially among Blacks (Chae et al. 2020; Liu and Kawachi 2017; Lu et al. 2019; Rej et al. 2019). These relationships hold after controlling for a variety of socio-demographic variables but may be modified by social support resources. Stress and allostatic load—acting via cortisol and associated pathways—are the likely proximate causes of this relationship (Tomiyama et al. 2012).

Another issue in the race–health relationship is the disproportionate emphasis placed on some diseases that are known to vary across populations. For example, sickle-cell anemia is a disease that is much more frequent in Blacks than in Whites, but it accounts for only 0.3% of excess deaths among Blacks (Cooper 1984). Similarly, Blacks are thought to be biologically more vulnerable to hypertension, a condition in which blood pressure is chronically greater than 140/90 mm Hg. In the United States, hypertension affects more than 40% of black adults, compared with just over 30% of whites, although both of these rates are high. Among Blacks it tends to occur earlier in life, be more severe, and result in mortality more often than in whites (Mozaffarian et al. 2015).

Some have suggested that blood pressure among Blacks is especially "salt sensitive," meaning it can be brought down significantly by reducing salt intake (Daniel and Rotimi 2003). Indeed the 2010 Dietary Guidelines for Americans singled out African Americans (as well as people older than 50 or with hypertension) for reduced sodium intake, but this, along with the UL for sodium, was removed in the 2015 version. There is no evidence that peoples of African descent are particularly vulnerable to hypertension in the absence of other contributors (such as discrimination). There does appear to be a latitudinal cline in genetic variants associated with salt retention, with higher frequencies found in lower latitudes relative to high latitudes, possibly because salt retention would have been adaptive in hot climates. This pattern is found across populations living in climatically variable environments, with alleles associated with salt retention not confined to African populations (Young et al. 2005). There is also a clear gradient in the frequency of hypertension among populations of West African descent, with the lowest rates found in West Africa, higher rates in the Caribbean, and the highest rates in the United States (Daniel and Rotimi 2003; Forrester 2004). And education, rather than genetic ancestry, was a better predictor of hypertension among African Americans (Non et al. 2012).

Group differences in hypertension could also derive from alterations in developmental pathways that occur as a function of early life environmental conditions (such as reduced birth weight, which is both more common among Blacks in the United States and associated with an increased risk of hypertension, Forrester 2004). Thus, salt-sensitive hypertension should not be viewed as a problem of Blacks, or of Africans more generally.

BiDil and "Racial Medicine" in the United States

In 2005 the U.S. Food and Drug Administration (FDA) approved the first drug for treatment of heart failure specifically in patients self-identifying as "Black." The pharmaceutical company NitroMed was awarded the patent for BiDil, which is a combination of two existing generic drugs (i.e., single drugs that are not covered by a patent that can be prescribed individually and used together) that enhance blood vessel dilation and blood flow. The combination drug was approved based on a study of Black patients who showed significantly reduced mortality when given this drug compared with a placebo. Heart failure is one outcome of hypertension. Importantly, there was no test of whether BiDil worked better in Blacks than in other groups such as Whites or Hispanics and the study provided no clear demonstration of why or how this drug is particularly effective among Blacks. Jones and Goodman argue that the patent on BiDil for non-race-specific use was about to expire, and approval for its exclusive use in blacks extended NitroMed's patent until 2020 (Jones et al. 1991). The patent request and approval were couched in the language of reducing social disparities in health, but its motivation may have been more purely economic.

There is substantial concern among public health, biomedical, and anthropological researchers about what this signals for the rise of a new "racial medicine" (Jones et al. 1991; Kahn 2013; Keita 2006; Temple and Stockbridge 2007). First, it should be noted that the individuals on whom BiDil was tested were self-identified Blacks, a heterogeneous set of individuals. Second, the embedded assumption about this race-specific drug is that it works specifically on some biological pathway that is different in Blacks than other populations. In other words, it suggests that there are genetic differences in heart disease susceptibility between blacks and other groups and that BiDil is tailored to Black genomes and Black biology (Kahn 2013). Third, this perspective serves to further naturalize differences in heart disease vulnerability that are clearly visible among racial and ethnic minorities in the United States. Health differentials can be attributed to genetic differences between groups rather than socioeconomic factors or experiences of discrimination that also differ between groups. The unanimous approval of BiDil by the FDA gives the impression of federal support for the use of race as a biological category, undermining a substantial body of work (reviewed earlier) that shows the myriad ways in which race is less a predictor of an individual's genetic makeup than it is an index of socially marked differences and life history challenges that can have negative impacts on health. Last, as Cooper, Kaufman, and Ward point out, "it is impossible for race as we recognize it clinically to provide both perfect sensitivity and specificity for the presence of a DNA-sequence variant. For this reason, race has never been shown to be an adequate proxy for use in choosing a drug; if you really need to know whether a patient has a particular genotype, you will have to do the test to find out" (Cooper et al. 2003, 1166).

With the mapping of the human genome and substantial resources being put toward understanding genetic contributions to disease, genes are again being highlighted as significant causes of disease. Understanding genetic underpinnings of disease (i.e., variants of genes that are associated with increased risk of disease X) and attributing group differences in rates of disease X to differences in genes (Frank 2007) are two distinct issues, requiring different kinds of investigation. Jonathan Kahn suggests that research seeking to understand population differences and genetic contributions to disease must have a "tight fit" between the population categories being used (which must be clearly defined and justified) and the genes of interest and their known relationship to a disease at the molecular level (Kahn 2006). It is also important to distinguish between membership in a particular ethnic or racial group as a risk factor and membership in the group as simply a "marker" of risk. In other words, it must be made explicit whether racial identity is a cause of disease or simply a correlate—meaning it serves as a surrogate for a series of (often social) factors that influence disease risk.

The FDA has defended its decision to approve BiDil for race-specific usage, citing the studies finding greater effectiveness in self-identified Blacks (Temple and Stockbridge 2007). But they also note, correctly, that there have long been calls for greater inclusion of women, minorities, and the elderly, among others, in clinical trials to ascertain whether treatments that had historically been tested only on white men would be effective or deleterious in other populations (Hudson and Collins 2017), and that the approval of drugs such as BiDil was a likely—and desirable—outcome of these efforts. In 1993, Congress mandated the inclusion of sufficient subpopulations in phase 3 clinical trials sponsored by the National Institutes of Health to be able to ascertain whether differences did indeed exist. As Temple and Stockbridge noted, "Given the long history of urgent interest in searching for racial and other demographic differences, which surely accepted the possibility that such differences might be discovered, it seems surprising that there would be so much discomfort when one was found" (Temple and Stockbridge 2007, 60).

It remains to be seen whether other drugs will be developed for use within specific "races." Economic forces may or may not support their further development and, of course, that is the critical issue for the pharmaceutical industry. As it turned out, BiDil was not widely prescribed, and in 2009 NitroMed sold the rights to BiDil to Arbor Pharmaceuticals. The FDA's willingness to approve BiDil suggests that it is open to approving other race-based treatments, although given the backlash toward and modest uptake of BiDil, pharmaceutical companies may be less likely to pursue this avenue.

The question is: How important is a biological predisposition with respect to the risk of hypertension and its related diseases? Importantly, salt-sensitive hypertension will only manifest in any group when exposed to a dietary environment in which salt is ubiquitous. The contemporary American diet contains an abundance of salt, which is present in virtually all prepared and preserved foods available in the supermarket or at restaurants (Moss 2013). As a result, Americans consume about 3,000–4,000 milligrams of salt each day compared with the 2015 Dietary Guidelines for America, which recommend less than 2,300 milligrams. Thus, the extent to which any population or individual is at risk for salt-sensitive hypertension depends primarily on the amount of salt in the diet, although it does appear that the salt-saturated environment may be more stressful for populations from low latitude regions than it is for other groups. Another factor to consider is that the dietary environment is not uniform in the United States. There is good evidence that poor neighborhoods have restricted access to fresh foods; that high-quality foods are more expensive for poor people; and that fast food, which is high in salt, fat, and refined carbohydrates, is more readily available and affordable for the poor (Baker et al. 2006). Thus, the dietary environment in which poor minorities live is characterized by a high frequency of a dietary stressor—salt. In addition, unequal access to opportunities for safe and enjoyable physical activity puts Blacks at greater risk of hypertension and the health risks that come with it (Cozier et al. 2007). In sum, one key to lowering the risk of salt-sensitive hypertension lies not so much in the identification of the genetic foundation of that syndrome as it does in changing an environment that puts people at risk of it in the first place.

Of course, increases in blood pressure are also part of the stress response. As we have seen, Blacks in the United States may be at increased risk of stress-related diseases such as hypertension because of experiences or perceptions of racism, social inequality, and economic deprivation. It is difficult to disentangle the contribution of stress from the contributions of salt in the diet and putative genes involved in the complex etiology of hypertension.

CONCLUSION

Stress is a generalized physiological response to a wide array of ecological, physiological, psychological, and social challenges. Although adaptive in the short run, exposure to chronic stress, especially that of psychosocial origin, can lead to a wide array of negative health outcomes. This chapter has specified some of the links between stress and health or disease and focused on the ways in which social and economic forces, such as poverty and various forms of discrimination, influence health through stress-mediated pathways. In the context of globalization, rising expectations for life often clash with economic realities, creating lifestyle incongruity, which is associated with a lack of control over one's ability to lead a fulfilling life. Likewise, in countries where there are strong status hierarchies, the experience of stress is heightened, especially among those of low status. Having the perception that you cannot control or improve your situation or fearing loss of status, having few social resources to draw on, or living in a society rife with divisions all contribute to stress and stress-related disease. Within this analysis, however, are examples of societies with high levels of social cohesion and egalitarianism, and they tend to have better health profiles as a result. This chapter also highlights how social conditions are strong influences on health, a theme echoed throughout this text, and how "healthy" societies, characterized by high-quality, meaningful social relations, are likely to be made up of healthy individuals. Although humans as primates may be primed to construct social hierarchies, the meanings we attribute to them and the ways in which we seek to ameliorate their effects or emphasize social distinctions have profound effects on our health.

We have also seen the ways in which health disparities among racial and ethnic groups in the United States are more appropriately seen as deriving from the compounding effects of discrimination and social and economic marginalization rather than inherent biological differences between groups. Any biological differences play very limited roles compared with the social factors in explaining variation in health between groups at this time. The experience of racism has negative effects on health, and these effects are in some ways mediated by the stress pathways. Despite the work of public health researchers demonstrating these greater disease burdens among racial and ethnic minorities, as the BiDil example illustrates, there is still a tendency to view population differences in health as outcomes of biological differences, while underestimating the social forces that contribute to health disparities that are important determinants of health.

STUDY QUESTIONS

1. What is a stressor? What is a stress response? How does allostasis differ from homeostasis?
2. What is the role of the autonomic nervous system in the stress response? What is the "fight or flight" response?
3. What is cortisol and what is its role in the hormonal stress response system?
4. What makes stress a more chronic rather than episodic issue for humans compared with other animals? How is social life itself a stressor for humans?
5. How is the cardiovascular system compromised by chronic stress?
6. How does cortisol influence energy metabolism?
7. Why is chronic stress associated with immunosuppression? How has this been demonstrated in "real-world" situations?
8. What evidence is there that stress is detrimental to children, both in utero and after they are born? What stressors in particular are children vulnerable to?
9. What did the Whitehall studies show about the relationship among stress, inequality, and health? What is the "status syndrome?" How does health vary among different countries according to levels of social equality and cohesion? What is lifestyle incongruity?
10. If race is a social construct, why is it important in health research dedicated in part to understanding the biological bases of disease? In the United States, how do mortality statistics vary across racial and ethnic groups, gender, and geography?
11. What is intersectionality, and how does it relate to stress and health?
12. What factors might explain the higher rates of hypertension among American Blacks? What is the contribution of "salt sensitivity?" What stressors may be important in variation in hypertension risk in the United States?

CRITICAL THINKING QUESTIONS

1. Is enough attention paid to alleviating stress in people's everyday lives? Should this be a major public health initiative?
2. In what ways is stress good? Is a totally stress-free life desirable?
3. What is your assessment of the role race and ethnicity plays in clinical practice and medical research today? Is enough attention paid to addressing disparities in health status among groups?
4. Consider the ways in which our need to understand biological differences (between sex, age, race/ethnic groups) runs into conflict with population stereotyping with respect to health. How does the BiDil issue fit into this potential conflict?

SUGGESTED BOOKS TO READ WITH THIS CHAPTER

William W. Dressler. 1991. *Stress and Adaptation in the Context of Culture: Depression in a Southern Black Community*. Albany: State University of New York Press.

Jonathan Kahn. 2013. *Race in a Bottle: The Story of BiDil and Racialized Medicine in a Postgenomic Age*. New York: Columbia University Press.

Michael Marmot. 2004. *The Status Syndrome: How Social Standing Affects Our Health and Longevity*. New York: Holt.

Michael Marmot. 2015. *The Health Gap: The Challenge of an Unequal World*. London: Bloomsbury Press.

Robert Sapolsky. 2004. *Why Zebras Don't Get Ulcers*. New York: Holt.

Richard G. Wilkinson and Kate E. Pickett. 2009. *The Spirit Level: Why More Equal Societies Almost Always Do Better*. New York: Penguin.

Mental Health and Illness

Chapter Goals

- To introduce the medical model of mental illness and its diagnosis in the context of a more general biocultural model of human health
- To establish the importance of distinguishing emic and etic perspectives in the cross-cultural study of mental illness
- To discuss examples of culture-bound syndromes and their definition and expression vis-à-vis the standard biomedical model
- To review eating disorders and reasons underlying their increase in prevalence in recent years
- To provide a biocultural perspective on mood disorders and schizophrenia

Human health and illness result from the interaction between our biological heritage and the cultural environment in which we live. Historically, mental illness has been the focus of intense debate about whether biology or culture (i.e., nature or nurture) has the more important influence. In general, biocultural anthropologists try to avoid nature–nurture-type debates—there is little sense in expecting that any complex human health phenomenon can be understood only in terms of genetics or the environment.

In this chapter we explore how a biocultural perspective on mental illness can take us beyond the false dichotomy of nature versus nurture. Such an exploration requires a historical perspective. Even today, we do not know the causes, nor do we have long-term cures, for many chronic, debilitating mental illnesses. Ideas about how to do best for patients with these conditions, or for how society can best control their behavior when it becomes problematic, naturally reflect broader cultural and intellectual traditions and trends. Too often, people with mental illness have lives that are characterized by cycles of recovery and relapse, undermining their ability to find a stable place in the societies in which they live. Although people with chronic physical ailments or disabilities face challenges, the uncertain status and stigma surrounding people with mental illness often make their lives uniquely precarious (Jenkins 2015).

During the twentieth century, mental illness became a focus of nature-nurture debates about human behavior. There were understandable historical reasons for researchers in the post–World War II era to turn toward the nurture perspective of mental illness. In the first half of the twentieth century, simplistic ideas about the Mendelian inheritance of mental illness and other conditions fueled the *eugenics movement*. Advocates for eugenics sought to "improve" the human species by preventing "undesirables," such as people with mental illness, from reproducing (Kevles 1985). The extreme eugenic views of the Nazis, who killed virtually all German mental patients as a prelude to genocide of Jews and Gypsies (Lifton 1986), prompted a postwar reaction against any genetic or biological perspectives of mental illness.

In the 1960s, antigenetics and antibiological perspectives on mental illness fueled a growing *antipsychiatry movement*. The antipsychiatrists, led by Thomas Szasz (1974) and R. D. Laing (2010 [1960]), portrayed mainstream psychiatry as a sometimes willing partner in the suppression of dissent, either indirectly (in developed Western countries) or directly (in the Soviet bloc nations) by labeling individuals with nonmainstream views deviant or mentally ill. Mental illness was seen to be less about the treatment of pathological behavior and more about the control of nonconforming behavior. The antipsychiatry movement was bolstered by the research of a new breed of cultural historians, such as Michel Foucault (Foucault 1971 [1961]). Foucault traced the factors that in seventeenth-century western Europe led to confinement becoming the "natural abode" of the "madman." Confinement remained the main way even liberal societies had for dealing with the severely mentally ill until the late twentieth century. Critical medical anthropology, which developed in the 1960s and 1970s, allied itself with antipsychiatry thinkers, sharing their critique of both biological explanations of mental illness and psychiatry in general.

At the same time as these antipsychiatry, antibiological views of mental illness were becoming popular, developments in mental illness treatment and research were laying the foundation for the emergence of modern, biologically oriented psychiatry. In the 1950s, the appearance of the first true antipsychotic medications lent support to the notion that major mental illnesses could be regarded as resulting from a "chemical imbalance" in the brain. Although far from being cures, in many countries, these new medications, which provided some measure of control over major psychiatric illnesses if not cures, precipitated the closing of asylums and other psychiatric facilities where patients were once housed indefinitely. Large and diagnostically sophisticated genetic studies in the 1960s also definitively showed that major mental illnesses such as schizophrenia were influenced in some way by genetic inheritance.

Since the 1970s, neuroscience studies conducted from the molecular to the structural and functional anatomical levels have shown that mental illness exists as a biological phenomenon. Clearly, the major mental illnesses—schizophrenia, bipolar disorder, major depression—have a genetic basis, although 60 years after this was established by pedigree studies, the exact genes involved have yet to be elucidated. Genome-wide scans have identified numerous candidate risk alleles for these conditions; the specific anatomical and physiological effects of these alleles are being enthusiastically investigated (Gatt et al. 2015; McIntosh et al. 2019). Contemporary psychiatry is increasingly biologically oriented, but it does not deny the importance of the family or larger sociocultural environment in developing or treating mental illness, and it sees both biological and environmental factors as critical for understanding mental illness.

The clinical treatment of mental illness at the individual level is done by psychiatrists and clinical psychologists. However, mental illness is a topic that transcends a narrow clinical perspective. By definition, a person with mental illness shows signs of "abnormal" behavior, and abnormal behavior can only be identified with reference to some standard of normal behavior. As we have seen with other definitions of health and the concept of biological normalcy (Chapter 2), normal behaviors are always expressed and defined in a cultural context. Thus, mental illness is an important research topic for anthropologists, sociologists, historians, and other researchers who are interested in how human societies work. Epidemiologists and evolutionary biologists also examine the expression of mental illness but focus on it at the population level rather than at the individual level. A topic as complex as mental illness must be approached from multiple perspectives. As we examine conditions such as eating disorders, depression, schizophrenia, post-traumatic stress disorder, and their expression in different cultures, we see that a biocultural perspective is essential for understanding them in the broader context of human health and disease.

THE MEDICAL MODEL IN BIOCULTURAL CONTEXT

The current medical model for the definitions and diagnostic features of mental illness is represented in the *Diagnostic and Statistical Manual of Mental Disorders*, Fifth Edition, otherwise referred to as the **DSM-5** (American Psychiatric Association 2013). This diagnostic compendium was produced by the American Psychiatric Association and represents the work of hundreds of clinicians and researchers to develop a consensus statement on the diagnosis of mental illnesses, from the mild to the severe.

The first version of the DSM was published in 1952. As a reflection of the collective clinical and scientific wisdom of the psychiatric community, the DSM has increased in importance and influence over the decades. The fifth edition of the DSM was published in 2013, and the process of producing this revision reflects the way Big Science and Big Medicine are done in the early part of the twenty-first century. The DSM-5 is the polished, depersonalized product of a community of scholars and clinicians (https://www.psychiatry.org/psychiatrists/practice/dsm). Dozens of work groups and committees, consisting of hundreds of researchers, spent years (1999–2008) preparing white papers and planning field trials. The field trial stage (2010–2011), testing the application of the new diagnostic criteria and categories, was conducted at 11 academic medical centers. In addition, a representative sample of 1,500 psychiatrists in "routine clinical practices" also tested components of the new manual. Furthermore, a volunteer sample of more than 3,000 psychiatrists, social workers, psychologists, and other clinical workers was also recruited and trained to participate in these field trials. Data from the trials were analyzed in 2011–2012, with the unveiling of the new DSM-5—14 years in the making—in 2013 at the annual meeting of the American Psychiatric Association.

The medical model of a mental disorder is reflected in this quote from the DSM-5:

> A mental disorder is a syndrome characterized by clinically significant disturbance in an individual's cognition, emotion regulation, or behavior that reflects a dysfunction in the psychological, biological, or developmental processes underlying mental functioning.

Mental disorders are usually associated with significant distress or disability in social, occupational, or other important activities. An expectable or culturally approved response to a common stressor or loss, such as the loss of a loved one, is not a mental disorder. Socially deviant behavior (e.g., political, religious, or sexual) and conflicts that are primarily between the individual and society are not mental disorders unless the deviance or conflict results from a dysfunction in the individual, as described above. (American Psychiatric Association 2013, 20)

The DSM defines both mental and physical illness in terms of the levels of disability and distress suffered by the individual. One of the critical issues in the diagnosis of mental illness arises when a patient does not have insight into his or her condition, fails to seek treatment, and thus becomes a danger to self or society. The medical model of mental illness must therefore address the relationship between the individual and society. The DSM-5 explicitly states that opposition to social norms—dissent and behaviors defined as socially "deviant"—does not correspond to mental illness. Thus, homosexuality is no longer seen as a form of mental illness (as it was, for example, in the DSM-II, American Psychiatric Association 1968) and the use of psychiatric confinement in cases of political dissent (as in the old Soviet Union) is strongly condemned.

An important point to remember is that according to its creators, what the various editions of the DSM seek to classify is not types of people but the diseases that people have. The anthropologist Sue Estroff (1989) has described the *I am* **illnesses** as chronic conditions that people do not simply have but also become. Physical illnesses, such as hemophilia or diabetes, fall into this category, as do the major mental illnesses, including schizophrenia and bipolar illness. For mental *I am* illnesses, it is often difficult to separate the disease from the self-identity of the person. Although some treatments for some forms of mental disorders require the development of this sort of self-perception (e.g., I am an alcoholic), most caregivers and researchers now avoid *I am* constructions. Hence, a person is not a "schizophrenic" but a "person with schizophrenia" or "someone who suffers from schizophrenia," not a "manic-depressive" but a "person with bipolar disorder." The diagnosis of a major mental illness is often a defining moment in a person's life, but the avoidance of *I am* constructions helps to prevent the illness from defining a person once the diagnosis is made.

The DSM is far from perfect, a fact that many critical anthropologists have been happy to point out. Psychological anthropologist Janis Jenkins summarizes these critiques: "Generally, among anthropologists there is a good deal of disdain for these diagnostic categories as historical inventions, biologically reductive, lacking in cultural validity, biased in relation to gender, ethnicity, and social class, and products of medicalization, potentially pernicious both socially and politically" (Jenkins 2015, 226). Psychiatrists have also pointed out the flaws in the DSM endeavor (e.g., Stein et al. 2013), although they are generally supportive of defining and validating diagnostic entities in support of clinical practice and research. Anthropologists have also found the DSM categories to be useful starting points for cross-cultural research, even if local and biomedical categories do not always align.

The DSM-5 does explicitly acknowledge that it is important to be sensitive to cultural issues around psychiatric diagnosis, especially in settings where the clinician and patient may have different cultural backgrounds. For example, religious practices or beliefs (such as hearing or seeing a deceased relative during a period of mourning) may be misinterpreted as a psychotic episode. Such potential cross-cultural misinterpretations are relatively obvious. However, there is debate concerning whether a diagnostic scheme like the DSM-5 can overcome more subtle but pervasive forms of cultural bias. For example, the class and cultural divisions between the caregiver and patient are not that important when diagnosing and healing a broken leg, but critics of the DSM-5 (and psychiatry in general) suggest that these divisions may play a much more significant role in the treatment of mental illness.

More than 100 years ago, when anthropologists and psychiatrists were first considering mental illness in "primitive" cultures, a commonly held view was that "madness" or any kind of mental illness was extremely rare or even absent in these cultures (Winston 1934). Mental illness was seen as a "disease of civilization," arising in susceptible individuals struggling with the demands of modern society. This view was replaced by the notion that mentally ill individuals could be found in primitive cultures, but that they were likely to fill the role of shaman or medicine man or woman (this did not mean that all such roles were filled by mentally ill individuals). This idea has been remarkably persistent despite several generations of critiques (Ackerknecht 1943; Peters and Price-Williams 1980; Stephen and Suryani 2000). As Erwin Ackerknecht wrote nearly 70 years ago, "We cannot any longer regard as abnormal a person only on the basis of certain fixed symptoms, disregarding the historical and cultural place of this person" (Ackerknecht 1943, 38). In other words, the "strange" behavior of the shaman, as observed by an outsider, should not be considered pathological until it is considered in its own cultural context. An observation of a Baffin Island Inuit makes the point more succinctly: "When the shaman is healing he is out of his mind, but *he is not crazy*" (in J. M. Murphy 1976, 1022). The behavior of a shaman is prescribed by his or her culture and must be consistent with the traditional expectations of other members of the culture. "Crazy" behavior is idiosyncratic and in some way violates cultural norms, which is not to say that such behavior is not shaped by cultural factors (e.g., many people with schizophrenia have the delusion that the government has implanted some sort of device into their head that controls their thoughts or actions).

Classic ethnographic studies of mentally ill people in their own cultures, such as Jane Murphy's (1976) work among Yupik-speaking Inuit on an Island in the Bering Sea and Egba Yorubas in Nigeria, Nancy Scheper-Hughes's (1979) analysis of schizophrenia in rural Ireland, and Sue Estroff's (1981) study of clients at a community mental health center in Madison, Wisconsin, provide a more nuanced picture of the mentally ill as the "other" within their own cultures. Mental illness is accepted as part of the personal narrative in the lives of some people and as part of the social fabric of most cultures.

Some medical anthropological studies of mental illness have attempted to reconcile the medical model with more culture-based forms of inquiry. The anthropologist and psychiatrist Edward Foulks's (1972) study of *pibloktoq*, or Arctic hysteria, looked at the expression of the condition in terms of the cultural context of Inuit life and in relation to the biopsychological status of individuals with the condition. Pibloktoq is characterized by manic episodes in which an individual may remove his or her clothing, run around wildly into water or roll around on the snow, make nonsense sounds, or speak uncontrollably. Foulks's analysis showed that individuals with pibloktoq actually possessed a range of conditions that corresponded to Western medical diagnoses (e.g., epilepsy or schizophrenia), but that there was no single condition that could be seen as a "Western equivalent," nor was there a biophysical correlate (e.g., calcium deficiency) for developing pibloktoq. Foulks argued that there was a combination of biological and psychological factors within individuals that could lead to the development of pibloktoq, the expression of which was shaped by the sociocultural environment of polar Inuit life (see below).

Carole Browner and her colleagues (Browner et al. 1988) have suggested that medical anthropological hypotheses about illness should incorporate both etic and emic perspectives (as described in Chapter 2). The etic perspective is provided by biomedical measures, whereas the emic perspective emerges from folk or ethnic categories of illness. Browner and colleagues analyzed a syndrome widely recognized in Latin America called *susto*, "a spiritual illness that occurs when one's vital essence, usually glossed in English as 'soul,' becomes separated from the body following a frightening or otherwise unsettling experience" (Browner et al. 1988, 685). Etic studies of susto sufferers showed that, as for pibloktoq, there was no specific Western medical disease that corresponded exclusively to the condition, although the DSM-5 (American Psychiatric Association 2013) relates susto to a variety of psychiatric illnesses, including depression and post–traumatic stress disorder. Susto patients were less healthy (from a combination of illnesses) and more likely to die than comparison subjects. Browner and her colleagues hypothesized that the obvious psychological stress of the susto sufferers serves to exacerbate the effects of their physical illnesses.

The examples of pibloktoq and susto demonstrate that different cultures can have different ways of identifying and defining mental illness. The DSM-5 is a "universalistic" diagnostic scheme, which is designed to be applicable across cultures, and is a valuable tool for all psychiatry researchers, including medical anthropologists. However, the role of culture in the expression of mental illness must be accounted for. As Steven Regeser López and Peter Guarnaccia write,

> Culture is important in all aspects of psychopathology research – from the design and translation of instruments, to the conceptual models that guide research, to the interpersonal interaction between researcher and research participants, to the definition and interpretation of symptoms and syndromes, to the structure of the social world that surrounds a person's mental health problems. (Lopez and Guarnaccia 2000, 590)

Careful research has also shown that some mental illnesses, such as schizophrenia or depression, appear in similar forms cross-culturally. Although the individual experience of mental illness varies depending on their cultural context, it is likely that many mental illnesses are rooted in neurobiology, and genetic factors may also be important in their expression. This suggests that evolutionary insights provided by a biocultural perspective may be useful as we try to understand the similar (or variable) expression of some mental illnesses across cultures.

CULTURE-BOUND SYNDROMES

Diseases such as pibloktoq and susto are sometimes referred to as **culture-bound syndromes**. These conditions are characterized by patterns of aberrant behavior or troubling individual experience, which are considered "illnesses" within a culture or set of cultures and which are given local names. They may or may not correspond to Western psychiatric diseases as outlined in the DSM-5. The term culture-bound syndrome has come under much anthropological scrutiny in the past two decades, especially for the way it has been used in various editions of the DSM (Hughes 1998; Nichter 2010). Although these critiques have several components, at their core is the idea that there is an intellectual, and ultimately clinical, disconnect between acknowledging the importance of culture on the one hand and then placing "cultural syndromes" (as they are now sometimes called) in a sort of waste-basket category outside of the main diagnostic scheme on the other.

Following the recommendations of a panel of cultural psychiatrists and medical anthropologists (Aggarwal 2013), the DSM-5 replaced the construct of the culture-bound syndrome with three concepts that may culturally inform clinical practice: (1) *Cultural syndrome* is introduced as a replacement for culture-bound syndrome; (2) *Cultural idiom of distress* is a phrase or "way of talking about suffering among individuals of a cultural group" that relates to shared concepts of pathology; and (3) *Cultural explanation or perceived cause* is a label or feature of an explanatory model that a culture uses to explain the origins of an illness or distress (American Psychiatric Association 2013, 14–15). As a guide to enhancing the cultural content of mental health assessment, the DSM-5 provides a Cultural Formulation Interview (CFI). The CFI has 16 questions designed to elicit pertinent cultural information—such as ideas about disease causality, social support networks, cultural background, and so on—from patients.

Because it is widely recognized, we will continue to use the term culture-bound syndrome, at least for this edition of this text, despite its apparent shortcomings. As Ronald C. Simons (1985a) points out, the concept of culture-bound syndromes is intrinsically ethnocentric, in that it privileges the Western medical model. Diseases such as anorexia nervosa (which we discuss in more detail later) or PMS (discussed in Chapter 6) have been described as Western culture-bound syndromes. Simons suggests that "petism"—living surrounded by large numbers of cats and dogs and their wastes and smells until the neighbors call the authorities—is an example of a culture-bound syndrome found in the United States and Europe (Figure 11.1). Like other culture-bound syndromes, it can be linked to a defined DSM-5 disease (namely, obsessive–compulsive disorder [OCD]), but it really stands on its own as a unique condition expressed in a specific cultural context.

A newly recognized condition in the DSM-5 is *hoarding disorder*, which now has its own diagnostic category, separate from OCD (Mataix-Cols et al. 2010). The DSM-5 working group that looked into the scientific and clinical literature on hoarding found that in its most serious manifestations, it certainly poses a threat to the health and well-being of people who exhibit the behavior. Although links to OCD are apparent in hoarding, they concluded that "the differences between hoarding and OCD outweigh the similarities" (Mataix-Cols et al. 2010, 570). They found that hoarding did not vary according to gender and that it is a universal phenomenon in that it is expressed in a

FIGURE 11.1 Some researchers have suggested that "petism" is a culture-bound syndrome of Western cultures. This Florida man has created a "cat ranch" for hundreds of cats. He has been labeled a hoarder and animal abuser.
Credit: © Lara Cerri/Tampa Bay Times/ZUMAPRESS.com.

wide range of cultural settings. A more recent study has shown that the DSM-5 criteria for hoarding disorder appear to be stable and valid across four diverse cultural settings (United Kingdom, Spain, Brazil, and Japan), indicating that it may be a universal form of psychopathology, although more research is needed in non-industrialized settings (Nordsletten et al. 2018).

A French Culture-Bound Syndrome

Over the past 200 years, clinicians have (sometimes reluctantly) recognized conditions for which chronic tiredness or exhaustion, in the absence of an obvious physical cause, is the primary symptom (Lian and Bondevik 2015). In the nineteenth century, this was called neurasthenia; currently in the United States, conditions such as chronic fatigue syndrome, myalgic encephalomyelitis, and fibromyalgia all share unexplained chronic tiredness as a symptom. Although these conditions can certainly in some cases arise from identifiable physiological factors (e.g., viral infection or autoimmune response), there is no known common underlying physiological etiology for them. As such, how these conditions are classified and treated by the medical and lay communities

is shaped strongly by wider cultural, rather than simply clinical, attitudes (Lian and Bondevik 2015).

The medical anthropologist Atwood Gaines (1992) studied a constellation of related conditions—*spasmophilie*, *fatigue*, and *triste/fatigue touts le temps*—that are widely recognized as diseases or medical conditions in France but not in other countries. In France, these are all considered somatic disorders, or diseases of the body, and they bear more than a passing resemblance to conditions such as chronic fatigue syndrome or fibromyalgia. Spasmophilie is a condition that was first recognized in the French medical literature in the 1950s; it showed a sevenfold increase in prevalence between 1970 and 1980. Symptoms include mild fatigue, body aches, mild nausea, listlessness, loss of appetite, sleep disturbances, and distractibility (many of these symptoms are associated with depression as defined in the DSM-5). Both health professionals and lay people recognize spasmophilie as a medical condition.

Stress is often thought to be the underlying cause of spasmophilie. According to Gaines, the French view that life is wearing, difficult, and burdensome is consistent with the existence of a disease that is directly related to the stresses of life. Vitamin deficiency is also considered a possible cause. For treatment, a physician is likely to recommend rest in secure surroundings or vitamins. Fatigue (literally "being tired") is an older version of spasmophilie (i.e., it was defined earlier), which recognizes tiredness itself as a disease state. For both blue- and white-collar workers, fatigue is (or was) an acceptable reason not to go to work, and a physician might prescribe rest for days or weeks as a cure. Again, Gaines sees fatigue as related to the French view of life as essentially burdensome; conditions like fatigue acknowledge that we all fall behind in our life struggles from time to time and need rest to catch up.

Finally, triste/fatigue touts le temps ("sad or tired all the time") is similar to the other two conditions, but with one important difference: there is a precipitating traumatic or stressful event that brings it on. The symptoms tend to be similar to those in spasmophilie or fatigue but more strongly expressed; the condition is also chronic and may last months or years. Gaines points out that following the DSM-IV, one could label this condition "chronic, reactive depression." The only problem with this, he argues, is that according to the DSM-IV, an otherwise healthy person cannot have a chronic, reactive depressive response to an event: a chronic response indicates a preexisting propensity toward depression. This is not the view of the disease in France.

In addition to their expression in the context of the pessimistic (by Anglo-American standards) worldview, Gaines (1992) links these conditions to others found in cultures throughout the Mediterranean region. He suggests that their origins as recognized disease states goes back to the notion of penance in the Catholic Church (i.e., the devoutly penitent were often thought to exhibit such signs) and to Aristotelian concepts of melancholia, which in Latin countries was a condition linked to the very bright and gifted. Gaines argues that over the centuries there has been a migration of these concepts from the religious and secular worlds to the medical world. The cultural importance of these "dejected states and dysphoria" was established in the religious realm, even positively so, which facilitated their reinvention as French ethnomedical concepts.

The culture-bound syndromes are essentially "folk illnesses," but they are no less real to the people suffering from them than those defined by Western medicine. Following the etic–emic model described earlier, the folk definition of a culture-bound syndrome can serve as a starting point for both biological and cultural investigations of mental illness in a given culture. Simons also emphasizes the importance of detailed observation in doing research on a culture-bound syndrome. After all, it is hard enough for an outside observer to understand normal behavior in another culture, much less behavior that is considered abnormal by that culture.

Amok and *latah* are two culture-bound syndromes that have attracted much attention from anthropological and psychiatric observers of other cultures (Murphy 1971). Amok has been known in the Western world for hundreds of years; the phrase "running amuck" has been in the English language since the mid-seventeenth century and amok itself has been mentioned in medical texts since the nineteenth century. The term is derived from Portuguese and originates in travelers' accounts of a specific group of courageous and suicidal South Asian soldiers. Over time, the term came to be used to describe a behavioral phenomenon seen in the Malay region and other parts of island Southeast Asia. In general, "amok" refers to a frenzied homicidal attack. In the Malay cultural context, however, an amok attack was seen to have a more specific form: (1) a period of brooding and depression before the attack occurs; (2) no connection between the outbreak and any provoking situation; (3) the subject committing amok acts with eyes closed; and (4) amnesia following the event. Amok attacks are almost always carried out by young men.

In the nineteenth century, amok came to be mentioned within the colonial Southeast Asian medical and legal literature with increasing frequency. At this time, the rate of amok was about 1 per 1,000 individuals per year, and thus even small cities would experience several incidents in a year (Murphy 1971). Numerous explanations for amok were offered, ranging from drug use to somatic abnormalities to a sense of frustration. By the 1920s, amok was more rare and often interpreted as a manifestation of cerebral malaria. In the 1930s, it was more likely to be interpreted as a local manifestation of a general psychotic condition, such as schizophrenia. In the 1950s and 1960s, reports of amok came in from other parts of Southeast Asia, including the Philippines and New Guinea, and again it was usually seen as a secondary result of a primary psychotic condition.

Henry B. M. Murphy, a pioneer in transcultural psychiatry, interpreted the decline in amok in the Malay region from the nineteenth century onward as reflecting basic changes in the expression and perception of the disease (Murphy 1971). Amok was most common during the initial period of European contact and colonization; it was a symptom of a society in transition. It is clear from the accounts of the time that the men who committed (and survived) amok attacks were not chronically mentally ill or psychotic. Amok was a consciously motivated behavior, occurring as a possible reaction to the stress associated with the loss of power and status during the beginning of the colonial period. Over time, amok became less common, as Malay society ceased to be a culture in transition and other avenues for alleviating social stress became available. Amok then became something that was undertaken only by the truly mentally ill, who were acting out a well-known cultural model of deviant behavior.

Murphy's scenario works well in the Malay cultural–historical context, but other researchers have pointed out that amok-type episodes occur in a wide range of cultures. Julio Arboleda-Flórez (1979) suggests that many mass-homicide events that have occurred in North America and elsewhere bear all the hallmarks of amok. These events (most commonly mass shootings) are almost always undertaken by men, usually in their twenties, who have no clinical history of mental disease. They had histories of impulsive behavior and poor emotional control, however, and at the time of the amok-like events, they were often in the midst of some sort of personal crisis or difficult life transition. Arboleda- Flórez argues that the amok individuals had an acute sense of the loss of control over their own lives and events surrounding them. The amok event was seen as a reassertion of control, even if the result was the complete obliteration of the life they once knew. Systematic research on amok-like cases (or "sudden mass assault by a single individual") indicate that across cultures, the men who perpetrate these crimes have similar personalities, indicating that amok itself is a local version of a more widespread phenomenon (Hempel et al. 2000).

Latah is another culture-bound illness from Southeast Asia. Unlike amok, however, no one is killed in a latah event, and indeed latah more often provokes amusement rather than fear. People with latah, or in a latah episode, may appear to be in a trancelike state, mindlessly mimicking the words and actions of people around them, obeying commands without thought, and hypersensitive to startle. It was first extensively noted by European observers in the nineteenth century, in many cases involving latah behavior among their Malay servants or assistants. In one case, "a cook was watching the cookhouse fire and was startled by the pot toppling over. A boy sitting with him made a grab to save the pot; but whereas the boy's hand stopped before reaching it, the cook's hand, in imitation, went into the fire, grasping the scalding metal" (Murphy 1971, 381). With deliberate cruelty, the boy repeated the motion, and the cook repeatedly imitated him, burning his hand each time.

In nineteenth-century Java, it was claimed that latah was so common that it could be observed every day in the streets. The expression of latah varied throughout the region; in some areas only women had it, in others, both men and women might exhibit it. People with latah were not considered mentally ill, and the condition was seen as separate from general mental functioning. By the twentieth century, it was in decline in urban areas but on the increase in rural areas. Murphy (1971) interpreted this pattern to be a result of the colonial transition beginning first in cities and then moving to the countryside.

Latah can still be observed in Malaysia. Ronald C. Simons (1985b) conducted fieldwork on latah in several Malay villages, each of which was home to several latah sufferers. Others in the villages found people with latah to be quite amusing, and they would deliberately provoke them, sometimes several times a day. Simons notes that latah-like conditions have been reported in many cultures. He suggests that latah and these other conditions are "culture-specific exploitations of a neurophysiologically determined behavioral pattern" (Simons 1985b, 44). The startle response is a basic human stimulus–response pattern. Some individuals are fast reactors and others are slow reactors. Simons argues that latah is a cultural manifestation of a "hyperstartle" condition, which may be found among individuals in all cultures throughout the world.

To test this idea, Simons attempted to find a group of "American hyperstartlers." He advertised in a local paper for people who startled easily and recruited 10 participants for his study. He found that although the individuals thought of themselves as unique, their experiences were similar. They were often and easily startled, which caused them to drop things or to swear. They tended to first notice this characteristic in adolescence, and others often startled them for amusement. Unlike latah, however, there were no reports of uncontrolled obedience or mimicking the acts of others. Nonetheless, although the condition was not given a label in American society, Simons did find a condition that resembled latah in several ways.

Simons made careful study of filmed latah events from Malaysia and Indonesia. He identified several subtypes of latah, including one that he called "role latah." People with role latah have the ability to take the initial uncontrolled startle response and mold it into a performance for others to enjoy. In some cases, the latah event starts as a performance, but during the performance, the emotional arousal it brings on leads to an actual hyperstartle response. "The 'silly' behaviors of *role latah* may include social commentary, teasing of others, and considerable wit and satire" (Simons 1985b, 51). In general, latah was seen among low-status individuals who could be teased with impunity. In Malaysia, the relative greater frequency of women with latah may reflect the fact that people feel safer provoking a woman rather than a man. Among the American hyperstartlers, they were most often provoked when they were younger.

Simons argues that latah and similar conditions arise out of individual variation in the universal capacity for startle. Although it may show cultural variation, it does not arise out of a specific cultural context. Simons finds Murphy's cultural transition model of latah to be a simplistic reading of Malay culture and history. The elaboration of the hyperstartle response into latah and the well-recognized role of the latah in Malay culture indicate that it cannot simply be explained as a manifestation of a culture in transition.

As discussed above, there is a growing consensus that the whole concept of a culture-bound syndrome leaves much to be desired. Although the term is still useful for identifying a group of conditions that have long been of interest to anthropologists and transcultural psychiatrists, more recent detailed analyses indicate that even "classic" culture-bound syndromes such as amok and latah are not strictly speaking "bound" to a specific culture. Pibloktoq, which we mentioned earlier, is another classic example of a culture-bound syndrome. Lyle Dick's (1995) reanalysis of the primary descriptions of the relatively few cases ever observed (around 40) casts doubt on its existence as a meaningful emic or etic category. Foulks's (1972) analysis showed that the condition, viewed from the etic perspective of biomedicine, was quite heterogeneous; Dick points out that term "pibloktoq" does not exist in Inuit dialects, and does not correspond to any emic category. He places the observations of pibloktoq episodes in the historical context of contact, colonization, and cultural disorganization experienced by Native circumpolar peoples beginning in the early part of the 20th century. Dick concludes that pibloktoq "did not constitute a specific disorder but rather encompassed a multiplicity of behaviors associated with Inuhuit psychological distress. These apparently included reactions of acute anxiety, symptoms of physical (and perhaps feigned) illness, expressions of resistance to patriarchy and possibly sexual coercion, and shamanistic practice" (Dick 1995, 23).

As it now stands, culture-bound syndrome is still a generic category for conditions that do not fit easily into Western classifications of mental illness such as the DSM-5. It is perhaps most useful as a conceptual and practical way of bridging between true emically defined conditions (such as susto and spasmophilie) and those that are defined by biomedicine. Clearly, as demonstrated by pibloktoq, and to some extent by amok, the historical and cross-cultural contexts in which some of these conditions were identified and imposed on cultures by observers need to be fully recognized and acknowledged.

EATING DISORDERS

In early 1983, media coverage of the death at the age of 32 of a well-known singer, Karen Carpenter, brought eating disorders to the attention of most of the American public for the first time. Included among the DSM-5 roster of eating disorders are **anorexia nervosa**, **bulimia nervosa**, and **binge-eating disorder**. Anorexia is characterized by the refusal to maintain a minimally normal body weight, whereas people with bulimia engage in repeated episodes of binge eating followed by compensatory behaviors such as self-induced vomiting, misuse of laxatives and diuretics, fasting, or excessive exercise. Binge-eating disorder is characterized by multiple episodes of eating more than most people would eat over a discrete time period, combined with a loss of the sense of control over eating. Bulimic behaviors combined with binge eating are often associated with anorexia. It is important to note that *excess* eating leading to the development of obesity is not currently included among the DSM-5 eating disorders, because there is no consistent association of obesity with a psychological or behavioral syndrome.

Anorexia—voluntary starvation—is a compelling condition, especially in a culture where access to abundant quantities of food is a given, and overconsumption is a much more widespread public health problem. The DSM-5 uses body mass index (BMI) (see Chapter 4) as a guideline for the identifying the "significantly low body weight" that is the primary physical symptom of anorexia nervosa. A BMI of 18.5 is generally considered the thin end of normal. Mild anorexia is indicated with a BMI of about 17; moderate anorexia, a BMI of 16 to 16.99; severe, 15–15.99; and extreme, below 15. Psychological factors in the diagnosis include an intense fear of gaining weight and the exhibition of significant disturbances in the perception of the shape and size of the individual's body.

Women with anorexia are typically amenorrheic (do not have menstrual periods). Dietary intake is severely limited, sometimes to a small number of foods, and purging or excessive exercise are often used to keep weight down. Self-esteem is strongly linked to body shape and weight gain. Weight loss is seen as an impressive achievement, and weight gain is considered a loss of self-control. Bulimia is more common than anorexia (prevalence rate of 1%–3% versus 0.5%–1.0% among adolescent and young adult females in the United States); bulimic individuals who are not anorexic also tend to have misperceptions about their body weight and shape. About 90% of all anorexia and bulimia sufferers are female, with onset typically in adolescence or early adulthood (Figure 11.2).

Beyond the obvious loss of weight, anorexia exacts a profound physical toll. At 6 to 12 years' follow-up, the mortality rate for anorexia is 9.6 times the expected age-specific rate; for bulimia, it is 7.4 times higher. Even at 20 to 40 years' follow-up, the anorexia mortality rate is 3.7 times the expected rate (Nielsen 2001). People with anorexia suffer from a wide range of skin, gastrointestinal, cardiovascular, and pulmonary problems; diminished bone mineral density; and multiple organ system dysfunctions (Mitchell and Crow 2006). They also suffer from a range of metabolic and hormonal dysfunctions. Neuroimaging studies indicate changes in gray matter volume of regions of the brain associated with regulating appetite (orbitofrontal cortex) and taste and body image (insula), along with loss in the structural integrity of the white matter (Frank 2015). Some studies also suggest temporary losses of overall brain gray and white matter volume while a patient with anorexia is ill with restoration of volume after recovery.

When anorexia came to widespread public attention in the 1970s and 1980s, there was focus on it as a new disease that predominantly affected white, middle-class girls. However, anorexia nervosa was first described in the medical literature in the 1870s, and "fasting saints," extremely religious women of medieval Europe (thirteenth to fifteenth century) who seemed to forego eating (save for a few herbs and communion wafers), had been celebrated for centuries (Brumberg 1989). There probably was a real increase in the rate of anorexia between 1950 and 1980 in the United States, along with an increase in reporting and diagnosis. In addition, women with anorexia in 1980s and 1990s weighed less than their counterparts in the 1930s, although they were taller as a result of better childhood nutrition (Brumberg 1989). Joan Jacobs Brumberg argues

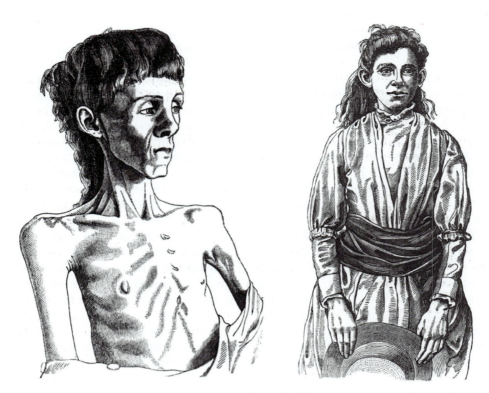

FIGURE 11.2 Anorexia nervosa has been in the medical literature since the nineteenth century, as demonstrated by these woodcuts of a "teenage girl suffering from anorexia nervosa" and of a "recovered anorexic patient" published in The Lancet in 1888.
Source: Courtesy of the National Library of Medicine.

that the intensification of anorexia in the 1980s was a result of a changing culture for women, in which physical fitness, self-determination, self-control, and a thinner standard of attractiveness combined to create a competitive environment conducive to the development of anorexia in increasing numbers of young women. As she writes,

> The way we experience anorexia nervosa in the 1980s is shaped by these recent and powerful accelerations in the imperative of female bodily control. The cult of strenuous exercise and the popularization of the "lite diet," for example, have had a clear effect on the symptom picture in anorexia nervosa. Although hyperactivity was associated with the condition in the nineteenth century, it was never, until very recently, a culturally sanctioned behavioral symptom. (Brumberg 1989, 255)

The power of the media to negatively influence eating behavior has been shown in a series of studies conducted by Anne Becker and her colleagues of adolescent girls from the Pacific island nation of Fiji (Becker 2004; Becker et al. 2002, 2007). Television was introduced to Fiji in 1995, during a period of rapid social and economic transition. Becker and her colleagues conducted two surveys of Fijian schoolgirls, one in 1995 before television was introduced and the other in 1998 (the average age of girls in both surveys was about 17 years). They found that significant changes in attitudes toward diet and body image occurred in just this relatively short period of time. Compared with girls in 1995, the girls who had been exposed to television were much more likely to be concerned with their weight and maintaining a thinner figure, modeled on the actresses they had seen on television. They were more likely to diet and engage in self-induced vomiting to maintain weight. As Becker and colleagues wrote, "The impact of television appears especially profound, given the longstanding cultural traditions that previously had appeared protective against dieting, purging, and body dissatisfaction in Fiji" (Becker et al. 2002, 511). Of course, the changes in attitude did not occur in a vacuum. Becker points out that the schoolgirls' changing attitudes were focused on "competitive social positioning . . . disordered eating among the Fijian schoolgirls in this study appears to be primarily an instrumental means of reshaping body and identity to enhance social and economic opportunities" (Becker 2004, 552). These goals indicate an obvious difference between Fijian and Western girls in terms of the attitudes underlying the development of eating disorders because the stereotypical Western sufferer is already someone from a privileged socioeconomic background.

It is important to remember that relatively few women develop eating disorders that can be defined as anorexia or bulimia (in contrast, "disordered" eating patterns are not unusual in the United States, where at any given time the majority of the population may be on a diet). Pedigree studies (family and twin) of anorexia and bulimia indicate that both conditions are genetically influenced. Heritability (the proportion of total variation resulting from genetic variation) for anorexia nervosa has been estimated to be 0.58 and for bulimia nervosa, 0.47 (Bulik et al. 2000; Wade et al. 2000). The fact that these numbers are substantially less than 1.0 indicates that there is also a sizeable environmental component in the etiology of eating disorders. Cultural influences play a role in affecting a proportion of the population (the size of which is currently unknown) that has an increased susceptibility to developing eating disorders.

Cross-cultural epidemiological studies indicate that anorexia can be found in populations throughout the world, albeit with somewhat different local expressions (Miller and Pumareiga 2001; Ritenbaugh et al. 1996). Although eating disorders were once thought to be rare or absent in minority populations in the United States, epidemiological data indicate that they are found among them, albeit at a lower rate than in European-derived populations. However, scores on tests that measure attitudes toward body image and dieting indicate that minority girls are developing attitudes that are more similar to those of "mainstream" U.S. culture. In other countries, anorexia tends to be found more commonly in more Westernized segments of the population, suggesting the role of cultural change or transition on the development of anorexia (Katzman and Lee 1997). For example, on the Caribbean island of Curaçao, cases of anorexia (nine in total) have been observed not among the majority Afro-Caribbean population, but among mixed-race, well-educated women, who saw themselves as part of the elite (mostly white) subculture and who actively distanced themselves from the black majority culture (Katzman et al. 2004). According to Melanie Katzman and her colleagues, these women were caught in "the crossroads of modern and traditional values." Their education provided them with an incentive and means to travel away from the island, but they discovered that they neither "fit in" off-island, nor were they comfortable within traditional Curaçao culture on reentry after time overseas. The an-orexic Curaçao women tended to have more anxiety and were more "perfectionist" than healthy comparison women in the culture (traits typical of anorexic women else-where), personality features that may have made this particular subgroup of women more susceptible to developing the disease (Forbush et al. 2007).

Anorexia is definitely present in urbanized Asian cultures (e.g., Hong Kong and Japan), although at a much lower frequency than in Western cultures (Miller and Pumareiga 2001). Increasing rates of anorexia in Japan have been ascribed to increases in urbanization, industrialization, and the breakdown of the family since World War II—in sum, Westernization. However, Kathleen M. Pike and Amy Borovoy (2004) suggest that local cultural conditions play a critical role in the expression of the dis-ease. Anorexic women in Asian cultures tend to exhibit less "fat phobia" and fear of weight gain than women in Western cultures (Katzman and Lee 1997). Pike and Borovoy (2004) argue that Japanese models of marriage, adulthood, and independence shape the expression of anorexia in Japan. For example, the thinness of an anorexic adolescent female may not only signify a desire to achieve an ideal of beauty but also represent a goal of delaying maturation and thereby rebelling against the "housewife" or other prescribed, dependent roles. In one of their case studies, Pike and Borovoy describe a Japanese woman who had gained weight while overseas and who subse-quently developed anorexia on her return. Although there is definitely a thin ideal of beauty in Japan, this woman's goal was not to achieve beauty but "sameness"—to fit in better with the population in general.

Despite the differences in rates and expression, the cross-cultural data reinforce the perspective that women are overwhelmingly the predominant victims of eating disorders. For Western cultures, it is generally accepted that the reason for this is that there is less of a societal emphasis on male body shape compared with that of females, but is this necessarily true of all cultures? In Western cultures, men who have sex with men have higher rates of eating disorders than heterosexual men (Miller and Pumareiga 2001), which could be evidence that within-culture gender role differences can account for sex differences in rates of eating disorders (this does not necessarily mean that homosexual men and heterosexual women share an un-derlying basis for developing anorexia, only that gender identity may be a factor). However, the cross-cultural pattern of a female bias in eating disorders suggests that there may be more basic factors underlying it (see later).

One way to examine attitudes toward body size and standards of attractiveness is to use a special kind of scaled questionnaire that consists of nine body silhouettes ranging from thin to fat (different ones for each sex), which can be used to survey people on their attitudes toward attractiveness in their own sex and the opposite sex. This method was pioneered by April Fallon and Paul Rozin in two classic studies from the 1980s (Fallon and Rozin 1985; Rozin and Fallon 1988). In their first study, Fallon and Rozin asked their subjects (American college students) to use the scale to point out their current figure, their ideal figure, and the figure they thought was most attractive to the opposite sex. In general, the males saw themselves as being close to the male ideal, which in turn was what they thought was close to what females found to be most attractive. The female students saw themselves as substantially heavier than their own ideal body size, the size they thought males would find attractive, and the size males identified as being the ideal for women. Women thought that men preferred a thinner body type than they actually did, and the women's ideal body type was even thinner than they thought men would like. Similar studies done in other cultural settings provide somewhat different results. African American women identify thinness as an ideal but tend to have less body dissatisfaction than European Americans even if their weights are higher. Rates of anorexia are lower in African Americans (Altabe 1998). Among contemporary Samoans, who come from a culture that traditionally identifies large body size as attractive, body image studies indicate that thinness is also an attractive ideal (Brewis et al. 1998).

There is no doubt that the attractive ideal for women in American society over the course of the later twentieth century became progressively thinner, as reflected in popular personalities and images of female beauty. What was driving this change toward thinness? The results from the Fallon and Rozin study (and others) indicate that it was not a matter of male preference changing, but female preferences. Miller and Pumariega (2001, 104) point out that eating disorders seem "more likely to develop during periods of affluence that were coupled with more egalitarian opportunities for women." Is the fact that increasing numbers of women were likely to see thinness—a proxy for self-control—as a personal ideal a consequence of the greater amount of self-control women were achieving in other domains? As conflicts still arise over traditional and nontraditional roles for women, even in Western industrialized nations, similar conflicts and anxieties for individual women may not be so dissimilar to those for women in transitional or Westernizing cultures (Katzman and Lee 1997).

Because eating disorders have a genetic component, evolutionary models have been offered to explain their prevalence. Like the cultural transition model, evolutionary models also tend to focus on environmental disruption as a triggering mechanism or stress that may lead to the development of eating disorders in susceptible individuals. Riadh Abed (1998) has proposed an evolutionary model of eating disorders based on sexual selection theory. Intrasexual competition, the way members of one sex compete with one another to gain reproductive access to members of the opposite sex, is at the core of his model. Abed points out that many surveys (e.g., Buss 2003) have shown that "nubile" females—younger women with high reproductive potential—are seen as most attractive by men across cultures (all other things being equal). Nubile women tend to be thinner than older women, even in societies where thinness per se is not considered an important feature of attractiveness. In contemporary Western societies, "pseudo-nubile" females abound; these are women of reproductive age who do not reproduce or who delay reproduction (as may be common in the very low fertility contexts of many developed countries) and who maintain on average a relatively thinner, more youthful figure. Abed argues that sexual selection in humans has led to women being particularly attuned to their own attractiveness; the presence of large numbers of pseudo-nubile and nubile females in low-fertility societies thus intensifies intrasexual competition among women. Such an environment is one in which the drive for thinness (as well as an overall youthful appearance) is intensified, encouraging the development of eating disorders in susceptible individuals.

Patienthood and Eating Disorders

In Western biomedicine, "patients" are individual wellness-seekers who consult with doctors or other health-care providers in order to receive treatment for ailments in their bodies. As anthropologist T.S Harvey writes, "biomedical 'patienthood' is neither a universal nor an intuitive way of being-in-the-world but, instead, a role produced and principally acquired in biomedical clinical interactions" (Harvey 2008, 578). In his research in Guatemala documenting encounters between Maya wellness-seekers and biomedical practitioners at government-sponsored clinics, Harvey observed patterns of interaction that were quite different from those one would expect in more typical biomedical settings. Maya might approach biomedical practitioners in groups of two to five, create narratives of ailments across multiple participants, present multiple bodies as the site(s) of sickness, or present themselves as standing in for physically absent "patients." Harvey pointed out that these interactions, which were more consistent with how Maya approached their traditional healers, were obviously quite different from typical biomedical consultations.

The definition and adoption of patienthood can vary cross-culturally (see Harvey 2008 for a broader discussion and other examples). In the biomedical treatment of mental illness, one of the main concerns is *resistance* to patienthood among those whom others may believe require treatment. Individuals exhibiting signs of mental illness are said to be lacking "insight" into their condition if they refuse to seek treatment; people who are addicted to drugs or alcohol are thought to need to acknowledge their condition before they can control it. Almost by definition, a person who is actively psychotic, delusional, or "crazy" cannot have insight, which becomes a major barrier to treatment—i.e., to becoming a patient.

The issue of patienthood is also relevant for the treatment of eating disorders. Many people with eating disorders might perceive that there is a narrow line between being lauded for weight loss and achieving a thin idealized body size or shape and receiving the medical diagnosis of anorexia that comes along with "excessive" weight loss. Other factors in which excessive dieting, exercise, or purging can also influence whether or not a person with an eating disorder sees themselves as a patient.

Ann M. Cheney and her colleagues (2018) interviewed young women in southern Italy who had histories of disordered eating. The morality of womanhood in this region is strongly influenced by Catholic traditions of self-sacrifice and selfless devotion to husband, family, and God. In the narratives of recovery, these young women told the investigators

the initial onset of disordered eating was not linked to a desire to lose weight or become thinner, but rather to emotional events or situations, such as the loss of a parent at a young age (necessitating greater responsibility to care for siblings) or taking on the responsibility to maintain an abusive relationship. The morality of self-sacrifice was embodied in food deprivation, while patienthood was rejected, sometimes explicitly so. What's important here, according to Cheney and colleagues, is that the road to recovery for these women was also morally centered and not framed in the context of a patient who is "cured." For one woman engaged in an abusive relationship, recovery from an eating disorder involved rejecting the moral burden of self-sacrifice placed on women, and instead embracing a feminist morality in which a woman's own needs were seen to be as important as those around her. For another, it was divine intervention that rescued her from the body-destroying affliction of anorexia and the soul-destroying habit of purging. She did not reject the self-sacrificing practices that led to her eating disorders, but in rebuilding her soul and regaining the ability to eat normally, she saw herself as arriving at a morally superior place, still dedicated to the ideal of serving others.

The culture of suburban southern California is quite different from that of traditional southern Italy, but moral imperatives still shape the experience of disordered eating. Susan Greenhalgh (2016) has documented some of the effects of the United States' "war on fat" on the eating and dieting habits of young college students in southern California. The surgeon general's initiative (so far, unsuccessful) was initiated at the end of the twentieth century to stem the alarming rise in obesity in the United States. Greenhalgh examined ethnographic essays written by hundreds of her students detailing the diet and weight-control experiences of themselves or someone close to them. Of the 160 informative enough to be analyzed, a full quarter of them described someone with anorexia or bulimia nervosa. However, Greenhalgh was more surprised by the patterns she observed among those who had not been diagnosed with an eating disorder:

I was struck by the difficulty differentiating between subjects with eating disorders and those who showed "merely" severely disordered diet, exercise, and thought patterns . . . troubled eating was so normalized among the young people featured as to be simply ordinary behavior, expected of anyone who falls outside the normative weight, or thinks he or she does . . . 74% of the subjects engaged at some point in potentially dangerous weight-loss practices such as self-starvation, binging and purging, use of extremely low calorie diets, use of weight-loss pills, laxatives, and/or diuretics, use of cocaine or other strong drugs, and severe dieting coupled with excessive exercising. (Greenhalgh 2016, 551)

Of course, there was individual variation in the dieting stories people told, reflecting their own ethnic, socioeconomic, family, and peer-group histories. But Greenhalgh argues that the war on fat helps to create an environment that intensifies the pressures to lose weight and engage in risky dietary behavior. As "pathological" behaviors are normalized, it is clear that the threshold for patienthood is shifting, which will put more people at risk for suffering from the more severe consequences of disordered eating.

A final issue that we will address in connection with eating disorders is that of *stigma*. Erving Goffman defined stigma in a sociological sense as "an attribute that is deeply discrediting" (Goffman 1963, 12). He pointed out that the attribute itself is not necessarily stigmatizing on its own but depends on who possesses it. A 300-pound man losing 100 pounds is congratulated by society, but a woman who starts at 120 pounds and loses 30 may be defined as having an eating disorder. Although there have been exceptions, mental illness has generally been a stigmatizing attribute in both Western and other cultures. Many efforts have been made over the past few decades to reduce the stigma associated with mental illness.

Stigma is relevant to eating disorders for two reasons. First, as the idea that thin is attractive has become more pervasive, the stigma associated with obesity has been increasing. Alexandra Brewis and her colleagues conducted a 10-nation survey (Samoa, Argentina, Iceland, United Kingdom, Mexico, New Zealand, Paraguay, Puerto Rico, United States, and Tanzania) to determine the level of fat stigma in each country, along with attitudes about personal responsibility toward obesity. They found that in all countries except Tanzania (the only African nation and one without obesity as a public health issue), fat and obesity were significantly stigmatized. In addition, they found cross-cultural support for the idea that fatness or obesity forms the basis for judging the personal qualities of an individual. Brewis and colleagues concluded, "These analyses suggest that norms about fat-as-bad and fat-as-unhealthy are spreading globally and that cultural diversity in conceptions of ideal or acceptable body size appears to be on the decline" (Brewis et al. 2011, 274).

Fat stigma may fuel the development of eating disorders, which in turn appear to be highly stigmatized themselves. Surveys show that people with eating disorders are ascribed far more negative and stigmatizing attributes than healthy people or those with a straightforward physical condition such as asthma, and they are also viewed more negatively than those with psychiatric illnesses such as depression or schizophrenia (Roehrig and McLean 2010; Stewart et al. 2006). Patients with eating disorders are more likely to be seen as responsible for their condition and more able to address the condition, if only they wanted to. They are also more likely to be seen as using their condition to get attention. One important consequence of this stigmatized view of eating disorders is that people suffering from them delay seeking help or treatment because of this negative perception (Becker et al. 2010). Stigma surrounding weight issues are complex, given that both morbid obesity and anorexia can be stigmatizing conditions. For men with eating disorders (although a proportional minority of the total sufferers, their absolute numbers would be more than a million in the United States alone), the stigma is doubled because they cope both with the condition and with the fact that they are of the "wrong" gender to be suffering from it.

ATTENTION DEFICIT HYPERACTIVITY DISORDER AND CULTURE

Attention deficit hyperactivity disorder (ADHD; also known as hyperkinetic disorder) has a worldwide prevalence rate of about 5% (Polanczyk et al. 2007). It is characterized by pervasive inattention, hyperactivity, and impulsivity and is associated with a broad range of negative social, academic, and economic outcomes in its sufferers. It is usually diagnosed in children rather than adults and is at least twice as common in boys as in girls. Although there is no cure for ADHD, the condition is often controlled with medication, usually an amphetamine-class stimulant. The most commonly prescribed drug for ADHD is Ritalin (methylphenidate), which is generally considered to be safe for children although there may be other medications with fewer adverse side effects (Padilha et al. 2018).

Concerns about the overdiagnosis of ADHD and the overuse of medications such as Ritalin are widespread both in lay and in scientific circles. In 2004 the *British Journal of Psychiatry* published a fascinating debate between two child psychiatrists centered on the topic "ADHD is best understood as a cultural construct" (Timimi and Taylor 2004). The "for" side was taken by Sami Timimi, an outspoken critic of the medicalization of childhood; the "against" side was represented by Eric Taylor, a prominent academic researcher in ADHD.

In arguing for the idea that ADHD should be understood primarily as a cultural construct, Timimi makes the following points:

1. There are no specific cognitive, metabolic, or neurological markers for ADHD.
2. Studies of ADHD prevalence vary from 0.5% to 26% of children, indicating widespread uncertainty about the clinical definition of the condition.
3. Neuroimaging studies have only looked at small samples and without appropriate, unmedicated, age- and sex-matched comparison groups.
4. Genetics show that ADHD is linked with being male and is associated with normal genetic variation, such as that associated with height.
5. There is no specific medication for the treatment of ADHD, and the medicines used for its treatment have been adopted without adequate research. The pharmaceutical industry has profited greatly from the widespread recognition of ADHD as a clinical condition.
6. That children are immature is a "biological fact," but culture dictates how we deal with that immaturity. ADHD propagates a simplistic idea that disengages parents, teachers, and doctors from their social responsibility to raise well-behaved children.
7. An ADHD diagnosis in an individual creates a potentially lifelong pattern of disability and medical dependence, discouraging efforts to develop proper problem-solving skills.

In arguing against the idea that ADHD is little more than a cultural construct, Eric Taylor makes the following points:

1. ADHD is a product of both genetic and social influences.
2. Consistent associations between brain structure and function and ADHD have been found in children with the condition, even those who are unmedicated.
3. Specific and robust genetic associations with the disease have also been found.
4. Severe hyperactivity is a strong predictor of poor psychosocial adjustment and is associated with an increase in accident rates, educational and occupational failure, and lack of constructive occupations or strong relationships. This is why it is important to treat the condition as early as possible.
5. Strong, specific environmental factors have not been shown to influence ADHD rates. In the United Kingdom, rates have been steady over decades, it is found in all social classes, and immigrant groups, who might be more likely to experience potentially stressful breakdown of family structures, do not show higher rates.
6. Social factors do affect the degree to which ADHD is seen as a problem. For example, in Hong Kong compared with England, there appears to be a lower threshold for the identification of "hyperactive" behavior in children, which may indicate that hyperactive behavior may be more disruptive in Hong Kong.
7. Careful clinical diagnosis of ADHD is always necessary; the diagnosis should not simply be made based on the reports of teachers or parents.
8. The absence of rigorous adherence to diagnostic criteria may lead to variation in rates of ADHD between countries. In the United States, some practitioners may be overdiagnosing the condition, as suggested by high rates of treatment for preschool-age children. The condition is probably undertreated in the United Kingdom.

The contrasting arguments of Timimi and Taylor are likely to leave an uncommitted observer more than a little confused. An epidemiological review by Guilherme Polanczyk and colleagues (Polanczyk et al. 2007) highlights the widespread variation in prevalence rates found in different studies but found no strong geographical patterning to explain the results. Rather, diagnostic criteria were the main source of variation. More recent meta-analyses indicate a "benchmark prevalence" of 7.2% for ADHD, with considerable variation among countries (Thomas et al. 2015).

The basic issue here is whether ADHD represents the medicalization of what is essentially normal child behavior. In some ways, the debate is reminiscent of concerns about the medicalization of pregnancy but with one big difference: there is no debate about whether a woman is pregnant! There probably is also no debate about the most extreme end of the spectrum in ADHD; there are children who unequivocally require medical treatment because their impulsive behavior is highly debilitating and disruptive and otherwise impossible to control.

However, most children diagnosed with ADHD are not at the extreme end of distribution of hyperactive behavior. If such behaviors are normally distributed in the population, then the vast majority by definition will be relatively mild cases. It is in the diagnosis and treatment of these cases that cultural factors potentially have their greatest impact. Parental attitudes about ADHD are shaped by multiple forces—the media, friends and relatives, health caregivers—which will play a large role in the decision about whether or not to treat a child pharmaceutically. In a qualitative study conducted by Manonita Ghosh and colleagues (Ghosh et al. 2016) among white, middle-class Western Australians, three themes concerning the decision to treat a child for ADHD emerged from parent interviews. The decision for treatment followed (1) the perception that ADHD was an impairment to school achievement; (2) a sense of relief that the condition was genetic and not the fault of the parents; and (3) the fulfillment of the responsibility to ensure that their child was "normal" and able to conform to social expectations. Underlying all three of these was a desire to enhance the self-esteem of their children. Parents were ambivalent about long-term stimulant use, but felt the benefits outweighed the costs. If the costs of ADHD were perceived to be not that high (e.g., if school achievement was not impaired), Ghosh and colleagues found that parents may not be as enthusiastic to pursue treatment. This suggests that ADHD is not necessarily perceived to be completely negative. Indeed, some parents expressed reservations about treating it for fear of losing the energy and creativity they thought it sparked in their children.

MOOD DISORDERS

Although no one really enjoys being sad, it is easy enough to appreciate how feeling sad may be good (Nesse 1991, 2000). In the short term, sadness may make our decision making more efficient, help us avoid unpleasant situations or circumstances, or even assist in clarifying in our own minds the nature of our attachments to other people or objects. However, being sad all the time helps us do very little: people who are sad for a long time ultimately become withdrawn and unable to muster interest in the world around them. In Western psychiatry, these people are called "depressed," although they could just as easily be called "withdrawn," because that is how they often appear to others.

Depression

Depression is the most common form of mood disorder, which is a category of mental illness in which a disruption in mood is the primary feature. The DSM-5 has nine criteria for "major depressive episode," of which a minimum of five are required for diagnosis. The criteria are as follows:

1. Depressed mood most of the day, nearly every day, as indicated by subjective report or observation made by others.
2. Markedly diminished interest or pleasure in all, or almost all, activities most of the day, nearly every day.
3. Significant weight loss when not dieting or weight gain (e.g., a change of more than 5% of body weight in a month) or decrease or increase in appetite every day.
4. Insomnia or hypersomnia nearly every day.
5. Psychomotor agitation or retardation nearly every day.

6. Fatigue or loss of energy nearly every day.
7. Feelings of worthlessness or excessive or inappropriate guilt (which may be delusional) nearly every day.
8. Diminished ability to think or concentrate, or indecisiveness, nearly every day.
9. Recurrent thoughts of death (not just fear of dying), recurrent suicidal ideation without a specific plan, a suicide attempt, or a specific plan for committing suicide.

According to the DSM-5, 80% of individuals recover from a depressive episode within a year with treatment. Thus, in the majority of cases, there is ultimately a remission of symptoms and a return to previous levels of functioning. However, in a significant proportion of cases, depression is ongoing or there are recurrent episodes. The risk of suicide in depression is about 30 to 80 times greater than for the general population (Goodwin and Jamison 1990).

Evidence for the biological basis of depression comes from multiple sources. Studies of brain anatomy and function using modern neuroimaging methods identify several areas that differ between depressed and nondepressed individuals (Lener and Iosifescu 2015). The actions of antidepressant medication point to two neurotransmitters, serotonin and norepinephrine, as being critical in the development of depression (Bleir 2001; Leonard 2000). Genetics also clearly plays a role. The first-degree relatives of people with depressive disorder are 2.0 to 4.0 times more likely to develop the condition than others in the general population (American Psychiatric Association 2013). However, depression is so common (lifetime risk of 10%–25% for women and 5%–12% for men) that it is clear that many people without an obvious genetic risk will develop the disorder at some point in their lives. The reason for this is that current molecular genetic studies point to major depression being a polygenic condition, with over 100 alleles contributing to its heritability (McIntosh et al. 2019). There is also substantial genetic correlation between depression and other psychiatric conditions, especially schizophrenia, bipolar disorder, and ADHD (McIntosh et al. 2019).

One problem with the word "depression" is that it is used to describe both an emotion and a disorder. As Arthur Kleinman and Byron Good point out, "depression then stands for two distinct states of persons: one normal, the other pathological" (Kleinman and Good 1985, 8). This causes confusion not only among researchers, especially those working in cross-cultural contexts, but also for people trying to deal with their depression or depression in someone close to them. Although there is some concern that depression has been overdiagnosed in recent years, the psychiatric community considers underdiagnosis of depression a graver problem than overdiagnosis. Studies show that depression is actually woefully undertreated, with only 30% or so of people suffering from depressive symptoms receiving adequate care (A. Young et al. 2001). This undertreatment must in part be caused by the difficulty in distinguishing normal from pathological depression, for both patients and caregivers alike. The problem of underdiagnosis is especially acute in older patients, where multiple medical conditions can obscure depressive symptoms (Morichi et al. 2015).

The fuzzy boundary between normal and pathological depression suggests that we should expect cross-cultural variation in the expression and diagnosis of depression.

Spero Manson (1996) has identified some of the basic conflicts that arise when trying to apply the Western, DSM concept of depression in a cross-cultural context.

1. Depression is characterized by both dysphoria (i.e., unhappiness) and somatic (bodily) symptoms. Whereas somatic symptoms, such as weight gain or loss, may be relatively easy to measure cross-culturally, dysphoria depends on a host of emotional factors that are likely to be influenced by local cultural conditions.

2. Cultures vary in terms of their definitions of self. Western cultures tend to be individualized and egocentric, with happiness and sadness defined in terms of the individual. Other cultures are more sociocentric, where happiness or sadness are based less on the individual, but rather are located in a web of social and familial interactions in which all people find themselves.

3. Words to describe mood vary tremendously among languages. Many languages do not have a term that corresponds exactly to depression.

4. Cultures vary in the expression of emotion, with some being highly expressive and others less so. There can be expressive variation within a culture according to gender or class. This makes it difficult to "calibrate" diagnostic practices across cultures.

5. Cultures vary in the proper context in which feelings, mood, and emotions are expressed. The psychotherapist's couch does not have an equivalent setting in many other cultures.

6. The somatic signs of depression will be described differently in different cultures. Somatic complaints (fatigue, restlessness, etc.) are important in the DSM definition of depression. Depressed patients from other cultures express somatic complaints in different ways. Nigerian patients complain of "heat in the head," "crawling sensations of worms and ants," "heaviness sensation in the head," or "biting sensation all over the body;" Mexican American patients with nervios (a culture-bound illness with a mood component) refer to "brainache" or the sensation that the brain is "exploding." (Manson 1996, 107)

Given these issues, substantial cross-cultural variation in the expression of depression should be expected. Lifetime rates of depression vary across countries, even where comparable diagnostic practices are used (Weissman and Olfson 1995). For example, rates in France and Lebanon are three to four times higher than rates in the United States or Korea. Despite variation in overall rates between countries, a consistent gendered pattern of depression has been observed: in each country surveyed by Weissman and Olfson (1995), the rate is significantly higher among women than among men, with the women's rate being on average about double that of men. Women's rates are higher beginning in the teenage years and continue to be higher across the life span. There is also the separate issue of depression associated with pregnancy. Around the world, 7% to 20% of pregnant women meet the criteria for major depression, with rates tending to be higher in lower-income countries (Biaggi et al. 2016). Depression treatment is complicated by the presence of the fetus. Studies of the impact on pregnancy of the most widely used class of antidepressants, serotonin reuptake inhibitors (which include fluoxetine [Prozac]), indicate that they may be associated with an increased rate of spontaneous abortion (Rahimi et al. 2006), and their use in the third trimester may increase the likelihood of the newborn experiencing a mild, transient *neonatal behavioral syndrome*, with central nervous system, motor, respiratory, and gastrointestinal signs (Moses-Kolko et al. 2005). The clinician and the expectant mother must evaluate the risks and benefits associated with the treatment of depression in pregnancy. Postpartum depression (ranging from postpartum blues to postpartum psychosis) is also relatively common. It is estimated that about 7% to 30% of new mothers experience depression in the months following birth (Parsons et al. 2012).

There is no generally accepted explanation for why women should have a substantially higher rate of depression than men. Certainly the increase in depression associated with pregnancy points to hormonal factors. As Myrna Weissman and Mark Olfson state, "Large shifts in progesterone, estrogen, cortisol, and beta-endorphin levels may contribute to postpartum depression" (Weissman and Olfson 1995, 800). However, although depression is a biological condition, it is also clear that multiple factors are important in its etiology. As discussed above, genetics are clearly a factor, as shown by twin studies and other genetic investigations (Kendler et al. 1993; McIntosh et al. 2019). However, stressful life events, previous history of depression, and neuroticism are also predictors of major depression (Kendler et al. 1993). Some researchers have argued that the particular stresses that women face in their lives (e.g., risk of being a victim of interpersonal violence, socioeconomic disparities compared with men, dealing with the changing role of women in society) make them more vulnerable to depression (Brandis 1998). However, there is little evidence to support the hypothesis that women's lives in general are more stressful than men's lives across cultures, and it is not well understood how this proposed stress actually leads to the increased rates of depression in women.

Evolutionary models for depression have been developed to account for sex differences in depression (McGuire and Troisi 1998), but they tend to predict higher rates in men than in women. Pleiotropic models in which depression is seen as the byproduct of genes selected for other reasons predict that reproductive-age females should have the lowest rates because depression would compromise their ability to attract mates or care for offspring. Another evolutionary model emphasizes low social status as a triggering mechanism for the condition (McGuire and Troisi 1998). Low or negative mood is an inevitable consequence of "losing" in the attempt to achieve social status; if this new status is not reconciled in some way, it could remain a chronic condition. This model again leads to the prediction that males will have more depression than females, because men, as good social primates, are generally more attuned to position in the rank hierarchy than women (McGuire and Troisi 1998). However, McGuire and Troisi also point out that the low-social-status model may be consistent with higher rates of depression in women, if in the context of interpersonal relationships, women are dominated by men, and depression occurs in the context of a "ritualized submissive response" (as a primatologist might describe it).

A variety of evolutionary explanations have been offered to explain how depressed and associated behaviors could be adaptive (Durisko et al. 2015). Such behaviors may lead to avoiding risks (being cautious), minimizing loses (giving up), promoting analysis (reasoning), recovering from sickness (resting), conserving energy (waiting), signaling social defeat (giving in), and soliciting resources (begging). Any of these normal depressive behaviors, combined with a genetic predisposition toward abnormal brain chemistry, extraordinary chronic or acute stress, physical injury, and so on, can lead to the development of clinical major depressive disorder. Zachary Durisko and colleagues (2015) suggest that identifying the underlying possible cause in terms of evolved function could help direct therapy for depressed patients.

From an evolutionary perspective, the high prevalence of pre- and postpartum depression is perhaps the biggest puzzle of all. It is common not only in Western countries, but also in industrialized societies around the world (Affonso et al. 2000). Postpartum depression undoubtedly has a detrimental influence on the survival of the infant and thus should be strongly selected against. Women from different cultures who suffer from postpartum depression often cite a lack of social support as a major precipitating factor in their illness (Stuchbery et al. 1998). In traditional cultures, birth and child care occur in a much more intensely social environment than in the contemporary world of medicalized delivery and nuclear families. Women in more traditional cultures may have experienced less postpartum depression than women today or had more social support when they did experience it; thus, the genes underlying postpartum depression persist without being selected out of populations.

Bipolar Disorder and Creativity

Bipolar illness, or manic-depressive disorder, is a widely known but relatively rare condition, with a prevalence rate of about 0.5% to 1.5% (Goodwin and Jamison 1990). It differs from depression (unipolar illness) in that the affected person experiences both depressive and manic episodes. A manic episode is defined as a "period of abnormally and persistently elevated, expansive, or irritable mood, and abnormally and persistently increased goal-directed activity or energy, lasting at least one week" (American Psychiatric Association 2013, 124). According to the DSM-5, it must include at least three of the following symptoms:

1. Inflated self-esteem or grandiosity;
2. Decreased need for sleep;
3. More talkative than usual or pressure to keep talking;
4. Flight of ideas or subjective experience that thoughts are racing;
5. Distractibility (i.e., attention too easily drawn to unimportant or irrelevant external stimuli);
6. Increase in goal-directed activity (either socially, at work or school, or sexually) or psychomotor agitation; or
7. Excessive involvement in pleasurable activities that have a high potential for painful consequences (e.g., engaging in unrestrained buying, sexual indiscretions, or foolish business investments).

Manic behavior can be delusional, as in cases of extreme grandiosity or in the attempt to carry out ambitious but unrealistic plans. Although most people with bipolar illness have manic and depressive episodes, a bipolar diagnosis can be given if a person has one or more manic episodes.

All the evidence points to a strong genetic component in developing bipolar illness (American Psychiatric Association 2013; Craddock and Forty 2006). Prevalence does not appear to vary across populations, although unlike unipolar depression, it has been relatively little studied cross-culturally. A reason for this may be that manic episodes are relatively rare and short in duration; several culture-bound syndromes incorporate manic behavior, so it may be reasonable to assume that something like bipolar illness is likely to be found across a wide range of cultures. As with depression, suicide risk is high in bipolar illness: about 35% of patients attempt suicide and completed suicide occurs in about 10% to 15% of cases (Goodwin and Jamison 1990). From a biocultural perspective, the most significant aspect of bipolar illness may be its possible association with the "artistic temperament." Kay Redfield Jamison, a psychologist who has written extensively about her own bipolar illness, has explained why such a connection may be warranted:

> The fiery aspects of thought and feeling that initially compel the artistic voyage—fierce energy, high mood, and quick intelligence; a sense of the visionary and the grand; a restless and feverish temperament—commonly carry with them a capacity for vastly darker moods, grimmer energies, and occasionally bouts of "madness." These opposite moods and energies, often interlaced, can appear to the world as mercurial, intemperate, volatile, brooding, troubled, or stormy. In short, they form the common view of artistic temperament, and as we shall see, they also form the basis of the manic-depressive temperament. (Jamison 1993, 2)

Three kinds of studies have been done to look for evidence for a connection between bipolar illness (and other forms of mental illness) and creativity (Figure 11.3). First, researchers have studied the biographies and autobiographies describing the lives of famous creative people to see whether they suffered from mood disorders

FIGURE 11.3   The poet and novelist Sylvia Plath detailed her own struggles with depression before committing suicide in 1963 at the age of 30.
Credit: Bettmann/Contributor

(Jamison 1993; Ludwig 1992). Second, detailed surveys have been conducted among creative people (such as writers attending a workshop) living today to see whether they suffer more than the general population from psychiatric disease (Andreasen 1987; Ludwig 1992). Third, researchers have looked at the close relatives of people with mental illness to see whether they can be found in creative professions (Karlsson 1970, 1984). In general, the results are consistent across these varied studies (keeping in mind that there may be a publication bias for positive results): creative people are much more likely to suffer from mood disorders, substance abuse, and other mental illnesses than people who are not in creative professions. One study showed that bipolar illness is particularly overrepresented (Andreasen 1987). The relatives of people with mood disorders are also more likely to be found in creative professions (writers, people with postgraduate degrees). A relatively recent review of the numerous studies conducted on the link between creativity and psychopathology concludes that there are many methodological issues in these kinds of studies that must be addressed to confirm a possible positive association, but that a link between bipolar disorder and creativity is supported (Thys et al. 2014).

Some authors have suggested that the reason bipolar illness is maintained in human populations is because of the compensating success of creative relatives of bipolar individuals (Richards 1981). One problem with this hypothesis is that there are few cross-cultural data available to test it. The link between madness and genius is especially poignant in Western cultures, and it is probably perceived in others as well, but there are undoubtedly limits on the extent to which it is possible to generalize the psychopathologies of Western writers, composers, and artists to other cultural settings. Individual creativity is a critical issue in human evolution, however, because our species is defined by extreme behavioral flexibility. This allows us access to "creative" solutions to problems that are not available to other animals. Bipolar illness or the genes underlying that condition may or may not be directly relevant to the evolution of creativity, but understanding cognition in bipolar illness may offer broader insights into how we developed our creative capacities as a species.

The Evolution of Substance Use and Abuse

The use of psychoactive substances, both licit and illicit, seems virtually ubiquitous, and the abuse of these substances is all too common. But why is drug addiction such a common human problem? Two different evolutionary analyses try to explain how people became addicted to drugs.

Randolph Nesse and Kent Berridge (1997) have provided an evolutionary analysis of psychoactive substance use that highlights the vulnerability of humans to the overall negative effects of these drugs. Their analysis is based on two premises: (1) neural systems that regulate human behavior and emotion have been shaped by millions of years of evolution to maximize fitness; these systems are exquisitely tuned to detect perturbations in the surrounding environment and to inform and direct appropriate responses

to environmental challenges; and (2) human exposure to abundant and readily available quantities of relatively pure psychoactive substances is relatively recent; they are a novel feature of the present environment compared with the environment of evolutionary adaptedness during which most of hominid evolution occurred.

Nesse and Berridge (1997) divide psychoactive drugs into two categories. First, there are those that stimulate positive emotions. These drugs affect the pleasure and reward centers of the brain to generate their effects. Drugs in this category include heroin, cocaine, alcohol, marijuana, and amphetamines. Taking these drugs can provide a sense of well-being or even a hedonic rush. In the past, these feelings were associated with fitness benefit. Thus, drugs that stimulate positive emotions are in fact sending a false signal to the brain of having achieved some sort of fitness-enhanced state. Nesse and Berridge point out that people who are less successful in social competition are more likely to use drugs of this kind, although there is individual variation in terms of drug-seeking behavior and susceptibility to long-term addiction. They argue that a "war" on drugs of this kind is likely to fail because they tap so directly into a fundamental component of the human nervous system and that it does not address the social situations that motivate people to seek out altered states.

A different class of psychoactive drugs includes those that can be used to block negative emotions. These are drugs (such as Prozac) that are widely used to control low mood or anxiety in people who are otherwise quite high functioning. Nesse and Berridge recognize that drugs used to fight depression or bipolar illness are necessary for some people, but they wonder about the widespread use of drugs to control relatively normal negative emotions. Anxiety and low mood are actually useful emotions in a variety of contexts, and they have been shaped by natural selection to facilitate appropriate responses to potentially negative situations. It is clear that some people are more prone than others to developing pathological depression, but Nesse and Berridge's analysis suggests that they represent one extreme of a continuum distributed across the whole population.

Nesse and Berridge emphasize the vulnerability of the human brain and its neural systems in the face of the recent introduction of psychoactive substances. Roger Sullivan and Ed Hagen (2002) take a rather different evolutionary view, at least in terms of the use (not necessarily the abuse) of drugs. Sullivan and Hagen argue that the use of psychoactive substances is nothing new in the human species. They point out that many traditional cultures, including hunter-gatherer groups, have long made use of psychoactive substances: Betel nut, the fourth most widely used drug in the world (after nicotine, ethanol, and caffeine), is chewed throughout Oceania, parts of South Asia, and East Africa, and the earliest evidence of its use goes back 13,000 years; Australian aborigines made use of nicotine-containing plants, perhaps dating back 40,000 years; tobacco was used throughout the Americas and was one of the earliest cultigens in the New World; chewing khat leaves is an ancient custom in Ethiopia and northeast Africa; and coca was domesticated in the Andes as long as 7,000 years ago. Most of these substances were taken orally and chewed, which allowed the active ingredients to directly enter the bloodstream via the mucosal layer lining the mouth (bypassing digestion in the intestines or metabolism in the liver).

Sullivan and Hagen note that in many cultures that use these substances, they are not considered "drugs" or medicinal, but rather "food." These substances are chewed for energy or to fight fatigue and not for their more subtle psychoactive effects. In fact, many have nutritional value beyond their psychological effects. For example, coca leaves are a good source of calcium, phosphorus, iron, and vitamins A, B_2, and E. The fuzzy boundary between food and drugs in traditional societies is evidence that the refined and purified form drugs take in contemporary societies is indeed an evolutionary novelty; however, people in traditional societies were able to maintain access to psychoactive substances even without modern processing techniques.

Sullivan and Hagen (2002) extend the evolutionary timeline of human–drug interaction well beyond the past 40,000 years. They point out that plant allochemicals (also known as secondary compounds), toxic chemicals that plants make to dissuade consumption by herbivores, have been a part of the environment over the entire course of human or even mammalian evolution. Over millions of years of coevolution, these allochemicals have come to mimic the form of mammalian neurotransmitters (and hence are available for us to exploit as psychoactive drugs). For example, the nicotine found in tobacco and pituri mimics the activity of the neurotransmitter acetylcholine (it is active at the "nicotinic receptors" of the system). In this sense, again, there is nothing novel about humans encountering and having to deal with psychoactive substances. Indeed, Sullivan and Hagen raise the possibility that the ability to absorb these substances through the mucosal lining of the mouth may be an adaptation to exploit the beneficial effects of some plant allochemicals.

Sullivan and Hagen propose that substance-seeking behaviors may have been selected for in humans and other mammals. Psychoactive substances may be just one category of "food" for which animals have evolved strategies for detection and exploitation. Sullivan and Hagen's view contrasts with that of Nesse and Berridge in that they see a great antiquity between humans and the psychoactive substances in their environment. Neither of these evolutionary models sees substance abuse as a problem that goes along with that. The two views differ in terms of the *motivation* for using psychoactive drugs: Nesse and Berridge see it fundamentally as a result of the mismatch between our neural machinery and the contemporary environment, whereas Sullivan and Hagen argue that the pursuit of neurotransmitter-rich substances may have been selected for long ago.

SCHIZOPHRENIA

The disease called **schizophrenia** is probably similar to what Yorubans traditionally refer to as *were*, Yupik-speaking Inuit call *nuthkavihak*, and Creole-speaking Papua New Guineans label *longlong* (Burton-Bradley 1973; Murphy 1976). Of course, in Western popular culture, schizophrenia is often thought—erroneously—to mean that a person has a split personality. Multiple-personality disorder is something quite different and substantially less common than schizophrenia. General estimates put the number of people with schizophrenia at about 1% of the population. There is clearly variation among populations in the rate of schizophrenia, although the reasons for this variation are not well understood at this point (Sass 1992; Torrey 1987). Careful diagnostic studies (Jablensky et al. 1992) conducted in a wide range of cultural settings make it clear that schizophrenia is a universal aspect of the human condition, in the sense that people with the disease can be found in almost any culture.

The DSM-5 diagnostic criteria include the following symptoms, each of which must be present for a significant period of time over a one-month period, for the diagnosis of schizophrenia:

1. Delusions;
2. Hallucinations;
3. Disorganized speech (e.g., frequent derailment or incoherence);
4. Grossly disorganized or catatonic behavior;
5. Negative symptoms: affective (emotional) flattening, alogia (poverty of speech), and avolition (lack of motivation or persistence to complete a task).

Only one of these symptoms is required if delusions are bizarre or hallucinations consist of a voice keeping up a running commentary on the person's behavior or thoughts or two or more voices conversing with each other.

People with schizophrenia may present with one predominant symptom category rather than all of them. For example, a person with paranoid schizophrenia would have predominantly delusional symptoms of a grandiose or paranoid nature and auditory hallucinations (also known as positive symptoms). Catatonic schizophrenia is dominated by negative symptoms, including immobility. It is important to keep in mind that the boundaries between schizophrenia subtypes are not rigid, and a person with schizophrenia may exhibit more than one subtype over the course of illness. The age of onset for schizophrenia is usually in the late teens or early twenties (women a little later than men typically). This is, of course, a particularly critical time during most people's lives, as they attempt to define an independent role for themselves in society.

Understanding of the neurological basis of schizophrenia was given a great boost in the 1950s with the discovery of reasonably effective antipsychotic medications (these improved the positive symptoms of schizophrenia; only in the 1990s were medications discovered that helped people with predominantly negative symptoms). For many researchers, the effectiveness of these medications represented proof that schizophrenia was not just a "psychological" disease. Extensive changes in the brain accompany the behavioral changes seen in schizophrenia (Bakhshi and Chance 2015; Pearlson 2000). There are both global (e.g., reduced gray matter and total brain volume) and regional changes in brain anatomy, including differences in the size and cellular organization of several regions and in the size of the cerebral ventricles, which tend to be larger in schizophrenia; functional neuroimaging studies show that there are multiple cognitive processing changes associated with schizophrenia; psychophysiological changes (such as eye movement abnormalities or differences in electrical signals generated by the brain) are prevalent; there are clearly differences at the neurochemical level. As Godfrey Pearlson states, "virtually every region of the brain is affected in schizophrenia" (Pearlson 2000, 558).

The genetic basis of schizophrenia has also been extensively studied. Results here mirror those of other major mental illnesses, such as bipolar disorder. Classical genetics studies looking at families, twins, or adoptions clearly demonstrate that people who are related to someone who has schizophrenia are themselves at significantly increased risk to develop the condition (Gottesman and Shields 1982). However, the search for a specific genetic basis for schizophrenia has turned up a host of possible candidate genes, with no definitive picture of the genetic basis of the condition yet to emerge (Craddock and Forty 2006; Lewis et al. 2003; Mantripragada et al. 2010). Almost all twin studies of schizophrenia indicate a concordance rate (percentage of twin pairs where both siblings are affected) of less than 50%, even for identical twins. This suggests that there is a large environmental component responsible for the development of schizophrenia. Exactly what factors in the environment, biological or psychological, might be relevant has yet to be determined, although many possibilities have been investigated (e.g., viral exposure, emotional environment of the family).

One of the most intriguing aspects of schizophrenia is the issue of how it is maintained at relatively high frequency (given its genetic basis) in human populations. Numerous studies looking at reproductive success in people who have schizophrenia (e.g., Erlenmeyer-Kimling and Paradowski 1966; Nimgaonkar et al. 1997) have shown that they substantially reduced reproductive rates; thus, there is a substantial fitness cost to having schizophrenia (there is not as convincing evidence for a fitness cost associated with bipolar disorder). This is especially true of men with the condition. For example, a study conducted in the Micronesian nation of Palau shows that of a group of 25 males diagnosed with schizophrenia (representing 40% of all known cases in the country), only 2 had married and they had produced a total of only four children (Sullivan et al. 2007). Not all studies show such a substantial fitness deficit associated with schizophrenia, but the trend is the same in other populations.

Schizophrenia thus poses an interesting evolutionary puzzle (see Brune 2004; Burns 2006 for reviews). As might be expected, there is no consensus on how schizophrenia evolved. All of the models posit that overt or clinical schizophrenia represents an extreme phenotype that is associated with genes that are also expressed (albeit less markedly) in nonafflicted individuals. In other words, there must be some avenue for compensating for the fitness losses associated with schizophrenia in nonafflicted individuals who possess some aspect of the schizophrenia genotype.

Three basic kinds of evolutionary models have been used to explain schizophrenia. First, heterozygous advantage models (similar to that used for sickle cell) proposed that heterozygous carriers of schizophrenia possessed some sort of fitness advantage. The problem with these models, which date to the 1960s, is that the genetics of schizophrenia do not correspond in any way to a simple Mendelian model. A second kind of model suggests that the schizophrenia genotype is maintained in populations because of increased fitness in related carriers, but that there is a frequency-dependent limit on the fitness advantage the carriers had. The advantage the carriers have (be it creativity or tendency to not engage socially) is only available to a relatively small proportion of the population at any one time; hence, there is a limit to how prevalent the genotype can become. The third kind of model is composed of essentially genetic load-type arguments. They suggest that the genes underlying schizophrenia are widely distributed throughout the human species and may be linked to the evolution of some fundamental aspect of human behavior, such as language or social cognition. In this view, schizophrenia is seen as a "cost" of social evolution: it arises as a result of relatively small perturbations (genetic and developmental) to the basic human neural plan, perhaps in conjunction with combinations of alleles that predispose an individual toward the lower end of the normal distribution in social competence.

The evolutionary models of schizophrenia inform us about schizophrenia at the individual level, in that they help us see human behavior as a continuum and not simply in terms of a clinical divide between normal and pathological. Anthropological studies of people with major mental illness provide us with a much more direct window into what it means to have schizophrenia. For example, in Palau (mentioned earlier), research by Roger Sullivan and his colleagues (Sullivan et al. 2007) suggest that differences in traditional gender roles may lead to differential outcomes for schizophrenia in men and women. In Palau, in the context of traditional patterns of reciprocal exchange and obligations, young women have a much more secure place in the household compared with young men (Figure 11.4). Women are expected to earn revenue for the clan in the course of marriage and childbirth, but the stresses associated with this are offset by maintenance of their traditional status in the home, even in the face of development and urbanization. If a young woman develops schizophrenic illness, she is likely to be cared for in the home and able to maintain at least some portion of her traditional obligations. In contrast to young women, young men in Palau are "floating." They have

FIGURE 11.4   The Palauan nurse Nancy Mengloi interviews a patient as part of a study of the expression of schizophrenia in this small Micronesian nation.
Credit: Roger Sullivan.

no meaningful social identity until they earn an income, marry, have children, and achieve meaningful political and economic status. Schizophrenic illness interferes with their ability to accomplish all of these socially prescribed roles and may contribute to the relatively poorer outcome in men with schizophrenia compared with women in Palau.

The nature of lives of people with major mental illness living in an urban U.S. community was described by Sue Estroff in her ethnography *Making It Crazy* (1981). Although this study was done decades ago, the community mental health care system she described is still the prevailing treatment model today. These community mental health centers developed following the introduction of antipsychotic medications in the 1950s. These medications led to the emptying of the large, state-run mental hospitals (asylums), which had provided the dominant means of housing and caring for the severely mentally ill since the nineteenth century (Figure 11.5). Estroff portrays the community of mental health patients (the majority of whom had diagnoses of schizophrenia) who made use of the services of a single community outpatient facility. She compared the center to a village arena; there was no confinement and the patients came and went as they pleased. At the center, patients received their medications, attended training meetings and recreational sessions, had holiday dinners, met for field trips, and so on. "Clients" were those identified as needing help with living skills; they interact with "staff," who recognize and seek to alter the behavior of clients (see box, Anthropologist in Action: Paul Brodwin).

FIGURE 11.5   The Central Ohio Lunatic Asylum, Columbus, Ohio, in an engraving from the 1840s. Until the 1960s, large numbers of severely mentally ill individuals were housed in facilities like this.
Credit: Courtesy of the National Library of Medicine.

Clients recognize that they have to survive ("make it") in the crazy identity role. A willingness to take on the crazy role is part of being able to survive in that system. Crazy is both a constellation of features identified by society and associated with a certain group of people; however, the crazy role is also defined by the people who inhabit it. Crazy can be defined as nonsensical, perverse, and contradictory. Estroff found that although the staff–client relationship was predicated on reducing craziness, there was still plenty of craziness to be had. Clients were described as acting crazy or being a crazy, but she points out the word crazy was not used as a pejorative in this setting.

Most of the patients Estroff interacted with had relatively poor work histories and almost all had a history of inpatient hospitalization (they were perhaps somewhat worse off than a more typical group of patients). Vocational and life-skills training were at the core of the center's mission, which emphasized social learning over psychotherapy. The center was reasonably well staffed with a psychiatrist, social worker, recreational therapist, psychologists, several nurses, and clerks. The clients lived in a variety of places: the local YMCA, halfway houses, apartments, or with parents.

Anthropologist in Action: Paul Brodwin

Health-care providers in a community mental health center work on a daily basis with chronically mentally ill individuals. These clients have severely debilitating conditions that make accomplishing everyday tasks, such as complying with medication and treatment schedules, difficult. In addition, the staff at these centers is caught in the middle between the clients and the bureaucratic administrators who (naturally enough) expect some form of quantifiable accounting for the funds (never truly adequate) that the center receives. The anthropologist Paul Brodwin's (2011) "ethnography of futility" captures the despair and helplessness that these health-care providers often feel as they deal with the same problems, pressures, and failures year after year.

For two years, Brodwin observed the work of a staff at a community mental health center in a poor neighborhood of a large U.S. city. The staff consisted of nine social workers and one part-time psychiatrist who were collectively responsible for about 75 clients living in the community. Although they ostensibly lived on their own, the vast majority of clients could not function without the help of the center's case managers. The treatment model the staff used is called Assertive Community Treatment (ACT). ACT is a well-respected method, endorsed both by government organizations and by advocacy groups for the mentally ill.

At the core of the ACT model is the treatment plan. During twice-weekly staff meetings, the staff reviews each client's case, going over his or her background, current status, and future treatment options. The staff identifies specific problems that each client must address, which are

FIGURE 11.6 Paul Brodwin.
Credit: Paul Brodwin/John Ruebartsch.

then linked to a multistep treatment plan reflecting specific goals and outcomes to address the problems. Some goals are short term and others long term. Short-term goals might involve regularly taking prescribed medications, meeting with the case worker, or letting the center's staff know about suicidal thoughts. Long-term goals could involve keeping a journal of thoughts and feelings and discussing them with the psychiatrist or improving a job or living situation. The treatment plan is not only for the client. It also serves as the official record of the clinic's interactions with the client for funding purposes. Ideally, over time, the fulfilled treatment plans developed for a client should become a narrative of that client's clinical and social progress.

Of course, in the real world, the narrative of progress almost never really develops. And this is what leads to the sense of futility experienced by the caregivers in the mental health center. Treatment plans are drawn up, but they do not mean much when clients refuse to meet with case workers or take medication, spend what little money they have on street drugs, lose access to housing and wind up in the streets, or when truly unexpected but inevitable emergencies or crises come up. Worst of all, many of the clients do not themselves embrace the idea of a narrative of progress: they have given up on any hope of bettering their situation. The treatment plans, which for bureaucratic reasons must always be maintained, can become a mocking reminder of the failure to progress. As one supervisor paraphrased a treatment plan for a particularly difficult, noncompliant client, "Take these [medications], stay in your housing. Take these, here's your food. Take these, don't die" (Brodwin 2011, 198).

Brodwin found that the caseworkers addressed their sense of futility in two different ways. Some caseworkers reach such a state of professional alienation that they ultimately have little choice but to move on. The majority, however, "reframe the time horizon." In other words, they look at what they do for the clients in the present and compare it with an even worse imagined future if they did nothing; or they look backward and focus on any evidence of improvement in the life or condition of the client. The only caregiver that Brodwin found who did not profess to a sense of futility was the center's psychiatrist. He could not accept that what he did could not make a difference. Partly, this was a function of his neurological model of mental illness: he strongly believes that each psychotic break or depressive episode contributes to on overall worsening of the client's condition. He sees psychiatric illnesses such as schizophrenia as progressive, degenerative diseases. Brodwin also points out that the psychiatrist is relatively empowered compared with the caseworkers, both by his ability to prescribe medication and by his education, which allows him a broader theoretical perspective on the course of illness.

The community model of mental health care will be around for a long time. There will be no return to the huge mental hospitals where patients are warehoused for decades on end. Just as unlikely is a great increase in financial support for the clients of the community mental health centers. Their treatment depends on those who do the difficult and often unrewarding work in these centers. Understanding the caregivers' attitudes and perspectives, and their extraordinary working conditions, could be one step in the direction of improving the care of their clients.

One of the most fascinating aspects of clients' lives that Estroff (1981) explored in detail concerned their attitudes toward medication. There are no cures for the major mental illnesses, only treatments to control the symptoms. Studies show that a significant proportion (25%–60%) of psychiatric patients is noncompliant for taking medications. There are many reasons for this—paranoia, side effects, loss of control to an authority, hostility and aggression transferred to medications, a tendency for patients to take less medication as they start to improve, and so on. Estroff found that about one-third of the clients she surveyed were positive about the medications, seeing their benefit, and, in some cases, deriving some satisfaction that their illness could be ascribed to a "chemical imbalance" that could be ameliorated by medication. Another third of the patients were more neutral about medication—they recognized their need for it and that it would be an ongoing part of their lives, side effects and all. The other one-third of the clients were strongly negative about medications. They expressed fears about the drugs they took, distrusted the psychiatrist's motivations for prescribing them, and in many cases refused to acknowledge that they had psychiatric problems that needed to be addressed.

Community mental health centers such as the one described by Estroff came into being after the introduction of antipsychotic medications in the 1950s and the subsequent emptying of most large residential psychiatric hospitals in the United States. The ongoing "homeless problem" is in part one of the results of this sequence of events. The relatively poor state of care of the mentally ill is not that much different today than it was described by Estroff 40 years ago. As she concludes,

> The real cultural craziness here is that not only do we describe these persons as pathologically dependent but we contribute to their dependencies. Not only do we view them as unintegrated within the community but we isolate them by constantly reminding them of their incompetencies and by introducing them to peers with whom they may be more comfortable.. . . We negatively value these persons, collectively and as individuals, for their differences and their dependencies, but we leave them with little chance to give us anything except "getting better" (which means being more like us). (Estroff 1981, 188–189)

Not all countries have embraced the community mental health model seen in the U.S. and elsewhere. Notably, Japan has been slow to adopt it, with the vast majority of patients with major mental illnesses, such as schizophrenia, still housed in mostly private psychiatric hospitals (Nakamura 2013). Japanese psychiatric patients have much longer (often lasting years) and more frequent hospitalizations than in countries with community-based treatment. The Japanese system is an outgrowth of a home- and family-based tradition of responsibility for psychiatric patients combined with government funding that favors the private hospital system.

Although the country has the highest number of in-patient psychiatric beds per capita in the world (Ng et al. 2010), Japan is beginning to develop community-based psychiatric services. Anthropologist Karen Nakamura (2013) has documented life in a pioneering community of care and support called Bethel, which has become widely known throughout Japan as a different way to help people with mental illness, especially schizophrenia. Bethel is located in a small, isolated, coastal town called Urakawa on the island of Hokkaido in northern Japan. Beginning in the 1980s, psychiatric patients from the local Red Cross hospital started to hold meetings in a church in the town, which formed the seed for the development of a unique community. The establishment of Bethel makes for a fascinating story, involving supportive reverends from the church, a charismatic and dynamic social worker, a psychiatrist from the local hospital who emphasized living with serious mental illness rather than curing or controlling it, and a core of enthusiastic and dedicated patients who helped get the operation up and running. Over a couple of decades, Bethel grew to own several buildings in Urakawa (which were cheap, since the area was economically depressed), operate businesses where patients could work, and put on an annual festival attended by visitors from all over Japan.

There are several ways in which Bethel differs from community mental health treatment in the United States. First and foremost, is the extent to which patients are involved in directing the activities of the community and how the structure of that community reflects the needs and desires of the patients. Although the patients are treated by a psychiatrist, helped by social workers and other caregivers, and receive guidance in financial and other practical matters, they are largely responsible for the paths they take, both collectively and individually. Their guiding principles, which Nakamura points out are largely inspired by their Christian faith or Alcoholics Anonymous, are as follows:

- Meeting is more important than eating.
- We want a workplace where we can goof off without fear.
- Move your lips, not your hands.
- We welcome prejudice and discrimination.
- From "auditory hallucinations" to "Mr. Voices."
- Trust in the power of the group.
- Weakness binds us together.
- Bethel's colors [diversity] make sales go up!
- We welcome the mixing of public and private.
- When you come to Bethel, your illness comes out.
- Let's value our lack of profits.
- Don't try too hard.
- Don't try to fix your illness by yourself.
- Just letting it be is good enough.
  (Nakamura 2013, 107)

It is obvious from these principles that the Bethel community members embrace their patienthood, but with some unique twists. For example, auditory hallucinations are referred to as *Gencho-sans* ("honorary voices"), and community members are encouraged not to hide the fact that they are hearing them but to share and receive advice about how to deal with them. Gencho-sans are distinguished from *Okyaku-sans* ("honorable visitors"), or negative self-thoughts, which anyone can have. Only people with schizophrenia have Gencho-sans. Anthropomorphized as a Pac-Man-like character, Gencho-sans have become a kind of mascot or symbol of the community, rendered on items sold to the public. Delusions are also encouraged to be shared with others and discussed (i.e., "mixing the public and private"). Every year at the festival, a grand prize is given for the best hallucination or delusion. The winners typically are those that foster group activity and support.

The success and fame of Bethel lead to increased demand and waiting lists to join the community. One change with the influx of new patients is that relatively fewer of them have schizophrenia, but rather personality, emotional, or mood disorders. A psychiatric social worker at Bethel told Nakamura that "she thought that while schizophrenia was easy to incorporate into the Bethel system, depression and personality disorders were more difficult . . . people with schizophrenia could learn to accept their illness and live with themselves. But people with emotional disorders had a much harder time . . . [because] they know what they could do if they were well" (Nakamura 2013, 203). If we look at the quote above from Sue Estroff, we can see why Bethel might be a particularly good home for people with schizophrenia: it is not a place where their "differences and dependencies" are negatively valued and there is no expectation that they be "more like us."

SLEEP

The final topic we will address in this chapter is generally regarded as sitting at the intersection between mental and physical health—and in many cultures, between the worlds of the living and of the dead—*sleep*. For all mammals and most other animals, including humans, sleep is a basic physiological requirement, although why this should be the case is still hotly debated. Sleep is regulated in the brain via two distinct processes (Lockley and Foster 2012). There is a *circadian cycle* that regulates daily sleep and wakefulness, which is influenced by exposure to light. A small collection of neurons (10,000 or so) in the hypothalamus called the *suprachiasmatic nucleus*, which receives inputs from the retinas of the eyes, is mostly responsible for this aspect of sleep regulation. We also sleep because we are tired and our bodies need to recover. This *homeostatic cycle* is regulated by pathways connecting multiple brain regions, involving several circulating substances and neurotransmitters that keep the brain and body in connection with one another. During a normal night's sleep, the brain is far from being totally at rest, and by measuring its electrical activity, different phases of sleep can be identified (Lockley and Foster 2012). The two main types of sleep we experience each night are *non-rapid eye movement* (NREM) and *rapid eye movement* (REM) sleep, cycling back and forth between the two forms every 90 to 100 minutes. The deepest sleep is obtained during NREM sleep, which is when problems such as bed wetting or night terrors can occur. During REM sleep, the body is rigid, except for the eyes, and there is a temporary paralysis. Dreaming can occur during either phase but is more vivid during REM sleep.

Although sleep is a basic aspect of human physiology and the negative impact on health and well-being caused by sleep has long been recognized, sleep was not really of clinical interest until the latter part of the twentieth century. To some extent, this was a result of sleep not being of widespread scientific interest until after World War II. For example, REM sleep was not discovered until the 1950s, which is the time when the sleep science pioneer William Dement began his groundbreaking work on the subject.

Following the basic science work, the end of the twentieth century saw a rapid and intense medicalization of sleep. The cultural anthropologist Matthew Wolf-Meyer (2012) has investigated the development of sleep medicine in the United States and conducted fieldwork among the staff and patients of a large midwestern sleep clinic. He summarizes how sleep problems went from being a personal to a clinical issue:

> In the nineteenth century, sleep's sovereignty was to be worked with on the part of the individual; through habitual practices one might allay whatever sleeping complaints he or she had. In the twentieth century, particularly in the latter half of it and the beginning of the twenty-first, sleep's sovereignty is met with an equal power, that of pharmaceuticals, of therapies . . . if sleep disrupts daily life, then it must be controlled. (Wolf-Meyer 2012, 77–78)

Wolf-Meyer makes it clear that people whose sleep habits differ from the prescribed eight continuous hours every night can have difficulty fitting in with normative work or school schedules. Managing sleep is to some extent about managing conformist lives. There can be no doubt that people with sleep disorders such as severe insomnia, narcolepsy, and sleep apnea (the repeated cessation of breathing during sleep, usually signaled by loud snoring) can benefit from pharmaceutical treatment or, in the case of sleep apnea, sleeping with a continuous positive air pressure (CPAP) device. Wolf-Meyer's case histories of people with these conditions show that many (but certainly not all) of them are satisfied with their clinical outcomes. With the growing medicalization of sleep, an increasing number of variant sleep patterns will be seen as pathological, leading to the situation in which "individuals come to understand their alternative orders as *disorders*" (Wolf-Meyer 2012, 127). This is a hallmark of medicalization.

Sleep disorders can lead to other health problems. For example, sleep apnea increases the risk for high blood pressure, stroke, heart attack, diabetes, and heart failure (http://www.nhlbi.nih.gov/health/health-topics/topics/sleepapnea). In certain extraordinary cases, sleep itself can cause death, or at least can appear to. During the 1970s and 1980s, a strange and deadly phenomenon was observed with alarming frequency, and almost exclusively, among Hmong immigrants (see Chapters 3 and 10) in the United States (Adler 2011; Young et al. 2013). This condition came to be known as **sudden unexplained nocturnal death syndrome** (SUNDS). At least 117 Southeast Asian immigrants died as a result of SUNDS, almost all of them otherwise healthy men, with a median age of 33 years and median time in the United States of 17 months. At the peak of the apparent epidemic (1981–1982), the death rate from SUNDS among Hmong men aged 25 to 44 years was 92/100,000; this meant that Hmong men were dying of SUNDS at a rate equivalent to the five leading causes of death for other American men in the same age group.

Later research has linked SUNDS to a genetic condition called *Brugada syndrome*, which is associated with cardiac abnormalities and death during the night (Young et al. 2013). Not everyone with Brugada syndrome dies from SUNDS, suggesting that other triggers, especially sleep abnormalities such as sleep apnea, may have a role in causing death. In general, the Hmong population has relatively high rates of sleep disorders (Young et al. 2013). Interestingly, SUNDS is no longer considered a problem among the Hmong (Adler 2011), suggesting that the initial stress of migration, transition, and assimilation played a role in the epidemic among the first wave of immigrants in the 1970s and 1980s. Later immigrants, arriving to an established community with more support services, did not experience an outbreak of SUNDS. This suggests a powerful role for the stress and anxiety of relocation on young Hmong men in the etiology of SUNDS.

The medical anthropologist Shelley Adler's (2011) research has placed SUNDS in the Hmong in a broader cultural, historical, and cross-cultural context. Adler begins with the phenomenon of **sleep paralysis**, a form of sleep disorder, typically occurring on wakening or falling asleep, in which an individual is fully aware but still experiencing REM-associated paralysis (or *atonia*). Adler refers to sleep paralysis as it is expressed cross-culturally as a *nightmare*, reflecting the term's original meaning as signifying a nocturnal visit by some being (Figure 11.7). Across cultures, the nightmare experience has several common features: a perception of being awake; a "realistic" perception of the surrounding environment (e.g., a bedroom where everything seems normal); an inability to move; an overwhelming sense of fear and dread; a sensed presence, often felt to be an "evil" presence; chest pressure—a common sensation that accompanies paralysis; difficulty breathing; supine position; and other odd auditory, olfactory, or

FIGURE 11.7 A visitor in the night compresses the chest of a sleeping maiden—a classic depiction of the nightmare/sleep paralysis. The Nightmare (1781) by John Henry Fuseli. *Credit:* Wikimedia Commons/Detroit Institute of Arts.

physical sensations. Given these features, it is not surprising that a nightmare is almost universally regarded as an unpleasant, if not terrifying, experience.

Adler demonstrates that sleep paralysis or nightmares are likely found in most human cultures. She lists more than 30 indigenous terms for describing variations on the same phenomenon. Some of these have historically been considered cultural-bound syndromes. For example, in Newfoundland, Canada, a condition known as *old hag* is widely known among the local population. People suffering from an old hag attack feel like they are being held down or someone is pressing on their chest, while they are dreaming or awakening, and they cannot move. The term "old hag" may have contributed to the word *haggard*, meaning to be tired looking, which is presumably how one would feel after a night following an old hag attack. In Japan, a nightmare-like experience is encompassed by the term *kanashibari*. Like old hag, kanashibari is perceived to be a kind of attack. The victims lie paralyzed while coming out of sleep and perceive a presence in the room. They then feel someone or something lying on their chests. Understandably, the victims feel an intense fear and anxiety.

In the Hmong, the term that corresponds most closely to nightmare is *dab tsog* (pronounced "da cho"). Adler (2011) describes this term as representing "the traditional

Hmong pressing spirit," one of many spirits and spiritual forces that inhabit the Hmong natural universe. In Laos, dab tsog spirits typically made their homes in caverns, which were avoided by women and girls for fear that they would be raped. Adler's interviews with Hmong in the United States demonstrate that dab tsog typically visit people in the night, "sitting or lying upon them, pressing down and squeezing them tightly, preventing their movement, and trying to suffocate them."

There can be little doubt that a dab tsog victim has suffered from a nightmare or an episode of sleep paralysis. The question is, how did dab tsog become SUNDS for a shockingly large number of refugee Hmong men in the United States? Adler's Hmong informants all agreed that they had never heard of someone dying from dab tsog back in Laos. Adler argues that a nocebo effect (Chapter 3) could have played a significant role in the expression of SUNDS at this particular time and place. With a high rate of sleep disorders, including sleep paralysis, coupled with a likely susceptibility to Brugada syndrome, the Hmong population carried with it a physiological vulnerability to SUNDS. The extraordinary and highly disruptive circumstances of their move from Laos to the United States put Hmong men especially under extreme and chronic stress. As Adler writes,

> In the United States, traditional support was disrupted by the tremendous social transformation that the early Hmong immigrants underwent in terms of hasty conversions to Christianity, the inability to practice traditional rituals, the dispersal of highly knit clans, the breakdown of the traditional age and gender hierarchy, and the need to learn a new language and to procure new means of employment. Hmong men suffered disproportionately from serious emotional stress due to changes in the traditional gender and generational hierarchy and the sudden inability to lead and provide for their families both financially and spiritually. (Adler 2011, 135–136)

With the loss of traditional religious practices, the Hmong lost effective traditional means to deal with a dab tsog attack. The stress of migration also lead to disordered sleep, increasing the likelihood of sleep paralysis and the expectation of a nightmare. When nightmare—a dab tsog attack—occurs, it manifests the worst fears of the victim, who feels exceptionally powerless to deal with it. The nightmare embodies a nocebo phenomenon, with the expectation of it occurring making it both more likely and more dangerous. Adler concludes "Like the nocebo, the night-mare cannot be categorized using conventional mechanistic models" (Adler 2011, 136). It reminds us not only that there is a connection between the health of the mind and that of the body, but how that relationship is influenced by the cultural environment in myriad ways.

CONCLUSION

Mental illness is found in all human cultures and recognized by ethnomedical systems throughout the world. In many different ways, our collective evolutionary heritage shapes the individual experience of mental disease. From depression to dementia, people are just as susceptible to developing mental illness at some point in their lives as they are to developing physical illness. We began this chapter by invoking the nature–nurture debate about human behavior and mental illness. The biocultural perspective shows that this dichotomy is false because determining causes and treatments for mental illness surely requires an understanding of both biological and cultural factors.

As we discussed earlier, people with mental illness bear the brunt of stigma—they are discredited not for anything they have done but for what and who they are. As Erving Goffman, in his groundbreaking analysis of stigma, has written (Goffman 1963, 2, 4): "Society establishes the means of categorizing persons and the complement of attributes felt to be ordinary and natural for members of each of these categories . . . people with a stigma are not quite human." Over the past few decades, great efforts have been made to reduce the stigma associated with being a member of a particular race/ethnic group or having a certain sexual orientation. The stigma of major mental illness has declined, but real progress seems to be elusive. Alexandra Brewis and Amber Wutich (2019) have detailed the five major ways that activists and other interested parties have tried to destigmatize mental illness. There have been attempts to *relabel* various psychiatric conditions (based on Goffman's insights), to *reframe* public perceptions of them directly, to *reeducate* the public in the hopes that increased knowledge would lead to decreased fear, to foster *connections* between individuals with and without mental illness to enhance empathy in the latter, and to engage in public *advocacy*, as seen when prominent individuals go public with their psychiatric diagnoses (e.g., the late Carrie Fisher and bipolar illness). Despite these efforts, stigma against the mentally ill very much still exists. Brewis and Wutich point out that this is particularly devastating for conditions such as depression, where the experience of stigma can exacerbate feelings of social and personal failure. The residents of the Bethel community in Japan embrace the very features of their illnesses that lead to stigma. They feel better about themselves even if social stigma still exists against them.

Though people are more educated about psychiatric illness now than they were in the past, it is just not enough. Depression medication is more widely prescribed than ever before, but it is apparent that there are many people with depression who do not receive treatment and many for whom medications are ineffective. Among celebrities, bipolar illness has become a sort of "hip," socially acceptable diagnosis, but schizophrenia remains in the shadows, hidden by phrases such as "nervous breakdown," "burned out," or "casualty of drugs." Substance abuse is recognized as a serious psychiatric issue, but the popular and legal attitudes toward the use of drugs and alcohol do little to anticipate the ultimate causes and consequences of abuse and addiction. With its acceptance of biological and cultural diversity—including "neurodiversity"—as characterizing features of the human species, the biocultural perspective supports a humanistic view of people who suffer from mental illness. The stigma associated with mental diseases has no basis in the larger evolutionary and cultural contexts in which human health and illness are expressed.

STUDY QUESTIONS

1. How is the medical model of mental illness expressed in the *Diagnostic and Statistical Manual of Mental Disorders?*
2. What is an *"I am* illness?"
3. What is pibloktoq? How does its expression intersect with biomedically defined diseases?
4. What are emic and etic perspectives? How are they important in the cross-cultural study of mental illness?
5. What is a culture-bound syndrome? Compare and contrast three examples.

6. What are anorexia nervosa and bulimia nervosa? How are they defined in the DSM-IV? How has the expression of eating disorders changed over the past 100 years? How can they be seen to be the result of both cultural and biological factors?

7. What are the most common forms of mood disorders? What complicates the conception and identification of depression?

8. What is the possible link between bipolar disorder and creativity? What evidence is there for this?

9. What is schizophrenia? Is it known in different cultures? Why is it an interesting evolutionary problem?

10. What does "making it crazy" actually mean? How do chronically mentally ill people adapt to the treatment regimes and practices required by society?

11. What is SUNDS? How does it relate to sleep paralysis among Hmong immigrants to the United States?

CRITICAL THINKING QUESTIONS

1. People with mental illness are sometimes characterized as being "others" within their own culture. In what sense is this perspective valid or invalid?

2. Are there any new emergent mental illnesses or new manifestations of old ones? How would you define them? What sort of treatments do they require?

3. How are the mentally ill stigmatized in our society? Or are they? Are there some kinds of mental illness that you would be willing to discuss freely with others and some kinds that you would not? Why or why not?

4. What has influenced your own experience of "patienthood?" Does your experience match up with biomedical expectations?

SUGGESTED ETHNOGRAPHIES AND OTHER BOOKS TO READ WITH THIS CHAPTER

Shelley R. Adler. 2011. *Sleep Paralysis: Night-Mares, Nocebos, and Mind–Body Connection*. New Brunswick: Rutgers University Press.

Alexandra A. Brewis and Amber Wutich. 2019. *Lazy, Crazy, and Disgusting: Stigma and the Undoing of Global Health*. Baltimore, MD: Johns Hopkins University Press.

Joan Jacobs Brumberg. 1989. *Fasting Girls: The History of Anorexia Nervosa*. New York: Plume Books.

Sue E. Estroff. 1981. *Making It Crazy: An Ethnography of Psychiatric Clients in an American Community*. Berkeley: University of California Press.

Kay Redfield Jamison. 1993. *Touched with Fire: Manic-Depressive Illness and the Artistic Temperament*. New York: Free Press.

Janis H. Jenkins. 2015. *Extraordinary Conditions: Culture and Experience in Mental Illness*. Berkeley: University of California Press.

Karen Nakamura. 2013. *A Disability of the Soul: An Ethnography of Schizophrenia and Mental Illness in Contemporary Japan*. Ithaca: Cornell University Press. (See also Nakamura's ethnographic film, *Bethel: Community and Schizophrenia in Northern Japan*, http://www.disability.jp/soul)

Susan Sheehan. 1983. *Is There No Place on Earth for Me?* New York: Vintage.

Matthew J. Wolf-Meyer. 2012. *The Slumbering Masses: Sleep, Medicine, and Modern American Life*. Minneapolis, University of Minnesota Press.

The Relevance of Medical Anthropology

In this book, we hope we have demonstrated that "getting sick" and "staying well" are truly biocultural phenomena. We have emphasized variation in health experiences across contemporary groups and across historical and evolutionary time. We have asked why health differs and why it changes. As biological and social scientists, we have analyzed health at the level of the population, society, and culture, as well as in a biological context that includes the evolutionary, developmental, and physiological bases of health. We have explored how cultures vary in locating and following the paths toward better health. The biocultural approach is also relevant to the health of individuals. After all, the clinical or therapeutic contexts in which individuals receive treatment are defined by their cultures, and the cultural environment defines in part the climate of risk for the development of ill health.

Patterns of health and ill health profoundly vary over time and across populations. This variation is a result of complex interactions among the environment, human behavior, and political and economic policies enacted at all levels of society, from the local to the global. Patterns of disease can be influenced by natural environmental changes, but social factors are far more influential in producing the variation in health status we observe in different populations today. For example, undernutrition influences health in myriad ways. Whether someone has a sufficient amount of food is not a biological issue, but a geopolitical and economic one. Thus, although in the very short term feeding can "solve" the problem, lasting solutions to chronic undernutrition will only come from social changes.

The biocultural perspective is essential for identifying the factors that contribute to variation in health between and within groups. It is only after we understand the complex interplay of these factors that we can begin to construct health policies targeting the factors that have the potential to affect health in sustained ways. There is no reason why health cannot be improved for all people, at least up to the levels of health and longevity enjoyed by the Japanese or the citizens of many Scandinavian countries that have favorable health statistics. Policies can act at the level of disease prevention, or once disease is established, they can ensure equal access to effective therapies. What are some of the salient factors that are at the forefront for achieving such a goal?

First, there is poverty. Looking across the spectrum of developed and developing nations, it is not hard to see that individuals in poorer countries have less access to adequate nutrition and clean water and less access to preventative and therapeutic medical treatment, and their governments lack the political and economic infrastructure to implement effective public health policies. Rapidly developing nations also suffer from the breakdown of traditional social networks and a loss of indigenous knowledge about healing. Furthermore, increased industrialization (which is often considered a means to alleviate poverty) may be coupled with increased exposure to air pollutants, other environmental toxins, and stress, all of which have widespread and potentially persistent negative health consequences.

Second, there is social inequality, a primary factor in determining health variability within cultures. Although social inequality is obviously linked to poverty, it is clear that patterns of health variability go beyond simple access to material goods. Social inequality dictates health-care priorities: Are the problems of men more important than those of women? Are those of adults worthy of more attention than those of children? In capitalist democracies, health-care priorities may be determined by those who have greater access to the media or direct access to legislators via paid lobbyists. Health care in the United States is in a slowly growing crisis because vast numbers of middle-class people (and poor people as well, of course) have inadequate or no health insurance; studies indicate that a substantial portion (just how substantial is a matter of debate) of all personal bankruptcies in the United States are precipitated by a medical crisis (Himmelstein et al. 2006; Dickman et al. 2017). Health systems reflect and embody more general patterns of social inequality. For example, although U.S. citizens are, on average, wealthier than those of Canada, access to health care is more limited for Americans in general, and disparities according to race and income are more pronounced (Lasser et al. 2006). The passage and implementation of the Patient Protection and Affordable Care Act (aka Obamacare) in 2010 has served to provide health-care insurance to more than 17 million Americans who had not had insurance before. Yet political and ideological debates about whether Obamacare or any form of publicly supported health insurance has a place in American society continue, reflecting wider disagreements about the role of government in substantively addressing social inequality in any way.

Then there is culture. The issue at hand is not whether cultures are intrinsically healthy (although some cultural practices may contribute to better or worse health), but how to use cultural knowledge to enhance individual and population health. Biomedical science has made great strides in understanding disease causation and prevention, but this knowledge is of little use if it cannot be disseminated and applied. What are the appropriate cultural channels for health education? How do biomedical practitioners complement and not simply supplant traditional healers? How do health-care providers maintain cultural safety? Specific cultures are the independent repositories of an abundance of knowledge about health and healing. Even from a strictly selfish perspective, everyone should support the preservation of such knowledge. After all, even a single medicinal discovery (such as quinine) can improve the lives of millions of people.

What about biological differences and their effects on health? At the group level, the most widely investigated variables are age, sex, and race (poorly defined according to a mix of sociological and biological characteristics), yet as we have seen, these are always shaped by sociocultural context. In industrialized societies, the association between age and disease risk has undergone a remarkable change over the past 100 years. Whereas once the mortality of the newborn and young because of infectious disease was the overriding factor in determining the health of populations, today the chronic illnesses (including cancer) associated with old age take center stage (i.e., the epidemiological transition). As we discussed earlier, aging is a fact of life, and we should be concerned that as biomedical science finds ways to prolong life, quantity of life takes precedence over quality of life. We can all hope to live as long as the average Okinawan today, but would it not be better to do so via lifestyle changes that prolong healthy adulthood rather than staving off death with medicine and multiple surgeries? Of course, it is important to keep sight of the fact that children in many countries are still at risk of dying from infectious disease and that the epidemiological transition is not yet a worldwide phenomenon. We must be particularly concerned with populations facing the "double burden" of chronic and infectious disease and recognize the ways in which traditional health intervention strategies may not be appropriate.

Sex is always an important variable in population health statistics. Beyond the different health concerns of men and women, it is reasonable to expect that sex differences will crop up in the expression of almost any disease or condition. However, the observation of a differential expression between men and women does not mean that it is solely the result of biological differences. Cultural gender roles dictate the size of social networks, work and activity patterns, access to food and treatment, and many other factors relevant to the health of boys and girls, men and women. There are significant biological differences between the sexes that influence health—for example, the bone biology of women makes them more susceptible to developing osteoporosis; conversely, men do not live as long as women when all else is more or less equal. What is important to keep in mind is that there are always overlapping experiences of health across the sexes.

Finally, there is race. Although anthropologists generally reject the formal use of the term for a host of good reasons, it is still used in society and in many clinical contexts. In this sense, how can race be profitably used to understand variability in health status? First, as a social construct, it is important to recognize that racial categories should only be used for understanding within-culture variability, not variability between cultures. When we use the term "African American" in a popular racial sense, we are referring to people who have experienced a particular population history. As we saw with the example of hypertension (Chapter 10), African Americans cannot be equated with Africans or Afro-Caribbeans, nor can they be defined in opposition to other recognized racial groups within American society. The term "African American" represents a group of people living today who share, to a greater or lesser extent, a common biological and cultural heritage. Today, that heritage is being actively explored and defined, in both biological and cultural terms. This is critical because it helps us move away from simply using African American and other social racial labels as a shorthand way of identifying people who look different from each other and instead allows us to see the U.S. population (for example) as the product of intersecting historical trends and events. However, it also forces us to consider the ways in which perceived biological differences lead to social differentiation that has important effects on health.

Geographic population variation is an essential tool for understanding the biocultural expression of health because geography encompasses genetic, cultural, and environmental factors important in the expression of disease. Racial categories have been used as a proxy for geographic variation, but they are not simply a replacement for understanding the particular factors associated with the expression of particular diseases. At the individual level, this can be critical because there are many people whose socially defined racial group is a poor match for their own biological or cultural history.

Although the biocultural perspective in medical anthropology takes population variation as a given, it does not lose sight of the fact that it is individuals who suffer from illness. The health of individuals is profoundly influenced by the groups to which they belong and the cultural and evolutionary histories of those groups. However, there is such tremendous individual variation caused by genetic inheritance, mixed with childhood experiences and adult behavior and living conditions, that understanding the causes of individual differences in health is terribly complex. Even most known risk factors contribute relatively little to an individual's likelihood of dying of a particular disease. For example, epidemiological studies show that smoking increases the likelihood that a person will die of a particular set of diseases (cancer, heart disease, emphysema, etc.), but at this point it is impossible to identify which disease will affect which smoker; indeed, despite the increased risk of contracting these serious diseases, many smokers die of causes entirely unrelated to smoking.

The world of health and illness is a dynamic one, and medical anthropologists have the tools to examine the effects of changes in health care and disease risk not only retrospectively but as they are happening. A fascinating example of this is an ethnographic study by Linda Hunt and colleagues (2017) on the impact of the recent introduction of electronic health records (EHRs) as an essentially required component of American medical care. In 2009 the Health Information Technology for Economic and Clinical Health Act (HITECH Act) was signed into law. This act encouraged and incentivized the use of EHRs, and by 2014 hospital use reached 93%. If you have visited a health-care professional in recent years, you may have noticed that the caregiver spends as much or more time looking at a computer screen as at you, the patient. That is because EHRs require the entry of health data into software, which requires the practitioner to follow a rigid series of screens, menus, and buttons to input coded health information.

EHRs work to the benefit of patients in that their health information is recorded in a standard, permanent, and easily transferrable form. But as critics have pointed out, they also work to help hospitals and insurance companies collect billing data and then mine that data to impose medical practice or to monitor the behavior of healthcare professionals. Hunt and colleagues (2017) observed interactions between providers and patients and noted that the amount of direct interaction with patients declined as more time was spent by providers looking at computer screens. Providers expressed ongoing frustration with the rigid way they had to enter information; sometimes they would not report potentially relevant information if the program did not let them do so easily. Even worse, the EHR software was clearly disempowering for the providers, as many of them felt that they spent more time trying to figure out what insurance would let them do rather than treating the patient as they were trained to do.

The changes brought about by the introduction of EHRs are relatively slow compared to the kind of action needed to respond to a health crisis or emergency, such as in an emerging epidemic or following a natural disaster. Medical anthropologists have the expertise to assist during these humanitarian crises, for example, in creating bottom-up responses to emerging situations and in finding ways to disseminate information (Abramowitz et al. 2015). However, as Sharon Abramowitz and her colleagues found in a survey of anthropologists concerning their involvement in medical humanitarianism, there was a sense in the anthropological community that they are on the outside when it comes to making and implementing humanitarian actions. Abramowitz and colleagues suggest that medical anthropologists should develop more of a focus on "policy and practice" in addition to "ethics and politics" when they enter humanitarian arenas (Abramowitz et al. 2015).

Like the subject matter it explores, medical anthropology is an always-expanding and -changing field. In sum, it is our hope that this book has provided you with new perspectives on problems of health and disease across populations and evolutionary time. For individuals and populations, health is primarily a function of historical, ecological, and sociocultural factors; when we see only the individual body as the sole locus of health or disease, valuable information about causation and potential solutions is lost. The many ways of understanding that context can only improve the well-being of all peoples and help individuals negotiate an ever-more-complex medical environment.

WHAT CAN I DO NEXT IF I AM INTERESTED IN MEDICAL ANTHROPOLOGY?

If this book has stimulated your interest in the field of medical anthropology, there are several ways of expanding your knowledge or applying the tools and perspective of medical anthropology in your career. The best resource for all matters related to medical anthropology is the Society for Medical Anthropology, a section of the American Anthropological Association (http://www.americananthro.org). The society maintains a website that is an invaluable source of information (http://www.medanthro.net) about medical anthropology news, funding, jobs, internships, and publications. Most jobs relevant to medical anthropology require training beyond the bachelor's degree.

Graduate Programs in Anthropology

If you are interested in pursuing medical anthropology training after completing an undergraduate degree, there are many anthropology graduate programs (master's and doctoral) that have a strong medical anthropology component. You can search for them on the main American Anthropological Association webpage (www.americananthro .org) or by simply searching for medical anthropology programs from an internet search engine. There are relatively few schools that actually offer a Ph.D. in medical anthropology, but there are some medical schools that have departments of social medicine, a closely allied field. Look for a program that lists medical anthropology as one of the key foci of the program and for faculty who have strong research interests in medical anthropology. Because medical anthropology is such a diverse field, look for a program that best matches your approach or topical interests. Many such programs are at universities that also have schools of public health, and these schools can provide additional training in epidemiology, biostatistics, and population health. Some schools offer joint anthropology and public health degrees. An anthropology master's degree usually takes up to two years; a Ph.D. is often about seven years (depending on the length of fieldwork). The Ph.D. is a useful degree for those wishing to pursue a research career, either in a university or health research center (such as the National Institutes of Health).

Some anthropology graduate programs emphasize applied anthropology work, as illustrated by the "medical anthropologists in action" described throughout the book. For those interested in applying the tools of medical anthropology to the development of health policy, interventions, or evaluation of existing programs, applied anthropology can provide these specific skills. For a good resource for programs and options in applied anthropology, see Consortium of Practicing and Applied Anthropology Programs (https://www.copaainfo.org).

Public Health Programs

Another option for graduate training is a master's of public health (M.P.H.), which you can get at a school of public health. The M.P.H. is a valuable degree for a variety of jobs in public health at the local, regional, state, national, or international level. As already noted, most universities with schools of public health have graduate programs in anthropology, so there may be opportunities to combine the M.P.H. course of study with some anthropology coursework. Like medical anthropology, public health is a diverse field; look for a school that offers coursework in areas of interest to you (infectious disease, chronic disease, international health, maternal and child health, mental health, etc.). For those considering a career in epidemiology, a Ph.D. in public health is the relevant degree.

Medical Schools and Clinical Health Professions

If you are considering going on to a professional training program in medicine, nursing, or one of the allied clinical medical fields, you can take the approach of medical anthropology into your clinical practice. If you would like to combine your clinical training with more training in medical anthropology, you might choose a joint M.D.–Ph.D. program. Having training in both clinical medicine and medical anthropology is a powerful combination, as Paul Farmer and Arthur Kleinman's careers exemplify. You can utilize your skills as an anthropologist while providing valuable clinical care to those you work with. Choose a medical school that has a department of social medicine or medical anthropology or one that has close ties to an anthropology department.

Work in Governmental and Nongovernmental Health Agencies

There are many health organizations around the world that you can get involved with, either now or after additional training. Among them are the World Health Organization, the United Nations, Amnesty International, Doctors without Borders, and Partners in Health (whose work you read about in Chapter 9; they also run a listserv for students interested in health and social justice—sign up for it at their website: http://www.pih .org). There are volunteer opportunities, as well as paid positions, that may require an M.P.H. or clinical degree. In the United States, the Centers for Disease Control and Prevention offers internships and jobs, and it conducts both national and international work on many different health topics. There is also the Peace Corps for U.S. citizens, which can place you in a health-related project, and the U.S. Agency for International Development. Do not forget about local health departments or clinics, which may also provide opportunities to gain experience. Be sure to check out the mission of any program you are interested in working for.

Genetic Counseling

Molecular genetics and genomics are having an ever-increasing impact on health care. Patients and family members need guidance dealing with genetic information that is not only complex but also associated with prophylactic treatments and interventions (such as a preventive mastectomy for those possessing the BRCA1/2 alleles) that would have been unheard of 20 years ago. New techniques may soon make modifications to the germline possible, which will open a whole new area of clinical intervention. The transition to a more fully genetic clinical medicine brings with it a host of potential conflicts and decisions, as patients must balance traditional with radically different therapies.

Genetic counselors must deal with people from all kinds of cultural, educational, religious, and socioeconomic backgrounds. An understanding of the biocultural nature of illness and treatment should be helpful in understanding how people reach health-care decisions and, in turn, helping them deal with the decision-making process. The website of the National Society of Genetic Counselors (http://nsgc.org) has information on genetic counselors and on genetic counseling as a career. A listing of accredited genetic counseling programs in the United States and Canada can be found here (http:// gceducation.org/Pages/Accredited-Programs.aspx).

As you can see, there are ample opportunities for students interested in medical anthropology. We hope that you will find the material in this book useful to you, whatever career you embark on.

GLOSSARY

ACUPUNCTURE A traditional Chinese medicine based on the insertion of fine needles, massage, or the application of heat at specific points on the body.

ADAPTABILITY Shorter-term, nonheritable physiological changes that occur in individuals when they are confronted with immediate challenges to their survival.

ADAPTATION A trait that confers some survival or reproductive advantage.

ADAPTIVE IMMUNE SYSTEM A part of the immune system found only in vertebrates. It involves recognition of specific pathogen characteristics (in contrast to the innate immune system, which recognizes general patterns).

ADRENAL GLAND A gland that sits just above the kidneys and secretes both epinephrine and cortisol.

AIDS Acquired immunodeficiency syndrome; the long-term consequence of HIV infection, in which immune function is impaired by infection and the individual becomes vulnerable to other opportunistic infections.

AIR POLLUTION Air in human environments that contains substances with harmful effects on health.

ALLERGY An immune response to antigens that are not, in and of themselves, deleterious. Characterized by release of IgE and inflammation of epithelial cells of the skin, respiratory, and gastrointestinal tracts.

ALLOSTASIS The ways in which "normal" function is maintained under different circumstances.

ALLOSTATIC LOAD The consequences of prolonged activation of the stress response, which usually are negative health outcomes.

ALZHEIMER'S DISEASE A form of senile dementia. Characterized anatomically by the accumulation of localized areas of neuronal cell death or damage (called plaques), which can only be seen microscopically.

AMOK A culture-bound syndrome known throughout Southeast Asia. Typically a frenzied homicidal attack performed by a young adult male.

ANOREXIA NERVOSA An eating disorder characterized by the refusal to maintain a minimally normal body weight. The DSM-IV diagnosis of the condition is given if a person is not maintaining at least 85% of his or her expected body weight, is intensely afraid of gaining weight, and exhibits significant disturbances in the perception of the shape and size of his or her body.

ANTAGONISTIC PLEIOTROPY THEORY OF AGING Genes that benefit an individual early in life and contribute to fitness but that may have longer-term deleterious effects are not selected against and may contribute to the increased morbidity and mortality associated with aging.

ANTHROPOLOGY A discipline that investigates the nature and causes of human variation and those aspects of life that are common to all of humanity.

ANTIBIOTIC RESISTANCE When bacterial species are not negatively affected by antibiotics (antibacterial compounds). Resistance can result from a number of different mechanisms.

ANTIBODIES Antigen-receptor proteins on the surface of B-cells. There are five classes of antibodies, each with a different function: IgA, IgD, IgE, IgG, and IgM.

ANTIGEN Any large molecule or cell that contains epitopes on its surface.

ANTIGENIC DRIFT The production of new antigens through mutations.

ANTIGENIC SHIFT Recombination of genetic material from multiple species. This is one means by which the influenza virus acquires new antigens.

APPLIED MEDICAL ANTHROPOLOGY A branch of medical anthropology that involves applying the principles and ethnographic knowledge derived from anthropological scholarship to the design or implementation of health policies and interventions.

ASSISTED REPRODUCTIVE TECHNOLOGIES (ARTS) Biomedical interventions designed to increase the likelihood of conception and a live birth, including in-vitro fertilization.

ASTHMA Constriction, inflammation, or both, of the bronchia (airways) of the lungs, usually resulting from an allergic reaction.

ATHEROSCLEROSIS Hardening of the arteries resulting from plaque buildup or inflammation.

ATOPY *See* allergy.

ATTACHMENT THEORY A psychological theory first proposed by the British psychiatrist John Bowlby in the 1950s that infants are born with a drive to "attach" to one caregiver, most often the mother.

AUTONOMIC NERVOUS SYSTEM The network of neurons involved in physiological changes that are largely unconscious (e.g., breathing, heart rate).

BACTERIA Single-celled prokaryotic microorganisms with cell walls.

B-CELLS Cells of the adaptive immune system that are made in bone marrow and that produce antibodies.

BIDIL A combination of two drugs that enhance blood vessel dilation and blood flow approved specifically for treatment of African Americans.

BINGE-EATING DISORDER Characterized by multiple episodes of eating more than most people would eat over a discrete time period, combined with a loss of the sense of control over eating.

BIOARCHAEOLOGY A field that focuses on biological remains to provide insight into past lifeways such as diet and activity patterns.

BIOCULTURAL PERSPECTIVE A perspective that considers the social, ecological, and biological aspects of health issues and, importantly, how these interact within and across populations and over evolutionary time.

BIOLOGICAL NORMALCY The assumption that all human biologies resemble those of one group. Historically, European biology has been considered the "norm" for the species and hence the "normal" type of biology. Others are hence "abnormal."

BIOMEDICINE The form of medicine that developed out of the scientific tradition in eighteenth-century Europe. It views disease as having a unique biological cause within the body.

BIPOLAR ILLNESS A widely known but relatively rare mental illness characterized by both depressive and manic episodes.

BODY MASS INDEX (BMI) Weight (kilograms)/height (square meters) (or to calculate it in pounds: weight (pounds)/height (square inches) × 703).

BRAIN DEATH Diagnosed when individual is in a coma (persistently unresponsive to stimuli) and unable to breathe on his or her own. There is no response to stimuli in the head: pupils are unresponsive; no sign of gagging, suckling, or swallowing; and no electrical activity in the brain.

BULIMIA NERVOSA An eating disorder characterized by repeated episodes of binge eating followed by compensatory behaviors such as self-induced vomiting, misuse of laxatives and diuretics, fasting, or excessive exercise.

CANCER Proliferation of malignant cells that, if they achieve broad distribution in the body, can fatally disrupt normal physiological function.

CARDIOVASCULAR DISEASE (CVD) Any dysfunction in the heart or circulatory system.

CAVITIES Tooth decay often brought on by a sticky, high-sugar diet.

CELIAC DISEASE An immunologically mediated sensitivity to gluten, a protein found in wheat, rye, and barley.

CHIROPRACTIC A clinical system developed at the end of the nineteenth century in the United States, which is based on manual manipulation of the musculoskeletal system to treat disease.

CHOLERA A waterborne bacterial disease caused by *Vibrio cholerae*. The bacterium produces a toxin that generates a profuse diarrhea, sometimes resulting in death from dehydration.

CIRCUMCISION In males, the removal of the foreskin of the penis.

CLITORIDECTOMY A form of female genital cutting in which the clitoris or clitoral hood is removed.

COMPLEMENT A "protein cascade" that is initiated on recognition of a pathogen.

CORTISOL A steroid hormone made from cholesterol that is secreted by the cortex of the adrenal gland. It is the main hormone that regulates the stress response.

CRITICAL MEDICAL ANTHROPOLOGY An analysis of how power differentials affect health.

CULTURAL RELATIVISM The evaluation of other cultures must not be in relation to another that is judged superior (which had often been Western civilization), but rather cultures must be understood or "made sense of" on their own terms.

CULTURE The beliefs, values, practices, and traditions of behavior of a group.

CULTURE-BOUND SYNDROME A condition characterized by a pattern of aberrant behavior or troubling individual experience, which is considered an illness within a culture or set of cultures, and which is given a local name. It may or may not correspond to a Western psychiatric disease described in the DSM.

CYSTIC FIBROSIS (CF) A genetic disease that is most common among populations of European descent. It is caused by altered chloride pumps in cell membranes, which result in a sticky mucus buildup outside of cells, especially in the lungs and gastrointestinal tract. Poor absorption of oxygen and nutrients results.

CYTOKINES Proteins involved in communication between immune cells.

CYTOTOXIC T-CELLS Cells that destroy cells with intracellular pathogens. They are involved in recognition, marking, and destruction of infected cells.

DEMENTIA Memory impairment, loss of decision making, judgment, and speech, among other symptoms.

DEPRESSION The most common mood disorder. Characterized by low mood, fatigue, thoughts of death, sadness, feelings of worthlessness, and diminished interest in pleasurable activities.

DIABETES (ALSO KNOWN AS DIABETES MELLITUS) A syndrome in which blood sugar levels remain high. There are two types: Type I (IDDM) appears to be immunologically mediated and caused by destruction of cells that produce insulin; Type II (NIDDM) is often caused by insulin resistance.

DIETARY REFERENCE INTAKES Standards for the recommended intake of nutrients.

DIRECT TRANSMISSION A means by which a pathogen spreads directly from one host to another (such as a respiratory pathogen).

DISEASE An alteration of physiology such that the function of a given physiological system is compromised.

DISPOSABLE SOMA THEORY OF AGING The idea that the somatic cells exist only to further the persistence of germ cells (eggs and sperm). The body is "disposable" because it only needs to be in a good condition through the normal reproductive life of the organism; there is no need to maintain it after that.

DSM-IV (*DIAGNOSTIC AND STATISTICAL MANUAL OF MENTAL DISORDERS*, FOURTH EDITION) A compendium of definitions and diagnostic features of mental illness, as developed by the American Psychiatric Association.

DUFFY BLOOD GROUP One of the red blood cell surface proteins. People without this protein appear to have resistance to *Plasmodium vivax*, a parasite that causes vivax malaria.

DYSMENORRHEA Painful menstrual periods.

EBOLA VIRUS DISEASE A filovirus that circulates in various places in sub-Saharan Africa and the cause of a large epidemic in West Africa in 2014–2015

EMBODIMENT The ways in which the environment in which humans live leaves traces in human biology or alters biological development in children

EMERGING (EMERGENT) INFECTIOUS DISEASES Diseases of infectious origin whose incidence in humans has increased within the past two decades or threatens to increase in the near future.

EMIC The perspective of members of a society.

ENAMEL HYPOPLASIA Bands of thin enamel in teeth indicate periods of growth disruption. Can be used to ascertain the relative duration of the growth stoppage, with wider bands indicative of more prolonged disruption compared with thinner bands, which indicate a shorter period of growth stoppage. Placement of bands also provides insight into the age at which the growth disruption occurred.

ENDEMIC A disease that has a long history in the population, with little change in either prevalence or incidence over time.

ENDOCRINE DISRUPTORS Any chemical (such as some pesticides or industrial chemicals) that alters hormonal function in ways that affect growth, maturation, and cognitive and behavioral development.

ENVIRONMENT OF EVOLUTIONARY ADAPTATION (EEA) The environment in which important aspects of an organism's evolution occurred and hence the environment to which they are best adapted.

EPIDEMIC A disease that dramatically increases its incidence and prevalence in a short period of time.

EPIDEMIC CURVE A typical course of an epidemic with a rapid rise in incidence followed by a decrease in incidence down to near zero.

EPIDEMIOLOGICAL TRANSITION A change in prevalence of diseases, such that one type of disease replaces another. Generally used in the context of a decline in infectious disease and a rise in chronic disease, as happened in wealthy countries over the course of the twentieth century.

EPIDEMIOLOGY The study of the distribution of disease in a population.

EPIGENETIC Changes in gene function or expression without changes to the gene itself (i.e., its nucleotide sequence).

EPITOPES Bits of proteins on cell surfaces that are identified by the host's immune system and possibly marked for distribution by immune cells.

ERECTILE DYSFUNCTION (ED) In males, the inability to achieve or maintain an erection.

ESTROGEN A hormone produced by the ovaries that is responsible for ovulation.

ETHNOGRAPHIC FIELDWORK Anthropological research that usually involves long-term residence in a community, speaking the local language, and participating in daily life as a member of that community.

ETHNOMEDICINE OR ETHNOMEDICAL SYSTEMS Healing traditions of a given culture.

ETHNOPHARMACOLOGY The study of indigenous medicines.

ETIC The perspective on a society from the view of an outsider.

EVIDENCE-BASED MEDICINE An intellectual movement within biomedicine initiated in the 1990s that advocates that patient care be based explicitly on the best available clinical research evidence; also recognizes that patients have rights in making clinical decisions about their care.

EVOLUTION Change in characteristics of a population over time.

EXCISION A form of female genital cutting in which the clitoris, along with part or all of the labia minora, is removed.

FAVA BEANS (VICIA FABA) A type of bean consumed in the Mediterranean that contains a compound called vicine, which is a potent oxidant that has antimalarial properties. People with glucose-6 phosphate dehydrogenase deficiency should not consume fava beans because it generates a profound oxidant stress that can be fatal.

FECUNDABILITY The ability to conceive.

FECUNDITY The ability to sustain a pregnancy.

FEMALE GENITAL CUTTING The removal of part of the female genitalia.

FERTILITY The production of a live birth.

FETAL ALCOHOL SYNDROME (FAS) A lifelong condition that causes physical and mental disabilities and is characterized by abnormal facial features, growth deficiencies, and central nervous system problems. It is caused by alcohol exposure during gestation.

FITNESS Reproductive success (in evolutionary terms).

FOOD INSECURITY A measure of the ability to access sufficient food.

FREE RADICALS Highly reactive molecules that contain at least one unpaired electron. These induce oxidative stress in cells and may contribute to the aging process.

FUNGI A diverse taxon of eukaryotic organisms; only a handful are significant pathogens of humans.

GERM THEORY OF DISEASE Robert Koch's demonstration that disease could be caused by microorganisms.

GERONTOLOGISTS Scientists who conduct research on aging.

GESTATIONAL DIABETES A form of diabetes (insulin resistance) that occurs during pregnancy and usually resolves after birth.

GLUCOSE-6 PHOSPHATE DEHYDROGENASE (G-6PD) An enzyme in a metabolic pathway that ultimately prevents hydrogen peroxide from building up in red blood cells. G-6PD deficiency results in higher levels of this potent oxidant and confers some resistance to malaria. The gene for G-6PD is on the X chromosome, and G-6PD deficiency is much more common in males.

HARRIS LINES Horizontal bands visible on the long bones that indicate periods of growth stoppage and an approximation of the age at which growth was disrupted.

HEALTH The World Health Organization defines health as "a state of complete social, psychological, and physical well-being." What constitutes health or a "healthy" state is variable cross-culturally.

HELMINTH HYPOTHESIS A hypothesis developed to explain the link between IgE and allergy. Suggests that reduced exposure to helminths results in IgE responding to nonpathogenic antigens with properties similar to those of helminths.

HELMINTHS Worms; three groups cause disease in humans: the roundworms (nematodes), the tapeworms (cestodes), and the flukes (trematodes).

HELPER T-CELLS   T-cells that bind to infected cells and mark the cell for destruction by phagocytes.

HEMOGLOBIN   A protein in red blood cells that aids in the transport of oxygen.

HERD IMMUNITY   When most of the population is immune to a pathogen because of vaccination or prior exposure. This makes it difficult for a pathogen to spread because there are few susceptible hosts.

HIV   Human immunodeficiency virus. An RNA retrovirus that infects T-cells.

HORMONE REPLACEMENT THERAPY (HRT)   The provisioning of postmenopausal women with either estrogen or estrogen and progesterone, usually to ameliorate uncomfortable symptoms of menopause or to reduce the risk of osteoporosis.

HOST   An individual either infected with or potentially infected with a parasite.

HUMAN LEUKOCYTE ANTIGENS   A set of genes that produce highly variable proteins involved in moving pieces of pathogenic proteins out to the surface of the cell where they can be recognized by T-cells. Also known as the major histocompatibility complex.

HUMORAL MEDICINE   Medical understandings of the body as a set of humors that must be in balance for health to be maintained.

HYGIENE HYPOTHESIS   A hypothesis developed to explain the rise in allergies in industrialized countries. Suggests that improvements in hygiene have resulted in less exposure to pathogens in childhood, which alters the development of the immune system in ways that cause it to respond inappropriately to nonpathogenic antigens.

HYPERTENSION   A blood pressure greater than 140/90 mm Hg.

***I AM* ILLNESSES**   Illnesses that become an intrinsic part of an individual's self-identity (e.g., I am a schizophrenic vs. I suffer from schizophrenia).

IDIOPATHIC   A disease or syndrome without a clear cause.

IGE   One of the classes of antibodies that responds to helminth infections. IgE appears to be involved in allergies and asthma.

ILLNESS   The subjective experience of symptoms and suffering, which motivates changes in behavior to alleviate this discomfort.

INCIDENCE   The number of new cases of a disease in a particular time period.

INFANT MORTALITY   Death in the first year of life.

INFECTIOUS DISEASE   A disease caused by a microorganism (virus, bacterium, protozoan, fungus, or helminth) that provokes an immune response in the host and that can be passed to another host. Identified using Koch's postulates.

INFERTILITY   The absence of conception after 24 months of regular, unprotected intercourse (WHO definition); more generally the inability to have a live birth.

INFIBULATION   A form of female genital cutting that involves the removal of the clitoris, the labia minora, and most or all of the labia majora.

INFLAMMATION   Part of the immune response to a pathogen that increases the blood supply to the site of damage or infection by promoting leakage of the blood vessels in the area.

INNATE IMMUNE SYSTEM   An evolutionarily old part of the immune system that involves recognition of some common patterns rather than specific characteristics of pathogens. It produces a relatively rapid response to a pathogen.

INSULIN   A hormone produced in the pancreas that is responsible for clearing glucose from the bloodstream by having cells take up glucose.

INSULIN-LIKE GROWTH FACTOR I (IGF-I)   A protein that induces cell division and inhibits cell death; it is active in many tissues in the human body including bone.

INTERNATIONAL CLASSIFICATION OF DISEASE   A globally recognized listing of standard definitions of disease.

INTERPRETIVE APPROACH   The attempt to understand medical systems, health, and disease strictly within their cultural contexts.

INTERSECTIONALITY   A concept advanced by black feminist theorists; the multiplicative, interacting effects of categories of identity such as sex/gender and race/ethnicity on individuals' lived experiences.

KOCH'S POSTULATES   The foundation of the germ theory of disease, used to establish whether a disease is caused by a microorganism. They are as follows: the pathogen must be found in all individuals with the disease; the organism must be isolated and grown in pure culture; the culture should cause the disease when introduced into another healthy individual; the pathogen can be isolated from the second individual and grown in culture.

KURU   A prion disease found among the Fore of New Guinea. It was transmitted through consumption of infected individuals after they died.

LACTASE PERSISTENCE   When the enzyme lactase (which digests the milk sugar lactose) continues to be produced into adulthood.

LACTATIONAL INFECUNDABILITY A period of time after birth during which a woman is unable to conceive while breastfeeding.

LACTOSE INTOLERANCE A syndrome that occurs in some individuals when they drink milk, characterized by gastrointestinal discomfort with nausea, cramping, gas, and diarrhea. Most often it is caused by lactase impersistence.

LATAH A syndrome known in Southeast Asia characterized by a trancelike state, mindless mimicking of words and actions of others, obeying commands without thought, and hypersensitivity to startle.

LEAD POISONING A condition that results from lead building up in the body, often over a period of months or years.

LIFE EXPECTANCY The average number of years an individual can expect to live, given his or her current age (usually calculated at birth, or age 0).

LIFE HISTORY THEORY A branch of evolutionary theory that attempts to understand the ways in which the stages of the life cycle and the behaviors associated with those stages are organized and the adaptive significance of that organization.

LIFESTYLE INCONGRUITY Inconsistency between one's lifestyle (or desired lifestyle) and one's education or occupation, such that the status that goes along with a particular lifestyle (i.e., accumulation of material possessions) is higher than what one's education or occupation can reasonably maintain.

LYMPHOCYTES White blood cells, which are key cells of the immune system. Includes T-cells and B-cells.

MAJOR HISTOCOMPATIBILITY COMPLEX (MHC) A set of genes that produce highly variable proteins involved in moving pieces of pathogenic proteins out to the surface of the cell where they can be recognized by T-cells. Also referred to as the human leukocyte antigens.

MALARIA A disease caused by the protozoan *Plasmodium spp.* and transmitted by Anopheles mosquitoes. Characterized by regular high fevers and parasitization of red blood cells. There are several known genetic adaptations to this disease, suggesting its importance in the evolution of many human populations.

MALNUTRITION Literally, "bad nutrition." Malnutrition is most often used as a synonym for undernutrition.

MAST CELLS Cells of the immune system that release granules of histamine and other molecules that increase vessel permeability. Part of the inflammatory response.

MEDICAL ANTHROPOLOGY The study of health-related issues from an anthropological perspective. It draws on social, cultural, biological, and linguistic anthropology to better understand those factors that influence health and well-being (broadly defined), the experience and distribution of illness, the prevention and treatment of sickness, healing processes, the social relations of therapy management, and the cultural importance and utilization of pluralistic medical systems.

MEDICALIZATION The defining of a condition as a disease, or a condition in need of medical surveillance.

MEDICAL PLURALISM When multiple healing systems exist within a single culture.

MORBIDITY Disease or the symptoms of disease.

MORTALITY Death.

MUTATION Mistakes that are made in the copying of DNA. Can lead to new antigens in pathogens, malignant cells, as in cancer, or new adaptive variants of a gene.

NATURAL KILLER CELLS Cells of the immune system that bind to the surface of recognized pathogens or infected host cells and "kill" them by poking holes in their membranes.

NATURAL SELECTION A process through which individuals with traits that enhance their survival or reproduction leave more offspring in subsequent generations such that those traits become more common over time.

NOCEBO EFFECT The causation of sickness (or death) by expectations of sickness (or death) and by associated emotional states.

NOSOCOMIAL INFECTIONS Pathogens that circulate in health-care facilities such as hospitals or nursing homes.

NOSOLOGY A system of disease classification.

NVP Nausea and vomiting of pregnancy; usually occurs in the first trimester of pregnancy.

OBESITY Having a body mass index of 30 or greater; more generally, having excess fat stores.

OLD FRIENDS HYPOTHESIS exposure to a diversity of microbes early in life stimulates regulatory T-cells that reduce the risk of allergy and asthma

ONCHOCERCIASIS (RIVER BLINDNESS) A helminth infection caused by *Onchocerca volvulus*, which uses the black fly (*Simulium damnosum*) as a vector. Its long-term effects include loss of sight and complete blindness, and the skin becomes unbearably itchy and chronically inflamed. Most common in West Africa.

OSTEOARTHRITIS   A condition resulting from repetitive use of joints, which results in visible modifications of these joints. The joints that show these bony distortions were likely those used routinely in hard work.

OSTEOPOROSIS   A thinning of bone tissue and loss of bone density, usually associated with aging.

OVERNUTRITION   A condition that exists when an individual takes in too many nutrients, most often defined by overconsumption of calories.

OVERWEIGHT   Having a body mass index of 25 to 30.

OVULATION   The release of an egg from the ovary around the midpoint of a woman's menstrual cycle.

PALEOPATHOLOGY   The study of health and disease using ancient skeletal materials.

PANDEMIC   An epidemic that occurs on a global scale.

PARASITES   Microorganisms that make use of the resources of other individuals, usually of a different, larger-bodied species.

PARASYMPATHETIC NERVOUS SYSTEM   The part of the autonomic nervous system that is activated during vegetative activities and suppressed during a stress response.

PARTICIPANT-OBSERVATION   The participation in, yet detached observance of, a group's behavior that is the hallmark of ethnographic fieldwork.

PATHOGEN   A microorganism that causes disease in a host.

PELVIC INFLAMMATORY DISEASE (PID)   A syndrome that may or may not be painful, in which the fallopian tubes are infected with a pathogen, usually a sexually transmitted bacterium. The fallopian tubes may become inflamed or scarred, preventing the fertilization of an egg or passage of the zygote to the uterus.

PERIOSTEAL REACTION   A rough outer layer of bone, indicative of infection and inflammation.

PHAGOCYTES   Cells of the immune system that destroy pathogens or infected cells. The most common form is the macrophage.

PHAGOCYTOSIS   When a phagocyte engulfs a pathogen or infected cell in the process of destroying it.

PHYTOCHEMICALS   Nonnutritive but biologically active compounds present in plants.

PIBLOKTOQ   Often translated as Arctic hysteria; a syndrome observed among Inuit peoples described as manic episode(s) in which an individual may remove his or her clothing, run around wildly into water or roll around on the snow, make nonsense sounds, or speak uncontrollably.

PLACEBO   A usually pharmacologically inert preparation prescribed more for the mental relief of the patient than for its actual effect on a disorder.

PLACEBO EFFECT   Improvement in the condition of a patient that occurs in response to treatment but cannot be considered caused by the specific treatment used.

PLEIOTROPY   When a gene has multiple effects in the body.

POLYCHLORINATED BIPHENYLS (PCBS)   A group of organic compounds with a similar chemical structure that are used and produced in industrial manufacture, associated with a number of health problems.

POROTIC HYPEROSTOSIS   An indicator of anemia (reduced oxygen-carrying capacity of blood). In response to anemia, red blood cell production increases, resulting in expansion of the bone marrow relative to the outer layer of bone. Outer bone is thin or nonexistent and the porous inner bone is exposed.

PREGNANCY-INDUCED HYPERTENSION (PIH)   When blood pressure rises above 140/90 mm Hg during pregnancy.

PREMENSTRUAL SYNDROME (PMS)   A cluster of negative emotional and physical symptoms before the onset of menstruation.

PREVALENCE   The total number of people with a disease in a particular time period.

PRIMARY INFERTILITY   The percentage of women who have not conceived after five years of marriage without contraceptive use.

PRIONS   Infectious proteins that cause neurodegenerative diseases such as Creutzfeldt–Jakob disease, Kuru (known from New Guinea), and other nonhuman forms that cause bovine spongiform encephalopathy (or mad cow disease) and scrapie, a similar disease of sheep.

PROBIOTICS   Helpful microorganisms that colonize the gastrointestinal tract.

PROLACTIN   A hormone that is released in the mother while a child is breastfeeding.

PROTEIN-ENERGY MALNUTRITION   A condition that exists when an individual shows deficiencies of protein and energy.

PROTOZOA   A taxon of single-celled eukaryotic microorganisms, many of which have complex lifecycles (such as *Plasmodium spp.*, which causes malaria).

PROXIMATE CAUSE OF DISEASE The immediate cause of some physiological disruption.

QUININE A bitter substance derived from the bark of the cinchona tree, which has antimalarial properties.

RACE Historically used to describe biologically distinct types of humans; now often used to refer to a group that is socially marked as biologically different.

RESURGENT INFECTIOUS DISEASES Infectious diseases whose prevalence had declined, but is now increasing or likely to increase.

SCHISTOSOMIASIS A helminth infection caused by *Shistosoma spp.*, which uses a freshwater snail as an intermediate host. The worms pair and establish themselves in the veins of the bladder or intestines, resulting in blood in the urine or feces and the buildup of scar tissue in these veins, which has long-term negative health consequences.

SCHIZOPHRENIA A mental illness found cross-culturally that includes delusions, hallucinations, disorganized speech, disorganized or catatonic behavior, and a variety of negative symptoms (emotional flattening, poverty of speech, lack of motivation or persistence to complete a task).

SCURVY A syndrome caused by a deficiency of vitamin C.

SECONDARY INFERTILITY The proportion of women with at least one child who do not go on to have another despite taking steps to do so.

SECULAR TREND A long-term historical trend in some variable. Increases in height and weight over the twentieth century are examples of secular trends.

SELECTIVE FORCES Factors that derive from the environment that ultimately pose threats to health and well-being, survival, and reproduction.

SENESCENCE The physiological decline associated with aging.

SICKLE-CELL ANEMIA A genetic disease in which an individual has two altered genes, resulting in all of their red blood cells having the sickle shape. This creates a profound anemia (inability to transport oxygen).

SICKLE-CELL HEMOGLOBIN A form of hemoglobin in which a single amino acid substitution creates an altered molecule (HbS) that causes the red blood cell to have a sickle shape.

SICKNESS Sometimes it is equated with disease, illness, or both, but has a sociological meaning as well (*see* sick role).

SICK ROLE A socially recognized set of different expectations for individuals with a socially recognized disease or illness.

SIT-AND-WAIT PATHOGENS Pathogens that are durable in the environment outside of the host. They tend to be among the most virulent pathogens.

SLEEP PARALYSIS A form of sleep disorder, typically occurring on wakening or falling asleep, in which an individual is fully aware but still experiencing REM-associated paralysis (or *atonia*).

SLEEPING SICKNESS A protozoan disease (*Trypanosoma spp.*) transmitted by the tsetse fly (genus: *Glossina*). Preferentially feeds on cattle, but also infects humans, generating chronic lassitude and ultimately coma and death.

SMALLPOX A virus (Variola) of the Orthopox family that causes pustules on the exterior and interior of the body, often resulting in disfigurement or death.

SOMATIC MUTATIONS Mutations that occur in somatic cells (all cells except ova and sperm).

SEXUALLY TRANSMITTED INFECTIONS (STIS) Infectious diseases that spread through sexual activity, such as gonorrhea or chlamydia.

STRESSORS Challenges to health and well-being, survival and reproduction, or anything that generates a physiological stress response.

STRESS RESPONSE A physiological response that involves both neurotransmitters (such as norepinephrine) and hormones (such as cortisol). Generally, it liberates energy to deal with a stressor and shuts down nonessential physiological processes.

STROKE A rupture of blood vessels in the brain.

SUDDEN INFANT DEATH SYNDROME (SIDS) A mysterious disease in which infants, mostly between the ages of two months and six months, simply stop breathing and die in their sleep.

SUDDEN UNEXPLAINED NOCTURNAL DEATH SYNDROME (SUNDS) First recognized among southeast Asian immigrants in the United States during the 1980s, death occurs during sleep in otherwise healthy young to middle-age adults, mostly men. May be linked to *Brugada syndrome*, a condition associated with abnormal cardiac function.

SUSTO In Latin America, a spiritual illness that occurs when one's vital essence (usually glossed in English as "soul") becomes separated from the body following a frightening or otherwise unsettling experience.

SYMPATHETIC NERVOUS SYSTEM The part of the autonomic nervous system that is activated during a stress response and suppressed for vegetative activities.

T-CELLS Cells of the immune system that are made in the thymus gland.

TELOMERES A length of repetitive nucleotide sequences at each end of a chromosome, which protects the integrity of the chromosome.

TUBERCULOSIS (TB) A highly infectious bacterial disease caused by *Mycobacterium tuberculosis.* It infects macrophages in the lungs and ultimately results in liquification of lung tissue.

ULTIMATE CAUSE OF DISEASE The more "distant" sociocultural, political–economic, historical, ecological, or evolutionary causes of disease.

UNDERNUTRITION A condition that exists when an individual receives too few nutrients.

VECTOR Any intermediate species or material that can take a pathogen from one host to the next.

VIRGIN SOIL EPIDEMIC An epidemic (usually of an infectious disease) that occurs in a previously unexposed population. Most often associated with high rates of mortality.

VIRULENCE A pathogen's ability to make a host sick; can be caused by a high reproductive rate of the pathogen, its ability to produce a toxin, or other attributes.

VIRUS Entities that contain hereditary material (either DNA or RNA) surrounded by protein. They must make use of a host's cellular replication mechanisms to reproduce.

WHITE COAT CEREMONY A ceremony at U.S. medical schools, promoted by the Arnold P. Gold Foundation, that is a self-conscious rite of passage for new medical students at the beginning of their training.

ZOONOSES Nonhuman animal infectious diseases, or animal diseases that derive from animals.

ZYGOTE A fertilized egg.

REFERENCES

Abarca-Gómez, Leandra, et al. (2017), "Worldwide trends in body-mass index, underweight, overweight, and obesity from 1975 to 2016: A pooled analysis of 2416 population-based measurement studies in 128.9 million children, adolescents, and adults," *The Lancet*, 390 (10113), 2627–42.

Abdullah, Asnawi (2015), "The double burden of undernutrition and overnutrition in developing countries: An update," *Current Obesity Reports*, 4 (3), 337–49.

Abed, Riadh T. (1998), "The sexual competition hypothesis for eating disorders," *British Journal of Medical Psychology*, 71, 525–47.

Abramowitz, Sharon, Marten, Meredith, and Panter-Brick, Catherine (2015), "Medical humanitarianism: Anthropologists speak out on policy and practice," *Medical Anthropology Quarterly*, 29 (1), 1–23.

Abreu, Ana Paula and Kaiser, Ursula B. (2016), "Pubertal development and regulation," *The Lancet Diabetes & Endocrinology*, 4 (3), 254–64.

Ackerknecht, E. (1943), "Psychopathology, primitive medicine, and primitive culture," *Bulletin of the History of Medicine*, 14, 30–67.

Adams, Kelly M., Butsch, Scott, and Kohlmeier, Martin (2015), "The state of nutrition education at U.S. medical schools," *Journal of Biomedical Education*, 2015, https://doi.org/10.1155/2015/357627

Adelson, Naomi (1998), "Health beliefs and the politics of Cree well-being," *Health: An Interdisciplinary Journal for the Social Study of Health, Illness and Medicine*, 2 (1), 5–22.

———— (2000), *"Being Alive Well": Health and the Politics of Cree Well-being* (Toronto: University of Toronto Press).

Adler, Shelley R. (1995), "Refugee status and folk belief: Hmong sudden deaths," *Social Science & Medicine*, 40, 1623–29.

———— (2011), *Sleep Paralysis: Night-Mares, Nocebos, and the Mind–Body Connection* (New Brunswick, NJ: Rutgers University Press).

Adomaityte, Jurga, Mullin, Gerard E., and Dobs, Adrian S (2014), "Anti-aging diet and supplements fact or fiction?," *Nutrition in Clinical Practice*, 29 (6), 844–46.

Affonso, D.D., et al. (2000), "An international study exploring levels of postpartum depressive symptomatology," *Journal of Psychosomatic Research*, 49, 207–16.

Aggarwal, Neil Krishan (2013), "Cultural psychiatry, medical anthropology, and the DSM-5 field trials," *Medical Anthropology*, 32 (5), 393–98.

Aidoo, Michael, et al. (2002), "Protective effects of the sickle cell gene against malaria morbidity and mortality," *The Lancet*, 359 (9314), 1311–12.

Aitoro, Rosita, et al. (2017), "Gut microbiota as a target for preventive and therapeutic intervention against food allergy," *Nutrients*, 9 (7).

Alfven, T., et al. (2006), "Allergic diseases and atopic sensitization in children related to farming and anthroposophic lifestyle—The PARSIFAL study," *Allergy*, 61 (4), 414–21.

Alizon, S., et al. (2009), "Virulence evolution and the trade-off hypothesis: History, current state of affairs and the future," *Journal of Evolutionary Biology*, 22 (2), 245–59.

Allen, J.S., Bruss, J., and Damasio, H. (2005a), "The aging brain: The cognitive reserve hypothesis and hominid evolution," *American Journal of Human Biology*, 17, 673–89.

Allen, J.S., et al. (2005b), "Normal neuroanatomical variation due to age: The major lobes and a parcellation of the temporal region," *Neurobiology of Aging*, 26, 1245–60.

Allen, John S. and Cheer, Susan M. (1996), "The non-thrifty genotype," *Current Anthropology*, 37, 831–42.

Allen, Lindsay H., Carriquiry, Alicia L., and Murphy, Suzanne P. (2020), "Perspective: Proposed harmonized nutrient reference values for populations," *Advances in Nutrition*. 11 (3), 469–483,

Allison, Anthony C. (1954), "Protection afforded by sickle-cell trait against malarial infection," *British Medical Journal*, 1, 290–94.

Allsworth, Jenifer E., Weitzen, Sherry, and Boardman, Lori A. (2005), "Early age at menarche and allostatic load: Data from the Third National Health and Nutrition Examination Survey," *Annals of Epidemiology*, 15, 438–44.

Almroth, L., et al. (2005), "Primary infertility after genital mutilation in girlhood in Sudan: A case-control study," *The Lancet*, 366 (9483), 385–91.

Aloia, John F. (2008), "African Americans, 25-hydroxyvitamin D, and osteoporosis: A paradox," *The American Journal of Clinical Nutrition*, 88 (2), 545S–550S.

Alonso, David, Bouma, Menno J., and Pascual, Mercedes (2011), "Epidemic malaria and warmer temperatures in recent decades in an East African highland," *Proceedings of the Royal Society B: Biological Sciences*, 278 (1712), 1661–69.

Altabe, M. (1998), "Ethnicity and body image: Quantitative and qualitative analysis," *International Journal of Eating Disorders*, 23, 153–59.

Altizer, Sonia, et al. (2013), "Climate change and infectious diseases: From evidence to a predictive framework," *Science*, 341 (6145), 514–19.

American College of Nurse-Midwives (2015), "Midwifery provision of home birth services," *Journal of Midwifery & Women's Health*, 61 (1), 127–33.

American Gastroenterology Association (2019), "Lactose intolerance," https://www.gastro.org/practice-guidance/gi-patient-center/topic/lactose-intolerance, accessed 26 October 2019.

American Psychiatric Association (1968), *Diagnostic and Statistical Manual of Mental Disorders* (2nd edition) (Washington: American Psychiatric Association).

———— (1994), *Diagnostic and Statistical Manual of Mental Disorders* (4th edition) (Washington: American Psychiatric Association).

———— (2013), *Diagnostic and Statistical Manual of Mental Disorders V* (Washington: American Psychiatric Association).

Anderson, Perry (2007), "Just the same capitalists as you," *Harpers*, 314 (1884), 22.

Andreasen, N.C. (1987), "Creativity and mental illness: Prevalence rates in writers and their first-degree relatives," *American Journal of Psychiatry*, 144, 1288–92.

Anis, Tarek H., et al. (2012), "Effects of female genital cutting on the sexual function of Egyptian women: A cross-sectional study," *Journal of Sexual Medicine*, 9 (10), 2682–92.

Arakawa, M., Miyake, Y., and Taira, K. (2005), "Hypertension and stroke in centenarians, Okinawa, Japan," *Cerebrovascular Disease*, 20, 233–38.

Arboleda-Florez, Julio (1979), "Amok," in RC Simons and CC Hughes (eds.), *The Culture-Bound Syndromes* (Higham, MA: D. Reidel Publishing), 251–62.

Armelagos, George J. (1990), "Health and disease in prehistoric populations in transition," in Alan C Swedlund and George J Armelagos (eds.), *Disease in Populations in Transition: Anthropological and Epidemiological Perspectives* (New York: Bergin and Garvey), 127–44.

Armstrong, G.L., Conn, L.A., and Pinner, R.W. (1999), "Trends in infectious disease mortality in the United States during the 20th century," *JAMA*, 281 (1), 61–66.

Ashley, Sarah, et al. (2015), "Food for thought: Progress in understanding the causes and mechanisms of food allergy," *Current Opinion in Allergy and Clinical Immunology*, 15 (3), 237–42.

Alzheimer's Association, (2016), "2016 Alzheimer's disease facts and figures," *Alzheimer's & Dementia*, 12 (4), 459–09.

Atlas, Ronald M. (2013), "One Health: Its origins and future," in John S. Mackenzie, et al. (eds.), *One Health: The Human-Animal-Environment Interfaces in Emerging Infectious Diseases: The Concept and Examples of a One Health Approach* (Berlin, Heidelberg: Springer Berlin Heidelberg), 1–13.

Atta, Callie A.M., et al. (2016), "Global birth prevalence of spina bifida by folic acid fortification status: A systematic review and meta-analysis," *American Journal of Public Health*, 106 (1), e24–34.

Aulino, Felicity (2017), "Narrating the future: Population aging and the demographic imaginary in Thailand," *Medical Anthropology*, 36 (4), 319–31.

Avis, Nancy E., et al. (2001), "Is there a menopausal syndrome? Menopausal status and symptoms across racial/ethnic groups," *Social Science & Medicine*, 52, 345–56.

Bachmanov, Alexander A., et al. (2011), "Genetics of sweet taste preferences," *Flavour and Fragrance Journal*, 26 (4), 286–94.

Bailey, Rahn K., et al. (2013), "Lactose intolerance and health disparities among African Americans and Hispanic Americans: An updated consensus statement," *Journal of the National Medical Association*, 105 (2), 112–27.

Bailey, Zinzi D., et al. (2017), "Structural racism and health inequities in the USA: Evidence and interventions," *The Lancet*, 389 (10077), 1453–63.

Baker, Elizabeth A., et al. (2006), "The role of race and poverty in access to foods that enable individuals to adhere to dietary guidelines," *Preventing Chronic Disease*, 3 (3), A76.

Baker, Paul T., Hanna, Joel M, and Baker, Thelma S. (eds.) (1986), *The Changing Samoans: Behavior and Health in Transition* (New York: Oxford University Press).

Baker-Austin, Craig, et al. (2013), "Emerging Vibrio risk at high latitudes in response to ocean warming," *Nature Climate Change*, 3 (1), 73–77.

Baker-Austin, Craig, et al. (2017), "Non-cholera vibrios: The microbial barometer of climate change," *Trends in Microbiology*, 25 (1), 76–84.

Bakhshi, K. and Chance, S.A. (2015), "The neuropathology of schizophrenia: A selective review of past studies and emerging themes in brain structure and cytoarchitecture," *Neuroscience*, 303, 82–102.

Bal, Munita Meenu and Saikia, Biman (2007), "Gender bias in renal transplantation: Are women alone donating kidneys in India?," *Transplant Proceedings*, 39 (10), 2961–63.

Balasubramanian, Priya, Howell, Porsha R., and Anderson, Rozalyn M. (2017), "Aging and caloric restriction research: A biological perspective with translational potential," *EBioMedicine*, 21, 37–44.

Balk, Deborah (2000), "To marry and bear children? The demographic consequences of infibulation in Sudan," in Bettina Shell-Duncan and Ylva Hernlund (eds.), *Female "Circumcision" in Africa: Culture, Controversy, and Change* (Boulder, CO: Lynne Rienner Publishers), 55–71.

Ball, Helen L. and Volpe, Lane E. (2013), "Sudden Infant Death Syndrome (SIDS) risk reduction and infant sleep location—Moving the discussion forward," *Social Science & Medicine*, 79, 84–91.

Barker, D.J. and Thornburg, K.L. (2013), "The obstetric origins of health for a lifetime," *Clinical Obstetrics and Gynecology*, 56 (3), 511–19.

Barker, David J.P. (1995), "Fetal origins of coronary heart disease," *British Medical Journal*, 311, 171–74.

———— (2004), "The developmental origins of adult disease," *Journal of the American College of Nutrition*, 23, 588S–595S.

Barnes, HM (2000), "Kaupapa Maori: Explaining the ordinary," *Pacific Health Dialog*, 7, 13–16.

Barreca, Alan and Schaller, Jessamyn (2020), "The impact of high ambient temperatures on delivery timing and gestational lengths," *Nature Climate Change*, 10 (1), 77–82.

Barrett, Ronald (2005), "Self-mortification and the stigma of leprosy in Northern India," *Medical Anthropology Quarterly*, 19 (2), 216–30.

Barros, Fernando C., et al. (2015), "Cesarean sections in Brazil: Will they ever stop increasing?," *Revista Panamericana de Salud Pública*, 38, 217–25.

Bastien, Joseph W (1985), *Mountain of the Condor: Metaphor and Ritual in an Andean Ayllu* (Prospect Heights, IL: Waveland).

Bauer, Greta R. (2014), "Incorporating intersectionality theory into population health research methodology: Challenges and the potential to advance health equity," *Social Science & Medicine*, 110, 10–17.

Beaton, G.H. (1989), "Small but healthy? Are we asking the right question?," *European Journal of Clinical Nutrition*, 43 (12), 863–75.

Becker, Anne E. (2004), "Television, disordered eating, and young women in Fiji: Negotiating body image and identity during rapid social change," *Culture, Medicine and Psychiatry*, 28 (4), 533–59.

Becker, Anne E., et al. (2002), "Eating behaviours and attitudes following prolonged exposure to television among ethnic Fijian adolescent girls," *British Journal of Psychiatry*, 180, 509–14.

Becker, Anne E., et al. (2007), "Facets of acculturation and their divers relations to body shape concern in Fiji," *International Journal of Eating Disorders*, 40, 42–50.

Becker, Anne E., et al. (2010), "A qualitative study of perceived social barriers to care for eating disorders: Perspectives from ethnically diverse health care consumers," *International Journal of Eating Disorders*, 43 (7), 633–47.

Begay, D.H. and Maryboy, N.C. (2000), "The whole universe is my cathedral: A contemporary Navajo spiritual synthesis," *Medical Anthropology Quarterly*, 14, 498–20.

Bellinger, David C. (2016), "Lead contamination in Flint—An abject failure to protect public health," *New England Journal of Medicine*, 374 (12), 1101–03.

Belloy, Michaël E., Napolioni, Valerio, and Greicius, Michael D. (2019), "A quarter century of APOE and Alzheimer's disease: Progress to date and the path forward," *Neuron*, 101 (5), 820–38.

Belsky, Jay, Houts, Renate M., and Fearon, R.M. Pasco (2010), "Infant attachment security and the timing of puberty: Testing an evolutionary hypothesis," *Psychological Science*, 21 (9), 1195–01.

Belsky, Jay, Steinberg, L., and Draper, P. (1991), "Childhood experience, interpersonal development, and reproductive strategies: An evolutionary theory of socialization," *Child Development*, 62, 647–70.

Bensoussan, A., et al. (1998), "Treatment of irritable bowel syndrome with Chinese herbal medicine," *Journal of the American Medical Association*, 280, 1585–89.

Benyshek, Daniel C. (2013), "The 'early life' origins of obesity-related health disorders: New discoveries regarding the intergenerational transmission of developmentally programmed traits in the global cardiometabolic health crisis," *American Journal of Physical Anthropology*, 152, 79–93.

Berchtold, N.C. and Cotman, C.W. (1998), "Evolution in the conceptualization of dementia and Alzheimer's disease: Greco-Roman period to the 1960s," *Neurobiology of Aging*, 19, 173–89.

Berkman, Lisa F. and Glass, T. (2000), "Social integration, social networks, and health," in Lisa F. Berkman and I. Kawachi (eds.), *Social Epidemiology* (New York: Oxford University Press), 158-162.

Bernstein, A.M., et al. (2004), "First autopsy of an Okinawan centenarian: Absence of many age-related diseases," *Journal of Gerontology: Medical Sciences*, 59A, 1195–99.

Bertranpetit, J. and Calafell, F. (1996), "Genetic and geographical variability in cystic fibrosis: Evolutionary considerations," *Ciba Foundation Symposium*, 197, 97–114.

Betti, Lia and Manica, Andrea (2018), "Human variation in the shape of the birth canal is significant and geographically structured," *Proceedings of the Royal Society B: Biological Sciences*, 285 (1889), 1–9.

Biaggi, Alessandra, et al. (2016), "Identifying the women at risk of antenatal anxiety and depression: A systematic review," *Journal of Affective Disorders*, 191, 62–77.

Bidlingmaier, M., et al. (2014), "Reference intervals for insulin-like growth factor-1 (IGF-I) from birth to senescence: Results from a multicenter study using a new automated chemiluminescence IGF-I immunoassay conforming to recent international recommendations," *Journal of Clinical Endocrinology & Metabolism*, 99 (5), 1712–21.

Bindon, James R. and Baker, Paul T. (1997), "Bergmann's rule and the thrifty genotype," *American Journal of Physical Anthropology: The Official Publication of the American Association of Physical Anthropologists*, 104 (2), 201–10.

Bird, Philippa K., et al. (2019), "Income inequality and social gradients in children's height: A comparison of cohort studies from five high-income countries," *BMJ Paediatrics Open Journal*, 3 (1), e000568–68.

Biswas, Aviroop, et al. (2015), "Sedentary time and its association with risk for disease incidence, mortality, and hospitalization in adults: A systematic review and meta-analysis," *Annals of Internal Medicine*, 162 (2), 123–32.

Black, P.H. (2006), "The inflammatory consequences of psychologic stress: Relationship to insulin resistance, obesity, atherosclerosis and diabetes mellitus, type II," *Medical Hypotheses*, 67 (4), 879–91.

Black, Robert E., et al. (2013), "Maternal and child undernutrition and overweight in low-income and middle-income countries," *The Lancet*, 382 (9890), 427–51.

Blair, P.S., Heron, J., and Fleming, P.J. (2010), "Relationship between bed sharing and breastfeeding: Longitudinal, population-based analysis," *Pediatrics*, 126 (5), e1119–26.

Bleir, P (2001), "Crosstalk between the norepinephrine and serotonin systems and its role in the antidepressant response," *Journal of Psychiatry and Neuroscience*, 26 (Supplement S), 3–10.

Bloomfield, Sally F., et al. (2016), "Time to abandon the hygiene hypothesis: New perspectives on allergic disease, the human microbiome, infectious disease prevention and the role of targeted hygiene," *Perspectives in Public Health*, 136 (4), 213–24.

Blurton Jones, Nicholas G, Hawkes, Kristen, and O'Connell, James F. (2002), "Antiquity of postreproductive life: Are there modern impacts on hunter-gatherer postreproductive life spans?," *American Journal of Human Biology*, 14 (2), 184–05.

Boas, Franz (1912), "Changes in the bodily form of descendants of immigrants," *American Anthropologist*, 14 (3), 530–62.

Bocquet-Appel, Jean Pierre, Naji, Stephan, and Bandy, Mathew (2008), "Demographic and health changes during the transition to agriculture in North America," in Jean Pierre Bocquet-Appel (ed.), *Recent Advances in Palaeodemography* (Dordrecht: Springer), 277–292.

Boehm, Christopher (1999), *Hierarchy in the Forest* (Cambridge, MA: Harvard University Press).

Bogin, B., et al. (2002), "Rapid change in height and body proportions of Maya American children," *American Journal of Human Biology*, 14 (6), 753–61.

Bogin, Barry (1999), "Evolutionary perspective on human growth," *Annual Review of Anthropology*, 28, 109–53.

Bogin, Barry and Loucky, J. (1997), "Plasticity, political economy, and physical growth status of Guatemala Maya children living in the United States," *American Journal of Physical Anthropology*, 102 (1), 17–32.

Bohren, Meghan A., et al. (2015), "The mistreatment of women during childbirth in health facilities globally: A mixed-methods systematic review," *PLoS Medicine*, 12 (6).

Boldin, Barbara and Kisdi, Éva (2012), "On the evolutionary dynamics of pathogens with direct and environmental transmission," *Evolution*, 66 (8), 2514–27.

Bonaporte, D. (2005), "The healing powers of the seventh son of a seventh son," *The People's Voice*, October 21.

Bonvillain, Nancy (2007), *Women and Men: Cultural Constructs of Gender* (Upper Saddle River, NJ: Pearson Prentice Hall).

Boulangé, Claire L., et al. (2016), "Impact of the gut microbiota on inflammation, obesity, and metabolic disease," *Genome Medicine*, 8 (1), 42.

Bowlby, John (1969), *Attachment and Loss: Volume I, Attachment* (New York: Basic Books).

Brandes, Stanley (2003), "Is there a Mexican view of death?," *Ethos*, 31, 127–44.

Brandis, M. (1998), "A feminist analysis of the theories of etiology of depression in women," *Nursing Leadership Forum*, 3, 18–23.

Brewis, A.A., et al. (1998), "Perceptions of body size in Pacific Islanders," *International Journal of Obesity and Related Metabolic Disorders*, 22, 185–89.

Brewis, Alexandra A. (2011), *Obesity: Cultural and Biocultural Perspectives* (New Brunswick, NJ: Rutgers University Press).

Brewis, Alexandra A., et al. (2011), "Body norms and fat stigma in global perspective," *Current Anthropology*, 52 (2), 269–76.

Brewis, Alexandra and Meyer, Mary (2005), "Marital coitus across the life course," *Journal of Biosocial Science*, 37 (4), 499–18.

Brewis, Alexandra and Wutich, Amber (2019), *Lazy, Crazy, and Disgusting: Stigma and the Undoing of Global Health* (Baltimore, MD: Johns Hopkins University Press).

Brives, Charlotte, Le Marcis, Frédéric, and Sanabria, Emilia (2016), "What's in a context? Tenses and tensions in evidence-based medicine," *Medical Anthropology*, 35 (5), 369–76.

Brodwin, Paul (2011), "Futility in the practice of community psychiatry," *Medical Anthropology Quarterly*, 25 (2), 189–08.

Brosch, R., et al. (2002), "A new evolutionary scenario for the Mycobacterium tuberculosis complex," *Proceedings of the National Academy of Sciences*, 99 (6), 3684–89.

Brown, Hannah and Nading, Alex M. (2019), "Introduction: Human animal health in medical anthropology," *Medical Anthropology Quarterly*, 33 (1), 5–23.

Brownell, Kelly (2004), *Food Fight: The Inside Story of the Food Industry, America's Obesity Crisis, and What We Can Do about It* (Chicago: Contemporary Books).

Browner, Carol H., Ortiz de Montellano, B.R., and Rubel, A.J. (1988), "A methodology for cross-cultural ethnomedical research," *Current Anthropology*, 29, 681–02.

Browner, Carole H. and Sargent, Carolyn F. (2011), *Reproduction, Globalization, and the State: New Theoretical and Ethnographic Perspectives* (Durham, NC: Duke University Press).

Brumberg, Joan Jacobs (1989), *Fasting Girls: The History of Anorexia Nervosa* (New York: Plume).

Brune, M. (2004), "Schizophrenia: An evolutionary enigma?," *Neuroscience and Biobehavioral Reviews*, 28, 41–53.

Brunson, Emily K. and Sobo, Elisa J. (2017), "Framing childhood vaccination in the united states: Getting past polarization in the public discourse," *Human Organization*, 76 (1), 38–47.

Brush, Stephen (1993), "Indigenous knowledge of biological resources and intellectual property rights: The role of anthropology," *American Anthropologist*, 95, 653–71.

Buckley, Thomas and Gottlieb, Alma (1988), *Blood Magic: The Anthropology of Menstruation* (Berkeley: University of California Press).

Bulik, C.M., et al. (2000), "Twin studies of eating disorders: A review," *International Journal of Eating Disorders*, 27, 1–20.

Burns, J.K. (2006), "Psychosis: A costly by-product of social brain evolution in Homo sapiens," *Progress in Neuro-Psychopharmacology and Biological Psychiatry*, 30, 797–14.

Burton-Bradley, B.G. (1973), *Stone Age Crisis* (Nashville: Vanderbilt University Press).

Buss, D.M. (2003), *The Evolution of Desire* (New York: Basic Books).

Butte, Nancy F. and King, Janet C. (2005), "Energy requirements during pregnancy and lactation," *Public Health Nutrition*, 8 (7a), 1010–27.

Byers, K.G. and Savaiano, D.A. (2005), "The myth of increased lactose intolerance in African-Americans," *Journal of the American College of Nutrition*, 24, 569S–573S.

Cabral, Christie, et al. (2014), "How communication affects prescription decisions in consultations for acute illness in children: A systematic review and meta-ethnography," *BMC Family Practice*, 15 (1), 1–13.

Campbell, Kenneth L. and Wood, James W. (1988), "Fertility in traditional societies," in Peter Diggory, Malcolm Potts, and Sue Teper (eds.), *Natural Human Fertility* (London: Macmillan Press), 39–69.

Campbell-Lendrum, Diarmid, et al. (2015), "Climate change and vector-borne diseases: What are the implications for public health research and policy?," *Philosophical Transactions of the Royal Society of London B: Biological Sciences*, 370, 20130552.

Cardini, F. and Weixin, H. (1998), "Moxibustion for correction of breech presentation: A randomized control trial," *Journal of the American Medical Association*, 280, 1580–84.

Carlsen, E., et al. (1992), "Evidence for decreasing quality of semen during past 50 years," *British Medical Journal*, 305, 609–13.

Carter, K.C. (1977), "The germ theory, beriberi, and the deficiency theory of disease," *Medical History*, 21 (2), 119–36.

Casadesus, G., et al. (2004), "Eat less, eat better, and live longer: Does it work and is it worth it?," in S.G. Post and R.H. Binstock (eds.), *The Fountain of Youth* (New York: Oxford University Press), 201–27.

Case, Anne and Deaton, Angus (2015), "Rising morbidity and mortality in midlife among white non-Hispanic Americans in the 21st century," *Proceedings of the National Academy of Sciences*, 112 (49), 15078–83.

Cassell, Joan (2005), *Life and Death in Intensive Care* (Philadelphia: Temple University Press).

Cassidy, Claire M. (1980), "Nutrition and health in agriculturalists and hunter-gatherers: A case study of two prehistoric populations," in Norge W. Jerome, Randy F. Kandel, and Gretel H. Pelto (eds.), *Nutritional Anthropology: Contemporary Approaches to Diet and Culture* (Pleasantville, NY: Redgrave Publishing Co.), 117–45.

Castle, Sarah E. (1994), "The (re) negotiation of illness diagnoses and responsibility for child death in rural Mali," *Medical Anthropology Quarterly*, 8 (3), 314–35.

Castro, Aruchu and Farmer, Paul (2007), "Medical anthropology in the United States," in Francine Saillant and Serge Genest (eds.), *Medical Anthropology: Regional Perspectives and Shared Concerns* (Malden, MA: Blackwell Publishing), 42–57.

Catassi, Carlo, et al. (2010), "Natural history of celiac disease autoimmunity in a USA cohort followed since 1974," *Annals of Medicine*, 42 (7), 530–38.

Catov, Janet M., et al. (2016), "Race disparities and decreasing birth weight: Are all babies getting smaller?," *American Journal of Epidemiology*, 183 (1), 15–23.

Cesario, Sandra K. and Hughes, Lisa A. (2007), "Precocious puberty: A comprehensive review of literature," *Journal of Obstetric, Gynecologic, & Neonatal Nursing*, 36 (3), 263–74.

Chae, David H., et al. (2020), "Racial discrimination and telomere shortening among African Americans: The Coronary Artery Risk Development in Young Adults (CARDIA) study," *Health Psychology* 39 (3), 209–219.

Chafen, Jennifer J. Schneider, et al. (2010), "Diagnosing and managing common food allergies," *JAMA*, 303 (18), 1848–56.

Chai, Bingli Clark, et al. (2019), "Which diet has the least environmental impact on our planet? A systematic review of vegan, vegetarian and omnivorous diets," *Sustainability*, 11 (15), 4110.

Chambers, Brittany D., et al. (2018), "Testing the association between traditional and novel indicators of county-level structural racism and birth outcomes among black and white women," *Journal of Racial and Ethnic Health Disparities*, 5 (5), 966–77.

Charlwood, Derek J., et al. (2003), "Raised houses reduce mosquito bites," *Malaria Journal*, 2 (1), 1–6.

Chavez-MacGregor, Mariana, et al. (2005), "Postmenopausal breast cancer risk and cumulative number of menstrual cycles," *Cancer Epidemiology and Prevention Biomarkers*, 14 (4), 799–04.

Chen, Lincoln C. (1983), "Child survival: Levels, trends, and determinants," in Rodolfo Bulatao and Ronald D. Lee (eds.), *Determinants of Fertility in Developing Countries* (New York: Academic Press), 199–32.

Cheney, Ann M., Sullivan, Steve, and Grubbs, Kathleen (2018), "The morality of disordered eating and recovery in southern Italy," *Medical Anthropology Quarterly*, 32 (3), 443–57.

Cheyne, A., et al. (2014), "Food and beverage marketing to youth," *Current Obesity Reports*, 3 (4), 440–50.

Childe, V.G. (1951), *Man Makes Himself* (New York: Mentor).

Childs, Stephen (1991), "'Cut out to do work": Recruitment experiences of a folk healer," *Anthropology of Consciousness*, 2, 25–31.

Chin, Nancy P. and Solomonik, Anna (2009), "Inadequate: A metaphor for the lives of low-income women?," *Breastfeeding Medicine*, 4 (s1), S-41–43.

Chisholm, James S. (1993), "Death, hope, and sex: Life-history theory and the development of reproductive strategies," *Current Anthropology*, 34 (1), 1–24.

Choung, Rok Seon, et al. (2017), "Less hidden celiac disease but increased gluten avoidance without a diagnosis in the United States: Findings from the National Health and Nutrition Examination Surveys from 2009 to 2014," *Mayo Clinic Proceedings* 92, 30–38.

Christakis, Nicholas A. and Fowler, James H. (2007), "The spread of obesity in a large social network over 32 years," *New England Journal of Medicine*, 357, 370–79.

Christensen, Kaare, et al. (2009), "Ageing populations: The challenges ahead," *The Lancet*, 374 (9696), 1196–08.

Clarke, Tainya C., et al. (2015), "Trends in the use of complementary health approaches among adults: United States, 2002–2012," *National Health Statistics Reports*, (79), 1–16.

Cleary-Guida, M.B., et al. (2001), "A regional survey of health insurance coverage for complementary and alternative medicine: Current status and future ramifications," *Journal of Alternative and Complementary Medicine*, 7, 269–73.

Closser, Svea, et al. (2016), "The global context of vaccine refusal: Insights from a systematic comparative ethnography of the global polio eradication initiative," *Medical Anthropology Quarterly*, 30 (3), 321–41.

Cockburn, T. Aidan (1971), "Infectious diseases in ancient populations," *Current Anthropology*, 12 (1), 45–62.

Cockerham, W.C., Hattori, H., and Yamori, Y. (2000), "The social gradient in life expectancy: The contrary case of Okinawa in Japan," *Social Science & Medicine*, 51, 115–22.

Cohen, Ed (2009), *A Body Worth Defending: Immunity, Biopolitics, and the Apotheosis of the Modern Body* (Durham, NC: Duke University Press).

Cohen, Lawrence (1995), "Toward an anthropology of senility: Anger, weakness, and Alzheimer's in Banaras, India," *Medical Anthropology Quarterly*, 9, 314–34.

_____ (1998), *No Aging in India: Alzheimer's, The Bad Family, and other Modern Things* (Berkeley: University of California Press).

Cohen, Mark Nathan (1989), *Health and the Rise of Civilization* (New Haven, CT: Yale University Press).

_____ (2009), "Introduction: Rethinking the origins of agriculture," *Current Anthropology*, 50 (5), 591–95.

Cohen, Mitchell L. (2000), "Changing patterns of infectious disease," *Nature*, 406 (6797), 762–67.

Cohen, S., et al. (2002), "Reactivity and vulnerability to stress-associated risk for upper respiratory illness," *Psychosomatic Medicine*, 64, 302–10.

Cohen, Sheldon, Tyrrell, David A.J., and Smith, Andrew P. (1991), "Psychological stress and susceptibility to the common cold," *New England Journal of Medicine*, 325 (9), 606–12.

Colborn, Theo, Dumanoski, Dianne, and Myers, John Peterson (1997), *Our Stolen Future* (New York: Plume).

Coleman-Jensen, Alisha, et al. (2019), *Household Food Security in the United States in 2018, ERR-270* (Washington, DC: U.S. Department of Agriculture, Economic Research Service.).

Collen, Alanna (2016), *10% Human: How Your Body's Microbes Hold the Key to Health and Happiness.* (New York: Harper Publishing).

Collins, Patricia Hill and Bilge, Sirma (2016), *Intersectionality* (John Wiley & Sons).

Colloca, Luana and Miller, Franklin G. (2011), "The nocebo effect and its relevance for clinical practice," *Psychosomatic Medicine*, 73 (7), 598–03.

Colson, Eve R., et al. (2013), "Trends and factors associated with bed-sharing: The National Infant Sleep Position Study (NISP) 1993–2010," *JAMA pediatrics*, 167 (11), 1032–37.

Colwell, Rita R. (1996), "Global climate and infectious disease: The cholera paradigm," *Science*, 274 (5295), 2025–31.

Conrad, Peter (2008), *The Medicalization of Society: On the Transformation of Human Conditions into Treatable Disorders* (Baltimore: Johns Hopkins University Press).

Cooper, R. (1984), "A note on the biological concept of race and its application in epidemiologic research," *American Heart Journal*, 108, 715–23.

Cooper, Richard S., Kaufman, Jay S., and Ward, Ryk (2003), "Race and genomics," *New England Journal of Medicine*, 348 (12), 1166–70.

Copelton, Denise A. and Valle, Giuseppina (2009), "'You don't need a prescription to go gluten-free': The scientific self-diagnosis of celiac disease," *Social Science & Medicine*, 69 (4), 623–31.

Cordain, Loren and et al. (2005), "Origins and evolution of the western diet: Health implications for the 21st century," *American Journal of Clinical Nutrition*, 81, 341–54.

Corder, E.H., et al. (1993), "Gene dose of apolipoprotein E type 4 allele and the risk of Alzheimer's disease in late onset families," *Science*, 261, 921–23.

Cozier, Yvette C., et al. (2007), "Relation between neighborhood median housing value and hypertension risk among black women in the United States," *American Journal of Public Health*, 97 (4), 718–24.

Craddock, N. and Forty, L. (2006), "Genetics of affective (mood) disorders," *European Journal of Human Genetics*, 14, 660–68.

Crenshaw, Kimberle (1989), "Demarginalizing the intersection of race and sex: A black feminist critique of antidiscrimination doctrine, feminist theory and antiracist politics," *University of Chicago Legal Forum*, 139.

Crooks, Deborah L. (1999), "Child growth and nutritional status in a high-poverty community in eastern Kentucky," *American Journal of Physical Anthropology*, 109, 129–42.

——— (2000), "Food consumption, activity, and overweight among elementary school children in an Appalachian Kentucky community," *American Journal of Physical Anthropology*, 112 (2), 159–70.

Crosby, Alfred W. (1986), *Ecological Imperialism: The biological expansion of Europe, 900–1900* (New York: Cambridge University Press).

Crowley-Matoka, Megan and Hamdy, Sherine F. (2016), "Gendering the gift of life: Family politics and kidney donation in Egypt and Mexico," *Medical Anthropology*, 35 (1), 31–44.

Csordas, Thomas J. (2000), "The Navajo Healing Project," *Medical Anthropology Quarterly*, 14, 463–75.

Csordas, Thomas J. and Lewton, Elizabeth (1998), "Practice, performance, and experience in ritual healing," *Transcultural Psychiatry*, 35, 435–12.

Cummings, A.J., et al. (2010), "The psychosocial impact of food allergy and food hypersensitivity in children, adolescents and their families: A review," *Allergy*, 65 (8), 933–45.

Currie, Candace, et al. (2012), "Is obesity at individual and national level associated with lower age at menarche? Evidence from 34 countries in the Health Behaviour in School-Aged Children Study," *Journal of Adolescent Health*, 50 (6), 621–26.

Curtis, Elana, et al. (2019), "Why cultural safety rather than cultural competency is required to achieve health equity: A literature review and recommended definition," *International Journal for Equity in Health*, 18 (1), 174.

Damoiseaux, Jessica S. (2017), "Effects of aging on functional and structural brain connectivity," *Neuroimage*, 160, 32–40.

Danaei, Goodarz, et al. (2010), "The promise of prevention: The effects of four preventable risk factors on national life expectancy and life expectancy disparities by race and county in the United States," *PLoS Medicine*, 7 (3), e1000248.

Danese, A., et al. (2009), "Adverse childhood experiences and adult risk factors for age-related disease: Depression, inflammation, and clustering of metabolic risk markers," *Archives of Pediatrics & Adolescent Medicine*, 163 (12), 1135–43.

Daniel, H.I. and Rotimi, C.N. (2003), "Genetic epidemiology of hypertension: An update on the African diaspora," *Ethnicity & Disease*, 13 (Suppl 2), S53–66.

Danubio, M.E., Amicone, E., and Varqui, R. (2005), "Height and BMI of Italian immigrants to the USA, 1908–1970," *Economics and Human Biology*, 3 (1), 33–43.

Daruna, Jorge H. (2004), *Introduction to Psychoneuroimmunology* (New York: Elsevier).

Das Gupta, Monica (1995), "Life course perspectives on women's autonomy and health outcomes," *American Anthropologist*, 97 (3), 481–91.

Davidson, Richard J., Jon Kabat-Zinn, Jessica Schumacher, Melissa Rosenkranz, Daniel Muller, Saki F. Santorelli, Ferris Urbanowski, Anne Harrington,

Katherine Bonus, and John F. Sheridan. 2003. Alterations in brain and immune function produced by mindfulness meditation. *Psychosomatic Medicine*, 65:564–70.

Davis, Dona (1996), "The cultural constructions of the premenstrual and menopause syndromes," in Carolyn F. Sargeant and Caroline B Brettell (eds.), *Gender and Health: An international perspective* (Upper Saddle River, NJ: Prentice Hall), 57–86.

Davis-Floyd, Robbie and Cheyney, Melissa (eds.) (2019), *Birth in Eight Cultures* (Waveland Press).

Davis-Floyd, Robbie, et al. (eds.) (2009), *Birth Models That Work* (Berkeley: University of California Press).

Dawson-Hughes, B. (2004), "Racial/ethnic considerations in making recommendations for vitamin D for adult and elderly men and women," *American Journal of Clinical Nutrition*, 80 (suppl), 1763S–1766S.

Day, Troy (2002), "Virulence evolution via host exploitation and toxin production in spore-producing pathogens," *Ecology Letters*, 5 (4), 471–76.

de Beer, Hans (2012), "Dairy products and physical stature: A systematic review and meta-analysis of controlled trials," *Economics & Human Biology*, 10 (3), 299–09.

de Menezes, Ehrika Vanessa Almeida, et al. (2019), "Influence of Paleolithic diet on anthropometric markers in chronic diseases: Systematic review and meta-analysis," *Nutrition Journal*, 18 (1), 41.

de Onis, Mercedes, et al. (2007), "Comparison of the WHO child growth standards and the CDC 2000 growth charts," *Journal of Nutrition*, 137, 144–48.

Deaton, Angus (2007), "Height, health, and development," *Proceedings of the National Academy of Sciences*, 104 (33), 13232–37.

Deaton, Angus and Arora, Raksha (2009), "Life at the top: The benefits of height," *Economics & Human Biology*, 7 (2), 133–36.

DeMaria, Andrea L., et al. (2019), "The myth of menstruation: How menstrual regulation and suppression impact contraceptive choice," *BMC Women's Health*, 19 (1), 125.

Denham, Aaron R., et al. (2010), "Chasing spirits: Clarifying the spirit child phenomenon and infanticide in Northern Ghana," *Social Science & Medicine*, 71 (3), 608–15.

Denham, M., et al. (2005), "Relationship of lead, mercury, mirex, dichlorodiphenyldichloroethylene, hexachlorobenzene, and polychlorinated biphenyls to timing of menarche among Akwesasne Mohawk girls," *Pediatrics*, 115, e127–34.

Dernini, S., et al. (2017), "Med Diet 4.0: The Mediterranean diet with four sustainable benefits," *Public Health Nutrition*, 20 (7), 1322–30.

Desai, Meghna, et al. (2007), "Epidemiology and burden of malaria in pregnancy," *The Lancet Infectious Diseases*, 7 (2), 93–104.

Desowitz, Robert (1981), *New Guinea Tapeworms and Jewish Grandmothers* (New York: W.W. Norton).

Desowitz, Robert S. (1991), *The Malaria Capers: Tales of Parasites and People* (New York: W.W. Norton).

Devitt, M. (2005), "Report: Insurance coverage for acupuncture on the rise," *Acupuncture Today*, 6, 1–3.

Devries, Stephen, Willett, Walter, and Bonow, Robert O. (2019), "Nutrition education in medical school, residency training, and practice," *JAMA*, 321 (14), 1351–52.

Dewey, K.G. (1998), "Growth characteristics of breast-fed compared to formula-fed infants," *Neonatology*, 74 (2), 94–105.

Dhabhar, Firdaus S. (2009), "Enhancing versus suppressive effects of stress on immune function: Implications for immunoprotection and immunopathology," *Neuroimmunomodulation*, 16 (5), 300–17.

Dhond, R.P., Kettner, N., and Napadow, V. (2007), "Do the neural correlates of acupuncture and placebo effects differ?," *Pain*, 128, 8–12.

Dhurandhar, E.J. and Keith, S.W. (2014), "The aetiology of obesity beyond eating more and exercising less," *Best Practice & Research Clinical Gastroenterology*, 28 (4), 533–44.

Diamond, Jared (1987), "The worst mistake in the history of the human race," *Discover*, May, 64–66.

Dick, Lyle (1995), "'Pibloktoq'(Arctic hysteria): A construction of European-Inuit relations?," *Arctic Anthropology*, 32 (2), 1–42.

Direkvand-Moghadam, Ashraf, et al. (2014), "Epidemiology of premenstrual syndrome (PMS)—A systematic review and meta-analysis study," *Journal of Clinical and Diagnostic Research: JCDR*, 8 (2), 106–09.

Dickman, Samuel L., Himmelstein, David U., and Woolhandler, Steffie (2017), "Inequality and the health-care system in the USA." *The Lancet*, 389:1431–1441.

Dobyns, Henry F. (1993), "Disease transfer at contact," *Annual Review of Anthropology*, 22, 273–91.

Dominguez-Bello, Maria G., et al. (2010), "Delivery mode shapes the acquisition and structure of the initial microbiota across multiple body habitats in newborns," *Proceedings of the National Academy of Sciences*, 107 (26), 11971–75.

Dossabhoy, Shernaz S., Feng, Jessica, and Desai, Manisha S. (2018), "The use and relevance of the Hippocratic Oath in 2015—A survey of U.S. medical schools," *Journal of Anesthesia History*, 4 (2), 139–46.

Dowse, G.K., et al. (1985), "The association between Dermatophagoides mites and the increasing prevalence of asthma in village communities with the Papua New Guinea highlands," *Journal of Allergy and Clinical Immunology*, 75, 75–83.

Drachman, D.A. (2006), "Aging of the brain, entropy, and Alzheimer disease," *Neurology*, 67, 1340–52.

Drenos, Fotios and Kirkwood, T.B. (2010), "Selection on alleles affecting human longevity and late-life disease: The example of apolipoprotein E," *PLoS One*, 5 (4), e10022.

Dressler, W.W. (1992), "Culture, stress, and depressive symptoms: Building and testing a model in a specific setting," in J.J. Poggie, B.R. DeWalt, and W.W. Dressler (eds.), *Anthropological Research: Process and Application* (Albany, NY: State University of New York Press), 19–34.

———— (1995), "Modeling biocultural interactions: Examples from studies of stress and cardiovascular disease," *Yearbook of Physical Anthropology*, 38, 27–56.

Du, Xueqin, et al. (2004), "School-milk intervention trial enhances growth and bone mineral accretion in Chinese girls aged 10–12 years in Beijing," *British Journal of Nutrition*, 92 (1), 159–68.

Dubois, L. Zachary (2012), "Associations between transition- specific stress experience, nocturnal decline in ambulatory blood pressure, and C- reactive protein levels among transgender men," *American Journal of Human Biology*, 24 (1), 52–61.

DuBois, L. Zachary, et al. (2017), "Stigma and diurnal cortisol among transitioning transgender men," *Psychoneuroendocrinology*, 82, 59–66.

Dubos, Rene J. and Dubos, Jean (1952), *The White Plague: Tuberculosis, Man, and Society* (Boston: Little & Brown).

Dufour, Darna L. and Piperata, Barbara A. (2008), "Energy expenditure among farmers in developing countries: What do we know?," *American Journal of Human Biology*, 20 (3), 249–58.

Dunlop, Joan H. and Keet, Corinne A. (2018), "Epidemiology of food allergy," *Immunology and Allergy Clinics*, 38 (1), 13–25.

Dunsworth, Holly M., et al. (2012), "Metabolic hypothesis for human altriciality," *Proceedings of the National Academy of Sciences of the United States of America*, 109 (38), 15212–16.

DuPont, Herbert L. (2018), "Gastric acid and enteric infections: Souring on the use of PPIs," *Digestive Diseases and Sciences*, 63 (4), 814–17.

Durisko, Zachary, Mulsant, Benoit H., and Andrews, Paul W. (2015), "An adaptationist perspective on the etiology of depression," *Journal of Affective Disorders*, 172, 315–23.

Eaton, S. Boyd, Eaton III, S.B., and Konner, Melvin J. (1999), "Paleolithic nutrition revisited," in Wenda Trevathan, E. O. Smith, and James J. McKenna (eds.), *Evolutionary Medicine* (New York: Oxford University Press), 313–32.

Eaton, S. Boyd and Konner, Melvin (1985), "Paleolithic nutrition: A consideration of its nature and current implications," *New England Journal of Medicine*, 312, 283–89.

Eaton, S. Boyd, et al. (1994), "Women's reproductive cancers in evolutionary context," *Quarterly Review of Biology*, 69 (3), 353–67.

Ehrenreich, Barbara and English, Deirdre (1978), *For Her Own Good: 150 Years of the Experts' Advice to Women* (Garden City, NY: Anchor Press).

Eisenberg, Dan T.A., Hayes, M. Geoffrey, and Kuzawa, Christopher W (2012), "Delayed paternal age of reproduction in humans is associated with longer telomeres across two generations of descendants," *Proceedings of the National Academy of Sciences*, 109 (26), 10251–56.

Eisenberg, Dan T.A. and Kuzawa, Christopher W. (2013), "Commentary: The evolutionary biology of the paternal age effect on telomere length," *International Journal of Epidemiology*, 42 (2), 462-465.

———— (2018), "The paternal age at conception effect on offspring telomere length: Mechanistic, comparative and adaptive perspectives," *Philosophical Transactions of the Royal Society B: Biological Sciences*, 373 (1741), 20160442.

Eisenberg, Dan T.A., Kuzawa, Christopher W., and Hayes, M. Geoffrey (2010), "Worldwide allele frequencies of the human apolipoprotein E gene: Climate, local adaptations, and evolutionary history," *American Journal of Physical Anthropology*, 143 (1), 100–11.

Ellaway, Rachel H., Cooper, Gerry, Al-Idrissi, Tracy, Dubé, Tim, and Graves, Lisa, (2014). "Discourses of student orientation to medical education programs." *Medical Education Online* 19:23714.

Emera, Deena, Romero, Roberto, and Wagner, Günter (2012), "The evolution of menstruation: A new model for genetic assimilation," *BioEssays*, 34 (1), 26–35.

Engler-Stringer, R., et al. (2014), "The community and consumer food environment and children's diet: A systematic review," *BMC Public Health*, 14, 522.

Epstein, M.B., et al. (2013), "Household fuels, low birth weight, and neonatal death in India: The separate impacts of biomass, kerosene, and coal," *International Journal of Hygiene and Environmental Health*, 216 (5), 523–32.

Ericksen, Karen and Brunette, Tracy (1996), "Patterns and predictors of infertility among African women: A cross-national survey of twenty-seven nations," *Social Science & Medicine*, 42 (2), 209–20.

Erlenmeyer-Kimling, L and Paradowski, W (1966), "Selection and schizophrenia," *American Naturalist*, 100, 651–65.

Espinoza, E., Hidalgo, L., and Chedraui, P. (2005), "The effect of malaria infection on maternal-fetal outcome in Ecuador," *Journal of Maternal-Fetal & Neonatal Medicine*, 18 (2), 101–05.

Estroff, S.E. (1981), *Making It Crazy: An Ethnography of Psychiatric Clients in an American Community* (Berkeley: University of California Press).

———— (1989), "Self, identity, and subjective experiences of schizophrenia: In search of the subject," *Schizophrenia Bulletin*, 15, 189–96.

Etkin, Nina L. and Ross, Paul J. (1991), "Recasting malaria, medicine and meals: A perspective on disease adaptation," in Lola Romanucci-Ross, Daniel E Moerman, and Laurence R Tancredi (eds.), *The Anthropology of Medicine: From Culture to Method* (2nd edn.; New York: Bergin & Garvey), 230–58.

Ettinger, Bruce, et al. (2012), "Evolution of postmenopausal hormone therapy between 2002 and 2009," *Menopause*, 19 (6), 610–15.

Eveleth, Phyllis B. and Tanner, James M. (1990), *Worldwide Variation in Human Growth* (2nd edn.; New York: Cambridge University Press).

Ewald, Paul W. (1994), *Evolution of Infectious Disease* (New York: Oxford University Press).

Fabrega, H. and Silver, D.B. (1973), *Illness and Shamanistic Curing in Zinacantan: An Ethnomedical Analysis* (Stanford: Stanford University Press).

Fabrega Jr., Horacio (1997), *Evolution of Sickness and Healing* (Berkeley: University of California Press).

Fadiman, Anne (1997), *The Spirit Catches You and You Fall Down* (New York: Farrar, Straus, and Giroux).

Fallon, A. and Rozin, P. (1985), "Sex differences in perceptions of desirable body shape," *Journal of Abnormal Psychology*, 94, 102–05.

Farmer, Paul (2001), *Infections and Inequalities: The Modern Plagues*, Updated Edition (Berkeley: University of California Press).

———— (2004), "An anthropology of structural violence," *Current Anthropology*, 45 (3), 305–25.

———— (2014), "Diary," *London Review of Books* [Online] 36 (20), 38–39.

———— (2019), *To Repair the World: Paul Farmer Speaks to the Next Generation*, California Series in Public Anthropology 29 (Berkeley: University of California Press).

Farrer, L.A., et al. (1997), "Effects of age, sex, and ethnicity on the association between apolipoprotein E genotype and Alzheimer disease: A meta-analysis," *Journal of the American Medical Association*, 278, 1349–56.

Fasano, Alessio, et al. (2015), "Nonceliac gluten sensitivity," *Gastroenterology*, 148 (6), 1195–04.

Feagin, Joe and Bennefield, Zinobia (2014), "Systemic racism and U.S. health care," *Social Science & Medicine*, 103, 7–14.

Fenner, Frank (ed.), (1988), *Smallpox and its Eradication* (Geneva: World Health Organization).

Fenske, Nora, et al. (2013), "Understanding child stunting in India: A comprehensive analysis of socio-economic, nutritional and environmental determinants using additive quantile regression," *PLoS ONE*, 8 (11), e78692.

Fessler, Daniel M.T. (2002), "Reproductive immunosuppression and diet: An evolutionary perspective on pregnancy sickness and meat consumption," *Current Anthropology*, 43 (1), 19–61.

Finch, C.E. and Sapolsky, R.M. (1999), "The evolution of Alzheimer disease, the reproductive schedule, and apoE isoforms," *Neurobiology of Aging*, 20, 407–28.

Finkel, T. and Holbrook, N.J. (2000), "Oxidants, oxidative stress and the biology of aging," *Nature*, 408, 239–47.

Finn, C.A. (1994), "The adaptive significance of menstruation," *Human Reproduction*, 9 (7), 1202–07.

Fiolet, Thibault, et al. (2018), "Consumption of ultra-processed foods and cancer risk: Results from NutriNet-Santé prospective cohort," *BMJ*, 360, k322.

Fitzgerald, Maureen H. (1990), "The interplay of culture and symptoms: Menstrual symptoms among Samoans," *Medical Anthropology*, 12 (2), 145–67.

Fitzsimmons, Colin Matthew, Falcone, Franco Harald, and Dunne, David William (2014), "Helminth allergens, parasite-specific IgE, and its protective role in human immunity," *Frontiers in Immunology*, 5, 61.

Flaxman, S.M. and Sherman, P.W. (2000), "Morning sickness: A mechanism for protecting mother and embryo," *Quarterly Review of Biology*, 75, 113–48.

Fleming, Peter J. and Blair, Peter S. (2015), "Making informed choices on co-sleeping with your baby," *BMJ*, 350.

Fleming-Dutra, Katherine E., Mangione-Smith, Rita, and Hicks, Lauri A. (2016), "How to prescribe fewer unnecessary antibiotics: Talking points that work with patients and their families," *American Family Physician*, 94 (3), 200–02.

Flesch, Hannah (2013), "A foot in both worlds: Education and the transformation of Chinese medicine in the United States," *Medical Anthropology*, 32 (1), 8–24.

Flinn, Mark V. and England, Barry G. (1997), "Social economics of childhood glucocorticoid stress response and health," *American Journal of Physical Anthropology*, 102 (1), 33–53.

Flöistrup, Helen, et al. (2006), "Allergic disease and sensitization in Steiner school children," *Journal of Allergy and Clinical Immunology*, 117 (1), 59–66.

Floud, Roderick, Wachter, Kenneth, and Gregory, Annabel (1990), *Height, Health and History: Nutritional Status in the United Kingdom, 1750–1980* (Cambridge University Press).

Forbush, K., Heatherton, T.F., and Keel, P.K. (2007), "Relationships between perfectionism and specific disordered eating behaviors," *International Journal of Eating Disorders*, 40, 37–41.

Ford, A.B., et al. (1990), "Race-related differences among elderly urban residents: A cohort study, 1975–1984," *Journal of Gerontology*, 45, S163–71.

Forrester, Terrence (2004), "Historic and early life origins of hypertension in Africans," *Journal of Nutrition*, 134 (1), 211–16.

Forsyth, Colin (2018), "From lemongrass to ivermectin: Ethnomedical management of Chagas disease in tropical Bolivia," *Medical Anthropology*, 37 (3), 236–52.

Foster, George M. and Anderson, Barbara G. (1978), *Medical Anthropology* (New York: John Wiley & Sons, Inc.).

Foucault, M. ([1963] 1994), *The Birth of the Clinic: An Archaeology of Medical Perception* (New York: Vintage Books).

Foucault, Michel ([1961] 1971), *Madness and Civilization: A History of Insanity in the Age of Reason* (London: Tavistock).

Foulks, Edward F. (1972), *The Arctic Hysterias* (Washington, DC: American Anthropological Association).

Fowden, A.L. and Moore, T. (2012), "Maternal–fetal resource allocation: Co-operation and conflict," *Placenta*, 33, e11–e15.

Frank, Guido K.W. (2015), "Advances from neuroimaging studies in eating disorders," *CNS Spectrums*, 20, 391–00.

Frank, Reanne (2007), "What to make of it? The (re) emergence of a biological conceptualizaiton of race in health disparities," *Social Science & Medicine*, 64, 1977–83.

Franke, Richard W. and Chasin, Barbara H. (1992), "Kerala State India: Radical reform as development," *International Journal of Health Services*, 22, 139–56.

Frassetto, L., et al. (2000), "Worldwide incidence of hip fracture in elderly women: Relation to consumption of animal and vegetable foods," *Journal of Gerontology Series A: Biological Science and Medical Sciences*, 55, M585–92.

Fredriksen-Goldsen, K.I., et al. (2014), "The health equity promotion model: Reconceptualization of lesbian, gay, bisexual, and transgender (LGBT) health disparities," *American Journal of Orthopsychiatry*, 84 (6), 653–63.

Freidenfelds, Lara (2009), *The Modern Period: Menstruation in Twentieth-Century America* (Baltimore: Johns Hopkins University Press).

Friel, Sharon and Marmot, Michael G. (2011), "Action on the social determinants of health and health inequities goes global," *Annual Review of Public Health*, 32 (1), 225–36.

Frisch, R.E. (1994), "The right weight: Body fat, menarche and fertility," *Proceedings of the Nutrition Society*, 53 (1), 113–29.

Froehlich, T.E., Bogardus, S.T., and Inouye, S.K. (2001), "Dementia and race: Are there differences between African Americans and Caucasians?," *Journal of the American Geriatric Society*, 49, 477–84.

Frohock, Fred M. (1992), *Healing Powers: Alternative Medicine, Spiritual Communities, and the State* (Chicago: University of Chicago Press).

Fujita, S. and Volpi, E. (2006), "Amino acids and muscle loss with aging," *Journal of Nutrition*, 136, 277S-80.

Fullerton, S.M., et al. (2000), "Apolipoprotein E variation at the sequence haplotype level: Implications for the origin and maintenance of a major human polymorphism," *American Journal of Human Genetics*, 67, 881–900.

Gaesser, Glenn A. and Angadi, Siddhartha S. (2015), "Navigating the gluten-free boom," *Journal of the American Academy of PAs*, 28 (8), 1–7.

Gaines, Atwood D. (1992), "Medical/psychiatric knowledge in France and the United States: Culture and sickness in history and biology," in A.D. Gaines (ed.), *Ethnopsychiatry* (Albany: State University of New York Press), 171–01.

Garfinkel, M.S., et al. (1998), "Yoga-based intervention for carpal tunnel syndrome," *Journal of the American Medical Association*, 280, 1601–03.

Garrett, Laurie (1994), *The Coming Plague* (New York: Penguin Books).

Gaskins, Audrey J., Toth, Thomas L., and Chavarro, Jorge E. (2015), "Prepregnancy nutrition and early pregnancy outcomes," *Current Nutrition Reports*, 4 (3), 265–72.

Gatt, Justine M., et al. (2015), "Specific and common genes implicated across major mental disorders: A review of meta-analysis studies," *Journal of Psychiatric Research*, 60, 1–13.

Gawande, Atul (2004), "The bell curve," *The New Yorker*. December 6, 82-91.

_____ (2008), *Better: A Surgeon's Notes on Performance* (New York: Picador).

Ge, Fangmin, et al. (2013), "Gender issues in solid organ donation and transplantation," *Ann Transplant*, 18 (508), 14.

Geronimus, Arline T. (1996), "Black/white differences in the relationship of maternal age to birthweight: A population-based test of the weathering hypothesis," *Social Science & Medicine*, 42 (4), 589–97.

Geronimus, Arline T. (2013), "Deep integration: Letting the epigenome out of the bottle without losing sight of the structural origins of population health," *American Journal of Public Health*, 103 (S1), S56–63.

Geronimus, Arline T., Bound, J., and Waidmann, T.A. (1999), "Health inequality and population variation in fertility timing," *Social Science & Medicine*, 49 (12), 1623–36.

Geronimus, Arline T., et al. (2010), "Do U.S. black women experience stress-related accelerated biological aging?," *Human Nature*, 21 (1), 19–38.

Gesing, Adam, et al. (2014), "Growth hormone abolishes beneficial effects of calorie restriction in long-lived Ames dwarf mice," *Experimental Gerontology*, 58, 219–29.

Ghosh, Manonita, et al. (2016), "'It has to be fixed': A qualitative inquiry into perceived ADHD behaviour among affected individuals and parents in Western Australia," *BMC Health Services Research*, 16 (1), 141.

Giblin, James Cross (1995), *When Plague Strikes: The Black Death, Smallpox, AIDS* (New York: HarperCollins).

Ginsburg, Faye and Rapp, Rayna (2013), "Disability worlds," *Annual Review of Anthropology*, 42, 53–68.

_____ (2020), "Disability/anthropology: Rethinking the parameters of the human," *Current Anthropology*, 61 (S21), S4-S15.

Giovannucci, Edward (2019), "A growing link—What is the role of height in cancer risk?," *British Journal of Cancer*, 120 (6), 575–76.

Glaser, R. and Kiecolt-Glaser, J.K. (eds.) (1994), *Handbook of Human Stress and Immunity* (New York: Academic Press).

Glover, Vivette, O'Connor, T.G., and O'Donnell, Kieran (2010), "Prenatal stress and the programming of the HPA axis," *Neuroscience & Biobehavioral Reviews*, 35 (1), 17–22.

Gluckman, Peter D., Hanson, Mark A., and Low, Felicia M. (2019), "Evolutionary and developmental mismatches are consequences of adaptive developmental plasticity in humans and have implications for later disease risk," *Philosophical Transactions of the Royal Society B*, 374 (1770), 20180109.

Goertz, C. (1996), "Summary of 1995 ACA annual statistical survey on chiropractic practice," *Journal of the American Chiropractic Association*, 33, 35–41.

Goffman, Erving (1963), *Stigma: Notes on the Management of Spoiled Identity* (Englewood Cliffs, New Jersey: Prentice-Hall).

Goldizen, Fiona C., Sly, Peter D., and Knibbs, Luke D. (2016), "Respiratory effects of air pollution on children," *Pediatric Pulmonology*, 51 (1), 94–108.

Goldstein, Joseph (2010), "The New Age caveman and the city," *New York Times*, January 8, 2010.

Goldstein, M.S., et al. (2002), "The impact of treatment confidence on pain and related disability among patients with low-back pain: Results from the University of California, Los Angeles, low-back pain study," *Spine Journal*, 2, 391–99.

Gomes, Nuno, et al. (2011), "Comparative biology of mammalian telomeres: Hypotheses on ancestral states and the roles of telomeres in longevity determination," *Aging Cell*, 10 (5), 761–68.

Goodman, Alan H. and Armelagos, George J. (1985), "Disease and death at Dr. Dickson's mounds," *Natural History*, 94 (9), 12–18.

Goodwin, F.K. and Jamison, K.R. (1990), *Manic-Depressive Illness* (New York: Oxford University Press).

Goosby, Bridget J., Cheadle, Jacob E., and Mitchell, Colter (2018), "Stress-related biosocial mechanisms of discrimination and African American health inequities," *Annual Review of Sociology*, 44 (1), 319–40.

Gosling, Anna L., et al. (2015), "Pacific populations, metabolic disease and 'just-so stories': A critique of the "Thrifty Genotype" hypothesis in Oceania," *Annals of Human Genetics*, 79 (6), 470–80.

Gottesman, II and Shields, J. (1982), *Schizophrenia: The Epigenetic Puzzle* (Cambridge: Cambridge University Press).

Goulet, Olivier (2015), "Potential role of the intestinal microbiota in programming health and disease," *Nutrition Reviews*, 73 (Suppl 1), 32–40.

Graignic-Philippe, R., et al. (2014), "Effects of prenatal stress on fetal and child development: A critical literature review," *Neuroscience & Biobehavioral Reviews*, 43, 137–62.

Grant, K.A., et al. (2009), "Maternal prenatal anxiety, postnatal caregiving and infants' cortisol responses to the still-face procedure," *Developmental Psychobiology*, 51 (8), 625–37.

Gravlee, Clarence C. (2009), "How race becomes biology: Embodiment of social inequality," *American Journal of Physical Anthropology*, 139 (1), 47–57.

Gravlee, Clarence C., Dressler, William W., and Bernard, H. Russell (2005), "Skin color, social classification, and blood pressure in southeastern Puerto Rico," *American Journal of Public Health*, 95 (12), 2191–97.

Greenburg, G. (2001), "As good as dead: Is there really such a thing as brain death?" *The New Yorker*, August 13, 36–43.

Greenhalgh, Susan (2016), "Disordered eating/eating disorder: Hidden perils of the nation's fight against fat," *Medical Anthropology Quarterly*, 30 (4), 545–62.

Grillenberger, Monika, et al. (2003), "Food supplements have a positive impact on weight gain and the addition of animal source foods increases lean body mass of Kenyan schoolchildren," *Journal of Nutrition*, 133, 3957S–3964S.

Gruenbaum, Ellen (1982), "The movement against clitoridectomy and infibulation in Sudan: Public health policy and the women's movement," *Medical Anthropology Newsletter*, 13, 4–12.

———— (2005), "Socio-cultural dynamics of female genital cutting: Research findings, gaps, and directions," *Culture, Health & Sexuality*, 7 (5), 429–41.

Gruenbaum, Ellen and Wirtz, Elizabeth (2015), "Female genital cutting debates," *The International Encyclopedia of Human Sexuality*, 369–26.

Guerra-Reyes, Lucia (2019), *Changing Birth in the Andes: Culture, Policy, and Safe Motherhood in Peru* (Nashville, TN: Vanderbilt University Press).

Guilmoto, Christophe Z., et al. (2018), "Excess under-5 female mortality across India: A spatial analysis using 2011 census data," *The Lancet Global Health*, 6 (6), e650–e58.

Gunnar, M.R., et al. (1996), "Stress reactivity and attachment security," *Developmental Psychobiology*, 29 (3), 191–04.

Gururaj, M.S., Siddapa, Anitha, and Kulkarni, A.G. (2015), "Sociodemographic determinants of low birth weight: A hospital based prospective case control study in rural south India," *International Journal of Tropical Medicine and Public Health*, 5 (1), 13–16.

Gutin, Iliya (2018), "In BMI we trust: Reframing the body mass index as a measure of health," *Social Theory & Health: STH*, 16 (3), 256–71.

Hagel, Isabel, et al. (2004), "The role of parasites in genetic susceptibility to allergy," *Clinical Reviews in Allergy & Immunology*, 26 (2), 75–83.

Hahn, R.A. (1998), "The nocebo phenomenon: Concept, evidence, and implications for public health," in PJ Brown (ed.), *Understanding and Applying Medical Anthropology* (Mountain View, CA: Mayfield), 138–46.

Hahn, Robert A. and Inhorn, Marcia C. (eds.) (2009), *Anthropology and Public Health: Bridging Differences in Culture and Society* (New York: Oxford University Press).

Haig, David (1993), "Genetic conflicts in human pregnancy," *Quarterly Review of Biology*, 68 (4), 495–32.

Haines, A., et al. (2006), "Climate change and human health: Impacts, vulnerability and public health," *Public Health*, 120 (7), 585–96.

Hales, Craig M., et al. (2017), "Prevalence of obesity among adults and youth: United States, 2015–2016," *NCHS Data Brief* (288), 1–8.

Hamilton, Jean A. (1996), "Women and Health Policy: On the inclusion of females in clinical trials," in Carolyn F. Sargeant and Caroline B Brettell (eds.), *Gender and Health: An International Perspective* (Upper Saddle River, NJ: Prentice-Hall), 292–25.

Hammer, M.D. and Crippen, D. (2006), "Brain death and withdrawal of support," *Surgical Clinics of North America*, 86, 1541–51.

Handelsman, David J. (2013), "Global trends in testosterone prescribing, 2000–2011: Expanding the spectrum of prescription drug misuse," *Medical Journal of Australia*, 199 (8), 548–41.

Hardin, Jessica (2016), "'Healing is a done deal': Temporality and metabolic healing among evangelical Christians in Samoa," *Medical Anthropology*, 35 (2), 105–18.

Harris, Marvin (1985), *Good to Eat: Riddles of Food and Culture* (Prospect Heights, IL: Waveland Press).

Harvey, T.S. (2008), "Where there is no patient: An anthropological treatment of a biomedical category," *Culture, Medicine, and Psychiatry*, 32 (4), 577.

Hausdorff, J.M., Rios, D.A., and Edelber, H.K. (2001), "Gait variability and fall risk in community-living older adults: A 1-year prospective study," *Archives of Physical Medicine and Rehabilitation*, 82, 1050–56.

Hawkes, Kristen (2003), "Grandmothers and the evolution of human longevity," *American Journal of Human Biology*, 15, 380–900.

Hawlena, Hadas and Ben-Ami, Frida (2015), "A community perspective on the evolution of virulence," in Serge Morand, Boris R. Krasnov, and D. Timothy J. Littlewood (eds.), *Parasite Diversity and Diversification: Evolutionary Ecology Meets Phylogenetics* (Cambridge, UK: Cambridge University Press), 376–400.

Hays, J.N. (1998), *The Burdens of Disease: Epidemics and Human Response in Western History* (New Brunswick, NJ: Rutgers University Press).

Hegsted, D. Mark (2001), "Fractures, calcium, and the modern diet," *American Journal of Clinical Nutrition*, 74, 571–73.

Heinemann, Laura Lynn (2014), "For the sake of others: Reciprocal webs of obligation and the pursuit of transplantation as a caring act," *Medical Anthropology Quarterly*, 28 (1), 66–84.

Hempel, A.G., et al. (2000), "A cross-cultural review of sudden mass assault by a single individual in the oriental and occidental cultures," *Journal of Forensic Science*, 45, 582–88.

Henderson, R. Max (2005), "The bigger the healthier: Are the limits of BMI risk changing over time?," *Economics and Human Biology*, 3, 339–66.

Hendrie, H.C. (2006), "Lessons learned from international comparative cross-cultural studies on dementia," *American Journal of Geriatric Psychiatry*, 14, 480–88.

Hendrie, H.C., et al. (1995), "Prevalence of Alzheimer's disease and dementia in two communities: Nigerian Africans and African Americans," *American Journal of Psychiatry*, 152, 1485–92.

Hennegan, Julie, et al. (2019), "Women's and girls' experiences of menstruation in low- and middle-income countries: A systematic review and qualitative metasynthesis," *PLoS Medicine*, 16 (5), e1002803–03.

Herforth, Anna, et al. (2019), "A global review of food-based dietary guidelines," *Advances in Nutrition*, 10 (4), 590-605.

Hering, Dagmara, Lachowska, Kamila, and Schlaich, Markus (2015), "Role of the sympathetic nervous system in stress-mediated cardiovascular disease," *Current Hypertension Reports*, 17 (10), 1–9.

Heritage, John and Maynard, Douglas W. (eds.) (2006), *Communication in Medical Care: Interaction between primary care physicians and patients* (New York: Cambridge University Press).

Hewlett, Barry S. and Hewlett, Bonnie L. (2007), *Ebola, Culture and Politics: The Anthropology of an Emerging Disease* (Boston: Cengage Learning).

Heyman, Melvin B. and the Committee on Nutrition (2006), "Lactose intolerance in infants, children, and adolescents," *Pediatrics*, 118 (3), 1279–86.

Heyneman, Donald (1984), "Development and disease: A dual dilemma," *Journal of Parasitology*, 79 (1), 3–17.

Hidaka, Brandon H., et al. (2015), "The status of evolutionary medicine education in North American medical schools," *BMC Medical Education*, 15 (1), 1–9.

Hill, Holly A., Elam-Evans, Laurie D, Yankey, David, Singleton, James. A., and Dietz, Vance (2016), "Vaccination coverage among children aged 19–35 months—United States, 2015," *Morbidity and Mortality Weekly Report*, 65(39), 1065-1071.

Himmelstein, D.U., et al. (2006), "Discounting the debtors will not make medical bankruptcy disappear," *Health Affairs*, 25, w84–88.

Hindell, J. (1999), "Transplant first in Japan," *BBC News*, February 28, http://news.bbc.co.uk/1/hi/health/287880.stm,.

Hinrichsen, G.A. and Ramirez, M. (1992), "Black and white dementia caregivers: A comparison of their adaptation, adjustment, and service utilization," *Gerontologist*, 32, 375–80.

Hirvonen, Kalle, et al. (2019), "Affordability of the EAT-Lancet reference diet: A global analysis," *The Lancet Global Health*.8 (1) e59-e66

Hoffer, Edward P. (2019), "America's health care system is broken: What went wrong and how we can fix it.

Part 3: Hospitals and doctors," *The American Journal of Medicine*, 132 (9), 1013–16.

Holmgren, Anton, et al. (2019), "Nordic populations are still getting taller–secular changes in height from the 20th to 21st century," *Acta Paediatrica*, 108, 1311-1320.

Holt-Lunstad, Julianne, Smith, Timothy B., and Layton, J. Bradley (2010), "Social relationships and mortality risk: A meta-analytic review," *PLoS Medicine*, 7 (7), e1000316.

Horie, Masayuki, et al. (2010), "Endogenous non-retroviral RNA virus elements in mammalian genomes," *Nature*, 463 (7277), 84–87.

Hosangadi, Divya (2019), The Global Rise of Dengue Infections. https://www.outbreakobservatory.org/outbreakthursday-1/3/21/2019/the-global-rise-of-dengue-infections

Hou, C.E., et al. (2006), "Frequency of dementia etiologies in four ethnic groups," *Dementia and Geriatric Cognitive Disorders*, 22, 42–47.

Howell, Nancy (1979), *Demography of the Dobe Kung* (New York: Academic Press).

_____ (2010), *Life Histories of the Dobe !Kung: Food, Fatness, and Well-being over the Life-span* (Berkeley: University of California Press).

Hrdy, Sarah Blaffer (1999), *Mother Nature: A History of Mothers, Infants, and Natural Selection* (New York: Pantheon Books).

_____ (2009), *Mothers and Others* (Cambridge: Harvard University Press).

Huard, Richard C., et al. (2006), "Novel genetic polymorphisms that further delineate the phylogeny of the Mycobacterium tuberculosis complex," *Journal of Bacteriology*, 188 (12), 4271–87.

Hudson, Kathy L. and Collins, Francis S. (2017), "The 21st Century Cures Act—A view from the NIH," *New England Journal of Medicine*, 376 (2), 111–13.

Huebbe, Patricia and Rimbach, Gerald (2017), "Evolution of human apolipoprotein E (APOE) isoforms: Gene structure, protein function and interaction with dietary factors," *Ageing Research Reviews*, 37, 146–61.

Hughes, Charles C. (1998), "The glossary of culture-bound syndromes" in DSM-IV: A critique," *Transcultural Psychiatry*, 35 (3), 413–21.

Hughes, J.J. and Keown, D. (1995), "Buddhism and medical ethics: A bibliographic introduction," *Journal of Buddhist Ethics*, 2, 105–24.

Hunt, Linda M., et al. (2017), "Electronic health records and the disappearing patient," *Medical Anthropology Quarterly*, 31 (3), 403–21.

Huq, Anwar, et al. (2010), "Simple sari cloth filtration of water is sustainable and continues to protect villagers from cholera in Matlab, Bangladesh," *mBio*, 1 (1), e00034-10.

Hursting, S.D., et al. (2003), "Calorie restriction, aging, and cancer prevention: Mechanisms of action and applicability to humans," *Annual Review of Medicine*, 54, 131–52.

Hurtado, A. Magdalena, et al. (2003), "Longitudinal study of tuberculosis outcomes among immunologically naive Ache natives of Paraguay," *American Journal of Physical Anthropology*, 121 (2), 134–50.

Hurwitz, E.L., et al. (2002), "A randomized trial of medical care with and without physical therapy and chiropractic care with and without physical modalities for patients with low back pain: 6-month follow-up outcomes from the UCLA low back pain study," *Spine*, 27, 2193–04.

Hurwitz, E.L., Morgenstern, H., and Yu, F. (2005), "Satisfaction as a predictor of clinical outcomes among chiropractic and medical patients enrolled in the UCLA low back pain study," *Spine*, 30, 2121–28.

Hurwitz, E.L., et al. (2006), "A randomized trial of chiropractic and medical care for patients with low back pain: Eighteen-month follow-up outcomes from the UCLA low back pain study," *Spine*, 31, 611–21.

Ianiro, Gianluca, Tilg, Herbert, and Gasbarrini, Antonio (2016), "Antibiotics as deep modulators of gut microbiota: Between good and evil," *Gut*, 65 (11), 1906–15.

Inhorn, Marcia C. (1996), *Infertility and Patriarchy: The Cultural Politics of Gender and Family Life in Egypt* (Philadelphia: University of Pennsylvania Press).

_____ (2003), "Global infertility and the globalization of new reproductive technologies: Illustrations from Egypt," *Social Science & Medicine*, 56, 1837–51.

Inhorn, Marcia C. and Patrizio, Pasquale (2015), "Infertility around the globe: New thinking on gender, reproductive technologies and global movements in the 21st century," *Human Reproduction Update*, 21 (4), 411–26.

Itan, Yuval, et al. (2010), "A worldwide correlation of lactase persistence phenotype and genotypes," *BMC Evolutionary Biology*, 10 (1), 36.

Jablensky, A., et al. (1992), "Schizophrenia: Manifestations, incidence and course in different cultures: A World Health Organization ten-country study," *Psychological Medicine*, 20 (Supplement), 1–97.

Jackson, G., Gillies, H., and Osterloh, I. (2005), "Past, present, and future: A 7-year update of Viagra (sildenafil citrate)," *International Journal of Clinical Practice*, 59 (6), 680–91.

Jamison, Kay Redfield (1993), *Touched with Fire: Manic-Depressive Illness and the Artistic Temperament* (New York: Free Press).

Janes, Craig R. and Corbett, Kitty K. (2009), "Anthropology and global health," *Annual Review of Anthropology*, 38, 167–83.

Jarvis, Judith K. and Miller, Gregory D. (2002), "Overcoming the barrier of lactose intolerance to reduce health disparities," *Journal of the National Medical Association*, 94 (2), 55–66.

Jeffery, Patricia, Jeffery, Roger, and Lyon, Andrew (1988), *Labour Pains and Labour Power: Women and Childbearing in India* (London: Zed Books, Ltd.).

Jeffery, Roger and Jeffery, Patricia (1997), *Population, Gender, and Politics* (New York: Cambridge University Press).

Jelliffe, D.B. (1972), "Commerciogenic malnutrition?," *Nutrition Reviews*, 30 (9), 199–05.

Jenkins, Janis H (2015), *Extraordinary Conditions: Culture and Experience in Mental Illness* (University of California Press).

Johns, Timothy and Duquette, M. (1991), "Detoxification and mineral supplementation as functions of geophagy," *American Journal of Clinical Nutrition*, 53, 448–56.

Johnson, Adiv A., Shokhirev, Maxim N., and Shoshitaishvili, Boris (2019), "Revamping the evolutionary theories of aging," *Ageing Research Reviews* 55 (November), 100947.

Johnson, Anna B., et al. (2018), "Attachment security buffers the HPA axis of toddlers growing up in poverty or near poverty: Assessment during pediatric well-child exams with inoculations," *Psychoneuroendocrinology*, 95, 120–27.

Johnson, T.M. (1987), "Premenstrual syndrome as a Western culture-specific disorder," *Culture, Medicine and Psychiatry*, 11 (3), 337–56.

Jones, C.P., LaVeist, T.A., and Lillie-Blanton, M. (1991), "'Race' in the epidemiologic literature: An examination of the *American Journal of Epidemiology*, 1921–1990," *American Journal of Epidemiology*, 134, 1079–84.

Jones, Gareth, et al. (2003), "How many child deaths can we prevent this year?," *The Lancet*, 362 (9377), 65–71.

Jordan, Brigitte (1993), *Birth in Four Cultures* (Fourth edn.; Prospect Heights, IL: Waveland Press).

Jutla, Antarpreet, et al. (2013), "Environmental factors influencing epidemic cholera," *American Journal of Tropical Medicine and Hygiene*, 89 (3), 597–07.

Kahn, Jonathan (2006), "Genes, race, and population: Avoiding a collision of categories," *American Journal of Public Health*, 96 (11), 1965–70.

_____ (2013), *Race in a Bottle: The Story of BiDil and Racialized Medicine in a Post-Genomic Age* (New York: Columbia University Press).

Kaiser, Bonnie and Bouskill, Kathryn (2013), "What predicts breast cancer rates? Testing hypotheses of the demographic and nutrition transitions," *Journal of Population Research*, 30 (1), 67–85.

Kalipeni, Ezekiel (2000), "Health and disease in southern Africa: A comparative and vulnerability perspective," *Social Science & Medicine*, 50, 965–83.

Kalofonos, Ippolytos Andreas (2010), "'All I eat is ARVs,'" *Medical Anthropology Quarterly*, 24 (3), 363–80.

Kaptchuk, Ted J. (2002), "Acupuncture: Theory, efficacy, and practice," *Annals of Internal Medicine*, 136, 374–83.

Karlsson, J.L. (1970), "Genetic association of giftedness and creativity with schizophrenia," *Hereditas*, 66, 177–81.

_____ (1984), "Creative intelligence in the relatives of mental patients," *Hereditas*, 100, 83–86.

Katz, Joanne, et al. (2013), "Mortality risk in preterm and small-for-gestational-age infants in low-income and middle-income countries: A pooled country analysis," *The Lancet*, 382 (9890), 417–25.

Katz, Solomon H. (1987), "Fava bean consumption: A case for the coevolution of genes and culture," in Marvin Harris and Eric B Ross (eds.), *Food and Evolution: Toward a Theory of Human Food Habits* (Philadelphia: Temple University Press), 133–59.

Katzman, M.A. and Lee, S. (1997), "Beyond body image: The integration of feminist and transcultural theories in the understanding of self starvation," *International Journal of Eating Disorders*, 22, 385–94.

Katzman, M.A., et al. (2004), "Not your 'typical island woman': Anorexia nervosa is reported only in subcultures in Curacao," *Culture, Medicine and Psychiatry*, 28, 463–92.

Kawachi, Ichiro and Subramanian, S.V. (2014), "Income inequality," in Lisa F. Berkman, Ichiro Kawachi, and M. Maria Glymour (eds.), *Social Epidemiology* (2nd edn.; New York: Oxford University Press), 126–51.

Keita, S.O.Y (2006), "BiDil and the possibility of a resurgent racial biology and medicine," *Anthropology News*, 46 (7), 31–32.

Kendler, K.S., et al. (1993), "The prediction of major depression in women: Toward an integrated etiologic model," *American Journal of Psychiatry*, 150, 1139–48.

Kent, George (2015), "Global infant formula: Monitoring and regulating the impacts to protect human health," *International Breastfeeding Journal*, 10, 6.

Keogh, Ruth H., et al. (2018), "Up-to-date and projected estimates of survival for people with cystic fibrosis using baseline characteristics: A longitudinal study using UK patient registry data," *Journal of Cystic Fibrosis*, 17 (2), 218–27.

Kevles, D.J. (1985), *In the Name of Eugenics* (New York: Alfred A. Knopf).

Khera, Rohan, et al. (2014), "Gender bias in child care and child health: Global patterns," *Archives of Disease in Childhood*, 99 (4), 369–74.

Kibret, Solomon, et al. (2015), "Malaria impact of large dams in sub-Saharan Africa: Maps, estimates and predictions," *Malaria Journal*, 14 (1), 339.

Kim, H.H., Li, P.S., and Goldstein, M. (2010), "Male circumcision: Africa and beyond?," *Current Opinion in Urology*, 20 (6), 515–19.

Kim, Kwang Soon, et al. (2016), "Dietary antigens limit mucosal immunity by inducing regulatory T cells in the small intestine," *Science*, 351 (6275), 858–63.

Kim, Kyoung-Nam and Hong, Yun-Chul (2017), "The exposome and the future of epidemiology: A vision and prospect," *Environmental Health and Toxicology*, 32, e2017009–09.

Kinch, Michael (2018), *Between Hope and Fear: A History of Vaccines and Human Immunity* (Pegasus Books).

King, Charles (2019) Gods of the Upper Air: How a circle of renegade anthropologists reinvented race, sex, and gender in the twentieth century. New York: Doubleday.

King, Janet C. and Garza, Cutberto (2007), "Harmonization of nutrient intake values," *Food and Nutrition Bulletin*, 28 (Suppl 1), S3–12.

Kirkwood, T.B.L. and Rose, M.R. (1991), "Evolution of senescence: Late survival sacrificed for reproduction," *Philosophical Transactions of the Royal Society of London (Series B)*, 332, 15–24.

Kirkwood, T.B.L. and Austad, S.N. (2000), "Why do we age?," *Nature*, 408, 233–38.

Kitzinger, Sheila (1998), "Letter from Europe: The Cesarean epidemic in Great Britain," *Birth*, 25 (1), 56–58.

Klaus, Marshall H. and Kennell, John H. (1976), *Mother–Infant Bonding: The Impact of Early Separation and Loss on Family Development* (St. Louis, MO: C.V. Mosby).

Klein, Elliot, et al. (2018), "Female genital mutilation: Health consequences and complications—A short literature review," *Obstetrics and Gynecology International* https://doi.org/10.1155/2018/7365715.

Kleinman, A. and Good, B. (eds.) (1985), *Culture and Depression* (Berkeley: University of California Press).

Kleinman, Arthur (1988), *The Illness Narratives: Suffering, Healing, & the Human Condition* (New York: Basic Books).

———— (2008), "Catastrophe and Caregiving: The failure of medicine as an art," *The Lancet*, 371, 22–23.

———— (2019), *The Soul of Care: The Moral Education of a Husband and a Doctor* (New York: Viking Press).

Kleinman, Arthur, Eisenbeg, Leon, and Good, Byron (1978), "Culture, illness, and care," *Annals of Internal Medicine*, 88 (2), 251–58.

Klonoff, Elizabeth A. and Landrine, Hope (2002), "Is skin color a marker for racial discrimination?," in Thomas A. LaVeist (ed.), *Race, Ethnicity, and Health* (New York: Jossey-Bass), 340–49.

Knight, Rob (2015), *Follow Your Gut: The Enormous Impact of Tiny Microbes* (New York: Simon and Schuster).

Kobayashi, Shunzo, et al. (2012), "Reproductive history and breast cancer risk," *Breast Cancer (Tokyo, Japan)*, 19 (4), 302–08.

Kohrt, Brandon A., et al. (2008), "Comparison of mental health between former child soldiers and children never conscripted by armed groups in Nepal," *JAMA*, 300 (6), 691–02.

Koidis, Anastasios (2016), "Developing food products for consumers on a gluten-free diet," In *Developing Food Products for Consumers with Specific Dietary Needs*, Steve Osborn and Wayne Morley, eds. (Cambridge, MA: Elsevier) 201–14.

Kolata, Gina (1999), *Flu: The Story of the Great Influenza Pandemic of 1918 and the Search for the Virus That Caused It* (New York: Simon & Schuster).

Komlos, John and Lauderdale, Benjamin E. (2007), "The mysterious trend in American heights in the 20th century," *Annals of Human Biology*, 34 (2), 206–15.

Kondo, Naoki, et al. (2008), "Do social comparisons explain the association between income inequality and health?: Relative deprivation and perceived health among male and female Japanese individuals," *Social Science & Medicine*, 67 (6), 982–87.

Konig, S. (2003), "An organ donor campaign targets Jews," *New York Times*, February 9. https://www.nytimes.com/2003/02/09/nyregion/an-organ-donor-campaign-targets-jews.html

Konner, Melvin and Worthman, Carol M (1980), "Nursing frequency, gonadal function, and birth spacing among the !Kung hunter-gatherers," *Science*, 207, 788–91.

Konner, Melvin and Eaton, S. Boyd (2010), "Paleolithic nutrition twenty-five years later," *Nutrition in Clinical Practice*, 25 (6), 594–02.

Koren, Gideon, Madjunkova, Svetlana, and Maltepe, Caroline (2014), "The protective effects of nausea and vomiting of pregnancy against adverse fetal outcome—A systematic review," *Reproductive Toxicology*, 47, 77–80.

Kramer, M.S. and Kakuma, R. (2012), "Optimal duration of exclusive breastfeeding (Review)," *Cochrane Database Systematic Reviews*, 8, CD003517.

Krieger, N., et al. (2015), "Age at menarche: 50-year socioeconomic trends among U.S.-born black and white women," *American Journal of Public Health*, 105 (2), 388–97.

Krieger, Nancy (2000), "Refiguring 'race'; Epidemiology, racialized biology, and biological expressions of race relations," *International Journal of Health Services*, 30 (1), 211–16.

———— (2002), "Shades of difference: Theoretical underpinnings of the medical controversy on Black-White differences in the United States, 1830–1870," in Thomas A. LaVeist (ed.), *Race, Ethnicity, and Health: A Public Health Reader* (San Francisco: John Wiley & Sons), 11–33.

———— (2005), "Embodiment: A conceptual glossary for epidemiology," *Journal of Epidemiology and Community Health*, 59 (5), 350–55.

———— (2011), *Epidemiology and the People's Health: Theory and Context* (New York: Oxford University Press).

———— (2014), "Discrimination and health inequities," *International Journal of Health Services*, 44 (4), 643–10.

Kumar, Ashwani, et al. (2007), "Burden of malaria in India: Retrospective and prospective view," *American Journal of Tropical Medicine and Hygiene*, 77 (Suppl 6), 69–78.

Kuzawa, Christopher W. (1998), "Adipose tissue in human infancy and childhood: An evolutionary perspective," *American Journal of Physical Anthropology*, 107 (Suppl 27), 177–209.

Lad, V (2002), *Textbook of Ayurveda: Fundamental Principles* (Albuquerque: Ayurvedic Press).

Laderman, Carol (1983), *Wives and Midwives: Childbirth and Nutrition in Rural Malaysia* (Berkeley: University of California Press).

Lafferty, Kevin D. and Mordecai, Erin A. (2016), "The rise and fall of infectious disease in a warmer world," *F1000Research*, 5.

LaFleur, W.R. (2002), "From agape to organs: Religious difference between Japan and America in judging the ethics of the transplant," *Zygon*, 37, 623–42.

Laing, Ronald (2010 [1960]), *The Divided Self: An Existential Study in Sanity and Madness* (London: Penguin).

Lamb, Sarah (2019), "On being (not) old: Agency, self-care, and life- course aspirations in the United States," *Medical Anthropology Quarterly*, 33 (2), 263–81.

Lamberts, S.W.J., van den Beld, A.W., and van der Lely, A.-J. (1997), "The endocrinology of aging," *Science*, 278, 419–24.

Landauer, Thomas and Whiting, John (1964), "Infantile stimulate and adult stature of human males," *American Anthropologist*, 66, 1007.

Landrigan, Philip J., et al. (2018), "Pollution and global health—An agenda for prevention," *Environmental Health Perspectives*, 126 (8), 084501.

Lane, M.A., et al. (2001), "Caloric restriction in primates," *Annals of the New York Academy of Sciences*, 928, 287–95.

Lang, Claudia and Jansen, Eva (2013), "Appropriating depression: Biomedicalizing ayurvedic psychiatry in Kerala, India," *Medical Anthropology*, 32 (1), 25–45.

Larsen, Clark Spencer, et al. (2019), "Bioarchaeology of Neolithic Çatalhöyük reveals fundamental transitions in health, mobility, and lifestyle in early farmers," *Proceedings of the National Academy of Sciences*, 116 (26), 12615–23.

Lassek, William D. and Gaulin, Steven J.C. (2006), "Changes in body fat distribution in relation to parity in American women: A covert form of maternal depletion," *American Journal of Physical Anthropology*, 131 (2), 295–02.

Lasser, K.E., Himmelstein, D.U., and Woolhandler, S. (2006), "Access to care, health status, and health disparities in the United States and Canada: Results of a cross-national population-based survey," *American Journal of Public Health*, 96, 1300–07.

Leclerc-Madlala, S. (2009), "Cultural scripts for multiple and concurrent partnerships in southern Africa: Why HIV prevention needs anthropology," *Sexual Health*, 6 (2), 103–10.

Lederberg, Joshua, Shope, Robert E., and Oaks Jr., Stanley C. (eds.) (1992), *Emerging Infections: Microbial Threats to Health in the United States* (Washington DC: Institute of Medicine, National Academy Press).

Lederman, S.A., et al. (2004), "The effects of the World Trade Center event on birth outcomes among term deliveries at three lower Manhattan hospitals," *Environmental Health Perspectives*, 112 (17), 1772–78.

Lee, J.M., et al. (2007), "Weight status in young girls and the onset of puberty," *Pediatrics*, 119 (3), 624–30.

Lee, Richard B. (1968), "What hunters do for a living, or, how to make out on scarce resources," in R.B. Less and I. DeVore (eds.), *Man the Hunter* (Chicago: Aldine), 30–48.

Leidy, Lynnette E. (1999), "Menopause in evolutionary perspective," in Wenda Trevathan, E.O. Smith, and James J. McKenna (eds.), *Evolutionary Medicine* (New York: Oxford University Press), 407–27.

Leidy Sievert, Lynette (2006), *Menopause: A Biocultural Perspective* (New Brunswick, NJ: Rutgers University Press).

Leighton, Gerald and Clark, Mabel L. (1929), "Milk consumption and the growth of school-children," *Lancet*, 213 (5520), 40–43.

Lener, Marc S. and Iosifescu, Dan V. (2015), "In pursuit of neuroimaging biomarkers to guide treatment selection in major depressive disorder: A review of the literature," *Annals of the New York Academy of Sciences*, 1344 (1), 50–65.

Leon, D.A., Vagero, D., and Olausson, P.O. (1992), "Social class differences in infant mortality in Sweden: Comparisons with England and Wales," *British Medical Journal*, 305 (6855), 687–91.

Leonard, B.E. (2000), "Evidence for a biochemical lesion in depression," *Journal of Clinical Psychiatry*, 61 (Supplement 6), 12–17.

Leslie, Charles (1992), "Interpretations of Illness: Syncretism in modern Ayurveda," in Charles Leslie and Allan Young (eds.), *Paths to Asian Medical Knowledge* (Berkeley: University of California Press), 177–08.

Lewis, C.M., et al. (2003), "Genome scan meta-analysis of schizophrenia and bipolar disorder, Part II: Schizophrenia," *American Journal of Human Genetics*, 73, 34–48.

Lewis, Ronald W., et al. (2010), "Original articles: Definitions/epidemiology/risk factors for sexual dysfunction," *Journal of Sexual Medicine*, 7 (4 Pt 2), 1598–607.

Lewis, Tené T. and Van Dyke, Miriam E. (2018), "Discrimination and the health of African Americans: The potential importance of intersectionalities," *Current Directions in Psychological Science*, 27 (3), 176–82.

Lewontin, Richard C. (1972), "The apportionment of human diversity," *Evolutionary Biology*, 6, 381–98.

Lian, Olaug S. and Bondevik, Hilde (2015), "Medical constructions of long- term exhaustion, past and present," *Sociology of Health & Illness*, 37, 920–35.

Lieberman, Jay A., et al. (2010), "Bullying among pediatric patients with food allergy," *Annals of Allergy, Asthma & Immunology*, 105 (4), 282–86.

Lifton, R.J. (1986), *The Nazi Doctors* (New York: Basic Books).

Linde, Klaus, et al. (2005), "Acupuncture for patients with migraine: A randomized controlled trial," *JAMA*, 293 (17), 2118–25.

Lindeberg, Staffan (2012), "Paleolithic diets as a model for prevention and treatment of Western disease," *American Journal of Human Biology*, 24 (2), 110–15.

Lindenbaum, Shirley (1979), *Kuru Sorcery: Disease and Danger in the New Guinea Highlands* (Palo Alto, CA: Mayfield Publishing Co.).

———— (1987), "Loaves and fishes in Bangladesh," in Marvin Harris and Eric B Ross (eds.), *Food and Evolution* (Philadelphia: Temple University Press), 427–43.

Lionetti, Elena, et al. (2015), "Celiac disease from a global perspective," *Best Practice & Research Clinical Gastroenterology*, 29 (3), 365–79.

Lipp, Erin K., Huq, Anwar, and Colwell, Rita R. (2002), "Effects of global climate on infectious disease: The cholera model," *Clinical Microbiology Reviews*, 15 (4), 757–70.

Liu, Sze Yan and Kawachi, Ichiro (2017), "Discrimination and telomere length among older adults in the United States: Does the association vary by race and type of discrimination?," *Public Health Reports*, 132 (2), 220–30.

Livingston, Julie (2003), "Reconfiguring old age: Elderly women and concerns over care in southeastern Botswana," *Medical Anthropology*, 22, 205–31.

Livingstone, Frank B. (1958), "Anthropological implications of sickle cell gene distribution in West Africa," *American Anthropologist*, 60, 533–62.

Lobo, Roger A. (2017), "Hormone-replacement therapy: Current thinking," *Nature Reviews Endocrinology*, 13 (4), 220–31.

Lobstein, Tim, et al. (2015), "Child and adolescent obesity: Part of a bigger picture," *The Lancet*, 385 (9986), 2510–20.

Lock, M. (1996), "Death in technological time: Locating the end of meaningful life," *Medical Anthropology Quarterly*, 10, 575–00.

——— (1998), "Menopause: Lessons from anthropology," *Psychosomatic Medicine*, 60, 410–19.

Lock, Margaret (2013), *The Alzheimer Conundrum: Entanglements of Dementia and Aging* (Princeton University Press).

Lockley, Steven W. and Foster, Russell G. (2012), *Sleep: A Very Short Introduction* (Oxford: Oxford University Press).

Loe, Meika (2006), *The Rise of Viagra: How the Little Blue Pill Changed Sex in America* (New York: New York University Press).

Lolli, Francesca, et al. (2017), "Androgenetic alopecia: A review," *Endocrine*, 57 (1), 9–17.

Longo, Valter D., et al. (2015), "Interventions to slow aging in humans: Are we ready?," *Aging cell*, 14, 497–01.

Lopez, S.R. and Guarnaccia, P.J. (2000), "Cultural psychopathology: Uncovering the social world of mental illness," *Annual Review of Psychology*, 51, 571–98.

Loudon, I. (2000), "Why are (male) surgeons still addresses as Mr?," *British Medical Journal*, 321, 1589–91.

Lovallo, William R. (2016), *Stress and Health: Biological and Psychological Interactions* (3rd edn.; Thousand Oaks, CA: Sage publications).

Lowsky, David J., et al. (2013), "Heterogeneity in healthy aging," *Journals of Gerontology Series A: Biological Sciences and Medical Sciences*, 69(6), 640-649.

Lozano, Rafael, et al. (2013), "Global and regional mortality from 235 causes of death for 20 age groups in 1990 and 2010: A systematic analysis for the Global Burden of Disease Study 2010," *The Lancet*, 380 (9859), 2095–28.

Lu, Darlene, et al. (2019), "Perceived racism in relation to telomere length among African American women in the Black Women's Health Study," *Annals of Epidemiology*, 36, 33–39.

Lu, Yao (2010), "Rural–urban migration and health: Evidence from longitudinal data in Indonesia," *Social Science & Medicine*, 70 (3), 412–19.

Ludwig, A. (1992), "Creative achievement and psychopathology: Comparison among professions," *American Journal of Psychotherapy*, 46, 330–56.

Lue, Tom F. (2000), "Erectile dysfunction," *New England Journal of Medicine*, 342 (24), 1802–13.

Lukachko, Alicia, Hatzenbuehler, Mark L., and Keyes, Katherine M. (2014), "Structural racism and myocardial infarction in the United States," *Social Science & Medicine*, 103, 42–50.

Maas, Angela H.E.M., et al. (2011), "Red alert for women's heart: The urgent need for more research and knowledge on cardiovascular disease in women: Proceedings of the workshop held in Brussels on gender differences in cardiovascular disease, 29 September 2010," *European Heart Journal*, 32 (11), 1362–68.

Maconochie, N., et al. (2007), "Risk factors for first trimester miscarriage—Results from a UK-population-based case control study," *British Journal of Obstetrics and Gynaecology*, 114 (2), 170–86.

Magiorkinis, Emmanuil, Beloukas, Apostolos, and Diamantis, Aristidis (2011), "Scurvy: Past, present and future," *European Journal of Internal Medicine*, 22 (2), 147–52.

Magkos, Faidon, et al. (2019), "A perspective on the transition to plant-based diets: A diet change may attenuate climate change, but can it also attenuate obesity and chronic disease risk?," *Advances in Nutrition*, 00, 1–9.

Mah, Timothy and Halperin, Daniel (2010), "Concurrent sexual partnerships and the HIV epidemics in Africa: Evidence to move forward," *AIDS and Behavior*, 14 (1), 11–16.

Mahley, R.W. and Rall, S.C. (2000), "Apolipoprotein E: Far more than a lipid transport protein," *Annual Review in Genomics and Human Genetics*, 1, 507–37.

Mainous, A.G., 3rd, et al. (2010), "Life stress and atherosclerosis: A pathway through unhealthy lifestyle," *International Journal of Psychiatry in Medicine*, 40 (2), 147–61.

Maizels, R.M. (2016), "Parasitic helminth infections and the control of human allergic and autoimmune disorders," *Clinical Microbiology and Infection*, 22 (6), 481–86.

Malekzadeh, Reza, Sachdev, Atul, and Fahid Ali, Ayman (2005), "Coeliac disease in developing countries: Middle East, India and North Africa," *Best Practice & Research Clinical Gastroenterology*, 19 (3), 351–58.

Manchanda, P., et al. (2005), "Understanding firm, physician and consumer choice behavior in the pharmaceutical industry," *Marketing Letters*, 16, 293–308.

Mangione-Smith, Rita, et al. (1999), "The relationship between perceived parental expectations and pediatrician antimicrobial prescribing behavior," *Pediatrics*, 103 (4), 711–18.

Mangione-Smith, Rita, et al. (2006), "Ruling out the need for antibiotics: Are we sending the right message," *Archives of Pediatrics & Adolescent Medicine*, 160, 945–52.

Mangione-Smith, Rita, et al. (2015), "Communication practices and antibiotic use for acute respiratory tract infections in children," *Annals of Family Medicine*, 13 (3), 221–27.

Manheimer, Eric W., et al. (2015), "Paleolithic nutrition for metabolic syndrome: Systematic review and meta-analysis," *American Journal of Clinical Nutrition*, 102 (4), 922–32.

Manson, Spero (1996), "Culture and DSM-IV: Implications for the diagnosis of mood and anxiety disorders," in J.E. Mezzich, et al. (eds.), *Culture and Psychiatric Diagnosis; A DSM-IV Perspective* (Washington: American Psychiatric Association), 99–113.

Manton, K.G., Gu, X., and Lamb, V.L. (2006), "Change in chronic disability from 1982 to 2004/2005 as measured by long-term changes in function and health in the U.S. elderly population," *Proceedings of the National Academy of Sciences*, 103, 18374–79.

Mantripragada, K.K., Carroll, L.S., and Williams, N.M. (2010), "Experimental approaches for identifying schizophrenia risk genes," *Current Topics in Behavioral Neuroscience*, 4, 587–10.

Marmot, Michael (2004), *The Status Syndrome: How Social Standing Affects Our Health and Longevity* (New York: Henry Holt and Company).

———— (2015), *The Health Gap: The Challenge of An Unequal World* (London: Bloomsbury Press).

———— (2017a), "Social justice, epidemiology and health inequalities," *European Journal of Epidemiology*, 32 (7), 537–46.

———— (2017b), "The health gap: The challenge of an unequal world: The argument," *International Journal of Epidemiology*, 46 (4), 1312–18.

Marmot, Michael and Wilkinson, Richard G. (eds.) (2006), *Social Determinants of Health* (New York: Oxford University Press).

Marquis, G.S., et al. (1997), "Association of breastfeeding and stunting in Peruvian toddlers: An example of reverse causality," *International Journal of Epidemiology*, 26 (2), 349–56.

Martin, Emily (1987), *The Woman in the Body: A Cultural Analysis of Reproduction* (Boston: Beacon Press).

———— (1988), "Premenstrual Syndrome: Discipline, work, and anger in late industrial societies," in Thomas Buckley and Alma Gottlieb (eds.), *Blood Magic: The Anthropology of Menstruation* (Berkeley: University of California Press), 161–81.

———— (1991), "The egg and the sperm: How science has constructed a romance based on stereotypical male–female roles," *Signs*, 16 (3), 485–01.

———— (1994), *Flexible Bodies: Tracking Immunity in American Culture from the Days of Polio to the Age of AIDS* (Boston: Beacon Press).

Martínez, Inés, et al. (2015), "The gut microbiota of rural Papua New Guineans: Composition, diversity patterns, and ecological processes," *Cell Reports*, 11 (4), 527–38.

Martins, Vinicius J.B., et al. (2011), "Long-lasting effects of undernutrition," *International Journal of Environmental Research and Public Health*, 8 (6), 1817–46.

Martorell, Reynaldo (1980), "Interrelationship between diet, infectious disease, and nutritional status," in Lawrence S. Greene and F. Johnston (eds.), *Social and Biological Predictors of Nutritional Status, Physical Growth, and Neurological Development* (New York: Academic Press), 81–106.

———— (1989), "Body size, adaptation and function," *Human Organization*, 15–20.

Mascarenhas, Maya N., et al. (2012), "National, regional, and global trends in infertility prevalence since 1990: A systematic analysis of 277 health surveys," *PLoS Medicine*, 9 (12), e1001356.

Matacin, M.L. and Simone, M. (2019), "Advocating for fat activism in a therapeutic context," *Women & Therapy*, 42 (1–2), 200–15.

Mataix-Cols, David, et al. (2010), "Hoarding disorder: A new diagnosis for DSM-V?," *Depression and Anxiety*, 27 (6), 556–72.

Matousek, R.H., Dobkin, P.L., and Pruessner, J. (2010), "Cortisol as a marker for improvement in mindfulness-based stress reduction," *Complementary Therapies in Clinical Practice*, 16 (1), 13–19.

May, P.A., et al. (2013), "Approaching the prevalence of the full spectrum of fetal alcohol spectrum disorders in a South African population-based study," *Alcoholism Clinical and Experimental Research*, 37 (5), 818–30.

May, Philip A., et al. (2017), "Replication of high fetal alcohol spectrum disorders prevalence rates, child characteristics, and maternal risk factors in a second sample of rural communities in South Africa," *International Journal of Environmental Research and Public Health*, 14 (5), 522.

McBurney, Michael I., et al. (2019), "Establishing what constitutes a healthy human gut microbiome: State of the science, regulatory considerations, and future directions," *Journal of Nutrition*, 149 (11), 1882–95.

McConnell, J.R. (1999), "The ambiguity about death in Japan: An ethical implication for organ procurement," *Journal of Medical Ethics*, 25, 322–24.

McDade, Thomas W. (2001), "Lifestyle incongruity, social integration, and immune function in Samoan adolescents," *Social Science & Medicine*, 53, 1351–62.

McEwen, Bruce S. (2002), *The End of Stress as We Know It* (Washington DC: Joseph Henry Press).

McEwen, Bruce S. (2013), "The brain on stress: Toward an integrative approach to brain, body and behavior," *Perspectives on Psychological Science: A Journal of the Association for Psychological Science*, 8 (6), 673–75.

McGuire, M. and Troisi, A. (1998), *Darwinian Psychiatry* (New York: Oxford University Press).

McIntosh, Andrew M., Sullivan, Patrick F., and Lewis, Cathryn M. (2019), "Uncovering the genetic architecture of major depression," *Neuron*, 102 (1), 91–103.

McKenna, James J. and Gettler, Lee T. (2016), "There is no such thing as infant sleep, there is no such thing as breastfeeding, there is only breastsleeping," *Acta Paediatrica*, 105 (1), 17–21.

McKenna, James J. (1986), "An anthropological perspective on the Sudden Infant Death Syndrome (SIDS): The role of parental breathing cues and speech breathing adaptations," *Medical Anthropology*, 10 (1), 9–53.

McKenna, James J. and Mosko, S. (1993), "Evolution and infant sleep: An experimental study of infant-parent cosleeping and its implications for SIDS: An experiment in evolutionary medicine," *Acta Paediatrica*, 389, 31–36.

McKenna, James J. and McDade, Thomas W. (2005), "Why babies should never sleep alone: A review of the co-sleeping controversy in relation to SIDS, bedsharing, and breastfeeding," *Paediatric Respiratory Reviews*, 6, 134–52.

McKeown, Thomas (1978), "Determinants of health," *Human Nature*, (April), 260–66.

_____ (1979), *The Role of Medicine: Dream, Mirage, or Nemesis?* (Princeton, NJ: Princeton University Press) 260–66.

McKerracher, Luseadra, Collard, Mark, and Henrich, Joseph (2015), "The expression and adaptive significance of pregnancy-related nausea, vomiting, and aversions on Yasawa Island, Fiji," *Evolution and Human Behavior*, 36 (2), 95–102.

McManus, Donald P., et al. (2010), "Schistosomiasis in the People's Republic of China: The era of the Three Gorges Dam," *Clinical Microbiology Reviews*, 23 (2), 442–66.

McMichael, Anthony J. (2013), "Globalization, climate change, and human health," *New England Journal of Medicine*, 368 (14), 1335–43.

_____ (2017), *Climate Change and the Health Of Nations: Famines, Fevers, and the Fate of Populations* (Oxford University Press).

McNeill, William H. (1976), *Plagues and Peoples* (Garden City, NY: Anchor Books).

McSorley, H.J. and Maizels, R.M. (2012), "Helminth infections and host immune regulation," *Clinical Microbiology Reviews*, 25 (4), 585–08.

Medawar, Peter B. (1952), *An Unsolved Problem in Biology* (London: H.K. Lewis).

Meibom, Karin L., et al. (2005), "Chitin induces natural competence in *Vibrio Cholerae*," *Science*, 310 (5755), 1824–27.

Melby, M.K. (2005), "Vasomotor symptom prevalence and language of menopause in Japan," *Menopause: The Journal of the North American Menopause Society*, 12, 250–57.

Melzack, R. and Wall, P. (1988), *The Challenge of Pain* (London: Penguin).

Mennini, Maurizio, et al. (2017), "Probiotics in asthma and allergy prevention," *Frontiers in Pediatrics*, 5, 165.

Mertens, Elly, et al. (2017), "Operationalising the health aspects of sustainable diets: A review," *Public Health Nutrition*, 20 (4), 739–57.

Meyer, Ilan H. (2003), "Prejudice, social stress, and mental health in lesbian, gay, and bisexual populations: Conceptual issues and research evidence," *Psychological Bulletin*, 129 (5), 674–97.

Mikolajczyk, Rafael T., et al. (2011), "A global reference for fetal-weight and birthweight percentiles," *The Lancet*, 377 (9780), 1855–61.

Millen, Barbara E, et al. (2016), "The 2015 Dietary Guidelines Advisory Committee scientific report: Development and major conclusions," *Advances in Nutrition*, 7 (3), 438–44.

Miller, M.N. and Pumareiga, A.J. (2001), "Culture and eating disorders: A historical and cross-cultural review," *Psychiatry*, 64, 93–110.

Miller, R.G., et al. (2005), "Disparities in osteoporosis screening between at-risk African-American and white women," *Journal of General Internal Medicine*, 20, 847–51.

Milne, D. and Howard, W. (2000), "Rethinking the role of diagnosis in Navajo religious healing," *Medical Anthropology Quarterly*, 14, 543–70.

Milner, George R. (2019), "Early agriculture's toll on human health," *Proceedings of the National Academy of Sciences*, 116 (28), 13721–23.

Minster, Ryan L., et al. (2016), "A thrifty variant in CREBRF strongly influences body mass index in Samoans," *Nature Genetics*, 48 (9), 1049.

Mintz, Sidney W. (1985), *Sweetness and Power* (New York: Penguin Books).

Mintzes, Barbara (2002), "Direct to consumer advertising is medicalising normal human experience," *British Medical Journal*, 324 (7342), 908–11.

Mishra, Vinod, Roy, T.K., and Retherford, Robert D. (2004), "Sex differentials in childhood feeding, health care, and nutritional status in India," *Population and Development Review*, 30 (2), 269–95.

Mistry, Ritesh, Galal, Osman, and Lu, Michael (2009), "Women's autonomy and pregnancy care in rural India: A contextual analysis," *Social Science & Medicine*, 69 (6), 926–33.

Mistry, S.K. and Puthussery, S. (2015), "Risk factors of overweight and obesity in childhood and adolescence in South Asian countries: A systematic review of the evidence," *Public Health*, 129 (3), 200–09.

Mitchell, J.E. and Crow, S. (2006), "Medical complications of anorexia nervosa and bulimia nervosa," *Current Opinion in Psychiatry*, 19, 438–43.

Moerman, Daniel E. (1983), "General medical effectiveness and human biology: Placebo effects in the treatment of ulcer," *Medical Anthropology Quarterly*, 14 (3), 13–16).

———— (1989), "Poisoned apples and honeysuckles: The medicinal plants of Native America," *Medical Anthropology Quarterly*, 3, 52–61.

———— (2002), *Meaning, Medicine, and the "Placebo Effect"* (Cambridge: Cambridge University Press).

Moffat, Tina (2010), "The 'childhood obesity epidemic,'" *Medical Anthropology Quarterly*, 24 (1), 1–21.

Mojola, Sanyu A. (2014), *Love, Money, and HIV: Becoming a Modern African Woman in the Age of AIDS* (Berkeley: University of California Press).

Mojola, Sanyu A. and Wamoyi, Joyce (2019), "Contextual drivers of HIV risk among young African women," *Journal of the International AIDS Society*, 22 (S4), e25302.

Molina, G., et al. (2015), "Relationship between cesarean delivery rate and maternal and neonatal mortality," *JAMA*, 314 (21), 2263–70.

Money, John and Annecillo, Charles (1987), "Crucial period effect in psychoendocrinology," in Marc H. Bornstein (ed.), *Sensitive Periods in Development: Interdisciplinary Perspectives* (New York: Psychology Press), 145–58.

Monk Jr., Ellis P. (2015), "The cost of color: Skin color, discrimination, and health among African-Americans," *American Journal of Sociology*, 121 (2), 396–44.

Monteiro, Carlos Augusto, et al. (2018a), "Household availability of ultra-processed foods and obesity in nineteen European countries," *Public Health Nutrition*, 21 (1), 18–26.

Monteiro, Carlos Augusto, et al. (2018b), "The UN Decade of Nutrition, the NOVA food classification and the trouble with ultra-processing," *Public Health Nutrition*, 21 (1), 5–17.

Moon, R.Y. (2011), "SIDS and other sleep-related infant deaths: Expansion of recommendations for a safe infant sleeping environment," *Pediatrics*, 128 (5), 1030–39.

Moore, J.S. (1993), *Chiropractic in America: The History of a Medical Alternative* (Baltimore: Johns Hopkins University Press).

Morales, A. (2004), "Andropause (or symptomatic late-onset hypogonadism): Facts, fiction and controversies," *The Aging Male*, 7, 297–03.

Morales, A., Heaton, J.P.W., and Carson, C.C. (2000), "Andropause: A misnomer for a true clinical entity," *Journal of Urology*, 163, 705–12.

Morgentaler, Abraham, Feibus, Allison, and Baum, Neil (2014), "Testosterone and cardiovascular disease–the controversy and the facts," *Postgraduate Medicine*, 127 (2), 159–65.

Morichi, V., et al. (2015), "Diagnosing and treating depression in older and oldest old," *Current Pharmaceutical Design*, 21 (13), 1690–98.

Morris, Brian J. and Krieger, John N. (2013), "Does male circumcision affect sexual function, sensitivity, or satisfaction?—A systematic review," *The Journal of Sexual Medicine*, 10 (11), 2644–57.

Moses-Kolko, E.L., et al. (2005), "Neonatal signs after late in utero exposure to serotonin reuptake inhibitors: Literature review and implications for clinical applications," *Journal of the American Medical Association*, 293, 2372–83.

Moss, Michael (2013), *Salt, Sugar, Fat: How the Food Giants Hooked Us* (New York: Random House).

Mouritsen, A., et al. (2010), "Hypothesis: Exposure to endocrine-disrupting chemicals may interfere with timing of puberty," *International Journal of Andrology*, 33 (2), 346–59.

Mowat, Andrew (2017), "Why does cystic fibrosis display the prevalence and distribution observed in human populations?," *Current Pediatric Research*, 21 (1), 164-171.

Moynihan, Ray and Mintzes, Barbara (2010), *Sex, Lies, and Pharmaceuticals: How Drug Companies Plan to Profit from Female Sexual Dysfunction* (Vancouver, B.C.: Greystone Books).

Mozaffarian, D., et al. (2015), "Heart disease and stroke statistics—2015 update: A report from the American Heart Association," *Circulation*, 131 (4), e29–322.

Mueller, Noel T., et al. (2015), "The infant microbiome development: Mom matters," *Trends in Molecular Medicine*, 21 (2), 109–17.

Mummert, A., et al. (2011), "Stature and robusticity during the agricultural transition: Evidence from the bioarchaeological record," *Economics and Human Biology*, 9 (3), 284–01.

Munro, Jenny and McIntyre, Lynn (2014), "'Why should I feed her less?': Challenging assumptions on daughter discrimination in the food provisioning values of ultrapoor Bangladeshi female heads of household," *Women's Studies International Forum*, 45, 1–9.

Murphy, Henry B.M. (1971), "History and the evolution of syndromes: The striking case of latah and amok," in R Littlewood and S Dein (eds.), *Cultural Psychiatry and Medical Anthropology* (London: The Athlone Press), 371–92.

Murphy, J.M. (1976), "Psychiatric labeling in cross-cultural perspective," *Science*, 191, 1019–28.

Musial, Frauke (2019), "Acupuncture for the treatment of pain-a mega-placebo?," *Frontiers in Neuroscience*, 13, 1110.

Mustillo, Sarah, et al. (2004), "Self-reported experiences of racial discrimination and black–white differences in preterm and low-birthweight deliveries: The CARDIA study," *American Journal of Public Health*, 94 (12), 2125–31.

Nachtigall, Robert D. (2006), International disparities in access to infertility services. *Fertility and Sterility*, 85:871–875.

Nahin, Richard L., Barnes, Patricia M., and Stussman, Barbara J. (2016), "Expenditures on complementary health approaches: United States, 2012."

Nakamura, Karen (2013), *A Disability of the Soul: An Ethnography of Schizophrenia and Mental Illness in Contemporary Japan* (Ithaca: Cornell University Press).

Natale, Valerie and Rajagopalan, Anuradha (2014), "Worldwide variation in human growth and the World Health Organization growth standards: A systematic review," *BMJ Open*, 4 (1), e003735.

Nations, Marilyn, et al. (2015), "Cumbered cries: Contextual constraints on maternal grief in northeast Brazil," *Current Anthropology*, 56 (5), 613–37.

Nazrun, Ahmad Shuid, et al. (2014), "A systematic review of the outcomes of osteoporotic fracture patients after hospital discharge: Morbidity, subsequent fractures, and mortality," *Therapeutics and Clinical Risk Management*, 10, 937.

Neel, James V (1962), "Diabetes mellitus: A 'thrifty' genotype rendered detrimental by progress?," *American Journal of Human Genetics*, 14, 353–62.

Nelson, Mia and Ogden, Jane (2008), "An exploration of food intolerance in the primary care setting: The general practitioner's experience," *Social Science & Medicine*, 67 (6), 1038–45.

Nelson, Robin G. (2016), "Residential context, institutional alloparental care, and child growth in Jamaica," *American Journal of Human Biology*, 28 (4), 493–02.

Nesse, R.M. (1991), "What good is feeling bad?," *The Sciences* (Nov/Dec), 30–37.

——— (2000), "Is depression an adaptation?," *Archives of General Psychiatry*, 57, 14–20.

Nesse, Randolph M. and Berridge, Kent C. (1997), "Psychoactive drug use in evolutionary perspective," *Science*, 278, 63–66.

Nesse, Randolph M. and Williams, George C. (1994), *Why We Get Sick* (New York: Times Books).

Nestle, Marion (2013), *Food Politics: How the Food Industry Influences Nutrition and Health*, Revised and Expanded 10th Anniversary Edition (Berkeley: University of California Press).

——— (2018a), *Unsavory Truth: How Food Companies Skew the Science of What We Eat* (New York: Basic Books).

——— (2018b), "Perspective: Challenges and controversial issues in the dietary guidelines for

Americans, 1980–2015," *Advances in Nutrition*, 9 (2), 148–50.

Neville, Margaret (2013), *Lactation: Physiology, Nutrition, and Breast-Feeding* (New York: Springer Science & Business Media).

Ng, Chee, et al. (2010), "The ongoing development of community mental health services in Japan: Utilizing strengths and opportunities," *Australasian Psychiatry*, 18 (1), 57–62.

Ng, Kimmie, et al. (2014), "Dose response to vitamin D supplementation in African Americans: Results of a 4-arm, randomized, placebo-controlled trial," *American Journal of Clinical Nutrition*, 99 (3), 587–98.

Nguyen, A. (2007), "Taking root," *Saveur*, (104), 48–61.

Nichter, Mark (1981), "Idioms of distress: Alternatives in the expression of psychosocial distress in South India," *Culture, Medicine and Psychiatry*, 5, 379–08.

———— (2010), "Idioms of distress revisited," *Culture, Medicine, and Psychiatry*, 34 (2), 401–16.

Nichter, Mark and Nichter, Mimi (1983), "The ethnophysiology and folk dietetics of pregnancy: a case study from South India," *Human Organization*, 42, 235–46.

Nielsen, S. (2001), "Epidemiology and mortality of eating disorders," *The Psychiatric Clinics of North America*, 24, 201–14.

Nii-Trebi, Nicholas Israel (2017), "Emerging and neglected infectious diseases: Insights, advances, and challenges," *BioMed Research International*, https://doi.org/10.1155/2017/5245021.

Nimgaonkar, V.L., et al. (1997), "Fertility in schizophrenia: Results from a contemporary U.S. cohort," *Acta Psychiatrica Scandinavica*, 95, 364–69.

Non, Amy L., Gravlee, Clarence C., and Mulligan, Connie J. (2012), "Education, genetic ancestry, and blood pressure in African Americans and Whites," *American Journal of Public Health*, 102 (8), 1559–65.

Nondo, Ramadhani S.O., et al. (2015), "Ethnobotanical survey and in vitro antiplasmodial activity of medicinal plants used to treat malaria in Kagera and Lindi regions, Tanzania," *Journal of Medicinal Plants Research*, 9 (6), 179–92.

Nordsletten, Ashley E., et al. (2018), "A transcultural study of hoarding disorder: Insights from the United Kingdom, Spain, Japan, and Brazil," *Transcultural Psychiatry*, 55 (2), 261–85.

Nyberg, Colleen H., et al. (2012), "Diurnal cortisol rhythms and child growth: Exploring the life history consequences of HPA activation among the Tsimane," *American Journal of Human Biology*, 24 (6), 730–38.

O'Fallon, Brendan D. and Fehren-Schmitz, Lars (2011), "Native Americans experienced a strong population bottleneck coincident with European contact," *Proceedings of the National Academy of Sciences*, 108 (51), 20444–48.

Ochoa, Enrique C. (2012), "Political histories of food," in Jeffrey M Pilcher (ed.), *The Oxford Handbook of Food History* (New York: Oxford University Press), 23–40.

Ogden, C.L., et al. (2014), "Prevalence of childhood and adult obesity in the United States, 2011–2012," *Journal of the American Medical Association*, 311 (8), 806–14.

Olaya, Beatriz, et al. (2015), "Country-level and individual correlates of overweight and obesity among primary school children: A cross-sectional study in seven European countries," *BMC Public Health*, 15 (1), 1–12.

Oldstone, Michael B.A. (1998), *Viruses, Plagues, & History* (New York: Oxford University Press).

Olshansky, S.J., Carnes, B.A., and Cassel, C. (1990), "In search of Methuselah: Estimating the upper limits to human longevity," *Science*, 250, 634–40.

Olshansky, S.J., et al. (2005), "A potential decline in life expectancy in the United States in the 21st century," *New England Journal of Medicine*, 352, 1138–45.

Ombelet, Willem (2014), "Is global access to infertility care realistic? The Walking Egg Project," *Reproductive Biomedicine Online*, 28 (3), 267–72.

Ombelet, Willem, et al. (2008), "Infertility and the provision of infertility medical services in developing countries," *Human Reproduction Update*, 14 (6), 605–21.

Omran, A.R. (1971), "The epidemiologic transition. A theory of the epidemiology of population change," *Milbank Memorial Fund Quarterly*, 49 (4).

Onyango, Adelheid W, et al. (2014), "Complementary feeding and attained linear growth among 6–23-month-old children," *Public Health Nutrition*, 17 (09), 1975–83.

Orr, J.B. (1928), "Milk consumption and the growth of school-children," *The Lancet*, 1, 202–03.

Padilha, Sarah COS, et al. (2018), "Efficacy and safety of drugs for attention deficit hyperactivity disorder in children and adolescents: A network meta-analysis," *European Child & Adolescent Psychiatry*, 27 (10), 1335–45.

Palmer, B.F. and Clegg, D J. (2015), "The sexual dimorphism of obesity," *Molecular and Cellular Endocrinology*, 402, 113–19.

Pannaraj, Pia S., et al. (2017), "Association between breast milk bacterial communities and establishment and development of the infant gut microbiome," *JAMA Pediatrics*, 171 (7), 647–54.

Paradies, Yin, et al. (2015), "Racism as a determinant of health: A systematic review and meta-analysis," *PLoS ONE*, 10 (9), e0138511.

Pariente, J., Frackowiak, R.S., and others (2005), "Expectancy and belief modulate the neuronal substrates of pain treated by acupuncture," *NeuroImage*, 25, 1161–67.

Parker, J.D., et al. (2005), "Air pollution and birth weight among term infants in California," *Pediatrics*, 115 (1), 121–28.

Parsons, Christine E., et al. (2012), "Postnatal depression and its effects on child development: A review of evidence from low-and middle-income countries," *British Medical Bulletin*, 101 (1), 57–79.

Parsons, Talcott (1979), "Definitions of health and illness in the light of American values and social structure," in E. Gartly Jaco (ed.), *Patients, Physicians and Illness* (New York: Free Press), 97–117.

Patel, Pavankumar and Abate, Nicola (2013), "Role of subcutaneous adipose tissue in the pathogenesis of insulin resistance," *Journal of Obesity*, https://doi.org/10.1155/2013/489187

Patel, Vikram, et al. (2015), "Assuring health coverage for all in India," *The Lancet*, 386 (10011), 2422–35.

Patton, George C., et al. (2016), "Our future: A Lancet commission on adolescent health and wellbeing," *The Lancet*, 387 (10036), 2423–78.

Patton, Stuart (2004), *Milk: Its Remarkable Contribution to Human Health and Well-Being* (New Brunswick, NJ: Transaction Publishers).

Paul, Benjamin J. (1955), "Introduction: Understanding the community," in Benjamin J Paul (ed.), *Health, Culture, & Community: Case Studies of Public Reactions to Health Programs* (New York: Russell Sage Foundation), 1–14.

Pawankar, Ruby (2014), "Allergic diseases and asthma: A global public health concern and a call to action," *World Allergy Organ Journal* 7 (1), 12..

Pawloski, Lisa (2006), "A comparison of nutritional indicators from Bambara and Fulai girls born in Paris, France and in the Segou Region of Mali," *Nutritional Anthropology*, 27–28 (1–2), 13–23.

Payer, Lynn (1996), *Medicine and Culture* (New York: Henry Holt and Co.).

Pearce-Duvet, Jessica M. C. (2006), "The origin of human pathogens: Evaluating the role of agriculture and domestic animals in the evolution of human disease," *Biological Reviews*, 81 (3), 369–82.

Pearlson, G.D. (2000), "Neurobiology of schizophrenia," *Annals of Neurology*, 48, 556–66.

Pelto, Gretel H. (2008), "Taking care of children: Applying anthropology in maternal and child nutrition and health," *Human Organization*, 67 (3), 237–43.

Pelto, Gretel H. and Armar- Klemesu, Margaret (2015), "Identifying interventions to help rural Kenyan mothers cope with food insecurity: Results of a focused ethnographic study," *Maternal & Child Nutrition*, 11, 21–38.

Pepper, Gillian V. and Roberts, S. Craig (2006), "Rates of nausea and vomiting in pregnancy and dietary characteristics across populations," *Proceedings of the Royal Society B*, 273, 2675–79.

Perera, Frederica P. (2017), "Multiple threats to child health from fossil fuel combustion: Impacts of air pollution and climate change," *Environmental Health Perspectives*, 125 (2), 141–48.

Peretz, Jackye, et al. (2014), "Bisphenol A and reproductive health: Update of experimental and human evidence, 2007–2013," *Environmental Health Perspectives*, 122 (8), 775–86.

Perkins, Jessica M., et al. (2016), "Adult height, nutrition, and population health," *Nutrition Reviews*, 74 (3), 149–65.

Perreira, Krista M. and Telles, Edward E. (2014), "The color of health: Skin color, ethnoracial classification, and discrimination in the health of Latin Americans," *Social Science & Medicine*, 116, 241–50.

Peters, L.G. and Price-Williams, D. (1980), "Towards an experiential analysis of shamanism," *American Ethnologist*, 7, 397–18.

Petersen, R.C. (2003), *Mild Cognitive Impairment* (New York: Oxford University Press).

Pickett, Kate E. and Wilkinson, Richard G. (2015), "Income inequality and health: A causal review," *Social Science & Medicine*, 128, 316–26.

Pickstone, J. (1996), "Medicine, society, and the state," in R. Porter (ed.), *Cambridge Illustrated History of Medicine* (Cambridge: Cambridge University Press), 304–41.

Pike, Ivy L. (2005), "Maternal stress and fetal responses: Evolutionary perspectives on preterm delivery," *American Journal of Human Biology*, 17 (1), 55–65.

Pike, K.M. and Borovoy, A. (2004), "The rise of eating disorders in Japan: Issues of culture and limitations of the model of 'westernization,'" *Culture, Medicine and Psychiatry*, 28, 493–31.

Pilver, Corey E., et al. (2011), "Exposure to American culture is associated with premenstrual dysphoric disorder among ethnic minority women," *Journal of Affective Disorders*, 130 (1–2), 334–41.

Polanczyk, G., et al. (2007), "The worldwide prevalence of ADHD: A systematic review and metaregression analysis," *American Journal of Psychiatry*, 164, 942–48.

Popkin, Barry M. (1993), "Nutritional patterns and transitions," *Population and Development Review*, 19 (1), 138–57.

_____ (2002), "An overview of the nutrition transition and its health implications: The Bellagio meeting," *Public Health Nutrition*, 5, 93–103.

_____ (2006), "Global nutrition dynamics: The world is shifting rapidly toward a diet linked with noncommunicable diseases," *American Journal of Clinical Nutrition*, 84 (2), 289–98.

Porter, Roy, ed., (1996), *Cambridge Illustrated History of Medicine* (Cambridge: Cambridge University Press).

Porter, Roy (1997), *The Greatest Benefit to Mankind* (New York: W.W. Norton).

Potts, Annie, et al. (2004), "'Viagra stories': Challenging 'erectile dysfunction,'" *Social Science & Medicine*, 59 (3), 489–99.

Poulter, N.R., et al. (1985), "Blood pressure patterns in relation to age, weight and urinary electrolytes in three Kenyan communities," *Transactions of the Royal Society of Tropical Medicine Hygiene*, 79 (3), 389–92.

Powell, Lisa M., Rebcca M. Schermbeck, and Frank J. Chaloupka (2013) Nutritional content of food and beverage products in television advertisements seen on children's programming. *Childhood Obesity*, 9(6), 524–31.

Pradeu, Thomas (2010), "What is an organism? An immunological answer," *History and Philosophy of the Life Sciences*, 32, 247–68.

Pradeu, Thomas and Carosella, Edgardo D. (2006), "On the definition of a criterion of immunogenicity," *Proceedings of the National Academy of Sciences*, 103 (47), 17858–61.

Prendergast, Andrew J. and Humphrey, Jean H. (2014), "The stunting syndrome in developing countries," *Paediatrics and International Child Health*, 34 (4), 250–65.

Prince, Ruth and Geissler, P. Wenzel (2001), "Becoming 'one who treats': A case study of a Luo healer and her grandson in western Kenya," *Anthropology and Education Quarterly*, 32, 447–71.

Profet, Margie (1992), "Pregnancy sickness as adaptation: A deterrent to maternal ingestion of teratogens," in J.H. Barkow, L Cosmides, and J Tooby (eds.), *The Adapted Mind* (New York: Oxford University Press), 327–66.

_____ (1993), "Menstruation as a defense against pathogens transported by sperm," *Quarterly Review of Biology*, 68 (3), 335–86.

Promislow, D.E.L. and Harvey, P.H. (1990), "Living fast and dying young: A comparative analysis of life-history variation among mammals," *Journal of Zoology (London)*, 220, 417–37.

Rahimi, R., Nikfar, S., and Abdollahi, M. (2006), "Pregnancy outcomes following exposure to serotonin reuptake inhibitors: A meta-analysis of clinical trials," *Reproductive Toxicology*, 22, 571–75.

Raichlen, David A., et al. (2017), "Physical activity patterns and biomarkers of cardiovascular disease risk in hunter- gatherers," *American Journal of Human Biology*, 29 (2), e22919.

Ratjen, F. and Doring, G. (2003), "Cystic fibrosis," *The Lancet*, 361, 681.

Ravanos, Konstantinos, et al. (2018), "Declining sperm counts … or rather not? A mini review," *Obstetrical & Gynecological Survey*, 73 (10), 595–05.

Ravenscroft, Julia, Schell, Lawrence M., and Cole, Tewentahawih'tha' (2015), "Applying the community partnership approach to human biology research," *American Journal of Human Biology*, 27 (1), 6–15.

Raz, N. (1999), "Aging of the brain and its impact on cognitive performance: Integration of structural and functional findings," in F.I.M. Craik and T.A. Salthouse (eds.), *Handbook of Aging and Cognition II* (Mahwah, NJ: Lawrence Erlbaum), 1–90.

Redler, Silke, Messenger, Andrew G., and Betz, Regina C. (2017), "Genetics and other factors in the aetiology of female pattern hair loss," *Experimental Dermatology*, 26 (6), 510–17.

Rej, Anupam, et al. (2018), "PWE-145 The role of a Gluten Free diet in 'Lifestylers'? The first double blind randomised study," *Gut* 67, Suppl 1.

Rej, Peter H., et al. (2019), "Shortened telomere length is associated with unfair treatment attributed to race in African Americans living in Tallahassee, Florida," *American Journal of Human Biology*, 32, e23375.

Renton, Alan E, Chiò, Adriano, and Traynor, Bryan J. (2014), "State of play in amyotrophic lateral sclerosis genetics," *Nature Neuroscience*, 17 (1), 17–23.

Revelas, Mary, et al. (2018), "Review and meta-analysis of genetic polymorphisms associated with exceptional human longevity," *Mechanisms of Ageing and Development*, 175, 24–34.

Rhodes, Lorna Amarasingham (1990), "Studying biomedicine as a cultural system," in Thomas M. Johnson and Carolyn F. Sargent (eds.), *Medical Anthropology: Contemporary Theory and Method* (New York: Praeger), 159–73.

Richards, R. (1981), "Relationships between creativity and psychopathology: An evaluation and interpretation of the evidence," *Genetic Psychology Monographs*, 103, 261–24.

Ricklefs, R.E. and Finch, C.E. (1995), *Aging: A Natural History* (New York: Scientific American Library).

Ritenbaugh, C., et al. (1996), "A cross-cultural review of eating disorders in regard to DSM-IV," in J.E. Mezzich, et al. (eds.), *Culture and Psychiatric Diagnosis: A DSM-IV Perspective* (Washington: American Psychiatric Association), 171–86.

Ritenbaugh, Cheryl (1982), "Obesity as a culture-bound syndrome," *Culture, Medicine and Psychiatry*, 6, 347–61.

Roberson, L.L., et al. (2014), "Beyond BMI: The 'Metabolically healthy obese' phenotype & its association with clinical/subclinical cardiovascular disease and all-cause mortality—A systematic review," *BMC Public Health*, 14, 14.

Robinson, Siân and Fall, Caroline (2012), "Infant nutrition and later health: A review of current evidence," *Nutrients*, 4 (8), 859–74.

Roca, Anna, et al. (2015), "Ebola: A holistic approach is required to achieve effective management and control," *The Journal of Allergy and Clinical Immunology*, 135 (4), 856–67.

Rodríguez, Leonor, Cervantes, Elsa, and Ortiz, Rocío (2011), "Malnutrition and gastrointestinal and respiratory infections in children: A public health problem," *International Journal of Environmental Research and Public Health*, 8 (4), 1174–05.

Rodriguez-Casado, Arantxa (2016), "The health potential of fruits and vegetables phytochemicals: Notable examples," *Critical Reviews in Food Science and Nutrition*, 56 (7), 1097–07.

Roehrig, James P. and McLean, Carmen P. (2010), "A comparison of stigma toward eating disorders versus depression," *International Journal of Eating Disorders*, 43 (7), 671–74.

Rohr, Jason R., et al. (2019), "Emerging human infectious diseases and the links to global food production," *Nature Sustainability*, 2 (6), 445–56.

Romero-Corral, Abel, et al. (2010), "Normal weight obesity: A risk factor for cardiometabolic dysregulation and cardiovascular mortality," *European Heart Journal*, 31 (6), 737–46.

Rook, Graham A.W., Martinelli, Roberta, and Brunet, Laura Rosa (2003), "Innate immune responses to mycobacteria and the downregulation of atopic responses," *Current Opinion in Allergy and Clinical Immunology*, 3 (5), 337–42.

Rosenberg, Karen and Trevathan, Wenda (2002), "Birth, obstetrics and human evolution," *BJOG: An International Journal of Obstetrics & Gynaecology*, 109 (11), 1199–06.

Roshanafshar, Shirin, and Emily Hawkins (2018), Food insecurity in Canada. https://www150.statcan.gc.ca/n1/pub/82-624-x/2015001/article/14138-eng.htm.

Rostila, Mikael (2013), "The social capital of welfare states and its significance for population health," in Ichiro Kawachi, Soshi Takao, and Sankaran Venkata Subramanian (eds.), *Global Perspectives on Social Capital and Health* (New York: Springer), 277–05.

Roumy, V., et al. (2007), "Amazonian plants from Peru used by Quechua and Mestizo to treat malaria with evaluation of their activity," *Journal of Ethnopharmacology*, 112, 482–89.

Rowland, L.P., ed. (2000), *Merritt's Neurology*, 10th edition (Philadelphia: Lippincott Williams & Wilkins).

Rowley, Jane, et al. (2019), "Chlamydia, gonorrhoea, trichomoniasis and syphilis: Global prevalence and incidence estimates, 2016," *Bulletin of the World Health Organization*, 97 (8), 548.

Roy, Jonathan, Chakraborty, Sanjoy, and Chakraborty, Tandra (2009), "Estrogen-like endocrine disrupting chemicals affecting puberty in humans—A review," *Medical Science Monitor*, 15 (6), RA137-45

Rozin, P. and Fallon, A. (1988), "Body image, attitudes to weight, and misperceptions of figure preferences of the opposite sex: A comparison of men and women in two generations," *Journal of Abnormal Psychology*, 97, 342–45.

Rupp, Stephanie, et al. (2016), "Beyond the cut hunter: A historical epidemiology of HIV beginnings in Central Africa," *EcoHealth*, 13 (4), 661–71.

Rutherford, Julienne N., Asiodu, Ifeyinwa V., and Liese, Kylea L. (2019), "Reintegrating modern birth practice within ancient birth process: What high cesarean rates ignore about physiologic birth," *American Journal of Human Biology*, 31 (2), e23229.

Rutstein, Shea O. and Johnson, Kiersten (2004), "The DHS wealth index," *DHS Comparative Reports No. 6.* (Calverton, Maryland, USA: ORC Macro).

Ryan, F. (1997), *Virux X: Tracking the New Killer Plagues: Out of the Present into the Future* (Boston: Little Brown).

Rymer, Janice, Brian, Kate, and Regan, Lesley (2019), "HRT and breast cancer risk," *BMJ*, 367, l5928.

Rytter, Maren Johanne Heilskov, et al. (2014), "The immune system in children with malnutrition—A systematic review," *PLoS ONE*, 9 (8), e105017.

Sackett, D.L., et al. (1996), "Evidence-based medicine: What it is and what it isn't," *British Medical Journal*, 312, 71–72.

Sadler, Michelle, et al. (2016), "Moving beyond disrespect and abuse: Addressing the structural dimensions of obstetric violence," *Reproductive Health Matters*, 24 (47), 47–55.

Šaffa, Gabriel, et al. (2019), "Is the timing of menarche correlated with mortality and fertility rates?," *PloS one*, 14 (4), e0215462–62.

Sahi, T. (1994), "Hypolactasia and lactase persistence: Historical review and the terminology," *Scandinavian Journal of Gastroenterology*, 29 (Suppl 202), 1–6.

Sahota, A., et al. (1997), "Apolipoprotein E-associated risk for Alzheimer's disease in the African-American population is genotype dependent," *Annals of Neurology*, 42, 659–61.

Salkeld, G., et al. (2000), "Quality of life related to fear of falling and hip fracture in older women: A time trade off study," *British Medical Journal*, 320, 341–46.

Salthouse, Timothy A. (2009), "When does age-related cognitive decline begin?," *Neurobiology of Aging*, 30 (4), 507–14.

Sandbach, F.R. (1975), "Preventing schistosomiasis: A critical assessment of present policy," *Social Science & Medicine*, 9 (10), 517–27.

Sankar, Mari Jeeva, et al. (2015), "Optimal breastfeeding practices and infant and child mortality: A systematic review and meta-analysis," *Acta Paediatrica*, 104, 3–13.

Sapolsky, Robert M. (2004), *Why Zebras Don't Get Ulcers* (3rd edn.; New York: Henry Holt and Company).

Sass, L.A. (1992), *Madness and Modernism* (New York: Basic Books).

Schabussova, Irma and Wiedermann, Ursula (2014), "Allergy and worms: Let's bring back old friends?," *Wiener Medizinische Wochenschrift*, 164 (19–20), 382–91.

Schell, L.M., et al. (2006), "Effects of pollution on human growth and development: An introduction," *Journal of Physiological Anthropology*, 25 (1), 103–12.

Schell, Lawrence M. and Gallo, Mia V. (2010), "Relationships of putative endocrine disruptors to human sexual maturation and thyroid activity in youth," *Physiology & Behavior*, 99 (2), 246–53.

Schell, Lawrence M. and Magnus, P.D. (2007), "Is there an elephant in the room? Addressing rival approaches to the interpretation of growth perturbations and small size," *American Journal of Human Biology*, 19 (5), 606–14.

Scheper-Hughes, N. (1979), *Saints, Scholars, and Schizophrenics* (Berkeley: University of California Press).

———— (1992), *Death Without Weeping* (Berkeley: University of California Press).

Scheper-Hughes, Nancy and Lock, Margaret M. (1987), "The mindful body: A prolegomenon to future work in medical anthropology," *Medical Anthropology Quarterly*, 1 (1), 6–41.

Schug, Thaddeus T., et al. (2016), "Minireview: Endocrine disruptors: Past lessons and future directions," *Molecular Endocrinology*, 30 (8), 833–47.

Schulman, Kevin, et al. (1999), "The effect of race and sex on physicians' recommendations for cardiac catheterization," *New England Journal of Medicine*, 340, 318–26.

Schulte-Herbrüggen, Björn, et al. (2013), "The importance of bushmeat in the livelihoods of West African cash-crop farmers living in a faunally-depleted landscape," *PLoS ONE*, 8, e72807.

Schulz, L.O., et al. (2006), "Effects of traditional and western environments on prevalence of type 2 diabetes in Pima Indians in Mexico and the U.S.," *Diabetes Care*, 29 (8), 1866–71.

Schulz, R. and Salthouse, T.A. (1999), *Adult Development and Aging* (Upper Saddle River, N.J.: Prentice Hall).

Schwarz, Flavio, et al. (2016), "Human-specific derived alleles of CD33 and other genes protect against postreproductive cognitive decline," *Proceedings of the National Academy of Sciences*, 113 (1), 74–79.

Seaman, Rosie, et al. (2019), "The increasing lifespan variation gradient by area-level deprivation: A decomposition analysis of Scotland 1981–2011," *Social Science & Medicine*, 230, 147–57.

Seckler, David (1980), "'Malnutrition': An intellectual odyssey," *Western Journal of Agricultural Economics*, 5, 219–27.

Sellen, Daniel W. (2007), "Evolution of infant and young child feeding: Implications for contemporary public health," *Annual Review of Nutrition*, 27 (1), 123–48.

Sembuya, Rita (2010), "Mother or nothing: The agony of infertility," *Bulletin of the World Health Organization*, 88, 881–82.

Setji, Tracy L., Brown, Ann J., and Feinglos, Mark N. (2005), "Gestational diabetes mellitus," *Clinical Diabetes*, 23, 17–24.

Shadlen, M.-F., Larson, E.B., and Yukawa, M. (2000), "The epidemiology of Alzheimer's disease and vascular dementia in Japanese and African-American populations: The search for etiological clues," *Neurobiology of Aging*, 21, 171–81.

Shapiro, Julie Teresa, et al. (2020), "Ebola spillover correlates with bat diversity," *European Journal of Wildlife Research*, 66 (1), 12.

Sharp, Lesley (2006), *Strange Harvest: Organ Transplants, Denatured Bodies, and the Transformed Self* (Berkeley: University of California Press).

Shell-Duncan, Bettina and Hernlund, Ylva (2000), "Female 'Circumcision' in Africa: Dimensions of the practice and debates," in Bettina Shell-Duncan and Ylva Hernlund (eds.), *Female "Circumcision" in Africa: Culture, Controversy, and Change* (Boulder, CO: Lynne Rienner Publishers), 1–40.

Shirakawa, T., et al. (1997), "The inverse association between tuberculin responses and atopic disorder," *Science*, 275, 77–79.

Sho, H. (2001), "History and characteristics of Okinawan longevity food," *Asia Pacific Journal of Clinical Nutrition*, 10, 159–64.

Sibley, Lynn M., Sipe, Theresa Ann, and Barry, Danika (2012), "Traditional birth attendant training for improving health behaviours and pregnancy outcomes," *Cochrane Database of Systematic Reviews*, 8, CD005460.

Silverberg, Rachael, et al. (2019), "Lack of measles vaccination of a few portends future epidemics and vaccination of many," *American Journal of Medicine*, 132 (9), 1005-1006.

Silverman, Eric K. (2004), "Anthropology and circumcision," *Annual Review of Anthropology*, 419–45.

Simondon, K.B., et al. (2001), "Children's height, health and appetite influence mothers' weaning decisions in rural Senegal," *International Journal of Epidemiology*, 30 (3), 481–84.

Simons, Mirre J.P. (2015), "Questioning causal involvement of telomeres in aging," *Ageing Research Reviews*, 24(Pt B), 191-196.

Simons, Ronald C. (1985a), "Sorting the culture-bound syndromes," in R.C. Simons and C.C. Hughes (eds.), *The Culture-Bound Syndromes* (Hingham, MA: D. Reidel Publishing), 25–38.

_____ (1985b), "The resolution of the latah paradox," in R.C. Simons and C.C. Hughes (eds.), *The Culture-Bound Syndromes* (Hingham, MA: D. Reidel Publishing), 43–62.

Singer, Merrill and Baer, Hans (eds.) (1995), *Critical Medical Anthropology* (Amityville, NY: Baywood Publishing Company).

Siroux, Valérie, Agier, Lydiane, and Slama, Rémy (2016), "The exposome concept: A challenge and a potential driver for environmental health research," *European Respiratory Review*, 25 (140), 124–29.

Smith, Katherine F., et al. (2014), "Global rise in human infectious disease outbreaks," *Journal of The Royal Society Interface*, 11 (101), 20140950.

Smith-Morris, Carolyn (2004), "Reducing diabetes in Indian country: Lessons from the three domains influencing pima diabetes," *Human Organization*, 63 (1), 34–46.

_____ (2006), *Diabetes among the Pima: Stories of Survival* (Tuscon, AZ: University of Arizona Press).

Snow, Loudell F. (1993), *Walkin' over Medicine* (Boulder: Westview Press).

Snowden, Frank M. (2019), *Epidemics and Society: From the Black Death to the Present* (New Haven, CT: Yale University Press).

Sobo, Elisa J. (2015), "Social cultivation of vaccine refusal and delay among Waldorf (Steiner) school parents," *Medical Anthropology Quarterly*, 29 (3), 381–99.

_____ (2016a), "Theorizing (vaccine) refusal: Through the looking glass," *Cultural Anthropology*, 31 (3), 342–50.

_____ (2016b), "What is herd immunity, and how does it relate to pediatric vaccination uptake? U.S. parent perspectives," *Social Science & Medicine*, 165, 187–95.

Sobo, Elisa J., et al. (2016), "Information curation among vaccine cautious parents: Web 2.0, Pinterest thinking, and pediatric vaccination choice," *Medical Anthropology*, 35 (6), 529–46.

Society for Medical Anthropology (2017) What is Medical Anthropology? http://www.medanthro.net/about/about-medical-anthropology/

Sokolow, Susanne H., et al. (2017), "Nearly 400 million people are at higher risk of schistosomiasis because dams block the migration of snail-eating river prawns," *Philosophical Transactions of the Royal Society B: Biological Sciences*, 372 (1722), 20160127.

Sommer, Marni, et al. (2016), "A time for global action: Addressing girls' menstrual hygiene management needs in schools," *PLoS medicine*, 13 (2), e1001962–62.

Sontag, Susan (1978), *Illness as Metaphor*. New York: Farrar, Straus and Giroux.

Sow, S., S. J. de Vlas, D. Engels, and B. Gryseels (2002, Water-related disease patterns before and after the construction of the Diama dam in northern Senegal. *Annals of Tropical Medicine and Parasitology*, 96:575–586.

Speakman, John R. (2013), "Evolutionary perspectives on the obesity epidemic: Adaptive, maladaptive, and neutral viewpoints," *Annual Review of Nutrition*, 33, 289–17.

Stahl, Ann Brower (1984), "Hominid dietary selection before fire," *Current Anthropology*, 25 (2), 151–68.

Steckel, Richard H. (1995), "Stature and the standard of living," *Journal of Economic Literature*, 33 (4), 1903.

Stefani, Aurélia, et al. (2013), "Land cover, land use and malaria in the Amazon: A systematic literature review of studies using remotely sensed data," *Malaria Journal*, 12 (1), 192.

Stein, Dan J., Lund, Crick, and Nesse, Randolph M. (2013), "Classification systems in psychiatry: Diagnosis and global mental health in the era of DSM-5 and ICD-11," *Current Opinion in Psychiatry*, 26 (5), 493.

Steinman, Judith L. (2006), "Gender disparity in organ donation," *Gender Medicine*, 3 (4), 246–52.

Stephen, M. and Suryani, L.K. (2000), "Shamanism, psychosis and autonomous imagination," *Culture, Medicine and Psychiatry*, 24, 5–40.

Steptoe, Andrew and Kivimaki, Mika (2012), "Stress and cardiovascular disease," *Nature Reviews Cardiology*, 9 (6), 360–70.

Stern, Y. (2002), "What is cognitive reserve? Theory and research application of the reserve concept," *Journal of the International Neuropsychological Society*, 8, 448–60.

Stewart, Christopher J., et al. (2018), "Temporal development of the gut microbiome in early childhood from the TEDDY study," *Nature*, 562 (7728), 583–88.

Stewart, Maria-Christina, Keel, Pamela K., and Schiavo, R. Steven (2006), "Stigmatization of anorexia nervosa," *International Journal of Eating Disorders*, 39 (4), 320–25.

Stinson, Sara (1985), "Sex differences in environmental sensitivity during growth and development," *American Journal of Physical Anthropology*, 28 (S6), 123–47.

Stocking, George W. Jr. (1982), *Race, Culture, and Evolution: Essays in the History of Anthropology* (Chicago: University of Chicago Press).

Stokes, J.R. and Casale, T.B. (2015), "The use of anti-IgE therapy beyond allergic asthma," *Journal of Allergy and Clinical Immunology in Practice*, 3 (2), 162–66.

Strachan, David P. (1989), "Hay fever, hygiene, and household size," *British Medical Journal*, 299 (6710), 1259.

Strassmann, Beverly I. (1996), "The evolution of endometrial cycles and menstruation," *Quarterly Review of Biology*, 71 (2), 181–20.

———— (1999), "Menstrual cycling and breast cancer: An evolutionary perspective," *Journal of Women's Health*, 8 (2), 193–201.

Stuchbery, M., Matthey, S., and Barnett, B. (1998), "Postnatal depression and social supports in Vietnamese, Arabic, and Anglo-Celtic mothers.," *Social Psychiatry and Psychiatric Epidemiology*, 33, 483–90.

Stuebe, Alison (2009), "The risks of not breastfeeding for mothers and infants," *Reviews in Obstetrics & Gynecology*, 2 (4), 222–31.

Sullivan, Roger J., Allen, John S., and Nero, Karen (2007), "Schizophrenia in Palau: A biocultural analysis," *Current Anthropology*, 48 (2), 189–13.

Sullivan, Roger J. and Hagen, Ed H. (2002), "Psychotropic substance-seeking: Evolutionary pathology or adaptation?," *Addiction*, 97, 389–400.

Sun, Hui, et al. (2019), "Global, regional, and national prevalence and disability-adjusted life-years for infertility in 195 countries and territories, 1990–2017: Results from a global burden of disease study, 2017," *Aging*, 11 (23), 10952–91.

Sun, Lena H. (2019), "CDC sends experts to fight measles outbreaks in Pacific islands neighboring Samoa," *Washington Post*, 11 December.

Susser, Ida (2009), *AIDS, Sex, and Culture: Global Politics and Survival in Southern Africa* (New York: John Wiley & Sons).

Swagerty, Daniel L., Walling, Anne D., and Klein, Robert M. (2002), "Lactose intolerance," *American Family Physician*, 65.

Szasz, Thomas (1974), *The Myth of Mental Illness: Foundations of a Theory of Personal Conduct, Revised Edition* (New York: Perennial).

Tanya, Vincent N., et al. (2012), *Recent Advances in Onchocerciasis Research and Implications for Control* (Yaounde, Cameroon: Cameroon Academy of Sciences).

Taylor, Janelle S. (2003), "The story catches you and you fall down: Tragedy, ethnography, and 'cultural competence,'" *Medical Anthropology Quarterly*, 17, 159–81.

Temple, Robert and Stockbridge, Norman L. (2007), "BiDil for heart failure in black patients: The U.S. Food and Drug Administration perspective," *Annals of Internal Medicine*, 146 (1), 57–62.

Terry, R.D. and Katzman, D.K. (2001), "Life span and synapses: Will there be a primary senile dementia?," *Neurobiology of Aging*, 22, 347–48.

Thernlund, G.M, et al. (1995), "Psychological stress and the onset of IDDM in children: A case control study," *Diabetes Care*, 18, 1323–29.

Thomas, Rae, et al. (2015), "Prevalence of attention-deficit/hyperactivity disorder: A systematic review and meta-analysis," *Pediatrics*, 135 (4), e994–1001.

Thompson, Amanda L., et al. (2019), "Water, food, and the dual burden of disease in Galápagos, Ecuador," *American Journal of Human Biology*, 32 (1), https://doi.org/10.1002/ajhb.23344.

Thompson, Ross A. (2014), "Stress and child development," *The Future of Children*, 24 (1), 41–59.

Thornton, Robert (2015), "Magical empiricism and 'exposed being' in medicine and traditional healing," *Medical Anthropology*, 34 (4), 353–70.

Thresia, C.U. (2018), "Health inequalities in South Asia at the launch of sustainable development goals: Exclusions in health in Kerala, India need political interventions," *International Journal of Health Services*, 48 (1), 57–80.

Thys, Erik, Sabbe, Bernard, and De Hert, Marc (2014), "Creativity and psychopathology: A systematic review," *Psychopathology*, 47 (3), 141–47.

Timimi, S. and Taylor, E. (2004), "ADHD is best understood as a cultural construct," *British Journal of Psychiatry*, 184, 8–9.

Timio, M., et al. (1999), "Blood pressure in nuns in a secluded order: A 30-year follow-up," *Mineral Electrolyte Metabolism*, 25 (1–2), 73–79.

Tindle, H.A., et al. (2005), "Trends in use of complementary and alternative medicine by U.S. adults: 1997–2002," *Alternative Therapies in Health and Medicine*, 11 (1), 42–49.

Tomes, Nancy (1998), *The Gospel of Germs* (Cambridge: Harvard University Press).

Tomiyama, A. Janet, et al. (2012), "Does cellular aging relate to patterns of allostasis? An examination of basal and stress reactive HPA axis activity and telomere length," *Physiology & Behavior*, 106 (1), 40–45.

Tomiyama, A. Janet, et al. (2018), "How and why weight stigma drives the obesity 'epidemic' and harms health," *BMC Medicine*, 16 (1), 123–23.

Toppari, Jorma and Juul, Anders (2010), "Trends in puberty timing in humans and environmental modifiers," *Molecular and Cellular Endocrinology*, 324 (1–2), 39–44.

Torrey, E.F. (1987), "Prevalence studies in schizophrenia," *British Journal of Psychiatry*, 150, 598–608.

Trevathan, Wenda (2015), "Primate pelvic anatomy and implications for birth," *Philosophical Transactions of the Royal Society of London B: Biological Sciences*, 370 (1663), 20140065.

Tsevat, Danielle G., et al. (2017), "Sexually transmitted diseases and infertility," *American Journal of Obstetrics and Gynecology*, 216 (1), 1–9.

Tulchinsky, T.H. and Varavikova, E.A. (1996), "Addressing the epidemiologic transition in the former Soviet Union: Strategies for health system and public health reform in Russia," *American Journal of Public Health*, 86, 313–20.

U.S. Cancer Statistics Working Group (2005), *United States Cancer Statistics: 1999–2002 Incidence and Mortality Web-Based Report* (Atlanta: U.S Department of Health and Human Services, Centers for Disease Control and Preventions and National Cancer Institute).

U.S. Centers for Disease Control (2019), Deaths: Final Data for 2017, *National Vital Statistics Reports*, Vol. 68. https://www.cdc.gov/nchs/fastats/leading-causes-of-death.htm

———— (2020), HIV. https://www.cdc.gov/hiv/default.html

Ulett, G.A., Han, S., and Han, J. (1998), "Electroacupuncture: Mechanisms and clinical application," *Biological Psychiatry*, 44, 129–38.

Ungar, Peter S. (2006), *Evolution of the Human Diet: The Known, the Unknown, and the Unknowable* (New York: Oxford University Press).

United Nations (2012), WomenWatch. https://www.un.org/womenwatch/feature/ruralwomen/facts-figures.html

———— (2020), The Sustainable Development Goals Report, 2019. unstats.un.org/sdgs/report/2016/goal-02

United Nations Children's Fund (UNICEF) (2013), *Female genital mutilation/cutting: A statistical overview and exploration of the dynamics of change* (New York: United Nations Children's Fund).

United Nations Children's Fund (UNICEF) (2018), *Breastfeeding: A Mother's Gift, for Every Child* (New York: United Nations).

United Nations Children's Fund (UNICEF) (2019), The State of the World's Children, 2019: Children, food and nutrition: Growing well in a changing world. (New York: United Nations Children's Fund). https://www.unicef.org/reports/state-of-worlds-children-2019

U.S. Census Bureau (2006), *Statistical Abstract of the United States: 2000* (Washington, DC: U.S. Government Printing Office).

U.S. Centers for Disease Control. 2019. Deaths: Final Data for 2017, *National Vital Statistics Reports*, Vol. 68. https://www.cdc.gov/nchs/data/nvsr/nvsr68/nvsr68_09_tables-508.pdf

U.S. Food and Drug Administration (2019), FDA approves new treatment for hypoactive sexual desire disorder in premenopausal women. https://www.fda.gov/news-events/press-announcements/fda-approves-new-treatment-hypoactive-sexual-desire-disorder-premenopausal-women

Van den Bergh, Bea R.H., et al. (2005), "Antenatal maternal anxiety and stress and the neurobehavioral development of the fetus and child: Links and possible mechanisms. A review," *Neuroscience and Biobehavioral Reviews*, 29 (2), 237–58.

Vassallo, Milo F., et al. (2010), "Season of birth and food allergy in children," *Annals of Allergy, Asthma & Immunology*, 104 (4), 307–13.

Vercellotti, Giuseppe, et al. (2014), "Exploring the multidimensionality of stature variation in the past through comparisons of archaeological and living populations," *American Journal of Physical Anthropology*, 155 (2), 229–42.

Vermeulen, Sonja J., Campbell, Bruce M., and Ingram, John S.I. (2012), "Climate change and food systems," *Annual Review of Environment and Resources*, 37, 195–222.

Victora, Cesar G., et al. (2016), "Breastfeeding in the 21st century: Epidemiology, mechanisms, and lifelong effect," *The Lancet*, 387 (10017), 475–90.

Vidra, Nikoletta, Trias-Llimós, Sergi, and Janssen, Fanny (2019), "Impact of obesity on life expectancy among different European countries: Secondary analysis of population-level data over the 1975–2012 period," *BMJ Open*, 9 (7), e028086.

Vilcins, Dwan, Sly, Peter D., and Jagals, Paul (2018), "Environmental risk factors associated with child stunting: A systematic review of the literature," *Annals of Global Health*, 84 (4), 551–62.

Villanueva-Russell, Y. (2011), "Caught in the crosshairs: Identity and cultural authority within chiropractic.," *Social Science & Medicine*, 72, 1826–37.

Vitzthum, Virginia J. (1989), "Nursing behaviour and its relation to duration of post-partum amenorrhoea in an Andean community," *Journal of Biosocial Science*, 21, 145–60.

_____ (2009), "The ecology and evolutionary endocrinology of reproduction in the human female," *American Journal of Physical Anthropology*, 140 (S49), 95–136.

Vitzthum, Virginia J. and Ringheim, Karin (2005), "Hormonal contraception and physiology: A research-based theory of discontinuation due to side effects," *Studies in Family Planning*, 36 (1), 13–31.

Vivier, Eric and Malissen, Bernard (2005), "Innate and adaptive immunity: Specificities and signaling hierarchies revisited," *Nature Immunology*, 6 (1), 17–21.

Voelker, Rebecca (2019), "Patients with cystic fibrosis have new triple-drug combination," *Jama*, 322 (21), 2068–68.

Vogel, Virgil J. (1970), *American Indian Medicine* (Norman, OK: University of Oklahoma Press).

Vrijheid, Martine (2014), "The exposome: A new paradigm to study the impact of environment on health," *Thorax*, 69 (9), 876–78.

Wade, T.D., et al. (2000), "Anorexia nervosa and major depression: Shared genetic and environmental risk factors," *American Journal of Psychiatry*, 157, 469–71.

Waldram, James B. (2013), "Transformative and restorative processes: Revisiting the question of efficacy of indigenous healing," *Medical Anthropology*, 32 (3), 191–07.

_____ (2015), "'I don't know the words he uses': Therapeutic communication among Q'eqchi Maya healers and their patients," *Medical Anthropology Quarterly*, 29 (3), 279–97.

Walker, Rob F., et al. (2019), "Association of testosterone therapy with risk of venous thromboembolism among men with and without hypogonadism," *JAMA Internal Medicine*, 180(2), 190-197.

Wallace, I.J., et al. (2016), "Worldwide variation in hip fracture incidence weakly aligns with genetic divergence between populations," *Osteoporosis International*, 27 (9), 2867–72.

Walton, David A. and Ivers, Louise C. (2011), "Responding to cholera in post-earthquake Haiti," *New England Journal of Medicine*, 364 (1), 3–5.

Wang, Mei, et al. (2015), "Fecal microbiota composition of breast-fed infants is correlated with human milk oligosaccharides consumed," *Journal of Pediatric Gastroenterology and Nutrition,* 60 (6), 825.

Watts, G. (1996), "Looking to the future," in R. Porter (ed.), *Cambridge Illustrated History of Medicine* (Cambridge: Cambridge University Press), 342–72.

Watts, Nick, et al. (2018a), "The Lancet Countdown on health and climate change: From 25 years of inaction to a global transformation for public health," *The Lancet,* 391 (10120), 581–30.

Watts, Nick, et al. (2018b), "The 2018 report of the Lancet Countdown on health and climate change: Shaping the health of nations for centuries to come," *The Lancet,* 392 (10163), 2479–14.

Wax, Joseph R., et al. (2010), "Maternal and newborn outcomes in planned home birth vs planned hospital births: A meta-analysis," *American Journal of Obstetrics and Gynecology,* 203 (3), 243.e1–243.e8.

Waynforth, D. (2007), "The influence of parent–infant cosleeping, nursing, and childcare on cortisol and SIgA immunity in a sample of British children," *Developmental Psychobiology,* 49 (6), 640–48.

Weaver, Lesley Jo (2017), "Tension among women in North India: An idiom of distress and a cultural syndrome," *Culture, Medicine, and Psychiatry,* 41 (1), 35–55.

Weaver, Lesley Jo and Hadley, Craig (2009), "Moving beyond hunger and nutrition: A systematic review of the evidence linking food insecurity and mental health in developing countries," *Ecology of Food and Nutrition,* 48 (4), 263–84.

Weissman, M.M. and Olfson, M. (1995), "Depression in women: Implications for health care research," *Science,* 269, 799–01.

Wellin, Edward (1955), "Water boiling in a Peruvian town," in Benjamin Paul (ed.), *Health, Culture, & Community: Case studies of Public Reactions to Health Programs* (New York: Russell Sage Foundation), 71–102.

Wells, Jonathan C.K. (2000), "Natural selection and sex differences in morbidity and mortality in early life," *Journal of Theoretical Biology,* 202 (1), 65–76.

Wentzell, Emily (2008), "Imagining impotence in America: From men's deeds to men's minds to Viagra'", *Michigan Discussions in Anthropology,* 17, 44–75.

———— (2013), "Aging respectably by rejecting medicalization: Mexican men's reasons for not using erectile dysfunction drugs," *Medical Anthropology Quarterly,* 27 (1), 3–22.

Whaley, Arthur L. (2003), "Ethnicity/race, ethics, and epidemiology," *Journal of the National Medical Association,* 95 (8), 736–42.

Whitaker, Elizabeth D. (2005), "The bicycle makes the eyes smile: Exercise, aging, and psychophysical well-being in older Italian cyclists," *Medical Anthropology,* 24, 1–43.

WHO Expert Consultation (2004), "Appropriate body-mass index for Asian populations and its implications for policy and intervention strategies," *The Lancet,* 363 (9403), 157–63.

Wilbert-Lampen, Ute, et al. (2008), "Cardiovascular events during World Cup Soccer," *New England Journal of Medicine,* 358 (5), 475–83.

Wilcox, Allen J. (2001), "On the importance—and the unimportance—of birthweight," *International Journal of Epidemiology,* 30, 1233–41.

Wild, Christopher Paul (2005), "Complementing the genome with an 'exposome': The outstanding challenge of environmental exposure measurement in molecular epidemiology," *Cancer Epidemiology Biomarkers & Prevention,* 14 (8), 1847–50.

Wiley, Andrea S. (1992), "Adaptation and the biocultural paradigm in medical anthropology: A critical review," *Medical Anthropology Quarterly,* 6, 216–36.

———— (2004a), *An Ecology of High Altitude Infancy: A Biocultural Perspective* (New York: Cambridge University Press).

———— (2004b), "'Drink milk for fitness': The cultural politics of human biological variation and milk consumption in the United States," *American Anthropologist,* 106 (3), 506–17.

———— (2012), "Cow milk consumption, insulin- like growth factor- I, and human biology: A life history approach," *American Journal of Human Biology,* 24 (2), 130–38.

———— (2016), *Re-imagining Milk,* Second Edition (Revised) (New York: Routledge).

———— (2018), "The evolution of lactase persistence: Milk consumption, insulin-like growth factor I, and human life-history parameters," *Quarterly Review of Biology,* 93 (4), 319–45.

Wiley, Andrea S., and Jennifer M. Cullin (2020), Biological normalcy. *Evolution, Medicine, and Public Health,* doi:10.1093/emph/eoz035.

Wiley, Andrea S. and Katz, Solomon H. (1998), "Geophagy in pregnancy: A test of a hypothesis," *Current Anthropology,* 39 (4), 532–45.

Wilkinson, Richard G. (1996), *Unhealthy Societies: The Afflictions of Inequality* (New York: Rutledge).

Wilkinson, Richard G. and Pickett, Kate E. (2009a), *The Spirit Level: Why More Equal Societies Almost Always Do Better* (New York: Penguin).

Wilkinson, Richard G. and Pickett, Kate E. (2009b), "Income inequality and social dysfunction," *Annual Review of Sociology*, 35 (1), 493–11.

Wilkinson, Richard G. and Pickett, Kate E. (2017), "The enemy between us: The psychological and social costs of inequality," *European Journal of Social Psychology*, 47 (1), 11–24.

Willcox, B.J., et al. (2006), "Siblings of Okinawan centenarians share lifelong mortality advantages," *Journal of Gerontology: Biological Sciences*, 61A, 345–54.

Willcox, Bradley J., Willcox, Donald Craig, and Suzuki, Makoto (2017), "Demographic, phenotypic, and genetic characteristics of centenarians in Okinawa and Japan: Part 1—Centenarians in Okinawa," *Mechanisms of Ageing and Development*, 165, 75–79.

Willcox, D.C., et al. (2006), "Caloric restriction and human longevity: What can we learn from the Okinawans?," *Biogerontology*, 7, 173–77.

Willcox, Donald Craig, Scapagnini, Giovanni, and Willcox, Bradley J. (2014), "Healthy aging diets other than the Mediterranean: A focus on the Okinawan diet," *Mechanisms of Ageing and Development*, 136, 148–62.

Willerslev, Rane (2009), "The optimal sacrifice: A study of voluntary death among the Siberian Chukchi," *American Ethnologist*, 36, 693–704.

Willett, Walter (2017), *Eat, Drink, and Be Healthy: The Harvard Medical School Guide to Healthy Eating* (New York: Simon and Schuster).

Willett, Walter, et al. (2019), "Food in the Anthropocene: The EAT–Lancet Commission on healthy diets from sustainable food systems," *The Lancet*, 393 (10170), 447–92.

Williams, George C. (1957), "Pleiotropy, natural selection and the evolution of senescence," *Evolution*, 11, 398–11.

———— (2000), "The quest for medical normalcy—Who needs it?," *American Journal of Human Biology*, 12 (1), 10–16.

Williams, Roger (1956), *Biochemical Individuality: The Basis for the Genototrophic Concept* (New York: Wiley).

Williams, Thomas N., et al. (2005), "An immune basis for malaria protection by the sickle cell trait," *PLoS Medicine*, 2 (5), e128.

Willyard, Cassandra (2018), "Could baby's first bacteria take root before birth?," *Nature*, 553, 264–66.

Wilson, Amie, et al. (2011), "Effectiveness of strategies incorporating training and support of traditional birth attendants on perinatal and maternal mortality: Meta-analysis," *British Medical Journal*, 343.

Winston, E. (1934), "The alleged lack of mental diseases among primitive groups," *American Anthropologist*, 36, 234–38.

Witt, Claudia, et al. (2005), "Acupuncture in patients with osteoarthritis of the knee: A randomised trial," *The Lancet*, 366 (9480), 136–43.

Wolf-Meyer, Matthew J. (2012), *The Slumbering Masses: Sleep, Medicine, and Modern American Life* (Minneapolis: University of Minnesota Press).

Wolfe, Nathan D., et al. (2005), "Emergence of unique primate T-lymphotropic viruses among central African bushmeat hunters," *Proceedings of the National Academy of Sciences*, 102 (22), 7994–99.

Wood, James W., et al. (1992), "The Osteological Paradox: Problems of inferring prehistoric health from skeletal samples," *Current Anthropology*, 33 (4), 343–70.

Woodward, Alistair, et al. (2014), "Climate change and health: On the latest IPCC report," *The Lancet*, 383 (9924), 1185–89.

Woolf, Steven H., et al. (2018), "Changes in midlife death rates across racial and ethnic groups in the United States: Systematic analysis of vital statistics," *BMJ*, 362, k3096.

World Health Organization (1981), *International Code of Marketing of Breast-Milk Substitutes* (Geneva: World Health Organization).

———— (2005), The World Health Report 2005 - make every mother and child count. https://www.who.int/whr/2005/en/

———— (2009), *WHO Guidelines on Hand Hygiene in Health Care: First Global Patient Safety Challenge. Clean Care Is Safer Care* (Geneva: World Health Organization).

World Health Organization (2018) The Top 10 Causes of Death. https://www.who.int/news-room/fact-sheets/detail/the-top-10-causes-of-death.

World Health Organization (2020a), Adolescent Health. https://www.who.int/health-topics/adolescent-health/#tab=tab_1.

World Health Organization (2020b), Tuberculosis: Key Facts. https://www.who.int/news-room/fact-sheets/detail/the-top-10-causes-of-death

World Health Organization and UNICEF (2014), *Global Nutrition Targets 2025: Breastfeeding Policy Brief*, https://www.who.int/nutrition/publications/globaltargets2025_policybrief_breastfeeding/en/.

Worthman, Carol M. (1999), "Evolutionary perspectives on the onset of puberty," in Wenda Trevathan, E.O. Smith, and James J. McKenna (eds.), *Evolutionary Medicine* (New York: Oxford University Press), 135–63.

Wrangham, Richard (2009), *Catching Fire: How Cooking Made Us Human*. New York: Basic Books.

Wright, Gerard D. (2007), "The antibiotic resistome: The nexus of chemical and genetic diversity," *Nature Reviews Microbiology*, 5, 175–86.

Wright, Nicole C., et al. (2014), "The recent prevalence of osteoporosis and low bone mass in the United States based on bone mineral density at the femoral neck or lumbar spine," *Journal of Bone and Mineral Research*, 29 (11), 2520–26.

Writing Group for the Women's Health Initiative Investigators (2002), "Risks and benefits of estrogen plus progestin in healthy postmenopausal women: Principal results from the Women's Health Initiative randomized controlled trial," *JAMA*, 288 (3), 321–33.

Wu, Xiaoxu, et al. (2016), "Impact of climate change on human infectious diseases: Empirical evidence and human adaptation," *Environment International*, 86, 14–23.

Xiao, Jianbo (2016), "Phytochemicals in food and nutrition," *Critical Reviews in Food Science and Nutrition*, 56 (sup1), S1–S3.

Xiong, X. and Fraser, W.D. (2004), "Impact of pregnancy-induced hypertension on birthweight by gestational age," *Paediatric and Perinatal Epidemiology*, 18 (3), 186–91.

Xu, Z. and Knight, R. (2015), "Dietary effects on human gut microbiome diversity," *British Journal of Nutrition*, 113 (Suppl), S1–5.

Yajnik, C.S. (2004), "Early life origins of insulin resistance and type 2 diabetes in India and other Asian countries," *Journal of Nutrition*, 134, 205–10.

Yajnik, C.S. (2014), "Transmission of obesity-adiposity and related disorders from the mother to the baby," *Annals of Nutrition and Metabolism*, 64 (Suppl 1), 8–17.

Yamori, Y., Miura, A., and Taira, K. (2001), "Implications from and for food cultures for cardiovascular diseases: Japanese food, particularly Okinawan diets," *Asia Pacific Journal of Clinical Nutrition*, 10, 144–45.

Yang, E.V. and Glaser, R. (2002), "Stress-associated immunomodulation and its implications for responses to vaccination," *Expert Review of Vaccines*, 1, 453–59.

Yang, X-Y, et al. (2015), "Dexamethasone alone vs in combination with transcutaneous electrical acupoint stimulation or tropisetron for prevention of postoperative nausea and vomiting in gynaecological patients undergoing laparoscopic surgery," *British Journal of Anaesthesia*, 115 (6), 883–89.

Yehuda, R., et al. (2005), "Transgenerational effects of posttraumatic stress disorder in babies of mothers exposed to the World Trade Center attacks during pregnancy," *Journal of Endocrinology and Metabolism*, 90 (7), 4115–18.

Yewhalaw, Delenasaw, et al. (2009), "Malaria and water resource development: The case of Gilgel-Gibe hydroelectric dam in Ethiopia," *Malaria Journal*, 8 (1), 21.

Young, A.S., et al. (2001), "The quality of care for depressive and anxiety disorders in the United States," *Archives of General Psychiatry*, 58, 55–61.

Young, Eric, et al. (2013), "Unique sleep disorders profile of a population-based sample of 747 Hmong immigrants in Wisconsin," *Social Science & Medicine*, 79, 57–65.

Young, J. Hunter, et al. (2005), "Differential susceptibility to hypertension is due to selection during the out-of-Africa expansion," *PLoS Genetics*, 1 (6).

Young, Sera (2011), *Craving Earth: Understanding Pica—The Urge to Eat Clay, Starch, Ice, and Chalk* (New York: Columbia University Press).

Zatonski, W.A. and Bhala, N. (2012), "Changing trends of diseases in Eastern Europe: Closing the gap," *Public Health*, 126 (3), 248–52.

Zemel, B.S. and Jenkins, C. (1989), "Dietary change and adolescent growth among Bundi (gender-speaking) people of Papua New Guinea," *American Journal of Human Biology*, 1, 709–18.

Zhou, B., et al. (2016), "Worldwide trends in diabetes since 1980: A pooled analysis of 751 population-based studies with 4·4 million participants," *The Lancet*, 387 (10027), 1513–30.

Zhou, Yi-Biao, et al. (2010), "Effects of low temperature on the schistosome-transmitting snail Oncomelania hupensis and the implications of global climate change," *Molluscan Research*, 30 (2), 102.

Zhou, Yi-Biao, et al. (2016), "The Three Gorges Dam: Does it accelerate or delay the progress towards eliminating transmission of schistosomiasis in China?," *Infectious Diseases of Poverty*, 5 (1), 63.

Zhu, K., et al. (2006), "Growth, bone mass, and vitamin D status of Chinese adolescent girls 3 y after withdrawal of milk supplementation," *American Journal of Clinical Nutrition*, 83 (3), 714–21.

Zung, A., et al. (2012), "Increase in the incidence of type 1 diabetes in Israeli children following the Second Lebanon War," *Pediatric Diabetes*, 13 (4), 326–33.

INDEX

Note: Page numbers followed by *t* or *f* indicate a figure or table on the designated page